Program Overview

Finding God

Our response to God's gifts

2

School Edition
Catechist Guide

Barbara F. Campbell, M.Div., D.Min.
James P. Campbell, M.A., D.Min.

LOYOLAPRESS.
CHICAGO

Nihil Obstat:
Reverend John G. Lodge, S.S.L., S.T.D.
Censor Deputatus
March 6, 2004

Imprimatur:
Most Reverend Edwin M. Conway, D.D.
Vicar General
Archdiocese of Chicago
April 14, 2004

The *Nihil Obstat* and *Imprimatur* are official declarations that a book is free of doctrinal and moral error. No implication is contained therein that those who have granted the *Nihil Obstat* and *Imprimatur* agree with the content, opinions, or statements expressed. Nor do they assume any legal responsibility associated with publication.

Finding God: Our Response to God's Gifts **is an expression of the work of Loyola Press, an apostolate of the Chicago Province of the Society of Jesus.**

Senior Consultants
Jane Regan, Ph.D.
Richard Hauser, S.J., Ph.D., S.T.L.
Robert Fabing, S.J., D.Min.

Advisors
Most Reverend Gordon D. Bennett, S.J., D.D.
George A. Aschenbrenner, S.J., S.T.L.
Paul H. Colloton, O.P., D.Min.
Eugene LaVerdiere, S.S.S., Ph.D., S.T.L.

Peg Bowman, M.A.
Gerald Darring, M.A.
Brian DuSell, D.M.A.
Teresa DuSell, M.M.
Bryan T. Froehle, Ph.D.

Thomas J. McGrath
Joanne Paprocki, M.A.
Daniel L. Snyder, M.Div., Ph.D.
Christopher R. Weickert
Elaine M. Weickert

Catechetical Staff
Jeanette L. Graham, M.A.
Marlene Halpin, O.P., Ph.D.
Thomas McLaughlin, M.A.
Joseph Paprocki, M.A.

Grateful acknowledgment is given to authors, publishers, photographers, museums, and agents for permission to reprint the following copyrighted material; music credits where appropriate can be found at the bottom of each individual song. Every effort has been made to determine copyright owners. In the case of any omissions, the publisher will be pleased to make suitable acknowledgments in future editions. Continued on page 455.

Cover Design: Think Design Group
Cover Illustration: Christina Balit
Interior Design: Three Communication Design

ISBN: 0-8294-1864-4
Copyright © 2005 Loyola Press, Chicago, Illinois.

Manufactured in the United States of America.

LOYOLAPRESS.
3441 N. ASHLAND AVENUE
CHICAGO, ILLINOIS 60657
(800) 621-1008
www.LoyolaPress.org
www.FindingGod.org

04 05 06 07 08 09 10 11 12 13 Banta 10 9 8 7 6 5 4 3 2 1

Finding God

Our response to God's gifts

The Year in Our Church

Prayers and Practices of Our Faith

Recorded Scripture Story Scripts

Recorded Guided Reflection Scripts

Blackline Masters

FindingGod

Our response to God's gifts

A Deeper Relationship With God and the Catholic Church

"The desire for God is written in the human heart."

Catechism of the Catholic Church (CCC 27)

We desire to know God in a personal way in order to find meaning in our lives. This is the aim of catechesis as expressed in the *General Directory for Catechesis*: "to put people, not only in touch, but also in communion with Jesus Christ" (*GDC* 80). Loyola Press carefully crafted *Finding God: Our Response to God's Gifts* to help Catholic school catechists and parish catechists as they invite children and the significant adults in their lives into a deeper relationship with God and the Catholic Church in service to the world.

"There must be a better way to help children and adults enter into a deeper dialogue of faith." This simple sentence sparked a conversation about faith formation that grew to include theologians, teachers, catechists, catechetical leaders, pastors, and professors. A burning desire to honor the role of the catechist— and an Ignatian commitment to recognize God and his love in all things—turned that conversation into a flame. Together, we took up the challenge to create a vehicle that would support all people who nurture a lived faith. Thousands of hours were spent creating tools and crafting resources that would spark meaningful dialogues and offer experiences that would authentically pass on the beauty and truth of our Catholic faith one person at a time. Being better together and holding to this simple call, we made the work that was named *Finding God: Our Response to God's Gifts*.

The Inspiration Behind the Title

The title, *Finding God: Our Response to God's Gifts*, reflects the inspiration of Saint Ignatius of Loyola and describes what Catholic faith formation calls us to do: recognize the presence of God in the sacraments and in our communities of faith, and realize the presence of God in our experiences of God's creation and in our lives as people for others. May all of your efforts as a catechist help others to recognize God in all things.

"The desire for God is written in the human heart."

Catechism of the Catholic Church (CCC 27)

"The desire to share the faith is written in the heart of the catechist."

An Authentic Expression of Our Catholic Faith

Finding God: Our Response to God's Gifts reflects a vision of our Catholic faith grounded in Scripture and Tradition and an Ignatian recognition of the presence of God in all things. The expression of that vision is based on our Catholic belief that effective catechesis

† reflects the love of the Father, the Son, and the Holy Spirit

† centers on the person of Jesus Christ

† proclaims the liberating good news of salvation through Jesus Christ

† leads the Christian into the world in mission and action

† addresses the needs of the culture in which it is presented

† invites believers to reflect on personal experience in light of growing in relationship with God

† leads to full, conscious, active participation in the liturgical life of the Church

† creates a climate of prayer and nurtures a faith that is expressed in prayer

The What and the How of Faith Formation

To foster effective catechesis, the Church has provided the *Catechism of the Catholic Church* and the *General Directory for Catechesis*. Put simply, the *Catechism* might be considered the "what" of our beliefs as Catholics and the *General Directory for Catechesis* might be the "how" of effective catechesis.

The *Catechism of the Catholic Church*
The *Catechism of the Catholic Church*, published in 1992, provides us with a clearly stated synthesis of Catholic teaching explained in four major parts, or "pillars":

† The Profession of Faith (Creed)

† The Celebration of the Christian Mystery (Sacraments)

† Life in Christ (Ten Commandments and Beatitudes)

† Christian Prayer (Prayer)

The *General Directory for Catechesis*
The *General Directory for Catechesis*, published in 1997, serves as a complement to the *Catechism of the Catholic Church*. The *GDC* reminds us that catechesis is "the process of transmitting the Gospel, as the Christian community has received it, understands it, celebrates it, lives it, and communicates it in many ways" (*GDC* 105). *Finding God: Our Response to God's Gifts* provides a process for transmitting the Gospel that is supported by the principles of the *GDC*.

Finding God: Our Response to God's Gifts coherently presents the Church's doctrine and Tradition "which are safeguarded by the bishops who teach with a unique authority." ("Guidelines for Doctrinally Sound Catechetical Materials," United States Catholic Conference)

Finding God: Our Response to God's Gifts is an authentic expression of the Catholic faith, found to be in conformity with the *Catechism of the Catholic Church* by the Ad Hoc Committee to Oversee the Use of the Catechism.

Direct references to the *CCC* and *GDC* are included in the Catechist Preparation section of each session.

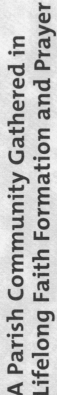

A Parish Community Gathered in Lifelong Faith Formation and Prayer

Every moment of every life is an opportunity to grow in a personal relationship with God. Each moment of each day God invites us to share in his love and his gifts. Our response to God's invitation is reflected in our relationships with others and in the way we serve and respect the dignity and beauty of all creation.

Finding God: Our Response to God's Gifts is rooted in the belief that a thriving parish gathers in community to nurture a lived faith for every person—that the shared relationships of all people of faith are the true support for catechesis. *Finding God: Our Response to God's Gifts* weaves together experiences in prayer, Scripture, Catholic social teaching, and liturgy for children and adults—as individuals, as families, and as learners on a faith journey.

> *"Every moment of every life is an opportunity to grow in our personal relationship with God."*

Prayer

We nourish a relationship with God through prayer—traditional prayer, reflective prayer, liturgical prayer, and praying with Scripture. Experiences of prayer in *Finding God: Our Response to God's Gifts* model and invite us to pray from within the truths we explore each time we gather. Our growing bond as a community helps each of us to enter into deeper communion with Jesus Christ through prayer.

Scripture

Finding God: Our Response to God's Gifts takes to heart the challenge that "easy access to Sacred Scripture should be provided for all . . ." (*Dogmatic Constitution on Divine Revelation* 22) Scripture sets the foundation for the truths that are reflected upon in each gathering of adults or children. The authentic teaching of the Church is revealed through both Scripture and Tradition.

Catholic Social Teaching

Our Catholic faith moves us to concern for others and a commitment to social justice. *Finding God: Our Response to God's Gifts* calls each of us to participate as people for others. Our faith is shared in our commitment to the principles of Catholic Social Teaching: Life and Dignity of the Human Person; Call to Family, Community, and Participation; Rights and Responsibilities; Option for the Poor and Vulnerable; The Dignity of Work and the Rights of Workers; Solidarity; and Care for God's Creation.

> *"A thriving parish gathers in community to nurture a lived faith for every person."*

Liturgy

Finding God: Our Response to God's Gifts echoes our belief that the celebration of the Eucharist is the "source and summit of the Christian life" (*CCC* 1324). *Finding God: Our Response to God's Gifts* helps children connect their faith to the celebration of faith at Mass and invites all of the faithful to join in a more meaningful participation in the Church's sacramental and liturgical life.

To Pray Without Ceasing

Saint Paul considered prayer so important that he told us to "pray without ceasing" (1 Thessalonians 5:17). As people of faith, we mentor each other to pray without ceasing and to know prayer as "a vital and personal relationship with the living and true God" (CCC 2558). We learn that prayer is a mutual revealing—we open ourselves to God and listen as he reveals the vastness of his love for us. As adults, we look for opportunities to share this lifetime nourishment of prayer with our children.

Mentoring Children Into a Life of Prayer

Adults support a child's prayerful, personal response to God by sharing their own very personal relationship with God and all of his creation. As catechists, we lead children to a personal relationship with God by helping them understand our Catholic faith and providing opportunities for them to talk about their faith with other children as well as adults. We mentor children to pray without ceasing by praying with them and by cherishing prayer as a deeply important, always present opportunity to grow in relationship with God.

Finding God: Our Response to God's Gifts invites adults and children to create a climate of prayerful faith sharing. The truths of our Catholic faith are affirmed and explored as the context and foundation of a personal relationship with God. We acknowledge that faith formation "includes more than instruction; it is an apprenticeship" (GDC 67). Catechists and all people of faith mentor children by "doing," by gently modeling and guiding children into the Catholic way of life, a life filled with the nourishment of meaningful prayer.

Opportunities for Prayer in Every Session

We learn to pray by opening ourselves to God. In *Finding God: Our Response to God's Gifts* we invite adults and children to open themselves to God's presence and to respond in prayer—traditional prayer, praying with Scripture, liturgical prayer, and personal reflective prayer.

Opportunities to pray are carefully woven into each session:

We invite children to join in a prayer of petition to ask for God's help on their faith journey.

We pray with them again in a reflective prayer that flows naturally from Scripture and Tradition. In this prayer, we guide them into sacred time and space, ask them to quiet themselves to enter into conversation with the Lord, or offer an opportunity to take to heart the basic prayers of the Catholic Church.

We invite the children to pray in gratitude for God's gifts and to ask for the grace to act on what they have learned.

In these ways children grow in their own personal and prayerful relationship with God.

> *"Rejoice always.*
> *Pray without ceasing.*
> *In all circumstances*
> *give thanks,*
> *for this is*
> *the will of God*
> *for you*
> *in Christ Jesus."*
> 1 Thessalonians 5:16–18

> *We mentor children to*
> *pray without ceasing*
> *by cherishing prayer*
> *as a deeply important,*
> *mutually revealing*
> *relationship with*
> *God.*

FindingGod

Our response to God's gifts

Developed from the start as a parish-wide program for catechesis, *Finding God: Our Response to God's Gifts* provides a wealth of support beyond the children's program for the program director, pastor, catechists, and facilitators who gather together adults, families, and children in faith formation.

To further support family faith formation, Gathering Sessions, the Pastor Guide, Parent Newsletters, and Video Sessions reflect the themes of the children's program:

**God
Jesus
The Church
The Sacraments
Morality**

Director Guide

Comprehensive yet concise, the Director Guide provides an overview of the program structure, catechist in-services, and materials for sessions with catechists, adults, and families participating in the program.

Pastor Guide

The Pastor Guide offers ways for the pastor to positively influence the quality of catechesis in the parish.

Gathering Sessions

Written by Jane Regan and Mimi Bitzan, five ready-to-use gathering sessions each year over a four-year cycle engage adults in meaningful conversation and prayer related to the themes of the children's program.

Gathering Together

Sacred Times

Sacramental preparation becomes family faith formation when using *Gathering Together* and *Sacred Times* with families preparing children for Reconciliation and Eucharist.

Toward an Adult Church

Jane Regan, co-author of *Gathering Sessions*, provides sound background and practical suggestions in her book *Toward an Adult Church.*

A Parent Guide to Prayer

A perfect resource for parents, this guide can be used as they pray with their children.

Family Learning Guide

Children's Book Parent Pages
(20 per year)

Take-home pages provide parents with background and activities to stay truly involved in their children's faith formation.

Families use the Children's Books and this guide to work together on faith formation at home.

Parent Newsletters
(5 per year)

Parent newsletters, by Tom McGrath, offer parents inspiration and motivation for personal and family faith formation. (Also available in Spanish.)

Raising Faith-Filled Kids
(with Discussion Guide)

Tom McGrath provides practical, from-the-heart advice on children's faith formation.

Videos with Leader Guides to Support Adult and Family Faith Formation

Videos for adult and family faith formation spark meaningful dialogues as adults meet to view topics of central issues such as "Why We Go to Mass."

www.FindingGod.org

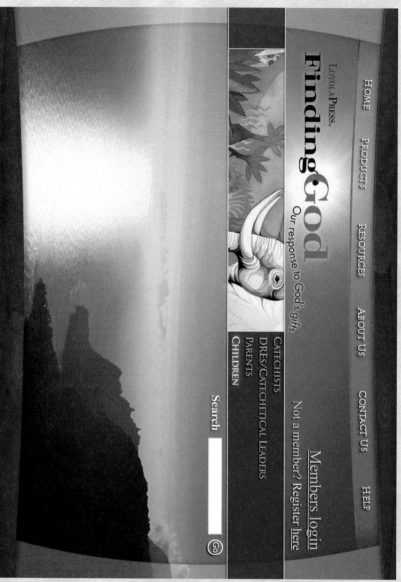

LOYOLAPRESS.

FindingGod
Our response to God's gifts

HOME · PRODUCTS · RESOURCES · ABOUT US · CONTACT US · HELP

Not a member? Register here

Members login

Search [ ] Go

CATECHISTS
DRES/CATECHETICAL LEADERS
PARENTS
CHILDREN

The Finding God Web site provides support for directors, catechists, parents, and children using the program and offers additional activities in English and Spanish.

FindingGod

Our response to God's gifts

Finding God: Our Response to God's Gifts offers catechists the materials needed to mentor children's faith formation within a climate of prayer. Soundly grounded in Scripture and Church Tradition, the content has been designed to support catechists of all experience levels and to offer all children meaningful faith experiences that are age-appropriate and relevant to their young lives.

Each Grade includes:

Children's Book

Brimming with fine art, illustrations, and photography, each Children's Book presents the truth and beauty of our faith in an engaging and age-appropriate way.

Five Overarching Themes

God
Jesus
The Church
The Sacraments
Morality

Catechist Guide

Providing complete catechetical background and clear plans, each Catechist Guide offers step-by-step support as we help children deepen their understanding of their faith and build a meaningful relationship with God.

Posters and Blackline Masters

Posters, Reproducible Activities, and Assessments serve as valuable tools and offer ways to extend each session and assess learning.

Vocal, Instrumental, and Reflective Music
(Music CD)

Songs of our faith recorded by the internationally known LA Children's Chorus draw children to listen and sing.

Reflective music offers calming beauty as we guide children in prayer.

Scripture Stories and Guided Reflections
(Spoken Word CD)

Dramatized recordings of Scripture Stories bring the Bible to life for adults and children alike. Recorded Guided Reflections offer support in mentoring children into a life of prayer.

Grade One

God is our Creator and loves us as our Father. Jesus came to tell us about God the Father and saves us through his life, death, and resurrection. The Holy Spirit shares the life of the risen Jesus Christ and forms the community of the Church. We know Jesus through personal prayer and by worshiping God together, especially in the celebration of the Eucharist. We can thank Jesus for the gift of himself and the Holy Spirit by obeying the Commandments, caring for one another, and caring for the world.

Grade Two

God loves each of us and we are called to act on God's love for us by loving one another, by living as Jesus wants us to live. As we prepare for the Sacraments of Penance and Eucharist, we give special attention to examination of conscience, how to make a good confession and importance of preparation to receive Jesus Christ in Holy Communion.

Grade Three

God creates us good and calls us to live in community. We emphasize the role of Jesus calling us to a new way of life—what it means to be a faithful follower of Jesus and how close Jesus wants us to be with our Father. We learn how each of the sacraments deepens our relationship with God and how the theological virtues of faith, hope, and charity are the foundation for the moral choices we make as we grow to be like Jesus.

Grade Four

God calls us to lead a moral life. He revealed the Ten Commandments to provide us with the parameters to live a life for God and others. Jesus taught us the Beatitudes and their relationship to living a Christian life. We give special attention to Sacraments of Healing and Sacraments at the Service of Communion as part of the moral dimension of our faith.

Grade Five

Strengthened in sacramental life of the Church, we are better able to live like Jesus in making choices for God and others. We enter into a new way of life when we celebrate the Sacraments of Initiation. Through the sacraments we live more fully in the Holy Spirit as members of the Church, united in diversity under the magisterium. The fullness of our life in Jesus Christ will find completion at the Last Judgment when we face our Savior.

Grade Six

We explore the history of salvation—from Creation, through the Old Testament, to its fulfillment in Jesus—as we share stories of our ancestors in faith: Abraham, Moses, David, and Solomon. We recognize the importance of the prophets as witnesses for God and their relevance to our own time. As followers of Jesus, we explore the meaning of the Psalms as the prayers of Jesus and the themes of Wisdom Literature that teach practical ways of living for God in everyday life. We find our connection to Christian worship from its roots in the Old Testament, and we learn of the special connection between the celebration of Passover and the celebration of the Eucharist. Important themes of Catholic Social Teaching call us to holiness, to care for the earth, and to act in the ways of justice.

Scope and Sequence Grade 1

Unit	Session	Theme	Scripture	CCC References
God Loves Us **1**	1. God Made Everything	God is the creator and loves all that he created.	Genesis 1:31 Psalm 96:11–13	287–289
	2. God Cares for Us	God loves us and wants nothing but the best for us.	Genesis 1:29 Psalm 27:13	356–358, 374–379
	3. God Is Our Father	Jesus tells us that God is his Father and our loving Father too.	Matthew 3:17 John 14:23	128–129, 238–240
	4. God Gives Us Peace	The Holy Spirit is God's presence among us.	John 20:19–22 Ephesians 6:23	691, 733–736
	5. Review		Genesis 1:3	
Jesus Loves Us **2**	6. God Sends Jesus	Jesus was born in Bethlehem.	Luke 2:4–14 Luke 2:19–20	437, 525–526
	7. Jesus Teaches Us	Jesus taught us how to pray to our Father as he prayed.	Luke 6:12 Matthew 6:9–10	2759–2772, 2779–2827
	8. Trust in God	Jesus taught us that God wants to know our needs.	Matthew 6:11–13 Luke 12:32	2828–2854
	9. Jesus Rises From the Dead	Jesus rose from the dead, making new life possible.	Matthew 28:1–10 Matthew 18:20	638–655, 988–1004
	10. Review			
All Are Welcome **3**	11. Following Jesus	Jesus gives us the Church as a sign of his love for us and for the whole world.	Mark 1:16–20 John 15:14	2–3, 774–776, 880–887, 949–953, 2419–2449
	12. Jesus Sends the Holy Spirit	The Holy Spirit gives us gifts of peace, strength, and joy.	Acts 2:1–4 Galatians 5:22	731–741
	13. Jesus Teaches Us to Share	Jesus calls us to share his love.	Acts 2:42–47 Philippians 2:18	2443–2449
	14. God Chose Mary	Mary, the mother of Jesus, loves and prays for us.	Luke 1:26–38 Luke 1:48	963–970
	15. Review			
Meeting Jesus **4**	16. Jesus in Our Lives	Jesus is with us in a special way through the Sacraments.	Mark 10:13–16 Psalm 34:9	5, 2225–2226
	17. Joining God's Family	In Baptism, we become members of God's family.	Acts 2:37–41 Matthew 28:19	1213–1274
	18. Celebrating Jesus	In celebrating the Mass, we remember what Jesus has done for us.	Luke 22:19–20 1 Corinthians 10:31	1329, 1334, 1340, 1382–1384, 1402–1403
	19. Listening to Our Father	When we pray, we are listening and talking to God.	1 Kings 19:9–13 John 6:45	2709–2719
	20. Review		Matthew 28:19	
Living Like Jesus **5**	21. Making Good Decisions	The Commandments help us make good decisions.	Exodus 20:1–17 Matthew 22:36–39	2052–2074
	22. Jesus Cares for Us	We are like Jesus when we care for one another.	Luke 15:3–7 John 10:11	2779–2785
	23. Jesus Loves Families	Jesus has given our parents to us, and we are called to honor and obey them.	Luke 2:41–51 Exodus 20:12	2201–2233
	24. God Loves the World	God wants us to care for the world he has given us.	Genesis 2:15,19–20 Psalm 67:7	2415–2418
	25. Review		Matthew 6:26–30	

A sixth unit in Grade 1 includes separate sessions for these seasons of the liturgical year: Advent, Christmas, Lent, Holy Week, Easter, Pentecost, and All Saints Day.

Catholic Social Teaching Themes · Words Learned · Saints and Holy People · Basic Prayers

Catholic Social Teaching Themes	Words Learned	Saints and Holy People	Basic Prayers
Family and Community, God's Creation	Amen, creator, God, saint	Saint Francis of Assisi, Saint Vincent de Paul	Sign of the Cross
Family and Community, God's Creation, Life and Dignity	liturgy, Mass		We praise you, we bless you, we thank you.
Family and Community, Solidarity	Bible, Jesus		
Family and Community, Rights and Responsibilities, Solidarity	Holy Spirit, Trinity		Glory Be to the Father
Family and Community, Work and Workers	angel, Christmas, Holy Family, Joseph, Mary	Saint Joseph, Mary	
Life and Dignity	heaven, Kingdom of God, prayer		Lord's Prayer
Family and Community	temptation, trespasses		Lord's Prayer
Family and Community	Christ, Resurrection	Saint Joseph	Lord's Prayer
Family and Community, Work and Workers, Solidarity	grace	Mary	Hail Mary
Family and Community	Catholic, Christian		Saint Richard of Chichester's Prayer
Family and Community	parish, Pentecost	Saint Peter, Saint Michael	Sign of the Cross
Family and Community, Life and Dignity	Church	Saint Peter	Sign of the Cross, Hail Mary
Family and Community	priest, sacrament	Saint Dominic Savio	
Family and Community, Solidarity	Baptism, godparent, holy water	Saint Peter	Sign of the Cross
The Poor and Vulnerable, Family and Community	Last Supper	Elijah	Prayer Before Meals, Prayer After Meals
Family and Community, Solidarity	commandment	Saint Ignatius of Loyola	Morning Prayer
Family and Community	forgiveness, sin	Mary, Saint Joseph	Glory Be to the Father
God's Creation		Saint Ignatius of Loyola	Evening Prayer

Scope and Sequence Grade 2

Unit	Session	Theme	Scripture	CCC References
1 God Loves Us	1. God Creates Us	God created the world to show us how much he loves us.	Genesis 1:1–31 / 1 Timothy 4:4	290–292, 307
	2. God Gives Us Jesus	Jesus is the Son of God who comes to save us.	Matthew 1:18–24 / Matthew 28:20	422–424, 430–432
	3. God Is Our Father	We call Jesus the Son of God because he reveals to us his loving Father.	Matthew 6:25–34 / 1 Peter 5:6–7	65, 2786–2793
	4. God's Life for Us	All good things we do and the good decisions we make come from the Holy Spirit.	Luke 2:25–32 / Isaiah 49:6	733–736, 739
	5. Review		Genesis 1:9	
2 Jesus Loves Us	6. Jesus Is Faithful	With God's help, we can follow the Commandments and live in peace with one another.	Luke 2:41–52 / Exodus 20:12	534, 2052, 2197–2246
	7. Jesus Saves Us	Jesus is the model for the love and goodness in our lives.	Luke 7:18–22 / Isaiah 35:5	427, 459, 520, 532, 581, 2607
	8. Jesus Calls Us to Love	Jesus calls us to the Kingdom of God.	Luke 14:16–23 / Matthew 4:23	541–556, 2632, 2816–2821
	9. Jesus Cares for Us	The parable of the lost sheep shows God's loving concern for us.	Matthew 18:10–14 / John 10:11	553, 861–862, 881, 896, 1465
	10. Review		Psalm 100:3	
3 All Are Welcome	11. We Worship God	The sacraments help us to worship God in a special way.	John 15:1–6 / Galatians 5:22	Part 2
	12. Celebrating Reconciliation	When we celebrate the Sacrament of Penance we are reconciled with God and others.	Luke 19:2–9 / Luke 12:33	1422–1484
	13. The Sacrament of Penance	In the Sacrament of Penance, our sins are forgiven.	Mark 2:1–12 / Luke 1:77	1468–1470, 1849–1869
	14. Mary Shows Us the Way	Mary is the great example of what it means to obey God.	Luke 1:39–55 / Luke 2:19	717, 2617–2619, 2676–2679
	15. Review		Psalm 51:3–4	
4 Meeting Jesus	16. New Life in Jesus	When we receive the Sacraments of Initiation, we receive new life in Jesus.	Acts 2:38 / Revelation 22:17	1212–1274, 1285–1314, 1322–1405
	17. Jesus Loves the Church	One way we can see God's love in the world is the way we celebrate the Eucharist.	Luke 24:13–31 / Acts 2:42	329, 1347
	18. Gathering for Mass	When we gather for Mass we hear the word of God.	2 Timothy 3:14–17 / Psalm 119:89	1348–1349
	19. Celebrating the Eucharist	Celebrating the Eucharist is central to Christian life.	Luke 22:14–20 / Hebrews 10:12	1350–1355
	20. Review		Mark 3:33–35	
5 Living Like Jesus	21. Being Like Jesus	Jesus shows us how to love through his words and deeds.	Luke 10:25–37 / Matthew 5:7	512–560
	22. We Share God's Life	God helps us follow our conscience so we can be truly free and happy.	Deuteronomy 30:16–18 / John 14:6	1749–1756, 1776–1794
	23. Following Jesus	We can be like Jesus by treating others fairly and with justice.	Matthew 5:1–10 / Matthew 22:37–38	1716–1719, 1725–1728
	24. Making Choices	God wants us to respect one another's good name and property.	1 Peter 3:10–12 / Psalm 34:12–15	1749–1756
	25. Review		John 14:27	

A sixth unit in Grade 2 includes separate sessions for these seasons of the liturgical year: Advent, Christmas and Epiphany, Lent, Holy Week, Easter, Pentecost, and All Saints Day.

Catholic Social Teaching Themes	Words Learned	Saints and Holy People	Basic Prayers
God's Creation, The Poor and Vulnerable, Work and Workers	creation, holy	Saint Isidore the Farmer	Glory Be to the Father
Family and Community	Blessed Sacrament, Emmanuel, genuflect, Savior, tabernacle	Saint Joseph, Mary, Holy Family	
God's Creation, Solidarity	petition, praise		Lord's Prayer
Solidarity	faith, Messiah, Temple	Simeon	Prayer to the Holy Spirit
Family and Community	conscience, Ten Commandments	Saints Anne and Joachim	
Solidarity	parable, pope	Saint John the Baptist	
The Poor and Vulnerable, Solidarity	bishop, crozier, deacon	Saint Martin de Porres, Saint Peter	Psalm 23
Family and Community, Solidarity	Magnificat	Saint Peter	
The Poor and Vulnerable, Solidarity		Mary, Saint Elizabeth	
Family and Community, Solidarity	Fruits of the Holy Spirit, original sin, rite	Saint Ignatius of Loyola	Act of Contrition
Solidarity	confession, contrition, examination of conscience, mortal sin, reconciliation, Sacrament of Penance, venial sin		
Family and Community	absolution, penance		
Family and Community, Solidarity	Body and Blood of Christ, Confirmation, consecration, Eucharist, Holy Communion, Sacraments of Initiation	Pope Saint Pius X, Saint Peter	
Family and Community, Solidarity	disciple, ministry, Sacrifice of the Mass		Prayer Before Meals
Family and Community	ambo, homily, Lectionary, Liturgy of the Word		
Family and Community, Solidarity	altar, Holy Days of Obligation, Liturgy of the Eucharist		
Family and Community	moral choice	Saint Martin of Tours	
God's Creation, The Poor and Vulnerable, Family and Community, Solidarity, Rights and Responsibilities			
Family and Community		Moses	
The Poor and Vulnerable, Family and Community, Solidarity	Beatitudes, Great Commandment, New Testament, Old Testament	Saint Elizabeth Ann Seton, Saint Peter	
Family and Community, Solidarity, Life and Dignity		Saint Francis Borgia, Saint Peter	

Scope and Sequence Grade 3

Unit	Session	Theme	Scripture	CCC References
Creator and Father **1**	1. Created to Be Happy	God wants us to know him.	Psalm 148:7–14 Genesis 1:31	41, 222–227
	2. Created to Be Together	The love of the Father, Son, and Holy Spirit is the source of the love we have for one another.	1 John 4:16 1 John 4:7–11	2196
	3. God Is Our Father	Jesus reveals to us that God is our loving Father, who calls us to live in peace with one another.	Matthew 6:9–14 2 Corinthians 1:3–4	2786–2796
	4. Jesus Is With Us	The Father sends Jesus to save us.	Matthew 1:18–23 Deuteronomy 31:8	430–433, 441–444
	5. Review		1 John 4:7–11	541–556
Son of God, Son of Mary **2**	6. Jesus' Good News	Jesus teaches us how to love the Father, others, and ourselves.	Matthew 13:31–32 Matthew 13:33	541–556
	7. Following Jesus	Jesus calls us to love God and others.	Mark 10:17–23 Matthew 6:21	2052–2055
	8. Jesus Gathers Disciples	Jesus invites his followers to enter the Kingdom of God.	Luke 5:1–11 Luke 10:2	2044–2046
	9. Jesus Dies and Rises	Through Jesus' death and resurrection, we receive salvation.	1 Corinthians 15:1–5 John 11:25–26	599–618, 638–655, 659–664, 731–732
	10. Review		Psalm 96:1–4	
Community of Jesus **3**	11. Jesus Sends the Holy Spirit	Jesus sends the Holy Spirit to bring life into the Church.	Acts 2:1–12 Galatians 5:22–23	731–741
	12. The Catholic Church	Jesus gives us leaders in the Church.	Matthew 16:18–19 John 21:17	858–862, 880–886
	13. The Church Prays	Jesus Christ is especially present in the celebration of the sacraments.	Luke 7:1–10 Luke 17:21	798, 947, 1088, 1097, 1118, 1123
	14. Mary Is Holy	Mary is the Church's model of faith and love.	Luke 1:46–54 Luke 1:45	717, 946–959, 971, 2617–2619, 2676–2679
	15. Review		1 Corinthians 12:4–7,11	
Meeting Jesus **4**	16. Sacraments of Initiation	Through the Sacraments of Initiation, we receive fullness of the Spirit and become members of the Church.	Acts 8:26–40 Ephesians 4:4	1212–1274, 1285–1314, 1322–1405
	17. Celebrating Reconciliation	When we fail to love God and others due to sin, Jesus calls us to forgiveness through the Sacrament of Penance.	Psalm 85:9 John 20:19–23	1422–1470
	18. Celebrating the Eucharist	The celebration of the Eucharist is at the center of parish life.	1 Corinthians 11:23–26 John 6:48	1396
	19. Christian Living	We are all called by God to do special work as a sister, brother, priest, married, or single person.	1 Corinthians 12:4–11 1 Peter 4:10	1350–1355
	20. Review		1 Corinthians 16:13–14 Ephesians 4:1–6	
Living Like Jesus **5**	21. Faith, Hope, and Charity	We live like Jesus when we practice the virtues of faith, hope, and charity.	1 Thessalonians 1:2–4 1 Corinthians 13:13	1812–1829
	22. Making Good Choices	Jesus gives us the help we need to make good moral choices.	Matthew 4:1–11 Colossians 3:17	2052–2074
	23. Living as God's Children	Jesus helps us to love and respect one another.	Philippians 1:3–11 Galatians 6:2	1878–1885, 2196
	24. All Life Is Sacred	Jesus calls us to share with one another in any way we can.	1 John 4:7 Psalm 8:6–10	2258–2262, 2415–2418
	25. Review		Psalm 119:1–3	

A sixth unit in Grade 3 includes separate sessions for these seasons of the liturgical year: Advent, Christmas, Lent, Holy Week, Easter, Pentecost, and All Saints Day.

Catholic Social Teaching Themes	Words Learned	Saints and Holy People	Basic Prayers
Work and Workers, God's Creation	apostle, Apostles' Creed, creed	Saint Ignatius of Loyola	Apostles' Creed (first line)
Family and Community, The Poor and Vulnerable, Solidarity, Life and Dignity		Saint Elizabeth of Hungary	Sign of the Cross Glory Be to the Father
Solidarity, Life and Dignity, Family and Community	Abba		Lord's Prayer
Family and Community, Work and Workers	Scriptures, Son of God	Mary Saint Joseph	Apostles' Creed (lines 2 and 3)
The Poor and Vulnerable, Family and Community	Paschal Mystery		Apostles' Creed (lines 4–8)
God's Creation, Family and Community, Solidarity	Gospel, mission	Saint Peter	
The Poor and Vulnerable, Family and Community, Solidarity	conversion		
The Poor and Vulnerable, Solidarity	monastery	Saint Scholastica Saint Benedict	
Life and Dignity, Solidarity	witness	Saint Katharine Drexel	Prayer to the Holy Spirit
Family and Community, Solidarity	apostolic, Marks of the Church, Mystical Body of Christ, one, pastor, Vicar of Christ	Saint Peter Pope Blessed John XXIII	Apostles' Creed (last lines)
Life and Dignity	blessing, sacramental		
Life and Dignity	Annunciation, Communion of Saints, Rosary, Visitation	Mary	The Rosary
Family and Community	People of God	Saint Paul the Apostle Saint Philip	baptismal promises
Family and Community	personal sin		Act of Contrition
Family and Community, Solidarity	epistle, worship		
Work and Workers, Family and Community	Holy Orders, Matrimony, vocation	Saint Andrew Kim Taegon	
The Poor and Vulnerable, Family and Community, Solidarity	charity, hope, virtue	Saint Monica, Saint Augustine, Blessed Jeanne Jugan	
Life and Dignity	moral law		Morning Offering
Family and Community, The Poor and Vulnerable	justice	Saint Paul, Saint Vincent de Paul, Saint Louise de Marillac	
God's Creation, Life and Dignity, The Poor and Vulnerable, Solidarity, Rights and Responsibilities		Blessed Frederic Ozanam	

Scope and Sequence Grade 4

Unit	Session	Theme	Scripture	CCC References
Creator and Father **1**	1. God Creates the World	God's love for us is seen in his creation.	Sirach 39:33 Psalm 65:10,14	296–298
	2. Our Father in Heaven	Jesus tells us that God is our loving Father.	Matthew 7:9–11 John 14:7	120–127, 2779–2783
	3. God's Plan for Salvation	God responds to the sin of Adam and Eve with the promise of a savior.	Genesis 3 Genesis 3:15	410–412
	4. God Calls Us to Obey	God speaks to us through our conscience.	Galatians 5:22–23 Matthew 6:10	1783–1794
	5. Review		Psalm 139	
Son of God, Son of Mary **2**	6. Jesus' Law of Love	Jesus' law of love allows us to live peacefully with one another.	John 13:34 1 Corinthians 13:13	1822–1826, 1889, 2011, 2083, 2196
	7. The Beatitudes	The Beatitudes show us how we can be truly happy and share happiness with others.	Matthew 5:1–10 Psalm 73:1	1716–1719
	8. Jesus Our Redeemer	Jesus redeemed us from our sins through his life, death, and resurrection.	Luke 23:39–43 Acts 1:9–11; 4:12	571, 601, 669
	9. Jesus Sends the Spirit	Jesus shares his new life with us through the power of the Holy Spirit.	Acts 9:32–35 Isaiah 11:2	731–732, 737–741
	10. Review		1 Peter 4:11	
Community of Jesus **3**	11. The People of God	Through the Sacraments of Initiation, we are made members of the Church.	Matthew 28:19–20 Acts 1:8	751–752, 1140–1141
	12. The Church Teaches Us	Jesus calls the Church to continue his mission.	Acts 1:21–26 Acts 2:42	888–892, 2041–2043
	13. God Is Our Friend	Jesus calls us to forgiveness and reconciliation when we sin.	Luke 15:11–24 Isaiah 49:15	1440–1442, 1854–1863
	14. Serving God and Others	Jesus calls Christians to be his disciples.	Luke 1:26–38 John 19:26–27	484–507
	15. Review		Luke 15:7	
Meeting Jesus **4**	16. Celebrating Reconciliation	Through the Sacrament of Penance, we renew our relationships with God and others.	Luke 15:4–7 Isaiah 40:11	1422–1470
	17. The Sacrament of the Eucharist	Jesus is really present to us in the Sacrament of the Eucharist.	Mark 6:34–44 1 Corinthians 10:16	1322–1405, 1548–1553, 2174–2188
	18. Anointing of the Sick	We celebrate the healing presence of Jesus in the Sacrament of the Anointing of the Sick.	James 5:14–16 Matthew 11:4–5	1499–1525
	19. Sacraments of Service	Matrimony and Holy Orders are Sacraments at the Service of Communion.	John 15:1–15 John 15:12–13	1536–1589, 1601–1658
	20. Review		Mark 11:25	
Living Like Jesus **5**	21. The Ten Commandments	By using the Ten Commandments as a guide for our actions, we are able to make good moral decisions.	Exodus 19:1–20:17 Matthew 5:17	2052–2074
	22. Loving God Above All	The first three commandments teach us to love God above all.	Mark 12:29–33 Luke 4:8	2084–2195
	23. Loving Our Family	The fourth through sixth commandments teach us to live in good relationship with others.	Matthew 5:43–48 Exodus 20:12–14	2201–2233
	24. Jesus Calls Us to Love Others	To choose to follow God's commandments is to choose life.	Deuteronomy 30:15–20 Exodus 20:15–17	2401–2557
	25. Review		Mark 12:30–31	

A sixth unit in Grade 4 includes separate sessions for these seasons of the liturgical year: Advent, Christmas and Epiphany, Lent, Holy Week, Easter, Pentecost, and All Saints Day and All Souls Day.

Catholic Social Teaching Themes	Words Learned	Saints and Holy People	Basic Prayers
God's Creation	free will, psalm, soul	Saint Teresa of Ávila	
Solidarity, Family and Community, The Poor and Vulnerable	Theological Virtues		Act of Faith
God's Creation	salvation, temptation		Act of Hope
Rights and Responsibilities, Life and Dignity	prudence	Saint Peter Canisius	
The Poor and Vulnerable, Solidarity, Family and Community	fortitude, Torah	Saint John Baptiste Vianney, Saint Vincent de Paul	Act of Love
Rights and Responsibilities, Solidarity, Family and Community	Sermon on the Mount	Saint Francis of Assisi	Peace Prayer of Saint Francis
The Poor and Vulnerable	Ascension, Redeemer, redemption		Apostles' Creed
The Poor and Vulnerable, Life and Dignity, Solidarity	Corporal Works of Mercy, Spiritual Works of Mercy	Blessed Mother Teresa, Saint Peter	Holy Spirit Prayer of Saint Augustine
Rights and Responsibilities, Family and Community	universal Church	Saint Louis IX, Saint Dominic	
Work and Workers, Family and Community	diocese, Precepts of the Church		Morning Offering
Family and Community,	capital sins, envy, pride, sloth		
The Poor and Vulnerable, Solidarity, Work and Workers		Mary, Blessed Miguel Pro	Hail, Holy Queen (Salve Regina)
Life and Dignity	repentance	Saint Ignatius of Loyola	Act of Contrition
Family and Community		Saint Hildegard of Bingen	
Solidarity, Family and Community	Anointing of the Sick, oil of the sick, viaticum	Venerable Pierre Toussaint	
Solidarity, Family and Community		Mother Mary Elizabeth Lange	
Life and Dignity	covenant	Saint Francis Xavier, Moses	Prayer to the Holy Spirit
Family and Community	obedience	Saint Thomas More	Divine Praises
Family and Community, Solidarity	temperance	Moses	
Family and Community			

Scope and Sequence Grade 5

Unit	Session	Theme	Scripture	CCC References
Creator and Father 1	1. God Creates Us	God creates and upholds the world through the power of his Word.	Genesis 1:1–2 Hebrews 11:3	36–38, 257–260
	2. God Saves Us	From the beginning, we have been promised a savior to free us from original sin.	Romans 5:12 1 Corinthians 15:21	402–408, 410–411
	3. God's Revelation	God's covenant with Abraham finds its fulfillment in Christ.	Genesis 12:1–17:16 Exodus 3:6	59–63, 1961–1964
	4. God Directs Our Lives	As a sign to the world of God's goodness, Jesus calls us to live in his kingdom.	Matthew 18:1–5 Mark 10:15	1716–1717, 1813–1829, 1965–1970
	5. Review		Genesis 1:24–28	461–478
Son of God, Son of Mary 2	6. New Life in Jesus	Jesus sends the Spirit to give us new life.	Ephesians 2:19–22 Isaiah 28:16	461–478
	7. Meeting Jesus	A sacrament is a sign by which Jesus shares God's life—grace—with us.	Mark 5:21–24,35–43 John 2:11	1210–1666
	8. Baptized Into Christ	In Baptism we enter into life in Christ.	Acts 2:1–15,22–38 Joel 3:1	1213–1274
	9. Growing in the Spirit	Confirmation strengthens our relationship with Christ.	Acts 2:2–4 John 3:8	1285–1314
	10. Review		Romans 6:3–5	
Community of Jesus 3	11. The Church Is One	The unity of the faith is expressed in a variety of ways.	1 Corinthians 12:12–13 Galatians 3:28	813–822
	12. Called to Holy Orders	Through the sacrament of Holy Orders, men are called to exercise ministerial leadership in the Church.	Acts 1:15–26 Matthew 16:18	1536–1589
	13. The Domestic Church	Jesus calls husbands and wives to form a domestic church with their children.	Luke 2:42–52 Ruth 1:16	1601–1658
	14. God Calls Us	Jesus calls everyone to serve God and others, and Mary is the model of how to respond.	1 Corinthians 12:27–29 1 Samuel 3:10	2013–2014
	15. Review		Ephesians 4:1–7,11–13	
Meeting Jesus 4	16. The New Passover	The Eucharist is the central celebration of Christian life.	John 6:1–15,34–35 John 20:29	1322–1405
	17. Celebrating the Eucharist	In the liturgy, Jesus Christ is present in his Word, in the assembly, and especially in the Eucharist.	1 Corinthians 11:27–29 Matthew 5:23–24	1345–1355
	18. Celebrating Reconciliation	In the Sacrament of Penance, we celebrate God's forgiveness, receive absolution for our sins, and are reconciled with ourselves, God, and the Church.	John 20:19–23 Matthew 6:14	1422–1484
	19. Jesus Heals Us	In the Sacrament of Anointing of the Sick, we celebrate Jesus' healing power.	Acts 3:1–10 Mark 6:13	1499–1525
	20. Review		Luke 15:11–24	
Living Like Jesus 5	21. Making Moral Decisions	Jesus is the foundation of a moral life.	Matthew 7:24–27 Proverbs 10:25	1776–1802
	22. Living a Moral Life	Jesus helps us to act responsibly toward others.	James 3:3–8,17–18 Matthew 5:9	2464–2513
	23. Growing in Holiness	Jesus' life in us makes us temples of the Holy Spirit.	Leviticus 11:44 1 Corinthians 6:19–20	2331–2363
	24. The Way to Jesus	Jesus calls us to live with our Father in heaven.	Matthew 25:32–46 Matthew 16:27	1023–1041
	25. Review		Psalm 34:12–23	

A sixth unit in Grade 5 includes separate sessions for these seasons of the liturgical year: Advent, Christmas and Epiphany, Lent, Holy Week, Easter, Pentecost, and All Saints Day and All Souls Day.

Catholic Social Teaching Themes	Words Learned	Saints and Holy People	Basic Prayers
God's Creation, Family and Community		Saint Augustine, Blessed Julian of Norwich	Sign of the Cross
Family and Community, Solidarity, Life and Dignity		Saint Peter Claver, Blessed Josephine Bakhita	
Solidarity, Rights and Responsibilities, God's Creation	Hebrews, Islam, Jews, Judaism, Muslims, Revelation	Abraham and Sarah	Lord's Prayer
Family and Community, Solidarity		Saint Philip Neri	Morning Offering
Rights and Responsibilities	Advocate, counsel, fear of the Lord, fortitude, Gifts of the Holy Spirit, holiness, knowledge, piety, understanding, wisdom		Prayer to the Holy Spirit
Life and Dignity, Family and Community	chrism, oil of catechumens, stewardship	Saint Peter, Saint Francis Xavier	
The Poor and Vulnerable, Family and Community, Solidarity			
Family and Community, Solidarity	Incarnation, mystery, sanctifying grace	Saint Alphonsus Liguori, Pope Blessed John XXIII	Apostles' Creed
Life and Dignity, Solidarity	clergy, evangelization, laity, priesthood, religious life, Stations of the Cross, vow	Saint Ignatius of Loyola, Saint Paul, Saint Gregory the Great	Prayer of Saint Ignatius of Loyola
Work and Workers	character, deacon, ordination, Sacraments at the Service of Communion	Saint Turibius of Mogrovejo	
Family and Community	domestic church	Blessed Luigi Beltrame Quattrocchi, Blessed Maria Corsine Beltrame Quattrocchi	Prayer Before Meals, Prayer After Meals
Family and Community	Assumption	Saint Paul, Mary	
The Poor and Vulnerable, Family and Community	assembly, liturgical year, Passover	Saint Bernadette Soubirous	
Solidarity, The Poor and Vulnerable	memorial, Real Presence, transubstantiation	Saint Thomas Aquinas	Tantum Ergo
Family and Community	miracle, Sacraments of Healing		Act of Contrition
Family and Community, Life and Dignity			
The Poor and Vulnerable		Saint Isaac Jogues and Companions, Saint Francis of Assisi	
Life and Dignity, Rights and Responsibilities	detraction, slander		
Life and Dignity	chastity	Blessed Kateri Tekakwitha	
The Poor and Vulnerable, Family and Community, Rights and Responsibilities	hell, indulgence, purgatory		

Scope and Sequence Grade 6

Unit	Session	Theme	Scripture	CCC References
Creator and Father **1**	1. The Bible, God's Story	In the Bible, God reveals himself to us especially in the life, death, and resurrection of Jesus Christ.	2 Timothy 3:16–17 2 Peter 1:20–21	121–123, 128–130
	2. God Creates the World	The human family is created in the image and likeness of God.	Genesis 1:1–2:4 Psalm 8:5–7	282–289
	3. Sin and Salvation	The root of sin is lack of trust in God and disobedience to his commands.	Genesis 6:5–9:17 Genesis 3:15	402–411
	4. Abraham Listens to God	God calls Abraham and Sarah to believe in him.	Genesis 15:1–5; 18:1–10 Galatians 3:7	59, 72, 165, 762, 992, 1819, 2571
	5. Review			
Son of God, Son of Mary **2**	6. God Is Faithful	God helps people overcome sinful choices.	Genesis 25:19–34; 27:1–45 Matthew 22:31–32	207, 211, 302–314
	7. Passover and the Eucharist	Jesus calls us to the new covenant.	Exodus 2:11–3:16 John 6:53–54	1322–1405
	8. God Leads His People	Exodus describes the covenant between God and the Israelites.	Exodus 14:10–30 Deuteronomy 6:4–5	2056–2063
	9. Being Faithful to God	David and Ruth made choices that helped to prepare the way for Jesus.	2 Samuel 11:1–17, Ruth 1–4, Matthew 20:30	1731–1738
	10. Review		Psalm 107:1–9	
Community of Jesus **3**	11. God's Presence in the Temple	The Church is the new temple of the Holy Spirit.	1 Kings 6:1–18; 8:1–26 John 2:19,22	308, 1373–1377
	12. Psalms, the Prayers of Jesus	The psalms help us learn how to pray, and Wisdom Literature gives us practical advice on how to live.	Psalm 23:1–4 Sirach 18:11–12	2585–2589
	13. The Mission of the Church	The mission of the Church is to proclaim Jesus' presence today.	Acts 2:14–41 Matthew 5:16	783–786
	14. The Marks of the Church	The Church is one, holy, catholic, and apostolic.	Ephesians 4:1–6,15–16 Luke 1:49	811–865
	15. Review		1 Corinthians 12:12–20	
Meeting Jesus **4**	16. Prophets Challenge the People	The prophets who called the Chosen People to repentance and conversion were powerful witnesses to God.	Isaiah 6:1–8 Matthew 1:22–23	61, 64, 218
	17. Prophets Give Hope	The prophets bring words of hope and encouragement.	Isaiah 40:1–2 Matthew 5:17	128–130
	18. Baptism and Confirmation	In Baptism we are born into the family of Jesus, a bond that is strengthened in Confirmation.	Ephesians 2:21–22 1 Peter 2:4–5	1213–1314
	19. Sacraments of Healing	In celebrating the Sacraments of Penance and the Anointing of the Sick, we find the healing presence of God in our everyday lives.	Luke 9:1–6 John 15:12	1420–1525
	20. Review		Isaiah 43:1–3	
Living Like Jesus **5**	21. Jesus' Way of Love	Jesus calls us to practice the virtues of faith, hope, and charity.	1 Corinthians 13:1–13 Deuteronomy 6:4–5	1812–1829
	22. Sacraments of Service	In the Sacraments of Holy Orders and Matrimony, Christians are called to holiness.	Leviticus 11:44 1 Peter 1:15–16	1536–1666
	23. Caring for the Earth	All of creation is a gift from God, and the goods of the earth are to be used in ways that honor God.	Genesis 1:28–31 Psalm 96:11–13	339–343, 2415–2418
	24. Jesus' Call for Justice	As Christians we are called to support the common good and the fundamental rights of each person.	James 2:14–26 1 John 4:21	1868–1869, 1905–1917
	25. Review		Ephesians 4:1–7,11–13	

A sixth unit in Grade 6 includes separate sessions for these seasons of the liturgical year: Advent, Christmas, Lent, Holy Week, Easter and Ascension, Pentecost, and All Saints Day and All Souls Day.

Catholic Social Teaching Themes · Words Learned · Saints and Holy People · Basic Prayers

Catholic Social Teaching Themes	Words Learned	Saints and Holy People	Basic Prayers
Family and Community	inspired, interpretation, Magisterium, scriptorium, Vulgate	Saint Jerome Saint Timothy	Prayer to the Holy Spirit
God's Creation, Solidarity, The Poor and Vulnerable, Life and Dignity	culture, exile, racism, sexism	Saint Frances Xavier Cabrini	
Life and Dignity			Hail Mary
Life and Dignity	Chosen People	Sarah and Abraham	Act of Hope
Solidarity		David Ruth	Psalm 51
Rights and Responsibilities	Exodus	Moses	
Solidarity		Moses	Psalm 23
Rights and Responsibilities, Family and Community	Divine Providence	Saint John Neumann Jacob	Morning Offering
Solidarity	Eastern Catholic Churches, Eucharistic liturgy; Israelite, Sabbath, Yahweh	Saint Helena Saint Roque Gonzalez	
Work and Workers	communal prayer, Liturgy of the Hours, personal prayer, Wisdom Literature		
Family and Community, Solidarity, Life and Dignity	Ark of the Covenant, discrimination, Holy of Holies, sacrifice	Saint Paul Mary	Nicene Creed
Solidarity			Lord's Prayer
Solidarity	Nicene Creed		
The Poor and Vulnerable, Rights and Responsibilities, Solidarity	prophet, reform, seraphim	Saint Ignatius of Loyola Amos, Jeremiah, Isaiah	Psalm 20
Life and Dignity			Prayer of Saint Richard of Chichester Act of Contrition
Family and Community	catechumen, Easter Vigil		
The Poor and Vulnerable, Family and Community	Promised Land	Saint Benedict of Palermo Saint Thérèse of Lisieux	Psalm 143:1–6
The Poor and Vulnerable	canonize, Doctor of the Church, eternal life	Saint Paul of the Cross	Act of Faith
Family and Community	presbyter		Act of Love
God's Creation, Solidarity	encyclical, solidarity		
Life and Dignity, Family and Community, Rights and Responsibilities	natural law	Saint Patrick	The Magnificat

FindingGod

Our response to God's gifts

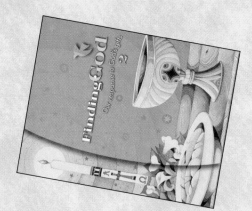

God's Invitation, Our Response

Each session of every *Finding God: Our Response to God's Gifts* Children's Book creates an environment in which children can recognize God's gifts, encouraging a response that arises from a deep sense of gratitude. Extraordinary fine art, folk art, illustrations, and photographs were sought out and selected to represent the rich diversity of the Church, to connect children to our Catholic identity, to articulate our Catholic heritage, and to develop Catholic literacy. All Children's Books follow the same organizational structure:

The Opening Prayer

A prayer as children open their books helps establish a prayerful climate for guiding children to a personal relationship with God.

Inside a Unit

Each unit begins with the story of a saint and explores one of five overarching program themes: God, Jesus, the Church, the Sacraments, and Morality in four sessions and a Unit Review.

Each unit features a saint whose response to God's love relates to the unit theme.

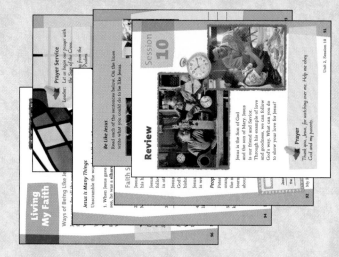

Sessions engage children in deepening their understanding of the Catholic faith as they explore, reflect on, and respond to God's invitation.

The Unit Review provides a faith summary, a prayer service, and multiple opportunities for children to review and discuss what they have learned.

Inside Every Session

Each of the 20 core sessions is covered over a five-day week. The five unit review sessions are covered over a four-day week. The sessions engage children by starting from typical moments in their own lives and inviting them to join in prayer. As children explore Scripture and Tradition, they discuss their faith and deepen their relationship with God in reflective prayer. Each session ends with a discussion of how to act upon what they have learned, and closes with a prayer of gratitude for God's gifts.

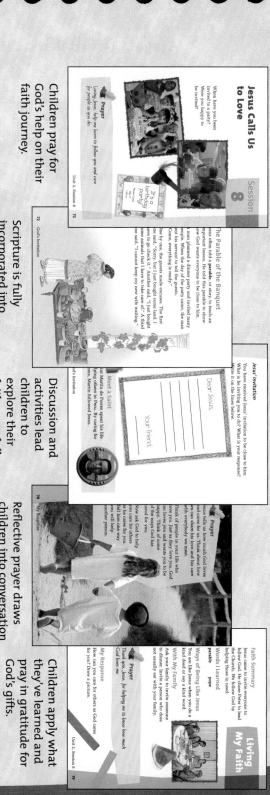

Children pray for God's help on their faith journey.

Scripture is fully incorporated into each session.

Discussion and activities lead children to explore their faith more fully.

Reflective prayer draws children into conversation with God.

Children apply what they've learned and pray in gratitude for God's gifts.

The Year in Our Church

Seven additional sessions highlight seasons and feasts of the liturgical year.

Prayers and Practices of Our Faith

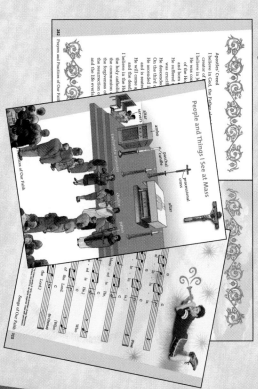

A final section serves as an age-appropriate reference to Catholic Prayers, Traditions, Beliefs, and Music, and also includes an extensive Glossary (English and Spanish).

Special Features in Every Children's Book

 Reading God's Word

 Link To Liturgy

 Did You Know?

 Meet a Saint/ Meet a Holy Person

 Sacred Site

Inside This Catechist Guide

Finding God

Our response to God's gifts

Catechist Preparation

Each Catechist Guide offers support for new and experienced catechists as they use *Finding God: Our Response to God's Gifts* with children.

The Effective Catechist

Pages EC1–EC24 of this Catechist Guide explore the role of a catechist as a mentor to children as they learn more about their faith and grow in a prayerful, personal relationship with God. Hints and suggestions throughout this section show us the ways an effective catechist might use *Finding God: Our Response to God's Gifts*.

Unit Preparation

Each of the five units begins with a two-page overview that identifies the focus of the unit and shows how the sessions are connected.

Description of the unit saint

Focus of the unit

Description of the sessions

Prayer opportunities in the unit

Catholic Social Teaching themes in the unit

Session Preparation

Each session begins with four pages to help you prepare. The first page is a 3-Minute Retreat that invites you to reflect prayerfully in preparation for the session.

The next two pages provide background information on Scripture and Tradition.

A brief description of the Scripture and Tradition that serve as the basis of the content

The Scripture passages in this session

References to the Catechism of the Catholic Church (CCC)

One or two questions for reflection

A short Scripture reading

A brief reflection on the Scripture reading

A prayer

A quotation from the documentary tradition of the Church

References to the General Directory for Catechesis (GDC)

An outline of the themes of Catholic Social Teaching

A description of the prayer or prayers in the session

Session title and theme

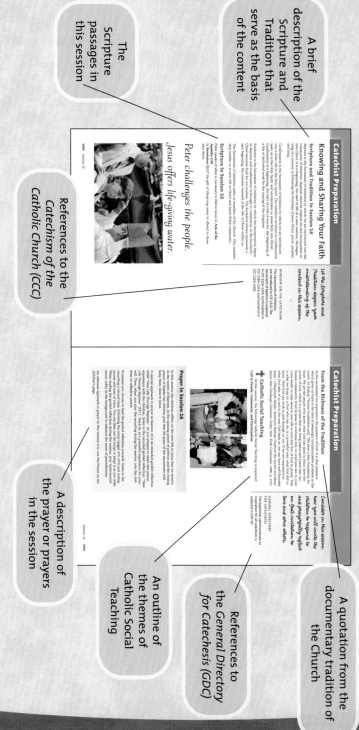

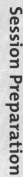

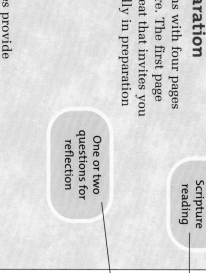

Get-Ready Guide

The fourth page of Catechist Preparation is a Get-Ready Guide.

An outline of the session content with outcomes for each step of the catechetical process

Suggested action to take before the session

A list of required and optional materials

Online resources

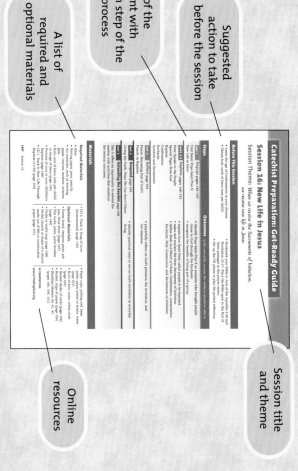

Step-by-Step Through a Session: A Four-Step Catechetical Process

Faith formation is most effective when the concepts being presented connect with the life of the learner. The catechetical process is a four-step process that helps make the connection between the life of the child and the teachings of the Catholic Church. In *Finding God: Our Response to God's Gifts* these four steps are Engage, Explore, Reflect, and Respond.

Each session of *Finding God: Our Response to God's Gifts* incorporates the following four steps that lead us and the children, under the guidance of the Holy Spirit, to an increased awareness of God's invitation to love him and one another.

Four-Step Process

God's Invitation

Explore

This step explores the teachings of the Church through Scripture, stories, and activities.

Days 1–3

Reflect

To help children internalize what they are learning, this step allows them to reflect prayerfully on God's invitation and their response.

Day 4

Respond

After reflection the children identify how they can respond to God's invitation as they live each day.

Day 4

Engage

This introductory step engages children in discussion or activities that relate the session theme to their lives.

Day 1

Our Response

Extending the Session

This page offers suggestions for additional activities and parent involvement.

Day 5

Step One: Engage

The Engage step is an opportunity to open the session by engaging the attention of the children. This step serves as a way to provide the children with a transition into this special time.

Engaging photographs to stimulate conversation

An activity or question inviting the children into conversation about an aspect of their lives that is connected to the theme of the session

Opening prayer of petition

Celebrating the Eucharist

Begin this session with the following activity. Bring a bowl of individually-wrapped candies. Pass around the bowl. Be sure none of the children are allergic to the candy. Say: *Please take one piece of candy. Sharing is one way that we show our love for others. We can share our time, possessions, and good will with others in our lives.*

Have the children open their books to page 177. Draw attention to the

photographs. Have the children describe what they see. (a father and son skiing, girls enjoying ice cream) Say: *Sharing and doing things with other people help bring people closer together. Sharing is also important at Mass. When we gather together as a parish community and when we celebrate the Liturgy of the Eucharist at Mass, we are sharing our faith with others.*

Read the title. Then read the questions, one at a time. Encourage volunteers to respond to the questions as they are asked.

Session 19

Celebrating the Eucharist

Have you ever given something to a friend? Have you shared something special with a relative? How did giving and sharing bring you closer to them?

Prayer

Jesus, my Savior, help me share your love with others.

Unit 4, Session 19 **177**

Prayer

Say: *Jesus loves everyone. He wants to share that love with all of us! Let's pray to him and ask his help as we learn how to share love. Together let's pray this prayer of petition. Then take a few moments to say whatever you would like to Jesus.*

Pray the prayer aloud. Then count to 10 silently, as you allow the children an opportunity to talk to Jesus. End the quiet time by praying *Amen.*

OPTION

POSTCARDS FOR PARISHIONERS

Remind the children: *When we reach out to others, we are acting like Jesus. There are members of the parish who are ill or homebound who would appreciate a greeting from us.*

Distribute a postcard to each child. Invite each of them to write a message of cheer for someone in the parish. Ask the children to use the heading "Dear Friend." Write on the board examples of what they could say in their notes. (We are praying for you. We hope you feel better soon. God loves you.) When the children have completed their work, collect the postcards. Give the cards to whomever is in charge of the parish ministry to the sick. Let the group know the cards will be sent to ill or homebound parishioners.

✝ *Family and Community*

Session 19 **177**

Step Two: Explore

In the Explore step the content of the session is presented in the context of a story or Scripture passage, the life of a saint or a holy person, or an aspect of the richness of Catholic tradition.

Comments on the features relating them to the focus of the session

Optional activities suggesting ways to adapt the session to the time available and offering a variety of approaches

Step-by-step instructions and suggestions for helping the children access the content in a variety of ways

Icons highlighting special features

✝ Catholic Social Teaching

🎵 Music CD

📖 Scripture passage

💿 Spoken Word CD

DAY 1
Explore

The Last Supper

Remind the children that previously they learned about the first part of the Mass, the Liturgy of the Word. Say: *Today we will continue learning about the Mass in our discussion of the Liturgy of the Eucharist.*

Read the title aloud. Ask the children: *Who has heard of the Last Supper? What do you know about it?* Allow the children to respond. Then explain: *The Last Supper was the last meal Jesus ate with his friends. They shared this meal the night before Jesus' death. It was a very special time Jesus shared with his friends.* Continue: *The story of the Last Supper is a very beautiful and meaningful one to Christians.*

Read the story aloud to the children. When you are finished, say: *Jesus actually broke the bread apart and shared it with everyone. When Jesus said "This is my body" and "This is my blood," he meant that he is giving himself to those who follow him. This is a very special gift.*

Have the children turn to the song "We Come to Your Table" in the Songs of Our Faith section in the back of their book. Play the song on Track 17 of CD 2 and have the children listen. Then play the song again, encouraging the children to sing along when they are comfortable. Finally, sing the song one last time, inviting the group to sing the entire song.

178 Session 19

Reading God's Word

Read the verse aloud. Then do a choral reading, dividing the verse into two parts. Have the girls say: *Jesus sacrificed himself for our sins.* Have the boys say: *He is with God forever.*

Point out the icon in the upper left-hand corner of the box and ask the children what it is. Explain that they may have noticed that whenever they see this icon, they know that something from the Bible is going to be read.

OPTION

LAST SUPPER PLACEMATS

Say: *Meals are special times we share with our families and others we care about, just as Jesus shared the Last Supper with his followers.* Have the children create placemats they can use at home. On construction paper, have the children draw their favorite foods and the people who are special to them. When they have finished, collect their work. Laminate the placemats, if convenient, before returning them to the children.

The Last Supper

Jesus sat at the table with his disciples. He said, "I want to share this supper with you."

Then Jesus took the bread. He blessed it and broke it. He gave it to them and said, "This is my body, which will be given for you. Do this in memory of me."

After the meal he took a cup of wine. He said, "This is my blood. It is given for you."

adapted from Luke 22:14–20

Reading God's Word

Jesus sacrificed himself for our sins. He is with God forever.

adapted from Hebrews 10:12

178 God's Invitation

Discussion questions (with possible responses) and activities to further engage the children

Explore

DAY 1

Liturgy of the Eucharist

Ask a volunteer to read the title and first paragraph for the children. Draw attention to the term *Liturgy of the Eucharist.* Say: *This is the next part of the Mass. In this part of the Mass, the bread and wine are presented, blessed, and become the Body and Blood of Christ. We receive the Body and Blood of Christ in Holy Communion.* This might be a good time to remind the children of the additional information in the section Order of the Mass at the back of their books.

Then point out the word *altar.* Encourage the children to look it up in the Glossary. Say: *The altar is the table where the bread and wine are offered to God and become the Body and Blood of Christ.* Draw attention to the photo at the top. Ask: *What is the family doing?* (presenting the gifts of bread and wine to the priest)

Read the second paragraph for the group. Ask the children if they remember the meaning of *consecration.* (the making of a thing or person special to God through prayer) Point out the illustration at the bottom. Say: *The bread and wine presented as gifts are consecrated and are received as Holy Communion.* Direct the children's attention to the We Celebrate the Mass (Part II) poster and point out the parts of the Communion rite, which include the Lord's Prayer and the sign of peace.

Then invite a child to read the third paragraph. Ask: *What two things are we supposed to do when we leave Mass?* (do good deeds and praise God for his goodness) Then call attention to the poster again. Point out the concluding rite, which includes the blessing and dismissal.

Did You Know

Read the last sentence aloud. Ask the children: *What do we do to celebrate the Lord's Day?* (celebrate Mass)

As your time together comes to an end, pray the Glory Be to the Father with the children. Remind them that the Mass gives glory to God. Then ask: *What will you do this Sunday to celebrate the Lord's Day? Talk about this with your family.*

Liturgy of the Eucharist

Suki and her family go to Mass together every Sunday. Last week as the **Liturgy of the Eucharist** began, they brought the gifts of bread and wine to the priest at the **altar.** Suki and her family listened as the priest asked God to accept and bless the gifts.

During the **consecration** the priest repeated the words of Jesus at the Last Supper. The bread and wine became the Body and Blood of Christ. The priest invited everyone to pray the Lord's Prayer and to share a sign of peace. Soon it was time to receive Holy Communion.

When the Liturgy of the Eucharist was over, the priest blessed everyone with the Sign of the Cross. He told them to do good works and to praise God for his goodness to them.

Did You Know?
Sunday is special because it is the Lord's day.

Unit 4, Session 19 **179**

OPTION

"WE CAN SERVE" SONG
Teach the children the song "We Can Serve," which is sung to the tune of "London Bridge Is Falling Down."

We can serve as Jesus served,
Jesus served, Jesus served,
We can serve as Jesus served,
We serve others!

OPTION

BLM 49: SHARING JESUS' LOVE
Blackline Master 49 asks children to create a book that shows how they can share Jesus' love.

Session 19 **179**

Option: Blackline Master
Suggestions for an appropriate time to use a Blackline Master found at the back of this Catechist Guide

Option
Suggestions for additional activities to extend the session

FYI
Additional background information related to the session provided where appropriate

Inside This Catechist Guide

Day 4

Step Three: Reflect

The Reflect step provides the opportunity for children to become more aware of God's presence in their lives. The reflective prayer presented in this step is more than just words; it is time spent forming a relationship with God. See pages EC6–EC9. The Reflect step always relates to the focus of the session and invites the children to internalize the concepts presented in the Explore step.

This step uses various forms of prayer: traditional prayers that are often taken to heart (memorized), psalms, saints' prayers, songs, or guided reflections that encourage children to talk and listen thoughtfully to God.

The side notes help to create a prayerful atmosphere, to create and use a prayer center, and to guide the children in reflective prayer.

The Review session in each unit includes a Prayer Service that invites the children to communal prayer.

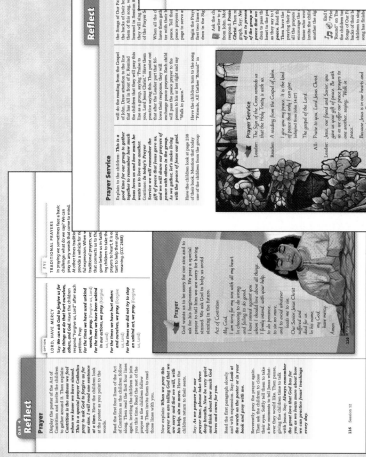

Traditional prayers, such as the Lord's Prayer, are often taken to heart (memorized).

Prayer Services engage the children in structured communal prayer, an essential part of our liturgical tradition.

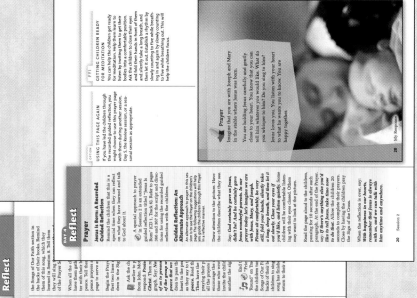

Guided reflections lead children into sacred time and space so they can talk and listen to God.

Step Four: Respond

The Respond step encourages children to demonstrate how the concepts learned in the session can make a difference in the way they live as they respond to God's invitation to love him and each other in their daily lives.

Faith Summary
A brief statement recapping the main content of the session

Words I Learned
An opportunity to review new words introduced in the session

Three features that invite the children to consider how they can apply what they learned to their lives

Living My Faith

Use the following activities to teach the children how to practice in their daily lives the concepts learned in this session. Have the children respond to each section as it occurs.

Faith Summary
Read the section aloud for the group. Ask the children: **What did Jesus do with the bread during the Last Supper?** (blessed it and broke it) **On what days are we to celebrate Mass?** (Sundays and Holy Days of Obligation) **Why do we attend Mass on Sunday?**

(because Sunday is the day Jesus rose from the dead)

Words I Learned
Call on volunteers to define each word. Have volunteers look the words up in the Glossary to double-check the definitions offered. Choose other volunteers to use the words in sentences.

Ways of Being Like Jesus
Ask: **What is the girl in the picture doing?** (pulling the little boy in the wagon) **Why?** (to help) **What are some of the ways you can help others?** (play with baby

sibling so mom will have time for other things) Read the section and say: **When one person helps another, that person is being like Jesus.**

✝ Family and Community

With My Family
Read the section. Ask the children: **What types of things could you give up so you would have time to help others?** (video games, TV, playing with friends)

✝ Family and Community

Living My Faith

Faith Summary
The Mass is the most important way Catholics pray.

Words I Learned
altar   Holy Days of Obligation

Liturgy of the Eucharist

Ways of Being Like Jesus
You are like Jesus when you give of yourself to help others.

With My Family
Give up one hour of your free time this week to help someone in your family.

Prayer
Thank you, Jesus, for giving yourself to me. Place in my heart a great love for the Eucharist.

My Response
Write a sentence telling how you can become closer to members of your parish.

Living My Faith

Unit 4, Session 19   **185**

Respond

DAY 4

Prayer
Say: **Now let's thank Jesus for giving himself to us. Please fold your hands and pray with me.** Then take a few moments to share with **God what is in your heart.**

Pray the prayer aloud. Then take two or three deep breaths as you give the children time to reflect. Conclude by praying the Sign of the Cross.

My Response
Read each section. Say: **When we are close to members of our parish, we become closer to Jesus because we are his followers and we are baptized members of God's family, the Church. Think about what you can do to become closer to the other members of your parish.** Then write a sentence about it. Some suggestions include: Greet them as you enter; Share the sign of peace with them; or Wish them a good day as you leave.

As you end this time together, say: **Let us be more like Jesus each day by helping whenever and wherever we are needed.**

Session 19   **185**

Prayer
Possible responses to the review questions to help you assess children's understanding of the concepts presented

Prayer
A closing prayer of gratitude

Extending the Session

The last page offers you some tips for providing closure to the session.

Preparation for Sunday Scripture Readings
Lead the children in a prayerful discussion of Sunday's Scripture readings. Visit www.FindingGod.org/Sunday for more information.

Seasonal Session
Consider the time of the liturgical year and use the appropriate seasonal session.

Unused Options and BLMs
Incorporate any unused options or Blackline Masters from the week's session.

Web Site Activities
Visit www.FindingGod.org to find additional activities for extending the session.

Additional Options
Choose from additional options provided on this page to extend the session or to reinforce concepts developed during the week.

DAY 5

Extending the Session

Choose from the following options to extend the session or to reinforce concepts developed during the week.

Family Involvement
Remind the children to take home the Raising Faith-Filled Kids page to share what they are learning with their families.

Preparation for Sunday Scripture Readings
Lead children in a prayerful discussion of Sunday's readings. Visit www.FindingGod.org/Sunday for more information.

Seasonal Session
Consider the time of the liturgical year and use the appropriate seasonal session. Seasonal sessions may be found on page 241.

Unused Options and BLMs
Incorporate any unused options or Blackline Masters from the week's session.

Web Site Activities
Visit www.FindingGod.org to find additional activities for extending the session.

OPTION

MY OWN MASS POSTER
Redistribute the My Own Mass posters from session 18. Invite the children to complete their posters using the bottom half of the paper. They can use the We Celebrate the Mass (Part II) poster displayed in the room as a guide in completing their own posters. Encourage creativity. When they are finished, invite the children to take their posters home and share what they have learned about the Mass with their families.

186 Session 19

OPTION

CLAY PLAYS
Form pairs of children. Have each pair work together to make the following out of clay: a table with bread and wine, Jesus, and several disciples. Have pairs reenact the Last Supper using the clay figures. Pairs can meet with other pairs to share their reenactments.

OPTION

EUCHARIST SCRAMBLE
Write each letter of the word *Eucharist* on different pieces of large construction paper. If you have a large class, consider making several sets and dividing the children into groups. Place the letters on the ground in random order. At a signal, have the children work together to place the letters in order to make a word. Give children clues as they go, such as *This is the sacrament we studied this week*, or *The part of the Mass where the priest repeats the words of Jesus at the Last Supper*. When the children unscramble the word, have them read it aloud. Invite volunteers to use the word in a sentence.

RAISING FAITH-FILLED KIDS
a parent page

Focus on Faith

The Eucharist, Our Home
He was a soldier overseas. On Sunday morning he went to the nearest Catholic church. The Mass was prayed in a language he did not understand, but the ritual was the same as at home. When he received Holy Communion, the soldier reflected on the parish community that had nurtured him. He realized that Jesus Christ is present in the same manner everywhere. As we go to Mass with our children we remember that we are celebrating with Catholics around the world.

Dinnertime Conversation Starter
Imagine that you and your family are attending Mass in a country where an unfamiliar language is spoken. What clues could you find in the church or in the celebration of the Mass that would indicate that it is Catholic?

Hints for at Home
Create a Jesus Sacrificed Himself for Us cross for your family. You will need poster board, scissors, photographs of your immediate and extended family, and glue. Draw a cross on the poster board and cut it out. Then invite your child to create a collage on the cross by cutting and attaching the photographs to fit. Display your completed cross in a prominent place.

Spirituality in Action
Be a role model for your child. Receive Holy Communion each time you are at Mass. Help your child understand that Jesus is present with us in many ways, especially in the Eucharist. In Holy Communion we receive the Body and Blood of Jesus Christ under the appearance of bread and wine.

Focus on Prayer
Your child is learning about the Liturgy of the Eucharist in Mass. The next time you are at Mass, guide your child to be attentive during this part of the liturgy. Call to your child's attention the offertory gifts, the Lord's Prayer, and the consecration.

186 www.FindingGod.org

Review Sessions

Each unit ends with a six-page Review session that summarizes the content of the unit and includes a Prayer Service.

1. As with the core sessions, each Review session begins with an engaging opening activity.

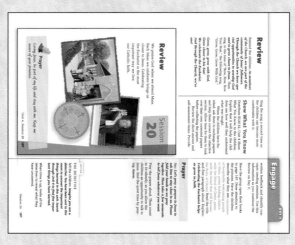

2. The Faith Summary page reviews the content of the entire unit.

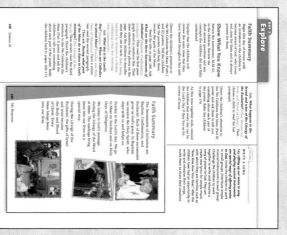

3. Additional activities, Options, and FYI features add flexibility and depth to the Explore step of the Review session.

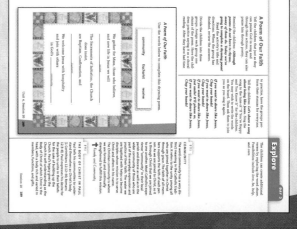

4. A variety of review activities enables you to reinforce and assess children's understanding of the key content as stated in the outcomes on the Get-Ready Guide.

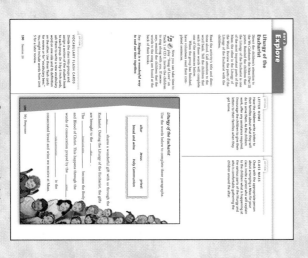

5. A Prayer Service provides an opportunity for communal prayer focused on the theme of the unit.

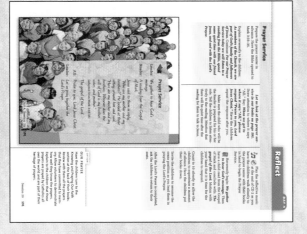

6. A variety of activities on the Living My Faith page helps you assess the children's understanding as they apply what they've learned to their lives.

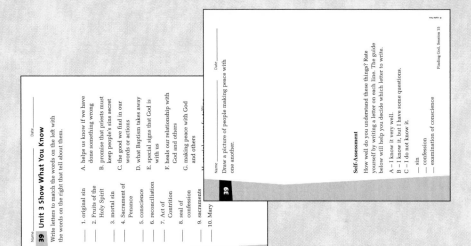

Assessment

As a Catholic school catechist, you seek to assess the formation that is taking place in the children and to offer feedback leading to further growth.

Because children learn in a variety of ways, a variety of forms of assessment is needed. In *Finding God: Our Response to God's Gifts* assessment takes the following forms:

Formal Assessment

A formal assessment asks the question *What do you know/understand?* A formal written assessment (quiz) is included within each unit's Review session (as a Blackline Master). The quiz items are consistent with the learning outcome statements in the Get-Ready Guide. This quiz also provides an opportunity for children to do a self-assessment.

Formal assessment provides you with an opportunity to identify which concepts need reinforcement, to affirm for children what they have learned, and to identify where specific assistance is needed.

Assessment of faith formation differs from assessment done in academic subject areas. In social studies, math, or science. In academic subject areas, knowledge and skills pertaining to the subject matter are assessed and used as a basis for determining a grade. In faith formation, assessment is used to discern growth into a way of life, namely discipleship. The assessment of knowledge in faith formation is part of the larger assessment of the child's formation into a life of liturgy, morality, prayer, and missionary activity.

Informal Assessment

Informal assessment asks the questions *What can you do with what you know, and how do you do it?* In *Finding God: Our Response to God's Gifts* this takes the shape of the following:

Ongoing Assessment—Each session offers many opportunities to assess children's grasp of concepts by observing their participation in discussions, group work, and their service to and care for others.

Specific Tasks—Many opportunities to evaluate verbal (oral and written) and nonverbal (drawn, crafted, etc.) expressions and responses are incorporated throughout the program.

The Year in Our Church

The Church celebrates the cycle of seasons and feasts that invites us, year after year, to deepen our faith commitment. Inviting children into these celebrations helps them grow in the Catholic way of life.

Each four-page seasonal session uses the same four-step catechetical process:

Engage
Explore
Reflect
Respond

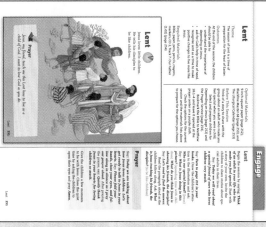

A Blackline Master of the Liturgical Calendar allows children to mark the seasons of the year in our Church.

Sessions focus on these seasons and feasts:

- Advent
- Christmas/Epiphany
- Lent
- Holy Week
- Easter
- Pentecost
- All Saints Day

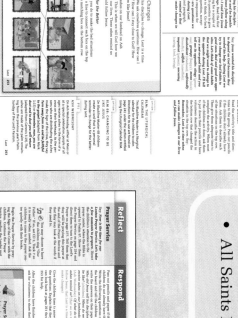

Seasonal sessions can be incorporated into your schedule at the appropriate times. You can use each session either alone, as part of another session, or as a Day 5 activity.

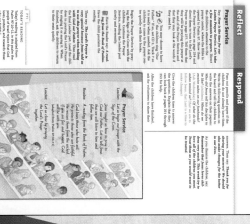

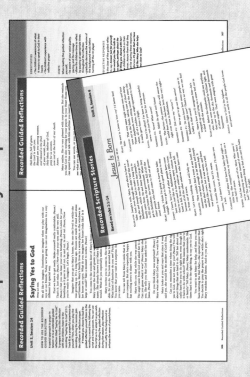

Prayers and Practices of Our Faith

The section at the back of the Children's Book contains a wealth of information.

Knowing and Praying Our Faith

Traditional prayers and ways of praying

Celebrating Our Faith

Liturgy and the sacraments

Living Our Faith

Catholic beliefs and practices

Songs of Our Faith

Lyrics and music for songs on the Music CD

Understanding the Words of Our Faith

Glossaries in English and Spanish

Catechist Resources

In addition to the prayers and practices in the Children's Book, the Catechist Guide contains the Blackline Masters, the scripts for the Audio Scripture Stories, and the Recorded Reflection Scripts.

Recorded Guided Reflection and Scripture Story Scripts

The Effective
Catechist

Go and Make Disciples

Jesus said these words to his disciples: "Go, therefore, and make disciples of all nations, baptizing them in the name of the Father, and of the Son, and of the Holy Spirit, teaching them to observe all that I have commanded you. And behold, I am with you always, until the end of the age." (Matthew 28:19–20) That call has remained alive throughout history. The church responds to that call today through our bishops, our pastors, and ourselves as people of faith.

What Is Catechesis?

Catechesis (from the Greek word meaning "to *echo* the teaching") is the Church's ministry of teaching and forming people in faith. True catechesis is the *process* of nurturing the Catholic faith and creating an environment in which faith can flourish. Each of us nurtures the Catholic faith simply by being a living example of faith.

Vocation of a Catechist

Finding God: Our Response to God's Gifts uses the term *catechist* to refer to those who serve in the parish religious education program as well as those who serve as teachers of religion in Catholic schools. As a Catholic school teacher, you are responsible for teaching a variety of subjects throughout the day. Faith formation, however, is more than a subject to be taught—it is an invitation to a way of life. *Finding God: Our Response to God's Gifts* recognizes and affirms that teachers of religion in Catholic schools are indeed *catechists*, called to form disciples of Jesus.

Our vocation as catechists opens us to grow in our own faith. Knowing that God is with us always, we freely accept the responsibility of mentoring others to find a deeper, more personal relationship with God.

As catechists, we assist pastors and bishops in guiding people to a living faith. We follow God's call to be disciples of Jesus and to proclaim his Good News through our words and actions. We grow in a deeper understanding of our faith and explore what it means to live as Catholics. We share in the community of the Church more fully by sharing with others what we know as people of faith. This School Catechist Guide is your companion on this mission. It will help you to grow in your own faith and to understand the hope that Jesus' message brings to the world. It will be your guide to help you effectively pass on the Catholic faith to others.

*"And behold,
I am with you always."*
Matthew 28:20

*"Knowing that God is
with us always, we freely
accept the responsibility of
mentoring others to find a
deeper, more personal
relationship with God."*

The Effective Catechist

A Catechist's Role

As catechists, we are a community of more than one million people in the United States who are dedicated to sharing the Good News of Jesus Christ. We work with adults, families, and children, passing on a lived faith one person at a time. We pray for grace in this mission. Sometimes it is the very children we are guiding who teach us through their examples of faith and love. We wonder at times what qualifies us to be catechists. We pray that we might be effective as we answer this call.

Qualities of an Effective Catechist

As catechists, we long to share the truth and beauty of our faith, yet, especially at first, we worry over our human limitations. As we grow as catechists, we realize that this combination of faith and humanity shared honestly makes our work personal and authentic. Each catechist shares faith in a very personal way. Effective catechists have these qualities in common:

† a desire to grow in and share our faith

† an awareness of God's grace and the desire to respond to that grace

† a commitment to the Church's liturgical and sacramental life and moral teachings

† a strength of character built on patience, responsibility, confidence, and creativity

† a generosity of spirit, respect for diversity, and a habit of hospitality and inclusion

Knowledge and Skills of a Catechist

Nothing in life prepares us to be catechists as fully as our life experience as faith-filled adults. As catechists, we yearn for the knowledge and skills that will help us gently nurture children to cultivate a lifelong relationship with God. We ground our efforts as catechists in these fundamentals:

† a basic understanding of Catholic teaching, Scripture, and Catholic Tradition

† honest and caring relationships with children

† effective teaching techniques and strategies

Finding God: Our Response to God's Gifts offers background and preparation in Church teaching, Scripture and Tradition, prayerful reflection, and session presentation support within each Catechist guide.

"As catechists, we yearn for the knowledge and skills that will help us gently nurture children to cultivate a lifelong relationship with God."

"Sometimes it is the very children we are guiding who teach us through their examples of faith and love."

The Work of a Catechist

Within a parish many roles join together to nurture a community gathered in lifelong faith formation. Pastors, principals, and religious education directors guide and support catechesis throughout the parish. Parents guide and support their children's faith formation. Our role as catechists is to join with pastors, principals, religious education directors, and parents in serving the faith formation of the children.

As catechists, we share our faith with children and accompany them on their faith journey. We care for children and support them as they grow in their own personal relationship with God and the Catholic Church. We guide children in their faith formation by teaching the truths of the Catholic faith, by being a model of Christian life, by praying with them, by calling them to service of others, and by giving them opportunities to discuss their learning with us and each other.

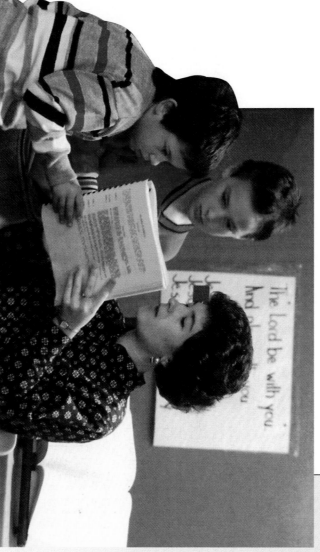

"Our role as catechists is to join with pastors, principals, religious education directors, and parents in serving the faith formation of the children."

"We care for children and support them as they grow in their own personal relationship with God and the Catholic Church."

Serving as a Catechist

The call to catechesis is an invitation to serve. True catechesis is based in mutually revealing relationships: our relationships with God, with others, and with all of creation. Our service is a response to God's invitation:

† to deepen our own individual and personal relationships with God

† to continue learning and growing as a person of faith

† to contribute to the faith formation of others

† to support pastors, principals, and religious education directors as they guide and support us

† to recognize and be grateful for all of God's gifts

To support catechists in this role, *Finding God: Our Response to God's Gifts* provides pastors, principals, and religious education directors with defined opportunities for training and faith formation to aid our growth as catechists, parents, and Catholics.

The Effective Catechist

> *"It takes the whole parish to form a living faith community—one person at a time."*

> *"Concretely, the community becomes a visible place of faith-witness. . . . It constitutes itself as the living and permanent environment for growth in the faith."*
>
> GDC 158

The Parish as a Faith Community

A famous African proverb says that "it takes a village to raise a child." For Catholics that village is the parish community. To rephrase the proverb, it takes a parish to form the faith of a child. To place the proverb in context, we might say that it takes the whole parish to form a living faith community—one person at a time.

The *General Directory for Catechesis* calls for the parish community to be "the living and permanent environment for growth in the faith." *(GDC 158)* As catechists, we work with the parish staff and each other to bring catechesis to the center of the parish faith community by invitation and example. Together we plan experiences and opportunities to involve the parish community in the catechetical process.

How to Support the Parish as a Faith Community

Put Faith Into Action

Work with your principal to select activities and service opportunities in which children, families, and adults can participate together.

Invite and Extend Support to Others

Encourage children to extend support and express care for others. Involve the children in activities such as designing and sending cards to parishioners—both adults and other children—who are sick or housebound. Encourage children to acknowledge others who are celebrating milestones in their lives. Invite parishioners to pray for and to honor the efforts of children of the parish.

Invite Parish Participation

Plan with your principal to invite and involve parishioners and parish staff members to serve as guest speakers and interviewees on topics and themes related to what the children are learning.

Think Public Relations

Publicize the parish work the children are doing. Work with your director and catechetical team to select appropriate ways to display children's work, post photographs of their activities, and include announcements in the parish bulletin about special events.

Connect to Parish Worship

Expand upon the Link to Liturgy feature and the seasonal sessions in the children's book to help lead the children to greater participation in the liturgical life of the parish. Keep the children and their families informed of the parish liturgical schedule.

Finding God: Our Response to God's Gifts provides many opportunities for involving the parish community in the catechetical process.

The Family as the Domestic Church

As catechists, we recognize and honor the role of the family in children's faith formation.

Since the early days of the Church, the family home has been considered a holy place. The home offers children the first proclamation of the faith and helps them learn human virtues, a life of prayer, and Christian charity. The Catholic Church reinforces this image by referring to the home as "the domestic church." (*CCC* 1666)

Parents share their faith with children in many ways—by reading Scripture, celebrating traditional family rituals, gathering the family for prayer, fostering communication, and faithfully living the gospel through social action. In doing so, they help to create a community of grace and prayer and a "school" for learning the Catholic way of life. We help parents recognize their own value and nurture their children by acknowledging them as leaders of the domestic church.

Together with the larger Christian community, the parish nurtures the domestic church and challenges us to live the Gospel in each moment of our daily lives.

How to Support Family Faith Formation

As directors and catechists, we seek out ways to support family members of all ages—both as individuals and as a family together. We seek out even the smallest opportunities for supporting family faith formation.

+ ***Prayer*** Pray for the parents of your children regularly, both privately and with the children when appropriate. Encourage children to pray for their families and for all the significant adults in their lives.

+ ***Communication*** Maintain regular contact with family members through phone calls, notes, and updates. Be available to parents should they wish to contact you. Encourage parents to take an interest in their child's learning.

+ ***Honor Families Always*** Speak often and with respect to children about the value of families and the role of elders in teaching us about our relationships with God and each other. Encourage children to pray for all families in the parish.

+ ***Invitation*** Invite parents to become involved in major activities such as a family day, a field trip, or a guest panel. Invite parents with expertise in areas such as art or music to assist you as you work with children.

Finding God: Our Response to God's Gifts supports adult and family faith formation. Support for family involvement extends the effectiveness of the family in raising faith-filled children.

"As catechists, we recognize and honor the role of the family in children's faith formation."

"Support for family involvement extends the effectiveness of the family in raising faith-filled children."

The Effective Catechist

Praying With Children

Faith is a living relationship with God that, like any relationship, requires communication to remain healthy. Another word for this communication with God is prayer. We invite children to pray in the context of the truths explored in the session and to respond gratefully to God's gift of grace.

As catechists, we know that praying with children can be an intimidating experience for some adults. Before you pray together, talk with children about prayer and about the place of prayer in your own life. Sharing prayer with reverence and sincerity each time we pray with children is the best way to model that each of us is called to develop our own personal relationship with God.

† Begin prayer with children by inviting them to still their hearts and minds so as to focus quietly on God's presence.

† As you pray traditional prayers, reverently pray each word, contemplating its meaning.

† As you lead children in reflective prayer, speak slowly, with feeling, and pause often so that children can reflect on what you're saying.

† After praying with children, give them a few moments to pray silently in their own words.

"Sharing prayer with reverence and sincerity each time we pray with children is the best way to model that each of us is called to develop our own personal relationship with God."

As we mentor children to "pray without ceasing," we guide them to know that they can strengthen their personal relationship with God by praying almost anywhere. Yet we want them to know prayer as something other than the hurried, task-oriented communication that makes up much of our busy days with others. Making a special place for children to gather in prayer shows them how much we value prayer and our relationship with God. Allowing children to participate in preparing the place where they pray together shows them how much we value them as people of faith.

Preparing a Prayer Center

Creating a prayer center helps everyone to grow in an awareness of the sacred. Invite children to help you create this sacred space. A prayer center can be a simple table draped with a cloth to show the liturgical season. On the table you can place a Bible, along with a crucifix, statue, icon, or another religious object. As we reserve this setting as a focal point, we demonstrate the value of prayer. If space permits, use it as a place for all to gather for prayer.

Enthroning the Bible

We show reverence for God's Word by "enthroning" the Bible—respectfully placing it in an open position in the prayer center. Enthroning the Bible becomes real to children if they are involved in placing the Bible in its open position. Invite them to participate in a procession led by a child holding the closed Bible high while children following sing a song or an "Alleluia." A second child might receive the Bible, open it, and reverently place it in the prayer center for all to see.

Taking Traditional Prayers to Heart: Memorization and Prayer

One of the ways that we sustain the "memory," the oral history, of the Church is through the memorization, or "taking to heart," of traditional prayers. Though we can and often do pray in our own words, traditional prayers are special in the same way that family heirlooms are. They have been passed on from generation to generation, linking children to basic truths of our faith, supporting personal prayer, and allowing groups of people to unite their minds, hearts, and voices in prayer. When children are taking traditional prayers to heart, it is important to be sure that they understand the meaning of the words in the prayers.

Prayer Services in the Review Sessions

Structured communal prayer is an essential part of our liturgical tradition. Classroom prayer services call children to unite with their peers in group prayer. In liturgical tradition, specific roles, such as Leader or Reader, are included in most prayer services. We guide children to participate actively in group prayer by encouraging them to try various roles at some time during the year, by explaining the purpose of each role, and by allowing them to rehearse and prepare beforehand.

"Making a special place for children to gather in prayer shows them how much we value prayer and our relationship with God."

"One of the ways that we sustain the 'memory,' the oral history, of the Church is through the memorization, or 'taking to heart,' of traditional prayers."

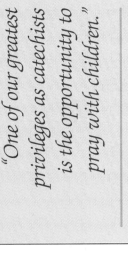

How to Lead Children in Reflective Prayer

The only way to learn how to pray is by praying.

One of our greatest privileges as catechists is the opportunity to pray with children. In the Reflect step of each session of *Finding God: Our Response to God's Gifts*, we pray with children, often using a reflective prayer that flows from the focus of the faith lesson of that session. As we share reflective prayer, we lead children to use reflection and imagination, to engage in prayerful conversation with God, and to recognize his presence in their daily lives.

The catechist notes for each session provide the words and the way to guide children to pray reflectively. In addition, each unit also has a recorded guided reflection on CD to use to prepare for, and to join together in, prayer with the children. Scripts for the recorded guided reflections are provided at the back of this catechist guide. Listening to these reflections beforehand will provide you with an example of how to lead reflective prayer—attending to quality of voice, pacing, and the message.

Getting Ready for Reflective Prayer

Invite the children to focus on God's presence. Establish a quiet, prayerful, and comfortable environment and mood to help them overcome the distractions of the everyday world.

Consider the following as you join children in reflective prayer:

Encourage a Comfortable Posture
If possible, move the children to the prayer center and invite them to find a position in which they can be comfortable yet alert. If space is limited, invite the children to get comfortable in their seats. Encourage children to close their eyes or to focus their attention on a symbol or a picture.

Invite Deep Breathing
Take two or three minutes to help children learn to relax and breathe deeply. Ask the children to rest their hands and to slowly, silently breathe in deeply and then breathe out gradually. Help them establish a rhythm to their breathing by counting slowly to three as they breathe in and asking them to breathe out as you count to three.

Use Reflective Music
Reflective (instrumental) music can help by covering distractions and providing a soothing setting in which to relax. Reflective music selected for this purpose can be found at the end of the Music CD for each grade.

"One of our greatest privileges as catechists is the opportunity to pray with children."

"As we share reflective prayer, we lead children to use reflection and imagination, to engage in prayerful conversation with God, and to recognize his presence in their daily lives."

Leading Reflective Prayer

Begin the reflective prayer with an invitation to reflect, or meditate, on an aspect of the theme of the session, often through a Scripture passage or a traditional prayer. Reflection time with children can be as brief as a few minutes or as long as 15 minutes.

Step-by-Step Directions

Through a series of age-appropriate "directions" in this catechist guide, you invite the children to engage their imagination and enter into a setting where they can encounter Jesus, dwell on his words, and converse with him.

Speaking Slowly and Pausing

By speaking slowly and pausing for emphasis after each line of the reflection, you invite the children to pray more reflectively.

Engaging Imagination

Finding God: Our Response to God's Gifts uses an approach inspired by Saint Ignatius of Loyola, inviting us to pray by using the gift of imagination—sight, sound, smell, taste, and touch. We thereby create a setting in our minds, a welcoming place — whether it be a biblical setting or a place of our own choice—to enter into conversation with Jesus. Saint Ignatius said that such conversation should resemble "the way one friend speaks to another." (*The Spiritual Exercises of Saint Ignatius #54*)

However you use the guided reflections, you may provide reflective music (tracks at the end of each Music CD) in the background.

Allowing Quiet Time With God

As the reflective prayer comes to a close, invite the children to spend time in silence with God, being aware of his presence. This is called contemplation.

Silent Prayer

To conclude the children's prayerful time with the Lord, you can now invite them to rest in God's presence. Allow one or two minutes for silent prayer, depending on the responsiveness of the group.

Transition

Finally, a few gentle words provide a gradual transition, taking the children into the next activity.

Respect

The children's thoughts and reflections in prayer are theirs alone. We show respect for their conversation with God by letting them keep these thoughts to themselves.

"Invite the children to engage their imagination and enter into a setting where they can encounter Jesus, dwell on his words, and converse with him."

Preparing the Learning Environment

When Jesus planned a special meal with his apostles during Passover, he sent Peter and John ahead of him, saying, "Go and make preparations for us." (Luke 22:8) In the same way, preparing the physical space for faith formation is important.

Seating Arrangement

The seating arrangement for faith formation may look different from the seating arrangement for other subjects. Desks lined up in uniform rows may not be the most conducive arrangement. If possible, seating arrangements such as a circle, semicircle, or clusters of tables can communicate that the time spent in faith formation is different from the time spent in other subjects. Create a seating arrangement that fosters a sense of community.

Prayer Center

A focal point with symbols that express the presence of the Word of God and communicate a sense of the sacred helps to create a prayerful atmosphere. A prayer center, which serves as such a focal point, may consist of a small table placed prominently in your classroom and covered by a cloth. The cloth could be the color for the liturgical season (see page 201 for colors of the liturgical seasons). On the table, place a Bible and one or more of the following: a bowl of holy water, a crucifix, a religious image or statue, a plant or flowers, or a candle. If space permits, the prayer center can serve as a gathering space for reflective prayer.

"A focal point with symbols that express the presence of the Word of God and communicate a sense of the sacred helps to create a prayerful atmosphere."

Visuals

Try to include visuals related to the session topic—such as posters, photographs, religious images, and statues—to engage the children. Change them regularly to stimulate visual learning and to mark movement into a new session topic. Take advantage of other equipment available to you: chalkboard, easel, overhead projector, CD player, television, and VCR and DVD players. Display the work that children have completed in the *Finding God* sessions. This will affirm the children, give them a sense of ownership of the classroom, and promote their Catholic identity.

Preparing for the Session

Jesus speaks of building a house on rock (Matthew 7:24–27) to teach about the importance of having a firm foundation for our lives. As a teacher, you know that preparation and planning serve as part of that firm foundation. In faith formation, preparation and planning enable you to develop a clear focus for the session; identify your expectations for the children; be more relaxed, flexible, and confident in delivery; and effectively engage children.

To help you in your planning and preparation, *Finding God: Our Response to God's Gifts* provides a Catechist Preparation section for each session (see pages PO28–PO29). As you use this resource to prepare effective sessions, keep in mind the following:

Pray and Reflect

Use the 3-Minute Retreat to take a few moments to reflect prayerfully before you prepare your session.

Place the Session in Context of the Unit

Consider how the session develops the theme of the entire unit and how it connects with previous sessions. Likewise, look ahead to see if you need to make any preparations for future sessions.

Understand the Background

Read and reflect on the Catechist Preparation section to deepen your understanding of the Scripture and Tradition that you will be presenting. Be sure to read the session's Scripture passages beforehand to become familiar with their focus.

Look Over the Get-Ready-Guide

Use the Get-Ready-Guide to get an overview of the session and to see how the Engage, Explore, Reflect, and Respond steps flow smoothly and connect effectively. The guide identifies the session outcomes, that is, what the children will know or be able to do as a result of the session. It also lists the required and optional materials you will need to lead the session, depending on the amount of time available to you.

Visualize the Session

As a final step, examine the directions in this catechist guide and visualize yourself presenting this session. This visualization will provide you with a sense of timing and flow and will help you to adapt and create contingency plans should anything unexpected occur.

"Beginnings are always important."

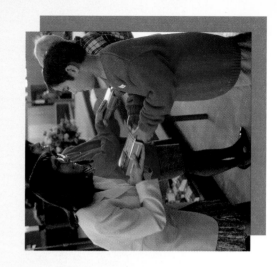

The First Session—Presenting the Books

Beginnings are always important. In the first session, you can help the children understand and appreciate the value and importance of the Children's Book by presenting it to them in a manner different from their other textbooks. Rather than distributing the Children's Books at the same time as other textbooks, hold on to the *Finding God: Our Response to God's Gifts* Children's Books until the first session. If the children already received the Children's Book and have written their names on the inside cover, collect them for this presentation.

† Play some instrumental music in the background.

† Option: Invite a child to read Isaiah 55:10–11, "So shall my word be that goes forth from my mouth." For children in grades one and two, read the following adapted version:

"The rain and the snow come down from the sky and do not return until they have watered all of the plants and flowers. In the same way, God's Word will not return to him until it has completed its work."

† Invite each child to come forward to receive a book as you call him or her by name and say: *May your life be changed by recognizing God in all things.*

† When the children have resumed their seats, turn off the instrumental music.

† Introduce the children to their books by explaining the meaning of the title, *Finding God: Our Response to God's Gifts.* (See page PO6, The Inspiration Behind the Title, for help.)

† Tell the children that their book will help to guide them through the sessions and into a deeper relationship with God.

† Invite the children to look at the cover of their Children's Books and to describe what they see. Together, read the prayer on the back cover.

† Have the children open the flap and together read the words "May God's Word be in my mind, on my lips, and in my heart." Explain that these are the words we pray silently before the Gospel as we use our thumb to trace a Sign of the Cross on our forehead, lips, and chest.

† Explain how the flap can be used as a book mark.

† Direct the children to open their books. If they have not yet printed their name on the inside cover, have them do so. Invite a volunteer to read the wording surrounding their name and the Scripture passage just below it.

† Explain that the Scripture passage on the inside cover is connected to the topic for this grade level.

† Slowly and prayerfully read each of the first four pages (beginning with "As I open this book . . .") aloud as a group.

† When you've finished, encourage the children to look through the pages and ask questions or reflect upon what they have read.

Communication Skills and Presence

The Gospel of Mark tells us that when Jesus spoke to the crowds, they "were astonished at his teaching, for he taught them as one having authority." (Mark 1:22) Jesus possessed the quality of positive *presence*, a quality that refers to the ability to communicate a sense of enthusiasm, confidence, authority, hospitality, and sensitivity. While presence may seem to be a rather elusive trait, it is a skill that can be acquired and improved upon. Here are a few of the elements of positive presence to pay attention to:

Body Language and Movement Around the Room

Since as much as two thirds of all effective communication is nonverbal, make sure your body language communicates your enthusiasm for proclaiming the Good News. Likewise, moving around the room instead of sitting in one place is an effective way of engaging children.

Eye Contact

Studies have shown that making eye contact actually increases brain activity! Eye contact can assist in conveying your message by enabling you to identify the children with wavering attention and to establish a connection between you and the children.

Facial Expression and Confidence

Since our faces, more than any other body part, reveal emotions, opinions, and moods, it is important for you to maintain a facial expression that shows how enthusiastic you are about the Good News of Jesus. Be aware also of how your face communicates your feelings about the children and your role as their catechist. To communicate a sense of confidence is important so that you exemplify what it means to trust in God's grace.

Voice: Volume, Variety, Pace, Tone, and Clarity

Voices are just as unique as faces. While some vocal qualities are genetic, you can develop vocal habits that can be used to your advantage. Speak loud enough for all to hear but not so loud as to be annoying. Speak slow enough to be understood but fast enough to avoid boredom. Speak clearly enough to avoid confusion. Speak with confidence and enthusiasm to inspire and with variety to avoid monotony.

"Moving around the room instead of sitting in one place is an effective way of engaging children."

Asking Questions and Leading Discussion

Jesus often used questions to engage people in discussion: "What is your opinion about the Messiah?" (Matthew 22:41); "Who do you say that I am?" (Mark 8:29); "Whose image and name does it bear?" (Luke 20:24). Jesus understood the connection between questioning and learning.

Asking effective questions allows you to ascertain what children know both before and after information is presented. Questioning is also an excellent way to get their attention and to invite children to think, become engaged, and remain on task. The Catechist Guide provides you with many thought-provoking questions to engage children effectively. Here are some tips for asking effective questions:

Preparing Your Questions

Before the session look over the questions you plan to use and anticipate the types of responses children might give. Questions in *Finding God: Our Response to God's Gifts* are simple, straightforward, and open-ended (cannot be answered with a simple yes or no). Be sure that any questions you prepare on your own follow this same model.

Asking a Question

When asking a question, pause and then, if necessary, repeat it. While awaiting a response, patiently allow time for the children to think (usually 3–4 seconds); resist the temptation to answer your own question. Direct a question to the whole group. Don't allow everyone else to avoid thinking about an answer by calling on one child before you pose the question.

Awaiting a Response

If the group is having difficulty answering a question, rephrase it and move around the room, making eye contact as you await a response (usually 3–4 seconds). Allow a few hands to go up since the same child is often the first to put his or her hand up. Then, if no one appears ready to give a response, call on someone and invite him or her to answer as well as possible and then proceed to engage others in the same manner.

Reacting to Responses

Affirm acceptable responses and invite other children to help if someone responds with incorrect information or has no response. Show enthusiasm for the responses so children feel encouraged to respond to further questions. Invite quiet children to participate by presenting them with nonthreatening questions.

Leading Discussions

Discussions are an important means of assessing children's understanding of a topic. The discussions promote active engagement in learning and allow the children an opportunity to express themselves. Initiate discussions by asking questions that go beyond retrieving information and invite individual thoughts, opinions, and feelings. Invite more than one response to a question and then ask for reactions to the earlier responses. Occasionally summarize what you heard and invite more discussion. Encourage respectful listening and assure confidentiality.

Keeping Children Engaged

When children are not engaged, discipline problems are more likely to occur. Keeping children engaged is the primary task of the catechist and, when done effectively, maintains *discipline*, which comes from the same root word as *disciple*, meaning "one who follows." To help children follow Jesus, you may wish to use some of these strategies for keeping them engaged and for responding when and if they become disengaged.

Create an Engaging Atmosphere

Create a comfortable and orderly atmosphere. Establish a few rules or guidelines for your group, display them, explain them, and enforce them consistently. Keep children on-task from the moment they enter the room. Vary the activities and keep children involved by calling on those with wavering attention, by assigning tasks and responsibilities, or by asking questions to reengage them.

Prepare

Prepare, organize, and provide clear expectations. Have all materials ready before the session and wait to distribute them until directions have been given and are understood. Check your seating arrangement and adjust it as needed. Children are more likely to become disengaged when they feel anonymous, so learn and use their names.

Respond Appropriately

Reinforce and affirm good behavior. Show respect, understanding, and a sense of humor when appropriate. Clearly identify any specific improper behavior you intend to address. Speak and act with confidence, firmness, and calmness. Avoid unwanted side effects by not panicking or losing your temper. Remain fair and flexible. Avoid using an ultimatum that would "paint a child into a corner" with no way out. Consult your principal, catechetical leader, parents, and colleagues in serious situations.

Use Nonverbal Communication

Move your gaze to all areas of the room and make eye contact with every child. Often eye contact alone can correct improper behavior and reengage a child. Move around the room and attempt to be present and proximate to all areas of the learning space. Avoid interrupting a session to confront misbehavior. Instead, use nonverbal communication such as tapping on the back of the chair, tapping on a table or desk, or standing next to or behind a child who seems disengaged.

"Show respect, understanding, and a sense of humor."

The Effective Catechist

Getting to Know a Second-Grade Child

As children mature, they become increasingly capable of comprehending more complex ideas and concepts. As catechists, we show our respect for God's creation by accepting all people for who they are and mentoring them as they grow in their personal relationship with God. *Finding God: Our Response to God's Gifts* links faith formation to a child's developmental level as a second grader by using language and activities appropriate to his or her age.

Profile of a Second-Grade Child (Ages 7–8)

"The second grade . . . can be considered part of the golden age of childhood."

The second grade, ages seven though eight, can be considered part of the golden age of childhood—a time of wonderful curiosity, changes, rapid growth, seemingly endless imagination, excitement, and enthusiasm. Though mostly positive and optimistic, some children occasionally can become moody and may prefer to spend time alone. Seven- and eight-year-olds love structure and order and work diligently at increasing skill in handwriting, computers, sports, and almost everything in which they are involved. This is also the time when many children prepare for First Penance and First Eucharist. With all the enthusiasm they have, these children are at a wonderful age for learning and faith development!

"With all the enthusiasm they have, these children are at a wonderful age for learning and faith development!"

Psychological and Intellectual Development

Children at this age . . .

★ love structure and routine

★ love to hear stories and to be read to

★ tend to learn best by doing

★ have vivid imaginations and short attention spans

★ like to work alone but, as the year goes on, increasingly will enjoy working in groups

★ are increasing their vocabularies rapidly and enjoy asking questions

★ have difficulty knowing the limits of their own abilities because these are expanding so quickly

★ begin to use logic

★ are interested in the natural world and in understanding how things work

Moral Development

Children at this age . . .

★ consider the right course of action to be the one that allows them to avoid punishment

★ begin to make moral decisions (although inconsistently) based on internal judgments

★ have a fairly well-developed sense of right and wrong and begin to form a conscience

★ need opportunities to develop a moral sense through their own experiences

★ need clear and direct instruction as well as the opportunity to observe sound moral behavior in the lives of significant adults (in their own lives and in the lives of saints and holy people)

Social Development

Children at this age . . .

★ are truly the center of their own worlds

★ like to spend significant amounts of time alone, engaged in their own thoughts and activities

★ are sensitive, respond strongly to both encouragement and criticism, and need a great deal of affirmation

★ have a tendency to underestimate the limits of their abilities but are able to recover quickly from mistakes and failures

★ need a sense of security and structure

★ rely heavily on parents, teachers, and significant adults

★ have a well-developed sense of humor and enjoy riddles and puzzles

★ consider being a part of a group, primarily of the same sex, extremely important

Spiritual Development

Children at this age . . .

★ love to celebrate and enjoy ritual

★ have a natural sense of wonder and are comfortable with prayer

★ enjoy quiet and are capable of reflecting for short periods of time

★ are capable of praying spontaneously in a conversational style

★ see nature as a reflection of God's love and greatness

★ view the Church as a community of friends who help one another

★ begin to appreciate the liturgical seasons, seasons of the year, and feast days

★ are capable of taking simple prayers to heart

"Children at this age have a natural sense of wonder and are comfortable with prayer."

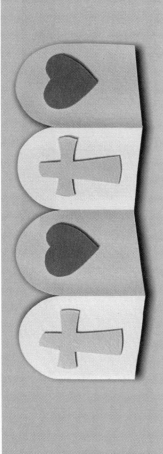

Paying Attention to Special Needs

Among the children you serve, some may have special needs. Through the positive recognition of the differences in individual abilities, you can enhance the unity of the Body of Christ. Contact your principal for assistance and visit **www.FindingGod.org** for more information.

Here are some suggestions for helping children with special needs:

Orthopedic (Physical) Impairment

Adapt activities to fit the needs of those with orthopedic (physical) impairment; develop a buddy system; anticipate and prepare in advance for situations in which a child's symptoms might be disruptive to the group; encourage social interaction; and use appropriate terminology when referring to physical disabilities.

Visual Impairment

Consider range of vision and lighting needs when seating a visually impaired child; provide large-print, audio, and manual materials; plan activities that use senses other than sight; allow the child to do work orally; and assign a partner for visual activities.

Deaf or Hearing Impairment

Seat the child with a hearing impairment near the front and face him or her when you speak; speak clearly, using a normal tone and pace; write key words and directions on the board; provide written materials; encourage social interaction; and work with your principal and the family to arrange for an interpreter if needed.

Speech or Language Impairment

Speak distinctly and in short phrases; use visual and written as well as oral instructions; work individually with the child or use an aide to work in a separate area with the child whose oral work needs attention; and allow extra time for the child to respond to questions and comments.

Social or Behavioral Problems, Attention Disorders, and Learning Disabilities

Work with the family and the principal to identify the type of disorder or disability; arrange the room to avoid distractions; provide structure and routine; give specific tasks that are interesting to the child; give, review, and clarify directions, expectations, and explanations; frequently monitor and affirm appropriate behavior; provide immediate feedback; develop nonverbal clues for unacceptable behavior; break down tasks into smaller, less overwhelming components; use flash cards; introduce skills one at a time; use visual aids and kinesthetic (movement, gestures) cues; request an aide for individualized attention; set up situations in which the child will experience success; frequently assess the child's understanding.

Mental Impairment

Adapt activities to the child's attention span and levels of coordination and skill; individualize learning with the help of an aide; simplify concepts and repeat periodically; arrange for gifted children to help the slower learners.

Giftedness

Challenge the gifted child through independent study, small-group work, enrichment activities, and discovery learning that is related to his or her interest; provide supplementary resources; use creative puzzles and games; ask the child to help with preparing session materials and with assisting slower or younger children; encourage high-level thinking skills.

The Effective Catechist

Celebrating Diversity

On the feast of Pentecost, the disciples boldly proclaimed the Word of God to people of many nations (Acts of the Apostles 2:5–13). *Finding God: Our Response to God's Gifts* celebrates the rich cultural and ethnic diversity of the Catholic Church and invites you to bring children of many different backgrounds together with the intention of building the Body of Christ. In doing so, you help the children to recognize themselves in the story of salvation history and to celebrate the Church's diversity. This diversity is reflected and celebrated throughout the children's book:

Mary

Joseph

Jesus

Peter

Art

Fine art that appears in *Finding God: Our Response to God's Gifts* depicts Catholic Tradition through a variety of ethnic and cultural images. As a result of extensive research, the illustrations of Jesus, Mary, Joseph, and Peter carefully and consistently reflect their Semitic heritage. Illustrations and photographs have been carefully designed and selected to depict people of various cultures, ethnicity, and economic status from all over the world so that the rich diversity of God's family is represented.

Saints and Holy People

Great care was given to the selection of the saints and holy people featured in the children's book in order to highlight the Church's diversity. Through stories of the experiences of some of the Church's great saints and holy people, *Finding God: Our Response to God's Gifts* honestly examines the successes and failures on the part of society and the Church to recognize and celebrate ethnic and cultural diversity.

Exploring Cultural Traditions

Numerous examples of the rich variety of traditions, popular devotions, and prayer expressions of various ethnic and cultural groups are integrated throughout the program. In the Respond step of many sessions, children are invited to identify strategies for affirming all people's gifts and for making their own communities and parishes more welcoming.

Songs

The songs chosen for *Finding God: Our Response to God's Gifts* (Music CD) reflect and celebrate the diversity of the Catholic Church.

Adjusting for Learning Styles

Children learn in different ways and need to be provided with varied learning experiences. *Finding God: Our Response to God's Gifts* incorporates approaches that focus on the following learning styles:

Word Smart

Some children learn best through reading, writing, and discussion. Have the children brainstorm ideas, quiz each other on new vocabulary and spelling, and summarize a session with a single word.

Music Smart

Some children have a good sense of rhythm and melody. Use music to create or enhance the desired atmosphere and encourage children to write their own songs or to write new lyrics for known tunes, based on the topic you are covering.

Logic/Math Smart

Some children tend to think in numbers and patterns. Ask the children to do surveys and interviews related to the theme you are covering, invent word or story problems about new material, or play questioning games such as "20 Questions."

Art/Space Smart

Some children tend to think in images and pictures. Summarize new learning by making posters or other displays and use diagrams, charts, and visual organizers to show a relationship between lessons.

Body Smart

Some children are well coordinated and enjoy using gestures, body language, and hands-on activities. Use athletic activities, role-play, simulation exercises, and other content-based games.

Nature Smart

Some children are keenly aware of the natural world and learn best when content is related to nature. Create observation notebooks, use microscopes, classify and categorize things in nature, or organize a scavenger hunt.

People Smart

Some children learn best by interacting with others. Peer-teaching activities, group projects, and small discussions are effective. You can also invite guest speakers to visit the class.

Self Smart

Some children are introspective and learn best when given time to process information. Have the children keep a reflective journal where they write regularly about what they are learning; incorporate independant learning activities and self-designed study projects into the curriculum.

(Source: This material has been adapted from the following book with permission from Kagan Publishing & Professional Development: Kagan, Spencer, and Kagan, Miguel. *Multiple Intelligences: The Complete MI Book.* San Clemente, CA: Kagan Publishing, 1998. 1 (800) 933-2667; www.KaganOnline.com/.")

The Effective Catechist

Creative Activities

To help you make the Word of God accessible to all children, whatever their learning style, *Finding God: Our Response to God's Gifts* provides creative activities for you to choose from. These activities also help you to assess in an ongoing manner the children's grasp of key concepts (see page PO38). Being aware of these activities and how to use them can greatly enhance your abilities as a catechist. Visit our Web site **www.FindingGod.org** for more activities.

This Catechist Guide also provides numerous optional activities to work "off the page" (depending upon the time available to you) while building upon the content covered in the text.

Speaking and Singing

The spoken or sung word allows children to assimilate, clarify, and understand concepts. Speaking and singing give them an opportunity to express themselves, articulate, and celebrate their faith while growing in the skill of social interaction.

Examples:

guest speakers

interviews

lectures

large-group discussions

panel discussions

questions and answers

singing (rounds, hymns, Mass parts, nursery rhymes, folk melodies)

small-group discussions

storytelling

Memorizing or "Taking to Heart"

Through catechesis we sustain the memory of the Church. When God gave Israel the Ten Commandments, he told them, "Take to heart these words which I enjoin on you today." (Deuteronomy 6:6) In addition to helping the children to take to heart certain doctrinal formulas, the memorization of commonly known prayers of the Christian tradition, appropriate to their age, is beneficial. Although memorization offers an essential support to the faith life of children, it is important to help them understand the meaning of what they are taking to heart.

Working With the Text

The *Finding God: Our Response to God's Gifts* Children's Book serves as the foundation upon which you can build your session. The session directions in this Catechist Guide suggest techniques for working with the text in order to engage children and focus their attention.

These techniques include the following:

- invite volunteers to read paragraphs aloud
- invite children to read independently and then summarize
- arrange children in small groups and assign paragraphs for each group to read and then summarize for the large group
- read aloud to the children as they follow along
- arrange a choral reading by dividing the large group into smaller groups to read assigned sections aloud as a group

Writing

Some children express themselves more easily in written form than in oral form. Writing is a powerful vehicle for self-discovery and prayer. Many of the greatest saints used writing to speak with God and to others, and to record their own thoughts. In writing, children have an opportunity to clarify their thoughts and to make visible the invisible.

Examples:

acrostics
crossword puzzles
e-mails
interviews
letters
litanies
logs
modern parables/stories
newspaper headlines/stories
paraphrases
poems
prayers
questions and answers
quizzes
raps
reports
riddles
skits
song lyrics
speeches
stories
slogans
summaries
telegrams
Web pages

Role-Playing and Dramatizing

Through the dramatic stories of our faith, children come to understand themselves and others as they begin to internalize the Christian message. Jesus used simple but dramatic stories and parables to invite people to enter into relationship with the Father.

Examples:

charades
children's literature
choral readings
dance
dramatic readings
gestures to songs
mime
pageants
plays
puppet shows
role-plays
shadow-play
storytelling
recorded Scripture stories on Spoken Word CD

Playing Games

Children naturally create and participate in games. Games allow children to build community, follow rules, and learn about cooperation and participation (as opposed to winning or losing), and to develop mentally, physically, and socially. Games encourage children to solve problems and to use their imagination. Of course, any game you choose should be adapted and used in a way that will reinforce or further the focus of your session.

Examples:

bingo
board games
card games
charades
drawing games
icebreakers
mixers
relays
skill games
spelling bees
team games
television quiz shows
tic-tac-toe
trivia games

The Effective Catechist

Audiovisuals

Although some children think and learn primarily through words, others do so through pictures, images, and sounds. Children who are visual-aural learners can develop a deeper appreciation of the message in each session when their visual-aural imagination is engaged.

Examples:

bulletin boards
CDs
chalkboards
colored chalk
charts
computers
concrete aids
DVDs
flannel boards
LCD projectors
maps
models
movies
music
pictures
Power Point presentations
recordings
scrapbooks
slides
transparencies
video or audio cassettes

greeting cards
holy cards
mobiles
models from clay or dough
mosaics
murals
paper dolls
paperweights from rocks
pennants
photo albums with
    pictures and captions
photo essays
placemats
plaques
portraits
posters
sculpture
sidewalk art with chalk
silhouettes
sponge paintings
stained-glass windows
texts lettered on objects
    (seashells, driftwood, rocks)
storybooks
t-shirts
yarn-and-cloth pictures

Drawing and Art

Faith goes beyond words. Many people express their faith through art and drawing. Children can grow spiritually by expressing their inner thoughts and feelings visually. Drawing and art can also help children to become more familiar with religious concepts and relate these to their own lives.

Examples:

album/CD covers
banners
booklets
bookmarks
bulletin boards
bumper stickers
buttons
cartoons
coats of arms
collages
comic books
commemorative stamps
dioramas
displays
doorknob hangers
finger paintings
fingerprint pictures from
    ink pads
flyers

Unit 1

Catechist Preparation

Unit 1: God Loves Us
Overview

Unit Saint: Saint Isidore the Farmer

Each unit begins with a Unit Saint, a person who showed people how to live in God's grace in their particular time and place. The focus of the first unit of the series is on creation. The Unit 1 saint is Saint Isidore the Farmer, a man who loved and cared for the earth and his fellow creatures very much. As we begin our unit and focus on God's creation and our responsibility to love and care for it, Saint Isidore serves as an excellent role model. He lived in Spain and is known for his kindness and compassion toward others, especially animals.

Consider how the focus of this unit is developed throughout the sessions.

Session 1: God Creates Us

The first session begins with God as our creator. God created us in his image, and he loves us and wants us to be happy. We return that love to God by living fully in his world and thanking him for all he gives us by sharing these gifts with one another. The children are continuing to learn to pray the Glory Be to the Father, or the Doxology.

Session 2: God Gives Us Jesus

We explore the greatest gift that God has given us—his own Son, Jesus Christ. Joseph and Mary are models of faith who listened to the Holy Spirit and placed their trust in God.

Session 3: God Is Our Father

We know of God's love for us as our Father through his Son, Jesus. Jesus reminds us that God is the creator of all life and that God loves all his children. We listen to Jesus' story of the birds of the air and the flowers of the field. This story reminds us to place our trust in God, our loving Father. The children review the Lord's Prayer.

Session 4: God's Life for Us

The focus of this session is on the Holy Spirit's presence in our lives. By listening to the Holy Spirit, we gain insight into ourselves, our relationships with others, and our world. We read the story of Simeon, who, guided by the Holy Spirit, recognized the infant Jesus as the Messiah. The children learn the Prayer to the Holy Spirit.

Session 5: Unit 1 Review

In this session we discuss the main ideas of the unit and have the opportunity to spend more time on any essential points that may need more attention.

God the Father Blessing, Gerard David

Catechist Preparation

Prayer in Unit 1

In this unit you will begin to establish the pattern and tone for prayer in the Engage, Reflect, and Respond steps of each session. The Engage step includes a short prayer of petition while the Respond step includes a similar short prayer of thanksgiving. These prayers include time for silent meditation. The Reflect step of each session includes a more extended prayer experience that invites the children to engage in a guided reflection, inviting them to pray in silence and relating the main focus to their own personal prayer.

As you guide the children through this unit, think about how you will help them to praise God through prayer and service.

✝ Catholic Social Teaching in Unit 1

In the story of the Good Samaritan (Luke 10:29–37), Jesus makes clear our responsibility to care for those in need. The Church articulates this responsibility in Catholic Social Teaching. The following themes of Catholic Social Teaching are integrated into this unit:

Care for God's Creation God is the creator of all people and all things, and he wants us to enjoy his creation. The responsibility to care for all God has made is a requirement of our faith. We are called to make the moral and ethical choices that protect the ecological balance of creation both locally and worldwide.

Call to Family, Community, and Participation Participation in family and community is central to our faith and to a healthy society. As the central social institution of our society, the family must be supported and strengthened. From this foundation, people participate in society, fostering a community spirit and promoting the well-being of all, especially the poor and vulnerable.

Solidarity Because God is our Father, we are all brothers and sisters with the responsibility to care for one another. Solidarity is the attitude that leads Christians to share spiritual and material goods. Solidarity unites rich and poor, weak and strong, and helps create a society that recognizes that we all live in an interdependent world.

The Dignity of Work and the Rights of Workers The Catholic Church teaches that the basic rights of workers must be respected: the right to productive work, to fair wages, to private property, to organize and join unions, and to pursue economic opportunity. Moreover, Catholics believe that the economy is meant to serve people, not the other way around. More than being just a way to make a living, work is an important way in which we participate in God's creation.

Option for the Poor and Vulnerable In our world many people are very rich, while at the same time, many are extremely poor. As Catholics, we are called to pay special attention to the needs of the poor. We can follow Jesus' example by making a specific effort to defend and promote the dignity of the poor and vulnerable and meet their immediate material needs.

Session 1: God Creates Us

3-Minute Retreat

Before you prepare for your session, pause for a few moments and be still. Take three deep breaths and be aware that our loving God is with you as you begin to lead the children through this journey of growth and discovery.

Genesis 1:27

God created man in his image;
in the divine image he created him;
male and female he created them.

Reflection

God created all things and has given the human family a unique role in his creation. Made in the image and likeness of God, we have a special relationship with God the Father, the Son, and the Holy Spirit. God made us to be like him and wants us to care for and love the world he created. Our Father, who loved us at the beginning, continues to love us today and always.

Questions

How do I see my special relationship with God and his creation? How can I best help the children see their special relationship to God and his creation?

Prayer

Speak to your heavenly Father using this prayer or one of your own. God, creator of all, help me to see your goodness in all of creation and your image in each person I meet, especially in the children who share this faith with me.

Take a few moments to reflect prayerfully before you prepare this session.

Catechist Preparation

Knowing and Sharing Your Faith

Scripture and Tradition in Session 1

We begin the program by reflecting on how God created the world and everything in it for us. Genesis 1:31 says that God proclaimed everything he made "very good." In the book of Genesis the goodness of things is described concretely. It is described in terms of ripe fields of grain ready for harvest. The world is for people to enjoy and use, but it is not to be exploited.

We are made in God's image and likeness, as living representatives of God on earth. As God's representatives, the human family has been given dominion over the earth. Human dominion is to be modeled on God's dominion. God's dominion is one that respects life. We can begin to appreciate the goodness and beauty of God by appreciating the goodness and beauty of the created world.

In this session we teach that God—the Father, the Son, and the Holy Spirit—creates, sustains, and loves all of creation. The created world is the result of God's decision to share his life and love with us. Should God forget the universe and everyone in it for an instant, it would lapse into nothingness.

Scripture in Session 1

God looks over what he has made in **Genesis 1:31.**
1 Timothy 4:4 relates God's word to the goodness of creation.

Let the scripture and Tradition deepen your understanding of the content in this session.

WINDOW ON THE CATECHISM

Creation as the loving work of the Holy Trinity is discussed in *CCC* 290–292. The human vocation to care for it is treated in CCC 307.

God creates everything good.

Everything created by God is good.

Catechist Preparation

From the Richness of the Tradition

In paragraph 23 of the Apostolic Letter of Pope Paul VI dated May 14, 1975, Pope Paul VI taught that "the more fortunate should renounce some of their rights so as to place their goods more generously at the service of others." This means we should care enough for others that we would be willing to make real sacrifices for them. We don't just offer to others things that we don't want or need. We actually give up things that we have a right to, and we do it because we sincerely care about the well-being of our neighbors.

✝ Catholic Social Teaching

In this session aspects of the following Catholic Social Teaching are integrated:

- **The Dignity of Work and the Rights of Workers**
- **Care for God's Creation**
- **Option for the Poor and Vulnerable**

Consider in this session how you will invite the children to respond to and prayerfully reflect on God's invitation to love and serve others.

GENERAL DIRECTORY
FOR CATECHESIS

Catechesis that is centered on Jesus leads us to understand the Father of all creation. This is discussed in GDC 100.

Prayer in Session 1

The first session establishes the pattern and tone for the prayers in each session. The short opening prayer of petition and the closing prayer of gratitude invite the children to reflect on the world God created. At the end of each prayer there is an opportunity for the children to engage in private reflection. In the Reflect step of this session, the children review both the Sign of the Cross and the Glory Be to the Father, or the Doxology.

Session 1: God Creates Us

Session Theme: *God created the world to show us how much he loves us.*

Before This Session

- In this first session, you will set up procedures and establish rules for the group. Begin to think about this. See pages EC10–24 for information and ideas.
- Prepare a prayer center in your room. For additional information on the prayer center see page EC7.
- Bookmark your Bible to Genesis 1:1–31 and 1 Timothy 4:4. Place the Bible in the prayer center open to the passage from Genesis.
- Set up the CD player ahead of time so you will be ready to play the songs and reflective music.

Outcomes   *At the end of the session, the children should be able to*

- identify Saint Isidore as someone who cared for God's creation.
- understand that God's creation is all around us.

- recognize and explain that God created everything out of love for us and that all of creation is good.
- explain that God wants us to be holy and to love one another.
- pray the Glory Be to the Father.
- define the words *creation* and *holy*.

- prayerfully reflect on God's presence, his invitation, and our response.
- pray the Glory Be to the Father.

- identify practical ways to act on God's invitation in everyday living.

Steps

DAY 1   Engage pages 1–3
Unit Saint: Saint Isidore the Farmer
God Creates Us

DAYS 2–3   Explore pages 4–9
God Made Heaven and Earth
God's Blessing
Our Loving God
A Center for Caring
Caring for God's Creation

DAY 4   Reflect page 10
Prayer: Sign of the Cross and Glory Be to the Father

DAY 4   Respond page 11
Living My Faith: Ways to Take Care of the World

DAY 5   Extending the Session page 12
Day 5 offers an opportunity to extend the session with activities that reinforce the session outcomes.

Materials

Required Materials

- Bible
- Writing paper, pens, pencils
- Art materials, such as drawing paper, crayons, markers, scissors, glue
- CD 2, Track 2: Song of Love (Instrumental) (page 1)
- CD 2, Track 3: "Echo" Holy, Holy (1:32) (page 7)
- CD 2, Track 1: Song of Love (4:00) (page 8)
- CD 2, Reflective music (page 10)

Optional Materials

- Butcher paper (page 5)
- World map or globe (page 5)
- Leaves, white paper or light-colored construction paper (page 5)
- Magazines, scalloped-edge scissors (page 9)
- Sentence strips (page 12)
- Slips of paper, bag (page 12)
- Blackline Master 1, washable inkpad, hand-cleaning supplies (page 4)
- Blackline Masters 2, 3 (page 6)

e-resources

www.FindingGod.org

God Loves Us

God Loves Us — Unit 1

Begin this first class by playing the instrumental music on CD 2, Track 2: "Song of Love." Ask the children to set aside material from any other subject that might distract them from today's session. You might allow a few minutes of friendly conversation so the children can relax before you begin.

Open this year with the Sign of the Cross. Ask the children to describe what it means to be a follower of God the Father and his Son, Jesus. Say: ***This year, we are going to learn many ways that we can be faithful followers of Jesus.***

Proceed with a formal book-opening ceremony as suggested on page EC 12 in the School Catechist Guide. Then invite children to turn to page 1.

Saint Isidore the Farmer

Saint Isidore the Farmer cared for the earth, the plants, and the animals. Although he was poor, Saint Isidore shared what he could with others.

Saint Isidore the Farmer

Note: Each unit begins with a Unit Saint, a person who showed others how to live in God's grace in a particular time and place. The saint was chosen because his or her contribution exemplifies the theme of the unit.

Focus attention on the picture of Saint Isidore the Farmer. Ask the group: ***What do you think the job of Saint Isidore (sănt iz´ ə dôr) was?*** (farming)

Read the caption aloud. Then remind the group: ***A saint is a person who has lived a life of special faith and goodness. A saint has been honored by the Church. Saint Isidore was a man who loved God. He also cared for the earth and his fellow creatures very much. This was one of the reasons the Church honored him.***

A DEVOUT FARMER (circa 1080–1130)

Note: This feature gives additional information about a topic or activity on the page on which it appears. It's intended for your own personal background and enrichment and need not be a part of the presentation of the session. You may, however, wish to share the information with the children as appropriate.

Saint Isidore was born in or near Madrid, Spain. He was a humble farmer who worked for the same employer for most of his life. Saint Isidore was a very devout man. Before going to work each morning, he would visit a church. While he plowed the fields during the day, he would pray. He also used to visit local shrines on pilgrimage. As illustrated in the picture, Saint Isidore is usually shown with a staff and a sheaf of grain. His wife, Maria de la Cabeza, was also later named a saint. Saint Isidore's feast day is May 15.

Engage

Saint Isidore the Farmer

Read the title. Draw attention to the bottom picture. Ask: *What do you see in this picture?* (a farmer taking young trees to be planted) *What name do we use for a person who cares for the land?* (farmer) *What do farmers do?* (grow fruits and vegetables, raise farm animals) Say: *Farmers care for the earth and grow healthful foods for us to eat.* Ask: *What are some ways we can care for the earth too?* (recycle, not waste food or water, plant our own garden)

✝ *Work and Workers*

Read the first paragraph. The pronunciation for Maria de la Cabeza is (mə rē´ə de lä ke bä´zä). Say: *God wants us to take good care of the earth. Saint Isidore can teach us about loving the earth.*

Read the second paragraph. Explain: *A patron saint watches over special groups of people, places, or animals.* Ask: *Which groups does Saint Isidore watch over?* (farmers, farm animals, farming communities) Explain: *Saint Isidore was special because he loved God and was kind toward others. He prayed from his heart, worked on a farm, and cared for his family.*

Read the last paragraph for the group. Say: *A feast day is a special day every year when we remember a particular saint.* Ask: *What are ways we could celebrate Saint Isidore's Day?* (have a picnic, give treats to animals or pets, work in a garden)

OPTION

CARING FOR GOD'S CREATION

Encourage the children to try to grow a potted plant at home. This experience will help them understand how special God's creation is and how to care for a living thing, the way Saint Isidore did.

✝ *God's Creation*

FARMING ANALOGIES IN THE GOSPEL OF MATTHEW

Jesus came from Galilee. The rich soils and valleys of Galilee made it an excellent farming district for fruits, grains, and vegetables. Jewish life in this area was centered in rural farms and villages.

The following are some examples from Matthew's Gospel of how Jesus used his experience of the agrarian way of life to teach.

A Tree and Its Fruits
(*Matthew 12:33–37*)
The Parable of the Sower
(*Matthew 13:1–9, 18–23*)
The Parable of the Mustard Seed
(*Matthew 13:31–32*)
The Curse of the Fig Tree
(*Matthew 21:18–22, 32–35*)
The Parable of the Tenants
(*Matthew 21:33–46*)

SAINT MARIA DE LA CABEZA

Maria de la Cabeza was the wife of Saint Isidore the Farmer. They had one son, who died while quite young. Both she and her husband were devoutly religious. Like Isidore, Maria was very concerned about the poor with whom she frequently shared her meals. The Church honors Saint Maria on her feast day, September 9.

Saint Isidore the Farmer

Saint Isidore and his wife, Saint Maria de la Cabeza, lived on a rich man's farm. Isidore worked for this man his whole life. He took care of the man's land with love. While Isidore worked, he prayed.

Isidore is the patron saint of farmers, farm animals, and farming communities. He is also the patron saint of picnics!

In many places farm animals and crops are blessed on Saint Isidore's Day.

2   God's Invitation

God Creates Us

Write this nursery rhyme on the board: *I see the moon and the moon sees me. God bless the moon and God bless me!* Underline the word *moon* each time it appears. Then point to the words as you read the rhyme aloud for the group. Invite the children to help you name some of the things in nature that God has made.

Use the rhyme as a model to name other things God has made. Call on a volunteer to say the first line of the rhyme, replacing the underlined word *moon* with another creation. For example: *I see the zebra and the zebra sees me.* Then have everyone say the second line: *God bless the zebra and God bless me.* Give several volunteers a chance to provide new words for the first line.

Have the group turn to page 3. Read the title of the session aloud. Ask volunteers what they see in the pictures. Then ask the group: *Who made the dog?* (God) *And who made the peacock?* (God) Say: *All of these were created by God. In this session we will learn more about God and creation.*

God Creates Us

Session 1

God is the Creator. He made heaven and earth. He created them to show how much he loves us.

God loves everything he makes. What are some things that God has made?

Prayer

God, help me know that you have made all things so I can see how good and wonderful you are.

Read the first two paragraphs aloud while the group follows along. Encourage the children to reply to the question. (birds, people, grass) Then ask: *Why did God make all of these things?* (because he loves us)

Ask the group to name other things God created. Have the children go to the window and point to God's creation. Encourage them to say: *God our Creator made _____.* Then have them return to their seats.

Prayer

Note: The Engage section of every session includes a prayer of petition in which children ask for God's help on their faith journey. In addition to the prayer in the book, always allow time for children to silently include their own prayers of petition.

Say: *God loves us and created the wonderful world where we live. Let's take some time to ask God to help us understand his world. Please close your eyes, fold your hands, and pray silently as I pray the prayer aloud for us. Then take some time to ask God for whatever is in your heart.*

Pray the prayer aloud slowly, emphasizing the goodness of God's world. Then pause for 5 to 10 seconds to give the group time to talk to God. Close by praying *Amen.* Ask the children to open their eyes.

GOD'S CREATIONS

Provide each child with a paper plate on which to draw and color one of God's creations. Attach crepe-paper streamers at the bottom. At the top, punch a hole and insert a length of string. Hang the plates around the room to celebrate God's creation.

Explore

God Made Heaven and Earth

Once again, pray with the children the prayer on page 3. Then have them turn to page 4 and look at the illustration. Have the children note some of its details, including the birds, sky, and clouds. Ask the children: *Who created, or made, these things?* (God)

Ask the group: *What do you think the world might be like without the sun, moon, and stars?* (dark, cold, dreary, without life)

 Draw attention to the Bible at the prayer center. Mention that it is bookmarked and opened to the scripture passage you will now read. Read the title and first paragraph aloud while the group follows along. Ask the group: *Does anyone remember learning in first grade about the three persons of the Trinity?* Congratulate them if they remember. Then say: *God the Father, the Son, and the Holy Spirit are the three persons of the Trinity.*

Read the second paragraph aloud. Then ask the children: *What are some animals that God created? Do you have any pets? What do you do to care for your pets?*

Then say: *God created all of these animals.*

✝ *God's Creation*

Say: *We just learned that God first created the world and then he made fish, birds, and other animals.* Ask: *What do you think God created next?* After they respond, tell them they will find out the answer as we continue with the story.

Read the first paragraph on the next page aloud. Ask: *What were the first man and woman supposed to take care of?* (the earth) Then ask: *How do you think God felt after he made the world and the first man and woman?* (happy)

Read the second paragraph. Then say: *God looked at all he had made, and he was pleased.*

What Did God Make?

Read the activity's title and directions aloud. Allow time for the children to complete the activity. When they have finished, invite volunteers to share their completed words with the rest of the group. Thank the volunteers for their participation.

OPTION

BLM 1: AMAZING ANIMALS

On Blackline Master 1 children use their thumbprints to create pictures of God's animals.

OPTION

FIRST MAN, FIRST FARMER

Read aloud this passage from Genesis 2:15: *The LORD God then took the man and settled him in the Garden of Eden to cultivate and care for it.* Explain: *This passage tells us that after he created the first man, God told him to take care of the world. So the first man was also the first farmer!* Remind the group: *Saint Isidore, about whom we learned at the beginning of the session, was also a farmer.* Ask: *Why is it important to care for the earth?* (because it is something that God created)

✝ *God's Creation*

God Made Heaven and Earth

At first there was no earth. There was no warm sun during the day. There was no glowing moon at night. No bright stars were shining in the sky. There was only God—the Father, the Son, and the Holy Spirit.

Then God made the world. He made the sky, the sun, and the moon. He made the sea. God filled it with different kinds of fish. He made the land. He filled it with many kinds of animals.

4   God's Invitation

GLIMPSES OF A NEW WORLD

Say: *God put man and woman in the world to enjoy it and to care for it. Imagine what the world first looked like a long, long time ago. What colors do you think the flowers were? What kinds of animals might there have been? What could the first man and woman have looked like?* Elicit a variety of responses and encourage the children to look at the picture on pages 4 and 5 to get a sense of what the world looked like. Then have the children draw a picture of what they think the world looked like. When they have finished, encourage the children to describe their pictures to

the group. Say: *When you go home, share with your family your picture of creation and tell them the story of how God created heaven and earth.*

LEAF RUBBING

Pass out leaves, two pieces of white paper or light-colored construction paper, and crayons. Have the children place two or three leaves between their papers. Then have them firmly hold their papers while they gently color over the paper in a back and forth motion. Soon the outline of their leaves will appear and they will have created an image of a part of God's creation!

THE SKY, THE LAND, AND THE SEA

Divide the children into three groups: Sky, Land, and Sea. Give each group a large sheet of butcher paper. Tell each group to draw beautiful things that God made that belong in their group. For example, the Sky group might illustrate birds or clouds, while the Land group might depict animals. The Sea group could draw fish and aquatic mammals. Walk around the room and help the groups come up with ideas. When they have finished, have each group stand and show their drawing to the rest of the group. One child could be chosen to describe the group's work.

STORYTELLING

Show the group a world map or globe. Call on volunteers to come forward and tell the story of creation in their own words. As they mention God's creations (earth, water, sky), have them point to whichever are visible on the map or globe. For the sky they might point outside to the sun, moon, or stars. Encourage them to mention the animals that God created too.

adapted from Genesis 1:1-31

Then God said, "Let us make someone special." So God made a man and a woman. He blessed them and told them to have children. He told them to take good care of the earth.

God looked at everything he had made. God was pleased with all he had done.

What Did God Make?

Fill in the blanks to name things God has made. These things are shown in the picture.

bi_r_d   _t_ ree   s_k_y   c_l_oud   s_u_n

THE CATHOLIC CHURCH'S COMMITMENT TO THE ENVIRONMENT

The Catholic Church has a tradition of safeguarding the environment. To learn more about the Church's efforts, visit the Web site for the United States Conference of Catholic Bishops: **www.nccbuscc.org/sdwp/international/globalclimate.htm.**

✛ *God's Creation*

Explore

God's Blessing

Ask: **What are some of the good things God has given us?** (the sun, water, fruits, plants, our families, our friends) Say: **God made these wonderful things for us because he loves us.**

Write the word *Abuela* on the board. Ask: **Does anyone know what Abuela means?** Explain that it is a Spanish word that means "Grandmother."

Read the title and the page aloud for the group. Draw attention to the word *creation* in dark type near the bottom of the page. See if anyone knows what it means. Then say: **Creation is everything that God has made. People are part of God's creation. He is full of love for his creation, and he wants us to love one another too.** Ask: **Why do you think God wants all people to love one another?** (because we are all part of his creation)

Point out the photo of Abuela, Rosa, and Juanita. Ask: **Can you tell which is Abuela, Rosa, or Juanita? What are they doing? How do you think they feel about one another? How can you tell?** Accept all reasonable responses.

Encourage children by saying: **Let's make a special effort to treat one another with care for the rest of this day.**

OPTION

BLM 2: GOD'S BLESSINGS

On Blackline Master 2 children write or draw answers to questions about God's blessings.

FYI

CATHOLIC RELIEF SERVICES

Catholic Relief Services (CRS) was founded in 1943 by the Catholic Bishops of the United States. One of its areas of concentration is working with local agencies to support some of the poorest farm families and rural communities in Asia, Africa, Latin America, and the Caribbean. In these communities CRS encourages agro-economic development with an emphasis on environmental awareness. To learn more about CRS, visit **www.catholicrelief.org.**

✝ *The Poor and Vulnerable*

OPTION

BLM 3: GOD'S CREATION

Blackline Master 3 is a fill-in-the-blank activity about God's creation.

OPTION

CLEAN-UP TOUR

Toward the end of the session, take the children outside or to a nearby park. Have them point out areas that could be cleaned up or improved upon. Encourage them to be mindful of treating the earth with respect.

✝ *God's Creation*

God's Blessing

Rosa asked her grandmother, "Abuela, why did God make us?"

"Because God is full of love," said Abuela. "He wanted someone to give his love to. He made the world and all things in it. The sun warms the day. Rain makes things grow."

"Yes," said Juanita, Rosa's sister. "There are fruits and plants to eat. There are many wonderful animals to see!"

"People are also part of God's **creation**," said Abuela. "God wants all people to love and care for one another."

Our Loving God

Allow some time for children to silently thank God for his gift of creation. Then review what the children have learned about God's creation. Ask: *Who is our Creator?* (God) *What did he create?* (heaven, earth, people) Say: *God has loved us from the beginning, and he will always love us. He wants us to love one another.*

Read the title and the first paragraph aloud as the group follows along. Ask the children: *Who are the three persons of the Trinity?* (Father, Son, and Holy Spirit)

Read the second paragraph for the group. Say: *God loves us and wants us to be happy. If we are friends with God and others, we can be happy.* Ask: *What are some things we can do to thank God for the beautiful world he has given us?* (respect his creation, praise him, love him, pray to him)

Draw attention to the word holy in dark type. See if any of the children know what it means. Say: *Because God loves us, we are "holy." That means we are sharing in the life of God and in his love.*

✚ *God's Creation*

✚ *recycle*

Reading God's Word

Note: This feature in each session contains a short Bible verse that is related to the session's theme and content. Each is brief enough to be easily remembered and used as a scriptural prayer.

Ask: *What are some of the good things that God created?* (trees, animals, people) Read the Bible verse aloud while the children follow along. Ask: *How can we show we are thankful for God's world?* (care for animals, recycle)

♪ Say: *Now we will hear a song called "Echo' Holy, Holy"* which talks about how wonderful and holy God is. Have the children turn to the song in the Songs of Our Faith section in the back of their books. Continue: *Listen carefully for the word holy. Listen at first, then sing along with the chorus as you hear the children sing it on the recording.*

Play the song "Echo' Holy, Holy" (CD 2, Track 3). Motion to the children when it's time for them to sing along with the chorus.

OPTION

ROLE-PLAY GOD'S CREATION

Invite the children to work in small groups to portray God's creation. If the group completed the Sky, the Land, and the Sea option on page 5, you may wish to have the same groups meet again. Tell the children to bring to life the sky, land, and sea. (The Sky group might pretend to be different planets rotating on their axes; the Land group could portray animals and people; the Sea group might pretend to be creatures in the sea.) Allow time for the children to work together to prepare their presentations. Encourage the children to share their skits with the other groups.

Session 1   7

Our Loving God

We have been created by a loving God. God is Father, Son, and Holy Spirit. This is called the Trinity. God loves us and cares for us. That is why he stays close to us and in our hearts.

Think of the beautiful story of creation. Picture the good things in the world. Remember that God has loved us from the beginning of the world. We can be **holy** because he loves us.

Reading God's Word

Everything that God made is good. We are thankful for all that God has given us.

adapted from 1 Timothy 4:4

Unit 1, Session 1   7

Explore

A Center for Caring

Draw the children's attention to the pictures and have them describe what they see. Encourage comments about the beauty in God's creation.

Say: **We are going to read about a special group of people working to help all of us care for God's creation.**

Ask children to follow along as you read the title and first paragraph. Call on a volunteer to find and read the sentence that tells what God wants us to do. (God wants us to care for his creation.)

Read the second paragraph and then explain: **Conservation means taking care of the things in our world to keep them safe from harm or waste.** Ask a volunteer to read the sentence that tells Mr. Jacobs's message. (His message is to treat the earth with respect.)

Read the last two paragraphs. Ask: **How can we show love for God?** (by respecting his creation) **As Catholics, what are we called to do?** (care for God's creation) Ask for children's suggestions about how we might do this. Then say: **When we read the next page, we will find out more about caring for creation; but first, we're going to learn a song about thanking God for his love for us.**

Invite the children to relax and to set their materials aside while they learn a new song that is called "Song of Love." Say: **As we learn more about God's love for us, we also learn how to share his love with others. Let's listen to this song about thanking God for his love for us and for showing us how to share it with others.** Ask the children to turn to "Song of Love" in the Songs of Our Faith section in the backs of their books so they can follow along with the words as they listen to the song.

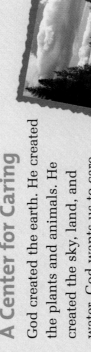

🎵 💿 Play the song (CD 2, Track 1). Play it again and invite the children to sing along. Then ask: **What does the song tell us about where we can find Jesus?** (in others, by reaching out to others, in our own heart, in our family and friends)

FYI

CATHOLIC CONSERVATION CENTER

The Web site for the Catholic Conservation Center is **conservation.catholic.org**. It contains links to many writings and resources about the environment and ecology from various Catholic sources. It has some beautiful illustrations to accompany Scripture passages and information about lives of saints concerned with ecology and conservation.

A Center for Caring

God created the earth. He created the plants and animals. He created the sky, land, and water. God wants us to care for his creation.

Members of the Catholic Conservation Center remind us to take care of God's creation. The Center was started by a Catholic named Bill Jacobs. His message is to treat the earth with respect.

The Catholic Conservation Center spreads this message. The Center reminds us that we show love for God by respecting his creation.

As Catholics, we all are called to care for God's creation. We all can follow Bill Jacobs's example of caring.

8   God's Invitation

Caring for God's Creation

Ask children to look at the picture for the activity. Allow children to work with partners to discuss and do the activity. When children have finished, ask them to keep their books open to this page.

Ask: *How can we be sure we have good water to drink?* (keep trash out of streams and rivers)
What can we do to make sure our streets and fields are clean? (not litter)

What Can You Do?

Read the title and the directions for the activity. Allow children to work with partners to discuss and do the activity. When children have finished, ask them to keep their books open to this page.

Say: *In the What Can You Do activity, we worked with partners to discuss our ideas for caring for the earth. Let's take a few moments to share our ideas with the class.*

Encourage children to share the ideas they have written or drawn and to tell how they will try to care for the earth this week.

End by praying these words with the children: *Thank you, God, for the beauty of creation, especially for _____.* Allow each child to add whatever he or she would like.

OPTION

CREATION LIST

God created the following things: land, water, sun, trees, plants, fish, birds, and land animals. On the board or on butcher paper, list these things horizontally. Below each word write what that creation does for us. For example, under *land* you would write *place to build homes*; under *water* you could write *provides drink.* As the list grows, help the children become more aware of God's love and generosity.

OPTION

PICTURE-PERFECT WORLD

Have some magazines available so children can browse for pictures of something beautiful in God's creation. Have them cut out a picture and glue it onto a piece of white paper. Have them trim the white paper to look like a photo edge. If you have scissors that cut scalloped or fancy edges, these would give a nice effect.

Then ask children to glue their pictures once more onto colored construction paper. During a sharing time, encourage children to talk about how the things in their picture have been cared for to preserve their beauty.

Caring for God's Creation

The Church teaches us to care for the earth. We love God, so we should not harm his creation. We should take care of all things found in nature.

We also help each other when we take care of the earth. We have better water to drink if we keep trash out of streams and rivers. We enjoy cleaner streets and fields if we do not litter.

What Can You Do?

With a partner think of three things you can do to take care of the earth. Write or draw your ideas.

Reflect

Prayer

Note: In the Reflect section of every session, children are invited to prayer and reflection that focus on an aspect of the session theme. If possible, have children gather around the prayer center for this prayer time.

Explain to the children that it is important to talk with God about what they have learned.

Before praying, review the Sign of the Cross with the children. First demonstrate it for the group. Then have them pray it with you. Make sure they touch their foreheads with their right hands as they say: *In the name of the Father.* Then they should touch their hearts and say: *and of the Son.* Then, as they touch their left shoulders, have them say: *and of the Holy.* As they touch their right shoulders, they should say: *Spirit.* Then they should bring their hands together and pray: *Amen.*

Now ask the children: *What do you see in the background photo?* (stars) Then ask: *Who made heaven and the stars?* (God)

♫ 💿 Softly play the reflective music at the end of CD 2 as you lead the children in reflection. Say: *Let's prepare for our special prayer time. Let's be quiet when we pray to God and listen to him in our hearts. Relax and take two deep breaths.* Pause for 10 seconds. Then read the first and second paragraphs slowly and reverently.

Say: *Repeat the words of the Glory Be to the Father after me as you follow along in your books.*

Pause for 10 seconds. Then read the final paragraph, pausing after each sentence. Say: *Let's close our prayer with the Sign of the Cross.*

Say: *With thankfulness in our hearts, let's learn more about how we can care for God's creation.*

FYI

GLORY BE TO THE FATHER

The Glory Be to the Father is called the Doxology, from the Greek word *doxa,* meaning "glory" or "praise." In the Doxology we praise God the Father, God the Son, and God the Holy Spirit.

Prayer

God made many things. We praise him with the Glory Be to the Father.

As you pray the Glory Be to the Father, think about how much God loves you and cares for you.

Glory be to the Father, and to the Son, and to the Holy Spirit. As it was in the beginning, is now, and ever shall be, world without end. Amen.

Think about the things we praise God for. Thank God for creating you. Thank him for loving you.

10   My Response

Living My Faith

Faith Summary
Read the section. Ask: **What things did we learn that God made?** (animals, heaven, earth, man, woman) Then ask: **Why did he make all these things?** (because he loves us)

Words I Learned
Ask volunteers to pronounce and define each word. Call on other volunteers to use each word in a sentence.

Ways of Being Like Jesus
Read the section. Ask: **What might we do to love God's people?** (be kind to them, use gentle words) **What can we do to take care of the earth?** (recycle, not waste, not litter)

 God's Creation

Respond

With My Family
Ask: **What is the family in the picture doing to enjoy God's world?** (having a picnic together) Encourage the children to invite their families to an indoor or outdoor picnic. Tell them to show their families various things in God's creation.

Prayer
Note: At the end of each session, children are invited to join in a prayer of thanksgiving and gratitude related to what they have learned about their faith. After praying the short prayer in the book with children, always give them a few moments to add their own prayers of thanks.

Give the children a few moments to speak with God in silence. Then say: **Let's close with the Sign of the Cross.**

Say: **Let's thank God for the beautiful world he made. Pray silently as I pray aloud for us. After the prayer think about what you can do today to care for God's world.**

My Response
Read the section. Say: **Take a moment to think of what you can do to care for the world. Then draw your idea.**

When the children have finished, ask volunteers to explain what they will do to take good care of the world when they leave today.

 God's Creation

Remind the children that they are part of God's creation and therefore are special to him.

Living My Faith

Faith Summary
Because he loves us, God made many things. All of them are good. God wants us to take good care of the world.

Words I Learned
creation   **holy**

Ways of Being Like Jesus
Jesus loves all of us and everything that God made. You are like Jesus when you love all of God's creation.

With My Family
Have a picnic with your family so you can enjoy God's world. Talk about God's creation.

 God's Creation

Prayer
Thank you, God, for all you have made. Help me love you by taking care of your creation.

My Response
Draw a picture showing what you will do to take good care of the world this week.

Living My Faith

Extending the Session

Choose from the following options to extend the session or to reinforce concepts developed during the week.

Family Involvement

Remind the children to take home the Raising Faith-Filled Kids page to share what they are learning with their families.

Preparation for Sunday Scripture Readings

Lead children in a prayerful discussion of Sunday's readings. Visit **www.FindingGod.org/Sunday** for more information.

Seasonal Session

Consider the time of the liturgical year and use the appropriate seasonal session. Seasonal sessions may be found on page 241.

Unused Options and BLMs

Incorporate any unused options or Blackline Masters from the week's session.

Web Site Activities

Visit **www.FindingGod.org** to find additional activities for extending the session.

OPTION

GOD MADE ME, AND I AM GOOD

Have each child draw a self-portrait and have him or her write *God made me, and I am good* below the picture. Invite each child to share his or her portrait with the class and tell one way that he or she is good. You might prompt the children by having them complete the following sentence: *I am good because _____.*

OPTION

SENTENCE PUZZLE

Write the sentence *God is the creator of everything* on separate sentence strips. Be sure to make enough for pairs or small groups of children. Cut apart each sentence strip between the words to create six pieces. Have each group work together to place the words in order to remake the sentence. When each pair or group has solved the puzzle, have them raise their hands. When all the groups are ready, have the children enthusiastically read the sentence aloud.

OPTION

HELPING OTHERS

Write each child's name on a separate slip of paper and place the slips in a bag. Have each child choose a name from the bag. Tell the children that at some point during the next week they should help the person whose name they chose. For example, a child might sharpen that person's pencil, offer assistance in spelling a word, share a crayon, or carry that person's backpack. At the end of the following week, invite children to tell what they did to help someone else.

RAISING FAITH-FILLED KIDS
a parent page

Focus on Faith

God Says That the World Is Good

Children love surprises. They soak up new experiences every day and ask many *why* questions about the way things work. It may not always benefit your child to hear these questions—such as "Why is the sky blue?"—answered only with scientific explanations. Instead, a story about how the blue color of the sky reminds us to honor Jesus' mother, Mary, might sound just right to your child. The first chapter of Genesis is filled with this kind of wonder. God is the great craftsman who created the sun, moon, and stars and said that they are very good. Perhaps even more amazingly, God keeps everything going day after day, and we awake each morning delighted to see that he has done it again. Children are God's happy surprises, and they remind us not to take things for granted.

Dinnertime Conversation Starter

Share your memories of a time when your family discovered something wonderful or beautiful about the world.

Spirituality in Action

Take your child to the zoo or a lush park. Encourage your child to use all of his or her senses to notice the surroundings. Ask your child to make observations about the animals or plants. Then share with one another an appreciation of these wonders that God has made.

Hints for at Home

Work with your child to create a collage representing the natural wonders that God has created. Use magazine clippings, poster board, and other materials to create the collage. Hang it in a special place in your home.

Focus on Prayer

Your child is learning to pray the Doxology, or Glory Be to the Father. Pray the prayer together often as a family to facilitate memorization. Begin the Glory Be to the Father with the Sign of the Cross.

Take a few moments to reflect prayerfully before you prepare this session.

Session 2: God Gives Us Jesus

3-Minute Retreat

Before you prepare for your session, pause for a few moments and calm yourself. Silently count to 10 and remember that you are in the loving presence of God as you continue helping the children on their faith journey.

Matthew 28:20

And behold, I am with you always, until the end of the age.

Reflection

God is not distant or aloof. He wants us to have a relationship with him, so he sent his only Son, Jesus, to lead us to salvation. Jesus fulfills God's promise to be with us always. In the last words from the Gospel of Matthew, Jesus assures his disciples that his love and presence are eternal. Even to this day, we receive Jesus in the Eucharist, our spiritual food, which strengthens us on our journey.

Question

In a world of broken promises, what does it mean to me to know that God's love and presence are eternal?

Prayer

Speak to God our loving Father, using this prayer or words of your own. Intimate and loving God, draw me continually closer to you and remain with me forever. Let me mirror your love and acceptance to all.

Catechist Preparation

Knowing and Sharing Your Faith

Scripture and Tradition in Session 2

Joseph was a just man who wanted to do the right thing when he found out that Mary was expecting a child. Joseph was told by the angel not to be afraid to take Mary as his wife, as she had conceived by the power of the Holy Spirit.

The angel told Joseph that Mary's son would be named Jesus, which means "God saves." Jesus would also be called Emmanuel, which means "God with us." The name *Emmanuel* is based on a promise from God: "Ever present in your midst, I will be your God, and you will be my people." (Leviticus 26:12)

Living in perfect obedience to his Father, Jesus saved us through his ministry to the poor and vulnerable and through his own suffering, death, and resurrection.

With the Father, Jesus Christ sends the Holy Spirit, the source of the grace we need to live as Jesus did. The Holy Spirit inspires us to recognize Jesus as Lord. As our Lord, Jesus receives all the praise, honor, and glory due to God.

Scripture in Session 2

An angel tells Joseph the name for Mary's son in **Matthew 1:18–24.** In **Matthew 28:20** the risen Jesus speaks to his disciples.

Let the scripture and Tradition deepen your understanding of the content in this session.

WINDOW ON THE CATECHISM

Jesus as the good news of our salvation is treated in *CCC* 422–424. The meaning of the name of Jesus is found in *CCC* 430–432.

Jesus is Emmanuel.

I am with you until the end.

Catechist Preparation

From the Richness of the Tradition

In "Pastoral Statement on the Handicapped" the American bishops stated on November 15, 1978, that prejudice begins with a recognition that others are different from us. People tend to understand these physical or psychological differences in moral terms, that is, "we" are not only different from "them" but are somehow better than "they" are. The solution to prejudice, then, requires an acceptance of the differences among people and a respect for others, not in spite of their differences but actually because of those differences. The answer is to eliminate the distinction between "us" and "them" so that we can respect one another as children of the same loving Father.

✝ Catholic Social Teaching

The following Catholic Social Teaching is woven into this session:

Call to Family, Community, and Participation.

Consider in this session how you will invite the children to respond to and prayerfully reflect on God's invitation to love and serve others.

GENERAL DIRECTORY FOR CATECHESIS

Jesus Christ not only transmits the word of God, he is the Word of God. This is explored in GDC 98.

Prayer in Session 2

The brief opening and closing prayers invite the children to reflect on God's gifts to us. The practice of genuflecting is also introduced.

A special approach to prayer in Session 2 is an extended guided reflection entitled "Jesus Is Born." As you prepare to share this prayer experience with the children, listen to the recorded guided reflection, "Jesus Is Born" (CD 1, Track 6), as a prayerful experience for yourself. Then, when you play the recording during the session, join the children in reflective prayer.

If instead you choose to lead the guided reflection yourself, listen to the recording a second time, following the script (pages 366–367) and noting pauses and tone of voice. You can then use the script or adapt it as you wish. When leading the guided reflection during the session, play instrumental music softly in the background to enhance the sense of prayerfulness.

An alternate approach to prayer in this session is to use the Prayer on the children's page.

Catechist Preparation: Get-Ready Guide

Session 2: God Gives Us Jesus

Session Theme: *Jesus is the Son of God who comes to save us.*

Before This Session

- You may wish to gather several baby-naming books for the children to look up the meanings of their names for the activity on page 16. Check the meaning of your name so you can share it as an example.
- Bookmark your Bible to Matthew 1:18–24 and Matthew 28:20. Place the Bible in the prayer center open to the first passage in Matthew.
- Set up the CD player so you will be ready to play the songs and the guided reflection. Listen to them prior to the session to become familiar with the content and pacing.
- Arrange a guided tour of your church for the option on page 22.

Steps

DAY 1	**Engage** page 13	
	God Gives Us Jesus	
DAYS 1-3	**Explore** pages 14–19	
	The Story of Joseph	
	Another Name	
	A Precious Gift	
	Jesus Cares for Us	
DAY 4	**Reflect** page 20	
	Prayer: Visiting Baby Jesus in the Stable	
DAY 4	**Respond** page 21	
	Living My Faith: Ways of Showing Respect for Others	
DAY 5	**Extending the Session** page 22	
	Day 5 offers an opportunity to extend the session with activities that reinforce the session outcomes.	

Outcomes *At the end of the session, the children should be able to*

- understand how it feels to receive a special gift.
- be able to tell the story of Joseph trusting the angel's message.
- identify Jesus as God's most precious gift and as our Savior, Emmanuel.
- explain that Jesus is present to us in the Blessed Sacrament.
- define *Blessed Sacrament, Emmanuel, genuflect, Savior,* and *tabernacle.*
- prayerfully reflect on God's presence, his invitation, and our response.
- identify practical ways to act on God's invitation in everyday living.

Materials

Required Materials

- Bible
- Writing paper, pens, pencils
- Art materials, such as drawing paper, crayons, markers, scissors, glue
- Baby-naming books (page 16)
- CD 2, Track 6: Jesus in the Morning (Instrumental) (page 13)
- CD 2, Track 5: Jesus in the Morning (1:37) (page 15)
- CD 1, Track 6: Jesus Is Born (11:00) (page 20)

Optional Materials

- Magazines, construction paper (page 15)
- Variety of trail mix ingredients, mixing bowl, spoon, napkins (page 22)
- Blackline Masters 4, 5, 6 (pages 13, 16, 17)

e-resources

www.FindingGod.org

God Gives Us Jesus

Have the children open their books to page 13. Read the title of the session. Have the children describe what they see in the pictures.

Ask: **How do you think the child feels about receiving a gift? How can you tell?**

Read the questions below the pictures. Encourage the children to respond to the questions.

Have the children list on paper at least three people they would like to give a gift to sometime during the year.

Encourage them to list gift ideas for each person next to his or her name. Say: **Gifts do not have to be "things." When we give a gift, it should come from the heart. For example, a gift for mom could be to help her with the dishes one night. A gift for your big sister might be to do one of her chores so she has time to spend with a friend. A gift could even be giving something you already have. For example, you could give your best friend one of your favorite toys that you know she likes. Any gift that you put time and thought into will be loved.** When the children have finished, have them place their materials aside.

God Gives Us Jesus

♪ Play the instrumental version of "Jesus in the Morning" (CD 2, Track 6) as a reminder that this is a special time together. Then ask: **What are some of the best gifts you have received for occasions such as birthdays and Christmas?** Invite volunteers to name some of these gifts and to share what made them so special. Say: **God gave us many special gifts too. In today's session we'll find out about the most precious gift of all.**

God Gives Us Jesus
Session 2

Prayer

Dear God, help me always remember the gifts you have given me.

Did you ever receive a special gift from a friend or family member? How happy did it make you?

Prayer

Say: **We've all received special gifts from our families and friends. This week we're going to talk about the amazing gifts we've received from God. Let's tell God we know that he gave us many wonderful gifts, especially his love for us.**

Then say: **Fold your hands and pray the prayer aloud with me. Then take a moment to say anything else you would like to share with God.**

Pray the prayer aloud. Pause and take three deep breaths to allow time for the children to pray silently. End by praying **Amen.**

BLM 4: PRECIOUS GIFTS
Blackline Master 4 is a cut-out-and-fold cube with a picture of Jesus.

Explore

The Story of Joseph

Read the title aloud. Ask: *Who remembers who Joseph is?* (Jesus' foster father) Ask: *Does anyone remember the story of Mary and the angel?* Say: *God sent the angel Gabriel to tell Mary she would have a son named Jesus.* Then say: *Now we will find out what happened when an angel came to Joseph.*

Read the first paragraph aloud. Ask: *Who remembers who the Holy Spirit is?* (the third person of the Trinity)

Read the second paragraph. Read the angel's dialogue with expression. Call on several volunteers to read the angel's dialogue with expression in their voices and on their faces. Then say: *God sent angels as messengers for him. This angel was sent to bring a special message from God to Joseph.*

Complete the reading on pages 14–15 in this guide before beginning Reading God's Word.

Reading God's Word

Read the verse aloud while the group follows along. Say: *These words tell us that Jesus promises to love us always and be with us.* Ask: *How does this promise make you feel?* (happy, safe, loved)

Divide the children into two groups. Explain that they will perform the verse in Reading God's Word as a choral reading. Assign the first group to read *I will be with you always* and the second group to read *until the end of the world!* Remind the children to read with feeling and expression as they speak these meaningful words.

Have the children describe what they see in the illustration. Explain that it shows the angel coming to Joseph in a dream. Say: *The angel told Joseph that Mary would have a child by the Holy Spirit.*

Read the first paragraph on the next page while the group follows along. Point out the word *Savior* in dark type. Say: *The name Jesus means "God saves."* Ask: *Why is Jesus our Savior?* (because he saves us from our sins)

Read the second paragraph aloud while the group follows along. Say: *The angel told Joseph that he shouldn't be afraid, and*

Joseph listened to the angel. Joseph had great faith in the angel's message.

Say: *Now we will listen to a song called "Jesus in the Morning" about Jesus being with us all day long—in the morning, afternoon, and when we go to bed. You will hear words that tell us what we can do for Jesus.* Have the children turn to the Jesus verses of the song in the Songs of Our Faith section in the back of their books. Continue: *Listen carefully, and I'll ask you what you heard after the song is over.*

The Story of Joseph

Before Joseph and Mary were married, an angel appeared to Joseph in a dream. The angel told Joseph that the baby which Mary was going to have would be from the Holy Spirit.

Joseph did not understand. Then the angel said, "Joseph, son of David, do not be afraid to take Mary as your wife."

adapted from Matthew 1:18–20

Reading God's Word

I will be with you always, until the end of the world!

adapted from Matthew 28:20

14   God's Invitation

Play the song "Jesus in the Morning" (Jesus verses) on Track 5 of CD 2. Afterwards, ask: **What words did you hear that told you what we can do for Jesus?** (praise, love) If time permits, play the song again and encourage the children to sing along.

Word Puzzle

Call attention to the activity and read the title and directions. Tell the children they can look back at the story for the correct spellings of the words. Give the children time to complete the activity. Invite volunteers to share their answers.

The angel told Joseph to name the child Jesus. The name *Jesus* means "God saves" or "God saves us." Because Jesus will save us from our sins, he is our **Savior**.

After Joseph woke up from his dream, he took Mary as his wife.

adapted from Matthew 1:21-24

Word Puzzle

Unscramble these letters to spell names from the Bible story you have just read.

Joseph   oJesp   J o s e p h
          suJes   J e s u s
          ryMa   M a r y

Unit 1, Session 2   **15**

OPTION

LITANY OF SAINT JOSEPH

Explain: *Saint Joseph was a good man who listened to God. Saint Joseph lived a life of faith.* Say: *A litany is a prayer that contains a verse and a response. We can ask Saint Joseph to pray for us.*

Explain that you will read some descriptions of Saint Joseph. Have the children respond, "Pray for us," after each. Read:

Foster father of the Son of God
Head of the Holy Family
Example for parents
Protector of the Church

OPTION

SAINT JOSEPH, PATRON SAINT

Tell the group that Saint Joseph is a patron saint of the Church. Ask: *Who remembers what a patron saint is?* (a saint who watches over a certain group of people) Remind the group: *Saint Isidore, whom we learned about at the beginning of this unit, is the patron saint of farmers.*

Tell the group: *In some pictures of Saint Joseph, he holds the infant Jesus. In other pictures he might hold tools, since he was a carpenter. Saint Joseph's feast day is March 19. In many parishes families celebrate this day by hosting a Saint Joseph's Table that features breads, pastries, vegetables, flowers, and perhaps the craftwork or artistry of the hosts.*

Ask the group: *What kinds of things could we include on a Saint Joseph's Table?* Distribute magazines, scissors, construction paper, markers, and glue. Have the children write *Saint Joseph's Table* at the top of their construction paper. Tell the children to cut out pictures of things they would include on a Saint Joseph's Table and to glue them onto their paper.

 Family and Community

FYI

ANGELS

Our oldest scriptures and earliest church traditions witness the existence of spiritual beings who glorify God. Angels in the Scriptures carried messages to the prophets, to Joseph, and to Mary, and angels announced the good news of Jesus' birth and resurrection.

Another Name

Begin by providing time for the children to speak with Jesus about whatever is on their minds. Then explain to the children the importance of names. Say: *Our names are our identification. They tell who we are. Let's see how Jesus' name tells us who he is.*

Call attention to the art. Ask the children: *Who is shown in the picture?* (Jesus, Mary, and Joseph) Then ask: *What is happening in the picture?* (Saint Joseph is very lovingly holding Jesus. Mary is working around the home.)

Write the names *Jesus, Christ, Savior,* and *Emmanuel* on the board. Call out each name and tell the children to raise their hands if they have heard the name. Make a check mark for each raised hand. With the children, count the check marks to determine totals for each name. Explain: *Christians all around the world use these titles for Jesus.*

Read the title and the first paragraph aloud. Focus on the name *Emmanuel* in dark type. Have the children practice pronouncing the name. Ask the group: *What does Emmanuel mean?* (It is Hebrew for "God with us.")

Say: *Many people are named after saints or other religious figures. Names can have special meanings. For example, Jessica means "wealth" in Hebrew, Rosa is "rose" in Spanish, and Shen means "spiritual" in Chinese.* Share the meaning of your name with the children.

Go around the room and ask the children if they know why they were given their names. If they are named after saints, suggest that they learn about those saints' lives. If children do not know the origin of their names, encourage them to ask their parents. If you brought

any baby-naming books, you might have the children look up the meanings of their names.

Names for Jesus

Read the section aloud for the group. Make sure the children understand the directions. Have them use their pencils to complete the activity. Check answers.

OPTION

BLM 5: JOSEPH

Blackline Master 5 requires children to fill in missing letters to complete sentences about Joseph.

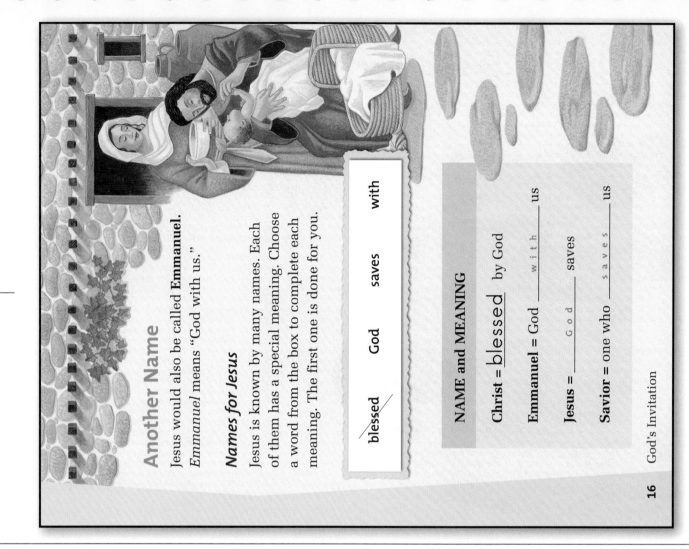

Another Name

Jesus would also be called **Emmanuel.** *Emmanuel* means "God with us."

Names for Jesus

Jesus is known by many names. Each of them has a special meaning. Choose a word from the box to complete each meaning. The first one is done for you.

blessed	God	saves	with

NAME and MEANING

Christ = blessed by God

Emmanuel = God with us

Jesus = God saves

Savior = one who saves us

16   God's Invitation

16   Session 2

A Precious Gift

Ask: *Have you ever given some-one a gift? What was it? How did it make the person feel?* Say: *God gave us a gift too. We'll learn more about that special gift now.*

Read the title and the first para-graph. Say: *God gave his Son to every person in the whole world.* Read the second paragraph aloud. Ask: *Who is God's Son who became man?* (Jesus) *Why do we call Jesus our Savior?* (He saves us from our sins.)

Read the third paragraph aloud while the group follows along.

Direct attention to the word *tabernacle* in dark type. Say: *The tabernacle is the container located near the altar where the consecrated bread is kept.* Have the children look at the picture. Say: *This is a tabernacle.*

Draw attention to the term *Blessed Sacrament.* Explain: *The Blessed Sacrament is the consecrated bread from Mass, which is kept in the tabernacle.*

Focus attention on the word *genuflect* in dark type. Say: *At Mass we do many things to show respect. When we enter or leave church, we genuflect. That means that we touch our right knee to the floor, before the Blessed Sacrament in the tabernacle.* Demonstrate the action and then have the children stand and prac-tice genuflecting together. Say: *What we are doing is called genuflecting. It is a sign of love and respect for the Blessed Sacrament.*

Link to Liturgy

Note: This feature, which appears in many sessions, introduces children to some aspect of our liturgy—the Mass and the sacraments. It helps children connect what they are learning about the Catholic faith to the celebration of that faith at Mass.

Read the section aloud. Say: *At the beginning of the Mass, the priest walks to the altar, bows, and leads the people in praying the Sign of the Cross. The priest then says, "The Lord be with you."* Ask: *What do we say in response?* ("And also with you.") Explain: *We call this the greeting. These words show that we believe that Jesus is with us.*

End by praying: *The Lord be with you.* Let the children respond: *And also with you.*

A Precious Gift

You know that God has given us many things. The most precious gift he has given us is his Son, Jesus. God gave Jesus to the whole world.

As God's Son who became man, Jesus wants to help us live good lives. Because of Jesus, we have been saved from our sins. He can help us live with God in heaven one day.

Jesus is with us in the **Blessed Sacrament.** We **genuflect** to honor the Blessed Sacrament inside the **tabernacle.**

Link to Liturgy

When the Mass begins, the priest says, "The Lord be with you." We respond by saying, "And also with you."

OPTION

BLM 6: BREAKING THE CODE

Blackline Master 6 is a code-breaking activity covering themes children have learned in this session.

FYI

THE BLESSED SACRAMENT

The celebration of the Eucharist is at the heart of the Church's life. We call the celebration of the Eucharist the *Most Blessed Sacrament.* This term refers to the consecrated bread that is reserved in the tabernacle, shown for adoration, or carried as communion to the sick.

Explore

Jesus Cares for Us

Remind the children that we can recognize God in the simplest of things. Invite them to close their eyes and think of a person or thing that reminds them of God's goodness. Then begin with the following: Write on the board *A friend is someone who_____.* Start a discussion about friendship by asking: *What is a friend?* (someone you like to be with, someone you can count on and who can count on you) Tell a friendship story of your own, and then encourage children to share a special time they have had with a friend and why it made them happy.

Ask the class to read with you the sentence on the board. Suggest how you would finish the sentence. (helps me when I have a problem, cares about me, is fun to be with) Encourage volunteers to take turns completing the sentence with their ideas.

Remind the children that earlier in the week you read from the Bible about how long Jesus promised to be with us. Ask if anyone remembers how long he said he would be with us. The children can turn to page 14 and look at Reading God's Word for the answer. (always, until the end of the world) Say: *Only a really good friend could make such a promise. Today we are going to read more about this special promise and what it means to us.*

Ask children to look at the picture on page 18 and tell why everyone seems so happy. (They are all friends. Jesus and the children are happy to be together.) Say: *Let's read more about our special friendship with Jesus.*

Read the title and first paragraph aloud. Ask: *What did Jesus promise?* (to love and care for us) *How long will Jesus be with us?* (until the end of time)

Read the next paragraph. Ask: *Because you are special to Jesus, what can you do?* (talk with him anytime) Say: *We can be as happy as these children when we spend time with our friend Jesus.*

OPTION

MY FRIEND JESUS

Invite children to draw a picture that includes them in a special scene with Jesus. Where would they be? What would they say to Jesus? What would Jesus say to them?

Jesus Cares for Us

Jesus told us, "Know that I am with you always, until the end." With these words, Jesus promised to love and care for us. He promised to be our Savior until the end of time.

With such a loving promise, Jesus has given you a precious gift. Jesus loves you. You are special. You can talk with Jesus anytime.

18   God's Invitation

Staying Close to Jesus

Read the title and first paragraph aloud for the group.

Invite comments about the picture of the child with a magnifying glass and how this suggests a mystery to be solved.

Read the second paragraph. Make sure the children understand what they are to do.

Suggest that the children work as detectives on their own to decode the message about Jesus. Give them time to complete the activity.

Say: **If you finish early, use the secret code to write your own name at the bottom of the page, as one of Jesus' special friends.**

When children have finished, ask a volunteer to read the message.

End your time together by praying the Glory Be to the Father with the children. Give them a few moments of silence to be with Jesus.

OPTION

CRACK THE CODE

Divide the class into groups. Using the secret code on page 19, ask the groups to encode a short message about something they learned in this week's lesson. They may look back in the session for ideas. (*Emmanuel* means "God with us." Jesus saves us from our sins.)

Assign each group a number and give each group two pieces of paper, one for the encoded message and one for the decoded message. Have the group put its number on both. Allow adequate time for the groups to prepare their encoded messages. Collect the decoded papers and hand out decoded messages so that the children can check their answers. Then have the groups read aloud the messages they decoded.

OPTION

SILENT TIME AT CHURCH

Take the children to a church at a time when it is relatively empty. Allow the children to scatter throughout the pews and spend some quiet time "staying close to Jesus."

Staying Close to Jesus

Jesus is always with you. You can talk to him often.

Use the code to reveal the message. It will remind you that Jesus is close to you.

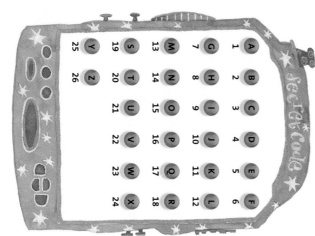

A	B	C	D	E	F
1	2	3	4	5	6

G	H	I	J	K	L
7	8	9	10	11	12

M	N	O	P	Q	R
13	14	15	16	17	18

S	T	U	V	W	X
19	20	21	22	23	24

Y	Z
25	26

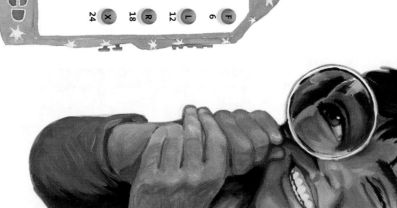

J E S U S
10 5 19 21 19

I S
9 19

W I T H
23 9 20 8

Y O U
25 15 21

I S
9 19

Reflect

Prayer

Jesus Is Born: A Recorded Guided Reflection

Remind the children that this is a special time when they can reflect on what they have learned and talk to God about it.

A special approach to prayer in Session 2 is an extended guided reflection titled "Jesus Is Born" (CD 1, Track 6). Refer to pages 366 and 367 for the script and directions for using the recorded guided reflection with the children.

Guided Reflection: An Alternate Approach

An alternate approach to prayer in this session is to use the Prayer on the children's page. The following suggestions will help you guide the children through this Prayer in a reflective manner.

Draw attention to the picture. Have the children describe what they see.

Say: *God certainly gave us Jesus, didn't he? And he certainly gave Jesus wonderful parents. In our prayer today let's imagine we are with Jesus, Mary, and Joseph. Please sit comfortably, be very still, fold your hands, silently take a long, deep breath, and then let it out slowly. Close your eyes if you'd like, and listen quietly.* Some children will be comfortable listening with their eyes closed. Others may want to look at the picture.

Read the page aloud to the children, pausing for 10 seconds after each paragraph. At the end of the Prayer, say: *If there's anything else you'd like to tell Jesus, take time now to do that.* Allow the children 20 seconds to complete their prayers. Close by having the children pray the Sign of the Cross.

When the reflection is over, say: *With happiness in our hearts, remember that Jesus is always with us, and we can talk with him anytime and anywhere.*

USING THIS PAGE AGAIN

If you have led the children through the recorded guided reflection, you might choose to use this prayer page with them during another session, Day 5, the Review session, or a seasonal session as appropriate.

GETTING CHILDREN READY FOR MEDITATION

You can help the children get ready for meditation. Help them learn to listen by inviting them to get their bodies into a comfortable position. Ask the children to close their eyes and fold their hands in front of them and silently take a long breath, and then let it out. Establish a rhythm by slowly counting to five while breathing in and again by slowly counting to five while breathing out. This will help the children focus.

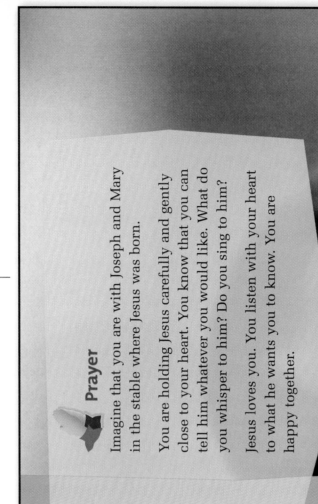

Prayer

Imagine that you are with Joseph and Mary in the stable where Jesus was born.

You are holding Jesus carefully and gently close to your heart. You know that you can tell him whatever you would like. What do you whisper to him? Do you sing to him?

Jesus loves you. You listen with your heart to what he wants you to know. You are happy together.

Living My Faith

Faith Summary

Read the section aloud. Ask: *What is God's greatest gift to the world?* (his Son, Jesus) *What are some names that Jesus is called?* (Christ, Emmanuel, Savior)

Words I Learned

Call on volunteers to pronounce and define each word. Choose other volunteers to use each word in a sentence. Invite the children to stand up and demonstrate how to genuflect.

Ways of Being Like Jesus

Read the section. Ask: *In what ways can we treat others with respect?* (use kind words, offer to help others, include others in what we do)

With My Family

Ask: *What is the girl in the picture doing to show her love for Jesus?* (making a card for someone)
Say: *God gave us the gift of his Son, Jesus. We can give gifts of love to others too.* Ask: *For whom might we each make a gift or card to show our love?* Elicit responses. Then encouragingly say: *Try to work on these gifts and give them to the person you choose before we meet again.*

✝ *Family and Community*

Prayer

Say: *We've talked a lot about the special gift that God gave us. Now let's thank him for this precious gift, Jesus. Let's pray the prayer aloud. Then think about how you can be like Jesus.*

Pause for 5 to 10 seconds, allowing the children a chance to continue to pray in silence. Close by praying *Amen.*

My Response

Read the section. Say: *To be more like Jesus, our Savior, we can show love to others by helping them.*

Allow the group ample time to work on this activity. When the children have finished their sentences, call on volunteers to read theirs.

As you end the day, say: *Remember, Jesus is with you now and always.*

Living My Faith

Living My Faith

Faith Summary

Because of God's great love for us, he sent his Son to become man. Jesus is God's greatest gift to the world. Jesus is our Savior.

Words I Learned

Blessed Sacrament   Emmanuel
genuflect   Savior   tabernacle

Ways of Being Like Jesus

We are blessed to be part of the human family. You are like Jesus when you love and respect people.

With My Family

Make a gift or card for someone in your family. On it write "I love you."

Prayer

Thank you, God, for sending us Jesus. Please show me how to be more like him.

My Response

Write a sentence about what you will do to help others.

Extending the Session

Choose from the following options to extend the session or to reinforce concepts developed during the week.

Family Involvement

Remind the children to take home the Raising Faith-Filled Kids page to share what they are learning with their families.

Preparation for Sunday Scripture Readings

Lead children in a prayerful discussion of Sunday's readings. Visit www.FindingGod.org/Sunday for more information.

Seasonal Session

Consider the time of the liturgical year and use the appropriate seasonal session. Seasonal sessions may be found on page 241.

Unused Options and BLMs

Incorporate any unused options or Blackline Masters from the week's session.

Web Site Activities

Visit www.FindingGod.org to find additional activities for extending the session.

OPTION
CHURCH TOUR

Arrange for the children to go on a guided tour of your church. Before the trip, review page 17 with the children. Remind them that Jesus is with us in the Blessed Sacrament, and that we honor the Blessed Sacrament inside the tabernacle. Be sure to point these out to the children as they follow the guide.

OPTION
GOD'S GIFTS MIX

Bring a mixing bowl, a mixing spoon, a variety of trail mix ingredients, and napkins to class. Place the materials on a table at the front of the room. Remind children that God gave us many gifts such as plants, seeds, and fruits for us to eat. Then call children one at a time to add the ingredients to the mixing bowl. Have other children stir the mix, pass out napkins, and serve some to each child. Then invite the children to eat and enjoy God's gifts.

OPTION
FRIENDSHIP TAG

Remind children of Jesus' promise to love and care for us. Tell them that by showing love and care to others we make and keep friendships. Then teach them how to play Friendship Tag. Bring the children to a big open playing area. Choose one child to be the tagger. As the tagger chases and taps children, the tagged hold hands with him or her, eventually forming a long chain. The chain then works together to tap the remaining children. When everyone is tapped and has joined the chain, have the children sit down to discuss the game. Ask them how it felt to be added to the chain, rather than be eliminated from the game. Then ask the children to share ways that they can include others when they are at play.

RAISING FAITH-FILLED KIDS *a parent page*

Focus on Faith

God Trusts Joseph With Jesus

The Gospel of Matthew tells us that Joseph was a man one could trust. He was open to hearing God's revelation that Jesus would be the one who saves us. God trusted Joseph to care for Jesus and Mary. Joseph may have helped Jesus take his first steps. We can imagine Joseph walking through the village with Jesus' hand firmly in his. Joseph taught Jesus about the history of their people and what it means to be faithful to God. As parents, we have been entrusted with children who are precious to God. We are their anchors in a hectic world, and our firm and loving hold on their hands as we walk together communicates to them the loving presence of the God who saves.

Saint Joseph Shadow of the Father, William Hart McNichols

Spirituality in Action

With your child prepare a package of nonperishable foods to deliver to a local food pantry. Explain to your child the importance of helping those who are less fortunate.

Dinnertime
Conversation Starter

Discuss what it must have been like for Jesus to learn from Joseph how to be a carpenter. What do you think Joseph would have taught him first? Discuss things that you learn from each family member.

Focus on Prayer

The story of Joseph reminds us of the immense love that the Holy Family had for God and for one another. As God directed him through an angel, Joseph took Mary as his wife and helped to bring up Jesus with great care. Through Joseph we learn the importance of family and of doing God's will. Spend a few moments together in quiet reflection, examining Joseph's dedication to God and to his family.

Hints for at Home

Work with your family to create an I Caught You Being Like Jesus bulletin board. Cut out hearts of colored paper and keep them in a special place, such as a basket with a marker tied to it. When one member of the family "catches" another being kind, loving, generous, or thoughtful, encourage him or her to write the name of the "caught" family member, along with a brief explanation of the Jesus-like act, on a heart. Post the hearts on a bulletin board.

22   www.FindingGod.org

Session 3: God Is Our Father

3-Minute Retreat

Before you begin preparing for your session, pause for a few moments and pay attention to your breathing. Take three deep breaths and be aware of the loving presence of God as you prepare to lead your group on their journey of spiritual growth.

Matthew 6:26

Look at the birds in the sky; they do not sow or reap; they gather nothing into barns, yet your heavenly Father feeds them. Are not you more important than they?

Reflection

Jesus explains that God is a loving Father. He assures us that God knows and cares about all of our needs. God takes care of the birds and flowers, so surely he will also take care of his people. Jesus assures us of the perfect and intimate love that God the Father has for us.

Questions

What worries of life could I place in the care of God, my heavenly Father? How can I share his love with others?

Prayer

With admiration in your heart, speak to the Father, using these words or others that come to mind.

Abba Father, you meet the needs of all creation. Be with me today and help me to be a sign of your love to the children.

Take a few moments to reflect prayerfully before you prepare this session.

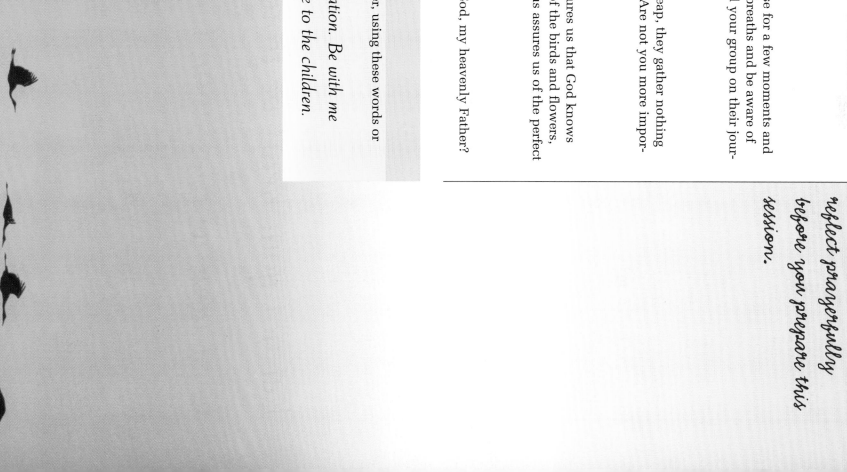

Catechist Preparation

Knowing and Sharing Your Faith

Scripture and Tradition in Session 3

In Matthew 6:26, Jesus explains that it is important to trust in God's care for us. Using the imagery of the birds of the air and the wildflowers in the field, Jesus tells us that God is our loving Father who is present for us.

Jesus taught us the Lord's Prayer. In praying the Lord's Prayer, we praise and glorify God and ask for what we need. In the first part of the Lord's Prayer, we give praise and honor to God:

Our Father, who art in heaven. Heaven is a state of complete happiness. Our goal is to be with God in the life that never ends. Living in the grace of Jesus Christ leads us to heaven.

Hallowed be thy name. God's name is holy. We are to treat God's name with reverence and respect.

Thy kingdom come. . . . God's Kingdom is present when we let God direct our lives and when we show others the same care and concern that God has shown us by sending his Son, Jesus.

In the second part of the Lord's Prayer, we ask for what we need. We ask for God's forgiveness as the first step toward forgiving others. We ask God to help us when our faith is tested. We end with *Amen,* expressing our acceptance of all that we have prayed.

Scripture in Session 3

In **Matthew 6:25–34** Jesus assures believers that God will take care of them. **1 Peter 5:6–7** counsels the young to be humble before God and to entrust him with their worries.

Let the scripture and Tradition deepen your understanding of the content in this session.

WINDOW ON THE CATECHISM

Jesus Christ is introduced in CCC 65. The principle that all prayer is addressed to God as Father is treated in CCC 2786–2793.

Let not your heart be troubled.

Cast your worries upon him.

Catechist Preparation

From the Richness of the Tradition

One way to combat injustice is to help children experience God as Father of us all so that they can see all people as members of one human family. In "Brothers and Sisters to Us," the November 14, 1979, pastoral letter on racism, the American bishops taught: "God's Word proclaims the oneness of the human family—from the first words of Genesis, to the 'Come, Lord Jesus' of the Book of Revelation. God's Word in Genesis announces that all men and women are created in God's image; not just some races and racial types, but all bear the imprint of the Creator and are enlivened by the breath of His one Spirit."

✝ Catholic Social Teaching

The following Catholic Social Teachings are emphasized in this session:

- **Solidarity**
- **Care for God's Creation**

Prayer in Session 3

This session continues the pattern of prayer in the brief opening and closing prayers that invite the children to reflect on God as their heavenly Father. At the end of each prayer, the children can pray quietly. This session presents two forms of prayer: petition and praise. The children also review the Lord's Prayer and the orans position as a prayer posture.

Consider in this session how you will invite the children to respond to children and prayerfully reflect on God's invitation to love and serve others.

GENERAL DIRECTORY FOR CATECHESIS

The relationship between Jesus and the Father is explored in *GDC* 100.

Catechist Preparation: Get-Ready Guide

Session 3: God Is Our Father

Session Theme: *We call Jesus the Son of God because he reveals to us his loving Father.*

Before This Session

- Bookmark your Bible to Matthew 6:25–34 and 1 Peter 5:6–7. Place the Bible in the prayer center open to the passage from Matthew.

- Set up the CD player so you will be ready to play the songs, Scripture story, and the reflective music.

Steps

Outcomes *At the end of the session, the children should be able to*

DAY 1	**Engage** page 23 God Is Our Father	• recognize that we are cared for by others.
DAYS 1-3	**Explore** pages 24–29 Trust in God God Cares for Us Christ the Redeemer Statue	• recognize and explain how God provides for his creation. • describe how Jesus wants us to know that God is our Father. • explain how we can praise and petition God. • define the words *petition* and *praise*.
DAY 4	**Reflect** page 30 Prayer: Lord's Prayer	• prayerfully reflect on God's presence, his invitation, and our response. • pray the Lord's Prayer.
DAY 4	**Respond** page 31 Living My Faith: Placing a Care in God's Hands	• identify practical ways to act on God's invitation in everyday living.
DAY 5	**Extending the Session** page 32 Day 5 offers an opportunity to extend the session with activities that reinforce the session outcomes.	

Materials

Required Materials

- Bible
- Writing paper, pens, pencils
- Art materials, such as drawing paper, crayon, markers, scissors, glue
- CD 2, Track 8: Our Father (Instrumental) (page 23)
- CD 1, Track 1: Trust in God (2:46) (page 24)
- CD 2, Track 7: Our Father (1:02) (pages 27, 30)
- CD 2, Reflective music (page 30)

Optional Materials

- World map or globe (page 23)
- Bubble solution and wand (page 23)
- White fabric tablecloth, colored fabric paints, empty tin pans, cardboard, hand cleaning supplies or moist towels (page 25)
- Slips of paper, hat or bowl (page 27)
- Small religious statues (page 28)
- Index cards or small pieces of paper (page 29)
- Blackline Masters 7, 8, 9 (pages 25, 27)

e-resources

www.FindingGod.org

God Is Our Father

As Session 3 begins, have the instrumental version of "Our Father" (CD 2, Track 8) playing in the background.

After turning off the music, pray the Lord's Prayer with the children. Refer to the back of the book for the words to the prayer if needed. Ask: *How many people are in your family?* Say: *Stand up if you have any brothers.* Then have them sit back down. Then say: *Now stand up if you have any sisters.* Have them sit back down, then say: *Now stand up if you are an only child.* Then have these children sit. Say: *All families are different and special. God loves all families and watches over them.*

Have the children open their books to page 23 and describe what they see in the picture. Ask: *What is the family doing? How do they feel about one another? For what might the family be thankful?* Accept all reasonable answers.

Read the title and the paragraph below the picture. Encourage the children to respond to the question.

Engage

Then ask: *What types of things does your family do together? What types of foods do you like to eat?* You might want to share things about your family first. Then invite volunteers to share too.

Prayer

Say: *God loves us very much, and we can tell him anything. Let's ask Jesus to help us learn how to love God as he did.*

Continue: *Pray the prayer aloud with me. Then take a moment to silently share whatever you would like with Jesus.*

Pray the prayer. Pause for 10 seconds so the children have time to speak with Jesus. End the prayer time by praying **Amen** and having the children open their eyes.

God Is Our Father

Session 3

God Is Our Father

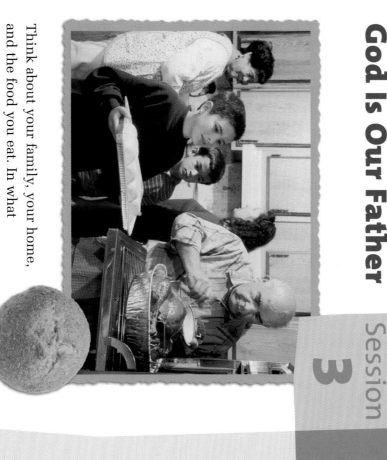

Think about your family, your home, and the food you eat. In what ways has God taken care of you?

Prayer

Dear Jesus, help me know and love God our Father as you did.

Unit 1, Session 3　23

OPTION

PEOPLE OF THE WORLD

On a world map or globe, show the children the continents and the oceans and then say: *God's world is huge, and he loves everyone in every country on every continent. God cares for every person in every place in the world.* Point to North America and show the children where they live. See if they know the names of any other continents.

✝ *Solidarity*

OPTION

BUBBLES OF LOVE

Gather outdoors for this activity. Blow hundreds of bubbles with your bubble solution and wand. Have the children try to count the number of bubbles. Say: *Look how the bubbles go all over! It's hard to count the number of bubbles, isn't it? These bubbles are like God's love. There is so much love, and God's love is for all people.*

Session 3　23

Explore

Trust in God

Ask: *What types of things do you see in this picture? What kinds of animals are there? Who created them?* (God) Then say: *These are part of God's creation. God takes care of them just like he takes care of us.*

Read the title and say: *We will now learn about trusting in God. Let's listen to how Jesus said we should trust in God.* Read the story on pages 24 and 25 aloud to the children. Be sure to read Jesus' words with expression.

Say: *Now we will listen to this story on CD so we can learn more about trusting in God.* The dramatized version of the Scripture passage developed for this session, "Trust in God," is based on Matthew 6:25–34.

Have the children sit comfortably as they prepare to listen to a Scripture story. Play the recording on Track 1 of CD 1. When the recorded passage ends, encourage the children to comment on what they heard.

Then ask: *What did Jesus tell us to do?* (trust in God) *What did he tell us not to do?* (worry) *What do you worry about?* (making good grades in school, scoring in a game) You might share things that you worry about as well. Say: *Jesus tells us that we can talk to him about our worries and that God will help us. Trusting in God will help us not to worry so much.*

Remind the children: *God gives food to the birds in the sky and sun and water to the flowers. He also provides wonderful things for us. He gives us the gift of his creation as well as parents who love and care for us.*

Tell the children that they can see how God cares for the flowers of the field with this fingerplay. Read each line and demonstrate the actions. Have the children repeat after you.

Five lovely flowers, standing in the sun.
(Hold up five fingers.)
Their heads are nodding, bowing one by one.
(Bend each finger individually.)
Down, down, down comes God's gentle rain.
(Raise both hands, wiggle fingers, lower hands.)
And the five lovely flowers lift up their heads again.
(Hold up five fingers.)

Trust in God

Jesus wants us to know that God our Father is close to us. Jesus helps us learn to trust in God.

Jesus said, "Do not worry about your life. Do not worry about what you will eat or drink or what you will wear. Worrying will not add one minute to your life.

"See the birds that fly and the flowers that grow. The birds in the sky do not work. Yet God gives them the food they need to live.

24   God's Invitation

Color God's Creatures

Read the directions for the coloring activity. After the group has finished, encourage the children to share their artwork.

Reading God's Word

Read this section while the group follows along. Say: *When we trust in God, we place our cares in his hands. We can feel as if we are being held in God's hands.* Have the children close their eyes for a moment. Then say: *Imagine being held in God's hands.* After a few moments, ask the children to open their eyes. Ask: *How did it feel to be held in God's hands?* (safe, comforted, loved) Say: *Thank God for his loving care often as you go through the rest of this day.*

OPTION
BLM 7: GOD TAKES CARE
For Blackline Master 7 children make paper quilt squares to add to a group quilt.

OPTION
BLM 8: NO MORE WORRIES
Blackline Master 8 asks children to write their worries on slips of paper and pray to God to take their worries away.

OPTION
TRUST IN GOD PRAYER TABLECLOTH
Lay a clean tablecloth on a table or on the floor. Put a piece of cardboard underneath the tablecloth so that the paints don't leak onto the table or floor. In large print write *Trust in God* on the tablecloth. Pour colored fabric paints into empty tin pans. Have the children put their hands in the paint and then press their hands on the tablecloth to make handprints. Have the children wash their hands. Then ask the group to use markers to print their names next to their handprints.

Explain: *Our handprints remind us that we are all unique and that God cares for every one of us.* Allow the tablecloth to dry and use it on the prayer table in the prayer center.

FYI
DIVINE PROVIDENCE
God cares for everything and everyone from the least to the greatest. Jesus asks us to trust in our heavenly Father who cares for us. Yet, God grants each of us the dignity of acting on our own. He does not superimpose his will on ours. Our response is to cooperate with God's plan for us which is life with him forever. Saint Peter tells us "Cast all your worries upon [God], because he cares for you." (1 Peter 5:7) We firmly believe that God is the master of the world. We don't always understand his ways, but one day when we see God "face to face," (1 Corinthians 13:12) we will fully know the ways by which he has guided his creation.

"Be like the flowers that grow wild. They do not work. But God helps them grow strong. God provides for all of them. And he will provide for you."

adapted from Matthew 6:25-34

Color God's Creatures
Color the birds and flowers in the picture.

Reading God's Word
Trust in the power of God. Place all your cares in his hands because he cares for you.

adapted from 1 Peter 5:6-7

God Cares for Us

Have the children look at the pictures. Ask: *What are the children in these pictures doing?* (praying) *How do you know?* (folded hands, closed eyes) Ask: *How do you think they feel inside?* (happy, calm)

Invite the children to imitate the prayer posture in the pictures and welcome God into their day. Ask the children: *What names do you use when addressing your father?* (daddy, papa) Explain: *Jesus called God Father the way we might say Dad.*

Read the title and the first two paragraphs aloud while the group follows along. Say: *Jesus wants us to know that God is our loving Father. We are very important to God. We can trust him to care for us the way he cares for the birds and flowers.*

Read the first paragraph on the next page. Draw attention to the word *petition* in dark type. Say: *To petition means to ask God for what we need. Please turn back to page 23 for a moment. The prayer at the bottom of the page is a prayer of petition because we are asking Jesus to help us.*

Tell the group: *Praying is talking and listening to God.* Ask the children: *What are some reasons we might pray a prayer of petition?* (to ask for help with our cares or worries, to ask God to bless our families)

Read the second paragraph aloud while the group follows along. Draw attention to the word *praise* in dark type. See if any of the children know what it means. Say: *Praise is an expression of the happiness we feel simply because God is so good.* Ask the children: *Have you ever been praised or thanked for a job well done, whether in school, at home, or in another area of your life? How does it feel to be praised?* Encourage a variety of responses. You may wish to share experiences of when you have been praised.

Complete the reading on pages 26–27 in this guide before beginning the Link to Liturgy.

Link to Liturgy

Read this section aloud. Explain: *During Mass we stand to pray the Lord's Prayer. This reminds us that we are God's children and members of his family. The first part of the Lord's Prayer is a prayer of praise because with these words we honor God for who he is in our lives. The second part of the Lord's Prayer is a prayer of petition because in it we ask God to help us.*

Review the orans position. Say: *The priest uses the orans position when praying the Lord's Prayer at Mass. You can pray this way too.* Demonstrate the orans position. (elbows slightly bent, hands open, palms up) Have the group stand and demonstrate it too. Say: *We can use the orans position when we pray to God. Watch for this prayer position when you go to Mass on Sunday.*

God Cares for Us

Jesus called God Father just as some children call their fathers Dad. Jesus reminds us that God is our Father too. God loves us and wants us to be happy. He wants all the best for us.

God gives birds the food they need to live. The flowers grow strong and lovely with God's care.

Link to Liturgy

During Mass, we stand to pray the Lord's Prayer. We pray this prayer together.

26   God's Invitation

Then explain: *We can praise God too. We can praise him for how wonderful he is.* Ask: *For what can we praise God?* (his goodness, his generosity, his love)

Read the last two paragraphs aloud while the group follows along. Explain: *Jesus was a good Son. He listened to his Father. He reminds us that we are to listen to God too. Jesus is a good model for us. He teaches us to trust in God.*

This might be a good time to remind the children of the additional information in Prayer and How We Pray section at the back of their books.

When we **petition** God in prayer, we ask him for what we need. We pray to God to help us. It is also good to **praise** God in our prayers. We tell him how wonderful he is.

God is our Creator and Father. We are his children. He cares for all people of the world because he is everyone's Father.

Jesus was a good Son. He listened to all that his Father said. Jesus had trust in God. He reminds us to trust God too.

OPTION
BLM 9: GOD IS OUR FATHER

For Blackline Master 9 children answer yes or no questions about the session.

OPTION
THE LORD'S PRAYER

Play Track 7 of CD 2, which has a musical version of the Lord's Prayer. Have the children turn to the "Our Father" song in the Songs of Our Faith section in the back of their books and encourage them to sing along. You may prefer, however, to sing a version used in your parish.

OPTION
PRAYER BUDDIES

Distribute a slip of paper to each child. Have each child write his or her name on it. Then collect all the names in a hat or bowl. Walk around the room and have each child pick a name. Then tell the children that the names they picked are their secret prayer buddies. Say: *Close your eyes, fold your hands like the children in the pictures, and take a few moments to pray to God for your prayer buddy. Ask, or petition, God to help your buddy in everything he or she does.* Give the children time to pray. Then quietly ask them to open their eyes. Encourage them to continue to pray for their prayer buddies during the next week.

OPTION
A HOLY PHRASE

Select a phrase from the Lord's Prayer (such as "Our Father, who art in heaven" or "thy kingdom come"). On the board create one blank space for each letter of the words in the phrase; include a blank space between the words of the phrase. Then have the children take turns calling out letters. Congratulate them when they figure out what the phrase is!

FYI
PRAYER OF PETITION

The prayer of petition acknowledges our dependence on God, who is our beginning and our end. This form of prayer springs from our heart's desire to serve God's kingdom here and to seek the realization of the kingdom to come. The Catechism of the Catholic Church reminds us that asking for God's forgiveness with a spirit of humility should be a prerequisite of a prayer of petition.

Explore

Christ the Redeemer Statue

Take a moment to invite the children to close their eyes and thank God for the many ways that God is present in our lives. Then say: *Yesterday we talked about how God is our Father and how he cares for us and all creatures.* Ask: *How can we show that we care for our friends and relatives who come to visit us?* (greet them happily, invite them in, embrace them)

Invite a few children to role play with you a welcoming scene. Ask one or two children to leave the room and knock on the door, pretending to be visitors. Welcome them with open arms, inviting them in warmly. Let a few children repeat the activity.

Say: *When we welcome our friends with open arms like you just did, they know we care for them. Today we will talk about Jesus' welcome to all of us.*

Read the title and the first paragraph aloud while children follow along. Ask: *What is a statue?* (a likeness of someone) *Why do you think Jesus' arms are outstretched in this statue?* Invite children to follow along as you read the last paragraph aloud to see if they were right. Say: *The statue shows Jesus welcoming the people, just as we welcomed each other with open arms.*

If you have a world map or globe, show the children the location of Brazil in relation to where they live. Say: *Jesus is with people everywhere in the world.*

STATUES HELP US REMEMBER

Display some small religious statues that you might have. Talk about their uniqueness and how they usually symbolize special aspects or qualities of the person represented. They help us remember something special about Jesus or Mary or whomever. (Examples: Jesus' welcoming arms, Mary with baby Jesus, Joseph with carpenter's tools) If there are statues in your school, take a walk to view them and discuss what you see. If possible, look at those in church also. Ask: *What statues do you have at home? Why are they special to your family?*

STATUE OF CHRIST THE REDEEMER

Brazilian engineer Heitor da Silva Costa sculpted this statue, which was inaugurated in 1931. The statue, located in Tijuca National Park, stands on Corcovado, or "Hunchback," Mountain. Its location affords spectacular views of the city, its mountains, and its beaches. There is a small chapel in the base of the statue. Christ the Redeemer's outstretched arms symbolize Christ blessing and protecting the city and its people.

Christ the Redeemer Statue

One of the world's largest statues is Christ the Redeemer. It overlooks the city of Río de Janeiro, or Río, in Brazil. This statue is almost 100 feet tall. It rests at the top of Corcovado Mountain. The mountain is leafy green with trees and other plants. It is a popular place for visitors; some like to have picnics there.

Jesus stands with his arms wide open. The statue shows how Jesus welcomes people into his loving embrace.

Close the session with this little song. Write the following rhyme on the board. Sing it with the children to the tune of "Twinkle, Twinkle, Little Star."

Jesus, Jesus, always near,
how I love that you are here.
You are with me in the day,
and at bedtime when I pray.
Jesus, Jesus, always near,
how I love that you are here.

Suggest that children think about how their actions at home tonight could show that they are remembering that Jesus is with them. What could they do that would make Jesus proud to be with them? (do a chore without being told, be cheerful to family members, help a brother or sister with homework)

On the board write *Tonight Jesus will be with me when_____.* Ask children to write the sentence on an index card or small piece of paper. Ask them to complete the sentence with something they will do at home tonight to make Jesus proud to be their friend. They may share their ideas if they wish.

Jesus Is With Us

Say: *Jesus watches over all people. He wants everyone to know that God loves them. Jesus is with us at all times to help us remember this.*

Invite the children to look at the picture and describe what they see. Ask: *What is the boy doing?* (listening to music) Read the title and paragraph aloud. Ask a child to read the words coming from the speakers. Encourage the children to share the way they would finish the sentence.

Give the children time to write their responses. After they have finished, call on volunteers to share their answers.

Jesus Is With Us

Jesus watches over the people of Río. Jesus is with us too. On the lines below, write about one time when you knew that Jesus was with you.

Jesus is with me when . . .

_____

_____

JESUS SURROUNDS US

Ask the children to stand. Explain that they are going to do an exercise called "Jesus Surrounds Us." Lead them in the following words and actions: *Jesus is above me* (stretch arms high into the air); *Jesus is below me* (stretch arms downward); *Jesus is beside me* (extend right arm); *Jesus is on each side of me* (extend left arm); *Jesus is behind me* (turn around); *Jesus is everywhere* (turn back around and wave arms in all directions).

End the exercise by having the children cross their hands over their hearts and say, "But most importantly, Jesus is within me."

Reflect

Prayer

Say: *It's now time for us to pray to God and quietly tell him whatever we would like. During this time we should be still so that we can hear God in our hearts.*

♪ Softly play the reflective music at the end of CD 2 as the children begin to reflect.

Read the first paragraph aloud. Then say: *We are so blessed that God wants to be with us. Let's take some time to praise God for his greatness and to petition him to care for us and our world. This prayer is called the Lord's Prayer. As I pray the prayer, think about how much God our Father loves each of us.*

Read the second paragraph for the group. Then pray the prayer aloud. Then say: *This is the most important prayer that Jesus has taught us. It is important to learn it by heart. I will help you. Please put your hands in the orans position. I will pray a line. Then I would like you to repeat it.*

With hands in the orans position and with a heartfelt voice, pray the prayer, line by line, while the group repeats after you. Then take a couple of deep breaths, giving the children a chance to pray in the quiet of their hearts.

♪ Track 7 of CD 2 has a sung version of the Lord's Prayer. Play this and encourage the group to sing along using the words on this page. You may prefer to sing the version used in your parish.

This may be a good time to have the children look through the Prayers and Practices of Our Faith section (pages 271–285). Ask them to look for prayers they have learned at home, at school, or at church.

THE LORD'S PRAYER

The Lord's Prayer is the quintessential prayer of the Church. In this prayer we address God as our Father since, through Baptism, we have become children of God. When we pray this prayer, we are one with the Father and Jesus Christ, his Son.

The Lord's Prayer, or Our Father, has seven petitions. The first three glorify God, his holy name, and speak of both the coming of the kingdom and the fulfillment of his will. The remaining four petitions present the Father with our needs and ask that he nourish our lives, heal us of sin, and help us overcome evil.

GESTURES IN THE LITURGY

Since the earliest days of the Church, gestures have been an important part of worship. Some gestures are positions for praying. The orans position is used by the priest during the liturgy. The people are welcome to use it, especially during the Lord's Prayer. The word *orans* comes from the Latin word for "praying." Genuflecting was originally used in the presence of rulers. We genuflect in front of the tabernacle as a sign of reverence for the Blessed Sacrament.

Prayer

In prayer we talk to and listen to God. We praise God, our loving Father, and we ask him for what we need. Jesus gave us the words to the Lord's Prayer, or the Our Father. You can praise God with this prayer and bring your needs to him.

As you pray, keep in mind how much God our Father loves us.

Lord's Prayer

Our Father,
who art in heaven,
hallowed be thy name;
thy kingdom come;
thy will be done on earth
    as it is in heaven.
Give us this day our daily bread;
and forgive us our trespasses
    as we forgive those
        who trespass against us;
and lead us not into temptation,
but deliver us from evil.
        Amen.

30   My Response

Living My Faith

Faith Summary
Read the section aloud. Say: **God cares for us and wants us to trust him and know that we are loved and safe.** Ask: **What does Jesus tell us we should do instead of worrying?** (trust in God)

Words I Learned
Call on volunteers to pronounce and define each word. Tell them to check their Glossaries if they need help. See if the children can use the words in sentences.

Ways of Being Like Jesus
Read the section for the group. Ask: **Why is it important to obey and listen to our parents?** (to be like Jesus, it makes God happy)

With My Family
Ask: **How are the mother and daughter in the picture caring for creation?** (making a bird feeder) Encourage the children to create a bird feeder with their families, just as the daughter and mother in the picture. Remind them: **We can help care for God's creatures,**

Faith Summary
Jesus helps us learn that God is our loving Father and is close to us. Jesus tells us to trust in God and place our cares in God's hands.

Words I Learned
petition   **praise**

Ways of Being Like Jesus
Jesus was a good son to God the Father. He obeyed his Father. You are like Jesus when you listen to your parents.

With My Family
Help care for the birds of the sky. Place a bird feeder in your yard.

Living My Faith

Prayer
Thank you, Jesus, for teaching me to trust in God and to place my cares in his hands.

My Response
Draw a picture or write a sentence to describe a care you would like to place in God's hands.

Respond

like birds. When we do this, it reminds us how God cares for us.

God's Creation

Prayer
Say: **We've learned about trusting God. Now let's thank Jesus for teaching us to place our worries in God's hands. Pray this prayer of thanks aloud with me. Then take a few moments to tell God about your worries and ask him to help you with them.**

Pray the prayer aloud. Then pause and give the group time to speak with God. Then say: **Let's close with the Glory Be to the Father.**

My Response
Read the section for the group. Say: **God wants us to trust him with our worries. Think about a worry that you have that you would like God's help with. Draw a picture or write a sentence about it. You could also just talk to God silently about your worries.**

Answer any questions the children may have, but respect each child's privacy regarding their cares and concerns.

Conclude enthusiastically by saying: **We are all God's children! Let's place ourselves in his hands.**

Extending the Session

Choose from the following options to extend the session or to reinforce concepts developed during the week.

Family Involvement

Remind the children to take home the Raising Faith-Filled Kids page to share what they are learning with their families.

Preparation for Sunday Scripture Readings

Lead children in a prayerful discussion of Sunday's readings. Visit www.FindingGod.org/Sunday for more information.

Seasonal Session

Consider the time of the liturgical year and use the appropriate seasonal session. Seasonal sessions may be found on page 241.

Unused Options and BLMs

Incorporate any unused options or Blackline Masters from the week's session.

Web Site Activities

Visit www.FindingGod.org to find additional activities for extending the session.

GOD CARES

Remind the children that God loves and cares for us and wants us to be happy. Review with them the meanings of the words *praise* and *petition*. Invite each child to take some time to praise or petition God. Tell the children to silently thank God for what he has given them. Say: *Ask him to help you love and care for others as he loves and cares for you. Talk to God in your own words.*

WHAT MAKES A GREAT DAD?

Organize the children into small groups. Have each group work together to make a list of words that could describe dads, such as *good listener, patient, fair,* or *funny.* Invite the groups to share their ideas. Then help students relate their ideas to God the Father, explaining that like fathers here on earth, God has all these attributes and more.

GIVE ME A G!

Help the children move away from tables or desks into a more open area. Tell the children that they are going to use their arms to spell some important words from the session. Begin by saying: *Give me a G.* Then ask the students to form a G with their arms. Continue with each letter in the word *God.* When done, ask the children what word they spelled. After the children name the word, ask them to tell how God is our Father.

RAISING FAITH-FILLED KIDS
a parent page

Focus on Faith

Teach Me to Pray

We are all beginners in prayer. No matter how many years we have been praying, we feel like rookies before God. We wonder what to say, what to do, what to say next, and whether we are being heard at all. This is what the disciples must have felt when they approached Jesus and asked him to teach them to pray. Jesus' response was to teach the Lord's Prayer. He would teach us the same thing today. Jesus wants us to know that no one loves us more than God does. God is always ready to listen, to forgive, and to help us forgive others. However we pray or teach our children to pray, prayer means to be open to love and to share that love with others.

Dinnertime Conversation Starter

Talk together about the things each of you would like to ask God for. Ask each family member to pray to God for one thing.

Hints for at Home

Help God take care of the birds of the sky. With your child create birdie treats. You will need peanut butter, birdseed, nylon netting, and twine. Combine a cup of peanut butter with a cup and a half of birdseed to form a thick, dry mixture. Divide the mixture into four pieces and roll each into a ball. Place each ball into a piece of nylon netting and tie the opening with a long piece of twine. Tie the opposite end of the twine to a tree branch and watch God's creatures enjoy your creation!

Focus on Prayer

Your child is learning to pray the Lord's Prayer, or the Our Father. Pray the prayer together often as a family to build memorization. At Mass help your child watch for the special gestures the priest uses during the Our Father. The words to the Lord's Prayer are found at www.FindingGod.org.

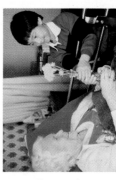

Spirituality in Action

As children of God, we are part of one human family. Take your child to visit a nursing home or a homebound member of your community. Explain to your child that showing concern and kindness for others is a way to remain connected to our larger human family.

Session 4: God's Life for Us

3-Minute Retreat

Before you prepare for your session, pause for a few moments and set aside any distracting thoughts. Slowly take three deep breaths as you clear your mind. Be aware that the Holy Spirit is with you and is helping you as you proceed in this journey of spiritual growth and discovery.

Luke 2:28–32

He [Simeon] took him [Jesus] into his arms and blessed God, saying:
"Now, Master, you may let your servant go
  in peace, according to your word,
for my eyes have seen your salvation,
  which you prepared in sight of all the
   peoples, a light for revelation to the Gentiles,
   and glory for your people Israel."

Reflection

No outward sign let Simeon know that the infant Joseph and Mary brought to the Temple was the Messiah. Simeon listened to the Holy Spirit and recognized the Messiah. The same Holy Spirit speaks to us to give us insight and guidance into our relationships with God, with others, and with ourselves. When we listen to the Holy Spirit, we can understand how God is present in our lives and make good decisions.

Questions

When am I most able to hear the promptings of the Holy Spirit? How can I best create an atmosphere that will also allow the children to be attentive to the Holy Spirit?

Prayer

Pray to the Holy Spirit using this prayer or one of your own.

Come, Holy Spirit, fill the hearts of your faithful.
And kindle in them the fire of your love.
Send forth your Spirit and they shall be created.
And you will renew the face of the earth.

Take a few moments to reflect prayerfully before you prepare this session.

Catechist Preparation

Knowing and Sharing Your Faith

Scripture and Tradition in Session 4

In the Scripture for this session, we see how God helps us recognize what is really important in our relationships. God promised Simeon, a righteous and devout man awaiting the Messiah, that he would not die before seeing him.

One day an ordinary-looking couple with a child entered the Temple. They had come to present their son to God, bringing with them an offering of two turtledoves. Simeon, by now an old man with tired eyes, probably did not see Mary, Joseph, and the infant Jesus very clearly. Simeon, however, recognized that this little child was the Messiah. Through the guidance of the Holy Spirit and with the eyes of faith, he saw beneath the surface and recognized in this infant God's promise fulfilled.

The teaching of the Church stresses the importance of recognizing the work of the Holy Spirit in all our relationships. The same Spirit who came to Mary, Joseph, and Simeon is with us and is helping us through his grace to recognize God's presence in our own lives. Grace invites, prepares, and calls us to act freely for God and others. By listening to the Holy Spirit we learn how to care for others and for ourselves.

Scripture in Session 4

We read the words of Simeon at the presentation of Jesus in **Luke 2:25–32.** In **Isaiah 49:6** the prophet speaks to the Jewish people in exile.

Let the scripture and Tradition deepen your understanding of the content in this session.

WINDOW ON THE CATECHISM

The work of the Holy Spirit in human life is in *CCC* 733–736, 739. The work of the Holy Spirit in our relationships is discussed in *CCC* 739.

Let your servant go in peace.

I will make you a light to the nations.

Catechist Preparation

From the Richness of the Tradition

The American bishops, on page 29 of their 1986 "Economic Justice for All: Pastoral Letter of Catholic Social Teaching and the U.S. Economy," spoke of the Church's call "to experience the power of God in the midst of poverty and powerlessness." Just as Simeon recognized the Messiah in the ordinary family that came to the Temple, so are we to experience God in our encounters with others. To have this experience, the bishops tells us, there must first be an emptying of self. We must become detached from material goods in order to see God in those who are poor, for only in our poverty is the power of God able to show itself to us.

✙ Catholic Social Teaching

The following Catholic Social Teaching is emphasized in this session: **Solidarity.**

Consider in this session: how you will invite the children to respond to and prayerfully reflect on God's invitation to love and serve others.

GENERAL DIRECTORY FOR CATECHESIS

Catechesis takes place within the Christian community. The role of the Holy Spirit in forming this community is covered in *GDC* 253.

Prayer in Session 4

In this session the children learn the Prayer to the Holy Spirit, which reinforces the belief that the Spirit guides them in the same way that it guided Simeon. In the opening prayer of petition and closing prayer of gratitude we acknowledge the importance of and our need for the Holy Spirit in our lives.

Catechist Preparation: Get-Ready Guide

Session 4: God's Life for Us

Session Theme: *All good things we do and the good decisions we make come from the Holy Spirit.*

Before This Session

- Bookmark your Bible to Luke 2:25–32 and Isaiah 49:6. Place the Bible in the prayer center open to the passage from Luke.
- Set up the CD player so you will be ready to play the song. Listen to it ahead of time.
- Invite someone who knows sign language to help your class with an option on page 42.

Steps

DAY 1	**Engage** page 33	
	God's Life for Us	
DAYS 1-3	**Explore** pages 34–39	
	Simeon of Jerusalem	
	The Holy Spirit	
	A Woman of Great Faith	
DAY 4	**Reflect** page 40	
	Prayer: Prayer to the Holy Spirit	
DAY 4	**Respond** page 41	
	Living My Faith: Ways of Caring for Others	
DAY 5	**Extending the Session** page 42	
	Day 5 offers an opportunity to extend the session with activities that reinforce the session outcomes.	

Outcomes

At the end of the session, the children should be able to

- appreciate the good things in our lives.
- explain how Simeon was able to recognize Jesus because he listened to the Holy Spirit.
- describe how the Holy Spirit guides us in decision-making.
- define the words *faith*, *Messiah*, and *Temple*.
- prayerfully reflect on God's presence, his invitation, and our response.
- pray the Prayer to the Holy Spirit.
- identify practical ways to act on God's invitation in everyday living.

Materials

Required Materials

- Bible
- Writing paper, pens, pencils
- Art materials, such as drawing paper, crayons, markers, scissors, glue
- CD 2, Track 10: Jesus in the Morning (Instrumental) (page 33)
- CD 2, Track 9: Jesus in the Morning (Spirit verses) (1:37) (page 37)

Optional Materials

- Magazine pictures of happy people doing good things (page 33)
- Life Savers candy (page 35)
- Feathers (page 37)
- Butcher paper (page 39)
- Construction paper, dice (page 42)
- Blackline Master 10, pushpins (page 35)
- Blackline Masters 11, 12 (page 35)

e-resources

www.FindingGod.org

As class begins, play the instrumental version of "Jesus in the Morning" (CD 2, Track 10).

When everyone is settled, ask: *What kinds of good things have you done recently?* You might share some good things you have done as well. Say: *All of these good things come from the Holy Spirit.*

Have the children open their books to page 33 and describe what they see in the pictures. Ask: *What are the children doing? How do they feel?* (happy) *How do you know?* Explain: *We've talked about God, our Creator, and about Jesus, his Son. Today we'll learn about the Holy Spirit.* Read the title of the session and the paragraph. Encourage volunteers to respond to the question.

Invite the children to offer words of praise to God for these good things in their lives. Ask individuals to complete the phrase: *For the _____.* For example: *For the warmth of the sun* or *For the love of my family.* Then invite the group response: *Praise be to God.*

Engage

Prayer

Say: *When we do good things for ourselves, others, and the world, the Holy Spirit helps us do this. Today we're going to take some time to ask God to help us be close to the Holy Spirit. Please pray this prayer of petition aloud with me. Then quietly tell God whatever is in your heart.*

Reverently pray the prayer aloud. Then pause for 5 to 10 seconds, allowing the children time to speak with God. Close by praying *Amen.*

DAY 1

God's Life for Us

God's Life for Us

Session 4

Prayer

Dear God, bring me closer to your Holy Spirit so that I can remember he is always with me.

We have received the gift of life. We celebrate it in many ways. How have you celebrated your gift of life lately?

Unit 1, Session 4   33

OPTION

PEOPLE OF THE SPIRIT

Divide the children into groups of three or four and have the children look through magazines and find pictures of people doing good things. When the groups have found a few pictures, ask them to choose one person to share their pictures with the rest of the group. Say: *These people are filled with the Holy Spirit!*

Session 4   33

Explore

Simeon of Jerusalem

Draw attention to the Bible in the prayer center. Tell the children that it is opened to the story they are about to read in their books. Explain to the children: *We will read a Bible story about Mary and Joseph bringing Jesus into the Temple to present him to God.* Have the children describe what they see in the painting.

Read the title and the first paragraph aloud. Pronounce the name Simeon for the children and have them repeat it after you. Then say: *The man with the white beard is Simeon.*

Slowly read the second paragraph. Say: *Simeon prayed to God for many years and had been promised by the Holy Spirit that he would not die before he saw the person chosen by God to save his people. He was able to listen to what the Spirit told him.* Ask the group: *Who else that we have learned about also listened to the Holy Spirit?* (Mary and Joseph)

Draw attention to the word *Messiah* in dark type. See if any children know what it means. Explain: *Messiah describes Christ.* Ask: *And who is Christ?* (Jesus) Say: *God made a promise to send Jesus to be the Savior.*

Read the last paragraph. Draw attention to the word *Temple.* Say: *The Temple is the place where the people worshipped God.*

Read the first paragraph on the next page. Say: *When most of the people saw Mary, Joseph, and Jesus, they probably thought they were a poor couple with an ordinary baby.* Then ask: *When Simeon looked at Mary, Joseph, and the infant Jesus, what did he see?* (the Messiah, the one who had come to save the people) *Why do you think Simeon was able to see*

that Jesus was the Messiah when the other people in the Temple could not? (Simeon listened to the Holy Spirit who helped him to see how important Mary, Joseph, and Jesus were to God and to the people.) Say: *Because Simeon listened to the Holy Spirit, he was able to see who Jesus really was—our Savior.*

Ask: *How do you think Simeon felt when he held the infant Jesus in his arms?* (happy because God's promise to him had been fulfilled)

Simeon of Jerusalem

There was a man named Simeon who lived in Jerusalem.

Simeon loved God. He listened to the Holy Spirit. The Spirit promised that Simeon would not die until he had seen the **Messiah.**

One day Simeon was in the **Temple.** Mary and Joseph came with the baby Jesus. Simeon saw them enter the Temple. Simeon saw that Mary was carrying Jesus.

34   God's Invitation

Simeon's Story

Read the activity title and directions on page 35. Make sure the children understand what to do. When they have finished, check answers.

Tell the children: *When we do all we can to care for and help others, we know that we are listening to the Holy Spirit—just as Simeon did.*

OPTION

BLM 10: THE HOLY SPIRIT

Blackline Master 10 asks children to contribute to a group Holy Spirit bulletin board.

OPTION

BLM 11: GOD LOVES US

Blackline Master 11 is a review of Unit 1 vocabulary words.

OPTION

BLM 12: THE STORY OF SIMEON

Blackline Master 12 asks children to order events from the story of Simeon.

OPTION

LIFE SAVERS CANDY

Lovingly give each child a Life Savers candy after checking to be sure that each child can safely eat it. Tell them:

May this Life Savers candy be a reminder to you that the Holy Spirit is an important part of our lives and that he is always with us to help us.

FYI

THE SYNOPTIC GOSPELS

Synoptic has at its root the Greek word "to see" (*optic*) and means "to see together." The Gospels of Matthew, Mark, and Luke can be placed side-by-side and seen somewhat together. This is because Matthew and Luke used the Gospel of Mark, the first gospel written, when they wrote their Gospels. While similar, there are stories and sayings unique to each. For example, the story of Simeon of Jerusalem is found only in Luke 2:25–35.

Simeon's Story

Guided by the grace of the Holy Spirit, Simeon knew that Jesus was the Savior.

Simeon took Jesus into his arms. He praised God and said, "Now, Master, you may let your servant go in peace. My eyes have seen the Savior. He is the one you have promised to all people."

adapted from Luke 2:25-32

Simeon's Story

Draw a line to match important words from the story of Simeon.

1. Simeon loved God and listened to the

2. God's promise to all people is

3. Simeon was in the

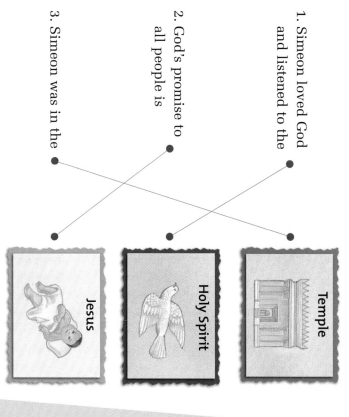

Jesus | Holy Spirit | Temple

Explore

The Holy Spirit

Remind the group: *The Holy Spirit guided Simeon so that he could recognize Jesus as the Messiah. Now we'll learn more about the Holy Spirit and how he helps us in our lives.* Make sure the children are on page 36. Read the title and paragraph aloud as the group follows along.

Draw attention to each picture individually and have the children describe what they see. Ask the following about each picture: *What are these people doing? Who are they with? How do they feel about the person they are with? How can you tell?* Call on volunteers to respond.

Then say: *The Holy Spirit is in each of these people. The love they are showing for others comes from the Holy Spirit. The Holy Spirit is with us in everything we do. When people do something kind or are happy, the Holy Spirit is alive in them.*

Read aloud the top paragraph on page 37 while the group follows along. Point out the word *faith* in dark type. See if anyone knows what it means. Say: *Faith is a gift from God that helps us believe in him and live as he wants us to live.* Ask: *How did Simeon show us he had faith?* (He listened to the Holy Spirit and believed he would see Jesus.)

Point to each picture individually and have the children describe what they see in each one. For example, in the top right picture you might ask: *Who do you see in the photograph? How is the boy holding the baby? How does he feel about the baby? How can you tell?* After the children have described all of the pictures, say: *God wants us to live like this—to show love to others and to care for creation. It is God's Holy Spirit that helps us live this way. All of the happy and good things we see in these pictures are happening because the Holy Spirit is with the children.* Explain that the good things we do are because of the Holy Spirit; we are showing faith that the Holy Spirit is with us and will always help us.

Ask the children: *What are some good things that people have done for you?* Elicit a variety of

Complete the reading on pages 36–37 in this guide before beginning Reading God's Word.

Reading God's Word

 Say: *We have been looking at all of the ways in which the Holy Spirit helps us to love one another. When people see us acting this way, they can think that something wonderful is happening. When the Bible says that we can be a light to the world, it is talking about how wonderful it is when people act in the same loving way people are acting in these pictures. Let's listen to the Bible saying that we are to be like a light to the world.*

Then read aloud the passage from Isaiah for the children while they follow along.

The Holy Spirit

The Holy Spirit is here to guide us, as he guided Simeon. The Spirit helps us know that God is always with us.

Reading God's Word

You will be my light to the ends of the earth so that all people may be saved.

adapted from Isaiah 49:6

responses. You might share some good things that people have done for you. Then say: *The people did these things because the Holy Spirit was with them!*

Tell the children that we can petition, or ask, the Holy Spirit to guide us. Have the group respond, *Holy Spirit, guide us* after each petition. Read:

Holy Spirit, open our hearts so that we may hear you.

Holy Spirit, open our minds so that we may listen to you.

The Holy Spirit also gives us **faith** in God. By listening to the Spirit, we learn to care for ourselves and others, as God wants us to.

Did You Know?

The name *Simeon* means "God has heard."

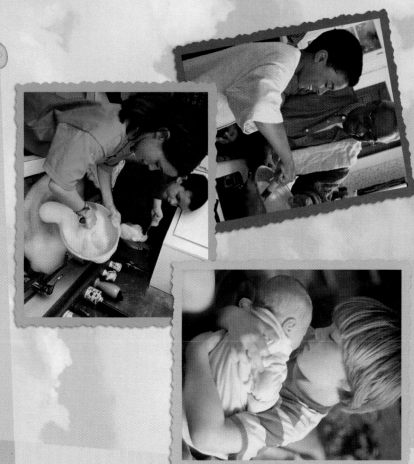
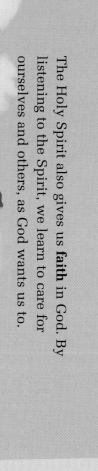

♪ Say: *Do you remember the song we sang about Jesus' always being with us? The Holy Spirit is always with us too. We're going to hear the song with verses about the Spirit.* Have the children turn to the Spirit verses of the song in the Songs of Our Faith section in the back of their books. Play "Jesus in the Morning" (Spirit verses) on Track 9 of CD 2 while the children listen. Then play the song again, asking the group to sing along.

Did You Know?

This feature contains interesting information related to the content of the session. It enriches the understanding of the topic of the page on which it appears.

Read the section aloud. Remind the children that they talked about names that have special meaning when discussing the name *Jesus,* which means "God saves," and *Emmanuel,* which means "God with us." Ask if any of them have discovered the meanings of their names.

Close by praying with the children the Glory Be to the Father—a simple prayer of praise for the Trinity.

OPTION

FRUITS OF THE SPIRIT

Read aloud this passage from Galatians 5:22–23: . . . *the fruit of the Spirit is love, joy, peace, patience, kindness, generosity, faithfulness, gentleness, self-control.*

List the qualities contained in the passage on the board. Then explain each and invite the children to think of how they can show each quality. Have them stand and complete a sentence with one of the qualities and a specific example. For example: *I show love when I _____.* (write letters to my grandparents)

OPTION

FEATHERS

Have a few volunteers come forward. Give them each a feather. Tell them to hold their feathers up high and then to let go of them so that they fall to the floor. Ask: *What controls the way the feathers fall to the floor?* (air) Say: *Even though we can't see the air, it exists and affects the feathers. The same is true of the Holy Spirit. We may not be able to see him with our eyes, but he is real and always with us, just like the air we breathe.*

Explore

A Woman of Great Faith

As you begin this time together, explain to the children that it's time for us to hear some Good News! Ask the children to think of a recent time when they received some good news. (family going someplace fun, special relative coming to visit, winning something) Encourage volunteers to share their stories. You may need to ask some guiding questions such as: *How did you get the news? How did it make you feel? What was the first thing you did after you heard? With whom did you share the news? How did you share it?*

Ask the children to recall the good news that Simeon received in the Temple. (that Jesus was the Messiah) Ask: *Why did Simeon receive the news?* (He listened to the Holy Spirit.)

Tell the children that today they are going to read about another person who was in the Temple that day and who also listened to the Holy Spirit.

Invite the children to comment on what they see in the picture on page 38. Tell them that the woman pictured is Anna.

Ask the children to read along as you read the title and the first paragraph aloud. Ask: *What is a widow?* (a woman whose husband has died) Ask: *How did Anna spend her time?* (praying in the Temple)

Read the second paragraph. Ask: *What did Anna see when she met the Holy Family?* (that Jesus was the Messiah) *What helped her know that?* (the power of the Holy Spirit)

Read the next paragraph with enthusiasm in your voice. Then invite volunteers to role play the part of Anna and say and do what Anna did after hearing the news. (shared the news, told everyone about the Savior)

Read the last paragraph. Ask: *Why was Anna a good example for others, like Simeon was?* (She was close to the Spirit. She obeyed God.)

FYI

A SANCTIFYING PRESENCE

At the heart of the Church's world-wide mission is the Holy Spirit's animating and sanctifying presence, making the Church the sacrament of the Holy Trinity's communion with all people.

✝ *Solidarity*

A Woman of Great Faith

You have read the story of Simeon in the Temple. Anna was another important person in the story. Anna was a widow who lived a long life. She prayed in the Temple very often.

Anna was in the Temple when Joseph and Mary came with Jesus. Anna was excited. She hurried over to meet them. The power of the Holy Spirit helped her see that Jesus was the Messiah.

Anna knew that her prayers had been answered. She left the Temple that day full of hope! She told the good news to all the people she met. Anna told them the Son of God had come to save them.

Anna was very close to the Holy Spirit. She obeyed God always. She set a good example for others to follow.

38 God's Invitation

A Letter to the Spirit

Ask the children how they feel when they receive mail from family and friends. (happy, excited) Ask: **Why do you feel this way?** (It means people care about them. They like to get news.)

Suggest that it is also fun to send letters. Ask if anyone can think of a time when they wrote a special letter to someone. Have a few volunteers share their experiences. Ask guiding questions such as: **Why did you write the letter? What kinds of things did you write about? Did the person answer your letter?**

Tell the children that today they will have a chance to write a letter to the Holy Spirit. Read aloud the title and the paragraph. Brainstorm with the children ideas of things they might say to the Holy Spirit.

Give the children time to think about and write their letters. Suggest that they may do a draft copy first on scratch paper, so their final copy in the book will be very neat. Walk around the room as the children work, helping with spelling and ideas. Remind the children to sign their letters!

Some children may wish to share their letters, but some may prefer that it remain between them and the Holy Spirit.

Remind the children of the people whose lives they read about this week who listened to the Holy Spirit for guidance. See if the children can name the people. (Simeon and Anna) Also remind them of Saint Isidore, the Farmer, and his wife, Saint Marie de la Cabeza, and of Saint Joseph. Ask: **Do you think they were guided by the Holy Spirit? How do you know?** (Saint Isidore was poor but shared what he had. Saint Joseph did what God wanted and took Mary as his wife.) Explain that when we let the Holy Spirit guide us, we too become holy. We are pleasing to God.

Close by giving children a few moments to thank the Holy Spirit for helping them become holy.

A Letter to the Spirit

You can talk to the Holy Spirit anytime. He is always with you. Complete this letter to the Holy Spirit. Thank him for being your guide. Ask him to help you in your life.

Dear Holy Spirit,

Thank you for guiding me when _____

_____

Please help me _____

_____

Thank you,

_____

LIFE-SIZE STORIES

Separate the children into four groups. Assign one of the following sets of characters to each group: Joseph and the angel; Simeon, Mary, Joseph, and the baby; Isidore and Maria; Anna and townspeople.

Provide each group with enough butcher paper to draw life-size versions of the characters they have been assigned. Encourage them to trace around a student's body for the characters' outlines. Have the groups color their figures based on the illustrations in their books. Depending on the number of children in each group, they can also create butcher-paper backgrounds.

Have the groups write scripts for their characters and perform dramatic re-enactments of the stories they learned. Keep in mind that this activity may require additional time on the following day.

DAY 4
Reflect

Prayer

Ask the children: *Have you ever had a hard time making up your mind about something?* Tell the children to think about it for a moment. Say: *When we listen to the Holy Spirit, we get help in making decisions.*

Then say: *Let's take time to speak with and listen to the Holy Spirit during our special prayer time. So let's be still as we begin our prayer.*

Say: *Now please close your eyes and fold your hands. After we pray the prayer, please continue to keep your eyes closed for a few moments so you can talk to the Holy Spirit and ask whatever you would like.*

Read the first paragraph aloud. Then say: *You can talk to the Holy Spirit the same way that you talk to God and Jesus. Please pray in your hearts as I pray this prayer aloud.*

Pray the prayer aloud. Then read the final paragraph in a soft voice. Then take two or three deep breaths so the children have a chance to talk to the Holy Spirit. Invite the children to open their eyes. Close with the Glory Be to the Father.

Say: *With the Holy Spirit as our guide, let's learn more about how we can recognize God in our lives.*

OPTION

JESUS IN THE MORNING

 Invite the children to provide gestures to accompany the spirit verses of "Jesus in the Morning" (CD 2, Track 9).

40   Session 4

FYI

THE HOLY SPIRIT

In art the Holy Spirit is often depicted as a dove. This is probably because in the New Testament we first meet the Holy Spirit at the baptism of Jesus. Some of the passages that depict the Holy Spirit as a dove include the following:

…and he saw the Spirit of God descending like a dove [and] coming upon him. (Matthew 3:16)

…and the Spirit, like a dove, descending upon him. (Mark 1:10)

…and the holy Spirit descended upon him in bodily form like a dove. (Luke 3:22)

FYI

THE HOLY SPIRIT'S PRESENCE

Jesus sent the Holy Spirit to his disciples to help them continue the work he had begun. The Holy Spirit remains with the Church today as she continues to respond to Jesus' mandate "Go, therefore, and make disciples of all nations." (Matthew 28:19) The Holy Spirit intends to renew the face of the earth.

✝ Solidarity

Prayer

The Holy Spirit is in your heart, waiting to guide you. Ask the Holy Spirit for help by praying this prayer.

Come, Holy Spirit, fill the hearts of your faithful. And kindle in them the fire of your love. Send forth your Spirit and they shall be created. And you will renew the face of the earth.

Ask the Holy Spirit to fill your heart with love. Thank him for being your guide.

40   My Response

Living My Faith

Use the following activities to help the children express what they learned in this session.

Faith Summary

Read the section for the group. Ask: **Whom did we learn about in this session who listened to the Holy Spirit?** (Simeon) **Where did Simeon see the infant Jesus?** (in the Temple)

Words I Learned

Call on volunteers to pronounce and define each word. Choose volunteers to use each word in a sentence.

Ways of Being Like Jesus

Read the section aloud for the group. Ask the children: **Can you name some ordinary things that show that God is all around us?** (family, the sun, trees)

With My Family

Ask: **What are the children in the picture doing?** (raking leaves) Then read the section aloud. Ask: **Why is it important to care for our families? What gift helps us show our love for God and others?** (the gift of faith)

Prayer

Say: **We've learned about the special place that the Holy Spirit has in our lives. Now let's ask the Holy Spirit to guide us. Please pray with me as I pray this prayer aloud. Then think about how you can listen to the Holy Spirit in your lives.**

Pray the prayer aloud. Then pause and give the children a moment to pray silently. End by saying: **Let's close the prayer with the Sign of the Cross.**

My Response

Read the sentence and say: **Think about what you can do for someone this week. Draw a picture of what you will do.**

While the children work, walk around the room and observe how well the children are able to apply what they have learned to their everyday lives.

Close by saying: **God has given us the gift of faith. Let's use this gift to love God and others.**

Living My Faith

Faith Summary

The Holy Spirit is present in our lives. When we listen to the Spirit, we recognize God in ordinary things around us.

Words I Learned

faith   Messiah   Temple

Ways of Being Like Jesus

Jesus knew that God is all around us in many ordinary things. You are like Jesus when you see God in the world around you.

With My Family

Show your care for your family. Rake leaves or do other yard work.

Prayer

Holy Spirit, thank you for being my guide. Help me to always listen to you and to do what you want me to do.

My Response

Draw a picture to show how you can take care of someone this week.

Extending the Session

Choose from the following options to extend the session or to reinforce concepts developed during the week.

Family Involvement

Remind the children to take home the Raising Faith-Filled Kids page to share what they are learning with their families.

Preparation for Sunday Scripture Readings

Lead children in a prayerful discussion of Sunday's readings. Visit **www.FindingGod.org/Sunday** for more information.

Seasonal Session

Consider the time of the liturgical year and use the appropriate seasonal session. Seasonal sessions may be found on page 241.

Unused Options and BLMs

Incorporate any unused options or Blackline Masters from the week's session.

Web Site Activities

Visit **www.FindingGod.org** to find additional activities for extending the session.

SHOWING OUR FAITH

Write *faith* on the chalkboard. Have each child write a sentence or two with the word *faith* in it, or have them draw a picture showing someone being faithful to God. Have volunteers read aloud their sentences or share their pictures with the class.

SIGN THE HOLY SPIRIT PRAYER

Invite a parish member who uses sign language, or an American Sign Language Instructor, to teach the class to pray the first sentence of the Prayer to the Holy Spirit in sign. As the children practice and become proficient in signing the prayer, have them pray that part of the prayer for other groups or for their families.

JUMP ON A WORD

Write each of the following terms on a separate piece of construction paper: *faith, Holy Spirit, Mary, Simeon, Messiah,* and *Temple*. Tape the papers on the floor in a line. Have a child roll a die and jump along the line the number of times that he or she rolled. Then help the child read the word on the paper on which he or she landed. Ask the child to tell something about the word. Invite each child to take a turn.

RAISING FAITH-FILLED KIDS
a parent page

Focus on Faith

Seeing People for Who They Are

We all live with stereotypes. It is easy to make assumptions and to label people according to their looks, clothes, or ethnic origins. In this session your child read about Joseph and Mary's coming with the baby Jesus to the Temple. Their humble offering of two turtledoves immediately labeled them as poor and unimportant, and this is how most people saw them. Simeon, inspired by the Holy Spirit, saw beneath the surface to recognize the promised Messiah in Jesus. The Holy Spirit also calls us to see everyone through the eyes of faith and to discover how each person is sacred and loved by God. When you look at your child today, whom do you see? How can you nurture the sacred person within your child?

Dinnertime Conversation Starter

Discuss a movie or television show you have all seen in which a character starts out looking like a villain but is revealed as a hero at the end. Explore together what this can tell us about looking beyond first impressions.

The Presentation of Christ in the Temple, Vittore Carpaccio

Focus on Prayer

Your child is learning the Prayer to the Holy Spirit. In this prayer we ask the Spirit to remain with us through everything we do, say, and think. The prayer reminds us to call on the Spirit for guidance when we are experiencing struggles or difficulties in our lives. Pray the prayer together and invite your child to discuss what it means to him or her. The words to the Prayer to the Holy Spirit are found at www.FindingGod.org.

Hints for at Home

Create and display a simple family tree. Include grandparents, aunts and uncles, and cousins. Talk about how your family members reflect God's presence in your lives. You might add items that reflect God's presence in the ordinary. For example, you might include pine cones, seashells, twigs, and leaves in the display. You might add pictures of your immediate and extended families as well as family pets. Over time, continue to add to your display.

Our Catholic Heritage

Your child has read the story of Simeon in the Temple (Luke 2:25–32). The message of the story is that Simeon, guided by faith, was able to recognize the presence of God in the ordinary. Although he saw a poor, helpless baby, Simeon, inspired by the Holy Spirit, recognized Jesus as the Messiah. Read the story with your child. Spend a few moments together thinking about the ways we might recognize God in the people we see every day.

Session 5: Unit 1 Review
3-Minute Retreat

Before you begin to prepare for your session, pause for a few moments and turn your focus inward. Take three deep breaths and rest in the loving presence of God as you prepare yourself to help the children grow strong in their Catholic faith.

1 Peter 5:6–7

So humble yourselves under the mighty hand of God, that he may exalt you in due time. Cast all your worries upon him because he cares for you.

Reflection

In the Scripture, to be humble means to recognize the true relationship between God and ourselves. We have been created by God. When we come to appreciate that God is our creator and that he cares for us, the appropriate response is one of humility. It is only through humility that we are capable of praising God. We bow humbly before God our Father, knowing that our relationship with him is one of intimacy. God cares for us and wants us to turn to him with all of our cares.

Questions

What cares can I bring to God today? In what ways can I best help the children appreciate God's blessings and respond with humility and praise?

Prayer

Reverently pray this prayer or one of your own.

Almighty God and Father of us all, thank you for your wondrous creation and for the way you care for me. I humbly bow before you and present my cares to you.

Take a few moments to reflect prayerfully before you prepare this session.

Catechist Preparation: Get-Ready Guide

Session 5: Unit 1 Review

Unit Theme: *God Loves Us*

Before This Session

- Fill a container with holy water from church.
- Display at the prayer center a bowl of holy water and cover the table with the tablecloth (if created earlier). Bookmark your Bible to Genesis 1:9. Place the Bible in the prayer center open to the passage from Genesis.
- Set up the CD player. Listen to the songs before the children arrive.

Outcomes *In this session, the children will review*

- how God created everything because he loves us.

- how and why God created the world.
- that Jesus came to save us.
- that Jesus reveals to us his loving Father.
- that the Holy Spirit helps us to make good decisions

- how to prayerfully reflect on God's invitation in everyday living.

- practical ways to act on God's invitation in everyday living.

Steps

| DAY 1 | **Engage** page 43 |

Review

| DAYS 1–3 | **Explore** pages 44–46 |

Faith Summary
Trinity Knots

| DAY 4 | **Reflect** page 47 |

Prayer Service: Water as a Reminder That God Created Everything

| DAY 4 | **Respond** page 48 |

Living My Faith: Thanking God for Many Good Things

Materials

Required Materials

- Bible
- Writing paper, pens, pencils
- Art materials, such as drawing paper, crayon, markers, scissors, glue
- Index cards (page 43)
- Green construction paper, 6-inch pieces of green ribbon, hole punch (page 46)
- Bowl of holy water; prayer tablecloth (if created earlier) (page 47)
- CD 2, Track 1: Song of Love (4:00) (page 45)
- CD 2, Reflective music (page 47)
- CD 2, Track 7: Our Father (1:02) (page 47)

Optional Materials

- Slips of paper with names of various parts of God's creation written on them, bowl or hat (page 45)
- Poster boards, magazines (page 45)
- Several pieces of rope or string (page 46)
- Blackline Master 13—Unit 1 Show What You Know (pages 43, 44)

e-resources

www.FindingGod.org

Say: **We have learned about God, his many gifts, and his love for us. Today we will review all the good things we've learned and praise God for all he has done for us.**

Have the children turn to page 43 and describe what they see in the pictures. Ask: **Who created all these beautiful animals?** (God) Remind them: **These are God's creatures. He loves them all.**

Read the title of the session and the paragraph. Encourage the children to respond to the question. They might thank God by praying to him or doing things to help his creation.

Distribute index cards. Have the children each write one thing for which they are thankful. Then have them save their index cards for use in the prayer service at the end of the week.

Show What You Know

Distribute BLM 13, Unit 1 Show What You Know, to the children. Explain that it will help the children see how well they understand what was taught.

When the children have finished, ask them to exchange papers and help them correct the objective section. Allow time for them to look over their own corrected papers before collecting the papers.

Session 5

Review

God is our Creator and Father. He created heaven and earth because of his great love for us. He gave us his only Son, Jesus Christ, as our Savior. How can we thank God for all he has given us?

Prayer

God, our Father, I thank you for your gifts. Help me love you so much that I think of you often.

Engage

Review the short-answer and self-assessment items. Provide written feedback and identify concepts needing attention. Use this information as you continue the Review on Day 2.

Prayer

Say: **Let's ask God to help us be grateful for his many gifts. Please close your eyes, fold your hands, and clear your minds as I pray this prayer. Then take a moment to say whatever you want to God.**

Reverently pray the prayer aloud, emphasizing God's gifts. Then take three deep breaths so the children have time to talk to God. End by praying **Amen** and asking the children to open their eyes.

OPTION

THANK YOU, GOD

Pass out paper. Have the children write a letter to God, thanking him for all his gifts. Tell them to be specific about the gifts they are grateful for. Review greetings and closings for letters. Encourage volunteers to share their letters with the group.

OPTION

GIFTS FOR EVERYONE

Divide the children into three groups—God's Gifts to Us, Our Gifts to God, and Our Gifts to Others. Give each group a sheet of paper and markers.

Have the groups work to identify and list the gifts that fall in their categories. For example, God's Gifts to Us might include life, love, and Jesus. Our Gifts to God might include prayer and praise, while Our Gifts to Others might include kindness and respect.

Tell them to write their ideas on the paper. Walk around the room and help the groups. When time is up, invite the groups to share their lists with the other groups.

Faith Summary

Begin by having the children pray with you the prayer on page 43. Then give them a little time to think about God as the prayer suggests.

Show What You Know

Return the assessment, BLM 13, to the children. Review the short-answer questions and any concepts the children did not fully understand.

Make sure the children are on page 44. Have them describe what they see in the picture. Ask: *What are the different things that God is holding in the picture?* Call on several volunteers to respond. Ask: *How do you think the creatures must feel to be in God's hands?* (happy, safe)

Tell the children that we will now review the main ideas they have learned in this unit. Ask: *Whom did God send to us because he loves us?* (Jesus) Then read the first paragraph so they can see if their answer is correct. Then ask: *Whom does Jesus help us learn more about?* (God) Then read the second paragraph to discover the correct answer. Ask: *Who is the third person of the Trinity who is always with us?* (Holy Spirit) Then read the final paragraph. Ask: *What can we learn from the Holy Spirit?* Encourage a variety of responses. Accept all reasonable answers.

Say: *Let's all go deep down in our hearts and thank the Holy Spirit for helping us learn so much.*

OPTION

KIND WORDS ROLE-PLAY

Invite the children to work with partners to carry on conversations or role-plays that contain only kind and gentle words. Their role-plays could

be about anything—siblings' deciding who will walk the dog, friends' deciding at whose house they will have a sleep-over, deciding if a baseball player is out or safe. Allow volunteers to share their conversations with the rest of the group.

✚ *Family and Community*

OPTION

BE AN EXPLORER

Tell the children: *Imagine you're an explorer and that you have come to this room to discover important things learned in this unit. Search through Unit 1 to collect evidence and report back.*

Have the children record what they discover along with its page number. Continue: *Begin looking at pages 1 through 41 and find three or four important things from this unit. Be ready to share your findings with the group.* Give the children time to review the pages in the book. Then call on volunteer explorers to share what they found.

Faith Summary

God made many good things because he loves us. He sent us his Son, Jesus. Jesus saves us from our sins.

Jesus helps us learn more about God. Jesus wants us to know that God is close to us. God is in our hearts. God loves us.

The Holy Spirit is always with us. Through the Holy Spirit, we can learn to care for others.

44   My Response

Review Search

Remind the children that it's a good thing the Holy Spirit is with us always, because there is more reviewing to do. Allow for a few moments of silence while the children ask for the help of the Holy Spirit.

Have the children look at page 45. Read the title and directions aloud while the group follows along. Make sure the children understand that the word search involves locating within the puzzle the individual words that are listed above the word search.

Encourage the children to keep track of which words they have found by checking off each word as they find it. Tell the group they can find the words running across the puzzle rows or running down them.

After the children have completed the activity, invite volunteers to show where in the word search they found a word from the key.

Then invite the children to relax and prepare to sing "Song of Love." Say: *As we learn more about God's love for us, we also learn how to share his love with others. Let's listen to this song about thanking God for his love and for showing us how to share it with others.* Ask the children to turn to "Song of Love" in the Songs of Our Faith section in the back of their books and follow along with the words as they listen. Play the song (CD 2, Track 1). Play it again and invite the children to sing along. Then ask: *What does the song tell us about where we can find Jesus?* (in others, by reaching out to others, in our own heart, in our family and friends) *How does the Holy Spirit show us how to "sing God's song of love"? What does that mean to you?* Encourage a variety of answers that focus on how the Holy Spirit invites us to spread God's love to others.

Review Search

Circle the important names and words in the puzzle. These words are found below.

| FAITH | GOD | HOLY | JESUS |
| JOSEPH | MARY | MESSIAH | PRAISE |

J	O	S	E	P	H	R	I
V	U	F	A	I	T	H	F
A	C	A	R	J	M	Y	B
J	I	K	M	I	E	R	U
E	P	R	A	I	S	E	R
S	O	K	L	E	S	N	U
U	A	G	B	O	I	I	L
S	H	O	K	M	A	R	Y
A	R	D	G	E	H	A	I
L	I	B	H	O	L	Y	C

Explore

OPTION
CREATION CHARADES

Play charades with the group. On slips of paper, write the names of various parts of God's creation. (birds, flowers, children, fish, elephants) Fold the slips of paper, and put them into a bowl or hat. Have volunteers come forward and draw a piece of paper. Then have them act out their words. See if the group can guess what parts of creation they are!

OPTION
CREATION COLLAGE

Divide the class into groups. Give each group a poster board, magazines, a marker, glue, and scissors. Have them write *God's Creation* at the top of their posters. Then encourage them to find and cut out pictures of things in God's creation. Tell them to glue these onto the poster board to create a collage. Walk around the room and help the groups find pictures. When they have finished, display the posters around the room. Ask each group to choose one member of the group to come to the poster and explain the group's creation collage.

Trinity Knots

Ask: *What is a knot? Has anyone ever tied a knot?* Say: *Today we're going to learn about a special kind of knot called a Celtic* (kel'tik; sel'tik) *knot.*

Read the first paragraph aloud while the group follows along. Have the children look at the picture. Say: *This is a Trinity Knot. It is a type of Celtic knot. Long ago, monks from Ireland made beautiful Bibles by decorating the pages with colorful Celtic knots. These knots were used in borders on the pages or were placed around the first letters of the first words on the pages.* Then read the second paragraph aloud for the group as they follow along.

Distribute green construction paper, glue, scissors, 6-inch pieces of green ribbon, and crayons or markers. Give the children time to color and decorate their knots. Have them cut out the frame surrounding their knots and glue them onto the green construction paper. Then punch a hole at the top of their construction paper. Have them string ribbon through the hole. After they have completed their knots, invite them to share their creations with the group. Tell the children: *Hang your Trinity Knots in a special place at home to remind you of the Trinity's love for you.*

Invite the children to recall the love of the Trinity by repeating the lines and actions from this fingerplay:

The three persons in the Holy Trinity,
(Hold up three fingers.)
God, his Son, and the Spirit care for me.
(Point to self.)
The Spirit helps me listen and know.
(Place hand behind ear.)
And helps my heart to grow and grow.
(Place hand on heart.)

OPTION

TYING KNOTS

Bring in several pieces of rope or string. Call on volunteers to come forward and show the group how they would tie a knot. Then say: *Look at the different ways people make knots! Let's remember that the Trinity Knot we see on page 46 has three knots and reminds us of the Trinity, which is composed of three persons—the Father, the Son, and the Holy Spirit.*

Trinity Knots

Celtic knots were used in art by monks in Ireland long ago. Each knot had a special meaning. The Trinity Knot represented the Holy Trinity.

This Trinity Knot will remind you that God—the Father, the Son, and the Holy Spirit—cares for you. Color the picture and cut it out. Hang it in a special place.

46 My Response

Note: The prayer services at the close of the review sessions are more structured prayers than those in the other sessions in the units. These services engage the children in a variety of patterns of liturgical prayer and, therefore, will help them become familiar with the Church's liturgical tradition. If it's feasible in your setting, have children gather around the prayer center for this prayer time.

Say: *We will have a special prayer today. As part of our prayer service, we will have a bowl of holy water to remind us that we became part of God's family when we were baptized with water. We will read from the Bible about God's creation and* pray the Lord's Prayer together. Then say: *Please look at the prayer service on page 47.* Draw attention to the parts that say "All." Explain: *I will read the parts that say "Leader," and you will read the parts that say "All."* Tell the children to bring their books and the index cards that they saved for the prayer service and gather around the prayer center.

[♪ CD] While they are gathering, play the reflective music at the end of CD 2. After the children have gathered, begin: *Praise*

Prayer Service

Leader: Praise be to God, who fills our lives with joy.

All: Amen.

Leader: Water was used when we were baptized. It reminds us that God created everything.

All: Amen.

Leader: A reading from the Book of Genesis.

Then God said, "Let the water under the sky be gathered into a single basin, so that the dry land may appear." [Genesis 1:9]

The Word of the Lord.

All: Thanks be to God.

Leader: Together let us pray the Lord's Prayer.

be to God, who fills our lives with joy. Motion for the children to pray: *Amen.* Hold up the bowl of holy water. Reverently say: *Water was used when we were baptized. It reminds us that God created everything.* Have the children reply: *Amen.*

[📖] Continue: *A reading from the Book of Genesis.* Pause for a moment, and continue the reading from Genesis. Then pause and say: *The Word of the Lord.* Invite the children to respond: *Thanks be to God.* Then say: *Together let us pray the Lord's Prayer.* Have the children put their books and index cards down. Then raise your hands in the orans position and have the children do the same. Lead the group in the Lord's Prayer.

[♪ CD] Instead of praying the Lord's Prayer, you might prefer to play the recorded version of "Our Father" (Track 7 of CD 2) or use a parish version of the song.

When the Lord's Prayer is completed, say: *Let's now close our eyes and share a moment of silence with God.* After 10 seconds, explain: *Please pick up your index cards. I will give you each a chance to read your card.* After each card is read, we will say: *"Thanks be to God."* Say: *God, we praise you for your many gifts of love. Let us thank you for _____.* Invite the children to individually read their cards, and have the group respond: *Thanks be to God.*

Have the children return to their seats. Say: *With love for God in our hearts, let's now think about what we can do to show this love through our actions.*

Respond

Living My Faith

The ideas below help the children apply what they learned in this unit to their everyday lives.

Ways of Being Like Jesus

Read the section. Ask: *How are the children in the picture showing kindness?* Ask: *Can you think of times when you can use gentle words?* (when helping little brother with homework he doesn't understand)

With My Family

Read the section. Ask: *What types of kind things can we say to our family members?* (politely thank parents for a delicious meal, tell dad he looks handsome in his new shirt) Tell the children: *Say something kind to the first family member you see after leaving today. Watch how happy he or she becomes.*

✝ *Family and Community*

Prayer

Say: *God loves us very much. Let's thank God for all he has given us. Please fold your hands and pray the prayer aloud with me. Then take a few moments to be alone with God.*

Pray the prayer aloud. Then pause for 5 to 10 seconds so the children have time to reflect. Then say: *Let's end with the Sign of the Cross.*

My Response

Read the section and say: *God has given each of us many blessings: our families, our friends, and our homes. Think about what you would like to thank God for and draw a picture and write a sentence about it.*

As they work, observe how well the children are able to apply the concepts of this unit to their everyday lives. As you walk around, affirm the children's ideas and artwork.

As your time together ends, say one kind thing about each child, emphasizing how they are being like Jesus. For example: *Joan, thank you for smiling during today's time together. When you do this, you are being like Jesus!*

Living My Faith

Ways of Being Like Jesus

Jesus knew the power of gentle words and actions. You are like Jesus when you speak to others with respect and show them kindness.

With My Family

Practice acting like Jesus with your family. Say a kind thing about each member of your family. Watch him or her smile!

Prayer

Dear God, thank you for all you have given me. Help me share your love with others.

My Response

What would you like to thank God for? Draw a picture and write a sentence to go with it.

48   My Response

Unit 2

Unit 2: Jesus Loves Us
Overview

Consider how the focus of this unit is developed throughout the sessions.

Unit Saints: Saint Anne and Saint Joachim

Saint Anne and Saint Joachim are the Unit Saints for the second unit. Tradition has named Anne and Joachim the parents of Mary and praises them for raising her to have strong faith and love for God. Saint Anne is the patron saint of mothers, especially those who are expecting babies, and Saint Joachim is the patron saint of fathers.

Session 6: Jesus Is Faithful

Jesus was faithful to the Ten Commandments. With God's help we can follow the Commandments and live in peace with one another. Jesus was obedient to God and to his parents. Jesus, Mary, and Joseph were faithful followers of the Jewish tradition and worshiped God both at home and at the Temple.

Session 7: Jesus Saves Us

Jesus is the model of the love and goodness in our lives. We bring love and goodness to others by following his example. Jesus showed great care for the sick and those in need. We are called to follow Jesus' example. The Ten Commandments guide us to love others.

Session 8: Jesus Calls Us to Love

We explore how Jesus invites us to be closer to God. In the parable of the Banquet, Jesus taught that all are welcome in God's kingdom. Jesus left us his Church to help us follow his example. We follow Jesus' example by welcoming all people and by helping those who need special care. Jesus chose Peter to be the first leader of the Church.

Session 9: Jesus Cares for Us

The parable of the Good Shepherd teaches us about God's loving care for every one of us. In this session Jesus teaches us about the Good Shepherd who searched until he found the lost sheep. Today the bishops have the responsibility to show this care and concern for all God's people.

Session 10: Unit 2 Review

In this session we review the main ideas of the session, reinforce ideas that need additional attention, and assess the children's understanding of the unit's main concepts.

Jesus Gives Sight to One Born Blind

Catechist Preparation

Prayer in Unit 2

In this second unit, continue using the established pattern and tone for prayer in each session. The brief opening prayer of petition and the closing prayer of gratitude invite the children to reflect on the focus of the session. After each prayer, continue giving the children an opportunity to add their own prayers.

In the Reflect step a guided reflection gives you the opportunity to help the children pray in silence. The children are also introduced to the practice of praying with Scripture, using Psalm 23. In the Prayer Service the children praise God for creating and caring for us.

As you guide the children through this unit, think about how you will help them to praise God through prayer and service.

✝ Catholic Social Teaching in Unit 2

The following themes of Catholic Social Teaching are integrated into this unit:

Call to Family, Community, and Participation Participation in family and community is central to our faith and to a healthy society. As the central social institution of our society, the family must be supported and strengthened. From this foundation, people participate in society, fostering a community spirit and promoting the well-being of all, especially the poor and vulnerable.

Option for the Poor and Vulnerable In our world many people are very rich, while at the same time, many are extremely poor. As Catholics, we are called to pay special attention to the needs of the poor. We can follow Jesus' example by making a specific effort to defend and promote the dignity of the poor and vulnerable and meet their immediate material needs.

Solidarity Because God is our Father, we are all brothers and sisters with the responsibility to care for one another. Solidarity is the attitude that leads Christians to share spiritual and material goods. Solidarity unites rich and poor, weak and strong, and helps to create a society that recognizes that we all live in an interdependent world.

Session 6: Jesus Is Faithful

3-Minute Retreat

Pause before you prepare your session. Take a few deep breaths and be aware of God's loving presence with you.

Luke 2:46,51–52

After three days they found him [Jesus] in the temple . . . He went down with them and came to Nazareth, and was obedient to them; and his mother kept all these things in her heart. And Jesus advanced [in] wisdom and age and favor before God and man.

Reflection

At 12 years of age, Jesus was a faithful Jewish boy who was devoted to the Ten Commandments. His interest in Scripture was enhanced by his discussion with the rabbis in the Temple. When everyone else headed for home, he stayed behind. Later, when found by his parents, he showed obedience to the Commandments by obeying his parents.

Questions

How do I strive to follow the Ten Commandments? In what ways am I being called to grow in wisdom, age, and grace?

Prayer

Speak to Jesus using this prayer or one of your own.

Jesus, lead me to love the law of God, teach me to be obedient and to help the children advance in wisdom and age and grace before God and others.

Take a few moments to reflect prayerfully before you prepare this session.

Knowing and Sharing Your Faith

Scripture and Tradition in Session 6

The Ten Commandments are revealed by God. They provide the basis for a faithful relationship between God and his people. The Commandments are a covenant based on the needs of the community and the survival of the people of God.

The Ten Commandments are unique because they include obligations not only to God but also to one another. Because Moses brought two stones with the Commandments on them down from the mountain, many believe that one stone contained the obligations to God and the other stone contained the obligations to others.

From the time of Saint Augustine in the fifth century, Catholic catechisms have used the Ten Commandments as the framework for discussions of Christian morality. The Commandments are binding on Christians because they are the basis for Jesus' command to love.

Scripture in Session 6

Luke 2:41–52 is a story of Jesus at the age of 12.
Exodus 20:12 names the Fourth Commandment.

Let the scripture and Tradition deepen your understanding of the content in this session.

WINDOW ON THE CATECHISM

The discussion of the Ten Commandments begins in CCC 2052. The Fourth Commandment is reviewed in CCC 2197–2246. The discussion of Jesus in the Temple is found in CCC 534.

Jesus is found in the Temple.

Honor your father and your mother.

Catechist Preparation

From the Richness of the Tradition

The story of Jesus in the Temple is the only story we have of Jesus' childhood. The story reminds us how important children are to us, not just because they represent the future but because they bring us special gifts today. Children are the sign of God's continual gift to the world. We need to respect children and make their rights a priority in our society and in our Church.

✝ Catholic Social Teaching

In this session aspects of the following theme of Catholic Social Teaching are integrated: **Call to Family, Community, and Participation.**

Consider in this session how you will invite the children to respond to and prayerfully reflect on God's invitation to love and serve others.

GENERAL DIRECTORY FOR CATECHESIS

The relationship between parents, their children, and the catechetical community is explored in *GDC* 226.

Prayer in Session 6

A special approach to prayer in Session 6 is an extended guided reflection entitled "Lost and Found." As you prepare to share this prayer experience with the children, listen to the recorded guided reflection, "Lost and Found" (CD 1, Track 7), as a prayerful experience for yourself. Then, when you play the recording during the session, join the children in reflective prayer.

If instead you choose to lead the guided reflection yourself, listen to the recording a second time, following the script (pages 368–369) and noting pauses and tone of voice. You can then use the script or adapt it as you wish. When leading the guided reflection during the session, play instrumental music softly in the background to enhance the sense of prayerfulness.

An alternate approach to prayer in this session is to use the Prayer on the children's page.

Catechist Preparation: Get-Ready Guide

Session 6: Jesus Is Faithful

Session Theme: *With God's help, we can follow the Commandments and live in peace with one another.*

Before This Session

- Bookmark the Bible to Luke 2:41–52 and Exodus 20:12. Display the Bible in the prayer center open to the passage in Luke.
- Set up the CD player so you will be ready to play the recorded Scripture story. Listen to the story ahead of time.
- Display the poster: Ten Commandments.
- Make the appropriate arrangements for the option on page 56, which requires a computer with Internet access.

Outcomes   *At the end of the session, the children should be able to*

- identify Saint Anne and Saint Joachim as Mary's parents.
- understand the importance of obeying our parents.

- describe how Jesus obeyed God and his parents.
- explain that conscience helps us recognize right from wrong.
- identify the Ten Commandments as a guide for how to follow Jesus.
- define *conscience* and *Ten Commandments*.

- prayerfully reflect on God's presence, his invitation, and our response.

- identify practical ways to act on God's invitation in everyday living.

Steps

DAY 1   **Engage** pages 49–51
Unit Saints: Saint Anne and Saint Joachim
Jesus Is Faithful

DAYS 2-3   **Explore** pages 52–57
Jesus With the Teachers
Jesus the Good Son
God's Special Rules
The Mafa Group

DAY 4   **Reflect** page 58
Prayer: Jesus in the Temple

DAY 4   **Respond** page 59
Living My Faith: Honoring God and Our Parents

DAY 5   **Extending the Session** page 60
Day 5 offers an opportunity to extend the session with activities that reinforce the session outcomes.

Materials

Required Materials
- Bible
- Writing paper, pens, pencils
- Art materials, such as drawing paper, crayons, markers, scissors, glue
- CD 1, Track 2: Jesus With the Teachers (4:11) (page 52)
- CD 1, Track 7: Lost and Found (8:43) (page 58)
- Poster: Ten Commandments

Optional Materials
- Chart paper (page 54)
- Box or basket (page 57)
- Blackline Master 14, craft sticks (page 52)
- Blackline Master 15, tape or safety pins (page 53)
- Blackline Master 16 (page 54)

e-resources
www.FindingGod.org

Jesus Loves Us

Unit 2

Tell the children that today they will begin Unit 2, which is all about Jesus. They will discover more about Jesus' great love for us. Say: *We will find out how Jesus cares for all people in the same way, whether they are rich or poor, healthy or sick. Jesus wants everybody to be part of God's family.* Ask the children to recall all the things family members do for each other. Invite them to thank God for their own families and for being a part of God's family.

Now talk to the children about their families. Ask: *How many of you are part of a big family?* Encourage volunteers to respond. Then say: *Jesus was part of a family.*

Talk to the group about how our parents are called to follow Jesus' example of love by teaching us and caring for us. Mention how they also are called to give us a strong religious foundation.

Say: *Mary was part of a family too. She had parents who loved her. Now we will learn about her parents. We will learn how they cared for her and helped her become a loving follower of God.*

Saint Anne and Saint Joachim

Anne and Joachim were Mary's parents. They raised Mary to have a strong faith and a great love for God.

49

Saint Anne and Saint Joachim

Draw attention to the picture of Saint Anne and Saint Joachim. Read the caption, pronouncing *Joachim* (jō´ə kim) for the children. Ask the group: *What are Anne and Joachim doing?* (holding a child in their arms) Say: *Saint Anne and Saint Joachim were the parents of Mary, who became the mother of Jesus.* Ask: *Who is the child in the picture?* (Mary) Say: *Saint Anne and Saint Joachim were loving parents. They helped Mary learn about God.*

FYI

SAINTS

Anne and Joachim are examples to us in our relationship with God and others. Saints are holy men and women who have lived lives that inspire and teach us. They are role models to be imitated. We are one with them in the Communion of Saints.

Engage

Saint Anne and Saint Joachim

Read the title and the first paragraph aloud. Explain: **Devotion means "faithful and loyal." Mary's parents were devoted to her and taught her to be devoted to God.**

Read the next two paragraphs aloud. Ask: **Who can remind us what a saint is?** (a holy person who has died as a good friend of God and now lives with God forever) Ask: **What is a patron saint?** (a saint who watches over a special group) Ask: **Why do you think Saint Anne is the patron saint of mothers and Saint Joachim the patron saint of fathers?** (because they were devoted parents of Mary, a very important person in our faith)

Draw attention to the illustration on the bottom of the page. Have the children describe what they see. Ask: **What is Anne doing in the picture?** (preparing thread to make clothing) **What is Joachim doing?** (reading a scroll) **How about Mary?** (doing embroidery)

FAMILY HELPERS

Invite the children to draw pictures of their families showing what each member does at home. Refer them to the illustration on page 50 as an example.

50 Unit 2

MARY'S LOVING PARENTS

We do not know much about Saint Anne and Saint Joachim, but we believe they reared Mary to be loving and faithful to God. Mary's willingness to follow God reflects the faith that she received from her family. The names of Joachim and Anne are found in early Christian writings. The feast of Joachim was celebrated in the Church from early times. Anne is the patron saint of childless women, expectant mothers, women giving birth to children, and homemakers. When we pray for our parents, we can ask Saint Anne and Saint Joachim to join us in praying to God for them. The feast day of Joachim and Anne is July 26.

THE DOMESTIC CHURCH

In speaking of the importance of the family, the Church frequently uses the term *domestic church.* This reflects the Church's high regard for the family as the primary place where faith is formed. The home is the first "school" in which the children of God learn the lessons of faith—belief, prayer, worship, and the importance of a life of love and service. This great mission of the family is rooted in the mutual love and fidelity of the husband and the wife.

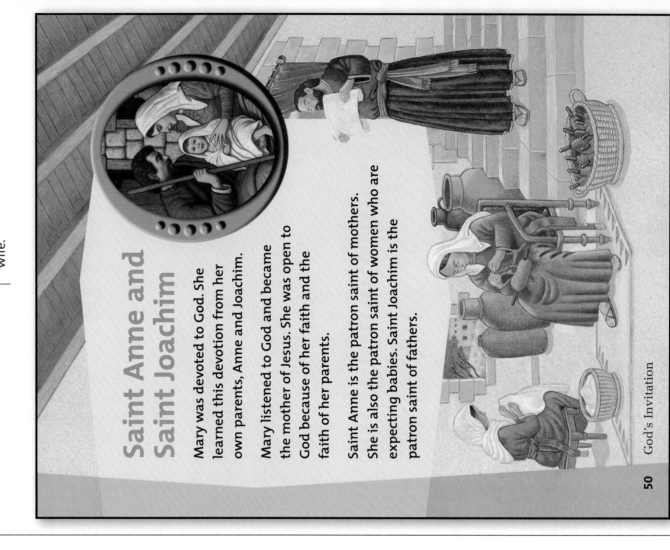

Saint Anne and Saint Joachim

Mary was devoted to God. She learned this devotion from her own parents, Anne and Joachim.

Mary listened to God and became the mother of Jesus. She was open to God because of her faith and the faith of her parents.

Saint Anne is the patron saint of mothers. She is also the patron saint of women who are expecting babies. Saint Joachim is the patron saint of fathers.

50 God's Invitation

Jesus Is Faithful

Ask the children: ***What are some of the best times you've had with your families? Have you gone on special trips together? Have you had fun times during holidays such as Thanksgiving and Christmas?*** Invite volunteers to share their favorite times and to explain why these times are important to them. Say: ***Jesus was part of a family too. In this session we will learn how Jesus was faithful both to God and to his parents.***

Say: ***Open your books to page 51.*** Read the title of the session. Ask: ***Does anyone know what faithful means?*** (devoted, true, loyal) Focus attention on the photographs. Have the children describe what they see. (a boy listening to his father, a child helping to wash the family car, a family brushing their teeth)

Read the questions while the group follows along. Call on volunteers to answer the questions. Explain: ***Listening to our parents is very important. Jesus listened to his parents.*** Ask: ***What are some ways that you listen to your parents?*** (do my homework when they tell me to; finish my chores; be nice to my brother, sister, or other relatives)

✝ *Family and Community*

Prayer

Say: ***This week we are talking about how to listen to and obey both God and our parents. Let's ask Jesus to help us love God and be faithful to him. Now, please close your eyes and fold your hands while I pray the prayer. When the prayer is finished, quietly tell God whatever you wish in your hearts.***

Pray the prayer aloud. Pause and take three deep breaths to allow time for the children to pray. End the prayer time by praying **Amen** and asking the children to open their eyes.

Jesus Is Faithful

What are some ways you have obeyed your parents? What are some chores you have helped with?

🔺 Prayer

Jesus, Son of God, give me the grace to love God and to be faithful to him.

HONORING YOUR PARENTS ROLE-PLAY

Have one child play the role of a parent and another the role of a child. Give the pair a situation to act out. For example, if a parent were walking into the house with a bag of groceries, what could the child do? You may have time to provide other situations for other volunteers to act out (a parent is sick). Tell the group: *Look for situations at home in which you can support the family by helping your parents.*

✝ *Family and Community*

Explore

Jesus With the Teachers

Begin the day by inviting the children to pray together the prayer on page 51. Then draw the children's attention to the illustration on page 52. Have them describe what they see. Explain: *This is a picture of a caravan. A caravan is a group of people and animals traveling together. In this story we will find out who the people in the caravan are and where they are going.*

Read the title and say: *Jesus and his parents were followers of the Jewish faith. We will learn about a story in which Jesus, Mary, and Joseph went on a journey in a caravan. Many people made the journey to celebrate a festival.* Then read the entire story on pages 52 and 53 to the children as they follow along.

Say: *Now we'll hear the story we just read. This will help us to learn more about Jesus with the teachers.* Have the children listen quietly as you play the recorded Scripture, Jesus With the Teachers, on Track 2 of CD 1.

Encourage the children to look at the pictures on pages 52 and 53 of the book as they listen to the story. When the story is finished, encourage them to say whatever they would like about what they heard.

Complete the reading on pages 52 and 53 before beginning Did You Know?

Did You Know?

Read this section aloud. Say: *As Jewish people, Mary and Joseph worshiped in the Temple.* Ask: *Today, as Catholics, where do we worship?* (church)

Ask: *How do you think Mary and Joseph felt when they could not find Jesus?* (scared, worried, concerned) Continue: *How do you think their feelings changed when they found Jesus?* (They were relieved.)

Explain with reverence: *Jesus had a special role to play for God. Mary and Joseph would learn more about that role. Mary and Joseph would never forget finding their lost child in the Temple. Jesus was obedient to his parents and returned home with them.* Ask: *How do you think your parents would react if they lost*

you? Allow the children to respond. Then say with emotion: *Mary and Joseph were very worried about their son. They must have been really happy when they found him.*

OPTION

BLM 14: JESUS IN THE TEMPLE
On Blackline Master 14 children create puppets to retell the story of Jesus in the Temple.

Jesus With the Teachers

When Jesus was 12 years old, he went with his parents to Jerusalem. They were celebrating a festival. When the festival was over, Mary and Joseph headed for home with their friends.

Mary and Joseph thought Jesus was traveling with them. They looked for him, but they could not find him. They became very worried.

Mary and Joseph returned to Jerusalem to look for Jesus. After three days they found him in the Temple.

adapted from Luke 2:41-46

Did You Know?

The Temple was the most important place of worship for the Jewish people.

52 God's Invitation

BLM 15: KEEPING A COMMANDMENT CLOSE

On Blackline Master 15 children make pockets to fill with reminders of ways they can obey their parents.

✝ *Family and Community*

Jesus was sitting with the teachers, listening to them and asking questions. When his parents saw him, they were amazed.

Mary asked, "Son, why did you do this to us? We were very worried about you."

Jesus said, "I must do what my Father wants me to do." His parents did not completely understand.

Jesus returned home with Mary and Joseph. Mary remembered what happened. Jesus grew older and wiser.

adapted from Luke 2:47–52

ROLE-PLAY THE BIBLE STORY

Divide the class into groups of four or five. Assign the children the roles of Jesus, Mary, Joseph, and one or two teachers in the Temple. Tell the groups to act out the Bible story of Jesus With the Teachers. Have the groups share their scenes with the rest of the children.

OUR CARAVAN

Tell the group they will pretend they are traveling in a caravan. Ask: *Where should we pretend we are going? What types of things do we need to take with us? For how long will we be gone?*

Then have the children line up and pretend to be carrying their supplies as they walk around the room several times, as if they were traveling. You may want to stop at times to pretend to cook food, build a fire, or rest.

When you have finished, you might lead a discussion in which you ask the children to compare traveling today (with hotels, cars, restaurants, etc.) to the hardships of traveling during Mary and Joseph's time.

LISTENING AND OBEYING

In the Bible the verbs *listen* and *obey* mean the same thing. This implies that obedience is the result of careful listening to the Word of God so that we can, with Jesus' help, trust in God and believe in his love for us.

Explore

Jesus the Good Son

Tell the children they will learn a song called "I Love Jesus" to remind themselves that they can be like Jesus. Sing the verses to the tune of "London Bridge Is Falling Down."

Sing the first verse while the group listens to the melody and the pattern of the song. Then have the group join you as you repeat the first verse. Sing the second verse and have the children join you. Do the same thing for the third verse.

Jesus was a faithful Son,
faithful Son, faithful Son.
Jesus was a faithful Son.
I love Jesus!

Jesus listened to God's Word,
to God's Word, to God's Word.
Jesus listened to God's Word.
I love Jesus!

Jesus knew God's rules for life,
rules for life, rules for life.
Jesus knew God's rules for life.
I love Jesus!

Read the title and the first and second paragraphs aloud while the children follow along. Then explain sincerely: *You can talk to Jesus whenever you wish. You can ask him to help you obey your parents.*

Finding Jesus

Read the activity's title and directions. Make sure the children understand what they are to do. Remind the children that each word is used only once. Walk around the room and offer help where needed. When the children have completed their work, ask volunteers to share their answers. End the day by inviting the children to ask God to help them obey their parents.

Ask them to work together to create a mural that shows their ideas. Help the groups come up with ideas if they are having difficulty. When the groups have completed their murals, display them.

✝ *Family and Community*

BLM 16: THE HOLY FAMILY

Blackline Master 16 is an activity for children to unscramble key words from this session.

OBEY YOUR PARENTS MURAL

Allow the children to work in groups. Distribute chart paper and markers or crayons. Invite the groups to discuss ways in which they can be obedient to their parents. (clean their bedrooms, be polite, don't argue or fight)

Jesus the Good Son

Jesus realized that he should obey his parents and not cause them to worry. That is why he went home with them and always did what they asked.

Like Jesus, you should listen to and obey your parents. Ask Jesus to help you obey them.

Finding Jesus

Use the words in the box to tell about when Mary and Joseph found Jesus.

Mary	Temple	three

1. the number of days that Jesus was missing

   t h r e e

2. the person who looked for Jesus

   M a r y

3. where Jesus was found

   T e m p l e

God's Invitation

54

God's Special Rules

Sing the last verse of "I Love Jesus" with the children:

*Jesus knew God's rules for life,
rules for life, rules for life,
Jesus knew God's rules for life.
I love Jesus!*

Then explain: *We follow rules in many situations. Can you name some of them?* (home, school, sports) Ask the children: *What are some of the rules we observe in these situations?* (not talking in class, completing chores, listening to the bus driver and the crossing guard, playing by the rules of a game)

Draw attention to the pictures. Ask: *What are the children in the pictures doing to observe the rules in their families?* (mom and son doing homework; mom, dad, and son doing dishes; daughter going to bed) Say: *Now we will learn about special rules from God.*

Read the title and the paragraph aloud. Say: *Jesus, Mary, and Joseph were devoted followers of the Jewish faith. They obeyed the Ten Commandments, God's Word.* Display the Ten Commandments poster.

Continue: *The Ten Commandments are God's special rules. They tell*

us how to live good lives. Say: *The Commandments are very important. When we follow the Commandments, we are being like Jesus.*

Ask the children: *How would you define the word conscience?* After they share their ideas, explain: *Conscience is the voice of God that guides us to do what he asks. It tells us when we are doing something that we should or shouldn't do.* Ask: *What did Jesus' conscience tell him?* (to obey his parents)

Say: *Each of us has a conscience. It will guide us as Jesus' conscience guided him.*

Reading God's Word

Read the section aloud. Explain: *Honoring, or respecting and obeying, our parents is very important. It is what God wants us to do, and it's one of his Ten Commandments.* Direct the children's attention to the Ten Commandments poster and point out the Fourth Commandment to them. Say: *We should obey our parents just like Jesus obeyed his.*

Remind the children that the Holy Spirit helps us make decisions. Say: *It is not always easy to follow Jesus' example of obeying our parents, but the Holy Spirit will help us.*

This might be a good time to remind the children of the additional information in the section The Ten Commandments at the back of their books.

THE TEN COMMANDMENTS Direct the children's attention to the poster of the Ten Commandments. Read each of the Commandments to the children and answer any questions they may have. The Commandments on the poster are adapted from Exodus 20:2–17.

God's Special Rules

Jesus, Mary, and Joseph were followers of the Jewish faith. They accepted the **Ten Commandments** and always obeyed them. As Catholics, we also are to follow the Ten Commandments. We follow Jesus when we obey the Commandments. Our **conscience** guides us to do what the Commandments tell us.

Reading God's Word

Honor your mother and father so that you may live a long life.

adapted from Exodus 20:12

Explore

The Mafa Group

Begin by asking the children if they know what it means to pose for a photograph.

Encourage them to share various circumstances in which they might have been asked to pose. (at their birthday party with friends, on a new bike, with family on vacation) Discuss why such photos are important to their families. (so special times can be remembered)

Tell the children that they are going to read about a group of people in Africa who posed for some very special pictures. If you have a world map or globe in your room, point out Cameroon in West Africa, southeast of Nigeria.

Ask the children to turn to page 56. Have them look at the picture and tell what they think might be going on. Say: **When we read this page, we will find out more about this picture.**

Read the title and the first paragraph aloud. Ask: **Why do you think the people wanted to see African people in the paintings?** (They wanted the people in the paintings to look like them.) Talk about Bible stories being for all people of all times and that we imagine people in the Bible looking like us.

Read the next paragraph while the children follow along. Ask: **What do the village people do?** (choose Bible stories, pose for pictures) **What does the photographer do?** (takes their picture)

Read the last paragraph aloud, then ask: **What happens to the photographs?** (An artist copies them to make paintings. They are shared with people in many countries.)

Tell the children you will talk more about the picture when you do the activity on the next page.

JESUS MAFA

To expose children to more Mafa paintings, visit **www.jesusmafa.com.** You could project the images onto a large screen. When you get to the menu, click on *miniposters or cards* to get a listing that includes all of the Bible story paintings. Children might enjoy seeing the paintings of the Scripture stories with which they are familiar. A Scripture citation accompanies each picture. You might read these verses from your Bible. Mention that children can access **www.jesusmafa.com** on their home computers as well.

The Mafa Group

In 1973 a Christian group in Cameroon, Africa, wanted to see African people in paintings of Bible stories. The group found a special way to do that.

Villagers from the Mafa group of Cameroon choose Bible stories. Then villagers play the parts of the people in the stories. A photographer takes pictures of them as they pose in their villages and in the countryside of Cameroon.

An artist then copies the photos to make beautiful paintings. Since 1977 these paintings have been shared with many countries of the world.

When the children have finished, check answers together by having volunteers read the questions and answers. Encourage various answers to the last question.

Say: *This painting helps us remember that Jesus is present to all of us, no matter who we are or where or when we live.*

Give each child a small piece of drawing paper. Tell the children that this will be for a special work of art that they will take home with them. Have them draw and color a special frame around the edge of the paper. As they work on their frames, remind them that this

week they learned that they can be like Jesus by following God's commandment to obey their parents. Ask them to draw a special picture inside their frame showing one thing they will do tonight at home to show love and obedience toward their parents. Allow time for sharing their works of art.

End this time together by saying: *Jesus wants us to follow God's commandments and obey our parents. Talk to Jesus now and ask him to help you follow his example.* Allow a few moments for quiet reflection.

Your Work of Art

Direct the children's attention to page 57. Read aloud the title, first paragraph, and directions.

Tell the children to follow along as you read each of the questions but not to write their answers yet. Tell them that you are reading it because some of the words are difficult to read. Encourage them to think about what their answers might be.

After reading all of the questions, have the children work with partners to complete the activity. Emphasize that they may look back at pages 52 and 53 for ideas and for help with spelling words.

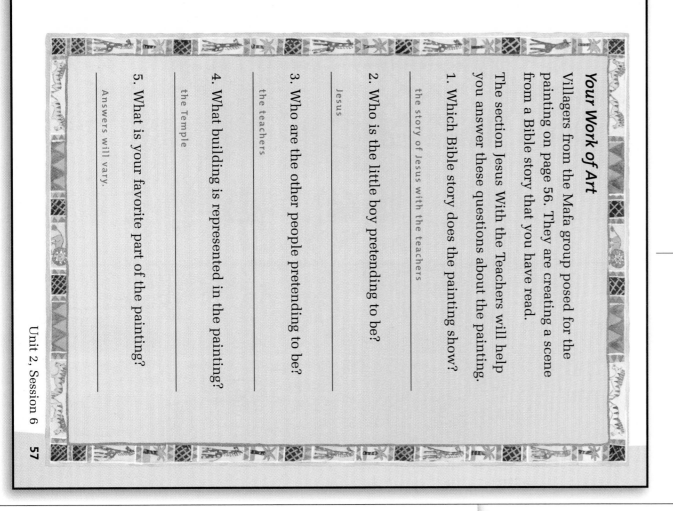

Your Work of Art

Villagers from the Mafa group posed for the painting on page 56. They are creating a scene from a Bible story that you have read.

The section Jesus With the Teachers will help you answer these questions about the painting.

1. Which Bible story does the painting show?

   the story of Jesus with the teachers

2. Who is the little boy pretending to be?

   Jesus

3. Who are the other people pretending to be?

   the teachers

4. What building is represented in the painting?

   the Temple

5. What is your favorite part of the painting?

   Answers will vary.

Unit 2, Session 6   57

QUESTION THE TEACHERS

Ask each child to take out a piece of paper and write a question about a topic that he or she might be having difficulty understanding. Questions could be about God, Jesus, the Holy Spirit, or anything else discussed in this session.

Place all the questions into a box or a basket. Gather the children into a circle and pull out the questions one at a time. Drawing on the wisdom of the group, answer as many questions as you can. If you cannot finish during this day, answer the remaining questions the following day. If there are questions that need further explanation, contact a priest or staff person for help.

Explain to the children that this activity is similar to the time that Jesus and the teachers were in the Temple, asking questions and listening to answers.

Reflect

Prayer

Lost and Found: A Recorded Guided Reflection

Prayer is one way we grow closer to God. Remind the children that our prayer today helps us understand what we have been learning.

A special approach to prayer in Session 6 is an extended guided reflection titled "Lost and Found" (CD 1, Track 7). Refer to pages 368 and 369 for the script and directions for using the recorded guided reflection with the children.

Guided Reflection: An Alternate Approach

An alternate approach to prayer in this session is to use the Prayer on the children's page. The following suggestions will help you guide the children through this Prayer in a reflective manner.

Say: *Let's prepare for our special time of prayer. Please sit comfortably, be very still, fold your hands, silently take a long, deep breath, and then let it out slowly. Do this several times. Close your eyes if you'd like, and listen quietly.* Wait until the children have settled comfortably.

Say: *Mary and Joseph were happy and relieved when they found Jesus in the Temple. The Temple was a special place. We have a special place too. Let's listen to learn more about it.*

Read the reflection aloud to the children, pausing after each paragraph. At the end of the prayer, say: *You might have something you still want to talk about with God. Take time to do that now.* Allow 20 seconds of quiet time. Invite all the children to open their eyes. Then pray the Sign of the Cross together.

Say: *Now, while remaining quiet and prayerful, let's learn more about how we can make Jesus' teachings part of our lives.*

OPTION

USING THIS PAGE AGAIN

If you have led the children through the recorded guided reflection, you might choose to use this prayer page with them during another session, Day 5, the Review session, or a seasonal session as appropriate.

Prayer

Jesus was at home in the Temple. This was the special place where he could worship God the Father.

You have a special place where you can go to worship God the Father too. The next time you go to church, take time to be quiet before or after Mass. Make this your special time and place to be with God your Father. Imagine how happy he is to be with you!

Picture yourself in church. Thank God that you are his child. Be still with your heavenly Father.

58   My Response

Living My Faith

Use the following activities to help the children express what they have learned in this session.

Faith Summary

After you have read the section, ask: **Whose words are the Ten Commandments?** (God's) Then ask: **Which commandment did we learn that Jesus obeyed?** (Honor your mother and father.)

Words I Learned

Call on volunteers to pronounce and define each word. Direct the children to the Glossary for help. See if other volunteers can use the words in sentences.

Ways of Being Like Jesus

Read the section. Then ask the children: **In what ways can you obey and help your parents?** (do as your parents ask, willingly do chores, speak to your parents with respect) Say: **When you do these things, you are being like Jesus.**

With My Family

Read the section and then tell the children: **Look at the picture on page 59. What is the boy doing?**

Imagine that someone in your family does something for you, and you want to do something nice in return. Ask: If, for example, your dad cooks dinner, what could you do in return? (wash the dishes, clear the table, tell him how delicious the food was)

✝ *Family and Community*

Prayer

Say: **We talked about the importance of listening to God and to our parents. Now let's take a moment to thank God for his Commandments and ask him to help us obey him. Pray this prayer of thanks aloud with me. Then think about how you can obey God.**

Slowly pray the prayer aloud as the children pray silently. Then take three deep breaths to give the children time to pray in silence. To close, say: **Let's close our prayer with the Sign of the Cross.**

My Response

Read the section. Say: **When we obey our parents, we are following God's Commandments. Think about ways you can obey your parents. Write a sentence about it.**

✝ *Family and Community*

Say: **You can be more like Jesus by following the Ten Commandments. Start today by obeying without giving excuses or saying, "Wait a minute." Be a happy follower of Jesus.**

Living My Faith

Living My Faith

Faith Summary

Jesus was faithful to the Ten Commandments. They help us love God and others.

Words I Learned

conscience   Ten Commandments

Ways of Being Like Jesus

Jesus honored his parents, obeyed them, and helped them. You are like Jesus when you follow his example.

With My Family

Show your love for your family. Every time someone does something nice for you, do something nice for another person.

Prayer

Thank you, God, for giving us your Commandments. Help me to obey you as Jesus did.

My Response

Write a sentence to show what you can do to obey your parents.

Extending the Session

Choose from the following options to extend the session or to reinforce concepts developed during the week.

Family Involvement

Remind the children to take home the Raising Faith-Filled Kids page to share what they are learning with their families.

Preparation for Sunday Scripture Readings

Lead children in a prayerful discussion of Sunday's readings. Visit www.FindingGod.org/Sunday for more information.

Seasonal Session

Consider the time of the liturgical year and use the appropriate seasonal session. Seasonal sessions may be found on page 241.

Unused Options and BLMs

Incorporate any unused options or Blackline Masters from the week's session.

Web Site Activities

Visit www.FindingGod.org to find additional activities for extending the session.

OPTION

TEN COMMANDMENTS ILLUSTRATION

Remind the children that Jesus, Mary, and Joseph followed the Ten Commandments. Invite the children to create an illustration for the Ten Commandments. They can refer to the Ten Commandments poster if they need to be reminded of the Commandments. After they are finished, ask volunteers to share their illustrations with the class.

OPTION

I'M IN A BIBLE STORY!

Remind the children of how the Mafa villagers play the parts of people in Bible stories. Then have the children illustrate a scene from the story of Jesus with the teachers using themselves and people that they know as characters in the story. For example, their own parents could be Mary and Joseph, or they could be one of the teachers in the Temple. Have children share their completed drawings with the class, explaining who they drew and why they chose that person.

OPTION

JESUS IN THE TEMPLE SKITS

Divide the class into small groups. Have one child in each group assume the roles of the following: Mary, Joseph, Jesus. Have the groups act out the story of Jesus with the teachers. Give each group time to practice, and then invite the groups to perform their skits for the class. After the skits, discuss what the children noticed about each performance and how they felt as they performed their skits.

RAISING FAITH-FILLED KIDS
a parent page

Focus on Faith

Jesus' Obedience and Ours

Jesus was a faithful Jewish boy who loved and obeyed his parents. We like to emphasize this when we talk to our children. We tell them that they should be obedient to their parents, just as Jesus was obedient to his. The root word for *obedience* means "to hear or to listen." As parents, we need to listen carefully to our children in order to recognize their concerns and respond to them. Becoming a good listener is one obligation we have if we are to raise our children in the ways that Jesus wants. As Christian parents, we have authority over our children. We are called to exercise this authority by nurturing our children's growth in the Christian life.

Dinnertime Conversation Starter

Explain to your children that you are always ready to listen, whether they have good or bad news. Tell them that their honesty is more important than any mistake they might make. Be sure not to criticize them when they are honest. Instead, discuss what they should do in the future to act according to Jesus' teaching.

Hints for at Home

Help your child create a Time for Prayer clock. You will need a paper plate, crayons or markers, construction paper, scissors, and a brass fastener. With crayons or markers, decorate the paper plate to look like a clock. Create praying hour and minute hands by tracing your child's hands, fingers together, onto the paper. Cut out the child's hands and attach them to the center of the clock with the fastener, and hang the clock in a special place. You may wish to designate a special family prayer time, such as before dinner or at bedtime. You may also allow time for prayer when the moment is appropriate, such as when asking for guidance or expressing special thanks.

Our Catholic Heritage

Catholicism has developed into a truly global religion. For example, in recent years Catholicism has shown tremendous growth in Africa. Approximately 390 million people in Africa are Christian; of those, roughly 115 million are Catholic. As recently as the early to mid 1990s, there were fewer than 100 million Catholics in Africa.

Focus on Prayer

The family provides a nurturing environment in which your child can learn to pray. Be a positive role model. Guide your child to understand that speaking and listening to God can be done at any moment.

Catechist Preparation

Session 7: Jesus Saves Us

3-Minute Retreat

Take a few moments before you begin preparing for this session. Pause and be aware of God's presence as you embark on this journey of teaching and learning.

Luke 7:22

And he (Jesus) said to them in reply, "Go and tell John what you have seen and heard."

Reflection

Jesus told the followers of John the Baptist that, through him (Jesus), the blind see, the crippled walk, the deaf hear, lepers are cleansed, the dead are raised, and the poor hear the good news of God's saving grace. Jesus' life and actions testify that he is the Savior. There are many ways people can be blind, crippled, deaf, dead, unclean, or poor. Jesus calls us to live a life that gives testimony to the presence of God, who brings healing to the world.

Questions

In what ways am I in need of the healing grace of Jesus? How can I share in Jesus' healing presence?

Prayer

Pray to Jesus, using this prayer or one of your own.

Lord, heal those things in me that keep others from discovering your presence.

Take a few moments to reflect prayerfully before you prepare this session.

Knowing and Sharing Your Faith

Scripture and Tradition in Session 7

Jesus was a traveling rabbi, a teacher who went from town to town sharing the scriptures with crowds of people as well as his close followers. Jesus is also our teacher, exemplifying through his words and deeds how to be a loving and caring person.

Jesus, a compassionate man, teaches us to be concerned for the sufferings of others and to do what we can to alleviate suffering. Jesus, the man of solidarity, teaches us to identify with people in need. The champion of the marginalized, Jesus wants us to stand with those who are forced to the fringes of society and promote their causes. Jesus, the healer, teaches us to be reconcilers in society and promoters of physical, mental, and spiritual health. Jesus, the servant, shows us how to look out for the interests of others. The rescuer of the lost, Jesus teaches us to rescue, rather than judge, people.

All of this means that Jesus teaches us to love. In obedience and total commitment to the work of his Father, Jesus shows us how to love.

Scripture in Session 7

John the Baptist questions Jesus' identity in **Luke 7:18–22.** The promise **Isaiah** speaks of in **35:5** is fulfilled in Jesus.

Let the scripture and Tradition deepen your understanding of the content in this session.

WINDOW ON THE CATECHISM

The following images of Jesus are presented in the CCC: Jesus as teacher, CCC 427, 2607; Jesus as rabbi, CCC 581; Jesus as model, CCC 459, 520; Jesus' obedience, CCC 532.

John the Baptist sends his disciples to inquire about Jesus.

The blind will see and the deaf will hear.

Catechist Preparation

From the Richness of the Tradition

Everyone has the right to adequate health care. A health care system must preserve and enhance the sanctity and dignity of human life, meet the most pressing health care needs of the poor, provide health care for everyone, and promote good health as well as care for persons who are chronically ill or dying.

✝ Catholic Social Teaching

In this session, aspects of the following theme of Catholic Social Teaching are integrated: **Solidarity.**

Consider in this session how you will invite the children to respond to and prayerfully reflect on God's invitation to love and serve others.

GENERAL DIRECTORY FOR CATECHESIS

Jesus calls us to conversion and faith. This is examined in *GDC* 53.

Prayer in Session 7

In this session the children are introduced to the practice of doing an examination of conscience as a prayerful way of discerning whether or not they are following God's will. The children will pray to Jesus in the opening prayer of petition and in the closing prayer of gratitude, confident that he will show them how to love. In the short, guided reflection the children will ask Jesus to help them care for others by following his good example.

Catechist Preparation: Get-Ready Guide

Session 7: Jesus Saves Us

Session Theme: *Jesus is the model for the love and goodness in our lives.*

Before This Session

- Bookmark the Bible to Luke 7:18–22 and Isaiah 35:5. Leave the Bible open to the passage from Luke at the prayer center.
- Set up the CD player ahead of time so you will be ready to play the reflective music at the end of CD 2.
- Prepare for the Parish Life option on page 67 by inviting someone to speak to your class about the roles of children in a parish.

Outcomes *At the end of the session, the children should be able to*

- understand the importance of helping our families.

- follow Jesus as a model of love and goodness.
- identify John the Baptist as a holy man who taught people about the coming of the Messiah.
- describe ways that Jesus showed his love for everyone.

- prayerfully reflect on God's presence, his invitation, and our response.

- identify practical ways to act on God's invitation in everyday living.

Steps

DAY 1 **Engage** page 61
Jesus Saves Us

DAYS 1–3 **Explore** pages 62–67
Jesus Heals
Jesus Cares for Everybody
Jesus Is Alive
Blessed Carlos

DAY 4 **Reflect** page 68
Prayer: Jesus Helps Those in Need

DAY 4 **Respond** page 69
Living My Faith: Reaching Out to Others

DAY 5 **Extending the Session** page 70
Day 5 offers an opportunity to extend the session with activities that reinforce the session outcomes.

Materials

Required Materials

- Bible
- Writing paper, pens, pencils
- Art materials, such as drawing paper, crayons, markers, scissors, glue
- Unlined index cards (page 67)
- CD 2, Reflective music (pages 61, 68)

Optional Materials

- Butcher paper, washable black marker, colored chalk (page 61)
- Construction paper (page 63)
- Red construction paper, white paper (page 65)
- Butcher paper (page 67)
- Slips of paper with a kind act written on each (page 70)
- Pictures of Jesus (page 70)
- Blackline Masters 17, 18, 19 (pages 61, 63, 64)

e-resources

www.FindingGod.org

Jesus Saves Us

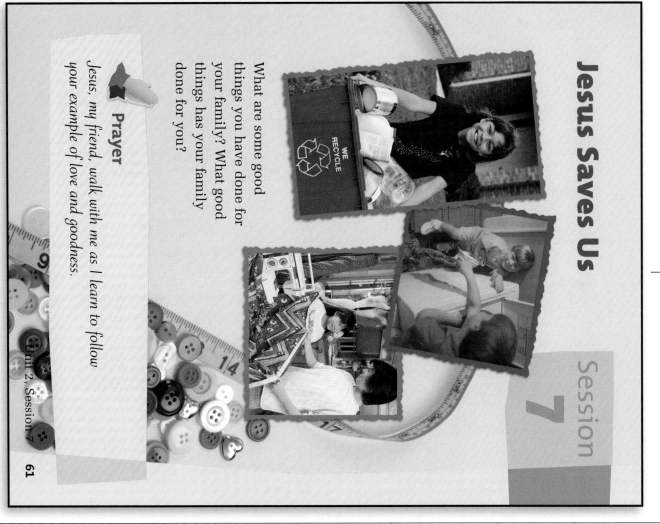

As the children settle, you may wish to play the reflective music at the end of CD 2.

Tell the children: *We are going to learn that Jesus loved everyone, especially people in need. We will find out how Jesus showed this love to them.*

Give them time to be with Jesus. Then say: *Take a moment to think about someone who loves you.* Ask: *In what ways does this person show his or her love?* Encourage volunteers to share.

Explain: *We carry the love of God and Jesus with us at all times. We also have the love of our families and those who care about us.* Ask: *How does their love make you feel?* (secure, happy, safe, loving)

Say: *Open your books to page 61.* Read the title of the session. Read the questions while the children follow along. Choose volunteers to respond.

Explain: *We can show love to those close to us—our families, friends, and neighbors.* Ask: *How is love shown through the actions of the people in the photos?* (a girl recycling, brothers doing laundry together, daughter helping her mother)

Prayer

Say: *Jesus loves everybody, especially those in need. Let's pray and ask Jesus to help us care for others, as he did.*

Pray along with me and then take a moment to talk silently to God.

Pray the prayer aloud. Then pause to give the children time to pray silently. End by praying **Amen.**

Jesus Saves Us

Session 7

Prayer

Jesus, my friend, walk with me as I learn to follow your example of love and goodness.

What are some good things you have done for your family? What good things has your family done for you?

Unit 2, Session 7 61

OPTION

BLM 17: JESUS AND THE BLIND MEN

Blackline Master 17 is a reader's theater for children to read parts aloud.

OPTION

WALK-IN-LOVE-WITH-JESUS MURALS

Invite the children to work in groups. Give each group butcher paper, a washable black marker, colored chalk, crayons, and/or markers. On the board, write *Walk in Love With Jesus.* Have the children copy the phrase onto their papers with a washable black marker. Invite them to use the black marker to trace the outlines of both of their shoes on the butcher paper and to write their names above the outlines. Have them decorate their murals with colored chalk, markers, or crayons.

When the groups have finished, have them display their murals.

Explore

Jesus Heals

Refer to the open Bible at the prayer center. Tell the children that it is opened to the story being read in this session.

Say: *Please follow along in your books as I read this story.* Slowly and with expression, read the title and the first paragraph of the story. Then ask the group what the illustration shows. (people who have been healed)

Read the second paragraph slowly and with expression. Explain: *John the Baptist was a holy man who wanted others to know that Jesus was the Messiah.* Ask the children: *Does anyone remember what Messiah means?* (anointed one, Savior)

Read the third paragraph aloud. Then ask: *Why do you think John sent his followers to ask Jesus if he was the one they were waiting for?* (John thought that Jesus was the Messiah, the one who saves us, and he wanted to be sure.)

Finish reading the story, reminding the group to follow along. Say: *John the Baptist told his followers to go and find out if Jesus was the Messiah. By Jesus' good deeds of healing people who were sick and curing people who were deaf and blind, John's followers learned that Jesus was truly the Messiah. Jesus told John's followers to tell John what they had seen and heard so that he would know who Jesus really was.*

How Can You Be Like Jesus?

Read the directions aloud for the children.

When the children have completed the exercise, invite volunteers to share their responses and to explain which choice shows that the person is acting like Jesus.

Ask: *Have you ever been in a situation like any one of these? What did you do?* Say: *There are many things we can do to be more like Jesus. I will give you a group of phrases and would like you to think of ways they can be completed to help others.*

Jesus Heals

Jesus helped many people who were in need. He gave sight to those who could not see. He healed people who could not walk.

At the same time there was a holy man named John the Baptist. He was teaching people about the coming of the Messiah.

Some of John's followers told him about Jesus. So John sent them to ask Jesus, "Are you the one we are waiting for, or should we keep looking?"

adapted from Luke 7:18-21

Did You Know?

Water is the most important symbol of Baptism.

62   God's Invitation

Complete the reading on pages 62 and 63 in this guide before beginning Did You Know?

Did You Know?

Read the sentence aloud to the children. Say: *Every time you go to church, you can remember your Baptism by placing your hand in the holy water and praying the Sign of the Cross.*

Discuss with the children different ways to complete the sentences.

Encourage the children to be aware of situations in which they can be helpful to one another.

End your time together by praying the Lord's Prayer for those who need God's help.

OPTION

BLM 18: HELPING TO HEAL OTHERS

Blackline Master 18 asks children to make healing bandages to give to different members of the group.

OPTION

HELPING THE SICK

Have the children recall times when they were sick. Ask: *Has anyone had the flu or a cold? How did you feel? What did your families do to help you feel better?* (make soup, give medicine) Tell the children: *We can help others who are sick by doing some of these things.* Ask: *What are some other things we could do to help those who are sick?* (let them rest, put blankets on them, rent their favorite video for them) Say: *When we help people who are sick, we are being like Jesus.*

✝ Solidarity

OPTION

CARDS FOR THE SICK

Pass out construction paper. Tell the children to fold the construction paper in half to create a card. Have the children draw a picture on the front. (smiley faces, sun, stars, animals)

On the inside have them write a loving message to someone who is sick. (We are praying for you. We hope you feel better soon.) They can address the letters to "Dear Friend." Walk around the room and help the children where needed.

Give these cards to a member of the parish staff who can arrange to have them delivered to parishioners in the hospital. Encourage the children to reach out to those who are not feeling well.

✝ Solidarity

Write the following phrases on the board:

Do you need . . . ?
(to borrow a pencil)
I can show you how to . . .
(ride a skateboard)
Are you having trouble with . . . ?
(your homework)
Let me help you with . . . .
(raking the leaves)
I have an extra . . .
(granola bar)

adapted from Luke 7:22

Jesus said to John's followers, "Go and tell John what you have seen and heard. The blind see again. The sick get well. The deaf hear, and the dead are raised. The poor hear the good news that God loves them."

How Can You Be Like Jesus?

Below are stories about people in need. Write a J on the line that shows what you can do to be like Jesus.

1. A person is caught in the rain with no umbrella.
___ Share your umbrella.
___ Turn your back and walk away.

2. Your father is fixing the front door at home.
___ Play video games.
___ Get tools for your father.

3. A friend from class does not understand the homework assignment.
___ Explain the assignment to your friend.
___ Tell everybody that your friend is going to fail.

Explore

Jesus Cares for Everybody

Invite children to reflect on ways they have been caring and helpful since yesterday's class. Then ask a volunteer to read the first paragraph aloud. Ask: **What did Jesus tell everyone?** (God loves him or her.) **For whom did Jesus have a special love?** (those who were sick) **How did Jesus show his love for those who were sick?** (He healed them.) Explain: **The Son of God became man to show us how much God loves us. When Jesus healed others, he was showing God's healing presence to the world.**

Have the children stand and join you in an action rhyme. Say each line and demonstrate the gestures. Tell the children to repeat each line after you.

The love in your heart
(form a heart with both hands)
Wasn't put there to stay.
(point to heart)
Love isn't love
(form heart again)
'Til you give it away.
(gesture outwards from heart)

Read the second paragraph. Ask: **How did some people show they were angry with Jesus?** (put him to death on a cross) If there is a crucifix in the room, you might want to draw attention to it.

Read the third paragraph aloud as the children follow along. Then ask: **Who raised Jesus from the dead?** (God)

OPTION

BLM 19: JESUS SAVES US

Blackline Master 19 is a matching exercise covering themes from this session.

OPTION

GROWING-IN-LOVE ACTION RHYME

Tell the children to stand for an action rhyme. Say each line of the following rhyme, demonstrate the action, and have the children repeat after you.

We can grow in love
(crouch down and pop up)
And bloom each day.
(gesture outwards)
We can care for others
(gesture to other children)
Through the words that we say.
(cup hands at mouth)
With all of our actions we can do good
(nod)
And live our lives the way we should.
(shake hands with another child)

Jesus Cares for Everybody

Jesus followed God, obeyed Mary and Joseph, and helped people in need. Jesus told people that God loved them. He had a special love for those who were sick. Jesus showed God's love for the sick by healing them.

But some people became angry with Jesus. They put him to death on a cross.

When Jesus died on the cross, everybody thought it was the end of his life. But God raised Jesus from the dead.

64   God's Invitation

Jesus Is Alive

In a clear voice read the paragraph aloud. Ask: **Where is Jesus now?** (in heaven and with us, always helping us and caring for us) Call on volunteers to respond to the questions in the paragraph. Accept all reasonable answers.

Tell the children: **Jesus showed us how to love others.** Teach the children the American Sign Language sign for "I love you," which is the thumb, index finger, and pinkie finger extended and the two center fingers tucked against the palm.

Remind the children of the "I Love Jesus" song they learned in the previous session. Tell them they will learn more verses today. Sing each verse to the tune of "London Bridge Is Falling Down" and ask the children to join in. Invite the children to make the "I love you" sign whenever they sing "I love Jesus."

Jesus helped the blind to see,
blind to see, blind to see.
Jesus helped the blind to see.
I love Jesus!

Jesus lived a life of love,
life of love, life of love.
Jesus lived a life of love.
I love Jesus!

Jesus helped people to walk,
people to walk, people to walk.
Jesus helped people to walk.
I love Jesus!

Reading God's Word

Read the section aloud as the children follow along. Ask: **According to the Bible, whom did Jesus heal?** (those who were blind and those who were deaf)

Explain that when we reach out to those in need, as Jesus did, we are being like him. Say positively: **When you help a friend with his or her homework, you are being kind like Jesus. When you cheer up a friend who is feeling sad, you are like Jesus.** Ask: **What are some other ways you can be like Jesus?** (saying hello to the cafeteria workers at school, going with our parents to visit someone who is lonely) End your time together. Say: **Let "I Can Be Like Jesus" be your motto for today.**

Jesus Is Alive

Now Jesus is alive in heaven. He is also with us, helping and caring for us. He wants us to love others as he loves us. How can you follow Jesus' example of love? How can you care for those around you?

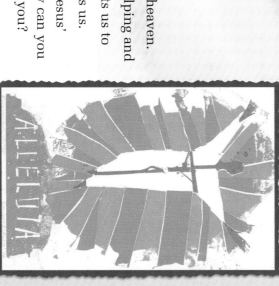

Reading God's Word

The eyes of the blind and the ears of the deaf will be opened.

adapted from Isaiah 35:5

OPTION

A LOVING SIGN

Pass out red construction paper and white paper. Have the children cut a heart out of their red construction paper. Then tell them to use their pencils to trace the hand they don't write with onto the sheet of white paper and then cut it out. Have them glue the palm of the hand to the heart. Then have them glue the two center fingers against the palm to create the "I love you" sign.

Explore

Blessed Carlos

Begin today's spiritual journey by reminding the children that they have talked this week about people who have helped them and about being helpers themselves. Ask: *Who are we like when we help others?* (Jesus) Say: *To follow Jesus, we must know him.*

Ask: *Who are some of the special people who have taught you about Jesus?* Encourage volunteers to share the people in their lives who have helped them to know Jesus. Make a list on the board of children's responses. (parents, teachers, priests, older siblings, grandparents, friends)

Discuss how all these people are special to us. Bring out the fact that they don't look alike, they are not the same age, but they share many of the same qualities. Say: *These people love Jesus and want to help us love him. They are happy to be Jesus' friends. They help others in the Church to know and love Jesus.*

Tell the children that today they will be reading about a special person who loved Jesus very much and told many other people about Jesus.

Invite children to look at the pictures on page 66. Read the title and first paragraph aloud as children follow along. The pronunciation for Rodríguez Santiago is (räd rē′gez sän′tē äg′ō). Ask: *Why do we call him Blessed Carlos?* (He lived a model life of goodness and love.) *Where was he born?* (Puerto Rico) If possible, show children on a world map the location of Puerto Rico in relation to where they live.

Read the next paragraph. Then ask: *What kinds of things did Carlos teach people?* (about the Mass, about Jesus' death and Resurrection)

Invite a volunteer to read the caption under the picture at the left. Mention that Carlos is an altar server in this picture.

Continue with the story of Blessed Carlos by reading aloud the first paragraph on page 67. Then see if children know what a *catechist* is. Explain that this is a person who teaches others about God, like the teachers in the parish religious education program. Ask: *I am also a catechist because I too pray with you, teach you about God, and encourage you to be a follower of Jesus.*

Read the next paragraph. Ask children what helped Carlos when he was very ill. (knowing God loved him) Ask: *What was Carlos named by the Church?* (blessed) Explain that the Church recognized that he lived a life of love and goodness, trying to be like Jesus, so they gave him the title of *blessed.* Invite a volunteer to read the caption next to the photo. Talk about this photo showing Pope John Paul II giving Carlos this title.

Being Like Carlos

Read the title and the paragraph, pausing for responses to the question. Make sure children understand the activity, and then give them time to write their sentences. Have a sharing time for those who would like to read their sentence aloud.

Blessed Carlos

There are people who live model lives of goodness and love. Carlos Rodríguez Santiago was one of those people. He was born in Puerto Rico. He was often ill during his lifetime, but he always remained cheerful.

Carlos wanted to tell people about Jesus. He did this by teaching them about the Mass. He taught them about the death and resurrection of Jesus.

Carlos spent his life doing what God asked of him.

Refer the children again to their sentence about being like Carlos.

Say: *You imagined yourself being a helper in the Church like Carlos was. Now imagine that someone took a photo of you, so you would be remembered as a helper.*

Give the children unlined index cards, and have them draw their photographs onto it. If you use 4-by-6-inch cards, you can mention that this is actual snapshot size. When they have finished, they may share their pictures with the group. Encourage the children to take home their photographs and put them where they will be a reminder to work hard to teach others about Jesus and to serve the Church.

Say: *We have many helpers in our lives to teach us about Jesus. The priests in our parish, teachers and catechists, our parents and families, even our friends can help us be true followers of Jesus. Remember them especially in your prayers today.*

To end the time together, say: *Remember, we followers of Jesus act in loving ways toward everyone!*

Carlos served the Church in many ways. He led the choir at his parish. He also served as a catechist. He taught many children about Jesus.

Carlos knew that God loved him. This helped him very much when he was in great pain from his illness. He told others that God loved them too. Carlos died from cancer. He has been named blessed by the Church.

Carlos was named blessed by the Church for his service to God and others.

Being Like Carlos

Imagine you are like Blessed Carlos. What could you do to help people in your parish or school? Write a sentence to explain how you would help others learn of God's love.

_____

_____

_____

Unit 2, Session 7   **67**

Explore

DAY 3

OPTION
A PARISH HELPER

Discuss with the children ways they can be like Blessed Carlos by volunteering in their parish. Ask them to list things they are already doing or could do, such as sing in the children's choir, pick up litter on the church or school grounds, pray for the priest, help with food and clothing drives, or donate some of their allowance to the Sunday collection.

Create a butcher-paper mural showing ways they choose to be involved in parish life.

OPTION
PARISH LIFE

Invite the pastor, a priest, a member of the parish staff, or a volunteer who coordinates parish outreach activities to speak to the children about their roles in the parish. Consider inviting another class to join your class for the presentation.

FYI
THE PROCESS OF CANONIZATION

The canonization process begins with an investigation by the local bishop of the life of a person who has lived a holy life or has died a martyr's death. The results of this investigation are sent to Rome where further investigation is carried out by the Congregation of the Causes of Saints. If the person is found to have died as a martyr or have lived a heroic life of grace, he or she is declared venerable. When a person has been venerable for a period of time and it can be shown that a miracle can be attributed to his or her intercession, the pope can declare the person blessed. When a second miracle is authenticated, the pope can declare the person a saint.

Carlos Rodriguez Santiago died in 1963. He was declared *blessed* by Pope John Paul II in April 2001.

Session 7   **67**

Reflect

Prayer

Play the reflective music at the end of CD 2. Adjust the volume so that it will be background music for the reflection.

Have the children describe what they see in the picture. Ask: *What are the children doing? How is the boy helping the girl?* Say: *It is a good thing to care for others. We are like Jesus when we care for others.*

Then say: *It is a special gift that we have Jesus to care for us. Please be still, close your eyes, fold your hands, and imagine that you were present when Jesus was healing all the people who came to him.* Pause for three deep breaths. Say: *Listen quietly as I begin our prayer. Then you will have a chance to pray to Jesus quietly in your heart.*

Read the first paragraph slowly and with expression. Afterwards, pause for five seconds so the children can imagine the scene. Slowly read the second paragraph. Pause so the children can think about their answers to the question. Now read the last paragraph, pausing for a few seconds after each sentence. Give the children time to speak silently with Jesus. Then say: *Please open your eyes when you are ready and together let us pray the Sign of the Cross.*

OPTION

LOVING PERSONS

Discuss with the children the social teachings of the Church found in the Showing Our Love for the World section on pages 308 and 309.

68 Session 7

FYI

PRAYER AND IMAGINATION

Saint Ignatius of Loyola, founder of the Society of Jesus, or the Jesuits, created the Spiritual Exercises. The exercises are a series of meditations that are to be read, using the gift of imagination. This might mean picturing Jesus in the Temple, on the shoreline of the Sea of Galilee, or in the garden of Gethsemane.

The purpose is to create a setting in which to encounter the Lord. This Ignatian method of praying scripture is incorporated into many of the guided reflections in this book, inviting children to use their imagination to enter into the Scripture passage being meditated upon and to encounter Jesus.

Prayer

The story of Jesus' healing those who were sick shows us that we should help people in need. Imagine how excited these people must have been when Jesus healed them.

Now imagine you are close to people who need help. What would Jesus want you to do for them?

Silently pray to Jesus. Ask him to show you ways to care for those in need. Tell him how you will help someone in your community.

My Response

68

Living My Faith

Use the following activities to help the children gain a fuller understanding of what they have learned in this session.

Faith Summary

Read the section; then ask the children: **What are some of the ways that Jesus helped others?** (cured those who were sick, deaf, blind, and crippled) Ask: **When we say Jesus is our example, what does that mean?** (We should be loving and good, as Jesus was.)

Ways of Being Like Jesus

After reading the section, direct the children's attention to the picture. Ask: **What is the older girl doing for the younger girl?** (helping her with homework) Ask: **In what ways might we be able to help the people in our lives who are in need?**

With My Family

Encourage the children to involve their families in caring for others. Ask: **In what ways might your families help someone who is elderly, sick, or alone?** (send a cheerful greeting card, take food to someone who is sick) Read the suggestion on the page and talk about this with the children.

Prayer

Say: **We've talked about following Jesus' example of helping people in need. Let's take some time to thank Jesus for being our example and showing us how important it is to care for others. Pray along with me as I pray this prayer of thanks. Then think about how you can help others as Jesus did.**

Pray the prayer aloud as the group prays along. Then take a couple of deep breaths to allow the children time to pray in silence. Close by saying: **Let's close our prayer with the Sign of the Cross.**

My Response

Read this section and then say: **There are many people you can reach out to. Some might need help with their homework while others might need food or clothes. There are many things we can do to help. Think about something you can do. Draw a picture about it.**

Say: **Remember, we followers of Jesus act in loving ways toward everyone!**

✝ Solidarity

Living My Faith

Faith Summary

Jesus is alive in heaven. He helps us to love others.

Ways of Being Like Jesus

Jesus helped those in need. Look around you at others who might need help. Can you help your brother or sister with homework?

With My Family

With your family, spend time visiting a local nursing home.

My Response

What is one thing you can do to reach out to someone else? Draw a picture.

Prayer

Thank you, Jesus, for showing me your loving ways, so that I can share your love with others.

Unit 2, Session 7   69

Extending the Session

Choose from the following options to extend the session or to reinforce concepts developed during the week.

Family Involvement

Remind the children to take home the Raising Faith-Filled Kids page to share what they are learning with their families.

Preparation for Sunday Scripture Readings

Lead children in a prayerful discussion of Sunday's readings. Visit www.FindingGod.org/Sunday for more information.

Seasonal Session

Consider the time of the liturgical year and use the appropriate seasonal session. Seasonal sessions may be found on page 241.

Unused Options and BLMs

Incorporate any unused options or Blackline Masters from the week's session.

Web Site Activities

Visit www.FindingGod.org to find additional activities for extending the session.

OPTION
REMINDER TO PRAY

Invite the children to think of someone they know who needs their prayers. Encourage them to draw a picture of that person. When they are finished, ask them to take the picture home and display it somewhere prominent as a reminder to pray for that person.

OPTION
DAILY KINDNESS

For each child, write a kind act on a slip of paper, such as *share a toy, give a hug, offer a compliment, do the dishes, set the table,* and so on. Place the slips of paper in a bag and have each child choose one. Challenge children to complete the kind act before the end of the day as a way to care for others as Jesus did.

OPTION
JESUS IS WITH YOU

Remind children that Jesus is with us, helping and caring for us. Then have them play a game called Jesus Is With You. Hide 10 to 12 pictures of Jesus around the classroom, both in plain sight and partially hidden. At a signal, invite the children to find the pictures. Once they are found, bring the class together and say: *Jesus is always with you—even when you aren't looking. Remember that you can talk to him anytime or anywhere.*

RAISING FAITH-FILLED KIDS
a parent page

Christ in the House of His Parents, Sir John Everett Millais

Focus on Faith

Jesus' Life and Ours

We do not know very much about Jesus' life on earth. We know about his birth, a little of his infancy, and of one event when he was about 12. Then we learn more about Jesus when he was about 30. Details of Jesus' life are quite scarce. Like any Jewish boy of his time, Jesus learned the traditions of his people. He learned a trade. He obeyed his mother and father. Most of his days, like most of ours, were probably filled with the ordinary things that people do. The simplicity of his life shows us that ordinary days are grace-filled days. In the midst of everyday life, Jesus prepared for his mission. God is also present in our everyday lives. In the loving families that we help God to nurture, ordinary life becomes sacred.

Spirituality in Action

Create an Every Penny Counts! can for your family to help those in need. Decorate a piece of construction paper, label it *Every Penny Counts!,* and glue it to an empty can. Invite members of your family to place a portion of their weekly allowances or earnings in the can. When the can is full, donate the money you have collected to a charitable group.

Hints for at Home

Jesus said,
"Do to others whatever you would have them do to you." (Matthew 7:12)

With your family, make a Being Good to Others cross as a reminder to treat people as Jesus teaches. You will need construction paper, scissors, crayons, and glue.

First, cut a cross out of the construction paper. Then have each family member draw and cut a heart shape from a separate sheet of paper. On his or her heart, each person should write one way to be good to others. Glue the hearts to the cross and discuss how each idea follows what Jesus teaches us about treating other people as we want to be treated.

Dinnertime Conversation Starter

Discuss a good deed that someone in your family observed today. Did someone help when an accident happened? Did someone share a snack? Did this deed inspire your family member to do something good?

Focus on Prayer

Your child has been reflecting on the ways in which Jesus led a life of total commitment to God. Spend a few quiet moments of reflection with your child as you think of ways you and your family might share the love of Jesus with one another.

Session 8: Jesus Calls Us to Love

3-Minute Retreat

Before you prepare for your session, pause for a few moments and pay attention to your breathing. Slowly take three deep breaths to clear your mind. Remember that God is with you as you continue to grow in faith.

Luke 14:23

The master then ordered the servant, "Go out to the highways and hedgerows and make people come in that my home may be filled."

Reflection

In the parable of the banquet, Jesus tells us that all people are invited to the Kingdom of God. The mercy and love of God are not reserved for a few, and the invitation to serve the Kingdom of God is not forced on anyone. Jesus invites us; we need only answer "yes." We share with Jesus the belief that all people are important to God, and we demonstrate this commitment through our service to others.

Question

How can I quiet myself to listen to Jesus' invitation to follow him?

Prayer

Pray to Jesus, using these words or words of your own.

Divine Master, thank you for the invitation to share in your bountiful blessings. I accept.

Take a few moments to reflect prayerfully before you prepare this session.

Knowing and Sharing Your Faith

Scripture and Tradition in Session 8

Jesus often referred to the Kingdom of God, knowing his listeners would understand him because they knew the Old Testament. People had an expectation that God would intervene in their lives in some way. Jesus surprised them, however, with his proclamation that the kingdom was near—in fact, already among them. He may also have disappointed some of them when he said that the coming of the kingdom would not be dependent upon any political order, nor would kingdom values have any political consequences.

The kingdom cannot be understood in this world's terms because it is the work of the Father. Jesus made no attempt to define it. Instead, Jesus spoke of it in parables comparing it sometimes to a banquet. In those parables, he makes it clear that all are welcome in the kingdom, including sinners, outcasts, and the despised. People will be part of the kingdom because they have responded to the call to conversion. It is true that some will be found unworthy of the kingdom, but this will be their own doing. It will be the result of their refusal to accept the invitation of the Father.

Scripture in Session 8

Jesus teaches about the Kingdom of God in **Luke 14:16–23**. In **Matthew 4:23**, Jesus is described as a teacher and healer.

Let the Scripture and Tradition deepen your understanding of the content in this session.

WINDOW ON THE CATECHISM

The rich imagery of the Kingdom of God is detailed in CCC 541–556. The petition "Thy kingdom come" is discussed in CCC 2632, 2816–2821.

Jesus shares the parable of the banquet.

Jesus teaches and heals people.

From the Richness of the Tradition

The parable of the banquet focuses on hospitality and welcoming strangers. "As Catholics we are called to take concrete measures to overcome the misunderstanding, ignorance, competition, and fear that stand in the way of genuinely welcoming the stranger in our midst and enjoying the communion that is our destiny as children of God." ("Welcoming the Stranger Among Us: Unity in Diversity," November 15, 2000, United States Conference of Catholic Bishops)

✠ Catholic Social Teaching

In this session, aspects of the following themes of Catholic Social Teaching are integrated:

- **Option for the Poor and Vulnerable**
- **Solidarity**

Consider in this session how you will invite the children to respond to and prayerfully reflect on God's invitation to love and serve others.

GENERAL DIRECTORY FOR CATECHESIS

When we proclaim the Kingdom of God, we are proclaiming the "gift of Salvation." This is highlighted in GDC 97.

Prayer in Session 8

The short, guided reflection gives you the opportunity to help the children pray in silence and reflect on sharing God's love with those they meet. For more ideas about leading guided reflection, see page 64. In the opening prayer of petition and in the closing prayer of gratitude, the children consider what it means to follow Jesus.

Catechist Preparation: Get-Ready Guide

Session 8: Jesus Calls Us to Love

Session Theme: *Jesus calls us to the Kingdom of God.*

Before This Session

- Bookmark the Bible to Luke 14:16–23 and Matthew 4:23. Display the Bible in the prayer center open to the passage from Luke.
- Set up the CD player ahead of time so you will be ready to play the song.
- Write notes for the children to bring home to their parents for the Sharing Party option on page 80.

Outcomes *At the end of the session, the children should be able to*

- recognize how it feels to be invited to a party.
- describe how Jesus used parables to teach lessons about how to be closer to God.
- explain the meaning of the parable of the banquet.
- identify Peter as the Church's first leader.
- define the words *parable* and *pope*.
- prayerfully reflect on God's presence, his invitation, and our response.
- identify practical ways to act on God's invitation in everyday living.

Steps

DAY 1   **Engage** page 71
Jesus Calls Us to Love

DAYS 1-3   **Explore** pages 72–77
The Parable of the Banquet
Jesus Invites Us
Jesus Chose Peter
Bread for the World

DAY 4   **Reflect** page 78
Prayer: Jesus Invites Us to Care for Others

DAY 4   **Respond** page 79
Living My Faith: Ways to Care for Others

DAY 5   **Extending the Session** page 80
Day 5 offers an opportunity to extend the session with activities that reinforce the session outcomes.

Materials

Required Materials
- Bible
- Writing paper, pens, pencils
- Art materials, such as drawing paper, crayons, markers, scissors, glue
- Flashlight, magnet, paper clips, bolts (page 71)
- CD 2, Track 11: Friends, All Gather 'Round (2:14) (page 72)
- CD 2, Reflective music (page 78)

Optional Materials
- Chart paper, colored chalk (page 73)
- Construction paper, large envelope (page 73)
- Chart paper, poster board, magazines (page 74)
- Shoe boxes, gift wrap, tape (page 80)
- Notes to parents, extra snacks (page 80)
- Blackline Master 20, tape (page 73)
- Blackline Masters 21, 22 (pages 73, 74)

e-resources
www.FindingGod.org

Jesus Calls Us to Love

Begin today with these words: *With Jesus as our example, we can learn to follow God's way. Jesus lights our path and welcomes us to be with God. We can all follow.*

Have the children form a single-file line. Dim the lights and then use a flashlight to lead the children around the room. When finished, you may wish to place the light in a special place, such as on your desk or at the prayer center. Turn up the lights.

Say: *Today you followed me. A flashlight was our guide. Every day and all the time we can follow Jesus. He is our light and our guide. Now, turn to page 71.* Direct the children's attention to the photographs. Have them describe what they see. Ask: *What are the children doing? What does the invitation say?*

Read the title of the session and the questions. Encourage the children to reply. After a reasonable amount of time, say: *Jesus is inviting us to follow him. When people include others, they are doing as Jesus wants. We all grow closer to Jesus. We all grow closer to others.*

Engage

Hold up a magnet and tell the children to pretend that it stands for Jesus. Show paper clips and bolts; tell the children that they stand for people. Ask: *What do you think will happen when the magnet gets near a paper clip? a bolt?* After they respond, bring the magnet near the paper clips. Then say: *Like the magnet, Jesus draws people to him. By coming close to Jesus, we learn to love God and others.*

Prayer

Say: *Let's ask Jesus to help us learn how to care for people as he did.*

Continue: *After we pray this prayer of petition aloud, take a moment to talk to God silently about what is in your heart.*

Slowly pray the prayer aloud. Then pause, giving the children time to talk to God. Close the quiet time by praying *Amen.*

Jesus Calls Us to Love

Session 8

When have you been invited to a party? Were you happy to be invited?

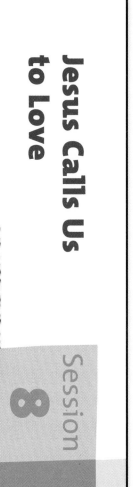

It's a birthday party!
Please Come!
July 14
1:00 P.M.

Prayer

Loving Jesus, help me learn to follow you and care for people as you do.

SECRET ACTS OF KINDNESS

Tell the group: *Jesus wants us to include people and think about what makes them happy. Try to do a secret act of kindness for someone during the week. For example, you could make your big brother's bed. Do your best to keep your good deed a secret.*

Ask: *What are some other secret acts of kindness you could do?* Have the children write the names of people for whom they would like to do a secret act of kindness. Then have them write what they would like to do for them. Encourage the children to do what is on their lists.

Explore

The Parable of the Banquet

Ask the children if they know the story of the three little pigs. Ask them what happened in the story. Then ask: *What's the lesson?* (Take time to build something strong, even if it takes longer.)

Say: *Jesus also told stories that have a lesson in them. We're going to read and talk about one of these stories today.*

Read the title and first paragraph aloud. Draw attention to the word *parable* in dark type in the first line. Have the children pronounce it. Explain: *Jesus was a great teacher. He wanted people to learn about God, and he worked hard to help them understand his teachings. Jesus often used parables, which are simple stories that show us what God wants for the world.*

Ask the children if they have ever heard the word *banquet*, and see if they can define it. Say: *A banquet is a big party or feast.*

Point to the open Bible at the prayer center. Say: *The story I am going to read you is from the Bible, which is opened to this story.* Read the second and third paragraphs. Read the dialogue with expression. Ask the group: *What does it mean to make an excuse?* (to give a reason for not being able to do something) Ask: *If you were the man giving the dinner party, how would you feel if everyone made an excuse and didn't come?* (sad, angry, disappointed)

Read the rest of the story aloud on the next page in the children's book while the children follow along. Say: *In the Bible story we read the last time we were together, we learned that Jesus helped people who were poor, sick, blind, and those who were crippled. Notice that the man in*

this story asks his servant to bring all of these same people to his dinner. Ask: *What might Jesus have wanted us to learn from this?* (God wants us to be close to everyone.)

Explain: *With this parable, Jesus wants us to know that he has invited all of us to join him, to be as he is, and to follow him.* Conclude reverently: *Jesus has a special place in his heart for those who need help.*

✝ *The Poor and Vulnerable*

♪ 💿 Say: *Now we're going to sing a song about gathering around the table of the Lord.* Ask the children to turn to the song "Friends, All Gather 'Round," in the Songs of Our Faith section in the back of their books. Play the song (Track 11 of CD 2) and encourage the children to listen to the verses and sing along with the refrain. Play the song again if time permits.

The Parable of the Banquet

Jesus often told a **parable**, or story, to teach an important lesson. He told this parable to show how God wants everyone to be close to him.

A man planned a dinner party and invited many people. When the day of the party came, the man sent his servant to tell the guests, "Come, everything is ready."

One by one, the guests made excuses. The first one said, "Sorry, but I just bought some land. I have to go check it." Another said, "I just bought some animals that I have to take care of." A third one said, "I cannot keep my new wife waiting."

72   God's Invitation

Jesus Invites Us

Invite the children to look at the illustration. Ask: *What is happening in the picture?* (People are gathering for the feast.) Ask: *Who was invited to the man's banquet?* (people who were poor, sick, blind, or crippled)

Ask a volunteer to read the title and paragraph aloud. Say: *We are invited to join Jesus. God loves everyone and wants everyone to be with him.*

OPTION
BLM 20: PARABLE OF THE BANQUET

For Blackline Master 20 children will make finger puppets for retelling the parable of the banquet to use in groups.

OPTION
BLM 21: COME TO GOD'S BANQUET

Blackline Master 21 is an invitation to God's banquet for children to decorate and take home.

OPTION
A DINNER INVITATION

Divide the class into groups. Provide the groups with chart paper, colored chalk, and crayons or markers. Invite them to create a dinner invitation, asking others to join them for a feast. Have them consider when and where the feast will occur.

Assist the groups in writing their invitations. When the groups have finished, allow them to present their invitations to the other groups.

✝ *Solidarity*

OPTION
MISSING-YOU CARDS

Remind the children: *It's important to include people in the things we do.* Say: *Look around the room for a moment.* Then ask: *Who is not here today?* After they respond, say: *Let's create cards for these children to let them know that they were missed.*

Distribute construction paper and crayons or markers and have the children make cards. If more than one child is absent, you might divide up the group and have one side of the room make a card for one child and the other side of the room make a card for another child. Put the cards into a large envelope and promise to deliver them to the absent classmate. If no one is absent, have each child make a card for a sick family member, friend, or parishioner. The children may bring these cards home and deliver the cards themselves.

Jesus Invites Us

The man in the story invited many guests. Jesus told this parable to teach us that God loves everyone. Everyone is invited to follow God.
adapted from Luke 14:16-23

The servant reported this to the master. The master got very angry. He said, "Go out quickly into the town. Bring the poor and the sick, the blind and the lane."

The servant returned and said, "Sir, I followed your orders. There is still room for more guests."

The master said, "Go out to the streets and highways. Have people come and fill my house."

Explore

Jesus' Invitation

As you begin, invite the children to spend a moment thanking God for including them in his family.

Read the title and paragraph aloud. Call on volunteers to respond to the questions. Jesus is inviting us to be close to God.

Give the children time to complete their responses. When they have finished writing and decorating, call on volunteers to share what they wrote.

Meet a Saint

Note: This feature, which appears in many sessions, introduces a saint whose life or work exemplifies the principles presented in the session.

Read the section aloud while the group follows along. Ask: *How did Saint Martin de Porres (sănt märt´ʻn də pôrz; or pôr´az) follow God?* (by caring for others) Explain: *In Peru, Saint Martin helped people who were sick and poor. Like Jesus, he cared for people who needed help the most. He wanted to help them to know that God cared for them.*

✦ *The Poor and Vulnerable*

BLM 22: JESUS CALLS US TO LOVE

Blackline Master 22 reinforces content learned in this session.

PRAYING COLLAGE

Have the children work in groups. Give the groups pieces of chart paper or poster board, magazines, glue, and scissors. Invite them to find pictures of people, places, and groups for whom they might pray. Tell them to cut out, arrange, and glue the pictures into a collage.

Go around the room and help the children create their collages. When the children have completed them, invite the groups to share their efforts. Collect the collages when you are finished and place them at the prayer center. Use them during the My Response section to remind the children of the importance of praying for others.

SAINT MARTIN DE PORRES

Martin was born in Lima, Peru, in 1875. He was recognized by the Church for his strong commitment to Christian virtue. He played a major role in establishing an orphanage and hospital in his native Peru, and he was known for taking great care of the African slaves who were brought to his native land. Martin's ultimate goal was to be a missionary in a foreign land, but he was never given the opportunity to spread God's message abroad. Eventually he became known as Saint Martin of the Americas. Saint Martin de Porres's feast day is November 3.

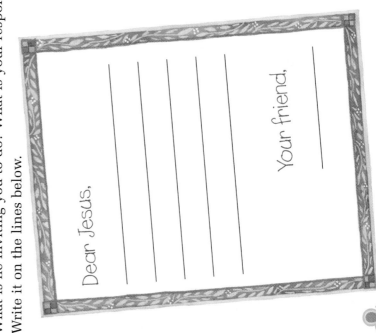

Jesus' Invitation

You have received Jesus' invitation to be close to him. What is he inviting you to do? What is your response? Write it on the lines below.

Dear Jesus,

Your friend,
_____

Meet a Saint

Saint Martín de Porres spent his life helping others in Peru. By caring for others, Martín followed Jesus.

Jesus Chose Peter

Ask: *Who are the important leaders in your lives?* (principal, teacher, priest, parents, catechist) Then say: *Take a moment to think about these leaders.* Pause and then ask: *What do you think makes them good leaders?* (listening, being encouraging, being helpful) Say: *Let's learn about a very important leader. His name was Peter.*

Read the title and the first paragraph aloud while the group follows along. Explain: *Peter knew that Jesus was the Messiah and our Savior. Jesus chose Peter to*

lead the Church. Then Peter could help others follow Jesus.

Read the second paragraph aloud, pointing out to the children that they are learning the word *pope* for the first time. Ask: *Who leads the Church now?* (the pope) Tell the children the name of the present pope. Draw attention to the photographs. Encourage the children to describe what they see. Say: *All three pictures are of popes.* Ask: *What color is the pope wearing in all three pictures?* (white) Then say: *The pope always wears white.*

Remind the group: *Jesus chose Peter to be the first leader of the*

Jesus Chose Peter

Peter was one of the first followers of Jesus. Peter knew that Jesus was the Messiah. Jesus chose Peter to become the leader of the Church.

Peter's role as leader of the Church has been passed on through the years. Today, the **pope** leads the Church as Peter did.

Reading God's Word

Jesus traveled through Galilee. He taught people, shared God's message, and cured those who were sick.

adapted from Matthew 4:23

Church. Today the pope leads the Church as Peter once did. Continue: *The pope is our most important leader. The pope asks us to do the things that Jesus wants us to do.*

Say: *We have other leaders in our lives too, like our teachers and parents. We should respect and follow our leaders. Let's practice what it is like to carefully listen to and follow a leader.*

To demonstrate this principle, play Follow the Leader. You might be the leader first and have the group follow what you do. (wink with your left eye, then put your right hand on your head) Then you might have a volunteer be the leader while the rest of the group imitates his or her actions.

Reading God's Word

Ask the children to listen as you read a short verse from Matthew 4:23. When finished, tell the children that the leaders of the Church today continue to teach and share God's message as Jesus did.

Remind the children that just as Jesus traveled through Galilee, they travel through their school, neighborhoods, and homes. It is in those places that they are called to share God's message.

FYI

SAINT PETER'S SQUARE

Piazza San Pietro, as Saint Peter's Square is known in Italy, is a gathering place for the faithful from around the world and is the area from which the pope speaks to the people.

Explore

Bread for the World

Take a moment to remind the children that living as Christians means that we reach out to those in need.

Ask the children what kinds of letters you and they have talked about this week. (invitations, responses) Ask: *What other kinds of letters do people write?* (friendly, business, apology) List the children's responses on the board.

Say: *Sometimes people write letters of petition.* Write the word petition on the board and ask if the children can guess what kind of letters these are. (asking for something) Say: *In an earlier lesson we learned about prayers of petition to ask God for what we need. Our opening prayer each session is a prayer of petition to ask Jesus to help us.*

Tell the children that today you will be reading about some people who write important letters of petition.

Ask: *In what prayer of petition do we ask God to give us our daily bread?* (the Lord's Prayer) *What does this mean?* (We are asking God to give us what we need to live.) Say: *Many people are concerned that all people in the world have enough to eat.*

Read the title and the first paragraph aloud. Ask: *What does the group called Bread for the World do?* (helps people who are hungry)

Read the second paragraph aloud, then ask: *Who do members of Bread for the World write letters to?* (government officials)

What kind of letters would you call these? (petition) *Why?* (They are asking for something.)

Read the third paragraph to the class. Ask: *What else do the members do besides write letters?* (pray, study)

Ask the children to look at the illustration. Explain that these are brochures and other materials that people can read to find out about Bread for the World. Some people may want to join and help the group.

Read aloud the first paragraph on page 77.

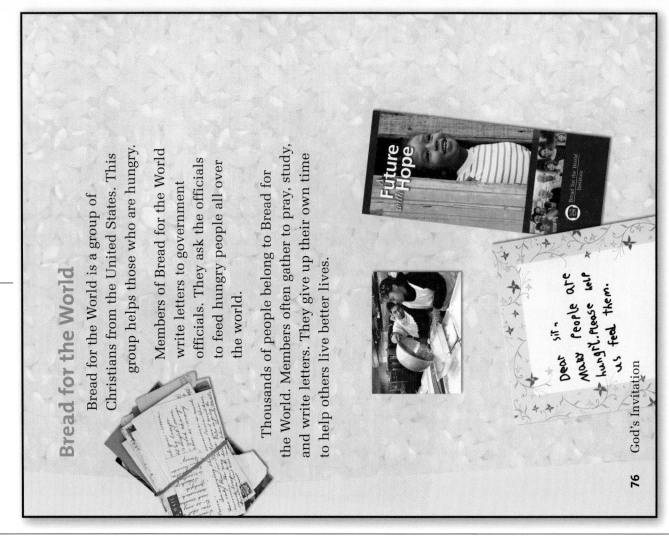

Bread for the World

Bread for the World is a group of Christians from the United States. This group helps those who are hungry.

Members of Bread for World write letters to government officials. They ask the officials to feed hungry people all over the world.

Thousands of people belong to Bread for the World. Members often gather to pray, study, and write letters. They give up their own time to help others live better lives.

76   God's Invitation

Ask: *How do some parishes support Bread for the World?* (Members and children write letters to officials.)

Read the second paragraph aloud. Ask: *How long has this group been helping people?* (more than 25 years)

In Your Own Words

Invite a volunteer to read the directions for listing reasons to help people who are hungry. Be sure children understand the activity.

Walk around the room as children work, helping them with ideas and spelling. When they have finished, have a sharing time for those who would like to read their lists to the group.

Say: *Even though there are organizations that provide food for those who need it, each one of us has a responsibility to do what we can as well.*

Thousands of parishes also support Bread for the World. Church members write letters to officials. Even children from these parishes get involved and write letters.

Bread for the World is more than 25 years old. The group always encourages new people to join.

In Your Own Words

Write a list that tells why it is important to help people who are hungry.

_____
_____
_____
_____
_____

OPTION

LEND A HELPING HAND

Ask: *Is there something we could do as a class to help those who are hungry?* Discuss possibilities with the children. (Collect non-perishables for the parish food pantry, put together a basket of foods for a family in need, collect canned goods for a local shelter.) If a decision is made to help out, organize and plan with the children what needs to be done.

OPTION

FEED THE HUNGRY

Give the children drawing paper. Ask them to draw a long loaf of bread lengthwise on the paper. Have them write *Bread for the World* above the loaf. Ask them to think for a moment about something they can do to help those who are hungry. It might be an idea that was discussed today or it could be something else. Tell them that when they have an idea, they should make a picture of it on their loaves of bread.

When the children have finished, invite volunteers to share their artwork with the group. Suggest that they take their pictures home so they can share with their families what they would like to do to help those who are hungry, like Bread for the World does.

OPTION

PRAYER FOR THOSE IN NEED

With the children, write a prayer asking God's blessing on those who do not have enough to eat. Have them copy the prayer onto a 4-by-6-inch index card to take home and pray with their families at mealtimes.

Reflect

Prayer

Invite the children to become aware of God, who is present to them at all times. Then have them open their books to page 78 and look at the picture. Ask them to describe what they see. (boy and girl walking together, hand in hand) Say: *These children are caring for each other, just as Jesus wants us to do.*

Say: *We learned about the parable of the banquet and how God wants everyone to be close to him. God loves us and cares for us. Now please fold your hands and close your eyes and pray along with me.*

Begin to play softly the reflective music at the end of CD 2. Then read the first paragraph, slowly pausing after each sentence.

In a soft, quiet tone read the second and third paragraphs. Pause for a couple of seconds after each sentence so the children have time to think. After each paragraph take four or five deep breaths, allowing the children time to talk with God. Ask all of the children to open their eyes.

Close the prayer with the Sign of the Cross. Say: *Even though our prayer time is over, God is always with you, watching over you.*

TAKEN TO HEART

Ask for volunteers to pray aloud any previously memorized prayers. Tell the children to refer to the Prayers and Practices of Our Faith section at the back of their books if they need help.

KINGDOM OF GOD

Probably the most predominant image in the preaching of Jesus in the Gospels of Matthew, Mark, and Luke is the Kingdom of God. The word *kingdom* may seem to imply a geographic location where God rules. But *kingdom* actually refers to God's rule, not to where he rules. When God rules, the poor are vindicated, the oppressed are liberated, and justice and peace are experienced by all. God's kingdom is like a hopeful sower who harvests far more than he imagined. God's kingdom is like a little mustard bush that overshadows a mighty cedar. It is like a banquet that you are invited to by surprise.

Prayer

Jesus tells us how much God loves and cares for us. Think about how we can share his love and his care with everybody we meet.

Think of people in your life who love you. Just as they love you, God too loves you and wants you to be happy. Think of some of the ways God has cared for you.

Now ask God to help you care for others as he cares for you. Tell him one way you will help another person.

78 My Response

Living My Faith

Use the activities that follow to assist the children in bringing into their lives what they have learned in this session.

Faith Summary

After you have read the section aloud, ask: *What lesson did we learn from the parable of the banquet?* (God loves all people and invites them to his kindgom.) Ask: *What do Jesus' parables teach us?* (how to be closer to God)

Words I Learned

Call on volunteers to pronounce and define each term. Ask: *Whom did Jesus choose as the first leader of the Church?* (Peter) *Who is the leader of the Church today?* (the pope) *What type of story teaches a lesson?* (parable) Choose volunteers to use the vocabulary words in sentences.

Ways of Being Like Jesus

Read the section and then direct the children to the picture. Ask: *What is happening?* (a family is having dinner with a guest) Say: *We can follow Jesus' teaching of caring for those in our lives by including them in the things we do. For example, we can invite neighbors to join us for a baseball game or say something kind to our grandparents.* Ask the group: *In what other ways can we do kind deeds and say kind words?* (invite someone to our home for a meal, tell people "thank you" when they help us)

✝ *Solidarity*

With My Family

Encourage the children to have their families invite someone to dinner. It would be nice to invite someone who is living away from his or her family, like a military person or a college student.

Prayer

Say: *We've learned about the importance of accepting people and showing them love. Now let's take a moment to thank Jesus for inviting us to follow him. Pray this prayer of thanks with me. Then think about what you can do to follow God.*

Pray the prayer slowly and with expression as the children pray along. Pause to give the children time to talk with Jesus. To conclude, say: *Let's pray Amen together.*

My Response

Say: *Jesus invited everyone to be part of God's kingdom.* Ask: *What could you do to care for someone in the community? Draw a picture that shows your idea. I'll walk around the room. If you have any questions, please ask.*

To end the time together, say: *Jesus is our light. Let's follow him.*

Faith Summary

Jesus came to invite everyone to follow God. He chose Peter to lead the Church. We follow God by helping those in need.

Words I Learned

parable   pope

Ways of Being Like Jesus

You are like Jesus when you do a kind deed or say a kind word.

With My Family

Ask your family to invite someone to dinner. Invite a person who does not usually eat with your family.

Living My Faith

Prayer

Thank you, Jesus, for helping me to know how much God loves me.

My Response

How can you care for others as God cares for you? Draw a picture.

Extending the Session

Choose from the following options to extend the session or to reinforce concepts developed during the week.

Family Involvement

Remind the children to take home the Raising Faith-Filled Kids page to share what they are learning with their families.

Preparation for Sunday Scripture Readings

Lead children in a prayerful discussion of Sunday's readings. Visit www.FindingGod.org/Sunday for more information.

Seasonal Session

Consider the time of the liturgical year and use the appropriate seasonal session. Seasonal sessions may be found on page 241.

Unused Options and BLMs

Incorporate any unused options or Blackline Masters from the week's session.

Web Site Activities

Visit www.FindingGod.org to find additional activities for extending the session.

WE NEED LOVE ACROSTIC

Remind the children that Jesus calls us to love. Have each child write the word *LOVE* vertically down the left side of a piece of drawing paper. For each letter in the word, have the children write one way that they can show a person love, such as *Leave a kind note, Open a door for the person, Vacuum without being asked, Eat what you are served without complaining.* Invite the children to share their ideas with family members when they go home.

GIFT OF LOVE

Have each child gift wrap the lid and the bottom of a shoebox separately. In the bottom of the box, have children write the word *love.* Invite children to give their "gift of love" to a special friend or family member and then tell the recipient the parable of the banquet and how it teaches us about God's love.

SHARING PARTY

Before Day 5, send the children home with notes asking their parents to send in snacks that can be shared with the class. Bring in a few extra snacks in case some children forget. Have the class reenact the parable of the banquet, displaying the snacks as food at the banquet. At the end of the reenactment, encourage the children to enjoy their snacks and discuss as a group why it was important that everyone was invited to enjoy the snacks.

RAISING FAITH-FILLED KIDS
a parent page

Focus on Faith

Welcoming the Stranger

What does it mean to serve the Kingdom of God? The following story helps us answer this question. A brother and sister were talking at a family reunion. The brother had drifted away from the Church but liked to argue points of Christian doctrine. The sister was a member of a prayerful religious community that cared for others. The brother tried to engage his sister in an intellectual debate about God and Christianity. She told him that she wasn't interested in debating these issues. She told him that if he wanted to discover what she thought about God, he should spend time with her community and join in her life of service. By extending this invitation, she was asking him to become a participant in serving the Kingdom of God.

Dinnertime Conversation Starter

Discuss with your child whom you might pray for today. How can you help others feel welcome after Mass or at school?

Hints for at Home

As God's creation, we are all reflections of his love. As we seek to be more like Jesus, we can spread God's love to others. Create a sign that reads "I am reflecting the love of Jesus!" Post the sign over a mirror in your home as a reminder that your family can spread love and kindness each day.

Spirituality in Action

Consider the needs of those in your parish who might require special care, particularly the elderly. Work with your child to create a special Bag of Cheer for an elderly person. Use a brown bag and decorate the outside with drawings or pictures from magazines. Invite your child to print a cheerful message on the bag. Then fill the bag with special gifts of cheer such as tea bags, cookies, holy cards, homemade bookmarks, and sample-size toiletry items. Deliver the package with your child.

Focus on Prayer

Help your child learn the importance of respecting people with special needs.

Session 9: Jesus Cares for Us

3-Minute Retreat

Before you prepare for your session, pause for a few moments and set aside any distracting thoughts. Take three deep breaths and know that you are in the loving presence of God as you help the children strengthen their faith.

John 10:11

I am the good shepherd. A good shepherd lays down his life for the sheep.

Reflection

The shepherd protects and guides his sheep. In the parable of the Good Shepherd, Jesus emphasizes that caring for only 99 out of 100 is not what God wants. God desires all people to be saved. The pope, bishops, and priests are responsible for shepherding the flock of Jesus. The bishop's crozier with its curved design reflects this role of shepherd much as a shepherd's staff does. Catechists and parents also carry out the responsibility of caring for God's children.

Question

How can I act in a way that reflects Jesus' care for his people?

Prayer

Speak to Jesus using this prayer or a prayer of your own.

Patient Shepherd, no matter where I wander, you never give up on me. Thank you for your love and help me guide those in my care.

Take a few moments to reflect prayerfully before you prepare this session.

Jonna Bjorklund, age 15, Sweden

Knowing and Sharing Your Faith

Scripture and Tradition in Session 9

Jesus said that he was the Good Shepherd, and he spent his public life caring for people. The Church learns from Jesus' example and seeks to provide pastoral leadership for the People of God. Bishops carry croziers, which resemble shepherds' staffs. The crozier is a symbol of pastoral authority exercised in service to God's people.

The pastor of the local church is the bishop, who provides pastoral leadership in worship, teaching, and governance. Priests who serve as pastors and associate pastors of parishes assist bishops in this ministry. Deacons, religious sisters and brothers, teachers, catechists, and other parish ministers also share responsibility for the care of God's people.

The pope has a special place in the Church, for he exercises pastoral leadership over the universal Church. He governs and teaches in a special way and symbolizes the unity of the People of God. People all over the world refer to him as "Holy Father" in recognition of the caring leadership he provides. The pope refers to himself as the "servant of the servants of God," the servant who leads all those who provide servant leadership within the Church.

Scripture in Session 9

In **Matthew 18:10–14** Jesus describes his Father's love for the sinner. Jesus reveals his willingness to lay down his life for others in **John 10:11.**

Let the Scripture and Tradition deepen your understanding of the content in this session.

WINDOW ON THE CATECHISM

Reference to the Good Shepherd is made in *CCC* 896. The role of the pope, bishops, and priests as shepherds can be found in *CCC* 553; pope, *CCC* 881; bishops, *CCC* 861–862, 896; priests, *CCC* 1465.

The heavenly Father wants no sheep to be lost.

Jesus is the Good Shepherd.

Catechist Preparation

From the Richness of the Tradition

Bishops feed their sheep in the name of the Lord, governing them, helping them become holy, and teaching them truths they need to understand in order to know Christ. Their teachings include things such as how to make proper use of material goods, how to create peace, and how to live together in harmony.

✝ Catholic Social Teaching

In this session, aspects of the following themes of Catholic Social Teaching are integrated:

- **Solidarity**
- **Call to Family, Community, and Participation**

Prayer in Session 9

In this session the children are introduced to the practice of praying with Scripture, in this particular instance with Psalm 23. The opening prayer of petition and the closing prayer of thanks center on our relationship to the Good Shepherd.

Consider in this session how you will invite the children to respond to and prayerfully reflect on God's invitation to love and serve others.

GENERAL DIRECTORY FOR CATECHESIS

The roles and relationship of the bishop, priests, parents, and catechists in the ministry of catechesis is examined in GDC 222–231.

Catechist Preparation: Get-Ready Guide

Session 9: Jesus Cares for Us

Session Theme: *The parable of the lost sheep shows God's loving concern for us.*

Before This Session

- Bookmark your Bible to Matthew 18:10–14 and John 10:11. Display the Bible open to the passage from Matthew in the prayer center.
- Set up the CD player. Listen to the reflective music in advance.
- For the Jigsaw Puzzle option on page 81, hide one puzzle piece from each puzzle so the children will have to search for it.
- Speak with a parish priest or sister about visiting your class for the option on page 85.

Steps

Outcomes *At the end of the session, the children should be able to*

DAY 1 — **Engage** page 81	• understand how it feels to find something that was lost.
Jesus Cares for Us	
DAYS 1-3 — **Explore** pages 82–87	• identify Jesus as the Good Shepherd who cares for us.
The Parable of the Lost Sheep	• explain the meaning of the Parable of the Lost Sheep.
Leaders of the Church	• describe how Jesus cares for us through the leaders of the Church.
Saint Patrick	• define the words *bishop, crozier,* and *deacon.*
DAY 4 — **Reflect** page 88	• prayerfully reflect on God's presence, his invitation, and our response.
Prayer: Psalm 23	• pray using the Psalms.
DAY 4 — **Respond** page 89	• identify practical ways to act on God's invitation in everyday living.
Living My Faith: Ways to Include Others	
DAY 5 — **Extending the Session** page 90	
Day 5 offers an opportunity to extend the session with activities that reinforce the session outcomes.	

Materials

Required Materials

- Bible
- Writing paper, pens, pencils
- Art materials, such as drawing paper, crayons, markers, scissors, glue
- Picture of your bishop with crozier (page 84)
- CD 2, Reflective music (page 88)

Optional Materials

- Several fairly simple jigsaw puzzles with large pieces (page 81)
- Green construction paper, cotton balls (two per child) (page 84)
- Parish bulletins (page 85)
- World map or globe (page 87)
- Large paint brushes, containers of water (page 90)
- Blackline Master 23, cotton balls, hole punch, string (page 83)
- Blackline Masters 24, 25 (pages 84, 85)

e-resources

www.FindingGod.org

Jesus Cares for Us

Jesus Cares for Us

Begin the day by reminding the children that they are special in God's eyes. Ask: *What are some things that are important to you that you would never want to lose?* (favorite toy, bicycle, video game system, dolls, CDs) *How do you take care of these things?*

Say: *Open your books to page 81.* Read the title of the session aloud. Tell the children: *Today we are going to learn about how Jesus cares for us.* Read the paragraph aloud while the group follows along. Ask volunteers to respond to the questions.

Draw attention to the pictures. Have the children describe what they see. (a boy who is sad because his dog is missing, boy looking for dog, boy finding dog) Ask: *How do you think the boy feels after finding his dog?* (happy, relieved)

Tell the children: *We will now sing a song that reminds us to keep Jesus close to us.* Sing the verse to the tune of "Mary Had a Little Lamb." Then have the children join in as you sing it a second time.

Jesus keeps me close to him, close to him, close to him. Jesus keeps me close to him, no matter where I go!

Tell the children that they will learn additional verses to the song later in this session.

Prayer

Say: *Jesus tells us that God cares for everyone. Let's pray to Jesus and ask him to help us understand how much God cares for us. Please fold your hands and pray the prayer of petition with me. When we have finished, quietly say whatever you like to Jesus.*

Pray the prayer aloud. Then take a couple of deep breaths to give the children time to pray. End by praying *Amen.*

Jesus Cares for Us

Session 9

Prayer

Jesus, help me recognize all the ways God cares for me.

Think of a time you lost something.
Where did you search for it?
How did you feel when you found it?

JIGSAW PUZZLE

Divide the class into groups. Have each group put together a simple jigsaw puzzle with large pieces. In advance, hide one piece from each puzzle somewhere in the room.

When the children realize they are missing one puzzle piece, ask: *How does it feel to have your puzzle incomplete? Do you want to look for the missing piece?*

Then say: *The missing piece is somewhere in the room. You will have to find it if you want it.* Give the children time to search. After someone finds it, ask: *How does it feel to have found the missing piece? How does it feel to have found the missing piece?*

Say: *Today we will learn that Jesus cares for us so much that he will look for us if we are ever lost.*

✝ Solidarity

Explore

The Parable of the Lost Sheep

Remind the children: *We have learned that Jesus was a great teacher.* Ask: *Who can recall the name of the special kind of story Jesus told to teach important lessons?* (parable) *Which parable did we learn the last time we met?* (parable of the banquet) Continue: *Today we'll learn another one of Jesus' parables, which will teach us about the great love God has for each of us.*

Read the title aloud. See if anyone knows the meaning of the word *shepherd*. Explain: *A shepherd is someone who takes care of sheep. A group of sheep is called a flock. A shepherd tends to a whole flock.*

✝ Read the first paragraph aloud. Say Jesus' words with expression. Remind the children: *God cares for every single person in the world and invites each of them to serve his kingdom.*

Read the second paragraph aloud. Say: *Imagine a shepherd with 100 sheep. Now imagine that one sheep has wandered away. The shepherd has gone to find it. What does that tell you about the shepherd?* (He loves his flock. He is concerned about every single sheep.)

Have the children describe what they see in the illustration. (the shepherd looking for the one lost sheep) Ask: *How do you think the shepherd will feel when he finds the sheep?* (excited, relieved)

Read the rest of the story on the next page in the children's book. Continue reading Jesus' words with expression. Explain: *In this parable Jesus used the sheep to represent all of us. He wants us to know that God will do whatever it takes to keep us close to him. Jesus wants us to realize that*

even if we stray, *God will always reach out to help us come back to him.*

Direct the children's attention to the illustration on page 83. Have the children describe what they see. Ask: *How do you think the shepherd feels after finding his lost sheep?* (happy, relieved)

Let's keep this story in our hearts.
(Touch heart.)
A shepherd has 100 sheep,
(Trace 1-0-0 in the air.)

Invite the children to stand and echo each line and action after you in this fingerplay.

And one little one wanders away.
(Hold up pinky.)
Though the shepherd still has 99,
(Trace 9-9 in the air.)
He cannot let the one little sheep stay lost.
(Shake head.)
He will search far and wide.
(Look from side to side.)
When he finds it, he will cheer!
(Clap hands.)
It is the same with God, our Father.
(Point up.)
He will keep every single one of us near.
(Hug self.)

The Parable of the Lost Sheep

Jesus said, "Always remember that each person is important to God. An angel in heaven watches over each of them."

Jesus continued, "What do you think about this? A man has a hundred sheep. If one of them gets lost, he will leave the other 99 and search for the one lost sheep."

Reading God's Word

[1] Ask a volunteer to read the verse aloud. Then have the group do a choral reading of the verse. Assign the first sentence to half of the group and the second sentence to the other half. Have the first group read: *I am the Good Shepherd.* Have the other group read: *A good shepherd lays down his life for the sheep.* Repeat this twice.

Conclude by reminding the children of God's great and constant love for them.

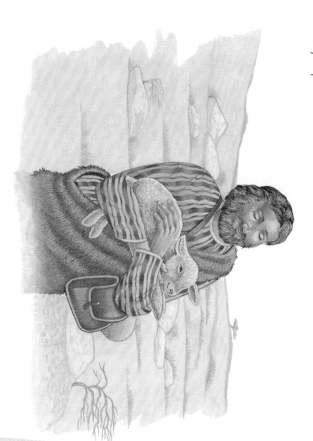

Jesus went on, "And if he finds that lost sheep, he is happier with it than he is with the other 99 sheep."

"That is also what your heavenly Father wants. He does not want one single person to be lost."

adapted from Matthew 18:10-14

Reading God's Word

I am the good shepherd. A good shepherd lays down his life for the sheep.

John 10:11

Unit 2, Session 9   83

OPTION

BLM 23: GOD IS MY SHEPHERD

On Blackline Master 23 children decorate a lamb to remind them of the parable of the Good Shepherd.

OPTION

"JESUS KEEPS ME CLOSE TO HIM" SONG

Teach the children two more verses to the tune of "Mary Had a Little Lamb."

*Jesus searches for each sheep, for each sheep, for each sheep.
Jesus searches for each sheep, no matter where it goes.*

*Jesus brings each lost sheep home, lost sheep home, lost sheep home.
Jesus brings each lost sheep home, he never lets it roam.*

OPTION

HIDIN' SHEEP

Have the group play this variation of Hide 'n Seek. Select one person to serve as the shepherd and the rest to act as sheep. Slowly and carefully remind the shepherd of the total number of sheep in his or her flock.

Then have the shepherd leave the room while the sheep hide. Have the shepherd return and search for every sheep until all of them are located. Repeat the game a few times so that several children have the opportunity to be the shepherd. Remind the children: *A good shepherd never allows any of the sheep to stay lost.*

Session 9   83

Explore

Leaders of the Church

Explain to the children that the leaders of the Church shepherd us today. Their mission is to keep us close to God. Say: **Close your eyes and ask God to bless the leaders of our Church. Now let's find out who these leaders are and what they do.**

Read the title aloud. Ask: **Who knows the different titles used to describe leaders of our Church?** (pope, bishop, priest, pastor) Invite the children to share those they know. Ask the group: **Who was the first leader of our Church—the person whose work others have continued?** (Peter)

Read the first paragraph aloud while the group follows along. Ask: **Who is the leader of the whole Church?** (the pope) **Does anyone know the name of our present pope?**

Read the second paragraph aloud. Draw attention to the words *bishop* and *crozier* (krōˊzhər). Have the children repeat them after you.

Invite the children to look at the photograph. Encourage them to describe what they see. Say: **The bishop is holding a crozier.**

Then have the children turn back to page 82. Ask: **Look at what the shepherd is holding in his hand. Do you see how it looks like the crozier?** Continue: **The bishop carries a crozier to remind him that he is to be like the Good Shepherd.**

Read the final paragraph on page 84. Draw attention to the word *deacons* in dark type. Say: **A deacon is a man who accepts God's call to serve the Church.**

Did You Know?

Read the section aloud. If you brought a picture of your bishop holding a crozier, show it to the children. If you didn't find such a picture, simply show the children

pictures of your bishop and tell them his name.

✝ *Family and Community*

BLM 24: JESUS LOVES US

Blackline Master 24 is a review of vocabulary words from Unit 2.

I AM THE GOOD SHEPHERD

Give each child a piece of green construction paper, two cotton balls, markers, scissors, and glue. Tell the children to use the green paper to symbolize a pasture.

Invite them to create a sheep out of the cotton and to glue it to the center of the pasture. Have them make legs and a face on their sheep with the marker. Go around and draw a heart around each child's sheep. Tell them to write *I Am the Good Shepherd* at the top of their pasture.

Walk around the room and work with any children who need help. Have the children put their names on their completed projects. Collect and place the children's artwork at the prayer center.

Leaders of the Church

Leaders of the Church

Like shepherds, leaders of the Catholic Church care for their people. The pope is the leader of the whole Church.

A **bishop** is another important Church leader. A bishop cares for many parishes. He tends to the needs of Catholics who belong to those parishes. Each bishop carries a shepherd's staff called a **crozier**.

Priests help the bishop with his duties. Priests and **deacons** serve the people in their parishes. They teach about God and lead the people in prayer. Religious sisters and brothers, teachers, and catechists also help people learn about God.

Did You Know?

The crozier that the bishop carries reminds us that he has a duty to care for his people. In this way, the bishop is like the Good Shepherd.

Find the Lost Sheep

Read the activity's title and directions. Make sure everyone was able to find his or her way through the maze. Say: **The Good Shepherd cares for his sheep and looks over them.** Ask: **Who cares for us in a similar way?** (God the Father)

End your time together by inviting the children to pray that they never stray from God their Father.

Find the Lost Sheep

A good shepherd cares about every sheep. Solve the maze to lead this good shepherd to his lost sheep.

BLM 25: JESUS CARES FOR US

On Blackline Master 25 children unscramble key words from this session.

OUR PARISH

Have the children think about the leaders in their parish. Ask the children: **Who is our priest? Do you know any religious sisters or brothers? What are their names?** Say: **We can talk to these Church leaders when we have problems in our lives that we need help with.**

Invite a parish priest or sister to visit with the children. If one agrees

to visit your group, then you will want to let the children know when you are having the special guest. Tell the children the guest's name and that when the guest arrives, they are to stand and say: **Welcome to our group, _____.**

Show the group your parish bulletin, pointing out where the name of your guest is printed.

PSALM 23

Psalm 23, "The Lord, Shepherd and Host," is probably the most familiar psalm and one of the most familiar passages in the Bible.

We associate this psalm with difficult times, especially with death. But it is also very much about being alive. The psalm challenges us to see all of our daily activities as God-centered, for it is God who keeps us alive. Because the Lord is our shepherd, we have food, drink, and security—there is nothing lacking.

Explore

Saint Patrick

As you begin, invite the children to help you make a list of the saints you have studied this year. List the names on the board as the children offer them. Encourage them to tell why each one is especially remembered. (Saints Isidore, Joseph, Anne, Joachim, John the Baptist, Martin de Porres) You might mention Blessed Carlos, who is not a saint yet but may be some day.

Ask: *Did all these saints live at the same time? Did they live in the same place? Did they have the same kind of job?* Say: *We answered "no" to all those questions, but these people were all alike in some way.* See if the children can conclude that they all dedicated their lives to sharing God's love with others.

Ask the children what they think of when they hear the name Saint Patrick. (Saint Patrick's Day, parades, everything green, shamrocks, parties, leprechauns) Say: *Many people celebrate the feast of Saint Patrick on March 17 with parades and fun times. Today we will learn about the life of this special saint.* Ask: *What do you think we will be able to say about this saint after we read?* (He dedicated his life to sharing God's love with others.)

Read the title and the first paragraph aloud. Ask: *What happened to Patrick when he was a teenager?* (He was kidnapped by pirates and forced to work as a shepherd in Ireland.)

Read the next paragraph for the group. Ask: *Why was Patrick unhappy in Ireland?* (cold and hungry, no freedom, homesick) *What did he do?* (prayed) *What happened when he prayed?* (He became happy. His love for God gave him strength.)

Continue reading the story on page 87. Read the first paragraph.

Ask: *Where did Patrick go when he escaped?* (back to family in Britain) *How did he feel when he was home?* (happy, but felt God was calling him back to Ireland)

Have a child read the last paragraph. Ask: *Did Patrick become a Church leader?* (yes, a priest and then a bishop) *Where did he work as a bishop?* (Ireland) *What did he do in Ireland?* (baptized people, taught people about God, shared God's love, made Ireland a Christian nation)

Saint Patrick

Patrick was the son of an important man. He was kidnapped from his home in Britain by pirates before he was 16 years old. He was forced to work as a shepherd in Ireland for six years.

Patrick suffered from cold and hunger while he worked in Ireland. He had no freedom, and he was homesick for his family. So Patrick began to pray. He became very happy when he prayed. His love for God gave him strength.

Ask: **How is Saint Patrick like the saints we talked about at the beginning of class?** (He dedicated his life to sharing God's love with others.) Say: **You were right! That's what you said we would be able to say about him. Sharing God's love is something all saints have in common.**

Invite the children's descriptions and comments on the four pictures on pages 86 and 87. (kidnapped by pirates, shepherd in Ireland, his escape, bishop of Ireland) Ask what Patrick is holding in the second and last pictures. (shepherd's staff—caring for sheep; bishop's crozier—caring for people)

Patrick escaped from Ireland when he was about 22 years old. Finally, he made it back to his family in Britain. He was happy there, but he believed God was calling him to return to Ireland.

In time Patrick became a priest and then a bishop and was sent back to Ireland. He traveled to all parts of Ireland to baptize people and to teach them about God. He was in great danger at times, but he continued to share God's love. He did many things to help Ireland become a Christian nation. Saint Patrick is the patron saint of Ireland.

Unit 2, Session 9   **87**

Divide the class into four groups to create a play in four acts about Saint Patrick. Lead the children to note that the four illustrations correspond with the four paragraphs on the pages. Assign each group a paragraph to dramatize; the illustrations can provide added inspiration. Encourage the children to use their imaginations to create dialogue as well as actions.

After the children's dramatization, remind them of your discussion about how saints share God's love with others. Say: **The saints' lives are examples to us of how we should live. They cared about** those close to them and then they reached out to more and more people.

Explore

OPTION
MY SAINT BOOK

Pass out drawing paper to the children. Have them look through their books to identify all of the saints they have learned about so far. Ask them to write the name of each saint and a description of what he or she did on separate sheets of drawing paper. As time allows, ask them to draw pictures of the saints as well. Have them finish their books by creating construction-paper covers with the words My Saint Book on them. Staple the pages together for them.

OPTION
THE IRISH BLESSING

You may want to read this prayer to the children. Tell them that the message is the wish many people pray for each other. They are praying that their friends will be watched over by God. Say: **When we think of God holding us in the palm of his hand, we think of God always being close to us and caring for us.**

The Irish Blessing

May the road rise up to meet you.
May the wind be always at your back.
May the sun shine warm upon your face,
The rains fall soft upon your fields,
And until we meet again,
May God hold you in the palm of his hand.

OPTION
WHERE IS IRELAND?

On a world map or globe, show children the location of Ireland in relation to where they live. Point out where Patrick had to go from Ireland to rejoin his family in Britain.

Session 9   **87**

Reflect

Prayer

Remind the children that this is their special time to pray about what they have been learning. Direct the children's attention to the background photograph on the page. Ask: **What do you see in the picture?** (meadow) **Would this be a good place for sheep? Why?** (There is grass and plenty of open space.) Say: **God has provided everything the sheep need to live. He has provided everything we need also. We feel safe because we are under God's protection.**

If you did the I Am the Good Shepherd option from page 84, draw attention to the children's completed projects. You may wish to play the reflective music at the end of CD 2 at this time.

Read the first paragraph. Say: **Let's take some time to pray to God, our Good Shepherd. I will pray each line from Psalm 23. This psalm is found in the Bible.** Then say: **Now please close your eyes or look at the picture or your art projects. Fold your hands and pray along with me silently.**

After praying the prayer, pause for 10 seconds. Then read the final paragraph. Pause for 10 more seconds to give the children time to speak quietly with God. Invite everyone to open his or her eyes if they were closed.

Close the prayer by reading the first two lines of Psalm 23 one line at a time and have the children repeat them after you.

Say: **Let's go on now and see how we can live what we have learned.**

PSALM 23

Place the children into two groups. Pray the psalms as a choral reading. Group 1 will pray the first line of each verse. Group 2 will pray the indented lines. Practice the lines before praying the psalm to make sure that the children can read all the words.

PSALMS

There are 150 psalms in the Bible. Psalms are songs that express the various emotions of people's lives. They have been an important part of Jewish and Christian worship throughout history. At Mass they are used during the Liturgy of the Word. During the Liturgy of the Word we call it a responsorial psalm because it is a response by the people to the first reading and because it is sung back and forth between the psalmist or cantor and the assembly.

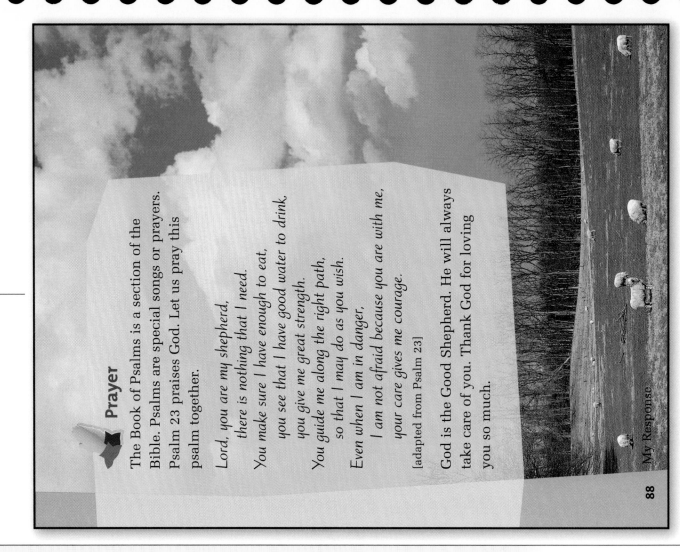

Prayer

The Book of Psalms is a section of the Bible. Psalms are special songs or prayers. Psalm 23 praises God. Let us pray this psalm together.

Lord, you are my shepherd,
     there is nothing that I need.
You make sure I have enough to eat,
     you see that I have good water to drink,
     you give me great strength.
You guide me along the right path,
     so that I may do as you wish.
Even when I am in danger,
     I am not afraid because you are with me,
     your care gives me courage.
[adapted from Psalm 23]

God is the Good Shepherd. He will always take care of you. Thank God for loving you so much.

My Response

88

Living My Faith

Work with the children to help them express what they have learned in the session.

Faith Summary

After reading the section aloud, ask the children: *Can you name the leaders of the Church who help God tend his flock?* (the pope, bishops, priests, sisters, brothers, teachers, catechists)

Words I Learned

Call on volunteers to pronounce and define each word. Refer to the Glossary for assistance. Choose a volunteer to draw on the board a picture of a crozier. Call on volunteers to use the words in sentences.

Ways of Being Like Jesus

Read the section and then ask the children: *What do you think is happening in the picture?* (two children are working together to make something in the kitchen) *What are some times when we can*

---

include others in our activities? (softball game, pizza party, doing homework together, playing together)

With My Family

Read the section. Ask: *Can you think of a way to plan a special day, such as a Thank-You Day or a Mom-Appreciation Day? What could you do on that day to make that person happy?* (rent Mom's favorite video and make her favorite snack, surprise the family by bringing something to eat while everyone watches a video)

✝ *Family and Community*

Prayer

Say: *Let's take a moment to thank Jesus for watching over us. Please pray along with me. After the prayer take a moment to thank Jesus for loving you and for whatever else you are thankful.* Pray the prayer aloud. Then take three deep breaths to give the group time to speak with God. Close by saying *Amen.*

My Response

Read the section. Say: *When we include others in the things we do, we are being like Jesus. Now take some time to think about what you will do to include others. Write a sentence about it.* Invite volunteers to share their sentences with the group.

As you end the day, say: *The Good Shepherd will watch over you wherever you are.*

Living My Faith

Faith Summary

Jesus teaches us about God's loving concern for us. The leaders of the Church help us to know and love God.

Words I Learned

bishop   crozier   deacon

Ways of Being Like Jesus

You are like Jesus when you include others in your work or play.

With My Family

Plan a special day for someone in your family. Let that person choose the activities.

Living My Faith

Prayer

Thank you, God, for being my Good Shepherd and for always staying by my side.

My Response

What can you do to include others in your work or play? Write a sentence.

Extending the Session

Choose from the following options to extend the session or to reinforce concepts developed during the week.

Family Involvement

Remind the children to take home the Raising Faith-Filled Kids page to share what they are learning with their families.

Preparation for Sunday Scripture Readings

Lead children in a prayerful discussion of Sunday's readings. Visit **www.FindingGod.org/Sunday** for more information.

Seasonal Session

Consider the time of the liturgical year and use the appropriate seasonal session. Seasonal sessions may be found on page 241.

Unused Options and BLMs

Incorporate any unused options or Blackline Masters from the week's session.

Web Site Activities

Visit **www.FindingGod.org** to find additional activities for extending the session.

OPTION

SAINT PATRICK SHAMROCK

Remind the children that Saint Patrick is the patron saint of Ireland, and that in sharing God's love with the Irish, he did many things to help Ireland become a Christian nation. Explain that one of the symbols for Saint Patrick is a shamrock. Invite the children to draw a large shamrock. Inside it have them write a short prayer to Saint Patrick asking him for his prayers and assistance in guiding them to share God's love.

Invite the children to take the shamrocks home and pray their prayers with their family.

OPTION

TAKING CARE OF SHEEP

Invite pairs or small groups of children to make a written or sketched list of things that shepherds do to care for sheep, such as feed them, make sure they have water, protect them from other animals, and so on. After the lists are complete, help the children compare their lists to ways God takes care of people. Accept all reasonable answers.

OPTION

PAVEMENT PAINTING

On a sunny day, take the children outside to some blacktop or sidewalk. Form pairs of children. Give each pair a large paintbrush and a container of water. Ask pairs to "paint" the following words or phrases with water, one at a time: *bishop, Saint Patrick, crozier, Jesus, deacon.* Challenge pairs to use each word in a sentence before washing them away with water.

The Good Shepherd, Elizabeth Lee Hudgins

Focus on Faith

Educators of Our Children

As parents, we are our children's primary teachers in the ways of the faith. This is a huge responsibility, and we have the tendency to think that it requires an extensive knowledge of every aspect of the Catholic Church. Thankfully, the entire burden does not fall on our shoulders. The Church has the support system of parishes, pastors, catechists, and religious education classes. Our role is to focus on the decisions we make every day. Our decisions should exemplify how a Christian should live. Are we honest in our dealings with our children? Do we keep our word with them? Do they see us dealing honestly with others? All decisions we make in daily life shape the religious growth of our children. We cannot help but be their primary teachers in the ways of our faith.

Dinnertime Conversation Starter

Discuss ways in which you as individuals can each be a source of blessing to one another and to others in the world.

Hints for at Home

Make a The Lord Is My Shepherd picture. You'll need felt, markers, scissors, a picture of your child, glue, a paper plate, and a small picture hook. Using the felt, help your child draw and cut out figures to represent a shepherd and a child. Include a crozier, or staff, for the shepherd. Glue the picture of your child's face onto the figure of the child. Draw a face on the shepherd.

Glue both figures to the inside of the paper plate. With the marker write the words *The Lord Is My Shepherd* around the outside of the paper plate. Attach a small hook to the back of the plate and hang it.

Our Catholic Heritage

Saint Patrick (380–461) was the son of a Roman nobleman. He was kidnapped by Irish pirates at age 16 and was taken to Ireland. Suffering from cold, hunger, and the loss of his freedom, he worked as a shepherd in Ireland. He eventually escaped and became a priest. He returned to Ireland as a missionary, or shepherd of the people. He established monasteries, convents, and parishes. Saint Patrick is one of the primary reasons that Ireland became a Christian nation.

Focus on Prayer

Your child has read an adapted version of Psalm 23, commonly known as The Lord Is My Shepherd. Read Psalm 23 with your child and discuss the feelings of safety and security that it provides us.

Session 10: Unit 2 Review

3-Minute Retreat

Before you prepare for your session, pause for a few moments and focus inward. Slowly take three deep breaths, relax, and recognize that you are in the loving presence of God as you help the children develop a close relationship with God our Father and Jesus.

Psalm 95:7

For this is our God,
    whose people we are,
    God's well-tended flock.
Oh, that today you would hear his voice.

Reflection

Jesus, the Good Shepherd, leads us safely to the Father. With so many voices vying for our attention, hearing his voice can be a challenge. We see Jesus' obedience to his parents, his faithfulness to the Ten Commandments, and his acceptance of his Father's will. Jesus leads us on a path to salvation. When we follow Jesus, we come to know more fully God's love for us. This, in turn, frees us to be more like Jesus.

Questions

In my day-to-day life what voices compete with the voice of Jesus the Good Shepherd? How can I respond to those other voices?

Prayer

Turn to Jesus and speak, using this prayer or one of your own.
Good Shepherd of my life, lead me from death into life.

Take a few moments to reflect prayerfully before you prepare this session.

Catechist Preparation: Get-Ready Guide

Session 10: Unit 2 Review

Unit Theme: *Jesus Loves Us*

Before This Session

- If you completed the prayer tablecloth during an earlier session, use it to cover the table in your prayer center.
- Bookmark the Bible to Psalm 100:3 and leave it open at the prayer center.
- Set up the CD player so you will be ready to play the songs.

Outcomes *In this session, the children will review*

- ways to live in love and goodness.

- that when we obey the Commandments, we are following Jesus.
- that Jesus is our model of love and goodness.
- that Jesus invites everyone to the Kingdom of God.
- that each person is important to God.

- how to prayerfully reflect on God's invitation in everyday living.

- practical ways to act on God's invitation in everyday living.

Steps

DAY 1 **Engage** page 91
Review

DAYS 2-3 **Explore** pages 92–94
Faith Summary

DAY 4 **Reflect** page 95
Prayer Service: Thanking and Praising Jesus

DAY 4 **Respond** page 96
Living My Faith: What We Thank Jesus For

Materials

Required Materials

- Bible
- Writing paper, pens, pencils
- Art materials, such as drawing paper, crayons, markers, scissors, glue
- CD 2, Track 1: Song of Love (4:00) (page 93)
- CD 2, Track 5: Jesus in the Morning (Jesus verses) (1:37) (page 95)

Optional Materials

- Long rope or jump rope (page 91)
- Mirror (page 93)
- 3 paper plates per child, 1 yard of ribbon per child, 6 inches of yarn per child, stickers, hole punch (page 94)
- Blackline Master 26—Unit 2 Show What You Know (pages 91, 92)

e-resources

www.FindingGod.org

Say: *Today we will review Unit 2 to remember all that we have learned.* Say: *We have learned about Jesus, our model of love and goodness. Let's praise him for showing us how much God loves us.*

Have volunteers stand and thank Jesus for something. Tell them to fill in the phrase *I want to thank Jesus for _____.* You might go first to provide an example. (for helping me in school, for my parents, for my home, for my best friend) Encourage the children to use their happiest voices when they praise Jesus.

Say: *Open your books to page 91.* Have the children describe what they see in the photographs. (grandfather and grandson building a clock; father and daughter cooking) Say: *By helping each other, these people are being like Jesus.*

Read the paragraph while the group follows along. Ask volunteers to respond to the question. Then ask: *What types of things can we do to be like Jesus and to show our love for others?* (pray, help people, be kind to new kids in school) Explain: *Jesus, our friend and Savior, has a special place in his heart for those in*

Review

Jesus is the Son of God and the son of Mary. Jesus is our friend and Savior. Through his example of love and goodness, we can follow God's way. What can you do to show your love for Jesus?

Prayer

Thank you, Jesus, for watching over me. Help me obey God and my parents.

---

need. He also has a special place for children—like all of you.

Show What You Know

Distribute BLM 26, Unit 2 Show What You Know, to the children. Explain that it will help the children see how well they understand what was taught.

When the children have finished, ask them to exchange papers and help them correct the objective section. Allow time for them to look over their own corrected papers before collecting the papers. Review the short-answer and self-assessment items. Provide written feedback and identify concepts needing attention. Use this information as you continue the Review on Day 2.

Prayer

Say: *Let's ask Jesus to help us.*

Pray the prayer. Give the children time to talk to Jesus. End by praying *Amen.*

OPTION

THANK YOU, JESUS

Have the children write a thank-you note to Jesus. Encourage the children to share their notes with the group, if they wish.

OPTION

JUMP FOR LOVE

On the floor arrange a long rope into the shape of a heart. Have the children stand outside the rope. Ask: *What is one thing you can do to show your love for Jesus?* (pray, clean bedroom, share video games with friends) When someone answers, have this child jump inside the rope. When everyone is inside the heart, say: *This heart is filled with love for Jesus. Let's remember to share love with others.*

Explore

Faith Summary

Tell the children to ask for the Holy Spirit to help as they continue reviewing.

Show What You Know

Return the assessment, BLM 26, to the children. Review the short-answer questions and any concepts the children did not fully understand.

Say: *We've learned that we can follow Jesus' example and become more like him. Let's review specific things we've learned about Jesus.*

Read the four paragraphs slowly and with expression while the group follows along. Say: *We've just heard some reminders of the special ways Jesus taught us about God. Let's see if we can remember the different stories from the Bible that have helped us learn about him.*

Ask: *Which Bible story told us about Jesus' searching his conscience and realizing that he should obey his parents?* (Jesus With the Teachers, Session 6)

Proceed: *Which Bible story reminds us that Jesus did all he could to help others, especially those who are sick?* (Jesus Heals, Session 7)

Ask: *Which parable reminds us of God's love and care for everyone?* (The parable of the banquet, Session 8)

Continue: *Which parable teaches us that God will search for us if we are lost?* (The parable of the lost sheep, Session 9) If time allows, go back to those sessions and read the parables again or place the children into four groups to dramatically re-enact the parables.

Conclude enthusiastically: *By reading the Bible, which contains stories about Jesus, we learn so much about him! We learn what we can do to be more like him.*

People Who Served God

Read the title and directions aloud. When the children have finished the activity, call on volunteers to share their work.

OPTION

LISTEN TO JESUS' WORDS

Explain that by reading the Bible, we learn the story of Jesus' life on earth.

Say: *We can be more like Jesus by listening to his words.*

Read aloud this passage from John 15:10: *If you keep my commandments, you will remain in my love, just as I have kept my Father's commandments and remain in his love.*

Ask the children: *What message does Jesus share with us in these words?* (God loves Jesus. Jesus loves us. Jesus followed the commandments. When we follow the commandments, we stay close to Jesus.)

Faith Summary

Jesus obeyed the Ten Commandments. He obeyed his heavenly Father and Mary and Joseph.

Jesus did all he could to help others. We can follow his example and discover the goodness in others.

Jesus told the parable of the lost sheep to show God's concern for us. He gave us our pope, bishops, and priests to care for us.

Jesus calls everyone to follow God. Everyone is welcome.

People Who Served God

Peter served God and others. The sentence in the orange box tells about Peter. In the blue box write the name of another important person you have learned about in this unit. Then write a sentence about this person.

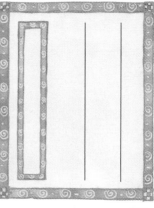

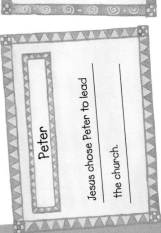

Peter

Jesus chose Peter to lead _____ the church.

Be Like Jesus

Explain with enthusiasm: **We've been working to be more like Jesus. Let's do an activity that will help us practice being more like him.**

Read the directions aloud. Make sure the children understand what they are to do. Then read the first situation. Say: **Now take some time to write what you would do in this situation to be more like Jesus.** Give the children time to complete their responses. Walk around the room and offer help where needed. Then invite volunteers to share what they would do in the first situation.

Read the second and third situations to the children. Give them time to write their responses. Then call on volunteers to share their answers. Thank the volunteers who responded.

Say: **Every time you do something kind for someone else, you are being like Jesus.**

Invite the children to stand and join you for this fingerplay. Ask them to repeat each line and its accompanying gesture after you.

I try to be like him more each day.
(point to self)

When I'm at home, at school, at play.
(mime throwing ball)
I remind myself to act with love.
(trace heart in the air)
To fill my heart with peace from above.
(point up toward the sky)
I will keep Jesus in my heart and mind.
(point to heart and head)
And try my hardest to be gentle and kind.
(shake hands with classmate)

♪ Play "Song of Love" on Track 1 of CD 2. Say: **This song teaches us how to be more like Jesus.** Encourage the children to sing along. The words to the song can be found in the Songs of Our Faith section in the back of the book.

Be Like Jesus

Read each of the sentences below. On the lines write what you could do to be like Jesus.

Your friend has broken her arm.

_____

_____

_____

You see your neighbor shoveling snow on a cold day.

_____

_____

_____

You see a little boy crying because he is lost.

_____

_____

Unit 2, Session 10   93

BEING-LIKE-JESUS IMPROVISATIONS

Explain to the children that an improvisation is a play that the actors make up as they go along. Often called improvs, these sketches involve hearing a situation, being assigned a character to play, and making up the scene as you go along.

Ask volunteers to present each situation in Being Like Jesus as an improv. Encourage those watching each sketch to observe the different ways we can become more like Jesus.

SEEING OURSELVES

Have the children pass around a mirror. Ask: **What do you see? Can you see the love of God in you? What can you do so that the qualities of Jesus inside of you will grow?** After they have had time to think, encourage volunteers to share their ideas. (listen to parents, follow rules at school, use gentle words with friends and siblings)

Explore

Jesus Is Many Things

Read the title and directions aloud. Give the children time to unscramble the words and write them on the lines. Tell them that they can look back through the unit if they need help.

Before starting, ask if anybody has questions about the activity. Answer any questions and ask the children to begin. Walk around the room and offer help where needed.

As your time together comes to an end, say: *I am amazed at all you have learned and how you have put it into action. God must surely be pleased with you.*

vertically, in their proper order, on the ribbon. Make a hole punch on the top plate of each child's wall hanging. Have the children put the yarn through the hole so that the artwork can be hung. Walk around the room and help the children with this activity.

Tell the children: *When you get home, put your art in a special place to remind yourselves to honor your parents.*

✝ *Family and Community*

CHURCH TOUR

With the children, tour your church to view stained-glass windows.

Remind the group that many stained-glass windows show scenes from Bible stories. See if the children recognize any Bible stories in the windows. Encourage a few volunteers to retell Bible stories from the unit to the group.

FATHER AND MOTHER WALL HANGING

Give each child three paper plates, a yard of ribbon, and six inches of yarn. Have them write *Honor* on one plate, *Your* on the second, and *Father and Mother* on the third. Invite the children to decorate each plate with drawings and stickers. Then ask them to glue the plates

---

Jesus Is Many Things

Unscramble the words to tell about Jesus.

1. When Jesus gave sight to those who could not see, he was a **elhare**. _____
   healer

2. When Jesus left Jerusalem with Joseph and Mary, he was a **dogo ons**. _____ _____
   good   son

3. When Jesus told parables, he was a **ecetahr**. _____
   teacher

4. When Jesus loves and cares for us, he is like the **dgoo hspehrde**. _____ _____
   good   shepherd

5. When Simeon saw Jesus in the Temple, he knew that Jesus was the **hsesiMa**. _____
   Messiah

My Response

Prayer Service

Prepare to play CD 2, Track 5, "Jesus in the Morning." Then say: *Now it's time to get ready for our prayer service. Please open your books to page 95 and look at the prayer service. Notice the places where it says "All." These are the places where you will respond. Look at the places marked "Leader." I'll be reading these sections.*

Direct the children's attention to the end of the prayer service. Say: *When I say, "Let us pray together the Lord's Prayer," please put your books on the floor and place*

your hands in the orans position to pray the Lord's Prayer. Remind the children of the orans position by demonstrating it. (hands open and facing up, held outward at your side)

Say: *We will also be singing the Jesus verses of "Jesus in the Morning" in our prayer service. Please turn to the song in the Songs of Our Faith section in the back of your books. Look at the words and listen as I play the song.* After listening to the song one time, invite the children to sing along with the CD.

Say: *Now we are ready for our prayer service. We know what we will sing and what we will say, but the most important thing is that we will be praying. To do this, please close your eyes and be very quiet.* Pause for about 10 seconds and then say: *Please come to the prayer center for our prayer service. Remember to bring your books, opened to "Jesus in the Morning."*

When the children are assembled, play the song and invite the children to sing along. When finished, say: *Now turn to page 95 for the prayer service, which we will begin by praying the Sign of the Cross.* Lead the children in doing so.

Say: *A reading from the Book of Psalms.* Then present the reading.

In an expressive and reverent tone continue to pray, motioning to the children each time they are to respond.

Immediately after the last Leader line, lead the children in putting the books on the floor, placing their hands in the orans position, and praying together the Lord's Prayer. Afterward pause for a moment of silence and lead the children in praying the Sign of the Cross. Then have them return quietly to their seats.

Prayer Service

Leader: Let us begin our prayer with the Sign of the Cross.

A reading from the Book of Psalms.

Know that God created us and watches over us. He cares for us always.

[adapted from Psalm 100:3]

Leader: Let us pray to Jesus.

All: Receive our thanks and praise.

Leader: Jesus, you are the Son of the living God.

All: Receive our thanks and praise.

Leader: Jesus, you are our teacher and friend.

All: Receive our thanks and praise.

Leader: Let us pray together the Lord's Prayer.

Respond

Living My Faith

Use these activities to help the children better comprehend what they have learned in this unit.

Ways of Being Like Jesus

After reading the section, ask the group: *For whom did Jesus have a special place in his heart?* (for those who needed help) *What did Jesus do for those in need?* (healed people who were sick and blind, made people who were crippled walk again) Ask: *What can you do to reach out to others as Jesus did?* (take flowers to a person who is sick, contribute clothing or food to a charity)

With My Family

Direct the children's attention to the picture and read the section. Tell them: *The next time you go to Mass, notice Bible scenes on the stained-glass windows. Ask your parents to explain any Bible scenes that are unfamiliar to you.*

Prayer

Say: *We've reviewed how wonderful Jesus is and how he cares for people. Let's thank God for giving Jesus to us to be our example. Please pray along with me this prayer of thanks. Then, take a few moments to think about how you can be more like Jesus.*

Pray the prayer aloud. Pause for 10 seconds to give the children time to be with Jesus. Close by saying: *Now let's close our prayer with the Sign of the Cross.*

My Response

Read the section. Ask: *What are some of the gifts Jesus has given you?* (family, home, food to eat) Then say: *Think about something Jesus has done for you for which you'd like to thank him.*

Allow sufficient time for the children to complete the activity. As they do so, move around the room to observe how well they can apply the main ideas of the unit to their daily lives.

Call each child forward for a blessing. While placing the Sign of the Cross on the child's forehead, softly say his or her name and the following: _____, *may you become more and more like Jesus.*

Living My Faith

Ways of Being Like Jesus

Jesus cares for all the people in the world. You are like Jesus when you do things to help others.

With My Family

Visit a church that has stained-glass windows. Enjoy the beautiful works of art with your family.

Prayer

Dear God, thank you for giving us Jesus to tell us about your goodness. Help me as I bring your goodness to those I meet today.

My Response

What would you like to thank Jesus for? Draw a picture or write a sentence to thank him.

96   My Response

Unit 3

Catechist Preparation

Unit 3: All Are Welcome
Overview

Unit Saint: Saint Ignatius of Loyola

The focus of this unit is staying close to Jesus through the sacraments. The saint for this unit is Saint Ignatius of Loyola. Born in Spain to a large family in 1491, Ignatius became a soldier. After being wounded in battle, Ignatius had only two books at his disposal during his rehabilitation, one about Jesus and the other about the saints. These books had a profound effect upon him. After his recovery, he went on retreat and began writing his *Spiritual Exercises*. Ignatius founded an order called the Society of Jesus, or the Jesuits. One of Ignatius' goals was to reform the Church through education and frequent reception of the sacraments. Ignatius is a good example of growing closer to Jesus through the sacraments.

Session 11: We Worship God

The children learn the parable of the vine and the branches, which teaches us that Jesus is our source of life. The sacraments help us to grow as children of God. In Baptism, we receive the forgiveness of original sin and personal sin. Baptism also gives us new life with the Father, the Son, and the Holy Spirit, as well as membership in Christ's Body, the Church.

Session 12: Celebrating Reconciliation

The story of Zacchaeus shows us how lives are changed when touched by the forgiveness of Jesus. As Christians we look to Zacchaeus as a model for taking responsibility for our offenses.

Session 13: The Sacrament of Penance

In this session, the children learn the story of Jesus offering forgiveness and healing the man who was paralyzed. While sin wounds and isolates us, the Sacrament of Penance brings us God's healing. In the Sacrament of Penance, we make peace with God and others.

Session 14: Mary Shows Us the Way

Mary is a model for following Jesus. The children learn about Mary's visit to Elizabeth and Mary's song of praise, the Magnificat. The Hail Mary expresses our love for Mary and asks her to pray for us so that we will trust God as she does.

Session 15: Unit 3 Review

In this session we review the main ideas of the unit, go over points that need more discussion, and evaluate the children's understanding of the main concepts.

Consider how the focus of this unit is developed throughout the sessions.

Catechist Preparation

Prayer in Unit 3

In this third unit continue using the same pattern and loving tone for the prayers in each session. The brief opening prayer of petition and the closing prayer of gratitude invite the children to reflect on staying close to Jesus. At the end of each prayer, the children have an opportunity to engage in silent meditation.

The children will be reminded that, while they can use their own words to pray, there are special prayers for them to learn. The Act of Contrition and the Magnificat will be introduced. The prayer service at the end of the unit brings together key unit themes of contrition, praise, and Mary, our model of prayer.

As you guide the children through this unit, think about how you will help them to praise God through prayer and service.

✝ Catholic Social Teaching in Unit 3

The following themes of Catholic Social Teaching are integrated into this unit:

Call to Family, Community, and Participation Participation in family and community is central to our faith and to a healthy society. As the central social institution of our society, the family must be supported and strengthened. From this foundation, people participate in society, fostering a community spirit, and promoting the well-being of all, especially the poor and vulnerable.

Option for the Poor and Vulnerable In our world many people are very rich, while at the same time, many are extremely poor. As Catholics, we are called to pay special attention to the needs of the poor. We can follow Jesus' example by making a specific effort to defend and promote the dignity of the poor and vulnerable and meet their immediate material needs.

Solidarity Because God is our Father, we are all brothers and sisters with the responsibility to care for one another. Solidarity is the attitude that leads Christians to share spiritual and material goods. Solidarity unites rich and poor, weak and strong, and helps to create a society that recognizes that we all live in an interdependent world.

Session 11: We Worship God

3-Minute Retreat

Before you prepare for your session, pause for a few moments and relax. Take three deep breaths and feel the closeness of God as you continue this journey of growth and discovery.

John 15:5

I am the vine, you are the branches. Whoever remains in me and I in him will bear much fruit, because without me you can do nothing.

Reflection

As cell phones and wireless devices grow in popularity, we talk about being connected. The same concept is found in the Gospel of John. Jesus, however, makes it clear that the only true life-giving connection is our relationship with God. The sacramental life of the Church helps us to live as Jesus did. Beginning with our Baptism, we are continually being renewed through our participation in the sacraments. The grace we receive through the sacraments keeps us connected to God so that our lives will bear fruit.

Questions

What, if anything, is keeping me from being connected to God? How can I help the children celebrate the life-giving power of the sacraments?

Prayer

Pray to Jesus using this prayer or one of your own.

Jesus, nurture me through the sacraments that I may live a fruitful life and share that blessing with others.

Take a few moments to reflect prayerfully before you prepare this session.

Knowing and Sharing Your Faith

Scripture and Tradition in Session 11

The sacraments are special encounters with Jesus. Baptism frees us from original sin and makes us members of the Body of Christ. Confirmation fills us with the Holy Spirit and strengthens us to do Christ's work in the world. In the Eucharist we are fed with the Body and Blood of Christ so that we will have nourishment as we follow in his footsteps. Penance brings us the forgiveness of Christ. Anointing of the Sick brings us the healing of Christ. Holy Orders gives a man a special participation in the priesthood of Christ so that he can celebrate the Sacrifice of the Mass and lead the Church in the celebration of the sacraments. A couple is brought together in Matrimony through the love of Christ, who sanctified marriage with his presence and miracle at the marriage feast of Cana.

It is through the sacraments that we experience the power of Christ in our lives.

Scripture in Session 11

Jesus uses the parable of the vine and the branches to teach the people in **John 15:1–6.**
Paul describes how the followers of Jesus are to live in **Galatians 5:22.**

Jesus is the vine; we are the branches.

The Holy Spirit leads us to love, joy, and peace.

WINDOW ON THE CATECHISM

The *Catechism* devotes a quarter of its pages to the sacraments (CCC, Part 2).

Let the Scripture and Tradition deepen your understanding of the content in this session.

Catechist Preparation

From the Richness of the Tradition

The Church finds in Jesus the main reason for its commitment to justice and peace, as well as its defense of human rights and the dignity of each and every person. "It is Christ's word that is the judgment on this world; it is Christ's cross that is the measure of our response; and it is Christ's face that is the composite of all persons, but in a most significant way of today's poor, today's marginal people, today's minorities." ("Brothers and Sisters to Us," November 14, 1979, United States Conference of Catholic Bishops)

✠ Catholic Social Teaching

In this session the following Catholic Social Teaching is integrated:
Call to Family, Community, and Participation.

Consider in this session how you will invite the children to respond to and prayerfully reflect on God's invitation to love and serve others.

GENERAL DIRECTORY FOR CATECHESIS

Communion with Jesus Christ as "the definitive aim of catechesis" is discussed in *GDC* 80.

Prayer in Session 11

A special approach to prayer in Session 11 is an extended guided reflection entitled "The Vine and the Branches." As you prepare to share this prayer experience with the children, listen to the recorded guided reflection, "The Vine and the Branches" (CD 1, Track 8), as a prayerful experience for yourself. Then, when you play the recording during the session, join the children in reflective prayer.

If instead you choose to lead the guided reflection yourself, listen to the recording a second time, following the script (pages 370–371) and noting pauses and tone of voice. You can then use the script or adapt it as you wish. When leading the guided reflection during the session, play instrumental music softly in the background to enhance the sense of prayerfulness.

An alternate approach to prayer in this session is to use the Prayer on the children's page.

Catechist Preparation: Get-Ready Guide

Session 11: We Worship God

Session Theme: *The sacraments help us to worship God in a special way.*

Before This Session

- Obtain a living ivy plant to show to the children on page 101.
- Bookmark your Bible to John 15:1–6 and Galatians 5:22. Place the Bible in the prayer center open to the passage from John.
- Set up the CD player so you will be ready to play the song and the guided reflection. Listen to them prior to the session.

Steps   Outcomes   *At the end of the session, the children should be able to*

DAY 1   Engage pages 97–99

Unit Saint: Saint Ignatius of Loyola

We Worship God

- identify Saint Ignatius of Loyola as someone who dedicated his life to God.
- recognize that gifts can make us happy.

DAYS 2–3   Explore pages 100–105

The Apple Orchard

Jesus Is the Vine

The Holy Spirit Comes to Us

The Sacrament of Baptism

Baptizing Baby Joshua

- recognize and explain the image of Jesus as the vine and our-selves as the branches.
- describe the sacraments as special signs that God is with us.
- identify Baptism as the first sacrament we celebrate.
- explain that through Baptism, we become children of God and members of the Church.
- define *Fruits of the Holy Spirit, original sin,* and *rite.*

DAY 4   Reflect page 106

Prayer: We Are Being Held Tightly to the Vine

- prayerfully reflect on God's presence, his invitation, and our response.

DAY 4   Respond page 107

Living My Faith: Ways to Use Kind Words This Week

- identify practical ways to act on God's invitation in everyday living.

DAY 5   Extending the Session page 108

Day 5 offers an opportunity to extend the session with activities that reinforce the session outcomes.

Materials

Required Materials

- Bible
- Writing paper, pens, pencils
- Art materials, such as paper, crayons, markers, scissors, glue
- Living ivy plant (page 101)
- CD 2, Track 2: Song of Love (Instrumental) (page 97)
- CD 1, Track 8: The Vine and the Branches (10:59) (page 106)

Optional Materials

- Various signs or symbols (paper heart, clock, picture of stoplight) (page 102)
- 9-by-12-inch construction paper, tape (page 105)
- Construction-paper vine with branches and fruit, 5 large paper leaves (page 108)
- Tag-board cards shaped like apples, paper clips, bucket or bowl (page 108)
- Blackline Masters 27, 28, 29 (pages 99, 100)

e-resources

www.FindingGod.org

All Are Welcome

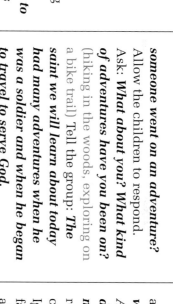

Softly play the instrumental version of "Song of Love" on Track 2 of CD 2. Say: *We begin our new unit listening to the melody of the song that calls us to be loving persons. Do you remember the name of the song?* Continue: *Let's take a little time to tell Jesus that we will try to be gentle and loving to all people we meet today.* Allow for quiet time.

Then ask: *Can you think of a television show or movie in which someone went on an adventure?* Allow the children to respond. Ask: *What about you? What kind of adventures have you been on?* (hiking in the woods, exploring on a bike trail) Tell the group: *The saint we will learn about today had many adventures when he was a soldier and when he began to travel to serve God.*

Saint Ignatius of Loyola

Have the children open their books to page 97. Focus attention on the picture of Saint Ignatius of Loyola. Pronounce *Ignatius* (ig nā´shes) for the children. Have them repeat it after you. Ask: *Who can tell us what a saint is?* Remind the group: *A saint is a holy person who has died as a good friend of God and now lives with God forever.* Then read the caption aloud as the children follow along. Just as Ignatius learned about the Catholic faith from his family, we can learn about it from our families too. We can also share what we learn with our families and grow closer to Jesus together.

All Are Welcome Unit 3

Saint Ignatius of Loyola

Ignatius of Loyola is an important saint. He learned about Jesus from his family.

97

FYI

SAINT IGNATIUS OF LOYOLA

Saint Ignatius of Loyola and many of his followers through the centuries have won recognition by the Church for their holiness. Many Jesuits are canonized saints; still more are among those whom the Church calls Blessed. Among the Jesuit saints are Ignatius of Loyola, Francis Borgia, Francis Xavier, and Peter Claver of Spain; Aloysius Gonzaga and Robert Bellarmine of Italy; Issac Jogues, Rene Goupil, and John de Brébeuf of France; Edmund Campion of England; Paul Miki of Japan; Roque Gonzalez of Paraguay; and Peter Canisius of Germany.

Engage

Saint Ignatius of Loyola

Draw attention to the picture of Saint Ignatius. Ask: *What is Saint Ignatius doing?* (reading) Say: *Saint Ignatius read many books.* Ask: *What kind of books do you think he read?* Say: *We'll soon find out the answer.*

Read the title and first paragraph aloud. Explain: *Saint Ignatius was brought up as a Catholic.* Ask: *What kind of job did he have?* (He was a soldier.) Read the next paragraph. Ask: *Why do you think Saint Ignatius wanted to be like Jesus and the saints he read about?* (He wanted to love and serve God as they did. They inspired him.) Explain: *We might not always know what God wants us to do, but as we grow in faith and learn to listen to God, we can find out how to follow God's way.*

FYI

MORE ABOUT SAINT IGNATIUS OF LOYOLA (1491–1556)

Saint Ignatius, one of 13 children, was part of a devoutly Catholic family. The photograph at the bottom of the page is a picture of the basilica and other buildings that have been built around the original home of Saint Ignatius. One of his brothers, Pedro, was an ordained priest. Maria Lopez Loyola, his aunt, was a Franciscan nun. After deciding to spend his life doing whatever God wanted of him, Saint Ignatius spent 10 months outside Manresa, Spain. There he prayed, served those who were sick, and came to know the Holy Spirit. At Manresa he wrote the *Spiritual Exercises*, a book that has two major elements: a systematized examination of conscience and a planned approach to meditation.

Saint Ignatius of Loyola

Ignatius was born in Spain to a large Catholic family. He became a soldier, but he never forgot his Catholic upbringing.

He returned home after being wounded in battle. He read books about Jesus and the saints. Ignatius wanted to be like them. He decided to spend his life doing whatever God wanted of him.

FYI

THE NORTH AMERICAN MARTYRS

In Auriesville, New York, is a hilltop shrine dedicated to the three North American martyrs who were martyred in New York: Saint Isaac Jogues, Saint Rene Goupil, and Saint John de la Lande. They remain America's first canonized saints and its only martyrs.

The Shrine to North American Martyrs in Midland, Canada, is located at the Mission of Sainte-Marie among the Hurons, where the Canadian martyrs had their mission. The eight North American Martyrs, who were canonized by Pope Pius XI on June 29, 1930, came to North America from France as missionaries. They are listed among the saints of the Society of Jesus, or Jesuits.

- Saint Isaac Jogues, SJ
- Saint Rene Goupil
- Saint John de la Lande
- Saint Anthony Daniel, SJ
- Saint John de Brébeuf, SJ
- Saint Gabriel Lalemant, SJ
- Saint Noel Chabanel, SJ
- Saint Charles Garnier, SJ

We Worship God

Focus attention on the photographs. Have the children describe what they see. Ask: **How do the children in the pictures look?** (happy) **Why?**

Read the paragraph aloud. Encourage the children to respond to the question.

Read the title. Ask: **What does worship mean?** Say: **Worship is honor given to God in public prayer. We come together as God's family to offer worship.**

✝ *Family and Community*

Ask: **Have you ever given a gift to someone? For what occasion? What was the gift? How did the person react?** Encourage responses. Say: **Today we'll learn about a special gift that God has given us that brings us closer to him.**

We Worship God
Session 11

Think of a favorite gift that somebody gave you. Maybe it was a birthday present or a Christmas present. How did you thank that person?

Prayer

Jesus, my friend, help me stay close to you so that I will grow in faith.

Engage

Prayer

Say: **Jesus loves us and is our friend. Let's pray a prayer of petition to him and ask him to teach us how to grow in faith. Please pray silently as I pray aloud.**

Pray the prayer aloud. Then say: **Now close your eyes, fold your hands, and follow in your hearts as I pray the prayer again. Then be still for a few moments and tell Jesus what is in your heart.**

Softly pray the prayer aloud. Then slowly count to 10 to allow the children time for reflection. Conclude the quiet time by praying **Amen** and asking the children to open their eyes.

OPTION

BLM 27: SAINT IGNATIUS OF LOYOLA

For Blackline Master 27 children draw pictures of Jesus on mock book pages.

OPTION

IT BRINGS ME HAPPINESS

Have the children draw and color activities, experiences, and people that bring them happiness. As they work, walk around the room and point out something special about each child's art.

FYI

GRACE

Grace is the gift of God that is freely given to us. Grace fills us with God's life and makes it possible for us to be his friends forever. Sanctifying grace is the Holy Spirit alive in us, helping us to live our Christian vocation. Actual grace is the help God gives so that the decisions we make every day can be consistent with his will.

Explore

The Apple Orchard

Begin today's class by praying with the children the prayer on page 99.

Have the children stand in a circle and join you for this fingerplay. Say each line and demonstrate the gesture. Invite the children to repeat after you. Say:

If I had two apples,
(Hold up two fingers.)
Here's what I'd do!
(Point to self.)
Keep one for me
(Hold in left hand and pretend to bite apple.)
And give one to you!
(Hand to child at your right.)

Read the title. Ask: *What is an orchard?* (a group of fruit trees) Have the children describe what they see in the bottom photograph. Say: *The children in the photo are in an apple orchard. Apples grow on trees.*

Read the first paragraph aloud. Ask: *What did the apples on the tree look like?* (red, shiny) Then read the paragraph below the picture. Ask: *Why did the farmer cut down some of the branches from the trees?* (They had stopped bearing fruit.) Say: *The farmer cut away the branches that could not grow fruit. He made room for the healthy branches to grow.*

Say: *Take a moment to imagine a healthy apple tree, its branches heavy with ripe, shiny fruit.* Pause for five seconds. Explain: *We can be like a healthy branch if we stay close to Jesus.* Ask: *Have you ever seen a plant that is dying? What does it look like?* Encourage volunteers to respond.

Say: *When a plant stops growing, its leaves become withered and brown. They fall off the branch.* Continue: *If people do not stay close to Jesus, they do not grow spiritually to be as strong, healthy, and happy as they might be.*

OPTION

BLM 28: GROWING GOOD FRUIT

Blackline Master 28 involves children in writing good deeds and coloring apples.

OPTION

BLM 29: WE WORSHIP GOD

Blackline Master 29 is a word puzzle that reveals an important word.

OPTION

"APPLE, APPLE, ON THE TREE" SONG

Sing the following song to the tune of "Twinkle, Twinkle, Little Star." Then invite the children to sing it with you a second time. You may want to write the words on the board so it will be easier for the children to sing.

Apple, apple, on the tree,
Red and ripe and growing free.
Follow God and you'll grow strong,
On his branches you belong.
Apple, apple, on the tree,
Red and ripe and growing free.

The Apple Orchard

Tiffany and her friend Joey walked through an apple orchard. They looked at the beautiful trees. They talked about how shiny the apples were and about how juicy they must be.

Tiffany noticed some branches on the ground. The farmer had cut these branches from the tree. He cut them because they did not grow fruit. The healthy branches on the trees are like people who choose God. God will help us if we invite him into our lives. We can ask him to guide us.

Jesus Is the Vine

Read the title aloud. Ask the children: *Does anyone know what a vine is?* Point out the illustration of the vine on page 101. Explain: *A vine is a plant with a long, bendable stem that helps many leaves and fruits grow.*

Say: *In the Bible, Jesus explains that he is the vine. Let's read these Bible verses now.* Hold up the Bible and point out that it is opened to the passage you are about to read from the children's book.

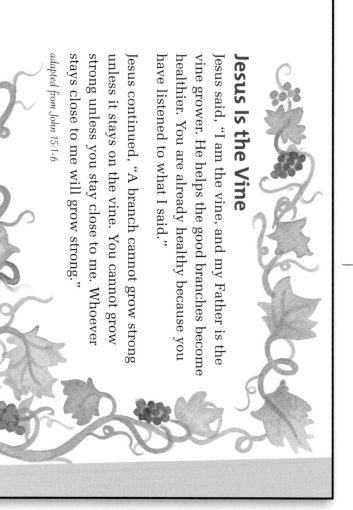

Read the two paragraphs. Ask: *What does Jesus mean when he calls himself the vine?* (He

gives us his life and keeps us strong.) *Why is God called the vine grower?* (He cares for us and helps us grow strong in faith; he helps us live good lives.)

Explain: *Just like a branch grows strong when it stays on the vine, we grow safe, strong, and happy when we stay close to Jesus.*

Display a living ivy plant. Have the children gather around the plant. Show them how its leaves are connected to the vines of the plant. Explain: *By staying on the vine and by getting water and sunlight, the leaves of the plant will grow full and strong. More and more leaves will be produced.*

Point out portions of the plant that are not flourishing or ask: *What would happen to one of the leaves if I pulled it off?* Explain: *When the leaves stop growing, they turn brown and crumble from the vine. By choosing to stay close to Jesus, we can grow, but by turning away from him, we will not grow.*

Reading God's Word

✝ Quiet the children. Slowly read the section with a joyful heart. Then tell the children to take a few moments to feel joy and peace in their hearts.

Jesus Is the Vine

Jesus said, "I am the vine, and my Father is the vine grower. He helps the good branches become healthier. You are already healthy because you have listened to what I said."

Jesus continued, "A branch cannot grow strong unless it stays on the vine. You cannot grow strong unless you stay close to me. Whoever stays close to me will grow strong."

adapted from John 15:1-6

📖 Reading God's Word

The fruit of the Spirit is love, joy, peace, patience, and kindness.

adapted from Galatians 5:22

Unit 3, Session 11   **101**

THE FRUITS OF THE SPIRIT

On the board draw a vine. Label the vine *Jesus.* Then draw branches coming from the vine and label them *us.* Say: *The Holy Spirit helps us stay close to Jesus, our vine. When we do, we will bear beautiful fruits. Our fruits are wonderful qualities, such as the ones listed in Reading God's Word.* Ask the children to name the qualities in the Scripture verse. As the children name them, write them on the board, so that they extend from the branches. Then ask the children to name other qualities that we exhibit when we stay close to Jesus; write these on the board, so that they stem from the branches. (politeness, sweetness, respect, helpfulness)

VINE IMAGERY

In the vivid imagery of this parable John shows clearly that it is God who tends the vine so that we can stay close to Jesus. While the image of the vineyard appears many times in the Scriptures, in John, Jesus is the vine. We remain fruitful as long as we remain connected to him.

Session 11   **101**

Explore

The Holy Spirit Comes to Us

Say: *Signs are things that stand for something else.* Raise your forefinger to your lips. Ask: *What does this sign mean?* (to be quiet) Then spread your fingers apart and raise your hand. Ask: *What does this sign mean?* (stop) Say: *Today we are going to learn about signs that help us grow closer to God.*

Read the title and first paragraph. Explain: *The sacraments help us grow closer to God.* Ask: *Who is the Holy Spirit?* (the third person of the Trinity)
Read the second paragraph. Draw attention to *Fruits of the Holy Spirit.* Say: *The Fruits of the Holy Spirit are ways we act when God is alive in us.* This might be a good time to remind the children of the additional information on Fruits of the Holy Spirit in the backs of their books. Then close this time with the Sign of the Cross.

OPTION

SIGNS

Bring in and demonstrate various signs for the children. Ask what these signs represent. For example, you could bring in a paper heart, a clock, and a picture of a red stoplight. Ask: *What does each of these signs stand for?* (love, time, stopping) You could also demonstrate various actions, such as clapping your hands. Ask: *What is the clapping of hands a sign for?* (enjoying something, praising someone) Say: *Signs stand for things. The sacraments are special signs that tell us God is with us.*

OPTION

FRUITS OF THE HOLY SPIRIT

Have the children draw their favorite fruits. Inside each fruit, have them write something nice they have done for someone. Then have them decorate their fruits with their

crayons or markers. Remind the children: *The Holy Spirit helps us act lovingly toward others.*

FYI

THE SEVEN SACRAMENTS

The sacraments are seven specific ways God's life enters our lives through the work of the Holy Spirit. Jesus gave the Church these sacraments. The sacraments are divided into three groups.

Sacraments of Initiation: Baptism, Confirmation, Eucharist

Sacraments of Healing: Penance, Anointing of the Sick

Sacraments at the Service of Communion: Matrimony, Holy Orders

FYI

THE RITE OF BAPTISM

During the Rite of Baptism, there are gestures and words which help us understand the richness of the sacrament. Dressed in white, the person being baptized is signed with the Sign of the Cross and hears the proclamation of the word of God. Then he or she is anointed with both the oil of catechumens and chrism. The initiate is also given a candle lit from the Easter candle. These signs, symbols, gestures, and words proclaim the faith into which the person is being baptized.

The Holy Spirit Comes to Us

Jesus gave us the sacraments. They are special signs that God is with us. In the sacraments we receive the Holy Spirit, who brings us God's special gift of grace. This helps us to be God's friends.

The Holy Spirit helps us to act as God wants us to. The good we find in our words or actions is called the **Fruits of the Holy Spirit.** We are able to be kind and loving because God is alive in us.

102   God's Invitation

The Sacrament of Baptism

Invite the children to recall that God is always with them. Then say: **Today we will learn about one of the sacraments.** Slowly read the first paragraph aloud. Ask: **What is the first sacrament we celebrate?** (Baptism) Draw attention to the word *rite* in dark type. Explain: **Rites are the special ways we celebrate each sacrament. According to the rite for the Sacrament of Baptism, a person can have water poured over his or her head or be immersed in the water.**

Direct attention to the photograph. Ask the group to describe what they see. (water being poured over an infant's head during Baptism)

Then read the second paragraph. Ask: **Does anyone know what the word sin means.** Give the children a chance to respond. Then say: **Sin is a choice we make that hurts our friendships with God and other people.** Ask: **Has anyone ever heard the words original sin?** Explain: **Original sin is the result of the sin of disobedience of Adam and Eve. It is important to remain close to God and choose to be his friend.** Explain happily: **When we celebrate the Sacrament of**

Baptism, original sin is forgiven. We become children of God and members of the Church.

✝ Family and Community

Did You Know?

Read the section aloud. Ask: **What do those words remind you of?** (the Sign of the Cross) **Who are the three persons of the Trinity?** (God the Father, the Son, and the Holy Spirit) Explain reverently: **Because we believe in the Trinity, we are baptized in the Trinity's name.** Ask the children: **Has anyone seen a brother, sister, relative, or other person being baptized?** Encourage them to share what they saw.

The Sacrament of Baptism

Baptism is the first sacrament we celebrate. We become children of God and members of the Church when we are baptized. In the **rite** of Baptism, a person is immersed in water or water is poured over the person's head. The grace we receive in the sacraments helps us stay as close to God as the vine is close to the branch.

Baptism takes away **original sin.** This sin is in the world because Adam and Eve chose not to obey God.

❓ Did You Know?
The words of Baptism that the priest says are "I baptize you in the name of the Father, and of the Son, and of the Holy Spirit."

The Sacrament of Baptism

Baptism is the first sacrament we celebrate. We become children of God and members of the Church when we are baptized. In the **rite** of Baptism, a person is immersed in water or water is poured over the person's head. The grace we receive in the sacraments helps us stay as close to God as the vine is close to the branch.

Baptism takes away **original sin.** This sin is in the world because Adam and Eve chose not to obey God.

❓ Did You Know?
The words of Baptism that the priest says are "I baptize you in the name of the Father, and of the Son, and of the Holy Spirit."

OPTION

THE SIGN OF THE CROSS

Ask the children: **Can you name times other than Baptism when we use the name of the Trinity?** (when we pray the Glory Be to the Father, when we pray the Sign of the Cross) Say: **When we pray the Sign of the Cross, we trace a cross on our bodies. You can pray the Sign of the Cross anytime you want to keep the Trinity close to you.** Invite the children to pray the Sign of the Cross with you.

Explore

Baptizing Baby Joshua

Begin by telling a story and showing pictures, if possible, about a Baptism in your family. Emphasize what a joyous occasion it was.

Encourage the children to share their stories as well.

After all have finished, ask: **Why is Baptism such a happy occasion?** (It is the first sacrament we receive. It takes away original sin. We become members of God's family.)

Say: **Thank you for sharing your happy stories. Today we will read about another family's Baptism celebration.**

Ask the children to look at the pictures on pages 104 and 105. Read the title aloud and ask the children to describe what they think is happening in the pictures.

Say: **Please follow along as I read the story about Joshua's Baptism. It will help you learn more about your own Baptism.** Read the first two paragraphs aloud. Ask: **How did the Bucca family feel?** (excited) **Why did the family members wear their best Sunday clothes?** (because Baptism is a very special celebration)

Read the next two paragraphs aloud. Ask: **What did Father Enright ask Mr. and Mrs. Bucca?** (what they wanted to name their child) **Can anyone read the words that Father said when he** *immersed Joshua in the water?* Have a volunteer read the priest's words.

Continue reading the story on page 105. Read the first paragraph aloud. Ask: **What did Father say about Joshua as a result of Baptism?** (that he was freed from sin and given new life through the Holy Spirit) Explain that Father anointed, or blessed, Joshua with oil.

Read the second paragraph and ask: **Of what was the white garment a sign?** (Joshua's new life; that he is clothed in Christ)

Read the last paragraph aloud. Say: **The candle is another sign that Father explained.** Ask: **What does the baptismal candle stand for?** (the light of Christ) Say: **Father asked Joshua's parents to keep Christ's light burning bright in Joshua's life.**

What Baptism Means

Read the questions and give the children time to draw or write their responses. Then invite them to share their artwork and ideas with the group.

Baptizing Baby Joshua

Everybody in the Bucca family was excited. Baby Joshua was going to be baptized.

Mr. and Mrs. Bucca wore their best Sunday clothes. Joshua's godparents were also ready for the celebration.

The celebration soon began. Father Enright asked Mr. and Mrs. Bucca what they wanted to name their child. "Joshua Michael," they said.

Later in the celebration, Father Enright immersed Joshua in water. Father Enright said, "I baptize you, Joshua Michael, in the name of the Father, and of the Son, and of the Holy Spirit."

Say: *The baptismal candle is a sign of Christ's light burning in your life. Can you let your light shine for others?* Ask children to make a large construction-paper flame. Suggest that they write on the flame one thing they can do to share their light with someone at home or in school today. Then have them write on the flame a thank you to God for giving them the grace of the Holy Spirit in Baptism. Display the flames in your classroom. Say: *Just think how bright our world will be when we all share the light.*

As your time together comes to an end, say: *Please pray with me by echoing my words:*

Lord Jesus,
we all need your light,
your example to follow.
With the grace of the Holy Spirit,
I will be a person of light
in my world today.

Father Enright said that Joshua was freed from sin and given new life through the Holy Spirit. Then he anointed Joshua with oil.

Next Joshua was dressed in a white garment. Father Enright said, "You have become a new creation and have clothed yourself in Christ." Joshua's godfather then lit a candle. Father Enright said that Joshua's parents were to keep the light of Christ burning brightly in their son's life.

What Baptism Means

What was your favorite part of the celebration? Why? Write or draw your answers.

MY BIRTH DAY IN GOD'S FAMILY

All the children no doubt know their birth dates. Suggest that they find out the date of their Baptism. Then have them make a construction-paper baptismal candle by writing their name and baptismal date on a piece of construction paper. They may also decorate the paper with signs and symbols of Baptism. Tell them not to write or draw within two or three inches of each side edge so the paper can be rolled to overlap. Roll and tape it into a tube shape. Stand it up and attach a paper flame. Suggest that the children share it with their families, telling them how they will share Christ's light.

SACRAMENTALS

The signs associated with the sacraments are called *sacramentals*. These include physical objects such as water, oil, bread, and wine. They also include gestures such as the laying on of the hands and blessings. The word *sacramental*, however, has a much broader meaning. It also encompasses objects such as statues, rosaries, holy water, scapulars, medals, and other objects and actions that remind us of God's presence in our everyday lives. Sacramentals such as these have their origins in the Church and prepare us to receive the fruits of the sacrament.

Reflect

Prayer

The Vine and the Branches: A Recorded Guided Reflection

As you prepare to spend this time together, remind the children that God is inviting them to know and follow him more closely.

A special approach to prayer in Session 11 is an extended guided reflection titled "The Vine and the Branches" (CD 1, Track 8). Refer to pages 370 and 371 for the script and directions for using the recorded guided reflection with the children.

Guided Reflection: An Alternate Approach

An alternate approach to prayer in this session is to use the Prayer on the children's page. The following suggestions will help you guide the children through this Prayer in a reflective manner.

Have the group look at the picture and describe what they see. Explain: *A vineyard is another place, like an orchard, where fruit grows. Grapes grow on the vine's branches.* Continue: *Jesus wants to hold us close to him just as the vine holds onto the grapes.*

Continue: *Please sit comfortably, be very still, fold your hands, silently take a long, deep breath, and then let it out slowly. Close your eyes if you'd like, and listen quietly.*

Read each paragraph slowly and with expression, pausing after each for 10 to 15 seconds to give the children time to reflect.

When the Prayer has been completed, softly say: *Jesus is with you. Take a moment to thank him.* Allow time for the children to do this. Close with the Sign of the Cross.

Say: *Let's now learn how we can share our love for Jesus with others.*

OPTION

USING THIS PAGE AGAIN
If you have led the children through the recorded guided reflection, you might choose to use this prayer page with them during another session, Day 5, the Review session, or a seasonal session as appropriate.

Prayer

Imagine that you are in your favorite place. Then imagine that Jesus is there with you. He wants to talk to you about the parable of the vine and the branches.

Jesus shows you a lovely vineyard. There are strong branches on the vine and clusters of ripe grapes. He shows you many healthy branches and how secure they are.

Jesus asks you to remember that he is the vine and you are one of the branches. He reminds you to stay close to him always. Invite him to look into your heart. You know that you can tell Jesus whatever you want. Place your cares in his hands and listen for what he wants you to know. Enjoy being together.

My Response

106

Living My Faith

Below are suggested activities to encourage the children to apply what they learned in this session.

Faith Summary

Read the section for the group. Call on a volunteer to tell the parable about the vine. Ask: *What is a sacrament?* (a special sign) *Whom do we receive in the sacraments?* (the Holy Spirit) *Which sacrament did we learn about this week?* (Baptism)

Words I Learned

Choose volunteers to pronounce the words and look them up in the Glossary. Invite other volunteers to use the words in sentences.

Ways of Being Like Jesus

Read the section aloud and say: *God helps us to be kind. When we are kind, it is a fruit of the Holy Spirit living in us.* Ask: *Can you name ways you can be kind when you play with others?* (share toys, set the table, dust) Then say: *When you help out at home, it is a fruit of the Holy Spirit living in you.*

✝ Family and Community

With My Family

Ask: *What are the children in the picture doing?* (using a chore jar) Say: *By sharing jobs with family members, we can work as a happy group. When God helps us to share, it is a fruit of the Holy Spirit living in us.* Ask: *What chores can you do at home to help your families?* (pick up toys, set the table, dust) Then say: *When you help out at home, it is a fruit of the Holy Spirit living in you.*

Prayer

Say: *We've learned about being close to God through Jesus. Now let's take some time to pray to God and thank him for Jesus. Pray with me. Then think about the ways that you can learn more about God.*

Pray the prayer aloud. Quietly count to five as you allow the children to reflect. Then say: *We'll conclude our prayer with the Lord's Prayer.*

My Response

Read the section aloud. Then ask: *Does anyone know the difference between honey and vinegar?* (Honey is sweet; vinegar is sour.) Ask: *Has anyone ever heard the saying "You can catch more flies with honey than with vinegar"?* Say: *That means that when we are sweet to people and use gentle words, they will become happy. God helps us be kind. Kindness is a fruit of the Holy Spirit living in us. Think about kind words you can use to make people happy. Then write them down.*

End this time together by saying: *Grow strong by staying close to Jesus.*

Living My Faith

Faith Summary

Jesus told the parable of the vine to teach us to stay with him. In the sacraments we receive the grace of the Holy Spirit to help us do this.

Words I Learned

Fruits of the Holy Spirit   original sin   rite

Ways of Being Like Jesus

Jesus calls us to act with kindness. You can use kind words. Speak with kindness when you are playing with your friends or family members.

With My Family

Make a chore jar for your family. Have family members pick jobs to do from the jar.

Help with dinner dishes

Prayer

Thank you, God, for giving me Jesus. Keep me close as I learn more about you and Jesus, your Son.

My Response

What are some kind words you can use this week? Make a list of three words, phrases, or sentences.

Living My Faith

Extending the Session

Choose from the following options to extend the session or to reinforce concepts developed during the week.

Family Involvement

Remind the children to take home the Raising Faith-Filled Kids page to share what they are learning with their families.

Preparation for Sunday Scripture Readings

Lead children in a prayerful discussion of Sunday's readings. Visit www.FindingGod.org/Sunday for more information.

Seasonal Session

Consider the time of the liturgical year and use the appropriate seasonal session. Seasonal sessions may be found on page 241.

Unused Options and BLMs

Incorporate any unused options or Blackline Masters from the week's session.

Web Site Activities

Visit www.FindingGod.org to find additional activities for extending the session.

OPTION

THE VINE AND THE BRANCHES

Play the recorded guided reflection "The Vine and the Branches" for the children. Depending on the activity you chose for Day 4, this may or may not be their first time hearing this reflection. After the reflection is finished, provide them with drawing paper. Have the children fold the paper into four equal quadrants and ask them to draw a picture in each quadrant to answer the following questions: *What is one special thing you saw during your experience? What is one thing that you smelled?*

What is one thing that you heard? What is one thing that you felt? Invite children to share their ideas with family members when they go home.

OPTION

FRUITS OF THE SPIRIT

Prepare a vine out of construction paper, with branches and fruit. Also prepare five large leaves. Organize the children into five groups, giving each group one leaf. Assign each group one of the following fruits of the Spirit: *love, joy, peace, patience, kindness,* and ask them to write on their leaf a way they can share their fruit of the Spirit with others. When the groups have completed their

---

OPTION

BOBBING FOR APPLES

Write the following words on separate tag-board cards shaped like apples: *Fruits of the Holy Spirit, original sin, rite, Jesus, Baptism.* Attach a paper clip to each apple and place them in a bucket or bowl. Make a bobbing rod from a yardstick, string, tape, and a strong magnet. Invite pairs of children to go "bobbing" for words. When a word is caught, ask the catcher to tell his or her partner a sentence using the word.

---

leaf, invite them to tape their leaves to the vine and display it in the room.

RAISING FAITH-FILLED KIDS
a parent page

Focus on Faith

God Makes Us His Own

When we send our children to school, we make sure that their possessions are marked so that they can be identified. In ancient times those in power used signet rings to place their seal of authority on documents so that people could identify the document with the authority of the ruler. This is the image that the Church uses to help us understand the meaning of the sacraments. In Baptism, Confirmation, and Eucharist we are sealed in the Holy Spirit. These seals identify us as belonging to God. The sacraments form us as God's people, so we can act in service to the world in the way Jesus did.

Dinnertime Conversation Starter

Discuss with your family the various ways in which Jesus served the world. Choose one way your family can effectively continue as Christians to identify you as Christians.

Our Catholic Heritage

Father James Keller (1900–1977) was a priest who believed that every individual had a contribution to make to society. In 1945 he founded the Christophers, a nonprofit organization that uses print and electronic media to spread the message of hope to all people. The motto Father Keller chose for The Christophers is "It is better to light one candle than to curse the darkness." The Christophers' work continues today with weekly television and radio programs, a daily radio message, newspaper columns, and brochures that provide resources for facing difficult life issues. You can find more information about the Christophers and their work at www.christophers.org.

Hints for at Home

Help your child nurture an ivy plant in your home. You will need an ivy plant, a clay pot, potting soil, paints or permanent markers, a watering can, and pruning shears.

Have your child decorate the clay pot, using the paints. Ask him or her to write *I am the vine* on the pot. Then plant the ivy in it. Water the plant regularly and invite your child to observe what happens over time. Show your child how to pull away leaves that become dried out. Use the pruning shears to show what occurs when you clip off a section of dead growth. (New growth takes place.) Relate this growth to the parable of the vine.

Focus on Prayer

Your child has reflected on the parable of the vine and on the security and comfort of knowing that Jesus holds us close to himself. Share with your child a moment when you felt Jesus was with you.

108 www.FindingGod.org

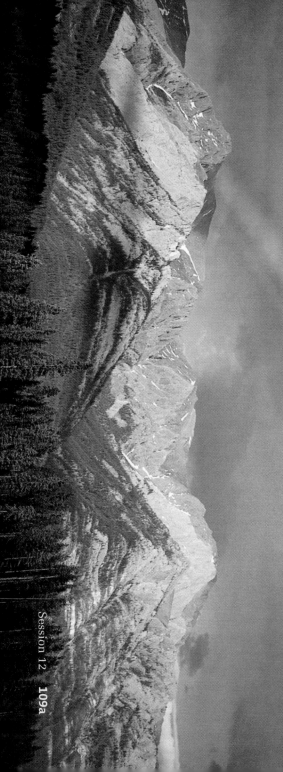

Session 12: Celebrating Reconciliation

3-Minute Retreat

Before you prepare for your session, pause for a few moments and quiet yourself. Take three deep breaths and remember that our loving Father is with you as you help the children become strong and loving Catholics.

Luke 19:5

Jesus looked up and said to him, "Zacchaeus, come down quickly, for today I must stay at your house."

Reflection

Zacchaeus was a man with many possessions and many problems. The wealthy Zacchaeus had a powerful position but was small in stature, both physically and in the community. Zacchaeus's reputation for dishonesty was well deserved. When Jesus called to him, Zacchaeus faced a pivotal moment in his life. He could have made excuses and turned Jesus away. Instead, Zacchaeus embraced Jesus and was transformed. When we embrace Jesus and turn away from sin, we too experience a transformation.

Question

What can I do so that my heart can become a more welcoming place for Jesus?

Prayer

Lovingly pray this prayer or one of your own.

Loving and forgiving Jesus, I run to you today. Come into my home, my heart, my life.

Take a few moments to reflect prayerfully before you prepare this session.

Catechist Preparation

Knowing and Sharing Your Faith

Scripture and Tradition in Session 12

The Sacrament of Penance is about confession, the open and public acknowledgment of our sinfulness. It is about forgiveness, the pardoning of our sins by God and the Church. It is also about repairing our relationships with God and others. The sacrament calls us to make our wrongs right and make restitution for the harm we have caused others. As a sacrament of healing, it is about reconciliation—bringing together those who have been separated by our sins.

The Sacrament of Penance is central to following Jesus, for he devoted his life to the forgiveness of sin. Even when he was not asked to do so, he forgave people their sins because it was integral to his mission. The Sacrament of Penance is also central to our being members of the Christian community, for there can be no love and peace within the community of believers if there is no forgiveness among us.

Scripture in Session 12

Jesus associates with a public sinner in **Luke 19:2–9**.
In **Luke 12:33** Jesus urges his listeners to embrace the Kingdom of God.

Jesus saves Zacchaeus.

Our treasure is with God.

Let the scripture and Tradition deepen your understanding of the content in this session.

WINDOW ON THE CATECHISM

Jesus' forgiveness, celebrated in the Sacrament of Penance, is discussed in CCC 1422–1484.

Catechist Preparation

From the Richness of the Tradition

The story of Zacchaeus tells us about Zacchaeus's reconciliation with God and others. Zacchaeus begins to respect the dignity of his clients and promises to treat them differently. Likewise, the story tells of a change of attitude in the people around Zacchaeus: Jesus challenges them to stop labeling Zacchaeus a sinner and to begin acknowledging the good things he does. This story shows us the way to true reconciliation in society: respect for everyone's dignity and an acceptance of others, free of judgment and stereotyping.

Over the last few decades Popes Paul VI and John Paul II have used their World Day of Peace messages to suggest approaches to peacemaking. If we want to be peacemakers, they have told us, we should do the following: work for justice, defend life, say no to violence, teach peace, respect freedom, respect minorities, respect the conscience of every person, reach out to the poor, offer forgiveness, and respect human rights. Indeed, there would be much more peace in the world if we heeded the advice of the popes.

✝ Catholic Social Teaching

We explore the following Catholic Social Teaching in this session: **Solidarity**.

Consider in this session how you will invite the children to respond to and prayerfully reflect on God's invitation to love and serve others.

GENERAL DIRECTORY FOR CATECHESIS

Catechesis for the Sacrament of Penance is at the heart of our ministry. The centrality of this sacrament to the gospel message is discussed in *GDC 102*.

Prayer in Session 12

In the opening prayer of petition and the closing prayer of gratitude in this session, we ask Jesus to teach us about forgiveness. The children are also introduced to the Act of Contrition as a way of asking for God's forgiveness and assistance in avoiding future sin.

Catechist Preparation: Get-Ready Guide

Session 12: Celebrating Reconciliation

Session Theme: *When we celebrate the Sacrament of Penance we are reconciled with God and others.*

Before This Session

- Create several footprints made of construction paper for use on page 109.
- Bookmark your Bible to Luke 19:2–9 and Luke 12:33. Place the Bible in the prayer center open to the first passage from Luke.
- Set up the CD player ahead of time so you will be ready to play the song.
- Display the posters: Act of Contrition, Ten Commandments.

Steps

DAY 1 **Engage** page 109
Celebrating Reconciliation

DAYS 1–3 **Explore** pages 110–115
Zacchaeus the Rich Man
Making Peace With God
Meet Mattie Stepanek
Peacemaker and Poet

DAY 4 **Reflect** page 116
Prayer: Act of Contrition

DAY 4 **Respond** page 117
Living My Faith: Ways to Forgive Someone
Who Treats Us Badly

DAY 5 **Extending the Session** page 118
Day 5 offers an opportunity to extend the session with activities that reinforce the session outcomes.

Outcomes   *At the end of the session, the children should be able to*

- understand how to become friends again.
- understand the story of Jesus forgiving Zacchaeus.
- explain mortal sin as a very serious wrong and venial sin as less serious.
- identify the Sacrament of Penance as the way in which we experience God's forgiveness when we confess our sins.
- understand contrition as sorrow for sins.
- define *confession, contrition, examination of conscience, mortal sin, reconciliation, Sacrament of Penance,* and *venial sin.*
- prayerfully reflect on God's presence, his invitation, and our response.
- pray the Act of Contrition.
- identify practical ways to act on God's invitation in everyday living.

Materials

Required Materials

- Bible
- Writing paper, pens, pencils
- Art materials, such as drawing paper, crayons, markers, scissors, glue
- CD 2, Track 14: A Man Named Zacchaeus (Instrumental) (page 109)
- CD 2, Track 13: A Man Named Zacchaeus (2:39) (page 111)
- Posters: Act of Contrition, Ten Commandments

Optional Materials

- Adhesive bandages (page 111)
- Construction paper (page 113)
- Books or poems by Mattie Stepanek (page 115)
- Sets of word cards (page 118)
- Blackline Masters 30, 31, 32 (pages 109, 111)

e-resources
www.FindingGod.org

109d Session 12

Celebrating Reconciliation

 Softly play the instrumental version of "A Man Named Zacchaeus" (CD 2, Track 14) while doing the following activity with the children:

Place construction-paper footprints on the floor to create a Walk-in-Peace pathway that winds around the room. Then invite children to walk in peace with you as you lead them on the pathway while the music plays.

When the children are seated explain: **God wants us to live in peace with one another. He gives us special ways to do this. He hopes that we will follow him and be as forgiving of others as he is of us.**

Tell the children to open their books to page 109. Read the title of the session. Read the paragraph aloud. Tell the children: **Think privately of a time when an unkind act hurt one of your friendships.** Then ask volunteers to share how they and their friends made up, or reconciled. Ask them not to use names.

Draw attention to the pictures. Ask: **What is happening in the left picture? How did the two boys become friends again?** Allow the children to respond.

Then explain happily: **Being friends again is what reconciliation is. Reconciliation, one of the words in the title on this page, means making friends again after a friendship has been broken by some word or action. We can be the kind of people that God wants us to be when we make peace with others. Today we are going to learn about this.**

Prayer

Say: **Jesus can help us learn about forgiveness. Let's meet Jesus in prayer and ask for his help.**

Then say: **Now please fold your hands. Let's pray together and then be still for a few moments and silently tell Jesus what is in our hearts.**

Reverently pray the prayer. Count to five silently as you allow the children time to be still with Jesus. Then say: **Let's close with the Sign of the Cross.**

Celebrating Reconciliation

Has a friend ever been unkind to you? Think of how it hurt your friendship. How did you become friends again?

Prayer

Jesus, my Savior, help me be aware of my sins. Teach me to ask for forgiveness when I am wrong.

OPTION

BLM 30: BECOMING FRIENDS AGAIN

Blackline Master 30 is a picture story for children to put together to show how they can forgive one another.

Zacchaeus the Rich Man

Make sure the children are on page 110. Read the title of the Bible story aloud. Pronounce the name Zacchaeus (zak´-ē əs) for the children. Have them repeat it after you.

Explain: *In this Bible story we will meet a man named Zacchaeus, who sinned but found a way to become closer to God with Jesus' help.*

Hold up the Bible that is at the prayer center and show that it is opened to the story you are about to read. Then read the first paragraph in the student book as the group follows along silently. Explain: *Zacchaeus collected money for the government. Sometimes he cheated people out of their money and took more of it than he was supposed to take. This made him rich. As you know, cheating people out of their money is stealing, and stealing is a sin.*

Read the second paragraph. Ask: *Why do you think Zacchaeus climbed the tree?* (He was not tall enough to see over the crowd around Jesus.) Explain: *Zacchaeus must have wanted to see Jesus very badly if he went through the trouble of climbing a tree!* Ask: *Why do you think Zacchaeus wanted to see Jesus so badly?* (He was curious to see this man he had heard so much about.)

Draw attention to the illustration. Have the children describe what they see. (Zacchaeus in the tree looking for Jesus) Ask the children: *How do you think the crowd will respond to Jesus' words when he says that he wants to stay at Zacchaeus's home?*

Read the rest of the story. Then ask: *Have any of you ever been in a large crowd? At a parade,*

perhaps? What was it like? Was it hard to see? Allow the children to respond. Then say: *This is probably how Zacchaeus felt when he couldn't see over the crowd.*

Ask: *Why do you think the crowd was angry that Jesus was staying at Zacchaeus's home?* (The people thought Jesus should stay away from sinners, and they knew Zacchaeus had cheated many people.) *What do we learn about Jesus from this story?* (Jesus was loving and forgiving of all people.) *How can we be more like Jesus?* (love and forgive others)

Ask: *What did Zacchaeus do that was wrong?* (He stole money

from others.) Explain: *Zacchaeus looked into his heart and knew that he had done wrong. He wanted to make it up to those he had hurt.* Ask: *What did he do to make his peace with them and God?* (He gave half his belongings to the poor and paid back those from whom he had stolen.)

Draw attention to the illustration and ask volunteers to explain what they see. (Jesus is having dinner at the home of Zacchaeus and his family.) Say: *In the Jewish tradition, eating with someone means you are reconciled and have made peace with him or her.*

Zacchaeus the Rich Man

Zacchaeus was a dishonest tax collector. He was very rich. One day he heard that Jesus was coming through town. Zacchaeus wanted to see Jesus very much. But Jesus was walking in a big crowd and Zacchaeus was not tall. He could not see over the crowd.

Zacchaeus ran ahead and climbed up a tree. Jesus saw him and said, "Zacchaeus, come down. I want to stay at your house today." This made Zacchaeus very happy.

110 God's Invitation

Invite the children to stand and join you in an action rhyme. Read each line and demonstrate the action. Then have the children repeat the line and action after you.

Little Zacchaeus had to climb a tree,
(Mime climbing up.)
For it was Jesus he longed to see.
(Put hands at eyes like binoculars.)
When Jesus asked him to come down,
(Mime climbing down.)
Zacchaeus turned his life around.
(Turn around.)
He made his peace with God, you see.
(Shake hands with people to your right and left.)

And walked in love through Christ's mercy.
(Put hands on heart.)

Display the Ten Commandments poster. Explain that, just like Zacchaeus, we are called to live at peace with God and others. Discuss with the children how the commandments help us do this.

Tell the children they will hear the story of Zacchaeus in a song called "A Man Named Zacchaeus." The children can find the words to the song in the Songs of Our Faith section at the back of their books. Have them follow the words as you play the song on Track 13 of CD 2.

The people in the crowd became angry. They wondered why Jesus was going to the home of a sinner.

Zacchaeus said to Jesus, "I will give half of everything I have to the poor. I will give money back to anyone I have cheated."

Jesus was pleased. He said that Zacchaeus was saved that day.

adapted from Luke 19:2–9

Reading God's Word

Sell what you have and give to those who do not have much. Your treasure is with the Lord. No thief can steal that from you.

adapted from Luke 12:33

Play the song to review the story of Zacchaeus and its lesson. Encourage the children to sing along.

Reading God's Word

Read the section aloud. Have the children perform the verse as a choral reading. Divide the children into three groups. Have each group read one sentence of the passage.

As this time together ends, remind the children that Jesus invites them to be forgiving people.

OPTION

BLM 31: ZACCHAEUS

Blackline Master 31 asks children to fill in blanks with words from the story of Zacchaeus.

OPTION

BLM 32: CELEBRATING RECONCILIATION

Blackline Master 32 is a crossword puzzle containing important words and themes about confession.

OPTION

GOD HEALS

Tell the group: **When we ask for forgiveness, God heals us of our sins.** Pass out bandages and markers. Have the children write *God Heals* on the bandages. Tell them to put an adhesive bandage on one arm as a reminder that God can make everything better.

Making Peace With God

Invite the children to ask Jesus to help them become better followers of him, just as Zacchaeus was. Tell children that they are about to begin learning about Penance, the sacrament of forgiveness. Say: *Jesus forgave Zacchaeus's sins, and Zacchaeus grew closer to Jesus and God. Because God loves and cares for us, he will forgive our sins. He says that when we tell him we are sorry, he will forgive us. Take a moment to privately think about something that you are sorry you have done. Ask God to forgive you.*

Remind the group: *As much as we try not to sin, there are times when we do. However, we can ask God to forgive us for these sins. He will always forgive us.*

Read the title and the first two paragraphs aloud. Explain the

difference between a mortal and a venial sin. Say: *A mortal sin is very, very bad. It is so bad that it breaks our relationship with God. When we commit a mortal sin, we turn our backs on God.* Add reassuringly: *Let's hope that most of us will never commit a sin so serious.*

Continue: *A venial sin is less serious. It hurts our relationship with God and others, but it is not so serious as a mortal sin.* Ask: *What is one thing that both kinds of sin have in common?* (They hurt our relationship with God and others.)

Slowly read the final paragraph on page 112 aloud while the

group follows along. Continue: *God gives us the wonderful opportunity to be forgiven through the Sacrament of Penance. We go to confession. When we confess our sins to a priest and tell God we are sorry, we receive God's forgiveness.*

Read the first paragraph on page 113. Draw attention to examination of conscience. Say: *Our conscience is the inner voice that helps us know what God wants us to do.* Say: *An examination of conscience is thinking about what we have said or done that may have hurt our friendship with God or with other people.*

Link to Liturgy

Read the section aloud. Explain: *When we gather for Mass, we admit to one another and to God that we do not always do what we should. We praise God for being merciful and ask for God's forgiveness and kindness.*

Continue: *At Mass the priest reminds us that God loves us and that he forgives us.*

Complete the reading on pages 112 and 113 before beginning Link to Liturgy.

Making Peace With God

We choose to turn away from God when we sin. We turn away from God when we commit a __mortal sin__ or a __venial sin.__

Mortal sin is a very serious wrong. Venial sin is a less serious wrong. All sin hurts our relationship with God and others.

Sin is forgiven when we celebrate the (**Sacrament of Penance.**) In (**confession**) we tell God we are sorry.(**Contrition**) is the name given to the sadness we feel when we know we have sinned. In (**reconciliation**) we make peace with God and with others. We promise God that we will try not to sin again.

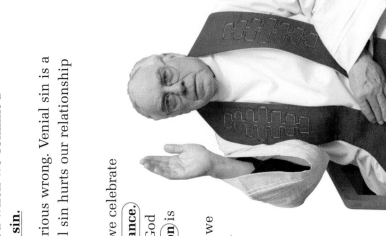

Link to Liturgy

Near the beginning of Mass, we pray special prayers to ask for God's forgiveness and mercy.

112 God's Invitation

Then read the second paragraph aloud. Ask: **How did Jesus feel when Zacchaeus felt sorry about cheating?** (happy) Then say: *If you sin and tell God you are sorry, he will forgive you. Zacchaeus thought about what he had done to hurt his relationships with others. In other words, he examined his conscience. When we examine our conscience, like Zacchaeus, we can choose to change.*

This might be a good time to remind the children of the additional information on An Examination of Conscience at the backs of their books.

Before going to confession it is important to make an **examination of conscience.** This will help us think about anything we have said or done that has hurt our friendship with God and with others. Your conscience will help you know if you have done something wrong.

Jesus was happy that Zacchaeus was sorry about cheating so many people. Jesus will be happy with you when you come to him in confession and tell him you are sorry for your sins. He will always forgive you.

God and You

Look at the words in dark type on these two pages, in the Making Peace With God section. Which of those words name ways to improve your relationship with God? Circle those. Which ones name things that harm your relationship with God? Underline those.

God and You

Read the title and directions aloud. Distribute green and red crayons. Give the group time to complete the activity. Go over the responses. The words in the first paragraph on page 112 should be underlined; those in the third paragraph should be circled.

Explore

OPTION

PEACE TO ALL WHO ENTER HERE

Have the children create a doorknob decorator that welcomes people. On construction paper, have the children draw and then cut out a doorknob decorator—long, thin, and with a hole at the top that is big enough for a doorknob to fit through. Have them write the word *Welcome* on it and decorate it. Invite them to hang the decoration on the doorknob of their bedrooms to remind themselves to live in peace with others.

OPTION

WALK IN PEACE

Distribute construction paper. Have the children trace one of their feet onto the paper, cut it out, and write one way they can live in peace with others. (say "I'm sorry," walk away from a fight) When finished, call on volunteers to share their ideas. Say: *We are in this room together and should walk in peace together. It will prepare us to walk in peace with our neighbors around the world.* Then have the children get up and place their footprints around the room as you did to begin yesterday's class.

✝ *Solidarity*

FYI

PENITENTIAL RITE

The purpose of the penitential rite at the beginning of Mass is to admit that we are in need of God's forgiveness. There are three options for the penitential rite at Mass, all of which include some form of the Greek litany: Kyrie eleison. Christe eleison. (Lord, have mercy. Christ, have mercy.) In this litany we praise the Lord and ask for God's mercy. The priest concludes this rite with a prayer asking God to forgive our sins and bring us to everlasting life.

Explore

Meet Mattie Stepanek

Help the children to recognize God in their daily lives by doing the following:

Tell them a personal experience about someone in your life who was a peaceable person—someone who avoided confrontations, made peace among those who were not getting along, was positive and saw the good in everyone. (parent, relative, friend) Then ask: *What might be a good name for a person who always makes peace?* (peacemaker) *Would anyone like to share a story about a peacemaker in your life? Remember, a peacemaker does not have to be an adult.* Encourage children to share their stories and to tell what kinds of things they might do to become peacemakers.

Talk about the qualities that the peacemakers they discussed seem to have in common. (kindness, caring, positive attitude, calm, good listener, forgiving)

Tell children that today they will read about a very special child who was a peacemaker.

Ask children to open their books to page 114. Read the title aloud and ask if any of them have ever heard of Mattie. Invite those who have to tell what they know about him. Then say: *The story about Mattie begins with a short passage from the Bible. See if you know why it starts this way.*

✝ Read the Bible passage. Ask: *Why do you think it starts with these words of Jesus?* (God wants all his children to be peacemakers. Mattie was a peacemaker.)

Read the second paragraph. Ask: *How was Mattie's life difficult?* (He had a rare disease. He used a wheelchair.) *What did he like to do?* (write poetry) *What did Mattie want to do?* (work for peace)

Invite children to comment on the photographs of Mattie. Read the caption.

Say: *Mattie appeared on television shows and was featured in newspapers and magazines, including Time Magazine for Kids.* Continue: *Just from the little we have read about him, what can you tell about the kind of person he was?* (didn't think of himself and his problems, wanted to help others, was happy)

FYI

MORE ABOUT MATTIE

Mattie was born in 1990 with a rare form of muscular dystrophy called dysautonomic mitochondrial myopathy. It caused muscle weakness and affected his body's "automatic" functions, so he needed a ventilator and extra oxygen and used a power wheelchair. He was the youngest of four children. His sister and two brothers died from the same condition. Mattie's mom, Jeni, has the adult onset form of the disability and uses a power wheelchair. Mattie received home schooling and studied a high school curriculum. His verse has been published in several books, the first of which is *Heartsongs* (Hyperion, 2002).

Meet Mattie Stepanek

Jesus said, "Blessed are the peacemakers, for they will be called children of God."

Matthew 5:9

Mattie Stepanek was a child who was a peacemaker. Mattie had a rare disease and used a wheelchair. He had been writing poetry since he was three years old. Mattie died on June 22, 2004, when he was 13 years old.

Above, Mattie and his mother hold his published book of poetry, *Journey Through Heartsongs.*

114 God's Invitation

Peacemaker and Poet

Read the title aloud. Say: *Mattie wrote thousands of poems. Many of them have been published in books. All of his books have the word "Heartsongs" in their titles. That's what Mattie wrote about— he said that his heartsongs were the songs in his heart that made him want to be a better person and to help others do the same.*

Read the sentence below the title. Slowly read the poem aloud as the group follows along. Then divide the class into two groups

and have them read the poem, alternating sentences. Invite children to share their ideas about the poem.

Say: *Jesus found the good in Zacchaeus. Mattie found the good things in life to celebrate each day. Can you find the good in people you meet? Can you be happy with the good things that happen each day? If you can, you can be a peacemaker too.*

MY HERO

OPTION

One of Mattie's wishes, which was granted to him, was to meet his hero, former U.S. President Jimmy Carter. When he spoke to Carter, he spoke with him about people and problems all over the world. Carter's peacemaking was an inspiration to Mattie.

Invite the children to write about their hero, someone who is an inspiration to them of how they would like to live helping others. It might be the peacemaker in their lives that they wrote about earlier or it could be someone else.

MATTIE'S POEMS

OPTION

If you have one of Mattie's books, you might read more of his verses aloud or invite children to read them. Many of his works can be found in various articles and stories about him online.

PEACE POETS

OPTION

Mattie wrote poems about peace because he wanted to be a peacemaker. Invite the children to write poems about things that are important to them such as love, joy, or courage. Indicate that their poems need not rhyme. Tell them to reread Mattie's poem for inspiration.

Peacemaker and Poet

With a partner, read Mattie's poem "Peace of Patience."

Peace of Patience

I cannot wait to become
A peacemaker.
I cannot wait to help
The world overcome
Anger, and problems of evil.
I cannot wait for the world
To be peaceful.
And for everyone
To live in harmony.
I cannot wait to grow
And be and overcome.
But, I will wait,
With patience,
And hope, and peace.

Reflect

Prayer

Display the poster of the Act of Contrition and invite the children to gather around it. Then explain: **Contrition is the sadness we feel when we know we have sinned. This is a special prayer Catholics pray to ask God to forgive us for our sins. I will read one sentence at a time.** Have the children look at the poster as you point to the words.

Read the first four lines of the Act of Contrition as the children follow along. Then read the first four lines again, inviting the children to join you this time. Read the rest of the prayer as the children follow along. Then invite them to read those lines with you.

Now explain: **When we pray this prayer we are telling God that we are sorry and that we will, with his help, sin no more.** Have the children return to their seats.

Say: **As we prepare for our prayer time, please take three deep breaths. Now be very quiet and think about how much God loves and cares for you.**

Read the first paragraph slowly and with expression. Say: **Look at the words on the poster or in your book and pray with me.**

Reverently pray the prayer again. Then ask the children to close their eyes. Softly tell them to take a few moments to tell Jesus whatever they would like. Then pause, giving the children time to talk with Jesus. Say: **Always remember the great love that God has for you as we learn more about how we can practice Jesus' teachings every day.**

OPTION

LORD, HAVE MERCY

Say: **We can ask God to forgive us for the things we do that hurt ourselves, others, and God.** Have the children respond "Forgive us, Lord" after each petition. Pray:

For the times we have used unkind words, we pray. (Forgive us, Lord)
For the times we have been unkind in our actions, we pray. (Forgive us, Lord)
For the times we have hurt others and ourselves, we pray. (Forgive us, Lord)
For the times we did not try to stop an unkind act, we pray. (Forgive us, Lord)

FYI

TRADITIONAL PRAYERS

In praying we sometimes face a basic challenge: what do we say? We can pray in any words that come to mind. At other times traditional prayers can provide a vehicle for rich and powerful expression. When we pray using traditional prayers, we affirm the link that connects us to those who have gone before us in faith. When teaching children to take these traditional prayers to heart, it is equally important to help them grasp their meaning. (CCC 2688)

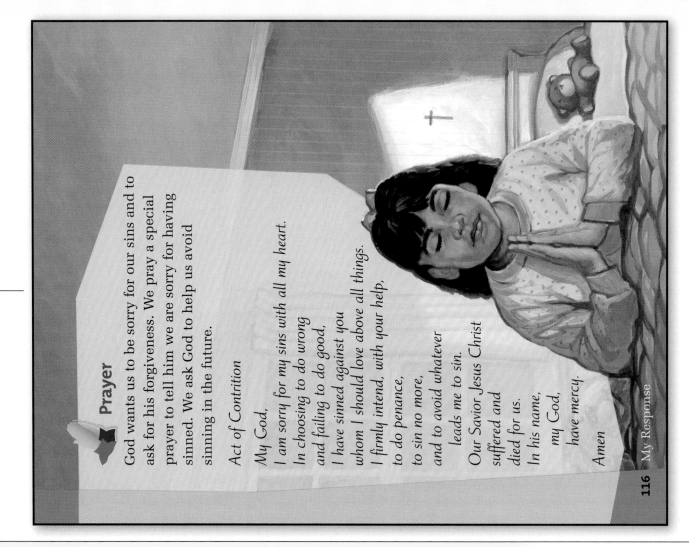

Prayer

God wants us to be sorry for our sins and to ask for his forgiveness. We pray a special prayer to tell him we are sorry for having sinned. We ask God to help us avoid sinning in the future.

Act of Contrition

My God,
I am sorry for my sins with all my heart.
In choosing to do wrong
and failing to do good,
I have sinned against you
whom I should love above all things.
I firmly intend, with your help,
to do penance,
to sin no more,
and to avoid whatever
leads me to sin.
Our Savior Jesus Christ
suffered and
died for us.
In his name,
my God,
have mercy.

Amen

116 My Response

Living My Faith

Use these suggestions to help the children apply what they learned in this session.

Faith Summary

Read the section. Ask the children: *What was Zacchaeus sorry for?* (stealing by cheating people out of their money) *What did he do to show he was sorry?* (gave money to the poor, gave money back to people he had cheated) Then say: *Imagine you are at Zacchaeus's home. How would you tell the story of meeting Jesus?*

Words I Learned

Call on volunteers to pronounce each word. Choose other volunteers to look up the words in the Glossary and read them aloud for the group.

Ways of Being Like Jesus

Read the section aloud for the children. Ask: *What kind of good things can you do for your classmates and relatives?* (share school supplies, remember to send cards for family birthdays)

✝ *Solidarity*

With My Family

Read the section and have the children describe what they see in the picture. Ask: *What does a welcome sign show?* (that everyone is included and should come in)

Prayer

Say: *God gives us his wonderful gift of forgiveness. Let's thank God for this gift and ask him to stay with us as we try to become forgiving people.*

Pray the prayer aloud with the children. Then say: *Ask God to look into your hearts now. Be still with him.* Slowly count to 10, allowing the children several moments of silence. Then say: *Let's close with the Sign of the Cross.*

Faith Summary

Zacchaeus opened his heart to Jesus. Our sins can be forgiven through the Sacrament of Penance.

Words I Learned

confession   contrition

examination of conscience   mortal sin

reconciliation   Sacrament of Penance   venial sin

Ways of Being Like Jesus

Jesus treated all people the same. You are like Jesus when you do good things for relatives and classmates.

Living My Faith

With My Family

Welcome people by creating a Welcome sign to put in your home.

My Response

Read the section aloud and then say: *Sometimes people aren't nice. Think about a time when someone wasn't nice to you. Ask: How did you make peace with him or her? Write a sentence about it.* Advise them not to use names and to keep their sentences general.

When they have finished, call on volunteers to share their sentence with the group.

Close the day with these words: *Remember to forgive others, because God has forgiven you.*

Prayer

Thank you, Jesus, for helping me to forgive others as you forgive me.

My Response

Have you treated someone badly? What steps can you take to apologize?

Extending the Session

Choose from the following options to extend the session or to reinforce concepts developed during the week.

Family Involvement

Remind the children to take home the Raising Faith-Filled Kids page to share what they are learning with their families.

Preparation for Sunday Scripture Readings

Lead children in a prayerful discussion of Sunday's readings. Visit www.FindingGod.org/Sunday for more information.

Seasonal Session

Consider the time of the liturgical year and use the appropriate seasonal session. Seasonal sessions may be found on page 241.

Unused Options and BLMs

Incorporate any unused options or Blackline Masters from the week's session.

Web Site Activities

Visit www.FindingGod.org to find additional activities for extending the session.

OPTION

NEIGHBORLY COUPONS

Remind the children of Mattie Stepanek and how he shared his message of peace through poetry. Invite each child to make a coupon for a neighbor that offers a "sharing service," such as an offer to share a bike or other toy, a service such as weeding the lawn, or time such as reading to another child. Encourage the children to present their coupons to neighbors and fulfill their offer. Explain that, like Mattie, they too can do their part to share God's gifts.

OPTION

SACRAMENT OF PENANCE ALPHABET GAME

Prior to the activity make five or six sets of word cards with the following words: *Penance, confession, contrition, examination of conscience, reconciliation, mortal sin, venial sin.* Form groups of six children and give each group a set. Have each child take a card. Challenge the groups to stand so their word cards are in alphabetical order. When the words are in order, have each child read his or her word aloud to the group and tell the group how it relates to the Sacrament of Penance.

OPTION

ZACCHAEUS THE RICH MAN

Form small groups. Have each group create a new skit based on "Zacchaeus the Rich Man." Ask children to expand on the story; for example, give reasons why Zacchaeus wanted to see Jesus, or have Jesus explain why Zacchaeus was saved. Allow the children to practice before presenting their skit to the class. After each group has performed, ask the audience: *Why do you think Jesus chose Zacchaeus? How do you think the angry crowd reacted to Jesus telling Zacchaeus he was saved?*

RAISING FAITH-FILLED KIDS

a parent page

Focus on Faith

Jesus Dines With Zacchaeus

When our children hurt one another, we can feel discouraged. We know that even though apologies are given and accepted, resentment can remain. Luke presents an account of reconciliation in the story of Zacchaeus, a tax collector whom people hated. Jesus did not scold Zacchaeus when they met, but rather asked Zacchaeus to invite him to dinner. Jesus' eating with Zacchaeus meant that Jesus forgave him and accepted him. Zacchaeus responded by vowing to pay back everyone he had cheated. Jesus teaches us that we can help our children be reconciled with God and with one another. The family dinner gives us the opportunity to share conversation and build relationships.

Dinnertime Conversation Starter

Arrange a time to invite to dinner someone with whom your family needs to rebuild a relationship.

Spirituality in Action

Your child is learning about reconciliation. Remind your child that we also pray for reconciliation among groups of people. Explain that criticizing others because of their appearance, religious beliefs, or way of life is not appropriate and is hurtful to them and to God. Encourage your child to get to know those who may be from other cultures or backgrounds.

Hints for at Home

Create walk-in-peace footprints for the entryway to each bedroom in your home. Make one pair for each room. You will need poster board, markers, scissors, and double-sided tape. Have your child trace his or her feet on the poster board once for every bedroom in your home. Decorate the outlines and write *Walk in peace* on them. Cut out the outlines. Use the tape to attach one pair to the floor outside each bedroom door, facing out from the bedroom. Remind your family members to walk in peace as they leave their bedrooms each morning.

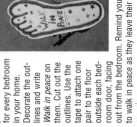

Focus on Prayer

Your child is learning to pray the Act of Contrition. Pray it with your child at bedtime after he or she reviews the good and hurtful things that were done that day.

Session 13: The Sacrament of Penance

3-Minute Retreat

Take a few moments to reflect prayerfully before you prepare this session.

Before you prepare for your session, pause for a few moments and pay attention to your breathing. Take three deep breaths and feel the loving presence of God as you lead the children on this spiritual journey.

Mark 2:5

When Jesus saw their faith, he said to the paralytic, "Child, your sins are forgiven."

Reflection

When Jesus approached the man who was paralyzed and had been lowered on a mat through a hole in the roof, he initially responded not only to the man's need for physical healing but also to his need for healing from sin. Our greatest suffering is caused by sin, which renders us unable to move toward a deeper relationship with God.

No matter what our offense may be, Jesus is always ready to forgive. Jesus shares his power to forgive sins with the bishops and priests of the Church through the Sacrament of Penance. This sacrament provides us with a way to receive the very same forgiveness offered to the paralyzed man.

Questions

What is preventing me from moving toward a deeper relationship with God? For what do I need to ask forgiveness so that I can experience the grace of Jesus' forgiveness?

Prayer

With a grateful heart, speak to Jesus, using this prayer or one of your own. Loving Jesus, you know my best and worst, and you love me. Give me the strength and courage to acknowledge my sin and seek your forgiveness in the Sacrament of Penance.

Catechist Preparation

Knowing and Sharing Your Faith

Scripture and Tradition in Session 13

Sin represents a break in our relationship with God. The Sacrament of Penance enables us to repair that break and gives us the grace to maintain a healthy relationship with God.

Sin also represents a break in our relationship with others. The Sacrament of Penance helps us to repair that break and live in harmony with others.

Sin is a rejection of God's love. Through the Sacrament of Penance, we become filled with God's love and become more responsive to God's loving action in our lives.

Sin is a refusal to listen to God and to obey his Commandments. The Sacrament of Penance makes us more obedient to God's will.

Sin represents an injustice, a wrong done to others and to ourselves as dignified human beings created in the image of God. The Sacrament of Penance helps us to restore justice, to rectify the wrong done to others, and to restore our human dignity.

Sin is an act of misdirection, pointing us away from God. The Sacrament of Penance helps to redirect our lives toward God and eternal salvation.

Scripture in Session 13

Jesus forgives a man's sins and heals his paralysis in **Mark 2:1–12.**
Luke 1:77 relates forgiveness and salvation.

Jesus cures the paralyzed man.

Forgiveness is a sign of salvation.

Let the Scripture and Tradition deepen your understanding of the content in this session.

WINDOW ON THE CATECHISM

The paralyzing effects of sin are discussed in CCC 1849–1869. The healing power of Penance is explored in CCC 1468–1470.

The Sick of the Palsy Brought to Christ by His Friends (detail)

From the Richness of the Tradition

In two of his messages for the World Day of Peace, Pope John Paul II made the connection between forgiveness and peace. The theme of his 1997 message was "Offer forgiveness and receive peace," and the theme of his 2002 message was "No peace without justice; no justice without forgiveness." Pope Paul VI also made the connection between forgiveness and peace.

In his 1970 message for the World Day of Peace, he wrote: "To preach the Gospel of forgiveness seems absurd to human politics, because in the natural economy justice does not often permit forgiveness. But in the Christian economy, which is superhuman, it is not absurd. Difficult, yes, but not absurd." (Message of His Holiness Pope Paul VI for the Celebration of the Day of Peace, January 1, 1970)

✝ Catholic Social Teaching

In this session the following Catholic Social Teachings are integrated:

- **Call to Family, Community, and Participation**
- **Solidarity**

Prayer in Session 13

In the opening prayer of petition and the closing prayer of thanks, we ask Jesus to teach us to be peaceful. In this session the children review the Act of Contrition and pray for peace in their families, communities, and world.

Consider in this session how you will invite the children to respond to and prayerfully reflect on God's invitation to love and serve others.

GENERAL DIRECTORY FOR CATECHESIS

The liberating forgiveness of sins that Jesus brings is explored in *GDC* 101.

Catechist Preparation: Get-Ready Guide

Session 13: The Sacrament of Penance

Session Theme: *In the Sacrament of Penance, our sins are forgiven.*

Before This Session

- Bookmark your Bible to Mark 2:1–12 and Luke 1:77. Place the Bible in the prayer center open to the passage from Luke.
- Set up the CD player so you are ready to play the song and the Scripture story. Listen to them before the session begins.
- Display the posters: We Celebrate Reconciliation, Act of Contrition.

Steps

DAY 1	**Engage** page 119
	The Sacrament of Penance
DAYS 1-3	**Explore** pages 120–125
	Jesus Heals
	Jesus Forgives
	Let It Begin With Me
DAY 4	**Reflect** page 126
	Prayer: Forgiving and Being Forgiven
DAY 4	**Respond** page 127
	Living My Faith: Ways to Be a Peacemaker
DAY 5	**Extending the Session** page 128
	Day 5 offers an opportunity to extend the session with activities that reinforce the session outcomes.

Outcomes
At the end of the session, the children should be able to

- realize that we can make it up to someone when we hurt them.
- understand the story of Jesus healing the paralyzed man and forgiving his sins.
- describe how Jesus is always willing to forgive us.
- identify the Sacrament of Penance as a way of celebrating Jesus' forgiveness of our sins.
- define the words *absolution* and *penance*.
- prayerfully reflect on God's presence, his invitation, and our response.
- identify practical ways to act on God's invitation in everyday living.

Materials

Required Materials

- Bible
- Writing paper, pens, pencils
- Art materials, such as drawing paper, crayons, markers, scissors, glue
- Envelope, tape (page 123)
- CD 1, Track 3: Jesus Heals (5:30) (page 120)
- CD 2, Track 15: Jesus, Jesus (1:04) (pages 122, 126)
- Posters: We Celebrate Reconciliation, Act of Contrition

Optional Materials

- Construction paper, plastic foam ring, hole punch, piece of ribbon (page 121)
- Several large word cards, slips of paper, bowl, music (page 128)
- Blackline Masters 33, 35 (pages 121, 123)
- Blackline Master 34, colored paper, hole punch, 4 strings per child (page 121)

e-resources

www.FindingGod.org

The Sacrament of Penance

Say: *We've been learning how Jesus forgives our sins. When we are forgiven, we feel peace in our hearts. Let's begin our time together by singing a song about peace.* Invite the children to stand for a song. Sing this song to the tune of "Bingo," and have the children join you when you sing it a second time. Then demonstrate the American Sign Language signs for each letter in the word *peace*, and repeat the song again, with the children using the signs.

Remind the children: *We sometimes sin and hurt our friendships with God and others.* Explain: *When we examine our conscience and recognize that we have done something wrong, we take a step toward making up for our mistake.*

P-E-A-C-E, (Spell out with ASL.)
P-E-A-C-E, (Spell out with ASL.)
P-E-A-C-E, (Spell out with ASL.)
Oh, I can live in peace, oh!

*Oh, I can learn to live in peace,
Oh, I can live in peace, oh!*

Have the children look at the illustration on page 119 and describe what they see. Ask: **What did the girl do that was unkind?** (cut the dress of the other girl's doll) **How did she try to make up for it?** (repaired the dress and gave the doll back)

Read the title of the session. Say: *Penance is a sacrament. We have learned that a sacrament is a special sign that God is with us.*

Read the paragraph. Tell the children: *Privately think of a time when you did or said something unkind to a friend or family member.*

Ask: **How did you realize that you had hurt someone you love? What did you do or say to make it up to the person you hurt? How did you feel after you made peace with that person?**

Prayer

Say: *Let's spend some time with Jesus now and ask him to teach us more about forgiveness. Pray along with me. Then take a few moments to talk to Jesus.*

Pray the prayer aloud. Afterward, pause and silently count to 10 as the children reflect. Say: *Let's close with the Sign of the Cross.*

The Sacrament of Penance

Sometimes we do or say something to hurt others. How can we make it up to them?

Prayer

Jesus, my friend, teach me about your forgiveness so that I may learn to make peace with God and others.

Explore

Jesus Heals

Read the title of the page aloud and see if any of the children know what the word *heal* means. Say: *To heal means "to cure, fix, or make well again."* Continue: *We have already learned about some of the people Jesus healed. Turn back to page 62 and look at the picture and words.* Ask the children: *Who were some of the people Jesus healed here?* (people who were blind, deaf, or crippled) Say: *Now please turn again to page 120, and we will learn another Bible story that shows the wonderful healing powers Jesus shared with others.* Point to the Bible and explain that it is opened to the passage they are about to learn.

See if the children know what it means to be paralyzed. Explain: *When people are paralyzed, they cannot move parts of their body, such as their arms or legs.*

Ask the children to follow along as you read the story aloud. When you have finished reading, tell the children they will now listen to a recorded version of this story. Have the children sit quietly and comfortably as you play the dramatized version of the passage "Jesus Heals," based on Mark 2:1–12, the Scripture cited in the children's book. Ask the children to listen carefully for new information that was not included in the story you read. Encourage them to look at the picture on page 120 as they listen.

Play Track 3 of CD 1. When it is finished, discuss the story with the children and answer any questions they have about the story.

Ask the children: *Who can remember what Zacchaeus did in order to see Jesus?* (He climbed a tree.) *What did the paralyzed man have to do to see Jesus?* (have friends lower him through the roof) Say: *The man who was paralyzed couldn't see Jesus without the help of his four friends. What did Jesus do for the man who was paralyzed?* (He forgave his sins. He allowed him to walk.) Explain: *The man needed Jesus because his body was injured and he could not walk. But he was hurting in another way too. It is a way that all of us hurt—from sin. Jesus forgave him. Jesus helped him in both ways.*

Who helped the man who was paralyzed get to Jesus? (his friends) Explain: *The man who was paralyzed was able to reach Jesus only because he received help from his friends.*

Just as the man who was paralyzed had friends who helped him get close to Jesus, so do we have special people in our lives who help us be close to God. Ask: *Who are some of these people?* (family, friends, priest, catechist)

✝ *Family and Community*

Jesus Heals

Jesus was talking with some people in a house. The people crowded the rooms and blocked the doorways.

Four men walked by carrying their friend. Their friend wanted to see Jesus. He was paralyzed and could not walk. The men climbed to the roof of the house and made an opening. They lowered their friend to Jesus.

Jesus saw their faith. He said to the man who was paralyzed, "Your sins are forgiven."

Some people in the crowd were surprised. They said, "Only God can forgive sins!"

Following the Story

Ask a child to read the activity's title and directions. Call on volunteers to describe what is happening in each box. When the children have finished their work, check answers. Call on a volunteer to retell the story according to the numbered pictures.

As the day ends, remind children that they can be healers by helping someone who is suffering from illness or hurt feelings.

Following the Story
Number the pictures in the order that they happened in the story.

adapted from Mark 2:1-12

Jesus told the people that he had the power to forgive sins. Then he turned to the man who was paralyzed and said, "Stand up and walk home." The man got up and walked away. The people were amazed. They knew that Jesus must be God.

BLM 33: MAKING PEACE
Blackline Master 33 asks children to write sentences about ways in which they can be peaceful.

BLM 34: JESUS HEALS
On Blackline Master 34 children create a mobile containing items from the story of the man who was paralyzed.

HELPFUL HAND WREATH
Explain to the children: *We can reach out to others with helpful hands just*

Explore

DAY 1

as the friends of the man who was paralyzed helped him. Distribute construction paper to the children. Invite each child to use pencil to trace one of their hands on the construction paper. Tell them to write their name on the hand with marker. Have each child cut out his or her paper hand. Then invite the children to glue their paper hands onto a circle made of poster board or onto a plastic foam ring to form a wreath. Use a hole-punch to make two holes in the hand at the top of the wreath. Then thread a piece of ribbon through it so that the wreath can be hung. The children may wish to give the wreath as a gift to their pastor showing that the group believes in lending a helping hand to others.

✝ *Solidarity*

FRIENDS ARE IMPORTANT
Tell the children: *It's good to have friends who help and encourage us, just as the paralyzed man's friends helped him. Now we will role-play situations in which we can learn to be a good friend to someone.* Divide the children into small groups. Give each group a situation to role-play. You may wish to give these situations to more than one group, or you may wish to create other situations.

A friend is worried about a sick pet at home.

A friend at school broke an arm and has difficulty holding things.

You were invited to a party, but your friend was not.

Give the children time to practice their skits. Then have the groups perform their role-plays for everyone.

Explore

Jesus Forgives

Begin today's class by praying the Lord's Prayer with the children. Point out the line that mentions receiving and offering forgiveness.

Use the We Celebrate Reconciliation poster while discussing the Sacrament of Penance with the children.

Read the title of the section. Say: **However sinful we may be, Jesus always forgives us.** Ask a volunteer to read the first paragraph. Say: **Jesus forgives us in the Sacrament of Penance. Ask: Through whom does Jesus continue to forgive our sins?** (priests) Read the second paragraph aloud for the group. Point to the word *absolution*. Explain: **Absolution is the forgiveness God offers us in the Sacrament of Penance when we say we are sorry for our sins.**

Draw attention to the picture. Have the children describe what they see. (priest and child in face-to-face confession) Explain to the children that when they go to confession the scene will be similar.

Have volunteers read page 123 in the children's book aloud while the rest of the group follows along. Draw attention to the word *penance.* Say: **Look at the word in dark type. Remember that the word Penance with a capital P is the name of the sacrament. This penance, with a small p, is what we do to show we are turning away from sin because we want to live as God wants us to live.**

Complete the reading on pages 122 and 123 before beginning "Reading God's Word."

Reading God's Word

Read the sentence. Explain to the children that when their sins are forgiven in the Sacrament of Penance, they are saved. They are reconciled with God.

Continue: **Penance is one of the sacraments. Because we want to live as God wants us to live, we can celebrate this sacrament.** Continue: **The priest gives us a penance, or something special we are to do or say to show that we are turning away from sin.**

A guide for celebrating the Sacrament of Penance, titled How to Go to Confession, can be found at the back of the book.

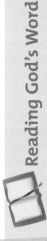

Say: **Now we will learn a song in which we celebrate Jesus' forgiveness and mercy.** Have the children turn to "Jesus, Jesus," in the Songs of Our Faith section in back of their books. Play the song on Track 15 of CD 2 as the group follows along. Then play the song again, inviting the children to sing along.

Jesus Forgives

Jesus forgave the sins of the man who could not walk. He forgives our sins too. Today Jesus does this through the priests who forgive our sins in his name.

Our sins are forgiven as the priest extends his hands over us and prays the prayer of **absolution.** The prayer ends with the words "May God grant you pardon and peace and I absolve you from your sins in the name of the Father, and of the Son, and of the Holy Spirit."

Reading God's Word

The people are given knowledge that they are saved because their sins have been forgiven.

adapted from Luke 1:77

122 God's Invitation

Did You Know?

Have a volunteer read the section aloud for the children. Ask: **What does it mean to keep something a secret?** Say: (not to tell anyone something you know) **Well, in confession the priest must keep everything he is told absolutely secret. This is very serious.**

Show the group an envelope with tape on both sides of it. Ask: **If you put a seal on a letter, what does that mean?** (that you put something on it so that it can't be opened) Say: **When the priest keeps everyone's confession a secret, it's called the seal of confession.**

As you finish, tell the children that it's a good idea to review their day before going to bed to make sure they were good followers of Jesus.

OPTION
BLM 35: THE SACRAMENT OF PENANCE

On Blackline Master 35 children order what takes place during the Sacrament of Penance.

OPTION
MAKING PEACE

Read aloud the following situations for the children, one at a time. Then ask the children how they can create peace in the situations. Allow a variety of responses.

You encourage your little brother to put his toys away. He says no and calls you bossy.

You go bike riding with a few kids in the neighborhood. A good friend from school gets angry that you didn't invite him to come along.

You are playing outside, and it starts to rain. You run into the house, dragging mud in on your shoes. Your mother becomes upset because there is mud all over the floor.

OPTION
STICKS AND STONES

Read aloud the following saying for the children: *Sticks and stones may break my bones, but words can never hurt me.* Ask: **Who has heard this saying before? Do you agree?**

Explain: *Sometimes, even though we try not to, we may hurt people with our words, and other people may hurt us with their words.* Ask: **When mean words hurt people, what are some nice words that can be used to heal the hurt?** (I'm sorry. Let's be friends again. I didn't mean it.) Say: *When others use these kinds of words to apologize, it is important to forgive them. The next time words hurt you or other people, remember how these words can heal.*

After we have confessed our sins, the priest gives us a **penance**. This is a prayer or a deed we do to make up for our sins. We tell God we want to live as his children.

The grace we receive in the Sacrament of Penance will strengthen us when we are tempted to sin. It will help us avoid sin and grow closer to God.

We leave confession knowing that we are at peace with God and with others.

Did You Know?

The priest must keep absolutely secret the sins that people have confessed to him. This is called the seal of confession.

Explore

Let It Begin with Me

Invite children to recognize God's forgiving presence in their lives by beginning with the following:

Ask children if they remember the name of the young peacemaker they read about in Session 12. (Mattie Stepanek) Ask: *What do you think was very special about Mattie?* (He forgot his own problems and wanted to help others. He was a young boy who knew how to live peaceably. He found the good in everything.) Say: *Today we will practice more situations that will help us learn how to be young peacemakers.*

Ask a volunteer to read the title aloud. See what children think "It" in the title refers to. Say: *Let's read and find out.*

Call on a child to read the first paragraph aloud. Ask: *Now what do you think "It" is?* (peace) *What are we called when we make peace with others, with God, and with the Church?* (peacemakers)

Read the next paragraph aloud. Invite volunteers to tell you in their own words what the directions tell them to do. Remind the children that since they are practicing being peaceable with all their classmates, it won't matter who is in each group. Randomly assign work groups.

How Can You Help?

Tell the groups to read and discuss among their members possible solutions to the first situation. Tell the children that each person should draw what he or she thinks is the best solution. All group members do not have to have the same solution. Walk around as groups work on the first situation, encouraging discussion and making sure they are following directions.

If all groups are working well, ask them to do the same with situations 2 and 3 on page 125. When all the children have had time to complete the activity, have a sharing time with the whole group. Encourage different peaceful endings, pointing out that there can often be more than one peaceable solution.

Let It Begin With Me

We can make peace with others, with God, and with the Church. When we do so, we are peacemakers.

The stories on these pages tell about times when people are not living in peace. Read each story with a small group. Create your own peaceful endings to the stories. Draw the endings in the empty space next to each picture.

How Can You Help?

1. Someone is teasing a child in your class because he is wearing a different kind of shirt. What would a peacemaker do?

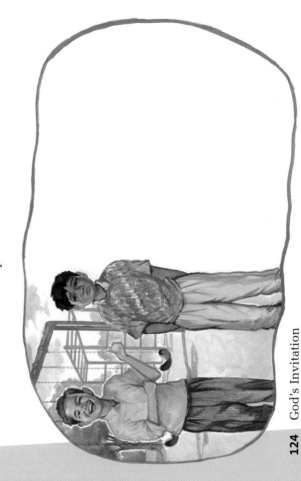

124   God's Invitation

Ask the children if working on the last situation was easier than the first. Say: ***The more practice we have being peacemakers, the easier it becomes to look for peaceful solutions and to spread peace wherever we go.***

Invite the children to write a short poem that summarizes what they have learned about forgiveness and that will serve as a reminder to be peaceful during difficult times. You might ask the children to begin by working in pairs to brainstorm a list of forgiving terms and then to write their own individual poems. Remind them that their poems can rhyme but they don't have to.

Example:
*If in peace
we want to live.
In our hearts
we must forgive.*

Poems could be shared and then put in a book that would be available in the classroom library.

Tell the children that sometimes it isn't easy to do and say the right thing. It is especially hard when others are not being peaceful. Encourage them to do what is right even if others tease them, become angry, or turn away.

End the day by having the children exchange handshakes of peace. Tell them to say to each other, while shaking hands: ***Peace be with you,*** and answering, ***And also with you.***

2. You yell at your sister for bothering you during a television show. Your sister is very upset.

3. You are playing a game with your friends. Another person comes along after the game has started. Someone says, "Go away!" What would a peacemaker do?

Unit 3, Session 13   125

OPTION

SUPER SLOGANS

Remind the children of a few memorable advertising slogans such as Coca-Cola, "The real thing" or Nike, "Just do it." Ask them to develop slogans for peace, such as "Peace works" or "Give peace a chance." Decorate the finished slogans and hang them around your classroom or in the school corridors.

Reflect

Prayer

Say: **It's our special prayer time. Know that the love of God is always in your hearts. We'll begin our prayer time by singing our song again.**

[music note] Play the song "Jesus, Jesus" on Track 15 of CD 2. The children sang the song earlier. For the words to this song, tell the children to turn to the Songs of Our Faith section at the back of their books.

Draw attention to the Act of Contrition poster, reminding the group: **We pray the Act of Contrition during the Sacrament of Penance. We can also pray it whenever we want to tell God we are sorry for something we have done and that we will try to do better with his help.**

Have the children fold their hands and close their eyes. Read the first two paragraphs in the book aloud very slowly. Then pause for 10 to 15 seconds to give the children time to respond in their hearts. Then slowly read the third paragraph. Pause for 15 seconds to allow the children time to be with Jesus.

Then say: **Now it's time to bring your attention back to the group. When you're ready, please open your eyes. Let's pray the Act of Contrition aloud together.** Draw attention to the Act of Contrition poster again. Point to the words as the children pray the prayer aloud with you.

Then say: **Always remember how much God loves you as we learn more about how we can live peacefully with others.**

PRAYER FOR PEACE

Invite the children to pray this prayer for peace with you. Ask them to respond "Lord, hear our prayer" each time after you say "we pray." Pray:

God, our Father, you created all the people of the world, we pray.
(Lord, hear our prayer.)
Help us to live in peace with our families, our neighbors, and our communities, we pray.
(Lord, hear our prayer.)
Guide us to recognize when we have sinned, we pray.
(Lord, hear our prayer.)

And help us to ask you for your forgiveness, we pray.
(Lord, hear our prayer.)
Guide us as we all work together to live as your children, your family, we pray.
(Lord, hear our prayer.)

Allow any child who wishes to add his or her own prayer to which the group will respond "Lord, hear our prayer." Then close by praying the Sign of the Cross.

[cross] *Solidarity*

Prayer

Contrition is the sadness we feel when we know we have sinned. We pray an Act of Contrition to tell God that we are sorry.

God wants us to make peace with him. He wants us to make peace with others. We ask forgiveness when we do something that is wrong.

Jesus knows what is in your heart. Know that you are safe with him. Be still and spend some time with Jesus. Listen to what Jesus wants you to know.

Living My Faith

Use the ideas below to encourage the children to put into practice the concepts learned in this session.

Faith Summary

Invite a child to read the section aloud for the group. Ask the children: *What did Jesus do for the man who could not walk?* (forgave his sins and healed his paralysis so he could walk) *In which sacrament do we receive God's forgiveness?* (Sacrament of Penance)

Words I Learned

Ask volunteers to pronounce each word. Ask other volunteers to read the definitions from the Glossary.

Ways of Being Like Jesus

Read the section aloud. Ask: *How are the mother and the child in the picture staying close to one another?* (showing their love by hugging) Ask: *What can you do to bring your family together?* (use gentle words, think about what would make the other person happy, obey parents)

✝ *Family and Community*

Respond

Words I Learned

Have a child read the section. Tell the children: *Take a few moments to think about someone in your family you need to forgive or someone you can ask to forgive you. Try to practice this forgiveness before we meet again.*

✝ *Family and Community*

Prayer

Say: *We have learned about forgiveness and the Sacrament of Penance. Let's continue to look inside ourselves, knowing that when we sin, we can ask for God's forgiveness. As children of God, let's pray this prayer together.*

Pray the prayer aloud. Then count to 10 silently, allowing time for silent reflection. Conclude: *Let's pray the Sign of the Cross.*

My Response

Read the section aloud for the children. Say: *There are many things we can do to create peace and love among our families and friends. Think about what you would like to do to be a peacemaker this week. Then write a sentence about it.*

As your time together ends, say: *We can be safe in knowing that God will always forgive us.*

Living My Faith

Faith Summary

When we celebrate the Sacrament of Penance, our sins are forgiven. We make peace with God and with others.

Words I Learned

absolution   penance

Ways of Being Like Jesus

Jesus worked to bring people together. Be a peacemaker with your family and friends.

With My Family

This week forgive a family member or ask someone to forgive you.

My Response

How will you be a peacemaker this week? Write a sentence to explain your idea.

Prayer

Thank you, God, my Father, for forgiving me. Help me to be a more peaceful child of yours.

Extending the Session

Choose from the following options to extend the session or to reinforce concepts developed during the week.

Family Involvement

Remind the children to take home the Raising Faith-Filled Kids page to share what they are learning with their families.

Preparation for Sunday Scripture Readings

Lead children in a prayerful discussion of Sunday's readings. Visit www.FindingGod.org/Sunday for more information.

Seasonal Session

Consider the time of the liturgical year and use the appropriate seasonal session. Seasonal sessions may be found on page 241.

Unused Options and BLMs

Incorporate any unused options or Blackline Masters from the week's session.

Web Site Activities

Visit www.FindingGod.org to find additional activities for extending the session.

JESUS HEALS

Play the audio scripture story "Jesus Heals" a second time and invite children to draw a picture based on the story. Encourage them to use their pictures to tell the story to family members at home.

SHARING GOD'S LOVE

Review pages 122 and 123 with the children. Then talk with them about what they might teach others about

the Sacrament of Penance. Form pairs of children and have each pair think of an aspect of the Sacrament of Penance that they might like to teach others. Have pairs meet to "teach" each other their ideas.

FRIENDS SHARE GIFTS

In advance, create several large cards that say *forgiveness, healing, loving, caring, grace* and *peace,* and tape them on the floor in a large circle. Cards can be repeated, as long as there are half as many cards as there are children. Write one set of the same words on slips of paper and place them in a bowl. Play music and have the children walk around the circle of cards. Stop the music after 10 to 15 seconds. When the music stops, have each child stand on a card with both feet. More than one child can share a card, and children may hang on to each other to stay on. Choose a slip of paper and ask children standing on the chosen word to use the word in a sentence. Take off one sign, start the music, and play again. This time, more children will have to share a sign. Play rounds, eliminating signs, until it is impossible for children to remain on any fewer signs.

RAISING FAITH-FILLED KIDS
a parent page

The Healing of the Paralytic, from the Manuscript of The Four Gospels

Focus on Faith

Jesus Forgives Us

The Gospel of Mark tells the story of the man who was paralyzed and could not reach Jesus. His friends helped him by carrying him to the top of the house where Jesus was staying, tearing open the thatched roof, and lowering the man's pallet. Jesus first forgave his sins and then told him to take up his pallet and walk. The man had dependable friends who helped him reach Jesus. Jesus helps us when we recognize our need to be forgiven of our sins. He has given us the Sacrament of Penance through which we can confess to a priest and receive absolution. Once we are forgiven and reconciled with God and one another, we can face the future with hope.

Dinnertime Conversation Starter

Like the man who was paralyzed, we often have trouble getting close to Jesus. Help your child talk about what he or she can do to stay close to Jesus.

Focus on Prayer

Your child was encouraged to live in peace. Pray with your child for a spirit of peace and forgiveness at home.

Spirituality in Action

Your child is learning that through the Sacrament of Penance we make peace with God and others. He or she is learning that God wants us to be reconciled with members of our community and our world. Notice words or actions that prevent peace or that build "walls" between people.

Discuss with your child small steps that he or she might take to be a peacemaker.

Hints for at Home

To remind your family that we can receive forgiveness for our sins, make healing bandages to use in your home. You will need plastic bandages of various sizes and shapes, permanent markers, and small stickers. Invite your child to write messages, such as *God is with me* or *Live in peace,* on the bandages with the markers. Decorate the bandages with the stickers. Use the bandages each time a skinned knee or cut finger needs care.

Catechist Preparation

Session 14: Mary Shows Us the Way

3-Minute Retreat

Before you prepare for your session, pause for a few moments and set aside any distracting thoughts. Take three deep breaths and know that God is with you as you help the children's faith grow stronger.

Luke 1:46–47

My soul proclaims the greatness of the Lord;
my spirit rejoices in God my savior.

Reflection

Filled with the grace of the Holy Spirit, Mary bursts into a song of praise during her visit with her cousin Elizabeth. Both women know of God's wonders. Elizabeth, pregnant with John the Baptist, praises Mary for her devotion to God, calling her blessed. Mary offers praise to God for his love of those who need him. Mary, Mother of God and Mother of the Church, shows us what it means to trust and love God. She was the first to accept Jesus into her life and remains a model for us today.

Questions

What moves my heart to sing praise to God or to call on him for help?
How can I develop a habit of gratitude and praise to God?

Prayer

Pray to our Father using Mary's words of praise or your own.

My soul proclaims the greatness of the Lord;
my spirit rejoices in God my Savior.

Take a few moments to reflect prayerfully before you prepare this session.

Knowing and Sharing Your Faith

Scripture and Tradition in Session 14

All of the popes of the 20th century proclaimed something wonderful about Mary. Pope Paul VI declared her the Mother of the Church. Just as mothers give birth, nourish, and educate their children, so does Mary guide our spiritual birth and development. She unceasingly prays to Jesus on our behalf and provides us with an example of how to live a holy life.

Mary's holiness was the result not only of a special gift from God but also of her continuous and generous cooperation with the action of the Holy Spirit. We contemplate Mary admiringly, Pope Paul VI said, because she was "firm in her faith, ready in her obedience, simple in humility, exulting in praising the Lord, ardent in charity, strong and constant in the fulfillment of her mission." ("Signum Magnum: Letter on the Blessed Virgin Mary," May 13, 1967)

Scripture in Session 14

The visit of Mary to Elizabeth is recounted in **Luke 1:39–55.**
Luke 2:19 describes Mary's response to the events surrounding Jesus' birth.

Mary visits Elizabeth.

Mary reflects on Jesus' birth.

Let the scripture and Tradition deepen your understanding of the content in this session.

WINDOW ON THE CATECHISM

The prayer of the Virgin Mary, the Magnificat, is discussed in *CCC 2617–2619.* The Visitation is treated in *CCC 717.* The Hail Mary is explored in *CCC 2676–2679.*

The Visitation, Mariotto Albertinelli

Catechist Preparation

From the Richness of the Tradition

The Fathers of the Second Vatican Council decided to place the teachings about Mary within the context of their treatment of the Church. Pope Paul VI, who played a major role in the council, pointed out the significance of this ecclesial perspective on Mary. The action of the Church in the world, he wrote, parallels Mary's concern for others, and her active love finds its extension "in the Church's concern for people in lowly circumstances and for the poor and weak, and in her constant commitment to peace and social harmony." When Christians show their love for others by working for justice and peace, they show themselves to be children of Mary and followers of Jesus. ("Marialis Cultus: Apostolic Exhortation for the Right Ordering and Development of Devotion to the Blessed Virgin Mary," February 2, 1974.)

Consider in this session how you will invite the children to respond to and prayerfully reflect on God's invitation to love and serve others.

GENERAL DIRECTORY FOR CATECHESIS

Mary's role as a model for catechetical renewal is explored in *GDC* 291.

Prayer in Session 14

In the opening prayer of petition and the closing prayer of thanks, we seek guidance in following Mary's example. In this session the children also review the Hail Mary, asking Mary the Mother of God and the Mother of the Church to intercede for them. They are also introduced to Mary's song of praise, the Magnificat, in the Reflect step.

✝ Catholic Social Teaching

In this session the following Catholic Social Teaching themes are explored:

- **Option for the Poor and Vulnerable**
- **Solidarity**

Catechist Preparation: Get-Ready Guide

Session 14: Mary Shows Us the Way

Session Theme: *Mary is the great example of what it means to obey God.*

Before This Session

- Find a picture of your mother or someone who took care of you and bring it to the session for use on page 129.
- Bookmark your Bible to Luke 1:39–55 and Luke 2:19. Place the Bible in the prayer center open to the first passage from Luke.
- Set up the CD player so you will be ready to play the reflective music. Listen to it ahead of time.

Steps

		Outcomes *At the end of the session, the children should be able to*
DAY 1	**Engage** page 129	• appreciate people who help us in difficult times.
	Mary Shows Us the Way	
DAYS 1–3	**Explore** pages 130–135	• retell the story of Mary visiting her cousin Elizabeth.
	Mary Visits Elizabeth	• identify the Magnificat as Mary's prayer of praise.
	Mother of the Church	• explain that we call Mary the Mother of the Church.
	Mary Teaches Us	• define the word *Magnificat*.
	Saint Bernadette	
DAY 4	**Reflect** page 136	• prayerfully reflect on God's presence, his invitation, and our response.
	Prayer: Hail Mary	• pray the Hail Mary.
DAY 4	**Respond** page 137	• identify practical ways to act on God's invitation in everyday living.
	Living My Faith: Ways to Help One Person This Week	
DAY 5	**Extending the Session** page 138	
	Day 5 offers an opportunity to extend the session with activities that reinforce the session outcomes.	

Materials

Required Materials

- Bible
- Writing paper, pens, pencils
- Art materials, such as drawing paper, crayons, markers, scissors, glue
- A picture of your mother or someone who took care of you (page 129)
- CD 2, Track 2: Reflective music (page 129)
- CD 2, Reflective music (page 136)

Optional Materials

- Globe or map of the United States (page 131)
- Rosary (page 131)
- Construction paper (page 138)
- Blackline Masters 36, 37 (pages 131, 132)
- Blackline Master 38, staples, stapler (page 132)

e-resources

www.FindingGod.org

Mary Shows Us the Way

Engage DAY 1

You may wish to quietly play the instrumental version of "Song of Love" (CD 2, Track 2) as the children rest in the knowledge that God loves them.

Bring in a picture of your mother, an aunt, or a grandmother. Show the picture to the children and tell them a story of something you and she did together. You may then want to ask: **What kinds of things do you do with your mother, aunt, or grandmother?** Explain: **Jesus'** mother, Mary, loved and cared for him deeply. She also loves us. **Today we will learn more about Mary and her love for us.**

Have the children open their books to page 129 and describe what they see in the pictures. Ask: **In what ways are the people helping one another?**

Read the title. Then read the questions aloud, one at a time. Encourage the children to respond to the questions. Ask: **Who usually helps you when you need help?** Call on volunteers to respond. Explain: **Mary is always ready to help us. She prays for us so that we will be open to all that God** offers us. **She was open to God and can help us be the same way.**

Prayer

Say: **Mary loved God and was obedient to him. Let's pray to God now and ask him to help us learn from Mary's example.**

Reverently pray the prayer. Then say: **God is with you. You can talk to him about anything you'd like. Spend some time talking to him. Ask for his help as you learn more about Mary.**

Give the children time for reflection. Count to 10 as they enjoy their silent time. End the quiet time by praying **Amen.**

Mary Shows Us the Way

Session 14

When do you need help with something in your life? Is there a subject in school that is difficult? Who usually helps you?

Prayer

God, my Heavenly Father, teach me about Mary so that I may learn to follow her example.

OPTION

PRAISING WOMEN

Remind the children: **Catholics around the world honor Mary.** Then say: **Take a moment to think about a special woman in your life and the things that she does for you.** Pause for 10 seconds to allow the children to think. Then ask: **What are some ways in which we can honor the special women in our lives?** (say "please" and "thank you" to Mom, send Grandmother a greeting card, take cookies to our teacher) Encourage a variety of responses. Then encouragingly say: **Try your best to do at least one special thing for a special woman in your life.**

Mary Visits Elizabeth

Ask: *Whom do you talk to when you have really important news to share?* (parents, friend) Explain: *When Mary had special news, she told her cousin Elizabeth. You might share your good news in person, by phone, or by e-mail. Mary had to travel a long way, riding on a donkey to tell Elizabeth her good news. Now we'll learn about this visit.*

Read the title. Explain: *After Mary learned that she was to be the mother of Jesus, she went to visit Elizabeth to share the news. In this story we will learn about their special visit.*

Draw attention to the illustration and ask the group to describe it. (Mary and others traveling by donkey to see Elizabeth, shepherd with sheep, trees, a woman carrying a water jar)

Have a child read the first two paragraphs. Ask: *What did Elizabeth call Mary?* (blessed) Say: *We use this word today to praise Mary. We say it in the prayer the Hail Mary, which you learned last year.* Ask: *Does anyone remember the part of the Hail Mary where we use the word blessed?* ("blessed are you among women")

Pray the Hail Mary together. If necessary, the children can find the words to the prayer in the Prayers to Take to Heart section at the back of their books.

Read the last paragraph. Explain: *Mary wanted Elizabeth and all of us to know that all praise belongs to God. Mary was grateful for all God had done for her and had given to her.*

Ask: *What is something God has given you?* (a healthy body, a home to live in, a good parent) Invite volunteers to share their responses.

You might begin the discussion by sharing what God has done for you. Then continue reading the last lines of the adaptation from Luke on the next page.

Read the final paragraph on page 131. Pronounce the word *Magnificat* (mag nif´i kät´; -kat´) for the children and invite them to repeat it. Explain: *The Magnificat is a special song of praise that Mary offered to God.* Explain: *Mary praised God for all he had done for her. God did a wonderful thing for her in choosing her to be Jesus' mother, and she offered words of thanks for this.*

Ask the group: *What can we learn about God by looking at his choice of Mary?* (He looks at what we are like as people. He doesn't look at the number of our possessions.)

✝ *The Poor and Vulnerable*

Draw attention to the illustration on page 131. Have the children describe what they see. (Mary and Elizabeth sitting at a table together, both look happy)

Then ask: *What kinds of things do you do when you are with your friend? How do you feel when you are together?* Say: *That's how Mary and Elizabeth felt when they were together.*

Mary Visits Elizabeth

The angel Gabriel told Mary that she was going to be the mother of Jesus. Soon after that, Mary went to visit her cousin Elizabeth.

Elizabeth was very happy to see Mary. She praised Mary for her love of God. She called her blessed.

Mary said to Elizabeth, "God is great. He is my Savior. All people will call me blessed. God has done great things for me."

130 God's Invitation

Did You Know?

Ask a child to read the section aloud. Explain: *Catholics through-out the world honor Mary.* Invite the children to share any individual cultural experiences of Mary in which they may have participated. (Example: the feast of Our Lady of Guadalupe) Say: *People around the world have read the same Bible stories of Mary that we have. Everyone calls her blessed as Elizabeth said they would.*

✝ Solidarity

End today by encouraging the children to be a blessing to their classmates and families.

Did You Know?

Catholics around the world honor Mary.

These words that Mary used to praise God have become a special prayer. Catholics call this prayer the **Magnificat**.

Then Mary said, "God's name is holy. His mercy will last forever."

adapted from Luke 1:39-55

Unit 3, Session 14   **131**

OPTION

BLM 36: ALL ARE WELCOME

Blackline Master 36 is a multiple-choice activity covering vocabulary words from Unit 3.

OPTION

VISITING FAMILY AND FRIENDS

Remind the group: *Mary traveled to visit Elizabeth to tell her the good news.* Ask: *Whom have you traveled to visit?* Hold up a globe or map of the United States and have the children name or point out states they may have visited or would like to visit. Then ask: *How did you get there? How long did it take?* Remind the children: *It took Mary a long time to travel to Elizabeth's home, but the trip was worth the effort so she could share her good news.*

OPTION

PRAYING THE ROSARY

Explain to the children: *When we pray the Rosary, we praise God and honor Mary. We pray the Sign of the Cross, the Glory Be to the Father, the Lord's Prayer, and the Hail Mary.*

Then display a Rosary. Say: *The Rosary is organized in decades (sets of 10). We pray the Hail Mary on each bead in the group of 10.* Divide the children into two groups and have them pray one decade of the Rosary with you. Have the first group pray: *Hail Mary, full of grace, the Lord is with you. Blessed are you among women, and blessed is the fruit of your womb, Jesus.* Then have the second group pray: *Holy Mary, Mother of God, pray for us sinners, now and at the hour of our death. Amen.*

This might be a good time to remind the children of the additional information on The Rosary at the backs of their books.

Session 14   **131**

Explore

Poem of Praise

Invite the children to stand, fold their hands, and pray the Hail Mary together. When they have finished, remind children that we praise people for something good that they have done. Ask them why Mary deserves our praise. Their responses will vary. Read the title and directions aloud. Call on volunteers to read the words in the box. Say: **Each of these words will be used one time in the poem. In a poem a paragraph has a special name—stanza.**

Read the first stanza. Tell the children to fill in the blank with a word from the box. Then read the second stanza. Have the children fill in the blank. Finally, read the last stanza and have the children write the correct word in the blank. Then review the responses. Read the poem aloud as a group. Have all the girls read the first stanza together, the boys read the second stanza, and the entire group read the last stanza. Encourage them to read with expression.

BLM 37: HONORING MARY

Blackline Master 37 asks children to color a picture of Mary and take it home to hang in a special place.

BLM 38: YOUR BOOK OF MARY

On Blackline Master 38 children create a book honoring Mary to take home to their families.

SPECIAL WOMEN

Tell the children: *Mary is a very special woman in our faith. We can pray to her and ask her for help. Think of women in your lives who are important to you and who help you. They could include your mother, grandmother, aunt, cousin, teacher, friend, or neighbor. Draw a picture of them. Above the picture write their names, and below the picture write why they are special to you.*

As the children work, ask each one individually whom he or she is drawing and why.

Poem of Praise

You should praise God as Mary did. Use the words in the box to complete this poem of praise.

Jesus	name	way

Mary praised God,
And we do the same,
For he is our Savior,
And holy is his _____ name _____.

Through actions and words,
Mary shows us the _____ way _____
To share God's great love,
With one another each day.

If we obey God,
As Mary shows us,
We stay with the Father
And his Son, _____ Jesus _____.

132   God's Invitation

Mother of the Church

Invite the children to name places where they have seen statues of Mary. (at church, at home, on lawns) Say: *Mary is very important to the Church. We display statues of her to honor her and to remind us that she is close to us.*

Draw attention to the photograph. Have the children describe what they see. (stained-glass window of Mary praying)

Ask a volunteer to read the title and first paragraph. Say: *Mary is the mother of Jesus and is our mother. She has the special* role of being the Mother of the Church. Explain: Read the second paragraph. Say: *The Church is the followers of Jesus around the world.*

Have a child read the third paragraph. Say: *We are the Church because we are Jesus' followers. So when we say Mary is the Mother of the Church, we are saying Mary is our mother.*

Read the final paragraph. Say: *Just as God gave Mary grace to be the mother of his Son, Jesus, so he gives us the grace we need to be his children. Remember to thank God often for his great gifts.*

Mother of the Church

Like Mary, the Church has a special relationship with God.

The Church is made up of people who are called by God. The Church shows the world how much God loves them. God loves everyone.

Mary is the Mother of the Church. She received God's help so she could follow him.

God gives us the same help, or grace. Mary prays for us so that we will listen to God.

Reading God's Word

Mary remembered all these things and kept them always in her heart.

adapted from Luke 2:19

Unit 3, Session 14   **133**

Explore   DAY 2

Reading God's Word

Read the Scripture verse aloud. Ask: *What are some of Mary's experiences that you think she kept in her heart?* (visit from the angel Gabriel telling her she would be the mother of Jesus, visiting Elizabeth, praising God in the Magnificat, the birth of Jesus)

Tell the children: *Take a moment to think of Mary and all the experiences she treasured and kept in her heart.*

OPTION
MOTHER MAY I

Play a modified version of Mother May I with the group. Have the children line up in a straight line. You can be mother and ask the children a question about Mary. The child who answers can take a step forward. Continue to ask questions about Mary and allow the children who answer to move forward. See who will reach you first! Here are possible questions:

Who is the mother of Jesus? (Mary)
What was the name of Mary's cousin? (Elizabeth)
How did Mary get to Elizabeth's home? (traveling on donkey with a caravan)
Who is Jesus' mother? (Mary)
Who told Mary that she would be Jesus' mother? (the angel Gabriel)
Who is Mary's husband? (the angel Gabriel) (Joseph)
What prayer do we pray to honor Mary? (Hail Mary)
What song of praise did Mary pray when she visited Elizabeth? (the Magnificat)

FYI
STAINED GLASS HONORING MARY

The Church interprets the image of Mary stepping on a snake as a reference to Genesis 3:15, which refers to the first promise of a savior. The half-moon in the artwork is a reference to Revelation 12:1, which the Church interprets as an image of Mary in heaven.

Session 14   **133**

Mary Teaches Us

Remind the children that we can find God's presence in the simplest things. Begin with the following:

Invite the children to play a game of mind pictures with you. Tell them you will say a word or phrase and they should picture it in their minds. Say that you will then call on a volunteer to describe their mind picture for the group. Suggest that they close their eyes and put their imaginations to work.

Say the word *apple*. Invite volunteers to describe their mind picture. Ask others to do the same when you say *shiny, red, delicious apple* and *rotten, half-eaten apple on the ground.* Discuss the different images, eliciting from the children that the describing words changed their picture of the apple.

Do a few other examples, including descriptions of people that tell what they are like inside as well as physical characteristics. Children may wish to suggest descriptions too.

Say: *Today we'll be thinking of some qualities to describe Mary.*

Ask a volunteer to read the title and the first paragraph aloud. Ask: *How did Mary obey God?* (by listening and trusting him)

Have someone else read the next paragraph. Ask: *Can someone read aloud the sentence that tells what Mary does for us?* (She prays for us so we will love God.)

Describe Mary

Read the title and the directions for the children. Say: *We're going to read some describing words, the kind of words we might have used in our game.*

Tell the children you will read each column of words slowly. Ask them to point to each word as you read it. Start with the "m" words and read all four columns. See if the children can figure out why there are "m" words, "a" words, and so on. Ask the children to look up at you and spell the name *Mary.*

Direct the children's attention to the lines on which they will write their words. Reread the "m" words and have the children write their choice. Ask volunteers to tell their words. Many will probably choose *mother,* but point out that all three words would be appropriate. Stress that there are no wrong answers. They should choose the words that match their mind pictures of Mary.

Reread the other three columns, pausing after each for the children to write their words. Then have a sharing time for children to read their four-word descriptions.

Mary Teaches Us

Mary shows us what it means to obey God. She listened to God and trusted him.

Mary loves God. She prays for us so we will love God.

Describe Mary

Use each letter in Mary's name to write a word that describes her. Choose from the words below.

marvelous	admired	ready	youthful
magnificent	awesome	radiant	young
mother	able	real	youth

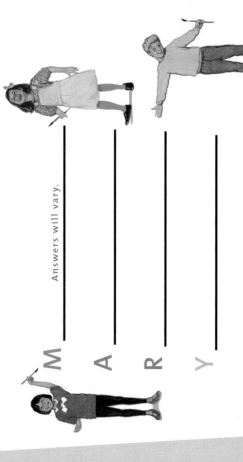

M _____

A _____

R _____

Y _____

Answers will vary.

Saint Bernadette

Tell the children that they are going to learn about a saint who had a great love for Mary. Read the title and ask the children to look at the top picture on page 135, which is a picture of Bernadette.

Have a volunteer read the first paragraph aloud. Ask: ***Where did Bernadette live?*** (France) ***What else did you learn about her?*** (She was sick as a child. Her family was not rich.)

Ask someone to read the second paragraph to the children. Ask: ***What happened when Bernadette was 14 years old?***

(The Virgin Mary appeared to her.) Explain: ***Bernadette could see Mary, but no one else could see her.*** Ask: ***What did Mary tell Bernadette to do?*** (drink from a stream) ***What happened?*** (A stream appeared where there had been none.)

Read the last paragraph. Ask: ***What do people do when they visit this holy place?*** (bathe in the water from the stream) ***What has happened to some people?*** (With Mary's help, they have been healed of their illnesses.) Explain: ***They believe and trust that God will cure them when Mary asks for God's help on their behalf.***

Recall with the children the poems and prayers of praise they have read this week. Say: ***Mary shows us how to praise and thank God for his gifts to us. Let's see if we can follow her example and praise God in prayer.***

On the board write *I praise God for ___* and *I thank God for ___.* Ask children to write their own prayer of praise by copying each of the sentence beginnings and completing them with their own ideas. Have a sharing time for those who would like to read theirs aloud.

Explore

Draw attention to the remaining pictures and have the children describe what they see. Then read the captions.

Remind the children: ***Just as God chose Mary for the person she was inside and not for her possessions, he chose Bernadette, whose wealth was in her goodness and not in riches.***

Saint Bernadette

Saint Bernadette was born in France a long time ago. Bernadette was ill and weak as a child. Her family was not rich.

Bernadette lived an ordinary life until she was 14 years old. At that time the Virgin Mary appeared to her. Mary told Bernadette to drink from a stream. There was no stream at first, but water soon appeared.

Many people still visit this holy place. They bathe in the water from the stream. Some have been healed of their illnesses with Mary's help. They are healed because Mary is with them in a special way.

Many people visit the holy place where Mary appeared to Bernadette.

Some people have been healed with Mary's help.

FYI

SAINT BERNADETTE OF LOURDES

Bernadette was born in Lourdes, France, in 1844, the oldest of six children in a very poor family. The Virgin Mary appeared to her on numerous occasions. When Bernadette asked Mary who she was, Mary replied, "I am the Immaculate Conception." During one of her appearances Mary encouraged praying the Rosary and doing penance for the conversion of sinners. Despite the doubt of others, Bernadette persisted in her belief in Mary, and eventually a chapel was built on the site as Mary had requested. Bernadette joined a religious order of sisters and died in 1879 at the age of 35. Her feast day is April 16.

Reflect

Prayer

Since Mary is the Mother of the Church and our mother, we can talk to her as a child talks to his or her mother. Ask: *What are the people doing in front of the statue of Mary?* (honoring Mary) Continue: *Do you have a statue of Mary at home? If you do, you can pray there and ask Mary to help you.* If there is a statue of Mary in your church or on your parish grounds, tell the children where it is and encourage them to look for it.

Say: *It's time for our special prayer time. During our prayer today we'll think about Mary. Take three deep breaths and then be still.*

As you lead the children in prayer, softly play the reflective music at the end of CD 2.

Continue: *Mary, the mother of the Church, loves each of us. She is our mother and she wants us to be close to God and to her Son, Jesus. Let's take some time to think about Mary and the special place she has in our hearts. Please close your eyes, fold your hands, and listen quietly as I read this page.*

Softly and lovingly read the reflection, pausing for 10 to 15 seconds after each paragraph. Then softly pray *Amen* and ask the children to open their eyes when they are ready. Close by inviting the children to pray the Hail Mary together. End by saying: *As we remember Mary in our hearts, let's try to follow her example every day.*

OPTION

MEMORIZING THE HAIL MARY

Group the children into pairs. Have them work together to help each other commit the Hail Mary to memory. Tell them to refer to page 278 if they need help with the words.

FYI

THE MAGNIFICAT

The Magnificat is Mary's song of thanksgiving and praise for what God did for her. In her, the poor and the lowly were lifted up. The might of God was seen in his concern for their troubles.

The word *Magnificat* is Latin and means "to magnify or give praise." It comes from the words of Mary's song in Luke 1:46–55. Another name for the Magnificat is the Canticle of Mary. A canticle is a song of praise found in the Bible that is not one of the psalms. The Canticle of Mary has a special place in our prayer life because it comes from the gospels. It is sung daily in the Church's Evening Prayer.

✝ *The Poor and Vulnerable*

Prayer

Mary had the courage and love to do what God asked her to do. In your imagination go to Mary and talk with her about saying yes to God. Ask her what it was like for her to do this.

Tell her it is not always easy for you to say yes to God. Stay with Mary for a while. Pray together to God to help you say yes too.

136   My Response

Living My Faith

The suggested activities below help the children apply the main concepts of the session.

Faith Summary

Read this section aloud for the children. Ask: **Who called Mary blessed?** (Elizabeth) **What is the name of the prayer that is made up of the words that Mary used to praise God?** (the Magnificat)

Word I Learned

Choose a volunteer to pronounce and define the word. Have someone look up the word in the Glossary to verify its definition. Call on another volunteer to use the word in a sentence.

Ways of Being Like Jesus

Invite a volunteer to read the section. Ask: **How can we honor Mary?** (pray to her, love Jesus, treat others well)

Faith Summary

Elizabeth called Mary blessed. We honor Mary in a special prayer called the Magnificat.

Word I Learned

Magnificat

Ways of Being Like Jesus

Jesus loved his mother very much. You are like Jesus when you honor Mary.

With My Family

Talk with family members about ways to honor Mary in your home.

Living My Faith

Prayer

Thank you, God, for the example of Mary. Help me say yes to you.

My Response

What can you do this week to show your love for Mary, our Mother?

Respond

With My Family

Read the section. Ask: **What is the child in the picture doing?** (placing flowers near a picture of Mary) **Why is the child doing this?** (to honor Mary) **How can your family honor Mary in your home?** (pray the Hail Mary, pray the Rosary, keep a special picture or statue of Mary in your home)

✝ *Solidarity*

Prayer

Explain: *We have learned that Mary wanted to do what God asked her. She wants us to do the same. She praised God for all he had done for her. Now we'll thank God for the example of Mary and ask for his help in being open to him. Pray this prayer of thanks with me. Then continue to tell God what is in your heart.*

Pray the prayer aloud. Then take two or three deep breaths, giving the children time to be with God. End the quiet time by praying *Amen.*

My Response

Read the section. Say: *Mary loved God very much. It is important that we try to be like her. Think about how you can be like Mary this week. Then draw a picture of what you will do.*

When they have finished, call on volunteers to explain how they will show love for Mary. Say: *As we finish up today, know in your hearts that Mary will watch over you as you try to be a helpful person.*

Choose from the following options to extend the session or to reinforce concepts developed during the week.

Family Involvement

Remind the children to take home the Raising Faith-Filled Kids page to share what they are learning with their families.

Preparation for Sunday Scripture Readings

Lead children in a prayerful discussion of Sunday's readings. Visit www.FindingGod.org/Sunday for more information.

Seasonal Session

Consider the time of the liturgical year and use the appropriate seasonal session. Seasonal sessions may be found on page 241.

Unused Options and BLMs

Incorporate any unused options or Blackline Masters from the week's session.

Web Site Activities

Visit www.FindingGod.org to find additional activities for extending the session.

MEET MARY

Arrange to take the children to church to "meet Mary." Invite them to search stained glass, statues, mosaics, paintings, and other artwork to find representations of Mary. Encourage children to talk about what they notice. Then invite each child to enter a pew and talk to Mary silently, using the words of the Hail Mary or words of their own.

MOTHERS

Form small groups of children. Ask each group to work together to create a list of character traits that an excellent mother has, such as patience, kindness, love, and so on. Invite each group to share their list with the class. Then guide the children to see that Mary was all those things to Jesus, and in many ways, is the same kind of mother for us.

I CHOOSE YOU AS A FRIEND

Have each child write his or her name in the center of a piece of construction paper. On the top of their paper, have them write *I choose you as a friend because you're . . .* Then have each child stand behind a desk that is not his or her own. Ask the children to write a describing word or phrase about the person whose name is on the paper in front of them, such as *funny, smart, cool, honest,* and so on. Have children move from paper to paper, until each child has written something kind about every other child.

Focus on Faith
a parent page

Incontro di Maria, Mariotto Albertinelli

Supporting One Another

We all need the help of others to become the people God wants us to be. After Mary said yes to becoming the mother of Jesus, she received love and support from her cousin Elizabeth. When Elizabeth saw Mary, Elizabeth shouted in joy and considered herself blessed that Mary came to visit her. Mary responded in joy with the Magnificat, her song of thanks to God. Elizabeth affirmed Mary and supported her faith in God. In the same way, we are called to support one another's faith. As parents we have the special responsibility to support our children's faith. We begin doing this by creating a positive environment in which their faith can grow.

Dinnertime Conversation Starter

Conduct a mental treasure hunt with your family. One by one, think of the rooms in your home. Are there statues, pictures, books, or crosses that identify your home as Catholic? What can be done to create a more Catholic environment?

In Our Parish

With your pastor's permission ask families to decorate bulletin boards in the church to honor Mary. Families might work together to create small works of art to show their reverence for Mary.

Spirituality in Action

Mary provides us with an example of how God loves the less fortunate in a special way. He looked beyond "his handmaid's lowliness" and lifted her up. When we assist the poor, we are acting as God calls us to act. Anything we do for them, we do for God.

With your child establish a special box containing items that your family can donate to a shelter in your community. Place things such as mittens, hats, socks, toothpaste, toys, and books into the box and donate the contents from time to time throughout the year.

Focus on Prayer

Your child has reflected on Luke 1:46–55, which contains the words of the Magnificat. Mary praised God for the great things he had done for her. Talk with your child about ways in which God has blessed your family.

Session 15: Unit 3 Review
3-Minute Retreat

Before you prepare for your session, pause for a few moments and focus inward. Breathe in deeply and count to 10. Exhale, relax, and recognize that you are in the loving presence of God as you help the children grow closer to Jesus.

Luke 19:10

For the Son of Man has come to seek and to save what was lost.

Reflection

In the story of Zacchaeus from the Gospel of Luke, Jesus dines with Zacchaeus, a man lost to greed and sin. After Zacchaeus's change of heart, Jesus states his mission to reconcile those who are lost to sin. The Body of Christ, the Church, continues this mission of reconciliation through the Sacrament of Penance. We turn to this sacrament to restore peace to our relationship with God and others. We also have the example of Mary who lived a life free from sin. Her continual choice to say yes to the will of God is a model of grace and obedience.

Questions

What does the decision of Zacchaeus challenge me to do in my life?
How does the example of Mary give me guidance and inspiration?

Prayer

Prayerfully speak to Jesus, using these words or words of your own.

Lord, you see me and love me wherever I am. Find me when I am hiding and save me when I am lost.

Take a few moments to reflect prayerfully before you prepare this session.

Catechist Preparation: Get-Ready Guide

Session 15: Unit 3 Review

Unit Theme: *All Are Welcome*

Before This Session

- If you completed the prayer tablecloth option during an earlier session, use it to cover your prayer table. Bookmark your Bible to Psalm 51:3–4. If possible, display a statue of Mary on the prayer table before the Prayer Service begins.
- Set up the CD player so you will be ready to play the reflective music for the Prayer Service.
- If you choose to do the Vocabulary Quiz option on page 141, come up with your sentences ahead of time.
- Invite a priest to speak with your class if you intend to do the Visiting With a Priest option on page 141.

Outcomes *In this session, the children will review*

- the ways we are members of one community of faith.
- how the sacraments help us stay close to God.
- Jesus' calling us to a relationship with God and others.
- the Sacrament of Penance and how it reconciles us with God and others.
- the ways Mary teaches us to obey God.
- how to prayerfully reflect on God's invitation in everyday living.
- practical ways to act on God's invitation in everyday living.

Steps

DAY 1 Engage page 139
Review

DAYS 2-3 Explore pages 140–142
Faith Summary
God's Community

DAY 4 Reflect page 143
Prayer Service: We Ask Mary to Pray for Us

DAY 4 Respond page 144
Living My Faith: Ways to Open Our Hearts to Forgiveness

Materials

Required Materials

- Bible
- Writing paper, pens, pencils
- Art materials, such as drawing paper, crayons, markers, scissors, glue
- Yarn, hole punch (page 140)
- Washable marker (page 144)
- CD 2, Track 1: Song of Love (4:00) (page 141)
- CD 2, Reflective music (page 143)

Optional Materials

- Ball of yarn (page 139)
- 11-by-17-inch paper (page 142)
- Parish bulletins (page 142)
- Blackline Master 39—Unit 3 Show What You Know (pages 139, 140)

e-resources

www.FindingGod.org

Review

Remind the children of the song "I Love Jesus," which they have sung in previous sessions to the tune of "London Bridge Is Falling Down." Sing these new verses. Invite the group to join you.

Jesus offered love to all,
love to all, love to all.
Jesus offered love to all,
and I love Jesus!
Jesus forgave everyone,
everyone, everyone.
Jesus forgave everyone,
and I love Jesus!

Jesus loves us from his heart,
from his heart, from his heart.
Jesus loves us from his heart,
and I love Jesus!

Have the children turn to page 139. Read the title and the first paragraph aloud. Draw attention to the first picture and have the children describe what they see. Say: **When we love and care for one another, we are acting as Jesus would.**

Show What You Know

Distribute BLM 39, Unit 3 Show What You Know, to the children. Explain that it will help the children see how well they understand what was taught.

Review

Session 15

Through the Church we are part of a community. The sacraments keep us close to God and to one another.

Prayer

Jesus, my model of goodness, guide me to seek forgiveness for my sins so that I may remain close to you.

Engage

DAY 1

When the children have finished, ask them to exchange papers and help them correct the objective section. Allow time for them to look over their own corrected papers before collecting the papers. Review the short-answer and self-assessment items. Provide written feedback and identify concepts needing attention. Use this information as you continue the Review on Day 2.

Prayer

Say: **We have learned that when we pray, we grow closer to Jesus. Please pray along with me.**

Slowly pray the prayer aloud with the children. Then say: **Please sit quietly and fold your hands. Close your eyes while I pray the prayer again. Then be still and tell Jesus anything else you'd like him to know.**

Pray the prayer aloud slowly and with feeling. Pause and count to five silently. End the quiet time by praying **Amen** and telling the children to open their eyes.

OPTION

COMMUNITY WEB

If possible, have the children sit in a circle, preferably on the floor. Have one child hold one end of a ball of yarn and then gently toss it to another child. That child then holds onto a piece of the yarn and throws the ball to someone else. Have them continue to do this many times until a web forms. Explain: **Even though each of us is an individual, we are connected by this community web and are all a part of one other! The Church is a community. We are all connected to one another.**

Faith Summary

Say: *Let's take a moment to ask the Holy Spirit to guide us as we continue our review.*

Show What You Know

Return the assessment, BLM 39, to the children. Review the short-answer questions and any concepts the children did not fully understand.

Read the title aloud. Explain that each of the paragraphs on this page summarizes one of the previous sessions. Ask the group: *Which parable reminds us that we can grow strong, happy, and healthy by staying close to Jesus?* (parable of the vine) Tell the group to read the first paragraph silently. Then congratulate the children for answering the question correctly.

Ask: *Which Bible story told us about a man who climbed a tree to see Jesus?* (the story of Zacchaeus) Have the children read the second paragraph to see if they answered correctly.

Now ask: *In which sacrament do we make peace with God and others?* (Sacrament of Penance) Read the third paragraph to check the answer.

Then ask: *Who is the Mother of God and helps us obey God?* (Mary) Read the final paragraph to check the answer.

Say enthusiastically: *As you know, many Bible stories tell us about Jesus and his loving ways.* Then invite volunteers to explain which of the unit's Bible stories was their favorite. Give them time to look back through previous sessions.

Keeping God Close

Read the activity title and directions. Say: *We'll make a wristband to wear. Whenever we look at it, we'll be reminded that God is great!* Distribute yarn. Give the children time to create wristbands.

As the children finish, punch holes at the ends of their bands. Help them put the yarn through the holes and tie the bands around their wrists.

Say: *Wherever you go today, with your wristband you will be spreading the message that God is great.*

MARY HAD A LITTLE LAMB

Divide the class into small groups. Tell them that they will make up a song to the tune of "Mary Had a Little Lamb." Everyone's song will begin with the same lines. They are to come up with a final line to the song.

This is what I learned this month,
Learned this month,
Learned this month,
This is what I learned this month,
(children fill in last line)

They can look on page 140 for ideas. For example, the last line could be "Jesus healed the sick man." After the groups have had time to come up with their last line, invite each one to sing its song.

Faith Summary

Jesus shared the parable of the vine to remind us that he wants us to remain close to him. Jesus comes to us in the sacraments.

Jesus forgave Zacchaeus his sins. He became a friend to Zacchaeus. Jesus does the same for us in the Sacrament of Penance.

The Church celebrates the Sacrament of Penance with us. When we celebrate the sacrament, we make peace with God and one another.

Mary shows us how to say yes to God.

Keeping God Close

Color and cut out the wristband.
Tie it on.

God Is Great

Explore

Vocabulary Word Puzzle

Say: *Everything we do can be an act of praise for God. So let's praise him by continuing our review. On this page we'll do a puzzle and a fill-in-the-blank activity to help us review some of the vocabulary words that describe the Sacrament of Penance.*

Read the activity title and directions aloud. Emphasize to the children that they should complete this in two steps: fill in the missing letters of the words in the box and then write the words on the lines at the bottom.

Have them first fill in the letters in the words in the box. Call on volunteers to share their answers.

Have the children begin completing the sentences. Slowly read the first sentence while the group follows along. Then give the group time to fill in the answer. Remind them that the answer is one of the words in the box. When they have finished with the first sentence, tell them to do the rest. When the children finish, ask volunteers to share their answers, and ask them to spell the words.

♫ 💿 Now take time to play CD 2, Track 1: "Song of Love." Ask the children to sing along with you. If necessary, the children can find the words in the Songs of Our Faith section at the back of their books.

OPTION
VISITING WITH A PRIEST

Invite a priest to talk with the children about the Sacrament of Penance and the act of going to confession. What will the children see? What will they do? How can they prepare? Encourage the children to listen carefully and ask the priest any questions they would like. This might be done in the reconciliation room of the church.

OPTION
VOCABULARY QUIZ

On the board, list vocabulary words from the unit. Then play a quiz game. Give the children a definition and see if they can figure out which word it goes with. For example:

This is a serious choice to turn away from God.
(mortal sin)

This is a choice we make that weakens our relationship with God or others.
(venial sin)

These are the special things we do to celebrate each sacrament.
(rites)

This is the way we find ourselves acting because God is alive in us.
(Fruits of the Holy Spirit)

This is thinking about what we have said or done that may have hurt our friendship with God or with other people.
(examination of conscience)

This is the forgiveness God gives us in the Sacrament of Penance.
(absolution)

Vocabulary Word Puzzle

Fill in the missing letters to spell words you learned in Unit 3. Use the words to complete the sentences below.

ri _t_ e

_c_ onfes _s_ ion

ve _n_ ial si _n_

mo _r_ tal _s_ in

_p_ enan _c_ e

1. You completely turn your back on God if you commit a _____ _____ .
   mortal   sin

2. Water may be poured over a person's head in the _____ of Baptism.
   rite

3. We tell God we are sorry in the Sacrament of _____ .
   Penance

4. Sins are forgiven in _____ .
   confession

5. A _____ _____ is a less serious wrong.
   venial   sin

God's Community

Read the title. Say: *As members of the Church, we are all part of God's community. Please follow along as I read the first paragraph aloud.* Continue: *We are all God's children, and we can live peacefully with one another.*

Bring God's Children Together

Have a volunteer read the title and directions aloud. Tell the children to use their crayons to color the letters and scissors to cut out the pictures. Once the pictures are cut out, have the children line up the pictures to spell a word.

When they have finished, invite them to share their creations with partners. Invite the children to respond as a group to your question: *What is the unscrambled word?* (church)

Invite the group to stand to join you in this fingerplay. Say each line and show children the accompanying gesture. As you say it a second time, have them join you.

Here's the church,
(Thread fingers together pointing down; join thumbs.)
Here's the steeple,
(Raise and join index fingers.)
Open the doors,
(Spread thumbs apart.)
And see all the people!
(Wiggle interlocked fingers.)

Ask: *What special message do you think we can learn from this fingerplay?* (People are the Church. The Church is a community of people.)

✝ *Family and Community*

OPTION
WHO'S WHO?

Have a number of parish bulletins available. Browse through the pages with the children pointing out people, committees, articles, and events that they should be aware of. Say: *It takes many people and a lot of time to create community in a parish.*

OPTION
OUR COMMUNITY

Ask the group: *Can you name people who are part of our parish community?* (priest, other parishioners, themselves, families) Then pass out 11-by-17-inch sheets of paper. Have the children fold their papers accordion-style and cut out a string of people by drawing an outline of half of a person on the folded paper and then cutting it out. Demonstrate this for them. Then have them write the names of people in their parish community on each of the people. Remind the group: *All these people are part of God's community, and God loves them all.*

God's Community

God is happy when we work together to be part of his community, the Church. He is happy when we remember that we are his children.

Bring God's Children Together

Color the letters and cut out the boxes. Unscramble the letters. What do they spell? CHURCH

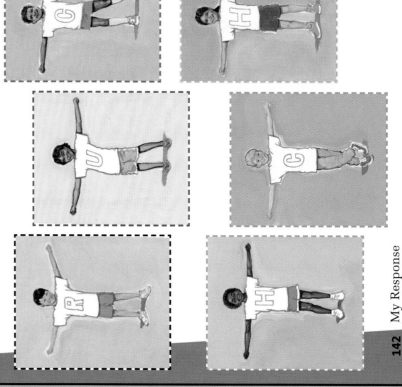

Prayer Service

Say: **It's time for our special prayer. In this prayer we're going to honor Mary. Begin by taking two deep breaths and exhaling slowly each time. Think about how much God loves Mary and remember how much Mary loves and cares for us.**

Say reverently: **God has given us so many things, and he promises to always forgive us. He wants us to stay close to him. We can ask Mary, the mother of Jesus and the Mother of the Church, to help us stay close to God.** Have the children look at the prayer service. Draw attention to the lines referring to Mary. Explain: **After each of these lines you will respond "pray for us." Now let us begin the prayer service.** Lead the children to the prayer center.

As a gathering song, play the reflective music at the end of CD 2. Have a statue of Mary in place. Begin: **We praise God by reading his word.**

Slowly and reverently proclaim the reading. Silently count to three and then read the next section and the litany. Motion to the children to respond **pray for us** after each line of the litany.

Say: **Let us pray the Hail Mary together.** If necessary, the children can find the words to the prayer in the Prayers to Take to Heart section at the back of their books. Lead the children in the prayer: **Hail Mary, full of grace, the Lord is with you. Blessed are you among women, and blessed is the fruit of your womb, Jesus. Holy Mary, Mother of God, pray for us sinners, now and at the hour of our death. Amen.**

Close by saying: **With honor and love for Mary in our hearts, let's review how we can be more like Jesus, her Son.** Then lovingly tell the children to return slowly to their seats.

Prayer Service

Leader: *We praise God by reading his word.*

A reading from the Book of Psalms.

Have mercy on me, God, in your goodness; wash away my guilt: keep me from sinning.

[adapted from Psalm 51:3–4]

Leader: *We can praise Mary and ask her to help us. After each phrase, say "pray for us."*

Mary, model of obedience,
Mary, mother of Jesus,
Mary, full of grace,
Mary, blessed among women,
Mary, full of love,

Let us pray the Hail Mary together.

FYI

THE HAIL MARY

The Hail Mary, our prayer in communion with the Mother of God, reflects two movements.

Hail Mary, full of grace, the Lord is with you. Blessed are you among women, and blessed is the fruit of your womb, Jesus: The first movement praises the Lord for all the great things he has done for Mary and, through her, for all human beings.

Holy Mary, Mother of God, pray for us sinners, now and at the hour of our death: The second movement entrusts our cares to Mary.

Respond

Living My Faith

Use these activities to help the children practice what they learned in this unit.

Ways of Being Like Jesus

Have a volunteer read the section aloud for the group. Tell the children: *Jesus always forgives us. While it might not always be easy to forgive others, we are to find forgiveness in our hearts. Think of someone you can forgive. Try to offer forgiveness to this person before next week.*

With My Family

Read the section. Have the children describe what they see in the picture. (mother and son having a peaceful moment) Say: *We should do our best to live in peace with our families. Ask: If you have been unkind to a family member, what can you do so that he or she will forgive you?* (say "I'm sorry," do something nice for them, say you won't do it again)

✝ *Family and Community*

Prayer

Say: *We have spoken about being sorry for our sins, about asking God to forgive us, and about our forgiving others. Let's thank Jesus and ask him to help us be forgiving people. Pray this prayer of thanks aloud with me. Know that Jesus is with us.*

Pray the prayer aloud. Allow the children time for reflection. In conclusion, invite them to pray the Sign of the Cross with you.

My Response

Say: *Enjoy a time of quiet reflection as you think about what you would like to have Mary ask God to grant you or someone else. Write a sentence or draw a picture of this.*

Give the children ample time to complete this section. Use this opportunity to assess how well the children are able to apply to their daily lives what they learned.

Congratulate the children on finishing their third unit and say: *Jesus wants us to offer others the same forgiveness that he offers us. He wants us to open our hands and reach out to help others; he wants us to open our hearts to forgiveness.*

Have each child come forward. Draw hearts with a washable marker in the palms of their hands. As you do this, say: ____, *remember to be helpful and forgiving.*

Living My Faith

Ways of Being Like Jesus

Jesus offers forgiveness to those who are hurting. You are like Jesus when you choose to forgive others.

With My Family

Talk about how Jesus helped everybody. Tell family members you are sorry if you treat them in an unkind way.

Prayer

Loving Jesus, thank you for helping me to be sorry for my sins. Help me to become a more forgiving person.

My Response

Mary will ask God to help us. What would you like Mary to ask God for you?

144   My Response

Unit 4

Unit 4: Meeting Jesus
Overview

Unit Saint: Pope Saint Pius X

The focus of this unit is on meeting Jesus in the Sacraments of Initiation. The saint for this unit is Pope Saint Pius X. Guiseppe (Joseph) Sarto was born to a poor family in Venetia, Italy, in 1835. He was elected pope in 1903, and as Pius X was noted for his charity and his desire to comfort those in need. He wanted Catholics to receive Holy Communion often and believed that children should be able to receive Holy Communion by age seven. Pius X serves as a model for what it means to meet Jesus in the sacraments, especially the Eucharist.

Session 16: New Life in Jesus

In this session we explore the Sacraments of Initiation: Baptism, Confirmation, and the Eucharist. Baptism is the beginning of our new life in Christ. Confirmation strengthens our commitment to Christ. The Eucharist nourishes us on our faith journey.

Session 17: Jesus Loves the Church

In this session we focus on the celebrations of Baptism and Eucharist. The Church celebrates the Eucharist, or the Sacrifice of the Mass, recalling that Jesus died for us and saved us from our sins. When we receive Holy Communion, we invite Jesus into our lives and recognize him in others.

Session 18: Gathering for Mass

The children learn that attending Mass is important and that the readings from the Liturgy of the Word are inspired by God. In the homily the priest explains the Scripture readings as they pertain to our lives.

Session 19: Celebrating the Eucharist

The Mass is the most important way we pray as Catholics. Jesus shared himself with the apostles at the Last Supper and continues to share himself with us today in the Eucharist. As Catholics, we attend Mass on Sunday, the Lord's Day. We also attend Mass on Holy Days of Obligation.

Session 20: Unit 4 Review

In this session we review the main ideas of the unit, reinforce ideas that need additional attention, and assess the children's understanding of the unit's main concepts.

Consider how the focus of this unit is developed throughout the sessions.

Catechist Preparation

Prayer in Unit 4

In this fourth unit, continue the established pattern and tone for prayer in each session. The short opening prayer of petition and closing prayer of gratitude invite the children to reflect on the focus of the session. Each also provides an opportunity for silent meditation.

Three of the Reflect pages in this unit invite the children into the experience of guided meditation. In the session on the Eucharist, the children reflect on the importance of family mealtimes and review the Prayer Before Meals. In the Prayer Service the children's prayer focuses on being part of Jesus' family.

✝ Catholic Social Teaching in Unit 4

The following themes of Catholic Social Teaching are integrated into this unit:

Call to Family, Community, and Participation Participation in family and community is central to our faith and to a healthy society. As the central social institution of our society, the family must be supported and strengthened. From this foundation, people participate in society, fostering a community spirit, and promoting the well-being of all, especially the poor and vulnerable.

Solidarity Because God is our Father, we are all brothers and sisters with the responsibility to care for one another. Solidarity is the attitude that leads Christians to share spiritual and material goods. Solidarity unites rich and poor, weak and strong, and helps to create a society that recognizes that we all live in an interdependent world.

As you guide the children through this unit, think about how you will help them to praise God through prayer and service.

Catechist Preparation

Session 16: New Life in Jesus

3-Minute Retreat

Take a few moments to reflect prayerfully before you prepare this session.

Before you prepare your session, pause for a few moments and reflect. Take three deep breaths and be aware that the loving presence of the Holy Spirit will help you as you continue to journey in faith.

Romans 6:4

We were indeed buried with him through baptism into death, so that, just as Christ was raised from the dead by the glory of the Father, we too might live in newness of life.

Reflection

In the sacraments we experience the truth that God desires to touch us and transform our lives with his love. The Sacraments of Initiation are transforming, drawing us into the Church and giving us grace to follow God's will. Cleansed of sin in Baptism, strengthened by the Holy Spirit in Confirmation, and nurtured by Jesus in the Eucharist, our lives change and we have a new life within us. Using ordinary elements of bread, wine, water, candles, oil, and white garments, we encounter in a physical way the invisible reality of God's grace.

Questions

How can I become more aware of the signs God gives me in the sacramental life of the church, and how can I nurture this awareness in others?

Prayer

Speak to God, using this prayer or one of your own.

Father, Son, and Holy Spirit, who entered into my life through the Sacraments of Initiation, continue your work of transformation in my life.

Resurrection of Christ, Raphael, c. 1503

Knowing and Sharing Your Faith

Scripture and Tradition in Session 16

Baptism is the Sacrament of Initiation by which we are introduced into the community of believers. Baptism removes original sin and incorporates us into Christ; it is a beginning, the start of life as a new creation, the beginning of a journey in following the footsteps of Jesus Christ, priest, prophet, and king.

Confirmation is the Sacrament of Initiation by which we are introduced into a fuller life in the Holy Spirit. The initiation involved in Confirmation seals us in the Holy Spirit and incorporates us more fully into Christ. Confirmation is a beginning, the start of a life of service, the beginning of a life of dedicated work for the coming of the kingdom.

Eucharist is the Sacrament of Initiation by which the incorporation begun in Baptism and Confirmation is brought to completion. In the Eucharist, Christ becomes food for our journey. The Eucharist always represents a new beginning, the constant renewal of the life of Christ within us.

The Sacraments of Initiation make us members of the Church. This membership entitles us to new life in Christ and Spirit-filled community.

Scripture in Session 16

Peter speaks of what is necessary to follow Jesus in **Acts of the Apostles 2:38.**
In **Revelation 22:17** the gift of life-giving water is offered to those who thirst.

Let the scripture and Tradition deepen your understanding of the content in this session.

WINDOW ON THE CATECHISM

The Sacraments of Initiation are introduced in CCC 1212. The Sacrament of Baptism is explored in CCC 1213–1274, Confirmation in CCC 1285–1314, and Eucharist in CCC 1322–1405.

Peter challenges the people.

Jesus offers life-giving water.

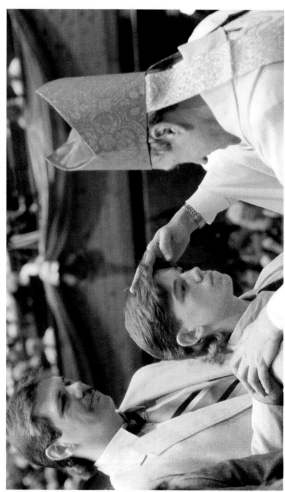

Catechist Preparation

From the Richness of the Tradition

In the sacraments we experience the presence of God. It is that presence which gives us hope in the face of seemingly insurmountable problems in the world. As Bishop Thomas Gumbleton said, "We have a firm foundation for hope. We are the people who know what God has done in Jesus: how the power of God, which is a power that can bring justice and peace into our human community, lived in Jesus to overcome evil, to overcome sin, to overcome death, to raise Jesus to new life as Lord and Son of God in power. That is what we hope in: a God who can do, in a powerful way, what God did in Jesus. That God can work in and through us, too. If we are responsive to what God asks of us and to the way God leads us, we can have well-founded hope." (*Shepherds Speak: American Bishops Confront the Social and Moral Issues that Challenge Christians Today*, New York: Crossroads, 1986, p. 213)

✝ Catholic Social Teaching

In this session, the following Catholic Social Teaching is explored:
Call to Family, Community, and Participation.

Consider in this session how you will invite the children to respond to and prayerfully reflect on God's invitation to love and serve others.

GENERAL DIRECTORY FOR CATECHESIS

The baptismal catechumenate as inspiration for all catechesis is explored in *GDC* 90.

Prayer in Session 16

In this session the children reflect on the new life in Jesus that we receive in the waters of Baptism. In the opening prayer of petition and the closing prayer of thanks the children pray that the grace of the sacraments will keep them close to Jesus.

A special approach to prayer in Session 16 is an extended guided reflection titled "New Life Through Baptism." As you prepare to share this prayer experience with the children, listen to the recorded guided reflection, "New Life Through Baptism" (CD 1, Track 9), as a prayerful experience for yourself. Then, when you play the recording during the session, join the children in reflective prayer.

If instead you choose to lead the guided reflection yourself, listen to the recording a second time, following the script (pages 372–373) and noting pauses and tone of voice. You can then use the script or adapt it as you wish. When leading the guided reflection during the session, play instrumental music softly in the background to enhance the sense of prayerfulness.

An alternate approach to prayer in this session is to use the Prayer on the children's page.

Catechist Preparation: Get-Ready Guide

Session 16: New Life in Jesus

Session Theme: *When we receive the Sacraments of Initiation, we receive new life in Jesus.*

Before This Session

- Learn the age of Confirmation in your diocese.
- Obtain holy cards of Jesus (one per child).
- Bookmark your Bible to Acts of the Apostles 2:38 and Revelation 22:17. Place the Bible open to the first of these passages in the prayer center.
- Set up the CD player to play the guided reflection.

Outcomes *At the end of the session, the children should be able to*

- identify Pope Saint Pius X as someone who brought people closer to God through the Eucharist.
- recognize the benefits of being part of a group.
- explain how Saint Peter called people to be baptized.
- name and explain the three Sacraments of Initiation.
- define *Body and Blood of Christ, Confirmation, consecration, Eucharist, Holy Communion,* and *Sacraments of Initiation.*
- prayerfully reflect on God's presence, his invitation, and our response.
- identify practical ways to act on God's invitation in everyday living.

Steps

DAY 1   Engage pages 145–147
Unit Saint: Pope Saint Pius X
New Life in Jesus

DAYS 2-3   Explore pages 148–153
Peter Speaks to the People
Special Signs from God
Baptism
Confirmation
Eucharist
Symbols and Sacraments

DAY 4   Reflect page 154
Prayer: Becoming Part of God's Family in Baptism

DAY 4   Respond page 155
Living My Faith: Ways We Can Serve Others

DAY 5   Extending the Session page 156
Day 5 offers an opportunity to extend the session with activities that reinforce the session outcomes.

Materials

Required Materials

- Bible
- Writing paper, pens, pencils
- Art materials, such as drawing paper, crayons, markers, scissors, glue
- Holy card of Jesus (one per child) or image of Jesus (page 145)
- Pictures of your or your children's Baptism (page 148)
- CD 1, Track 9: New Life Through Baptism (11:35) (page 154)
- CD 2, Track 2: Song of Love (Instrumental) (page 145)

Optional Materials

- Poster board, tempera paint, pie pan, blow dryer (page 147)
- Flat rocks, paint, paint brushes (page 148)
- Globe or world map (page 148)
- Model church or shape of a church made out of felt or construction paper (page 151)
- Paper cups, potting soil, bean seeds, paper plates or bowls, water (page 151)
- Bowl of holy water, white cloth (page 153)
- Several decks of cards (page 156)
- Bucket, slips of paper (page 156)
- Blackline Masters 40, 41, 42 (pages 145, 149, 151)

e-resources
www.FindingGod.org

Meeting Jesus

Meeting Jesus
Unit 4

Pope Saint Pius X

Pope Saint Pius was an important pope. He helped the Church bring people closer to God.

145

♪♫ 💿 As your time together begins, play CD 2, Track 2: "Song of Love." Give each child a holy card of Jesus. If you do not have holy cards, display an image of Jesus instead. Encourage the children to spend a few minutes asking Jesus to help them understand and live what they will be learning in this new unit.

Ask: *Where are places that we meet people?* (at school, at the store, at the parish) Then say to the children: *We meet people in all different places. When we are open to them and welcome them warmly, it is possible that we can become friends.*

Invite the children to work in pairs. Have them interview their partners to learn three facts about them that nobody else in the class knows; for example: What is your favorite food? Where were you born? Where do you want to travel one day? What do you want to be when you grow up? Then have the children share with the group the interesting facts about their partners.

When they have finished, ask the children to look at their holy cards

or the image you displayed. Remind them that Jesus is their friend, role model, and Savior. Tell the children: *You can meet Jesus and learn more about him, as you just learned about one another. We will learn more about Jesus today. Remember that he is always with you.*

Then have the children open their books to page 145. Draw attention to the picture of Pope Saint Pius X. Ask: *What color is Pope Pius (pōp pī´əs) X wearing?* (white) Say: *Only the pope wears white.* Have the children turn back to page 75 to see the popes there wearing white too. Ask: *Do you know of any other people who wear special clothes or uniforms?* (police, firemen, postal carriers)

Have the group return to page 145. Read the caption aloud. Ask: *Who remembers what a saint is?* Say: *A saint is a holy person who has died as a good friend of God and now lives with God forever.*

Explain to the group: *Since Pius X was a pope who later became a saint, he has both the titles Pope and Saint in his name. X is the Roman numeral that stands for the number 10. That means that he was the tenth pope named Pius.*

OPTION

BLM 40: POPE SAINT PIUS X
Blackline Master 40 reinforces content about Pope Saint Pius X.

Unit 4   145

Pope Saint Pius X

Have one of the children read the title and the first paragraph aloud. Explain: **Pope Saint Pius's primary concern was that all Catholics receive Holy Communion more frequently. He was also concerned that Catholics start receiving Holy Communion at an earlier age. He wanted children to be close to God. So Pope Pius X decided that children around the age of seven should be able to receive Holy Communion.**

Ask a volunteer to read the second paragraph for the group. See if anyone knows what the word *charities* means. Explain: **Charities are organizations that help the poor and those in need, such as the Saint Vincent de Paul Society.** Also ask: **Who remembers who the pope is?** (the successor of Saint Peter and the leader of the Roman Catholic Church) **Where does the pope live?** (in Vatican City in Rome, Italy)

Ask: **How was Pope Pius X like Jesus?** (He spent his life in service to others.) Say: **When we help others, we too are being like Jesus.**

Point out the illustration at the top right. Have the children describe what they see. Ask: **Why do you think Pope Pius X is pictured with children?** (He cared about them. He wanted them to be close to God. He made it possible for them to receive Holy Communion at age seven instead of waiting until they were adults.)

FYI

POPE SAINT PIUS X

Pius X, one of 10 children, was born in Venetia, Italy, in 1835. He became a priest when he was 23 years old and was later named a bishop. When he became pope, he instituted changes regarding children and the Eucharist. He believed that children should receive Holy Communion not too long after they reached the age of discretion, or age seven. Today the changes he instituted are still observed.

Pope Saint Pius X

Pius X wanted Catholics to receive Holy Communion often. He believed that children should be able to receive Holy Communion around age seven. He wanted them to be close to Jesus.

Pope Pius X spread God's love to the world. He spent his life helping others. He created charities to care for people who were poor.

146   God's Invitation

New Life in Jesus

Have the children create a story as a group. You can begin the story with "Once upon a time" and have each child add a sentence. See what kind of crazy story the group will come up with! Then say: **We created this story as a team! Everyone added something special and important to the story.**

Read the title and questions aloud. Encourage the children to respond to the questions. Then ask: **What makes a good team member?**

(being fair, giving everyone a turn, listening to other people's ideas)

Draw attention to the photographs. Call on volunteers to describe what they see. (children playing the violin, children singing in a choir)

Ask: **Has anyone here ever been a part of groups like these or any other kind of group? If so, please tell our group about it.** Allow several responses. Then say: **These are all great activities to be a part of. Now we will learn about being a part of, or a member of, the Church. The sacraments help us to become a member of the Church and to stay a good member.**

Engage

Prayer

Say: **We've talked about what it takes to be a good group member. Now let's spend some time with Jesus and ask him to help us be good members of the Church. Then say: Please close your eyes, fold your hands, and be still as I pray the prayer. Then you will have time to tell Jesus what is in your heart.**

Pray the prayer aloud. When finished, count to 10 silently. Conclude the quiet time by praying **Amen** and asking the children to open their eyes.

New Life in Jesus

Session 16

Have you ever been a member of a group? Are you part of a choir or a sports team? What are the good things about being a member of a group?

Prayer

Jesus, my friend, help me learn about the sacraments so that I may appreciate what you are giving me.

OPTION

HELPING HANDS

Give each child an 8½-by-11-inch piece of poster board and markers. Pour tempera paint into a pie pan, and invite each child to place his or her hands into the paint. Then have the children place their handprints on their poster boards, pointing their hands outward. Have them wash their hands. Give the paint time to dry. You can speed up the drying process by using a blow dryer. After the paint has dried, have the children use the markers to draw pictures of themselves between their hands, which serve as angel wings. With their markers, have them write their names and *Helping Hands Angel* at the top of their posters.

When the children have completed their projects, place the posters aside. Say: **When we are part of a group, we offer helping hands to our teammates. Your family is a team. In what ways can you offer your helping hands at home?** (make bed, help fold laundry) Give the children time to share ways to use their helping hands at home.

✝ *Family and Community*

Explore

Peter Speaks to the People

Pray the prayer on page 147 with the children before you begin. Ask the children: **What have we already learned about Peter?** (He was called by Jesus to be his follower. Jesus chose him to be the first leader of the Church. The name *Peter* means "rock.")

Read the title and the first and second paragraphs aloud. Mention that the words in the second paragraph are from the Bible, and show that the Bible is opened to this passage. Then invite a strong reader to stand and read the second paragraph again. Encourage him or her to read with a great deal of expression and to try to speak as they think Peter would have spoken.

Draw attention to the art. Call on volunteers to describe what they see. (Peter talking to men, women, and children) Then explain: **Peter encouraged people to be baptized so that they could live in a new way with Jesus. He wanted them to know that they would receive forgiveness for their sins and that the Holy Spirit would be with them.** Then say: **Many of you were baptized when you were babies.** Ask: **Have any of you seen pictures of your Baptism? What have your families told you about your Baptism?**

If you have pictures of your or your children's Baptism, you might want to show them to the children. If the children have brought pictures of their Baptisms, have them share those with the group.

Did You Know?

Ask a volunteer to read the sentence aloud. Then have the children turn to page 146 and look at the picture at the bottom. Say: **This is a photograph of Vatican City. It is the home of the pope. About 1,000 people live in Vatican City,**

and another 4,000 or so work there every day.

OPTION

"UPON THIS ROCK" PAPERWEIGHT

Read aloud this passage from Matthew 16:18: **You are Peter, and upon this rock I will build my church.** Then say: **Now we will make special rocks to remember how special Peter is to the Church and to us.** Distribute paint, paint brushes, and large flat rocks. Tell the children to use the paints to write *Upon This Rock* on their rocks. Tell them that they can use the completed project as a paperweight for their desks at

home to remind themselves of the strength they receive through the Church.

OPTION

WORLD MAP

Refer to a world map or globe if either is available. Explain that Vatican City is located in Italy, in Rome. Point out the location. Say: **Vatican City is a very special place. People from all over the world visit it every day because it is the home of the pope and it is a very important city for Catholics from all over the world. Perhaps one day you too will visit Vatican City!**

Peter Speaks to the People

Jesus chose Peter to lead the Church. He wanted Peter to keep showing people how to be close to God.

Peter said to the people, "Change your lives and be baptized in the name of Jesus Christ. Then your sins will be forgiven. You will receive the gift of the Holy Spirit."

adapted from Acts of the Apostles 2:38

Did You Know?

Vatican City is the home of the pope. It is located in Italy.

148   God's Invitation

Special Signs From God

Ask a child to read the title and first paragraph aloud. Ask: *What are sacraments?* (special signs that show that God is with us)

Ask: *Who gave the sacraments to the Church?* (Jesus)

Say: *Now let's learn about Baptism, Confirmation, and Eucharist. They are called the Sacraments of Initiation.*

Print the new vocabulary words on the board. Practice pronouncing them with the children. Ask: *Does anyone know what initiation means?* Say: *Initiation means "beginning." We celebrate the Sacraments of Initiation as* we begin our lives as members of the Church.

Then slowly read the second paragraph. Say: *The Sacraments of Initiation bring us into God's family, which is the Church.* Review the meaning of grace, saying: *In first grade you learned that grace is a gift from God that fills us with his life and makes us his friends. Now you are learning that, because God's grace makes us holy, it is called sanctifying grace.*

Draw attention to the photograph on the upper right. Ask the children what they see. Say: *Water is the most important symbol of Baptism.* Then point to the second picture. Say: *Oil is the symbol for both the Sacraments of Baptism* and Confirmation. Have the children look at the third picture. Explain: *This is bread on the plate and wine in the cup. At Mass, through the words of the priest, they become the Body and Blood of Christ. This is the Sacrament of Eucharist.*

Baptism

Have the children look at the picture at the bottom of the page and have them describe what they see.

Have the children turn back to page 103 and review the two paragraphs that discuss original sin and grace.

Then have the children return to page 149. Ask a volunteer to read the rest of the page aloud. Say: *Another symbol in Baptism is the white garment. White is a sign used by the Church on special happy occasions, such as a Baptism or at Christmas or Easter.*

OPTION

BLM 41: SACRAMENTS OF INITIATION

Blackline Master 41 asks children to create a mobile to remind them of the Sacraments of Initiation.

FYI

AGE OF CONFIRMATION

In November 2001 the United States Conference of Catholic Bishops addressed the age for the reception of the Sacrament of Confirmation for the Latin Rite dioceses of the United States. The bishops determined the range of age to be between the age of discretion, usually considered to be about seven, and about sixteen years of age. This new norm was approved by the Vatican and took effect on July 1, 2002. In conformity with this norm, each bishop can set a more specific policy in his own diocese.

Special Signs From God

A sacrament is a special sign. It shows that God is with us. Sacraments were given to the Church by Jesus.

The **Sacraments of Initiation** are Baptism, **Confirmation**, and **Eucharist**. These sacraments bring us into God's family. They give us grace. Grace is a gift we receive from God.

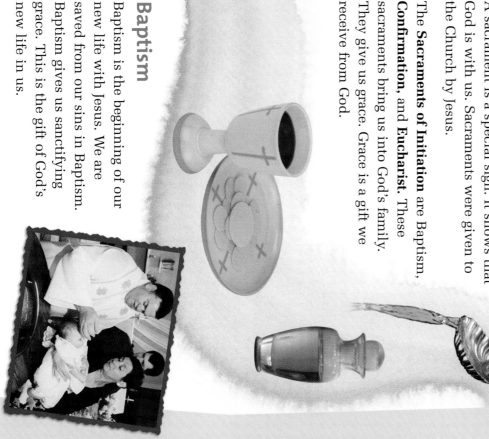

Baptism

Baptism is the beginning of our new life with Jesus. We are saved from our sins in Baptism. Baptism gives us sanctifying grace. This is the gift of God's new life in us.

We become a member of the Church when we are baptized. We become part of God's family.

Explore

Confirmation

Say: *Now we will learn about the other two Sacraments of Initiation—Confirmation and Eucharist.* Read the title and the first paragraph aloud. Tell the children at what age they will celebrate Confirmation in their diocese. Then say: *In the Sacrament of Confirmation, as in Baptism, we receive God's gift of grace, which helps us become his holy children.*

Eucharist

Ask a child to read the title and the first paragraph aloud. Draw attention to the terms in dark type. Say: *At Mass, the bread and wine become the Body and Blood of Christ that we receive in Holy Communion.* This might be a good time to remind the children of the additional information in the section Receiving Communion at the back of their books.

Have a volunteer read the final paragraph aloud. Draw attention to the word *consecration* in dark type. Say: *Consecration makes a thing or person special to God through prayer.* Say: *When we celebrate the Sacrament of the Eucharist, we receive the Body and Blood of Christ, which has been consecrated by the words of the priest during Mass.*

Reading God's Word

✝ Reverently read aloud the passage. Say: *Water is a symbol of new life in Baptism. The life we receive in Baptism is life as a member of God's family, the Church.* Then invite the children to read the passage aloud with you.

Ask: *When you're really thirsty, what do you want?* (water) Say: *Water is very important for our bodies, and we can't live long without it. Jesus is as important to us spiritually as water is to us physically.*

RECEIVING JESUS

Teach the children how to carry themselves as they receive Holy Communion. Explain that they are to hold their hands out reverently when they receive the Body of Christ. With their palms facing upwards, they should place their dominant hand below their other hand. If they are receiving Holy Communion on the tongue, they are to join their hands together. Tell them that when the priest or Eucharistic minister says *the Body of Christ* they are to respond *Amen.* When the cup is offered to them with the words *the Blood of Christ,* they are to respond *Amen* before drinking from the cup. If your parish has certain procedures for receiving Holy Communion, explain these to the children.

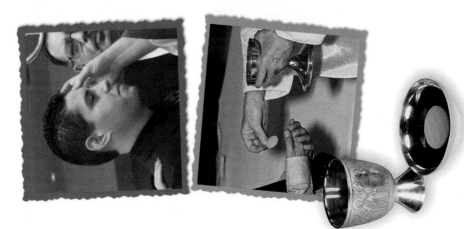

Confirmation

Confirmation makes us stronger in faith. It helps us become better Christians. God's sanctifying grace does this for us.

Eucharist

We receive the **Body and Blood of Christ** in the Eucharist. This is called **Holy Communion.**

The bread and wine of the Eucharist become the Body and Blood of Christ. This happens through the words of **consecration** prayed by the priest.

📖 Reading God's Word

The Spirit says, "Come." Whoever is thirsty may come forward and receive life-giving water.

adapted from Revelation 22:17

A Walk on the Beach

Before you begin, pray the Glory Be to the Father with the children.

Invite a child to read the activity's title and directions. Walk around the room and help the children. Encourage them to look back to pages 149–150 for the answers. When they have finished, check answers.

OPTION

BLM 42: MEETING JESUS

On Blackline Master 42 children finish sentences to review concepts from this session.

OPTION

FIND THE CHURCH

Create the shape of a church out of felt or construction paper, or use a small model of a church. Select a child to step outside the room. Ask another child to hide the church. Then bring the child waiting outside back in and ask him or her to find the church. The children can provide clues by saying *hot*, *warm*, or *cool*, depending on how close the searcher is to the church. When someone finds the church, have him or her say one thing that person knows about the church. Play the game a few times with different children. When finished, say: *The Church is very special*

to us. *It is there that we celebrate the sacraments Jesus gave us.*

OPTION

NEW LIFE

Say: *Through Baptism, we have new life in Christ.*

Then tell the children they will have the chance to watch new life bloom. Give each child a bean seed, a paper cup filled halfway with potting soil, and a sturdy paper plate or bowl to put under the paper cup. Tell the group to push their seeds into the soil carefully, covering them entirely with soil. Help the children water their seeds. Remind them: *Water is a sign of new life, and your seeds will need water to grow.* Ask the children to take their seeds home, place them in sunlight, give them a small amount of water each day or so, and watch new life grow! Say: *Just as these seeds will grow, so will we grow as children of God.*

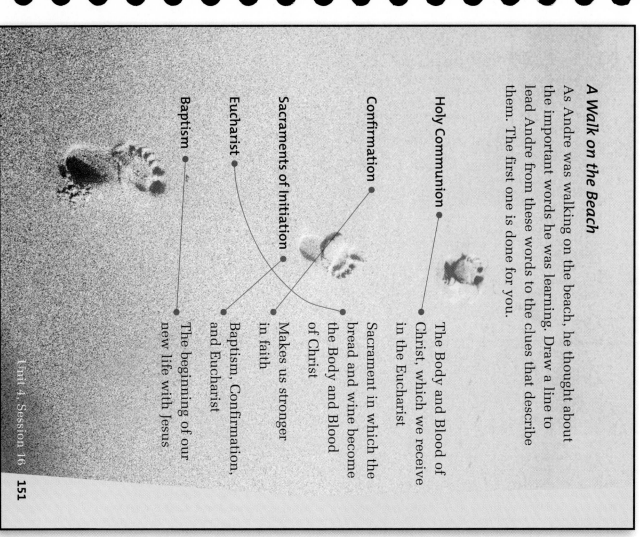

A Walk on the Beach

As Andre was walking on the beach, he thought about the important words he was learning. Draw a line to lead Andre from these words to the clues that describe them. The first one is done for you.

Baptism — The beginning of our new life with Jesus

Eucharist — Baptism, Confirmation, and Eucharist

Sacraments of Initiation — Makes us stronger in faith

Confirmation — Sacrament in which the bread and wine become the Body and Blood of Christ

Holy Communion — The Body and Blood of Christ, which we receive in the Eucharist

Symbols and Sacraments

Begin by reminding children of signs and symbols that they see in their everyday lives. (street lights, billboards, storefront signs) Say: *Just as signs and symbols serve as reminders in our everyday lives, the Church uses signs and symbols to remind us about important things.*

Ask children about some of the religious symbols that you have discussed with them. Ask questions such as these: *What do we think of when we look at a cross?* (Jesus died to save us.) *What does the bishop's crozier look like and what is its meaning?* (the shepherd's staff; that the bishop cares for his people like a shepherd) *Of what does the Celtic Trinity Knot remind us?* (the Trinity—Father, Son and Holy Spirit) *And the vine and branches in the vineyard?* (that Jesus is the vine that nourishes us, the branches)

Say: *Today we will learn more about the special signs of the Sacraments of Initiation.*

Read the heading and first paragraph aloud. Ask: *What are symbols?* (special signs) *Why does the Church use symbols in the Sacraments of Initiation?* (to help us understand the meaning of the sacraments)

Choose a volunteer to read the second paragraph. Ask: *What is the most important symbol of Baptism?* (water) *Of what is it a sign?* (new life) Have a child describe what is happening in the top picture. (a child being immersed in water at Baptism)

Read the third paragraph aloud. Ask: *Can someone tell us the words the priest says when he baptizes us?* ("I baptize you in the name of the Father, and of the Son, and of the Holy Spirit.")

After a volunteer reads the next paragraph aloud, ask: *What is the most important symbol of Confirmation?* (oil) *What is the bishop doing in the second picture?* (making the sign of the cross with oil on the person's forehead)

Read the last paragraph aloud. Ask: *What are the symbols of the Eucharist?* (bread and wine) *What happens to them when the priest prays the words of consecration?* (They become the Body and Blood of Christ.) *What is happening in the last picture?* (The priest is saying the words of consecration.)

Say: *Through these symbols the Church helps us to know and remember that the sacraments give us sanctifying grace to help us be holy.*

Symbols and Sacraments

Symbols are special signs. Symbols are used in the Sacraments of Initiation. These symbols help us understand the meaning of the sacraments.

Water is the most important symbol of Baptism. It is a sign of new life.

The person being baptized may be lowered into the water. The water may also be poured on the person's head. We are baptized in the name of the Father, the Son, and the Holy Spirit.

The bishop anoints us with oil in Confirmation. With the oil, he makes the sign of the cross on the forehead of the person being confirmed. Oil is the most important symbol of Confirmation.

Bread and wine are symbols of the Eucharist. The bread and wine become the Body and Blood of Christ. This happens through the words of consecration prayed by the priest.

152 God's Invitation

Sacraments and the Church

Remind the children that they have learned a lot about the Sacraments of Initiation this week. Say: *Now we'll do a word game to write down some of our thoughts about the sacraments.*

Read the heading and the directions for the group. Use the example sentence to show the children that the words *The sacraments . . .* begin each sentence. Give the children time to complete the sentences independently. Walk around the room as the children work, giving help as needed and praising their responses.

When most have finished, have a sharing time with volunteers reading various responses for each sentence starter.

Say: *Our actions can be a sign to others that we are members of God's family. When we accept God's grace in the sacraments, we try to act toward others as Jesus would have acted.* Ask the children to think of something they can do for someone in their families when they go home today to show that they are living as God wants them to. Have them write a sentence about it, possibly on an index card or Post-It note so they can take it with them as a reminder. Invite them to share their ideas with the group if they would like.

In closing, tell the children that they are living as followers of Jesus when they act in a loving manner toward one another.

OPTION

MORE SENTENCE STARTERS

Use other sentence starters and acrostic words to review additional concepts. Some possible combinations might include: *New life . . .* with the acrostic word *CHRIST; God's grace . . .* with the acrostic word *GIFT; Symbols . . .* with the word *SIGNS.*

Have children work with partners to create a sentence acrostic and then have the pairs share with the group.

OPTION

HOLY WATER BLESSING

Place a bowl filled with holy water on a white cloth on your prayer table at the prayer center. Say: *The water in the bowl is not ordinary water but is water from the church. It has been blessed by the priest, and we call it "holy water." Water is a symbol of new life. When we were baptized the priest said these words: "I baptize you in the name of the Father, and of the Son, and of the Holy Spirit." Let's bless ourselves with this water today to remind us that on the day of our Baptism we received new life as members of God's family, the Church. Come forward, one by one, dip your fingers into the water, and pray the Sign of the Cross.*

Demonstrate this for the children. Then have them come to the prayer center one by one. Tell them: *You can remember your Baptism every time you enter or leave the church by blessing yourselves with the holy water.*

Sacraments and the Church

Finish the sentences by writing something about the sacraments. The third one is done for you.

The sacraments . . .

Can bring _____
Answers may vary.

Celebrate our _____.

Reach out _____.

Help us _____.

Unite us in Jesus.

Have special _____.

Reflect

Prayer

New Life Through Baptism: A Recorded Guided Reflection

🔵 Say: *The sacraments draw us into the life of God. Let's reflect on the new life we have received through Baptism.*

A special approach to prayer in Session 16 is an extended guided reflection titled "New Life Through Baptism" (CD 1, Track 9). Refer to pages 372 and 373 for the script and directions for using the recorded guided reflection with the children.

Guided Reflection: An Alternate Approach

An alternate approach to prayer in this session is to use the Prayer on the children's page. The following suggestions will help you guide the children through this Prayer in a reflective manner.

Have the children describe what they see in the photo. Say: *We have talked today about the Sacraments of Initiation. When you were baptized, you received new life with Jesus. Today you are going to hear a reflection about Baptism. Please sit comfortably, be very still, fold your hands, silently take a long, deep breath, and then let it out slowly. Close your eyes if you'd like, and listen quietly.* Some children will be comfortable listening with their eyes closed. Others may want to look at the illustration.

Read the reflection aloud, pausing where appropriate. At the end of the Prayer, say: *If there's anything else you'd like to tell Jesus, take time now to do that.* Allow children 20 seconds to complete their prayer. Close by praying the Sign of the Cross.

OPTION

USING THIS PAGE AGAIN

If you have led the children through the recorded guided reflection, you might choose to use this prayer page with them during another session, Day 5, the Review session, or a seasonal session as appropriate.

FYI

PRAYING CONSTANTLY

Saint Paul advises that we should "pray constantly"(adapted from 1 Thessalonians 5:17).

In the Christian tradition, there are three major expressions of the prayer life: vocal prayer, meditation, and contemplative prayer. Vocal prayer invites us to express our interior prayer externally. Meditation is the turning of our attention to a deeper understanding of the Christian life, aided by Scripture, sacred books, and writings. Contemplative prayer is total awareness of and communion with God.

🔖 Prayer

We know that God gave us water to drink because we need it to live.

Think about the many things you can do with water. Maybe you like to go swimming or make water balloons. You can take a long, cool drink of water on a hot day. What other things do you do with water?

Now think about the water that was poured over you when you were baptized. You were given new life with Jesus. You became part of God's family. In your imagination meet Jesus in your favorite place. Tell him how happy you are to be God's child. Listen with your heart to what he tells you.

154   My Response

Living My Faith

Faith Summary

Read the section aloud. Ask the children: *What is a sacrament?* (special sign from God, special way in which God enters our lives)

Who gave us the sacraments? (Jesus) *What gift of God do we receive in the sacraments?* (grace)

How many Sacraments of Initiation are there? (three) *Can you name them?* (Baptism, Confirmation, Eucharist)

Why are these called the Sacraments of Initiation? (We celebrate the Sacraments of Initiation as we begin our lives as members of the Church.)

Words I Learned

Call on volunteers to define each word. Refer the children to the Glossary. Choose volunteers to use each word in a sentence.

Ways of Being Like Jesus

Choose a volunteer to read the section. Ask: *What is the boy in the picture doing?* (shoveling snow) *Why?* (to help his family) Invite children to role-play with partners ways in which they might do good deeds for others. (helping someone

With My Family

Remind the children that they can care for others by asking their families to do something for a charity. (riding bikes in a bike-a-thon, visiting the elderly)

bring the groceries in from the car, delivering homemade cookies to a new neighbor)

Prayer

Say: *We've learned that we receive the grace of God in the sacraments. Grace is a gift from God that fills us with new life. Now let's spend time with God and thank him for his gift of grace. Pray this prayer of thanks aloud with me.*

Pray the prayer aloud. Say: *Take this time to enjoy being still with God.* Allow the children time to reflect. Then pray: *Amen.*

My Response

Read the section. Say: *Through the sacraments we grow closer to God. Being close to God helps us serve others better. Think about how you can help others. Maybe you could pick up litter from a neighbor's yard or help wash your family's car. Draw your idea.*

When the children have finished, call on volunteers to share their drawings with the group, explaining how it shows them serving others.

Say: *You are very fortunate to have the life of God within you. You are a privileged person.*

Living My Faith

Faith Summary

Baptism, Confirmation, and Eucharist are the Sacraments of Initiation.

Words I Learned

Body and Blood of Christ

consecration

Holy Communion

Confirmation

Eucharist

Sacraments of Initiation

Ways of Being Like Jesus

You are like Jesus when you do good deeds for neighbors and others.

With My Family

As a family, volunteer your time or money to a charity.

Prayer

Thank you, God, for your gift of grace. Help me to always stay close to you.

My Response

Jesus came to serve you.
How can you serve others?

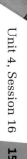

Extending the Session

Choose from the following options to extend the session or to reinforce concepts developed during the week.

Family Involvement

Remind the children to take home the Raising Faith-Filled Kids page to share what they are learning with their families.

Preparation for Sunday Scripture Readings

Lead children in a prayerful discussion of Sunday's readings. Visit www.FindingGod.org/Sunday for more information.

Seasonal Session

Consider the time of the liturgical year and use the appropriate seasonal session. Seasonal sessions may be found on page 241.

Unused Options and BLMs

Incorporate any unused options or Blackline Masters from the week's session.

Web Site Activities

Visit www.FindingGod.org to find additional activities for extending the session.

WATER IS IMPORTANT

Encourage the children to write a few of the uses for water. Play the recorded guided reflection "New Life Through Baptism" (CD 1, Track 9). After playing the reflection, remind the children of how water relates to Baptism. Then invite the children to choose one of the uses for water they have written and draw a picture of themselves using water in that way. Encourage the children to take the pictures home as a reminder to thank God for the gift of Baptism.

156 Session 16

SYMBOLS AND SACRAMENTS MATCHING

Prior to the session, create several decks of cards for Symbols and Sacraments Matching using unlined note cards. Write one of the following words or phrases on each card: *Baptism, Confirmation, Eucharist, water, oil, Bread and Wine.* Form groups of two or three children, and give each group a shuffled deck of cards. Ask the groups to lay the cards facedown and take turns trying to match each symbol to the sacrament it is used in.

FOUR SACRAMENTS CORNERS

Mark each corner of the room Baptism, Eucharist, Confirmation, and Sacraments of Initiation. Choose one person to hold a bucket with the names of each of the four corners written on slips of paper. Pick a song from the unit to play and stop for the game. When the music starts, invite the group to walk around the room. When the music stops, everyone should run to a corner. Then invite the person with the bucket to choose a slip of paper. The group in the corner called should name something about that term. Play until all the slips of paper have been used.

RAISING FAITH-FILLED KIDS
a parent page

Focus on Faith

New Life in God

From the window of their house, the mother and her children could see a pair of birds building a new nest. As time passed, they could see tiny eggs in the nest and the careful way they were kept warm. They noticed how the birds chirped in warning if an animal came too close. Then tiny birds came out of their shells. As spring turned into summer, the tiny birds grew and learned how to fly. One day they were gone, leaving the empty nest behind. Nature has many examples of life's transitions. As Christians, we celebrate these transitions in our spiritual lives in the sacraments. The sacraments that bring us new life in God are Baptism, Confirmation, and Eucharist.

Dinnertime Conversation Starter

What significant transitions or changes are your family facing? Explain to your child how the sacraments will provide the grace to help the family cope with these changes.

Hints for at Home

With your child create a "Jesus, Light My Way" switch-plate cover for a light switch. You will need a plain switch-plate cover, a permanent marker, and stickers, sequins, and other decorative items. Have your child use the marker to write *Jesus, light my way* on the switch-plate cover. Then have him or her use the stickers, sequins, and other items to decorate the plate. Attach the completed plate in a prominent room in your home.

Spirituality in Action

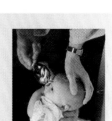

Jesus lived a life of service. Guide your child to find new ways to help others. Begin a family service project for the children's ward of a local hospital. With your family create placemats to deliver to the children there. You will need cardboard, scissors, fabric, glue, construction paper, permanent markers, and clear adhesive or laminate covering. Use the cardboard to form the bottom of the placemat. Cut the fabric to fit over the cardboard and glue it on top of the cardboard. Then write cheerful greetings on the construction paper and glue it to the fabric. Place the clear covering over the top of the placemat. Deliver the finished products to the children's ward.

Focus on Prayer

Share with your child the story of his or her Baptism. Look at photos or videos of the Baptism and explain how you felt on the day they were taken. With your child praise Jesus for the new life he gives us.

Session 17: Jesus Loves the Church

3-Minute Retreat

Before you prepare your session, pause for a few moments and quiet yourself. Relax and call to mind that you are in the loving presence of God who calls you to journey in faith.

Acts of the Apostles 2:42

They devoted themselves to the teaching of the apostles and to the communal life, to the breaking of the bread and to the prayers.

Reflection

In the breaking of the bread and in the prayers, the early Church experienced the risen presence of Jesus Christ. In the Eucharist, we come to know and experience the fullness of Jesus as they did. The Eucharist is spiritual food that not only allows us to receive Jesus more intimately into our lives but also strengthens us to serve the needs of others. Parish ministries, including the ministry of catechesis, are strengthened by Jesus' presence in the Eucharist and in the faithful who receive him.

Questions

How do I prepare myself to welcome Jesus Christ in the Eucharist? How does my welcoming of others parallel the way I welcome Jesus in the Eucharist?

Preaching of Saint Peter,
Hans Süss von Kulmbach

Prayer

Speak to Jesus in these or similar words.

Jesus, companion on my journey, I know you are present to me in the breaking of the bread. Nourish my heart and spirit so that I will always be willing to welcome and serve others.

Take a few moments to reflect prayerfully before you prepare this session.

Knowing and Sharing Your Faith

Scripture and Tradition in Session 17

Jesus, whose parents were unwelcome at the inn in Bethlehem and who was himself unwelcome in Judea at the time of King Herod, welcomed everyone into his presence during his public life. Against the objections of others, he welcomed children, outcasts, and sinners. He made himself welcome in the house of Zacchaeus, and he accepted the welcoming invitation of the two disciples on the road to Emmaus.

The Church that Jesus founded strives to be a welcoming community in faithfulness to the example of Jesus. Most parishes have welcoming committees and a catechumenal process, designed specifically for welcoming new members into the Church. Parish life is always centered around the celebration of Mass, when Jesus welcomes us to the table and molds us into a welcoming community.

The welcome that we receive in the Sacraments of Initiation gives us hope in another welcome—that which awaits us in the fulfillment of the Kingdom of God as Jesus welcomes those who have lived faithful lives.

Scripture in Session 17

Jesus reveals himself to two disciples in the breaking of bread in
Luke 24:13–31.
Acts of the Apostles 2:42 describes how the early Christian community chose to follow Jesus.

Let the Scripture and Tradition deepen your understanding of the content in this session.

WINDOW ON THE CATECHISM

The story of Emmaus as it relates to the celebration of Eucharist is discussed in CCC 329 and 1347.

The disciples recognize Jesus.

The early Christians break bread.

Catechist Preparation

From the Richness of the Tradition

"As Catholics we are called to take concrete measures to overcome the misunderstanding, ignorance, competition, and fear that stand in the way of genuinely welcoming the stranger in our midst and enjoying the communion that is our destiny as Children of God. We commit ourselves, accordingly, to working to strengthen understanding among the many cultures that share in our Catholic faith, to promoting intercultural communication among our people, and to seeing that those in ministry to our communities gain the language and cultural skills necessary to minister to the immigrants in our midst." ("Welcoming the Stranger Among Us: Unity in Diversity," November 15, 2000, United States Conference of Catholic Bishops)

✝ Catholic Social Teaching

In this session, aspects of the following Catholic Social Teaching themes are explored:

- **Solidarity**
- **Call to Family, Community, and Participation**

Prayer in Session 17

In the opening prayer of petition and the closing prayer of gratitude, the children welcome Jesus into their lives. In the Reflect step the children reflect on the importance of sharing meals with their families and review the Prayer Before Meals as a form of family prayer.

Consider in this session how you will invite the children to respond to and prayerfully reflect on God's invitation to love and serve others.

GENERAL DIRECTORY FOR CATECHESIS

The place of Eucharist as a Sacrament of Initiation is discussed in *GDC* 115.

Catechist Preparation: Get-Ready Guide

Session 17: Jesus Loves the Church

Session Theme: *One way we can see God's love in the world is the way we celebrate the Eucharist.*

Before This Session

- Bookmark your Bible to Luke 24:13–31 and Acts of the Apostles 2:42. Display it in the prayer center open to the passage from Luke.

- Set up the CD player so that you will be ready to play the Scripture story and the reflective music.

Steps

DAY 1	**Engage** page 157	Welcoming a New Neighbor

DAYS 1-3	**Explore** pages 158–163	Inviting Jesus to Dinner Welcoming Jesus Welcome to Mass Serving Your Parish

DAY 4	**Reflect** page 164	Prayer: Prayer Before Meals

DAY 4	**Respond** page 165	Living My Faith: Ways to Help a New Person

DAY 5	**Extending the Session** page 166	

Day 5 offers an opportunity to extend the session with activities that reinforce the session outcomes.

Outcomes   *At the end of the session, the children should be able to*

- realize the importance of welcoming people.

- tell the story of what happened on the road to Emmaus.
- explain that when we show hospitality to others, we welcome Jesus into our lives.
- explain that the Mass is the most important way we remember Jesus.
- pray the Prayer Before Meals.
- define *disciple, ministry,* and *Sacrifice of the Mass.*

- prayerfully reflect on God's presence, his invitation, and our response.
- pray the Prayer Before Meals

- identify practical ways to act on God's invitation in everyday living.

Materials

Required Materials

- Bible
- Writing paper, pens, pencils
- Art materials, such as drawing paper, crayons, markers, scissors, glue
- Various items that suggest chores children might do (page 162)
- CD 2, Track 2: Song of Love (Instrumental) (page 157)
- CD 1, Track 4: Inviting Jesus to Dinner (4:53) (page 158)
- CD 2, Reflective music (page 164)

Optional Materials

- Roll of crepe paper (page 157)
- Assortment of breads of the world, world map or globe (page 159)
- Oversized craft sticks (2 per child), glitter (page 160)
- Magazines, construction paper (page 161)
- Large piece of poster board or butcher paper (page 166)
- Photocopies of the Glory Be to the Father in Italian (page 166)
- Blackline Master 43, brass fastener (page 158)

- Blackline Masters 44, 45 (pages 159, 160)

e-resources

www.FindingGod.org

Jesus Loves the Church

♪ 💿 Softly play CD 2, Track 2, "Song of Love."

Say: *There are many times that people show their love. Can you name some times when people do this?* (friends wishing you a happy birthday or sharing a toy with you) Explain: *Jesus loves all of us. He wants us to love one another. Today we'll find out ways that we can show our love as followers of Jesus.*

Have the children open their books to page 157. Read the title and paragraph aloud. Encourage the children to respond to the questions. Call on volunteers to describe what is happening in the picture. (a new family moving into a neighborhood, neighbor welcoming new neighbor) Ask the children if they have ever moved into a new neighborhood or had new people move into their neighborhoods. Discuss with them different things that they could do to be welcoming to newcomers. Say: *When someone new comes to our neighborhood, school, or parish, we should try to make them feel welcome.*

Prayer

Say: *Jesus loves everyone. We can be like him when we act in a loving way toward others. Let's invite our friend Jesus into our hearts and lives. Please pray aloud with me. Then quietly tell Jesus what is in your heart.*

Pray the prayer. When finished, allow the children time to talk to Jesus. Then say: *Let us close by praying the Sign of the Cross together.*

Jesus Loves the Church

Session 17

Imagine that a new child has moved into your neighborhood. How can you welcome your new neighbor? What can you do to make him or her feel at home?

Prayer

Jesus, my friend, help me welcome you into my heart and my life. Help me do good for others.

CIRCLE OF KINDNESS

Invite the children to sit or stand in a circle. Begin the activity by naming an act of kindness that you can do for others. Then pass a roll of crepe paper, unrolling it a bit, to the child to your right. Ask him or her to name another act of kindness and then to pass the crepe paper along to the next child. Continue until each child has had a turn. Point out that you are wrapped in a circle of kindness. Say: *Remember how this connectedness feels and remember to perform acts of kindness as often as you can.* Have the children roll the paper back up to gather up all their acts of kindness.

Explore

Inviting Jesus to Dinner

Read the title of the page to the children. Then direct their attention to the open Bible at the prayer center. Say: *The story we are about to read is from the Bible. It took place in a village not far from the city of Jerusalem. The story is about two of Jesus' disciples. Does anyone know what a disciple is?* (a follower of Jesus) Explain: *These two disciples were very sad because Jesus had died. Let's find out what happened to them.* Ask the children to follow along silently while you read the story aloud.

When you have finished, discuss the story briefly with the children. Then say: *Now we will listen to a recording of this story.*

Have the children sit quietly as you prepare to play the dramatized version of Inviting Jesus to Dinner. It is based on Luke 24:13–35, the Scripture story cited in the children's book.

Draw the children's attention to the picture on page 158. Ask them to look at the picture and try to figure out when in the story this scene takes place. Also ask them to pay close attention to any details in the recording that weren't included in the version you read.

[CD icon] Play CD 1, Track 4. When the story is finished, lead the children in a discussion of what they heard. Encourage them to share their comments or questions with the group.

Reading God's Word

[cross icon] Read the verse aloud. Say: *When you are having dinner with your family, you can remember how special sharing a meal was for Jesus and his followers.* Invite the children to read the verse aloud as an action piece, using the following gestures:

Jesus' followers came together to learn (form a book of two hands and pretend to read), *to pray* (join hands and bow head in prayer), *and to break bread* (mime eating).

OPTION
BLM 43: TIME FOR DINNER
On Blackline Master 43 children create a clock to remind their families about the story of Jesus' breaking bread with the apostles.

FYI
STORY OF EMMAUS
The story of Emmaus beautifully shows the disciples' journey into faith after the death and resurrection of Jesus. The disciples are walking away from Jerusalem, discouraged by the events that led to Jesus' death. Jesus joins them on the walk and explains the Scriptures to them. They are interested but not convinced. Finally they arrive at an inn. The disciples offer hospitality and Jesus accepts. They realize who he is when he breaks bread with them.

Inviting Jesus to Dinner

After Jesus died, two of his **disciples** were walking along a road. They met a man. The disciples did not know who he was. The disciples told him about all that had happened to Jesus. They invited the man to join them for dinner.

The man sat down with the disciples at the dinner table. He broke bread, blessed it, and gave it to them. When he did this, they knew that he was Jesus. They knew that Jesus had risen.

adapted from Luke 24:13-31

[book icon] ### Reading God's Word

Jesus' followers came together to learn, to pray, and to break bread.

adapted from Acts of the Apostles 2.42

A Message for Jesus

Read the activity's title and directions aloud. Help the children write a message of welcome for Jesus on the four steps leading to the door of the house. Then have them color the house in bright colors. Encourage them to decorate the house with curtains, flowers, and others things that will make it feel welcoming. When the group has finished, call on volunteers to share their messages and artwork. Thank the children who volunteer.

Explain: *When we show hospitality to one another, we are welcoming them and Jesus into our lives.* Then sing, to the tune of "Row, Row, Row Your Boat," the following song:

Hospitality,
Hospitality,
Welcoming, welcoming,
welcoming, welcoming
You into my life!

Say: *When we welcome others into our lives, we are welcoming Jesus. Make a special effort today to be welcoming by including others in your games and conversations.*

✚ *Solidarity*

BLM 44: GOD'S GRACE

Blackline Master 44 asks children to create a banner containing ways to show love to others.

BREADS OF THE WORLD

Remind the children that different kinds of bread are eaten by people all over the world. Then have a festival featuring breads of the world. You might include pita and flat bread from the Middle East, challah from Israel, tortillas from Mexico, focaccia from Italy, and a baguette from France. Before you have the children taste the breads, make sure they are not allergic to wheat or gluten.

On a map or globe show the children the locations of the areas where each kind of bread is eaten. Then encourage them to sample each bread and choose their favorites. Remind them that Jesus chose to bless the bread when celebrating the first Eucharist.

ROLE-PLAY MEETING JESUS

Divide the class into groups of three or four. Have someone in each group act as Jesus. Have the others play the role of a family that Jesus is visiting. Have the children role-play welcoming Jesus to their home. How would they treat him? What would they talk about? What would they offer him? How would Jesus act? What would Jesus say? Give the children time to develop their skits. Then have them perform them in front of the group.

A Message for Jesus

Like the disciples in the story, you can invite Jesus into your life. Imagine that Jesus is coming to visit your home. Welcome him by writing a message on the stairway. Write one word on each step.

Unit 4, Session 17   159

Explore

Welcoming Jesus

Tell the children: *Today we will learn about how the grace of the Holy Spirit helps us welcome Jesus into our lives.* Read the title aloud. Ask: *Who is the Holy Spirit?* (the third person of the Blessed Trinity) Then read the first paragraph aloud. Say: *When we are baptized, we receive the Holy Spirit. The Holy Spirit stays with us throughout our lives. The grace of the Holy Spirit helps us to love others. When we love others, Jesus comes into our lives. We can call on the Spirit whenever we need help in loving others.*

Invite a volunteer to read the second paragraph aloud. Then draw attention to the term *Sacrifice of the Mass* in dark type. Say: *The Sacrifice of the Mass helps us remember the sacrifice of Jesus on the cross.*

Draw attention to the pictures on the page. Have the children describe what they see and what the pictures are showing about each of the sacraments. Say: *The top picture is about Baptism. The hand is a symbol of God our Father, the water is the water of Baptism, and the dove signifies the Holy Spirit whom we receive in Baptism. The bottom picture is about the Eucharist. We see a priest holding up the Eucharist.*

BLM 45: INVITING JESUS TO DINNER

Blackline Master 45 asks children to put events in order from the story of Jesus breaking bread with the disciples.

160 Session 17

Baptism makes us followers of Jesus. As Jesus served others, so should we also serve others.

A MINISTRY OF HOSPITALITY

Did you ever consider your work as a catechist as a ministry of hospitality? Especially with young children, it is just that. As their catechist, you represent the faith community. It is, therefore, important to be open, warm, and welcoming when interacting with the children.

HOSPITALITY CROSS

Distribute two oversized craft sticks, glue, a permanent marker, and glitter to each child. Invite the children to create a Hospitality Cross. Tell the children to glue the sticks together in a cross formation. Then invite them to write *HO_PITALITY* on the vertical stick. Tell them to leave out the letter S. Then have them write *JESUS* on the horizontal stick, using the first S to fill in the missing one on the other stick. Have the children decorate their crosses. Explain: *Once we are baptized, we are called upon to serve others and show them hospitality.*

Welcoming Jesus

The Holy Spirit comes to us in Baptism and stays with us throughout our lives. Every day the grace of the Holy Spirit helps us to love others. When we love others, we welcome Jesus into our lives.

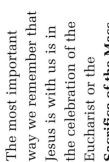

The most important way we remember that Jesus is with us is in the celebration of the Eucharist or the **Sacrifice of the Mass.** The Mass helps us remember that Jesus died for us and saved us from our sins.

160 God's Invitation

Welcome to Mass

Read the title aloud. Then remind the children: *Just as the two disciples on the road invited Jesus to join them for dinner, so does the Church welcome us to Mass. During Mass we remember that Jesus died for us and saved us from our sins.*

Read the next paragraph aloud. Ask: *How do you think Nikki's family felt when Devin invited them to sit with his family?* (happy, because it's hard to be a newcomer) Explain: *Welcoming others into our lives is an important way of showing our love for the family of God.*

Read the final paragraph. Draw attention to the word *ministry* in dark type. Explain: *A ministry is a service or work done for others. There are many kinds of ministries that people do in our parish community.* Ask: *Can you think of examples?* (choir, usher, altar servers, catechists)

Have a volunteer read the first paragraph aloud. Ask: *How did Devin feel as he was waiting for Mass to begin?* (close to his family and to God) Continue: *Attending Mass is a special way of staying close to Jesus and others who are baptized members of the Church.*

Mass is a way of sharing that closeness with those we love.

Link to Liturgy

Read the section aloud. Explain: *Here is an example of one kind of ministry. Ministers of hospitality welcome those who are coming to Mass.* Call attention to the picture. Ask the children to describe what they see.

Say: *The family members who are welcoming other parishioners are ministers of hospitality.* Ask: *How would you feel if you were a new person and you were welcomed like this?* (happy, as if I belonged)

End this time together by saying: *Our hospitality should extend beyond church. Let us be welcoming to everyone we meet.*

✝ Family and Community

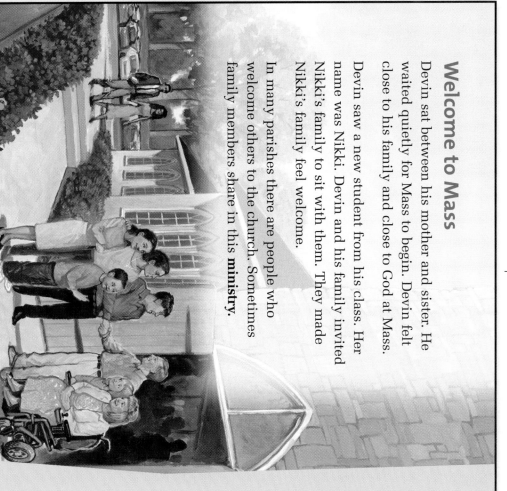

Welcome to Mass

Devin sat between his mother and sister. He waited quietly for Mass to begin. Devin felt close to his family and close to God at Mass.

Devin saw a new student from his class. Her name was Nikki. Devin and his family invited Nikki's family to sit with them. They made Nikki's family feel welcome.

In many parishes there are people who welcome others to the church. Sometimes family members share in this **ministry**.

Link to Liturgy

Many churches have ministers of hospitality who welcome people to the parish church for Mass.

OPTION

WELCOMING ROLE-PLAY

Divide the class into three groups and give each group a setting: at lunch, at recess, and after school. Have the groups role-play situations featuring new children being welcomed by others. Give the children time to develop their scenes, and then invite them to present their skits to the rest of the group. Lead the children in a round of applause for each group after they perform. Say: *By participating in and watching the performances, you can get great ideas for ways to welcome others into your lives.*

OPTION

WELCOME COLLAGE

Distribute magazines, construction paper, scissors, and glue. Invite the children to cut out pictures and words from the magazines and create a collage that describes how they might welcome others into their lives. Have them glue their pictures and words onto the construction paper. When the children have finished, ask them to share their collages and explain them to the group.

Explore

Serving Your Parish

Take a moment to remind children that God invites us to care for one another every day.

Display some items that suggest chores children might do to help their families. (dustpan, cloth, oven mitts) Ask the children if they ever use things like these to help out at home. Ask what kinds of chores children do to contribute to their families' well-being. Encourage discussion by asking the children to respond to these or similar questions: *How does doing your chores help your family? Why is it important that each person does his or her part to help? Do you think these things are a way of showing hospitality?*

Continue by saying: *Yesterday we talked about some ministries in which families in a parish can take part.* Ask: *What were some of the ministries we mentioned?* (choir members, altar servers, ushers) *Can you think of any other parish ministries, maybe some in which your families or people you know have participated?* (bringing the Eucharist to the sick and elderly, babysitting during Mass, reading the Scripture at Mass, planning social events for the parish)

Say: *Just as our families at home and our classroom families depend on all the members to be welcoming and gracious, our Church family depends on all of us to welcome one another.*

Focus the children's attention on the picture. Ask a volunteer to read what the man is saying. Say: *Yesterday we talked a little about ministers of hospitality. Let's read more about what ministers of hospitality do in a parish.*

Read the title and the first two paragraphs aloud. Ask: *What do ministers of hospitality do at Mass?* (welcome people as they enter the church, help people find seats)

Read or invite a volunteer to read the third paragraph aloud. Ask: *How do ministers of hospitality help people who are new to the parish?* (They make them feel at home.) *What are some ways you could make people feel welcome in our parish community?* (greet them when you see them at church, ask them to sit with you, invite them to parish events)

Ask a few volunteers to role-play participating as a minister of hospitality. They might act out greeting others at the door, showing visitors to their seats, or inviting them to join a group.

Serving Your Parish

People serve their parishes in many ways. They share their time and talents with their parish communities.

Some people serve their community by welcoming people to Mass. They are called ministers of hospitality. They help welcome people who are entering the church. They help people find seats when the church is crowded.

Some ministers of hospitality welcome newcomers to the parish community. They make people feel at home.

Welcome to our church!

Ask the children to think about how they could act as ministers of hospitality in their own families. Show them again the objects you displayed at the beginning of class today. Say: **Maybe one of these will give you an idea of something you do or can offer to do for your family.**

Ask the children to write a sentence or draw a picture to show what they might do. When they have finished, ask volunteers to share their ideas.

As the day draws to an end, say: **Let's keep the spirit of welcome and hospitality alive in our classroom and our homes.**

Say: **We've talked about ways to participate in the life of our parish. Let's see how many ways we can name.** Invite as many volunteers as possible to contribute ideas. List the children's suggestions on the board as they are given. (ministers of hospitality, readers, those who bring the gifts to the altar, choir members, altar servers, ushers, those who decorate the church, ministers of care, those who plan social events and charity drives)

 Family and Community

Have a volunteer read the first paragraph aloud. If your parish has ministers of hospitality who welcome people to Mass, ask the children to talk about their experiences with those ministers. Ask: **Did anyone's family members ever volunteer to be ministers of hospitality? What did it feel like to participate?**

Read the last paragraph aloud. Ask the children to identify how the people in the pictures are participating in parish life. (The woman is a hospitality minister who is helping the family that is bringing the gifts to the altar.)

In some parishes whole families can serve as ministers of hospitality. A family may volunteer to greet people as they enter church.

Parish members also volunteer to present the gifts of bread and wine at Mass. Ministers of hospitality help these parishioners too.

This family is presenting the gifts.

Session 17   **163**

OPTION

WELCOMING OCCUPATIONS

Ministers of Hospitality at church are volunteers. For some people, however, welcoming is part of their everyday jobs. See how many of these jobs the children can name. Here are some examples: waiters, airline attendants, receptionists, restaurant hostesses, and teachers. Discuss with the children how people demonstrate hospitality and create a welcoming environment.

OPTION

CLASSROOM HOSPITALITY

Say: **Imagine that someone in your classroom had the job of being a Minister of Hospitality. Write a job description, listing the responsibilities that person would have.** This activity can be done in small groups. Create a final description based on the groups' reports. You may even want to create such a position, providing each child with an opportunity to act as Minister of Hospitality in the classroom for a week.

Reflect

Prayer

Remind the children that prayer is a way to stay in touch with God and to talk with him about what they've been learning.

Make sure the children are on page 164. Have them look at the picture. Ask the children: *What is the family doing before they eat?* (praying) Tell the children: *When Jesus ate with his friends, he blessed the food they were going to eat. Now we'll learn a prayer of blessing. You can pray it with your family before every meal you eat together!*

Softly play the reflective music at the end of CD 2 to help create a prayerful and peaceful environment for the children.

Say: *Please close your eyes and fold your hands as I begin our prayer.* Read the first two paragraphs, pausing for a few seconds after each sentence so the children have time to think. Then say: *We pray the Prayer Before Meals to thank God for the food we are about to eat.*

Slowly pray the prayer with a sense of gratitude. Pause for 10 seconds and then invite the children to open their eyes. Say to the children: *Now I will help you pray the prayer. Repeat after me as I pray. Look at the picture and imagine that this is your family as you sit down together to enjoy a lovely meal.* Pray the prayer again, pausing after each comma so the group can repeat after you. Pray the prayer a third time with the children. Then encourage the children to pray this prayer with their families at mealtimes.

OPTION

PRAYER BEFORE MEALS

Provide the children with white drawing paper on which to copy the Prayer Before Meals. Allow them time to decorate their papers. Encourage them to take the prayer home to remind their families to pray before meals.

FYI

THE DOMESTIC CHURCH

The term *domestic church* is applied to our own families. It reflects the Church's high regard for the family as the primary place where the People of God are formed. The home

is the first "school" in which the children of God learn the lessons of faith: belief, prayer, worship, and the importance of a life of charity and service. This great mission of the family is rooted in the mutual love and fidelity of the husband and the wife. Since the well-being of the family is so important to the well-being of society and the Church as a whole, it is crucial that both provide meaningful support for the family unit.

Prayer

Mealtime is a good time to share. You can help set the table or help make the meal. You can also share thoughts with your family during meals.

Praying is another important part of gathering for meals. Before eating, take time to thank God for the food you have. With your family pray this prayer before meals.

Prayer Before Meals

Bless us, O Lord,
and these your gifts
which we are about to receive
from your goodness.
Through Christ our Lord.
Amen.

164   My Response

Living My Faith

Use the suggestions given on this page to encourage the children to apply the main ideas of this session to their daily lives.

Faith Summary

Read this section aloud for the children. Ask: **Who comes to us in the sacraments?** (the Holy Spirit) **Whom does the Holy Spirit's grace help us love?** (Jesus and others)

Words I Learned

Call on volunteers to define each word. Encourage them to look in the Glossary to check the definitions. Choose other volunteers to use the words in sentences.

Ways of Being Like Jesus

After reading the section, ask: **What are some things you can do to welcome new children?** (play with them, introduce them to your friends, eat with them at lunch)

✝ Family and Community

Living My Faith

Faith Summary

The Holy Spirit comes to us in the sacraments. His grace helps us love Jesus and others. At Mass we remember that Jesus died to save us from our sins.

Words I Learned

disciple   ministry   Sacrifice of the Mass

Ways of Being Like Jesus

Jesus welcomed new people into his life. You are like Jesus when you welcome new students at school.

With My Family

As a family, take a treat to a new neighbor.

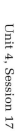

My Response

Draw a picture to show how you can help a new person in your school, neighborhood, or parish.

  Prayer

Loving Jesus, you are always welcome in my life. Help me to welcome others.

Respond

DAY 4

With My Family

Have a volunteer read the section. Ask the children: **What is something special and delicious that you and your family might bake for a new neighbor?** Accept all reasonable answers. Continue: **Ask your mom or dad to take you with them to deliver your special treat.**

✝ Family and Community

Prayer

Say: **We've talked about welcoming others, the way that we welcome Jesus when we celebrate the Eucharist. Let's tell Jesus how we welcome he is in our lives. Please fold your hands and pray with me.**

Lovingly pray the prayer. Take two deep breaths to give the children a few moments of silence. Then say: **Let's end our prayer by praying Amen together.**

My Response

Read the section. Say: **When we make others feel special and welcome, we make Jesus happy. Think about what you can do to help a new person. Then draw a picture of your idea.** When the children have finished their drawings, display them around the room. Tell the children that you are displaying the pictures so that others will know that they are a welcoming group.

As your time together comes to an end, encourage the children to be welcoming to everyone, not just new people in their lives.

Extending the Session

Choose from the following options to extend the session or to reinforce concepts developed during the week.

Family Involvement

Remind the children to take home the Raising Faith-Filled Kids page to share what they are learning with their families.

Preparation for Sunday Scripture Readings

Lead children in a prayerful discussion of Sunday's readings. Visit **www.FindingGod.org/Sunday** for more information.

Seasonal Session

Consider the time of the liturgical year and use the appropriate seasonal session. Seasonal sessions may be found on page 241.

Unused Options and BLMs

Incorporate any unused options or Blackline Masters from the week's session.

Web Site Activities

Visit **www.FindingGod.org** to find additional activities for extending the session.

OPTION

PRAY LIKE POPE SAINT PIUS X

Explain to the children that they are going to learn the *Glory Be to the Father* in Italian, Pope Saint Pius X's native language. Pray each line slowly, allowing time for the children to work on pronunciation.

*Gloria al Padre al Figlio
allo Spirito Santo.
Come era nel principio e
ora e sempre,
nei secoli dei secoli.*

166 Session 17

OPTION

WELCOME! SIGN

Teach children how to say "welcome to our church" in American Sign Language. *Welcome* (hold right hand palm up and slightly cupped at waist level and bring in toward body on a slight upwards arc) *to our* (begin with right hand, palm facing left, at the right shoulder and swing around to left shoulder, palm now facing right) *church* (curl right hand into "C" shape and tap on the top of flattened left hand). Visit **commtechlab.msu.edu/sites/aslweb /browser.htm**, for video instructions of these words. Practice with the children until they understand the movements.

OPTION

WE WELCOME YOU SIGN

Invite the children to gather around a large piece of poster board or butcher paper. At the top of the paper, write *___'s Second-Grade Class Welcomes You!* in large letters. Encourage the children to write welcoming messages or draw welcoming pictures on the sign. Remind them to write their name under their message. Arrange to hang the sign in the lobby of your church for a week or two to welcome parishioners to Mass.

After the children have prayed the entire prayer, hand out photocopies of it so that they can take the prayer home and practice with their families.

RAISING FAITH-FILLED KIDS
a parent page

Supper at Emmaus, Ivo Dulcic

Focus on Faith

Welcoming Jesus Into Our Lives

The young boy could not help but notice that his friend was not available to play on Sunday mornings. When he asked, he discovered that the family went to Sunday Mass. Intrigued, the boy asked his parents' permission to attend Mass with his friend's family. His parents agreed, and he attended Mass with the family regularly. The young boy was attracted to the faith through the hospitality of his friend's family. The story of the two disciples walking with Jesus after the Resurrection is also a story of hospitality. At the end of the walk, the disciples asked Jesus to dine with them, welcoming him into their lives. (*Luke 24:13–35*)

Dinnertime Conversation Starter

Discuss ways in which your family can welcome people into your lives.

Hints for at Home

Development of children's sacramental living starts at home, and a parent's blessing each day can play a big part in fostering this development. For example, you can express yourself in a loving manner when greeting your child or saying goodbye. You can also teach your children to greet others in a Christian manner. With your child bake a loaf of bread, using a favorite recipe. At a family meal ask your child to serve as a minister of hospitality and help your family members to their seats. Then cut a piece of bread for each member of the family. Invite each person to say a blessing and pass a piece to the person seated at his or her right. Conclude by praying as a group, "Let us remember Jesus, the bread of life."

166 www.FindingGod.org

Our Catholic Heritage

Vatican II gave us the Rite of Christian Initiation of Adults, or RCIA, which describes how the Church helps those who are searching for God. With God's help many adults enter the way of faith and conversion as the Holy Spirit opens their hearts. Every Holy Saturday thousands of men and women celebrate the Sacraments of Initiation—Baptism, Confirmation, and Eucharist. They become new members of the Catholic Church through these sacraments.

Focus on Prayer

Your child has reflected on the story of two of Jesus' disciples who recognized him during the course of a meal. Also, your child has learned the Prayer Before Meals. Use this simple mealtime prayer. You may wish to expand on it by asking the members of your family to add a word of personal thanks. The words to this prayer can be found at www.FindingGod.org.

Session 18: Gathering for Mass

3-Minute Retreat

Before you prepare your session, pause for a few moments and pay attention to your breathing. Silently count to 10 and remember that God is with you as you share the journey of faith with the children.

Psalm 119:89

Your word, LORD, stands forever;
it is firm as the heavens.

Reflection

Please. Thank you. I'm sorry. I love you. Words have great power in our lives. They define us, confine us, and at times release us to be our best selves. In the celebration of the Mass, we are enriched by the Word of God. The readings from Scripture, the homily, the prayers of the assembly, and the words of consecration prayed by the priest all unite in an act of worship and praise. The great challenge is that, in order for words to have any real transformative power, they not only need to be spoken but need to be heard and acted upon as well.

Question

How can I listen with greater openness and concentration at Mass and pray with an awareness of the words I speak?

Prayer

Prayerfully speak to God in the silence of your heart or by using this prayer.

God of creation, by your word all came into existence. Guide me so that I will receive your word proclaimed through the Scriptures with an open heart and mind.

Take a few moments to reflect prayerfully before you prepare this session.

Catechist Preparation

Knowing and Sharing Your Faith

Scripture and Tradition in Session 18

When we take into account that Jesus is the Word of God, that the Scriptures are the Word of God, that Jesus is present in the assembly from the moment of its gathering in his name, and that the liturgy is presided over by a priest, an *alter Christus* (another Christ) acting in the person of Christ, we must acknowledge that the Liturgy of the Word is a Christ-filled event. We do not have to wait until after the Liturgy of the Word to be nourished by the presence of the Lord, for as the "Constitution on Divine Revelation" declared, "The Church . . . receives and offers to the faithful the bread of life from the table both of God's word and of Christ's body."

We prepare for the Liturgy of the Word by gathering in a spirit of forgiveness, acknowledging our own sinfulness before God and others and praising God for his mercy. Then and only then are we ready to hear the word of God proclaimed and its message explained to the community in the homily.

The Liturgy of the Word is an act of worship in which we show reverence for God's Word and for the God who speaks that word. It is also an act of preparation for the sacrifice that will follow in the Liturgy of the Eucharist, the sacrifice of Jesus Christ who is Lord and Master in word and in deed.

Scripture in Session 18

2 Timothy 3:14–17 speaks of the need for fidelity to the teachings of Jesus.
Psalm 119:89 praises God for the permanence of his Word.

Let the scripture and Tradition deepen your understanding of the content in this session.

WINDOW ON THE CATECHISM

The gathering for Mass and the Liturgy of the Word are discussed in *CCC* 1348–1349.

We are to remain faithful to God's Word.

God's Word lasts forever.

From the Richness of the Tradition

The presence of Jesus in the Eucharist has great implications for justice and peace. So too does the presence of Jesus in the Scriptures, as was acknowledged by Pope Pius XII in his encyclical "On Promoting Biblical Studies" on September 30, 1943: "There those who are wearied and oppressed by adversities and afflictions will find true consolation and divine strength to suffer and bear with patience; there—that is in the Holy Gospels—Christ, the highest and greatest example of justice, charity and mercy, is present to all; and to the lacerated and trembling human race are laid open the fountains of that divine grace without which both peoples and their rulers can never arrive at, never establish, peace in the state and unity of heart; there in fine will all learn Christ."

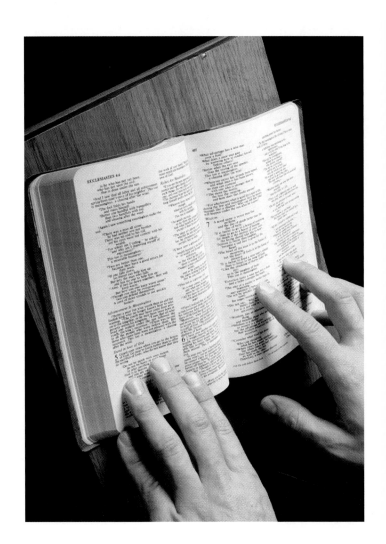

✠ Catholic Social Teaching

Aspects of the following Catholic Social Teaching themes are brought up in this session:

- **Call to Family, Community, and Participation**
- **Solidarity**

Prayer in Session 18

In this session the children will be introduced to some of the responses of the Liturgy of the Word. Likewise, they will reflect upon how they are called to listen to God's messages during the Liturgy of the Word and live these messages in their lives. In the opening prayer of petition and in the closing prayer of thanks, the children pray for a greater appreciation of the Mass.

Consider in this session how you will invite the children to respond to and prayerfully reflect on God's invitation to love and serve others.

GENERAL DIRECTORY FOR CATECHESIS

The need for disciples of Christ to be "constantly nourished by the word of God" is discussed in *GDC* 50.

Catechist Preparation: Get-Ready Guide

Session 18: Gathering for Mass

Session Theme: *When we gather for Mass we hear the Word of God.*

Before This Session

- Bookmark the Bible to 2 Timothy 3:14–17 and Psalm 119:89. Place it open to the passage from 2 Timothy in the prayer center.
- Display the poster: We Celebrate the Mass (Part I).
- Set up the CD player so that you will be ready to play the reflective music.
- Arrange for your class to visit the church for the option on page 169.

Steps

	Outcomes *At the end of the session, the children should be able to*
DAY 1 **Engage** page 167 Getting Ready to Have Friends Over	• recall the excitement of preparing for a special event.
DAYS 1–3 **Explore** pages 168–173 The Mass Begins Hearing God's Message Responding to God's Word We Praise God	• identify the Bible as the book which contains God's special messages. • explain that we hear the Word of God during the Liturgy of the Word. • explain that the priest helps us learn how to apply the readings to our lives. • define *ambo, homily, Lectionary,* and *Liturgy of the Word.*
DAY 4 **Reflect** page 174 Prayer: Asking God to Help Us Understand His Special Messages	• prayerfully reflect on God's presence, his invitation, and our response.
DAY 4 **Respond** page 175 Living My Faith: Making a List of People to Pray For at Mass	• identify practical ways to act on God's invitation in everyday living.
DAY 5 **Extending the Session** page 176 Day 5 offers an opportunity to extend the session with activities that reinforce the session outcomes.	

Materials

Required Materials

- Bible
- Writing paper, pens, pencils
- Art materials, such as drawing paper, crayons, markers, scissors, glue
- CD 2, Reflective music (page 174)
- Poster: We Celebrate the Mass (Part I)

Optional Materials

- Church bulletins (page 170)
- Paper plates, craft sticks, magazines (page 171)
- Tag-board strips (page 173)
- Large pieces of butcher paper (page 176)
- Blackline Master 46, colored paper (page 170)
- Blackline Master 47, hole punch, brass fasteners (page 170)
- Blackline Master 48 (page 171)

e-resources
www.FindingGod.org

Gathering for Mass

As you begin this time together, encourage the children to be open to God's invitation to gather with the parish family for Mass. Give them some quiet time to thank Jesus for the gift of Mass, our Eucharistic celebration. Say: *Think about all the times you gather with others. We gather here to learn. You get together with your friends at school. Then, after school, you might see your classmates at sports activities. You might also gather with friends at a birthday party.*

Tell the children to open their books to page 167. Read the title and questions aloud one at a time. Encourage the children to respond to each question as it occurs.

Direct attention to the photographs. Call on volunteers to explain what they see. (mother and daughter cleaning the house for a sleepover, girl going shopping for food with her mother, friends coming to the sleepover) Explain: *This family is sharing a good time together getting ready for a sleepover.*

Prayer

Say: *When we gather together at church for Mass, we go to a familiar place that is special to us. Please pray with me.*

Pray the prayer aloud. Then count to 10 silently as you allow children time to talk to God. End the quiet time by praying **Amen.**

Engage

Session 18

Gathering for Mass

Have you ever invited friends to a sleepover? What did you have to do to get ready for them? Was it exciting to prepare for this fun time?

Prayer

God, my Father, help me discover the many ways I can praise you and ask for your blessings at Mass.

Unit 4, Session 18   **167**

SPECIAL DAYS

Tell the children: *Sunday is the Lord's Day. Other special days are holy days. Holy Days of Obligation are days when we remember special events in the lives of Mary and Jesus.* On the board create two columns. Label one column "Special Days" and list under it the six Holy Days of Obligation (see page 180 of your guide). Label the other "Ways to Celebrate." Ask the children how they would like to celebrate the day and write it in the second column. (go to Mass, receive Holy Communion, do a good deed for someone else) Say: *We want to remember to attend Mass with our families on the Holy Days of Obligation.*

PREPARING FOR CHURCH

Tell the children to draw pictures of their families preparing for church. They may wish to draw their families eating breakfast, putting their coats on, or getting into their cars. When they have finished, call on volunteers to share their pictures and explain how their families prepare for Mass.

Session 18   **167**

Explore

The Mass Begins

Explain to children that the Mass is the greatest celebration of the Church community. The more they understand what is happening, the greater their appreciation of the Mass will be.

Read the title and the first paragraph. Ask the children if they have known anyone who was a reader at Mass.

Then choose a child to read the second paragraph aloud and ask: *What happens at Mass during the entrance song?* (The priest and ministers come to the altar.) *What happens at Mass after the entrance song?* (The priest greets everyone and leads the people in asking God to forgive their sins.)

Then ask for a volunteer to read the third paragraph. Ask: *To whom does the Gloria give glory?* (God the Father, Jesus, and the Holy Spirit.)

Display the We Celebrate the Mass (Part I) poster. Point to the introductory rites and say: *In the introductory rites we sing the entrance song. As part of the greeting, we pray the Sign of the Cross. We ask God's forgiveness and then we pray the Gloria.* Keep the poster on display for use later in the session.

Teach the children this "Here is the church" fingerplay.

Here is the church,
(Thread fingers together pointing down; join thumbs.)
Here is the steeple,
(Raise and join index fingers.)
Open the doors,
(Spread thumbs apart.)
And see all the people!
(Wiggle interlocked fingers.)

Then say: *I'd like to teach you a little more of the fingerplay, since we're learning more about*

the Church today. Demonstrate the following. Then repeat it and invite the children to join you.

Close the doors,
(Join thumbs.)
And hear them pray,
(Fold hands in prayer.)
Open them always,
(Spread thumbs apart.)
On the Lord's Day!
(Gesture outwards with both hands.)

LITURGY OF THE WORD

The Liturgy of the Word is rich in the quantity and variety of its readings.

It provides the priest and people alike with an abundance of material for prayer and reflection. It is an opportunity for the richness of the Bible to be opened to all. In the three readings from sacred Scripture, God is speaking to his people.

Among the readings, the Gospel is set aside by marks of honor. For example, the faithful stand, an acclamation is sung, and the book of the Gospels is incensed. The Liturgy of the Word prepares and leads the assembly forward to the Liturgy of the Eucharist. Together the Liturgy of the Word and the Liturgy of the Eucharist form one single act of worship.

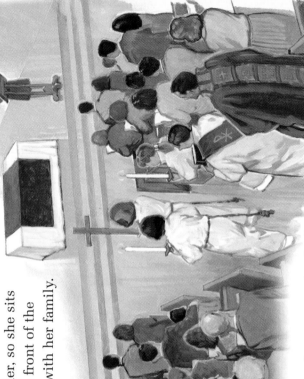

The Mass Begins

The O'Malley family attends Mass every Sunday and on special days. Mrs. O'Malley is a reader, so she sits near the front of the church with her family.

Mrs. Li leads everyone in singing the entrance song. Father Diego comes to the altar during the song. He greets the people. Then everyone prays that God will forgive their sins.

Next, the Gloria is prayed. This prayer gives glory to God the Father, and Jesus, his Son, and the Holy Spirit.

Hearing God's Message

Read the title for the children. Then read the first paragraph aloud as they follow along silently. Draw attention to the words *Lectionary* and *ambo* in dark type. Say: **The Lectionary is the book that contains special stories from the Bible which have been selected to be read at every Mass. In these readings we hear messages from God. The ambo is the platform from which these stories are read.** Draw attention to the art at the top of the page. Have the children describe what they see. (Mrs. O'Malley reading at the ambo) Say:

All the readings from Scripture that are read at Mass are read from the ambo.

Point out the attribution at the bottom of the second paragraph and say: **The letter is to a man named Timothy and comes from the Bible.** Show that the Bible at the prayer center is opened to this passage from Timothy. Then read the paragraph aloud. Ask the children: **What does this verse tell us?** (why the Bible is so important to Christians) **Why is the Bible so important to us?** (It contains messages from God.) **What are some of the things Jesus has taught us in the Bible?**

(to love God, to follow the Ten Commandments, to love others) Say to the children: **Because of our faith in Jesus, we believe what we have been taught. The Bible is the Word of God. It contains messages that teach us to live good lives, the kinds of lives God wants us to live.**

Have a volunteer read the third paragraph aloud as the group follows along. Draw attention to the word *homily* in dark type. Explain: **The homily is the explanation of what God is saying to us in the Mass. The homilist is the person who helps us understand how the Bible readings we hear during Mass have meaning for our lives. The homilist is a priest or a deacon. Learning more about these readings helps us draw even closer to Jesus and know him better.**

This might be a good time to remind the children of the additional information in the section People and Things I See at Mass at the back of their books.

At the end of your time together, say: *Tomorrow we will learn more about the Mass.*

THE LECTIONARY AND AMBO

Before the group meets, you may want to arrange a visit to the church to show the group the Lectionary and the ambo.

When you arrive in church, take the children to the ambo and hold up the Lectionary so that the children can see it; then ask: **How does this book look?** (pretty, heavy, important, fancy) Say: **This book should be treated with care and respect because the words in it have come to us from the Bible, and the messages in the Bible come from God.** Open the Lectionary and show the children the readings inside. Remind the children to look for the Lectionary and the ambo the next time they go to Mass.

Session 18   169

Hearing God's Message

Mrs. O'Malley walks to the place where she will read. This is the **ambo**. She will read Bible stories for everyone from a special book. It is called the **Lectionary**.

"You have known about God's messages since you were a child. These messages help you realize what is important."

adapted from 2 Timothy 3: 14-17

Then Father Diego goes to the ambo to read a story about Jesus' life. After this, Father Diego explains how all of the readings have an important message for our daily lives. This is called the **homily**.

Unit 4, Session 18   169

Responding to God's Word

Remind the children that together you have discussed the entrance rite and the readings that are part of the Mass. Ask the children what they can tell you about each. Then say: *Now we will look at ways we respond during Mass.* Ask a volunteer to read the first paragraph aloud. Ask the children: *With what words do you say that you believe in the teachings of the Church?* ("I believe.") Then slowly read the second paragraph. Point out the term *Liturgy of the Word* in dark type. Explain: *The Liturgy of the Word is the part of the Mass during which we listen to God's word from the Bible.*

This might be a good time to remind the children of the additional information in the section Order of the Mass at the back of their books.

Reading God's Word

Reverently read the verse aloud. Then invite the children to read it aloud in two groups, with the first group reading *The Word of the Lord* and the second reading *will last forever.* Repeat this two more times to help the children learn the verse.

170   Session 18

Say: *The church bulletin gives information for the whole church community. It can include information such as when meetings will be held, the name of your priest, times of Baptisms, names of children who have been baptized, families who are new to the parish, which parish activities are approaching, and the readings that will be used at Mass.*

Divide the class into small groups and give each group a copy of the church bulletin. Invite the children to look through the bulletins to find information about the church community, particularly those things that will enhance what they are learning. Ask the children in the groups to take turns writing down the facts they discover. When they have finished, have the groups read what they have learned. If you think they have missed something important, point it out to them.

✝ *Family and Community*

Responding to God's Word

After the homily the people express their belief in the teachings of the Church. They do this by saying, "I believe."

The Bible readings and the homily are part of the **Liturgy of the Word.** This is the time in the Mass when we listen to God's Word from the Bible. The Liturgy of the Word ends when the people pray together in need of their prayers.

Reading God's Word

The word of the Lord will last forever.

adapted from Psalm 119:89

170   God's Invitation

The First Part of the Mass

Read the activity's title and directions aloud. Encourage the children to look at the We Celebrate the Mass (Part I) poster for help. When they have finished, call on volunteers to read their numbers from top to bottom. Make sure all the children have their answers in the correct order.

Link to Liturgy

Draw attention to the icon in the upper left-hand corner of the Link to Liturgy box. Say: *You may have already noticed this icon. Whenever we see this icon, it means we are learning something about the liturgy or public prayer of the Church. The liturgy celebrates all the good things God has done for us through the life of his son, Jesus.* Have the children turn to page 161 and notice that they learned something else about the Mass at the bottom of the page where the same icon appears again.

Return to page 171 and read the section aloud. Say: *You might have noticed that we use this response often during our prayer services when we have readings from the Bible. When the priest or deacon proclaims the Gospel, he says, "The gospel of the Lord."*

We respond, *"Praise to you Lord Jesus Christ."*

Say: *A good way to end our time together is to pray: "Praise to you, Lord Jesus Christ." Let's pray it together as a reminder that everything we do can be an act of praise to God.*

Link to Liturgy

We are asked to respond to each reading during the Liturgy of the Word. When the reader says "The Word of the Lord," we say, "Thanks be to God."

The First Part of the Mass

Below are parts of the Mass that you have read about. They are in a jumbled order. Write numbers in the spaces to show the correct order.

4 _____ The priest reads a story about Jesus' life.

6 _____ The people say "I believe" to the teachings of the Church.

5 _____ The priest explains the readings in the homily.

2 _____ The people pray the Gloria, a prayer praising God.

7 _____ The people pray to God to help those in need.

1 _____ The people sing as the priest comes to the altar.

3 _____ A reader reads stories from the Bible.

OPTION

BLM 48: GOING TO MASS

Blackline Master 48 is a crossword puzzle that reinforces key words and themes from the session.

OPTION

FAN OF GOODNESS

Distribute a paper plate, a craft stick, magazines, scissors, and glue to each child. Invite the children to use the magazines and scissors to locate pictures of places or words that bring them joy. Then have them cut out these pictures or words. Encourage them to look also for pictures of churches and family activities that make them happy. Have them use the pictures and words to create a collage on the paper plate. Ask them to glue the craft stick to the back of the plate to make their own Fan of Goodness. When the children have finished, choose volunteers to stand and explain their collages.

We Praise God

Remind the children that in previous sessions this year you and they talked about how good it is to give and receive praise. Ask the children what it means to give praise. (to express approval or admiration for something someone has done)

Praise a few individuals in the class for recent accomplishments and encourage the children to turn to the nearest child and express praise for each other.

Ask volunteers to share words they used to express praise.

Continue: *The words you chose show that you admire and respect each other. At Mass we show our respect and love for God in our words of praise and in our actions. We will learn more about praising God today.*

Say: *First, let's begin by asking God, our Father, to help us know how best to praise him for all that he does for us.*

Ask the children to pray aloud the following prayer after you:

God, my Father, help me discover the many ways I can praise you and ask for your blessings at Mass.

Conclude the prayer by praying *Amen* together.

Ask children to think of the different ways they praise God, at Mass or anytime. List their suggestions on the board. (say prayers; talk to God in their own words; love him; genuflect; sing songs of praise)

Have children open their books to page 172 and look at the pictures of the people praising God at Mass. Ask children to describe the people's actions. (genuflecting to show respect to God; praying the Lord's Prayer in the orans position) Say: *Let's read about some of the ways we praise God when we go to Mass.*

Choose a child to read the heading and the first paragraph aloud. Ask: *What is our most important act of praise to God?* (the Mass) *How do we praise God before Mass begins?* (by greeting parish members) *How do we praise God during Mass?* (listen to readings, pray responses)

Read the second paragraph aloud and ask children to name some of the actions we do at Mass that show our respect for God. (kneel, stand, sit)

Ask the children to look at the photograph on page 173. Ask what they think another way of praising God might be. (singing)

Read the first paragraph on page 173 aloud. Ask: *How do you think singing shows our love for God?* (When we sing from our hearts, God knows we love him.) *What do all of our words, songs, and actions at Mass do?* (praise God)

We Praise God

The Mass is our most important act of praise to God. Even before Mass begins, we praise God as we greet the other members of our parish community. During Mass we continue to praise God as we listen to the readings and pray the responses.

Sometimes we kneel.
Sometimes we sit.
Sometimes we stand.
Everything we do shows our respect for God.

172   God's Invitation

Ways to Praise God

Read the activity heading and directions aloud. Invite volunteers to read aloud the words they will be searching for in the puzzle. Give children time to complete the word search independently.

When the children have finished, ask volunteers to use each of the words in a meaningful sentence about the Mass. Walk around to make sure the children have located all five words.

Say: *We know how good it makes us feel when someone praises us. We praise God with our words, songs, and actions at Mass. We praise God when we talk to him in our own words and through our actions.*

Ask the children to think about something they could do to praise God through their actions toward others. Say: *What could you do when you go home today to show that you are living as God wants you to?* (help a brother or sister with homework, help with the dishes, clean up without being told) Invite volunteers to share their ideas.

End the day by telling the children: *We want all that we say and all that we do to praise God.*

WE PRAISE GOD

You might want to use the children's suggestions for ways to praise God that you listed on the board as the beginning of an ongoing bulletin board. Write each suggestion on a tag-board strip and invite a volunteer to make a picture to illustrate each one. As you discuss other ways to praise God at Mass or in everyday life, add appropriate phrase strips and pictures.

ORDER PLEASE!

Write the statements about the order of the Mass from page 171 on separate strips of paper. Make four copies of these statements and place one of each into four envelopes. Place the children into four groups. Have the groups race to see which group can arrange the statements in the correct order. Make sure that their student books are closed.

PICTURE THIS

Divide the class into seven groups. Assign each group one part of the Liturgy of the Word (listed on page 171) to illustrate. Make a picture chart showing the order of the first part of the Mass.

Ways to Praise God

In the box are ways we praise God at Mass. Circle these words in the puzzle.

kneel	learn	listen	pray	sing

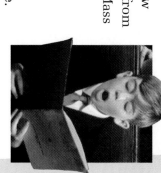

S	B	C	T	Q	E	A	K	Z
K	L	E	A	R	N	H	X	U
N	O	M	W	A	Z	O	S	N
E	P	Q	S	V	P	C	I	B
E	T	O	U	W	J	I	N	E
L	I	S	T	E	N	B	G	W
G	N	P	R	A	Y	T	U	Q
M	N	E	T	H	J	L	A	P

Ways to Praise God

Singing at Mass is another way to show our love for God. We can sing to God from our hearts. Everything we do during Mass praises God.

Reflect

Prayer

To begin the reflection this day, say: *Even though all we do and say can praise God, it is important to set aside time to praise him in prayer.*

Ask the children to look at the picture. Say: *Stained glass is little pieces of colored glass arranged carefully to create a beautiful pattern. It is often found in the windows of a church.* Ask: *What colors are in this stained glass? What book do you think this is?* (Bible) Say: *The first part of the Mass is a special time when we pray for the forgiveness of our sins, ask for God's blessings, and listen to God's messages from the Bible.*

Then invite the children to open their eyes and join you in praying the Sign of the Cross.

FYI

GENERAL INTERCESSIONS

The general intercessions, or the prayer of the faithful, concludes the Liturgy of the Word.

It is so placed because this prayer is the fruit of the working of the Word of God in the hearts of the faithful. It has been part of the Mass since the first century, when Pope Saint Clement wrote about "prayers for the people of God, the afflicted, pardon for sins, for peace and for rulers."

The general intercessions are addressed to God and ask for his blessing. The prayers of intercession are prayed for the needs of the Church, for national and world affairs, for the oppressed, and for the local community. On special occasions the intercessions may include prayers for those receiving the sacrament. The general intercessions have been called "a hinge between the two parts of the Mass" because this prayer ends the Liturgy of the Word and begins the Liturgy of the Eucharist.

✝ Solidarity

Play the reflective music at the end of CD 2. Keep the volume low so that it supports the reflection and doesn't distract from it. Continue: *Let's take some time to think about the Mass. Please close your eyes, fold your hands, listen attentively, and be with Jesus in your hearts.* Pause for several seconds to allow the children time to become quiet.

Say the following softly and slowly, pausing after each question: *Take a moment to use your imagination and picture yourself in your pew, waiting for Mass to begin. What do you see? Whom do you see around you? As the church fills with people, do you see any of your friends?* Pause for 10 seconds, allowing the children time to imagine.

Now begin reading the first paragraph, pausing briefly after each sentence. Then read the next two paragraphs, pausing for a few seconds after each sentence to give the children time to reflect. Read the last paragraph slowly and with expression. When finished give the children time to be with Jesus.

Prayer

At Mass we gather to praise God. We also receive messages from him. Mass brings us closer to God. It helps us do what God wants.

We can praise God in our everyday lives too. Think about something you want to tell God. Maybe you want to praise him for a good thing that has happened to you.

Think about how you can live God's message every day. What can you do to bring God's message into your life?

Now spend some quiet time with God. Ask him to help you understand his special message for you. Listen for what he wants you to know. Then just be still with him awhile.

174 My Response

Living My Faith

Have the children respond to each section as it occurs. Use the activities on this page to invite the children to apply to their daily lives the concepts learned in this session.

Faith Summary

Read the section. Say: *Imagine that I have never been to Mass before. I want to know why you go, what you do, and what you're listening to when people read from that special book. What would you tell me?* Call on volunteers to respond.

Words I Learned

Choose volunteers to pronounce and define each word. Have them use the Glossary to check the definitions. Ask other volunteers to use the words in sentences.

Ways of Being Like Jesus

Have a volunteer read the section aloud for the group. Ask the children: *What can we do in our everyday actions to show that we are like Jesus?* (pray for others, treat others with respect, help others)

With My Family

Read the section aloud. Ask the children: *What is the family in the picture doing? Why is it important to greet the priest at Church?* (He is an important part of the parish community. He led us in the celebration of the Mass.)

 Family and Community

Prayer

Say: *We've talked about gathering as Jesus' followers for Mass. Let's thank Jesus for giving his message of love to all of us.*

Pray the prayer aloud with the children. Then take three deep breaths, allowing the children several moments to reflect. Then say: *Let's close our prayer with the Sign of the Cross.*

My Response

Read the section and then say: *We can pray for our families and friends and ask God to help them. Think about people you would like to pray for. Then write down their names and what you would like God to do for them. Take your list with you the next time you go to Mass. Remember to pray for each of the named and what they need.*

As you end your time together, encourage children to join with their families and the parish community at Sunday Mass.

Living My Faith

Faith Summary

At Mass we praise God and ask for his blessing. The readings make Jesus present to us in a special way.

Words I Learned

ambo   homily   Lectionary

Liturgy of the Word

Ways of Being Like Jesus

You are like Jesus when your actions show that God is with you.

With My Family

As a family, greet the priest after Mass.

⭐ Prayer

Thank you, Jesus, for giving us your message. Help me listen carefully. I want to follow you.

My Response

Make a list of people you want to pray for. Take it with you the next time you go to Mass.

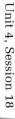

Extending the Session

Choose from the following options to extend the session or to reinforce concepts developed during the week.

Family Involvement

Remind the children to take home the Raising Faith-Filled Kids page to share what they are learning with their families.

Preparation for Sunday Scripture Readings

Lead children in a prayerful discussion of Sunday's readings. Visit www.FindingGod.org/Sunday for more information.

Seasonal Session

Consider the time of the liturgical year and use the appropriate seasonal session. Seasonal sessions may be found on page 241.

Unused Options and BLMs

Incorporate any unused options or Blackline Masters from the week's session.

Web Site Activities

Visit www.FindingGod.org to find additional activities for extending the session.

MY OWN MASS POSTER

Pass out one large piece of butcher paper to each child. Instruct the children to fold their sheets in half. They will use the top half for this activity, and the bottom half for an activity next week. Invite the children to create My Own Mass posters. Tell them that they can use the We Celebrate the Mass (Part I) poster displayed in the room as a guide in creating their own posters. Encourage creativity. When they are finished, collect the posters and store them for use next week.

WAYS TO PRAISE GAME

Organize groups of three or four children. Ask each group to come up with ways to praise God at Church. Some examples are *singing, praying, kneeling, listening to the homily,* and so on. Invite children to count how many examples they come up with and lead a round of applause for the group that figures out the most ways to praise.

PRAISE GOD WITHOUT WORDS

Form small groups of children. Invite each group to think of two or three ways we praise God without using words. (kneel, fold hands, fold arms, bow heads, make the Sign of the Cross) Invite the groups to demonstrate the gestures they have come up with. After each demonstration, ask the class if they can name a time during the Mass that the demonstrated gesture is used. Accept all reasonable answers. Remind children that all of these gestures show our respect for God.

RAISING FAITH-FILLED KIDS
a parent page

Focus on Faith

Jesus Is With Us

The little boy asked his mother whether it was true that God is inside us. She answered yes. Later she heard her son walking around the dining room table. "What are you doing?" she asked. "I am giving God a ride," he answered. A few moments later she heard him running around the table. When she asked, "What are you doing now?" he answered, "I am giving God a fast ride!" Our children have a wonderful sense of God in their lives. Attending Sunday Mass gives them the opportunity to hear God's word in their Scripture readings, to share songs of faith with their parish community, and to discover friends in faithful families. The people of their community keep God alive in their hearts.

Dinnertime Conversation Starter

Does your family have a special Sunday routine—Mass and a bike ride, Mass and a visit with grandma, Mass and a big breakfast? Discuss ways that you and your family can make the Lord's day special.

Hints for at Home

Read these Scripture passages with your child. Discuss what Jesus wants us to learn from them.

"Let the children come to me. Do not prevent them, because the kingdom of God belongs to them."
adapted from Mark 10:14

"Jesus spoke to them again, saying, 'I am the light of the world. Whoever follows me will not walk in darkness, but will have the light of life.'"
John 8:12

"Pray without ceasing."
1 Thessalonians 5:17

Spirituality in Action

Create a special bulletin board or a place on the refrigerator to post prayer intentions. Encourage family members to think of friends, neighbors, and others who need their prayers. When you go to Mass, take along your special intentions and offer them to God.

Focus on Prayer

Your child has started to learn the parts of the Mass. In this session your child has been introduced to the Liturgy of the Word: entrance, Gloria, readings, homily, and general intercessions. The next time you go to Mass, help your child identify the different parts of the Liturgy of the Word. Lead him or her to respond "Thanks be to God" when the lector says "The Word of the Lord."

Session 19: Celebrating the Eucharist

3-Minute Retreat

Take a few moments to reflect prayerfully before you prepare this session.

Before you prepare for your session, pause for a few moments and set aside any distracting thoughts. Feel the loving presence of God as you prepare to help the children grow spiritually.

Luke 22:19

Then he took the bread, said the blessing, broke it, and gave it to them, saying, "This is my body, which will be given for you; do this in memory of me."

Reflection

The greatest gift you can give to anyone is the giving of yourself. Jesus gives this truth a new level of meaning in the institution of the Eucharist during the Last Supper. He offers himself completely for all people for all time. God is not bound by time and space, and our celebration of the Mass brings the sacrifice of Jesus to the present time. As we receive the Body and Blood of Christ in the Eucharist, we are united in an intimate way with Jesus, one another, and all believers.

Question

How can I experience the Mass as not just a recollection of an event in the past but as the reality of Jesus Christ present in this moment?

Prayer

Prayerfully speak to Jesus in these or similar words.

Jesus, teacher, friend, and Savior, thank you for sharing yourself with me in the Eucharist.

The Last Supper, Andrea del Sarto

Catechist Preparation

Knowing and Sharing Your Faith

Scripture and Tradition in Session 19

The celebration of the Mass is the most important activity of the Church, "the source and summit of the Christian life" (*Catechism* 1324). It is an action of Christ and his Church that memorializes the Last Supper at which Jesus shared his body and his blood with his disciples. It is an action that makes present the death and resurrection of Christ, the Paschal Mystery that brought redemption to the entire world. It is an action of Christ and his Church in which Jesus is offered as a sacrifice to his Father for the sins of the world and in which God's people offer up their lives as a sacrifice to God. It is an action in which the living community of today is united with the Paschal Mystery and brought into direct contact with the saving acts of Jesus Christ.

Through all this action and through the power of the priest acting in the name of Christ, Jesus is truly present on the altar, surrounded by the community. As the celebration comes to a conclusion, the community is fed with the divine food and is sent into the world to serve God and to carry out the mission of the Church.

Scripture in Session 19

Jesus shares the Last Supper with his apostles in **Luke 22:14–20.** **Hebrews 10:12** reminds us that Jesus' sacrifice was for everyone.

Let the scripture and Tradition deepen your understanding of the content in this session.

WINDOW ON THE CATECHISM

The Liturgy of the Eucharist is covered in *CCC* 1350–1355.

This is my body and my blood.

Jesus offers a sacrifice for our sins.

Catechist Preparation

From the Richness of the Tradition

The Church recognizes the uniqueness of the presence of Christ in the Eucharist but also recognizes the presence of Christ elsewhere, such as in the Scriptures, in the Christian community, and in the presiders at liturgy. Christ is recognized in other places as well, and the American bishops have called on us to "recognize in the poor, the afflicted, and the oppressed the presence of the Lord summoning the Christian community to action." ("Resolution on the Pastoral Concern of the Church for People on the Move," United States Conference of Catholic Bishops, November 11, 1976)

"This holy Mass, this Eucharist, is clearly an act of faith. This body broken and blood shed for human beings encouraged us to give our body and blood up to suffering and pain, as Christ did—not for self, but to bring justice and peace to our people." (Archbishop Oscar Romero of San Salvador, homily of March 24, 1980)

✝ Catholic Social Teaching

The group will learn about the following Catholic Social Teaching in this session: **Call to Family, Community, and Participation.**

Prayer in Session 19

In this session the children reflect on Jesus' gift of himself to us in the Liturgy of the Eucharist, our central prayer as Catholics. The children thank Jesus for the Eucharist and pray for Jesus' help in sharing his love with others.

Consider in this session how you will invite the children to respond to and prayerfully reflect on God's invitation to love and serve others.

GENERAL DIRECTORY FOR CATECHESIS

The importance of liturgical education in catechesis is explored in *GDC* 85.

Catechist Preparation: Get-Ready Guide

Session 19: Celebrating the Eucharist

Session Theme: *Celebrating the Eucharist is central to Christian life.*

Before This Session

- For the welcoming activity, you will need to pass around a bowl of individually wrapped candies. Make sure that no children are allergic to the candies.
- Bookmark your Bible to Luke 22:14–20 and Hebrews 10:12. Place it open to the passage from Luke in the prayer center.
- Set up the CD player ahead of time so you will be ready to play the song and the reflective music.
- Display the posters: We Celebrate the Mass (Parts I and II).
- Arrange to take the class to visit the church for the option Our Church on page 183.

Steps

DAY 1   **Engage** page 177

Sharing Brings Us Closer to Others

DAYS 1–3   **Explore** pages 178–183

The Last Supper
Liturgy of the Eucharist
Our Most Important Prayer
Eucharist Around the World

DAY 4   **Reflect** page 184

Prayer: Lord, I Am Not Worthy to Receive You . . .

DAY 4   **Respond** page 185

Living My Faith: Thanking Jesus for Giving Himself to Us

DAY 5   **Extending the Session** page 186

Day 5 offers an opportunity to extend the session with activities that reinforce the session outcomes.

Outcomes   *At the end of the session, the children should be able to*

- understand how giving and sharing brings us closer to one another.
- understand the story of the Last Supper in relation to the Eucharist.
- explain how the Liturgy of the Eucharist prepares us to receive Jesus in Holy Communion.
- explain why we attend Mass on Sundays and Holy Days of Obligation.
- define *altar, Holy Days of Obligation,* and *Liturgy of the Eucharist.*
- prayerfully reflect on God's presence, his invitation, and our response.
- identify practical ways to act on God's invitation in everyday living.

Materials

Required Materials

- Bible
- Writing paper, pens, pencils
- Art materials, such as drawing paper, crayons, markers, scissors, glue
- Bowl of individually wrapped candies (page 177)
- Beach ball (page 180)
- CD 2, Track 17: We Come to Your Table (2:12) (page 178)
- CD 2, Reflective music (page 184)
- Posters: We Celebrate the Mass (Parts I and II)

Optional Materials

- Postcards (page 177)
- Construction paper, stickers (page 178)
- Gift box, slips of paper (page 184)
- Clay (page 186)
- Pieces of large construction paper (page 186)
- Blackline Masters 49, 50, 51 (pages 179, 180, 181)

e-resources

www.FindingGod.org

Celebrating the Eucharist

Begin this session with the following activity. Bring a bowl of individually-wrapped candies. Pass around the bowl. Be sure none of the children are allergic to the candy. Say: **Please take one piece of candy. Sharing is one way that we show our love for others. We can share our time, possessions, and good will with others in our lives.**

Have the children open their books to page 177. Draw attention to the photographs. Have the children describe what they see. (a father and son skiing, girls enjoying ice cream) Say: **Sharing and doing things with other people help bring people closer together. Sharing is also important at Mass. When we gather together as a parish community and when we celebrate the Liturgy of the Eucharist at Mass, we are sharing our faith with others.**

Read the title. Then read the questions, one at a time. Encourage volunteers to respond to the questions as they are asked.

Celebrating the Eucharist

Session 19

Have you ever given something to a friend? Have you shared something special with a relative? How did giving and sharing bring you closer to them?

🔺 **Prayer**

Jesus, my Savior, help me share your love with others.

Engage

Prayer

Say: **Jesus loves everyone. He wants to share that love with all of us! Let's pray to him and ask his help as we learn how to share love. Together let's pray this prayer of petition. Then take a few moments to say whatever you would like to Jesus.**

Pray the prayer aloud. Then count to 10 silently, as you allow the children an opportunity to talk to Jesus. End the prayer by praying **Amen.**

Prayer

DAY 1

OPTION

POSTCARDS FOR PARISHIONERS

Remind the children: **When we reach out to others, we are acting like Jesus. There are members of the parish who are ill or homebound who would appreciate a greeting from us.**

Distribute a postcard to each child. Invite each of them to write a message of cheer for someone in the parish. Ask the children to use the heading, "Dear Friend." Write on the board examples of what they could say in their notes. (We are praying for you. We hope you feel better soon. God loves you.) When the children have completed their work, collect the postcards. Give the cards to whomever is in charge of the parish ministry to the sick. Let the group know the cards will be sent to ill or homebound parishioners.

✝ *Family and Community*

The Last Supper

Remind the children that previously they learned about the first part of the Mass, the Liturgy of the Word. Say: *Today we will continue learning about the Mass in our discussion of the Liturgy of the Eucharist.*

Read the title aloud. Ask the children: *Who has heard of the Last Supper? What do you know about it?* Allow the children to respond. Then explain: *The Last Supper was the last meal Jesus ate with his friends. They shared this meal the night before Jesus' death. It was a very special time Jesus shared with his friends.* Continue: *The story of the Last Supper is a very beautiful and meaningful one to Christians.*

Read the story aloud to the children. When you are finished, say: *Jesus actually broke the bread apart and shared it with everyone.* Continue: *When Jesus said "This is my body," and "This is my blood," he meant that he is giving himself to those who follow him. This is a very special gift.*

Have the children turn to the song "We Come to Your Table" in the Songs of Our Faith section in the back of their book. Play the song on Track 17 of CD 2 and have the children listen. Then play the song again, encouraging the children to sing along when they are comfortable. Finally, sing the song one last time, inviting the group to sing the entire song.

Reading God's Word

Read the verse aloud. Then do a choral reading, dividing the verse into two parts. Have the girls say: *Jesus sacrificed himself for our sins.* Have the boys say: *He is with God forever.*

Point out the icon in the upper left-hand corner of the box and ask the children what it is. Explain that they may have noticed that whenever they see this icon, they know that something from the Bible is going to be read.

OPTION

LAST SUPPER PLACEMATS

Say: *Meals are special times we share with our families and others we care about, just as Jesus shared the Last Supper with his followers.* Have the children create placemats they can use at home. On construction paper, have the children draw their favorite foods and the people who are special to them. When they have finished, collect their work. Laminate the placemats, if convenient, before returning them to the children.

The Last Supper

Jesus sat at the table with his disciples. He said, "I want to share this supper with you."

Then Jesus took the bread. He blessed it and broke it. He gave it to them and said, "This is my body, which will be given for you. Do this in memory of me."

After the meal he took a cup of wine. He said, "This is my blood. It is given for you."

adapted from Luke 22:14-20

Reading God's Word

Jesus sacrificed himself for our sins. He is with God forever.

adapted from Hebrews 10:12

Explore

Liturgy of the Eucharist

Ask a volunteer to read the title and first paragraph for the children. Draw attention to the term *Liturgy of the Eucharist*. Say: *This is the next part of the Mass. In this part of the Mass, the bread and wine are presented, blessed, and become the Body and Blood of Christ. We receive the Body and Blood of Christ in Holy Communion.* This might be a good time to remind the children of the additional information in the section Order of the Mass at the back of their books.

Then point out the word *altar*. Encourage the children to look it up in the Glossary. Say: *The altar is the table where the bread and wine are offered to God and become the Body and Blood of Christ.* Draw attention to the photo at the top. Ask: *What is the family doing?* (presenting the gifts of bread and wine to the priest)

Read the second paragraph for the group. Ask the children if they remember the meaning of *consecration*. (the making of a thing or person special to God through prayer) Point out the illustration at the bottom. Say: *The bread and wine presented as gifts are consecrated and are received as Holy Communion.* Direct the children's attention to the We Celebrate the Mass (Part II) poster and point out the parts of the Communion rite, which include the Lord's Prayer and the sign of peace.

Then invite a child to read the third paragraph. Ask: *What two things are we supposed to do when we leave Mass?* (do good deeds and praise God for his goodness) Then call attention to the poster again. Point out the concluding rite, which includes the blessing and dismissal.

Did You Know

Read the last sentence aloud. Ask the children: *What do we do to celebrate the Lord's Day?* (celebrate Mass)

As your time together comes to an end, pray the Glory Be to the Father with the children. Remind them that the Mass gives glory to God. Then ask: *What will you do this Sunday to celebrate the Lord's Day? Talk about this with your family.*

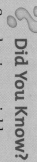

Liturgy of the Eucharist

Suki and her family go to Mass together every Sunday. Last week as the **Liturgy of the Eucharist** began, they brought the gifts of bread and wine to the priest at the **altar**. Suki and her family listened as the priest asked God to accept and bless the gifts.

During the consecration the priest repeated the words of Jesus at the Last Supper. The bread and wine became the Body and Blood of Christ. The priest invited everyone to pray the Lord's Prayer and to share a sign of peace. Soon it was time to receive Holy Communion.

When the Liturgy of the Eucharist was over, the priest blessed everyone with the Sign of the Cross. He told them to do good works and to praise God for his goodness to them.

🤔 Did You Know?

Sunday is special because it is the Lord's day.

Unit 4, Session 19 **179**

OPTION

BLM 49: SHARING JESUS' LOVE

Blackline Master 49 asks children to create a book that shows how they can share Jesus' love.

OPTION

"WE CAN SERVE" SONG

Teach the children the song "We Can Serve," which is sung to the tune of "London Bridge Is Falling Down."

We can serve as Jesus served,
Jesus served, Jesus served,
We can serve as Jesus served,
We serve others!

Explore

Our Most Important Prayer

Invite the children to stand and form one large circle as they join you for the Receiving and Sharing Game. Explain that you will start the game by passing a beach ball to one of them. You will say: *I'm sharing the ball with _____* and name the child. That child will then say: *I'm receiving the ball from _____*, filling in first your name and then the person to whom he or she tosses the ball. Continue until each child has had a turn. At the end of the game, explain: *At Mass, when we get to know one another, we become a group or community. When we go to Mass, we may not know everybody's name, but we are a community because we are all baptized members of the Church.* Then ask the children to be seated, close their eyes, and thank God for the privilege of being a part of the Church community.

Say: *We'll read more about Mass now.* Read the title. Ask a volunteer to read the first paragraph aloud. Explain: *After baptized Catholics have celebrated their First Communion, the Church encourages them to receive Holy Communion every time they go to Mass.* Continue: *The prayers we say here, at meals, and at bedtime are very important, but the Mass is the most important way that Catholics pray.* Remind the children of Suki and her family, who presented the gifts at Mass.

Have another child read aloud the next paragraph. Draw attention to the term in dark type, *Holy Days of Obligation.* Say to the group: *These are days other than Sunday on which we attend Mass and celebrate the great things God has done for us.* Say: *Mass is very important to the Church. It's so important that it's celebrated every day. We are to attend Mass*

on Sundays and on Holy Days of Obligation.

Tell the children that you would like to teach them a song to remember that Sunday is special. Sing the song to the tune of "Are You Sleeping?" and then ask the children to join you as you sing it a second time.

It's the Lord's Day,
It's the Lord's Day,
Yes, it is, Yes, it is!
Sunday is the Lord's Day,
Sunday is the Lord's Day,
It is his, It is his!

OPTION

BLM 50: MEETING JESUS

Blackline Master 50 is a review of vocabulary words learned in Unit 4.

FYI

HOLY DAYS OF OBLIGATION

There are six six Holy Days of Obligation celebrated in the United States: (1) Mary, Mother of God, January 1; (2) Ascension, Thursday of the sixth week of Easter or the following Sunday; (3) Assumption of the Blessed Virgin Mary, August 15; (4) All Saints, November 1; (5) Immaculate Conception, December 8; (6) Nativity of Our Lord Jesus Christ, December 25.

Our Most Important Prayer

The Mass is the most important way that Catholics pray. It is so special that Mass is celebrated every day. As Catholics, we should attend Mass every Sunday. The Church wants us to receive Holy Communion at every Mass we attend.

The Church also wants us to attend Mass on **Holy Days of Obligation.** These are days when we go to Mass to remember great things God has done for us.

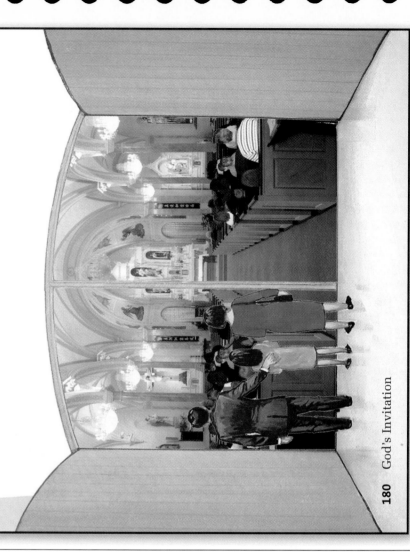

180 God's Invitation

Sharing Jesus' Love

Read the title and first two paragraphs. Make sure the children understand what they are to do. When they have finished their work, review their selections. Call on volunteers to share their sentences.

On the board draw an outline of a person. Say: *Now we must use our bodies to serve others, do good works, and praise God.* Ask: *How can we use our hands to do these things?* (pick up our toys, hold our little siblings' hands) Write their ideas inside the outline of the hand. Then ask: *How can we use our feet to serve?* (help someone cross the street, run errands) *How can we use our minds?* (help our siblings with their homework) Write our children's ideas in the appropriate part of the outline. To the tune of "If You're Happy and You Know It," sing this song, "If You Want to Share Like Jesus." Have the children first listen and then join in with you:

*If you want to share like Jesus,
Wave your hand!
If you want to share like Jesus,
Wave your hand!
If you want to share like Jesus,
Just smile! If I'll please us,
If you want to share like Jesus,
Wave your hand!*

You can add other verses, if you wish. Replace "wave your hand" with "blink your eyes," "pat your head," or "touch the ground."

Conclude by saying: *Let us remember to show our love for God and others every day and in every way we can.*

Sharing Jesus' Love

Jesus shares the wonderful gift of himself in the Eucharist. We can follow Jesus' loving example by sharing ourselves with others. All of these pictures show examples of sharing.

Mark the two examples that you think are the best. Under these pictures write a sentence explaining why you think they are the best examples of sharing.

Unit 4, Session 19   **181**

Session 19   181

OPTION

AT MASS

On drawing paper, have the children make a simple outline of a church. You may want to demonstrate this on the board. Then ask the children to divide the inside of their churches into four squares. In one square, have them print *Why I Go to Mass,* in the next, *When I Go to Mass,* in the third, *What I Do at Mass,* and in the last, *Who I Pray For.* Have them fill in their squares with their answers.

OPTION

BLM 51: CELEBRATING THE EUCHARIST

Blackline Master 51 asks yes-or-no questions about the Eucharist.

Eucharist Around the World

Help the children begin today's experience by inviting them to join you in an activity to examine the similarities and differences in things and events they are familiar with. Show the group two pencils of different lengths, one red and one regular lead pencil. Ask: **What are these?** (pencils) **Are they exactly alike?** (no) **How are they different?** (size, color) **How are they alike?** (both used to write)

Use another example, such as the same storybook in two different languages or ways different families might have of celebrating a birthday.

Tell the children that you will name some other things for comparison and they may add some of their own for the group to consider. (families, classrooms, foods, holiday celebrations) Lead the children to conclude that although there are differences, the things being compared are the same in important ways.

Say: **Today we will talk about what is alike and different about Eucharist celebrations.**

Read the title. Choose a child to read the first paragraph aloud. Ask: **Why do you think you can understand what is happening at Mass even if you cannot understand the language being spoken?** (We know that the bread and wine become the Body and Blood of Christ. The actions of the priest are the same.)

Invite the children to look at the photos of the two churches on the page. Encourage comments about how these churches are alike and different from each other and from theirs. Then ask the children to read the second paragraph quietly to themselves. Have a volunteer summarize the paragraph. Then ask: **Why do churches look different in various places in the world?** (People build and decorate them differently.)

Read the paragraph on page 183. Invite the children to describe and comment on each of the pictures. Then have them compare the similarities and differences among the churches. You might want to list the children's ideas on the board in two columns as they offer them.

Say: **Even though people all over the world have different ideas of what churches look like, they know, as we do, that the celebration of the Eucharist is always the same. We know that Jesus shares himself in the Eucharist with all people. It is good to know we are part of God's one family.**

Give the children drawing paper and invite them to design a church they would like. Will it be big? Small? Fancy? Plain? Ask them to draw just the outside of the church.

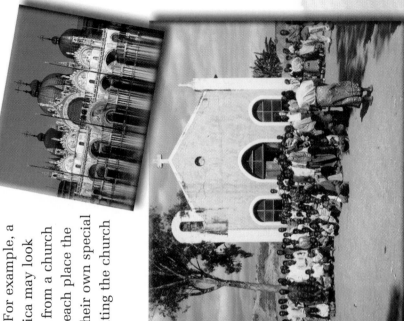

Eucharist Around the World

The Eucharist is celebrated all over the world. Wherever you go, you can understand what is happening during the Mass. You can understand even if you do not speak the language of that country.

Churches may look different in many places. For example, a church in Africa may look very different from a church in Europe. In each place the people have their own special way of decorating the church and the altar.

182   God's Invitation

When they have finished, ask the children to hold up the pictures of their churches so you can see them. Say: *All of your churches are so beautiful and so different. Now let's make a picture of something that will happen inside all your churches that is the same.* Ask: *What do you think that picture will be?* (Eucharist celebration)

Have the children draw a picture on the other side of their papers of the altar in their church and a picture of the priest during the consecration. Invite the children to share their pictures with each other and then to take them

home to share with their families what they learned about celebrating the Eucharist.

Say: *Please join me in a prayer of thanks to Jesus. Echo each part after me.*

Thank you, Jesus,
for giving yourself to me.
Place in my heart
a great love for the Eucharist.

Invite children to pray the Sign of the Cross with you.

This page shows how the Eucharist is celebrated in different places around the world. Study the pictures. What is different about how the Eucharist is celebrated from place to place? What is the same?

A CAREFUL LOOK

Tell the children that even in our country, church styles are different as are Mass celebrations. (Examples: kneelers, statues, stained-glass windows, participation of congregation, communion procedures)

Ask children to share their experiences attending Mass at other churches. Suggest that they try to visit another church, perhaps with grandparents or friends, and report back on what they discover as they look and listen carefully.

OUR CHURCH

Arrange with the appropriate person to take the children to church. Point out to the children the various design elements—statues, stained glass, the altar, a crucifix, and any changing seasonal decorations. Explain again that though the churches in the area may all look different, the Mass celebrated within is the same act of worship.

Reflect

Prayer

Today we are going to prayerfully think about Jesus' great gift to us, the Eucharist.

Say: **Please close your eyes, fold your hands, and be with Jesus.**

♫ Pause for five seconds as the children become quiet. Softly play the reflective music at the end of CD 2 to help create a prayerful environment.

Slowly and with expression, read the first two paragraphs, giving the children time to listen to the words of the prayer. Then read the last two paragraphs, pausing for several seconds after each sentence. When finished, count to 20 to allow the children time for reflection. Ask the children to open their eyes. Close by praying the Sign of the Cross together.

Ritual is described: the people of Israel were to procure a year-old male lamb without blemish, to apply its blood to the doorposts and lintels of their homes, and to eat the lamb in preparation for their escape from Egypt.

In biblical tradition it is the stated belief that it was because of the lamb's blood that the Hebrews were freed from their slavery and led into freedom.

In the book of the prophet Isaiah 53:7, the suffering servant of God, whose death will pay for the sins of the people, is described as a man whose appearance was "like a lamb led to the slaughter."

The writer of 1 Peter 1:19 reminds early Christians that they were ransomed "with the precious blood of Christ as of a spotless unblemished lamb."

In the Gospel of John 1:29, it is John the Baptist who, upon seeing Jesus, proclaimed, "Behold, the Lamb of God, who takes away the sin of the world."

During the communion rite of the Mass, when we pray for the Lamb of God to have mercy on us and to grant us peace, we are echoing a tradition of which we are a part.

Prayer

The Liturgy of the Eucharist helps prepare us to receive Jesus. The priest says, "This is the Lamb of God who takes away the sins of the world. Happy are those who are called to his supper."

We respond by praying, "Lord, I am not worthy to receive you, but only say the word and I shall be healed."

Think about these words. How special is Jesus' gift of the Eucharist? How can you thank him for giving himself to you?

Now spend some time with Jesus. Imagine you are talking to him. Talk to him about what you are thinking. Listen to what he wants you to know.

184 My Response

GIFT BOX

Pass out slips of paper. Have the children think about what good deeds they have done over the past week that they can offer to Jesus. (making their beds without being told, playing with younger siblings, setting the table) Have them write down their deeds on their papers. Then have them come forward and put them in a box. Tell the children you will bring this gift box to the Prayer Service at the end of the unit so that they can remember the gifts they are offering to Jesus.

LAMB OF GOD

Lamb of God is a designation for Jesus as the sacrificial victim who died for our sins.

Referring to Jesus as the Lamb of God has deep roots in Scripture. In Exodus Chapter 12, the Passover

Living My Faith

Use the following activities to teach the children how to practice in their daily lives the concepts learned in this session. Have the children respond to each section as it occurs.

Faith Summary

Read the section aloud for the group. Ask the children: *What did Jesus do with the bread during the Last Supper?* (blessed it and broke it) *On what days are we to celebrate Mass?* (Sundays and Holy Days of Obligation) *Why do we attend Mass on Sunday?*

Words I Learned

Call on volunteers to define each word. Have volunteers look the words up in the Glossary to double-check the definitions offered. Choose other volunteers to use the words in sentences.

Ways of Being Like Jesus

Ask: *What is the girl in the picture doing?* (pulling the little boy in the wagon) *Why?* (to help) *What are some of the ways you can help others?* (play with baby

---

(because Sunday is the day Jesus rose from the dead)

sibling so mom will have time for other things) Read the section and say: *When one person helps another, that person is being like Jesus.*

✝ *Family and Community*

Ways of Being Like Jesus

You are like Jesus when you give of yourself to help others.

With My Family

Read the section. Ask the children: *What types of things could you give up so you would have time to help others?* (video games, TV, playing with friends)

✝ *Family and Community*

With My Family

Give up one hour of your free time this week to help someone in your family.

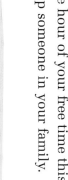

Words I Learned

altar

Liturgy of the Eucharist

Holy Days of Obligation

Faith Summary

The Mass is the most important way Catholics pray.

Prayer

Thank you, Jesus, for giving yourself to me. Place in my heart a great love for the Eucharist.

My Response

Write a sentence telling how you can become closer to members of your parish.

185

Respond

DAY 4

Prayer

Say: *Now let's thank Jesus for giving himself to us. Please fold your hands and pray with me. Then take a few moments to share with God what is in your heart.*

Pray the prayer aloud. Then take two or three deep breaths as you give the children time to reflect. Conclude by praying the Sign of the Cross.

My Response

Read each section. Say: *When we are close to members of our parish, we become closer to Jesus because we are his followers and we are baptized members of God's family, the Church.* Think about what you can do to become closer to the other members of your parish. Then write a sentence about it. Some suggestions include: *Greet them as you enter; Share the sign of peace with them;* or *Wish them a good day as you leave.*

As you end this time together, say: *Let us be more like Jesus each day by helping whenever and wherever we are needed.*

185

Choose from the following options to extend the session or to reinforce concepts developed during the week.

Family Involvement

Remind the children to take home the Raising Faith-Filled Kids page to share what they are learning with their families.

Preparation for Sunday Scripture Readings

Lead children in a prayerful discussion of Sunday's readings. Visit www.FindingGod.org/Sunday for more information.

Seasonal Session

Consider the time of the liturgical year and use the appropriate seasonal session. Seasonal sessions may be found on page 241.

Unused Options and BLMs

Incorporate any unused options or Blackline Masters from the week's session.

Web Site Activities

Visit www.FindingGod.org to find additional activities for extending the session.

OPTION

MY OWN MASS POSTER

Redistribute the My Own Mass posters from session 18. Invite the children to complete their posters using the bottom half of the paper. They can use the We Celebrate the Mass (Part II) poster displayed in the room as a guide in completing their own posters. Encourage creativity. When they are finished, invite the children to take their posters home and share what they have learned about the Mass with their families.

OPTION

CLAY PLAYS

Form pairs of children. Have each pair work together to make the following out of clay: a table with bread and wine, Jesus, and several disciples. Have pairs reenact the Last Supper using the clay figures. Pairs can meet with other pairs to share their reenactments.

OPTION

EUCHARIST SCRAMBLE

Write each letter of the word *Eucharist* on different pieces of large construction paper. If you have a large class, consider making several sets and dividing the children into groups. Place the letters on the ground in random order. At a signal, have the children work together to place the letters in order to make a word. Give children clues as they go, such as *This is the sacrament we studied this week,* or *The part of the Mass where the priest repeats the words of Jesus at the Last Supper.* When the children unscramble the word, have them read it aloud. Invite volunteers to use the word in a sentence.

RAISING FAITH-FILLED KIDS
a parent page

Focus on Faith

The Eucharist, Our Home

He was a soldier overseas. On Sunday morning he went to the nearest Catholic church. The Mass was prayed in a language he did not understand, but the ritual was the same as at home. When he received Holy Communion, the soldier reflected on the parish community that had nurtured him. He realized that Jesus Christ is present in the same manner everywhere. As we go to Mass with our children we remember that we are celebrating with Catholics around the world.

Dinnertime Conversation Starter

Imagine that you and your family are attending Mass in a country where an unfamiliar language is spoken. What clues could you find in the church or in the celebration of the Mass that would indicate that it is Catholic?

Spirituality in Action

Hints for at Home

Create a Jesus Sacrificed Himself for Us cross for your family. You will need poster board, scissors, photographs of your immediate and extended family, and glue. Draw a cross on the poster board and cut it out. Then invite your child to create a collage on the cross by cutting and attaching the photographs to fit. Display your completed cross in a prominent place.

Focus on Prayer

Your child is learning about the Liturgy of the Eucharist in Mass. The next time you are at Mass, guide your child to be attentive during this part of the liturgy. Call to your child's attention the offertory gifts, the Lord's Prayer, and the consecration.

Session 20: Unit 4 Review

3-Minute Retreat

Take a few moments to reflect prayerfully before you prepare this session.

Before you prepare for your session, pause for a few moments and turn your focus inward. Take a deep breath. Exhale. Relax and recognize that you are in the loving presence of God as you continue your journey of spiritual growth.

Matthew 12:50

For whoever does the will of my heavenly Father is my brother, and sister, and mother.

Reflection

Jesus cares about relationships. In this Gospel passage Jesus indicates that his family has room for us. We, through obedience to God and our reception of the Sacrament of Baptism, enter into the family of God. Jesus, our brother, gives himself completely both for and to us in the Eucharist. We are strengthened for the Christian life by the Gifts of the Holy Spirit received more fully in Confirmation. The Sacraments of Initiation do what they promise and draw us into a deep relationship with the family of God.

Questions

What do I think of when I hear the word *family*? What difference would it make if I incorporated Jesus as my brother into my concept of family? How can I communicate this relationship to others?

Prayer

Lovingly speak to God, using this prayer or one of your own.

Heavenly Father, brother Jesus, and Holy Spirit, my help and guide, thank you for welcoming me into the family of God. Help me to love all my brothers and sisters.

Catechist Preparation: Get-Ready Guide

Session 20: Unit 4 Review

Unit Theme: *Meeting Jesus*

Before This Session

- If you completed the prayer tablecloth option during an earlier session, use it to cover your prayer table.
- If you completed the Gift Box option last week, bring it to the session and place it on the prayer table. During the Prayer Service, remind the children of the good deeds they offered to Jesus.
- Speak with a priest about having a class Mass for the option on page 190.

- Choose a child to do the reading from the Bible in the Prayer Service. Practice the reading with the child.
- Open the Bible to Mark 3:33–35. Place it in the prayer center for the Prayer Service on page 191.
- Display the posters: We Celebrate the Mass (Parts I and II).
- Set up the CD player ahead of time so you will be ready to play the song and the reflective music.

Outcomes *In this session, the children will review*

- the significance of the Eucharist and the Mass in celebrating our Catholic faith.

- how we receive new life in Jesus.
- the word of God at Mass and how we hear it.
- the Eucharist and how we celebrate it.
- the Eucharist as a central part of Christian life.

- how to prayerfully reflect on God's invitation in everyday living.

- practical ways to act on God's invitation in our everyday lives.

Steps

| DAYS 1–2 | **Engage** page 187 |
Review

| DAYS 2–3 | **Explore** pages 188–190 |
Faith Summary

| DAY 4 | **Reflect** page 191 |
Prayer Service: We Are All Members of God's Family

| DAY 4 | **Respond** page 192 |
Living My Faith: We Participate in Mass

Materials

Required Materials

- Bible
- Writing paper, pens, pencils
- Art materials, such as drawing paper, crayons, markers, scissors, glue
- CD 2, Track 1: Song of Love (4:00) (page 190)
- CD 2, Reflective music (page 191)
- Posters: We Celebrate the Mass (Parts I and II)

Optional Materials

- Simple musical instruments such as triangles, bells, drums, tambourines, whistles (page 188)
- 3-by-5-inch cards (page 190)
- Blackline Master 52—Unit 4 Show What You Know (pages 187, 188)

e-resources

www.FindingGod.org

Engage

written feedback and identify concepts needing attention. Use this information as you continue the Review on Day 2.

Have the group open their books to page 187. Draw attention to the pictures. Have the children describe what they see. (ministers of hospitality welcoming people to Mass, priest holding chalice with the Blood of Christ, paten with the bread that will become the Body of Christ) Read the title and first paragraph aloud. Explain: *Celebrating the Eucharist helps us grow in faith.*

Prayer

Say: *Let's pray a prayer to Jesus to ask him to stay close to us. Please fold your hands as we pray together. Then take a few moments to tell Jesus whatever you want.*

Pray the prayer aloud. Then count to 10 silently, as you allow the children an opportunity to talk to Jesus. End the quiet time by praying **Amen.**

Review

Remind the children: *As members of the Church, we are part of the community of Jesus' followers. Through the Church we have special opportunities to worship God and to grow closer to Jesus.* Then sing, to the tune of "Row, Row, Row Your Boat," the following song, "Grow, Grow, Grow With God."

Grow, grow, grow with God,
Grow closer to his Son!
We celebrate the Eucharist,
And through the Church, we're one!

Show What You Know

Distribute BLM 52, Unit 4 Show What You Know, to the children. Explain that it will help the children see how well they understand what was taught.

When the children have finished, ask them to exchange papers and help them correct the objective section. Allow time for them to look over their own corrected papers before collecting the papers.

Review the short-answer and self-assessment items. Provide

Sing the song a second time so the children can become more comfortable with it.

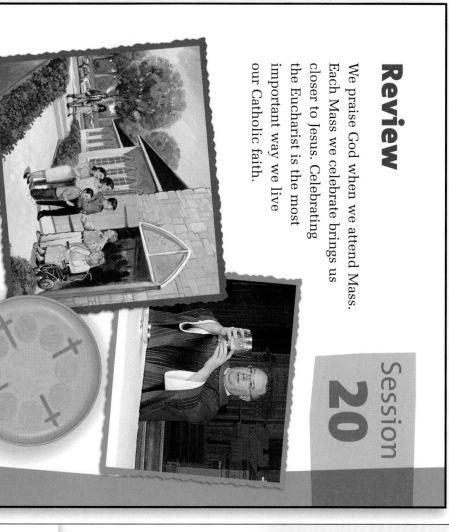

Session 20

Review

We praise God when we attend Mass. Each Mass we celebrate brings us closer to Jesus. Celebrating the Eucharist is the most important way we live our Catholic faith.

Prayer

Loving Jesus, be part of my life and stay with me. Keep me aware of your presence.

OPTION

THE DETECTIVE

Tell the children: *Imagine you are a detective. You have been sent to this room to uncover the important things learned in this unit. Search through Unit 4 to find five important things you have learned.*

When time is up, invite all the detectives to reveal what they have uncovered.

Explore

Faith Summary

Begin this day of review with an invitation to the children to become aware of God, who loves and cares for them and is always present for them.

Show What You Know

Return the assessment, BLM 52, to the children. Review the short-answer questions and any concepts the children did not fully understand.

Explain that the children will review the main ideas that they have learned throughout this unit.

Direct the children's attention to the We Celebrate the Mass (Parts I and II) posters. Tell the children that the posters will help them review the parts of the Mass.

Read the title on page 188. Ask: **What are the three Sacraments of Initiation?** (Baptism, Confirmation, Eucharist.) Then read the first paragraph aloud to reinforce this. Then draw attention to the photos on the page. Ask the children to describe what they see in each. (baby being baptized by immersion, a bishop confirming a boy, boy receiving Holy Communion)

Ask: **What day is the Lord's Day?** (Sunday) **When are Catholics to attend Mass?** (Sunday and Holy Days of Obligation) Have a volunteer read the second paragraph.

Then ask: **During what part of the Mass do we listen to God's messages?** (the Liturgy of the Word) Then slowly read the third paragraph. Direct the children's attention to the We Celebrate the Mass (Part I) poster and ask the children to tell you something about each part of the poster. Refer the children back to pages 168–171.

Ask: **What happens to the bread and wine at the Liturgy of the Eucharist?** (They become the Body and Blood of Christ.) Then choose a child to read the last paragraph.

Direct the children's attention to the We Celebrate the Mass (Part II) poster and ask them to tell you something about each part of the poster. Refer the children to page 179.

As this time together ends, remind the children that every day can be the Lord's Day if they live as followers of Jesus.

OPTION

WRITE A SONG

Say: *Lifting up our voices in song and playing musical instruments are special ways of offering praise to God.* Invite the children to work in small groups. Distribute simple musical instruments to each group. Challenge the children to work together to write and rehearse a song of praise to God. They can create new lyrics for simple music with which they are familiar, such as "Row, Row, Row Your Boat." After the children have had an opportunity to write and rehearse their songs, invite them to share their creations.

Faith Summary

The Sacraments of Initiation are Baptism, Confirmation, and Eucharist. Each of these sacraments gives us God's grace. In Baptism we receive the Holy Spirit, who stays with us and helps us.

Sunday is the Lord's day. We go to Mass on Sundays and on Holy Days of Obligation.

We listen to God's message during the Liturgy of the Word at Mass. The readings bring Jesus into our lives in a special way.

During the Liturgy of the Eucharist, the gifts of bread and wine become the Body and Blood of Christ. Every Mass brings Jesus into our lives.

188   My Response

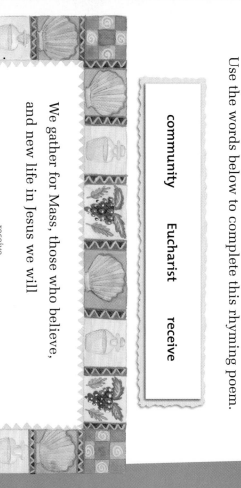

A Poem of Our Faith

Tell the children that just as they can praise God in song and through their actions, they can also praise him through poetry.

Remind the children: **Although poems do not have to rhyme, many of them do. Today we're going to complete a rhyming poem!**

Read the activity's title and directions. When the group has finished, review the answers.

Divide the children into three groups. Assign each group one stanza of the poem. Have the children practice saying it as a choral reading. After they have had time to practice, have the groups perform their stanzas for everyone.

Tell the children: **Let's share a song about being like Jesus.** Sing the song to the tune of "If You're Happy and You Know It" for the children. You may wish to write the words on the board. Then ask them to join you as you sing it again.

If you want to share like Jesus,
Clap your hands!
If you want to share like Jesus,
Clap your hands!
If you want to share like Jesus,
Just smile! It'll please us,
If you want to share like Jesus,
Clap your hands!

The children can create additional verses by replacing the word *share*. Possibilities include *love, be, help,* and *care*.

FYI

COMMUNITY

The word *community* has a very distinct meaning in the Catholic tradition. It refers to the unity among all who are joined together in Christ through grace. The faith of all members supports the faith of each person. As we are joined to Christ, so it is through Christ that we are joined to one another. Most Catholics experience "community" in their local parish and diocese as well as in the wider community of those who are part of the everyday expression and practice of their faith. The water we are baptized with helps us become disciples whose mission is to serve Christ and others in his name. The Christian community is where we are formed and continually strengthened to fulfill this mission.

✝ *Family and Community*

FYI

THE BODY OF CHRIST IN PAUL

Paul tells his communities to understand themselves as Christ's body (1 Corinthians 12:12–30; Romans 12:3–8). Paul expresses his desire for the people to unite in their beliefs for the sake of building up the Church. Paul's legacy gives the Church its self-understanding as the Body of Christ of which Christ is the head, with a body rich and varied in members, functions, and gifts.

A Poem of Our Faith

Use the words below to complete this rhyming poem.

> community   Eucharist   receive

We gather for Mass, those who believe,
and new life in Jesus we will _____ .
receive

The Sacraments of Initiation, the Church
does insist,
are Baptism, Confirmation, and _____ .
Eucharist

We welcome Jesus with hospitality
and join with others
in God's _____ .
community

Explore

Liturgy of the Eucharist

Direct the children's attention to the We Celebrate the Mass (Part II) poster. Remind the children that the Liturgy of the Eucharist is one of the most important parts of the Mass; the other is the Liturgy of the Word. Review the parts of the Liturgy of the Eucharist with the children.

Read the activity's title and directions aloud. Call attention to the word bank. Tell the children that each of these words will complete one of the sentences below.

When the group has finished, have volunteers read their completed sentences.

🎵 💿 Now you can take time to play "Song of Love" on Track 1 of CD 2. Invite the children to sing along with you. If necessary, remind the children that the words to the song are found at the back of their books.

Say: *Singing is a wonderful way to end our time together.*

OPTION

VOCABULARY FLASH CARDS

Divide the class into groups and assign a section of the student book to each group. On 3-by-5-inch cards, ask them to write a new vocabulary word on one side and its definition on the other. Use these flash cards for review or for "vocabulary bees." You might include words from Unit 5 for a later review.

OPTION

LETTER HOME

Have the children write a letter to their families about what they will do to serve them. As the children work, offer any assistance required. Encourage the children to give their letters to their families when they get home.

OPTION

CLASS MASS

Check with the appropriate person about arranging a Mass for your class. Invite a priest who will explain to the children what is happening at the various parts of the liturgy and who is comfortable gathering the children around the altar.

Liturgy of the Eucharist

Use the words below to complete these paragraphs.

> altar   Jesus   priest
>
> bread and wine   Holy Communion

Jesus shares a wonderful gift with us through the Eucharist. During the Liturgy of the Eucharist, the gifts are brought to the _altar_ .

The _bread and wine_ become the Body and Blood of Christ. This happens through the words of consecration prayed by the _priest_ .

Holy Communion is the consecrated bread and wine we receive at Mass.

My Response

Prayer Service

Prepare the prayer center in advance. Have the Bible opened to Mark 3:33–35.

Explain reverently to the children: **As members of the Church, we are part of God's family and followers of Jesus.** Continue: **For our Prayer Service today we will listen to a reading from the Bible, spend some quiet time with our friend Jesus, and end with the Lord's Prayer.**

Let us look at the prayer service in our books on page 191. Draw attention to where it says "All." Say: **When we get to where it says "All," please respond "Praise to you, Lord Jesus Christ."** Have the children repeat the response after you.

Make sure the child who will be the Reader is prepared for his or her role. Tell the children to listen attentively to the reading. Mention that there will be quiet time after the reading for them to talk to Jesus.

♪ 💿 Play the reflective music at the end of CD 2 as you have the children walk silently to the prayer center with their books in hand to begin the Prayer Service.

✝ Reverently begin: **We gather to hear God's message.** Then have a child read from the Gospel of Mark and conclude with: **The gospel of the Lord.** Motion with your hand that it is time for the children to respond.

Count to 10 silently to allow the children to experience a moment of silence. Have the children put their books down.

Invite the children to assume the orans position as you lead them in praying the Lord's Prayer.

After the Lord's Prayer is completed, ask the children to return to their seats.

Prayer Service

Leader: We gather to hear God's message.

Reader: A reading from the Gospel of Mark.

Jesus said to them in reply, "Who are my mother and my brothers?" He looked at those sitting around him and said, "Here are my mother and my brothers. Whoever does the will of God is my brother, and sister, and mother."

[adapted from Mark 3:33–35]

The gospel of the Lord.

All: Praise to you, Lord Jesus Christ.

Leader: Let us pray together the Lord's Prayer.

OUR PRAYER

Have the children turn to the Knowing and Praying Our Faith section at the back of their books. Review with them all the prayers that they have committed to memory. Allow volunteers to demonstrate how well they know the prayers. Explain to the children that these prayers are prayed by Catholics all over the world and are part of their heritage of prayers.

Respond

Living My Faith

Use the activities on this page to help the children practice what they learned in this unit.

Ways of Being Like Jesus

Read the section aloud. Say: *Since Mass is our most important prayer, it's a good time to ask God to guide and bless the people in our lives. Say a special prayer for the priest who is leading you in the celebration of the Mass.*

✝ *Family and Community*

With My Family

Read the section. Ask: *What are the children in the picture doing to serve their community?* (painting over graffiti) *What are some things you and your family can do together to help people in your community?* (bake a cake for a new neighbor, volunteer at parish clothes drive, prepare a meal for a family that just had a new baby)

✝ *Family and Community*

Prayer

Say: *We've talked about the ways that we can grow closer to Jesus as we grow in faith through the Church and especially through the sacraments. Let's pray to Jesus now and ask for his help as we continue to grow closer to him through the Church. Please fold your hands and pray this prayer of thanks aloud. Then take a few moments to share what is in your heart with Jesus.*

Pray the prayer aloud. Pause for several seconds to give the children time to talk with Jesus. Then conclude by praying the Sign of the Cross.

My Response

Read each section. Say: *When we give of ourselves, we are being true followers of Jesus. Think about what you can do to help a family member or friend. For example, you could help your parents around the house or help a friend with homework if he or she was absent from school.*

Allow the children time to write their sentences. As they work, walk around and see how well they are able to apply the main ideas in this unit to their daily lives.

At the end of the day, say: *Congratulations on completing Unit 4. Remember to live what you have learned.*

Living My Faith

Ways of Being Like Jesus

Jesus served God and others. You are like Jesus when you pray for others during Mass.

With My Family

Join your family in giving up some of your free time to serve members of your community.

Prayer

Dear Jesus, thank you for being with me as I grow closer to you through your Church.

My Response

Write a sentence describing a way you will help a friend or a member of your family.

Unit 5

Unit 5: Living Like Jesus
Overview

Unit Saint: Saint Martin of Tours

The focus of this unit is living like Jesus. The saint for this unit is Saint Martin of Tours. Martin was born in what is now modern-day Hungary probably in about A.D. 336 and entered the Roman army at the age of 15. One day, while serving in France, he met a man who was freezing. Martin cut his coat in two and gave half of it to the man. That same night he dreamed that he saw Jesus wearing that half of his coat. The very next morning Martin decided to become Christian. He eventually became a great bishop in France. Saint Martin of Tours is an example of someone who was like Jesus.

Session 21: Being Like Jesus

Saint Martin of Tours and the Good Samaritan are examples of people who reached out to help those in need. Jesus showed us how to love others through his words and actions. He wants us to love our neighbors and to care for those who are forgotten by others.

Session 22: We Share God's Life

We sometimes have to make difficult choices. We focus on how—with the help of the Holy Spirit, the Church, the Bible, and special people in our lives—we can make good moral choices.

Session 23: Following Jesus

Jesus teaches us his Great Commandment and the Beatitudes in order to guide us in our decision making and to help us to become holy. We examine God's love for the Jewish people in the Old Testament. We review the story of Jesus' life and the life of the early Church in the New Testament.

Session 24: Making Choices

Love of God and love of others are inseparable. In this session we learn how Jesus teaches us to respect people and their belongings. God wants us to live in mutual kindness and to be respectful of others in our words and actions.

Session 25: Unit 5 Review

We will review the main concepts of the previous four sessions, stressing the key points and reinforcing any areas in which the children may not have a clear understanding.

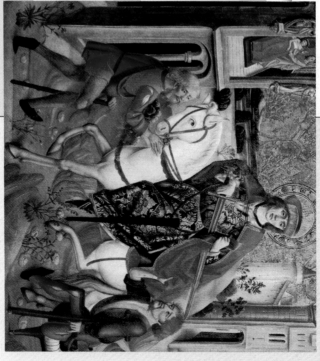

Saint Martin of Tours Sharing His Cloak With the Poor, 1490

Consider how the focus of this unit is developed throughout the sessions.

Catechist Preparation

As you guide the children through this unit, think about how you will help them to praise God through prayer and service.

Prayer in Unit 5

In this fifth unit continue using the established pattern and tone for prayer in each session. The short opening prayer of petition and the closing prayer of gratitude invite the children to reflect on the focus of the session. Each prayer also provides an opportunity for silent meditation.

In three of the guided reflections the children will imagine meeting Jesus, talking to him, and listening for his response. In a fourth reflection the children pray to the Holy Spirit for guidance in making good choices. The Prayer Service at the end of the unit encourages the children to think of themselves as peacemakers.

✝ Catholic Social Teaching in Unit 5

The following themes of Catholic Social Teaching are integrated into this unit:

Call to Family, Community, and Participation Participation in family and community is central to our faith and to a healthy society. As the central social institution, the family must be supported and strengthened. From this foundation, people participate in society, fostering a community spirit, and promoting the well-being of all, especially the poor and vulnerable.

Option for the Poor and Vulnerable In our world many people are very rich, while at the same time, many are extremely poor. As Catholics, we are called to pay special attention to the needs of the poor. We can follow Jesus' example by making a specific effort to defend and promote the dignity of the poor and vulnerable and to meet their immediate material needs.

Solidarity Because God is our Father, we are all brothers and sisters with the responsibility to care for one another. Solidarity is the attitude that leads Christians to share spiritual and material goods. Solidarity unites rich and poor, weak and strong, and helps to create a society that recognizes that we all live in an interdependent world.

Care for God's Creation God is the creator of all people and all things, and he wants us to enjoy his creation. The responsibility to care for all God has made is a requirement of our faith. We are called to make the moral and ethical choices that protect the ecological balance of creation.

Life and Dignity of the Human Person The Catholic Church teaches us that all human life is sacred and that all people must be treated with dignity. As Catholics, we strive to value people over material goods. We are called to ask whether our actions as a society respect the life and dignity of the human person. Our belief in the life and dignity of the human person is the foundation of our moral vision.

Rights and Responsibilities The Catholic Church teaches that every person has a right to life as well as a right to those things required for human decency. As Catholics, it is our responsibility to protect these fundamental human rights in order to achieve a healthy society. The only way to protect human dignity and to live in a healthy community is for each of us to accept our responsibility to protect those rights in our own interactions.

Catechist Preparation

Session 21: Being Like Jesus
3-Minute Retreat

Before you prepare for your session, pause for a few moments, take three deep breaths, and be aware of the loving presence of God, who is with you during your journey of growth and discovery.

Luke 10:36–37

"Which of these three, in your opinion, was neighbor to the robbers' victim?" He answered, "The one who treated him with mercy." Jesus said to him, "Go and do likewise."

Reflection

Help comes from unexpected places. For the injured man in the parable of the Good Samaritan, help came from someone who was outside the community of believers. As we live as children of God, our choice to do what is right comes from a decision to do what is good, just, and merciful out of love for God. With God's grace we can be an unexpected source of mercy for those who suffer.

Question

How can I be an instrument of healing and mercy in my relationships?

Prayer

Pray to God, using this prayer or one of your own.

My Lord and my God, I want to love you with all my heart, all my soul, and all my mind. Help me to love my neighbor as I love myself.

Take a few moments to reflect prayerfully before you prepare this session.

Catechist Preparation

Knowing and Sharing Your Faith

Scripture and Tradition in Session 21

Jesus modeled love for us in concrete ways. He was born and lived his life in humble circumstances and modeled for us the kind of simple and humble lifestyle that all of us are called to live. He was a model of obedience to his parents but more importantly to his heavenly Father. He was a model of service. He showed concern for others, and through his many acts of compassion and service, he taught us how to love. He opposed the stereotyping of tax collectors, Samaritans, and women and was a model of how we should accept one another. He spent much time in prayer and was a model to us of a prayer-filled life. He never made wrong moral choices and was a model to us of the moral person. He was faithful in his relationships with his Father and with others, even though that faithfulness cost him his life. He showed us how to be faithful in life and in death.

Scripture in Session 21

In **Luke 10:25–37** Jesus teaches about mercy by telling a parable. **Matthew 5:7** is the beatitude about being merciful.

Let the scripture and Tradition deepen your understanding of the content in this session.

WINDOW ON THE CATECHISM

In order to live like Jesus, we need to reflect upon his life. "The Mysteries of Christ's Life" are discussed in CCC 512–560.

The Good Samaritan shows love.

The merciful shall receive mercy.

Catechist Preparation

From the Richness of the Tradition

"As believers, we find our reason and direction for action in the life of Jesus and the teaching of his Church. We are reminded by the gospel that the first human problem Jesus faced on earth was a lack of shelter. There was 'no room in the inn' for the Holy Family in Bethlehem. Today, we see in the faces of homeless men, women, and children, the face of Christ. We know that in reaching out to them, standing with them in defending their rights, in working with them and their families for decent housing, we serve the Lord." ("Homelessness and Housing: A Tragedy, A Moral Challenge," March 24, 1988, United States Conference of Catholic Bishops)

✦ Catholic Social Teaching

In this session the following Catholic Social Teachings are explored:

- **Option for the Poor and Vulnerable**
- **Rights and Responsibilities**
- **Care for God's Creation**
- **Call to Family, Community, and Participation**
- **Solidarity**

Consider in this session how you will invite the children to respond to and prayerfully reflect on God's invitation to love and serve others.

GENERAL DIRECTORY FOR CATECHESIS

As catechists, it is our task to show the children who Jesus Christ is so that others may follow him. This task is explored in *GDC* 41.

Nativity Scene, fresco from the Church of San Francesco at Assisi, Simone Martini and others

Prayer in Session 21

In this session the children will reflect on the Good Samaritan story as a model for loving one's neighbor. This will be done as part of a short, guided reflection. In the opening prayer of petition and in the closing prayer of thanks the children will pray to become more loving, as Jesus was.

Catechist Preparation: Get-Ready Guide

Session 21: Being Like Jesus

Session Theme: *Jesus shows us how to love through his words and deeds.*

Before This Session

- Bookmark Luke 10:25–37 and Matthew 5:7. Place the Bible in the prayer center open to the passage from Luke.
- Set up the CD player so you will be ready to play the song, the Scripture story, and the reflective music.
- Display the poster: We Celebrate the Mass (Part II).
- Visit the Web site mentioned in the option on page 193.

Outcomes   *At the end of the session, the children should be able to*

- identify Saint Martin of Tours as a saint who was generous and caring.
- understand the importance of helping others.
- explain the story of the Good Samaritan.
- follow the Good Samaritan's example of caring for others.
- give examples of ways to reach out to other people.
- prayerfully reflect on God's presence, his invitation, and our response.
- identify practical ways to act on God's invitation in everyday living.

Steps

DAY 1 Engage pages 193–195
Unit Saint: Martin of Tours
Being Like Jesus

DAYS 2–3 Explore pages 196–201
The Good Samaritan
Reaching Out to Others
Acting as Jesus Would
Many Good Samaritans

DAY 4 Reflect page 202
Prayer: Being Merciful to Others

DAY 4 Respond page 203
Living My Faith: Thanking Those Who Act With Kindness

DAY 5 Extending the Session page 204
Day 5 offers an opportunity to extend the session with activities that reinforce the session outcomes.

Materials

Required Materials

- Bible
- Writing paper, pens, pencils
- Art materials, such as drawing paper, crayons, markers, scissors, glue
- CD 1, Track 5: The Good Samaritan (4:06) (page 196)
- CD 2, Track 19: Jesus' Hands Were Kind Hands (2:07) (page 196)
- CD 2, Reflective music (page 202)
- Poster: We Celebrate the Mass (Part II)

Optional Materials

- 30 building blocks (page 194)
- Poster board, magazines, newspapers (page 197)
- 6-by-1½-inch strips of construction paper (page 197)
- Construction paper, bandages (page 198)
- Paper plates or construction paper, newspapers, magazines (page 200)
- Shoeboxes, clay (page 204)
- Small paper bag, ribbon, construction-paper hearts, "compassionate gifts" (page 204)
- Blackline Masters 53, 54, 55 (pages 195, 197, 198)

e-resources
www.FindingGod.org

Living Like Jesus

♪ 💿 As you begin this last unit, play CD 2, Track 1: "Song of Love." Invite the children to sing along. Let this be a class prayer.

Remind the children that they learn about God so that they can live as God wants. Introduce the new unit by asking the following question: *What do you think when you see someone wearing a bandage?* (They've been hurt, and the bandage is helping the wound to heal.)

Then ask: *Who are people who help you when you are hurt?* (parents, families, catechists, teachers, friends, neighbors)

Say: *We are blessed to have so many people in our lives who help us. We can show we care for others too. When we reach out to others, we are acting as Jesus would and are living the kinds of lives God wants us to live.*

Then say: *Please turn to page 193 in your books.* Have the children focus attention on the picture of Saint Martin of Tours. Explain: *Saint Martin of Tours was a loving, caring man who reached out to*

help others. He acted as Jesus did. As we learn more about him, we will learn more about what it means to act as Jesus would. Then read the caption aloud as the group follows along.

Engage

OPTION

STICKING OUR NECKS OUT FOR OTHERS

Tell the children about the Giraffe Project, an organization based in Langley, Washington, that encourages children to serve their communities. To learn more about the organization, visit www.giraffe.org.

Say: *The Giraffe Project is a group that encourages people to stick their necks out for others.* Ask: *What can you do to stick your neck out for someone?* (make a new child at school feel welcome, donate something that is special to you to someone in need, recycle, pray for someone who is sick)

On the board write *I will stick my neck out for someone by _____.* Have the children copy the sentence onto the top portion of a piece of paper and fill in the blank with what they will do. Below their sentence, have the children draw a picture of a giraffe. On the bottom part of their papers, have the children draw a picture of what they will do to help someone.

When they have finished, call on volunteers to share their pictures and explain what they will do to help another person. End by saying: *When we stick out our necks for others, we are showing our love for them, as Jesus wants us to do.*

Living Like Jesus
Unit 5

Saint Martin of Tours
Saint Martin of Tours cared for others. Martin's kind acts helped him find out what God wanted him to do.

193

Unit 5   193

Saint Martin of Tours

Read the title and the first two paragraphs aloud. Explain: *Martin saw that the man was freezing and needed help. He reached out to help the man at a personal sacrifice to himself. We should try to notice when others need our help.* Ask: *Why do you think Martin saw Jesus wearing half of his coat in his dream?* (Jesus told us that anything we do for others, we do for him.)

Ask a child to read the final paragraph aloud. Ask: *What is a Christian?* (one who believes in and follows the teachings of Christ) *How was Saint Martin like Jesus?* (He helped many people.) Say: *When we help others, no matter who they are or where they live, we are being like Jesus too.*

✝ *The Poor and Vulnerable*

OPTION

SHARING BLOCKS

Divide the class into three groups. Explain that you will give each group blocks with which to build whatever they would like.

Give the first group 15 blocks, the next group 12 blocks, and the last group 3 blocks. Then invite the children to begin building.

The children may inquire about why the groups have different numbers of blocks. The group with only 3 blocks may say they can't build much with only 3 blocks. Ask all the groups: *What can we do so that we can all build something?* (The groups with more blocks can share.) *When Saint Martin saw a freezing man without a coat, what did he do?* (shared his coat) *What qualities does this show that Saint Martin had?* (unselfishness, generosity) Ask the groups that have 15 and 12 blocks: *Would you be willing to share your blocks with the group that has only 3 blocks?* Hopefully, they will be willing. If the group with 15 blocks gives 5 blocks to the

group that has 3 blocks, and the group that has 12 blocks gives them 2, everyone will have 10 blocks.

After the blocks are shared, praise the children and say: *When you share, you are being like Jesus.* Then give the children time to create something with their blocks and share their creations with the group.

FYI

SAINT MARTIN OF TOURS

Martin, born in about A.D. 336, was interested in Christianity at an early age, even though both of his parents were pagan. One day, he met a man who was freezing. Martin cut his own coat in half and gave half of

it to the man. The same night, he dreamed that Jesus was wearing the other half. The next morning Martin decided to be baptized.

After being drafted into the army, Martin was thrown into prison by Caesar Julian but was later released. Martin became a monk and in time was made the bishop of Tours.

Martin founded the abbey of Marmoutier, located outside of the city of Tours. The focus of this abbey, as well as other monastic communities Saint Martin founded, was to bring Christianity to rural areas. Martin played a major role in strengthening Christianity in France. His feast day is November 11.

Saint Martin of Tours

Martin lived a long time ago. He became a soldier at a young age.

One cold night Martin met a man who was freezing. Martin cut his coat and gave half of it to the man. That same night Martin saw Jesus in a dream. Jesus was wearing half of Martin's coat.

Martin became a Christian after his dream. Later he was made a bishop in France. As bishop, he helped many people. Saint Martin became one of the most important Church leaders of his time.

194 God's Invitation

Being Like Jesus

Remind the children: *God is merciful to us, and he wants us to show mercy to others. To be merciful is to act with kindness and compassion toward another. The story of Saint Martin of Tours and the freezing man shows us someone who is showing kindness and compassion toward another person. God wants us to follow the example of Jesus, who was merciful to everyone.*

Read the title aloud. Draw attention to the pictures. Have the children describe what they see. Say to the children: *Jesus was helpful and kind to others. The people in the picture are being kind and helpful. Think of a time when someone was helpful or kind to you.* Ask volunteers to briefly share their stories. Then say: *That person was being like Jesus. You can be like Jesus too!*

Read the questions aloud as the children follow along. Encourage the children to respond to the questions.

Engage
DAY 1
Prayer

Say: *We are learning about how we are to follow Jesus' example of love and goodness. Let's pray to Jesus and ask for his help as we discover ways to be like him. Pray with me. Then take time to tell Jesus silently what is in your hearts.*

Pray the prayer. Then pause and give the children time to reflect. End the quiet time by praying *Amen.*

Being Like Jesus

Being Like Jesus

Session 21

Have you ever helped someone who was sad or hurt?
How did you help this person?
How did it make you feel about yourself?

Prayer

Jesus, my model of love, help me learn about the things you said and did so I can become more like you.

OPTION
BLM 53: SAINT MARTIN OF TOURS

Blackline Master 53 is a puzzle containing key words about Saint Martin of Tours.

OPTION
CHART OF HEALING EXPERIENCES

Create a three-column chart on the chalkboard. Label the columns *Person, Action,* and *Feeling.* Tell the children that charts can help us organize information. Then ask volunteers to name people they helped, the action they took to help these people, and the way the action made them feel. Complete the chart as children share their experiences. Remind them: *When we help other people, we are being like Jesus.*

The Good Samaritan

Begin by praying together the prayer on page 195. Then explain to the children that many of the stories in the Bible show them ways to act as Jesus would want them to.

Direct the children's attention to the open Bible at the prayer center. Say: *This story comes to us from the Bible. It is a parable.* Ask: *Who remembers what a parable is?* (one of the stories Jesus told that shows us what God wants for the world) Read the title and say: *The parable of the Good Samaritan is a very popular Bible story that you will now hear. Samaritans were people who lived in Palestine. The Jewish people and the Samaritans hadn't liked one another for a long time. In this parable about the Good Samaritan, Jesus tells us how we should treat everyone. Please follow along as I read this story aloud.* After reading the story, say: *Now sit quietly and comfortably as we listen to this story on a CD. Listen for any other information you can find out about the Good Samaritan.*

The dramatized version of The Good Samaritan is based on Luke 10:25–37, the Scripture cited in the children's book.

Draw the children's attention to the pictures on pages 196 and 197. Tell them to look at the pictures as they listen to the story.

Play the recording on Track 5 of CD 1. When the story of the Good Samaritan is finished, encourage the children to say whatever they would like about what they heard.

Ask: *How did Jesus say we are to treat others?* (love our neighbors as much as we love ourselves) *What does it mean to show mercy?* (to be kind to others and help those in need) Then say: *The Samaritan helped the Jewish man*

even though the Jewish people and the Samaritans were enemies. Who does Jesus tell us to be like? (the Good Samaritan) *Why?* Accept all reasonable answers. Tell the children: *We should try to be like the Good Samaritan and help others in need. When we do this, we are being like Jesus.*

✝ *Rights and Responsibilities*

Remind the children that though Jesus wants them to care for people who need help, they can also be good Samaritans by caring for God's other creatures.

Tell the children of a time when you may have cared for a sick or injured animal. Then ask them if they have ever taken care of an animal in need. Then say: *When you cared for this animal, you were caring for one of God's creatures and were being a Good Samaritan.*

✝ *God's Creation*

🎵 💿 Have the children turn to the words of the song "Jesus' Hands Were Kind Hands" in the Songs of Our Faith section in the back of their book. Say: *In this song we will sing about how Jesus used his kind hands to help*

The Good Samaritan

A man asked Jesus, "What must I do to live with God forever?"

Jesus answered, "What does the law say?"

The man said, "You should love the Lord with all your strength. You should love your neighbor as much as you love yourself."

Jesus told the man that he had given the right answer. Jesus told him that he would go to heaven if he did these things.

Then the man asked Jesus, "Who is my neighbor?"

196 God's Invitation

people. Have them follow along, reading the words and listening to the melody as you play the song on Track 19 of CD 2. Then play the song again and have the children sing along. Say: *We should try to use our hands to do good deeds, as Saint Martin and the Good Samaritan did. Saint Martin used his hands to give half of his coat to the freezing stranger, and the Good Samaritan used his hands to help the injured man.*

✝ *Rights and Responsibilities*

Jesus answered by telling this story. "A Jewish man was traveling on a road. He was attacked by robbers. They left him hurt in the road. A Temple official walked by and ignored the hurt man. Another man passed by and did not help him.

"Then a good man from Samaria saw him. He wanted to help. So the Good Samaritan bandaged the man's wounds, lifted him onto his donkey, and took him to an inn."

Then Jesus asked, "Which of these three men acted like a good neighbor?"

"The one who showed mercy," said the man who was questioning Jesus.

"Yes," said Jesus. "Go and be like this man."

adapted from Luke 10:25-37

OPTION

BLM 54: THE GOOD SAMARITAN

On Blackline Master 54 children use a code to finish the story of the Good Samaritan.

OPTION

LOVE YOUR NEIGHBORS COLLAGE

Have the children work in pairs to create a collage of pictures and words that describe how we can love our neighbors wherever they may be. Distribute poster board, magazines, newspapers, scissors, and glue. Invite the children to cut out and arrange pictures and words on the

✝ *Family and Community*

OPTION

GOOD SAMARITAN CHAIN

Give each child a strip of construction paper (6-by-1½-inch). On the construction paper strip have the children write one way in which they might be a Good Samaritan. Call on volunteers to share what they wrote. Then have the children glue the ends of their strips together to create a chain. Hang the chain at the prayer center and say: *When we love our neighbors and care for them, we grow closer to Jesus and become linked to him.*

poster board. When the children have finished, have them share their collages with the group, explaining the reason for their choices and words.

Explore

FYI

THE SAMARITANS

The Samaritans were members of a group of people who lived in Israel at the time of the New Testament. They were the descendants of the people left behind when many of the Jewish people were exiled to Babylon in 587 B.C. They intermarried with non-Israelites who were brought into the country by the Assyrians. When the Jewish nation was restored after 536 B.C., the Samaritans were not welcomed back into the Jewish community. The Jews in Jesus' time looked down on the Samaritans as not being true followers of the Jewish religion. The Samaritans thought otherwise.

In telling the story of the Good Samaritan, Jesus was confronting his listeners with their own prejudices and emphasizing the universal nature of God's love. The priest and the Levite were Israel's spiritual leaders. They are examples of law-observing people who did not aid the injured man because they were afraid of becoming defiled and unable to fulfill their religious duties. The question Jesus is asking here is, What is a religious person's true duty to God and others?

Explore

Reaching Out to Others

Read the title aloud. Say: *We've learned about Saint Martin of Tours and the Good Samaritan. Now let's read about a girl who is a Good Samaritan!* Read the story as a miniplay. Ask for volunteers to be narrator, Chris, and Leyla.

Then draw attention to the illustration and call on volunteers to describe what they see. (Leyla helping Chris walk back home) Ask: *In what way was Leyla being a Good Samaritan?* (Leyla helped Chris even though they didn't always get along.) Ask the children: *Have you ever been a Good Samaritan? Or has someone ever been a Good Samaritan to you?* Encourage the children to share their experiences.

Reading God's Word

Refer to the Bible at the prayer center. Read the scripture passage aloud. Then say: *Jesus tells us that God will be merciful to people who are merciful, kind, and caring to others. We should help all people in need, even if they are not our friends.*

End the day by encouraging the children to be merciful, kind, and caring.

OPTION

BLM 55: BEING LIKE JESUS
Blackline Master 55 is an activity in which children complete sentences that cover content from the session.

OPTION

I CARE FOR YOU

Tell the children: *Take a few moments to think of the parable of the Good Samaritan. Imagine how the injured man felt as he lay in the road and was ignored by the first two men. The man was hurt in his body. Then his heart hurt when the men passed by him without helping.* Pass out construction paper, crayons or markers, scissors, and a bandage to each child. Have the children draw and cut out a paper heart. Then have them write a word or phrase that describes how they think the injured man felt. Have them carefully make a tear halfway down the heart. Explain: *When we hear unkind words or experience unkind actions, we hurt inside our hearts. God wants us to use kind words and actions. He wants us to help those who are hurt.*

Invite each child to mend the torn heart by removing the backing on the bandage and placing the bandage over the tear. Say joyfully: *We can mend hearts when we are merciful.*

✝ Solidarity

Reaching Out to Others

Leyla saw Chris fall off her bike. The two girls did not always get along, but Leyla began to run toward her. Chris slowly stood up and brushed herself off.

"Are you OK?" Leyla asked.

"I think I twisted my ankle," Chris moaned.

"Take my arm," Leyla said, as she reached to help Chris. "I will help you get home. Then I will come back and get your bike for you."

"Thanks," said Chris. "I feel better already."

Reading God's Word

Blessed are people who show mercy. God will have mercy on them.
adapted from Matthew 5:7

Acting as Jesus Would

Begin the day by saying: *We can be like Jesus and reach out in love and kindness to others. When we notice that someone else is hurting, we should try to help.* Invite the children to close their eyes and pray for the courage to offer help to anyone—not just friends and family—who needs it.

Ask a volunteer to read the title and paragraph aloud. Then say: *All three people we've read about this week—Saint Martin of Tours, the Good Samaritan, and Leyla—acted as Jesus would. They showed mercy and love toward others. We should try to do the same.*

✝ *The Poor and Vulnerable*

Making a Difference

Read the activity's title and directions aloud. Say: *This is a good time for us to see how much we've learned about how to be more like Jesus.* When the children have finished, ask: *What is happening in the first picture?* (The children are helping their mother by opening the door and carrying some of the groceries.) Then ask: *What is happening in the second picture?* (The children are ignoring their mother who could use help.) *In which picture is someone being like Jesus?* (the first picture) Ask: *Have any of you been in a situation like this one? What did you do?* Encourage the children to respond.

Link to Liturgy

Say: *The priest says these words to remind us to be like Jesus and to reach out to others. These words are said during the concluding rite of the Mass, at the end of the Mass. Listen for these words the next time you attend Mass.* Have a child read the section. Draw attention to the We Celebrate the Mass (Part II) poster. Note that these words are said at the dismissal, which, along with the blessing, form the concluding rite of the Mass.

Link to Liturgy

At the end of Mass, the priest reminds us to be like Jesus. The priest says, "Go in peace to love and serve the Lord."

Acting as Jesus Would

Saint Martin of Tours reached out to a suffering stranger. The Good Samaritan acted with love and mercy. Leyla helped Chris walk home. All of these people acted as Jesus would want.

Making a Difference

Check the box that shows an example of someone acting as Jesus would.

NOW IT'S MAKING A DIFFERENCE!

Remind the children of the Making a Difference activity that they completed in their books. Say: *We checked the box in the first picture because the children were acting as Jesus would. Let's draw our own pictures to show examples of people acting as Jesus wants.*

Have the children draw two illustrations—one that shows a person in need and another that shows how that person can be helped. Brainstorm ideas with the children. For example, they may wish to draw a picture of a child who forgot to bring lunch. In the second picture, they could draw themselves sharing their lunch with the child. If needed, help the children with other ideas. When the children have finished, call on volunteers to hold up their papers and explain how their second picture shows people acting like Jesus.

Good Samaritan Award

Ask the children what it means to receive an award. (that you are being rewarded for doing something well) Encourage the children to share stories of awards they have received themselves or their family members and friends have received. Ask: *How does it make someone feel when they receive an award?* (proud, happy, thankful)

Invite the children to turn to page 200 to look at a very special award. Say: *This is a Good Samaritan Award.* Ask: *What do you think a person might do to earn this award?* (act with love and mercy toward another, help someone in need)

Ask the children to read along as you read the heading and paragraph aloud. Suggest that the children sit quietly for a few moments and think of someone in their lives who deserves this special award because he or she acts like Jesus and helps others.

Give the children sufficient time to complete their awards. You might suggest that they make a practice copy on paper first so you can help them with their ideas and with spelling as they work. Then they may copy it onto the award, sign it, and cut it out. If time allows, glue the award onto colored construction paper.

Say: *Think of how happy this person will be to know that his or her caring acts are recognized and appreciated by you. Thank the person for showing you how to live as a helping friend.*

OUR NEIGHBORS

Invite the children to make a neighbor collage to help them remember that God tells us that all people are our neighbors, even those who look different than we look, live in different places, and may disagree with us. Tell the children they will need their scissors, glue, and a crayon or marker. Distribute newspapers and magazines to the children. Ask them

Give each child a paper plate or a piece of construction paper. Tell the children they will need their scissors, glue, and a crayon or marker. Distribute newspapers and magazines to the children. Ask them

to look for and cut out pictures of people who seem to need help—the homeless, the poor, the sick, the hungry. Encourage them to include pictures of people of various races. Have the children make collages by gluing their pictures on their plates or papers. Have a sharing time when the collages are completed. You might collect and display them on a bulletin board titled *Our Neighbors*.

Good Samaritan Award

You can make a Good Samaritan Award for somebody you know or have heard about.
Fill in the form and sign your name.
You may want to cut it out and give it to your Good Samaritan.

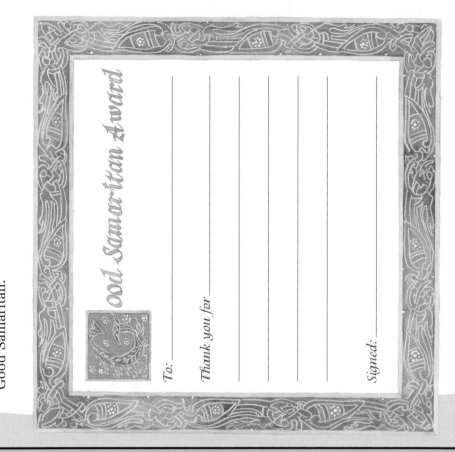

Good Samaritan Award

To: _____

Thank you for _____

_____

_____

Signed: _____

Many Good Samaritans

Tell the children that they are going to learn about a special group of people who help group of people whose help reaches out to people all over the world. Direct the children's attention to page 201. Read the heading and first paragraph aloud as the children follow along. Ask: **What is the name of this special group of helpers?** (Jesuit Volunteers) **Why do you think the little girl in the photo looks so happy?** (She is receiving help; she knows she is loved and cared about.) Say: *Notice how happy her helper looks too. It makes us happy when we are able to help those who need us.*

Have a volunteer read the second and third paragraphs. Ask: **What people do these volunteers help?** (children, the elderly, those who are ill) **Who can become members of the Jesuit Volunteers?** (people who want to help others)

Read the last paragraph, pausing after each question for the children's responses.

Say: *This week we read and talked about many people who lived or live their lives like Jesus did—Saint Martin, the Good Samaritan, Leyla, the Jesuit volunteers, and ourselves as we are told of helping friends. In doing this we used many special words that we might call "Jesus Words."*

Invite the children to help you make a list of these words. Suggest that they can be describing words, action words, or person or thing words—anything that would remind them of reaching out to others. Make a list on the board as children offer words. (*mercy, kindness, love, caring, volunteer, unselfish, help, compassion, need, sharing*)

Ask children to choose one word from the list and use it in a sentence to tell what they will do when they go home today to make a difference in someone's life. Those who wish may share their sentences.

Conclude this time together with these words: **God wants us to be loving and kind people. Remember what we read in the Bible, "Blessed are people who show mercy, God will have mercy on them."**

FYI

THE JESUIT VOLUNTEERS

More than 7,000 members of the Jesuit Volunteer Corps have committed themselves to working with the needy since its beginning in 1956. It has become the largest Catholic lay volunteer program in the country.

Groups of volunteers work in the five geographical regions of the United States. Internationally there are volunteers making a difference in Central America, South America, the Caribbean, Africa, Asia, and elsewhere.

For more information about this group and for pictures and stories about individual volunteers, visit www.jesuitvolunteers.org.

Many Good Samaritans

Many Catholic groups are made up of Good Samaritans. The Jesuit Volunteers is one of these groups. Members of the group help people all over the world. They have been helping people for about 50 years.

Members of the Jesuit Volunteers serve many different people. They serve people who do not have money or a place to live. They serve children, elderly people, and those who are ill.

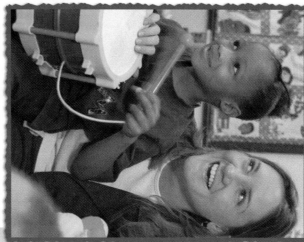

Jesuit Volunteers help children and adults throughout the United States.

The Jesuit Volunteers is one of the largest Catholic volunteer groups in the United States. Anyone who wants to help others can become a member of the Jesuit Volunteers. This is one way a person can be a Good Samaritan.

How can you be a Good Samaritan? Does someone need your help? What can you do for this person?

Reflect

Prayer

Begin by saying: *Now let's get ready for our very special time of prayer. Please get comfortable as we prepare to listen to and talk to God.*

Draw attention to the picture. Say: *Think of a peaceful place where you would like to meet Jesus.* Continue: *Jesus lived a life of love and concern for others. He wants us to live in the way he did. Let's spend some special time with Jesus now and ask him to help us be more like him. Follow along silently as I read to you aloud.*

♫ 💿 In the background softly play the reflective music at the end of CD 2. Then read the page aloud, pausing for two to three seconds after each sentence so that the children have time to think. After you read the last paragraph, pause to allow the children time to reflect and listen to what Jesus will say to them. Close the prayer by praying the Sign of the Cross together.

If you did the Good Samaritan Chain option on page 197, have the children read the chain links that have been placed on the prayer center that give examples of ways to be like the Good Samaritan.

of the page. Call on a volunteer to read the Meet a Saint section. Ask the children: *In what way was Saint Martin being a Good Samaritan?* (He cared for others.) Remind them: *Saint Martin established orphanages and hospitals in Peru. He was being like Jesus by helping others.* Then ask: *Are there people you know or have heard of who are Good Samaritans?* Allow a variety of responses.

OPTION

DO TO OTHERS

Read aloud this passage from Luke 6:31: *Do to others as you would have them do to you.* Tell the children: *It is important to treat others in the way in which we wish to be treated. This*

is called the Golden Rule. Then read aloud the following situations and call on volunteers to explain what they would do in the situations in order to follow the Golden Rule.

You and your friend both want to buy the newest video game, and there is only one left in the store.

Your little sister wants to watch her favorite television show, and you want to watch yours.

Your mom wants you to do your homework, but you want to play outside.

My Response

Prayer

Jesus asks us to show mercy in what we do and say. He wants us to act as the Good Samaritan did.

In your imagination meet Jesus in a place where you like to be. Tell Jesus you know he wants you to be kind and good to others.

Tell him about something nice that you did for someone. Then tell Jesus when it is hard for you to be nice. Ask him to help you. Listen to what Jesus will say to you.

OPTION

OTHER GOOD SAMARITANS

Have the children turn back to page 74 in their books. Draw attention to Saint Martin de Porres at the bottom

Living My Faith

Use the activities that follow to help the children better understand how they can apply what they have learned in this session to their daily lives.

Faith Summary

Ask a child to read the section. Ask: *In which parable did Jesus teach us about loving others?* (the parable of the Good Samaritan) *In what way did the Good Samaritan show mercy toward the injured man?* (The Samaritan bandaged the man's wounds, lifted him onto a donkey, and took him to an inn to be cared for.) *What is so different about the Good Samaritan that his story has been remembered for 2,000 years?* (The injured man was Jewish. Samaritans and Jews did not get along.)

Ways of Being Like Jesus

Read the section aloud. Have the children look at the picture and describe what they see. (a boy making a card) Invite the children to be Good Samaritans and show their concern for someone else by creating a get-well card for someone who is ill.

✝ *Family and Community*

With My Family

Have the children read the section silently. Encourage them to notice when someone in their family is unhappy. Ask: *What are some kind words you can use to cheer them up?* (I love you. God loves you. How can I help you feel better? Tell a joke to make them laugh.)

✝ *Family and Community*

Prayer

Say: *Let's thank Jesus for showing us how to treat others and ask for his help as we continue to try to be kind and loving. Please pray this prayer aloud with me. After we pray, take a few moments to think about how you can be merciful like Jesus was.*

Lead the children in praying aloud. Pause and give the children time to be with Jesus. Close by saying: *Let's close our prayer with the Sign of the Cross.*

My Response

Read the section. Say: *We have all had Good Samaritans in our lives who have helped us when we really needed it. Think about someone who has been a Good Samaritan to you. Then write that person a thank-you note.*

Encourage the children to give their notes to the person who was their Good Samaritan and to pray for that person often.

Living My Faith

Living My Faith

Faith Summary

Jesus shows us how to love others through his words and actions. He wants us to help our neighbors. He wants us to care for people whom others may have forgotten.

Ways of Being Like Jesus

Be a Good Samaritan. Make a get-well card for someone who has been ill.

With My Family

Offer kind words to a family member who may be unhappy about something in his or her life.

My Response

Think of the people in your life who have been kind to you. Write a thank-you note to one of them.

Prayer

Thank you, Jesus, for being my guide. Help me be a Good Samaritan for others.

Choose from the following options to extend the session or to reinforce concepts developed during the week.

Family Involvement

Remind the children to take home the Raising Faith-Filled Kids page to share what they are learning with their families.

Preparation for Sunday Scripture Readings

Lead children in a prayerful discussion of Sunday's readings. Visit www.FindingGod.org/Sunday for more information.

Seasonal Session

Consider the time of the liturgical year and use the appropriate seasonal session. Seasonal sessions may be found on page 241.

Unused Options and BLMs

Incorporate any unused options or Blackline Masters from the week's session.

Web Site Activities

Visit www.FindingGod.org to find additional activities for extending the session.

OPTION

I CAN BE LIKE SAINT MARTIN!

Remind the children of the story of Saint Martin of Tours. Ask the children to think of ways that they can help someone less fortunate than they are. Invite them to draw a picture illustrating one of these ways. At the bottom of the drawing, ask them to copy the scripture passage at the bottom of page 198, *Blessed are people who show mercy.* Encourage the children to display their drawings at home as a reminder to care for others, as Saint Martin did.

OPTION

THE GOOD SAMARITAN SHADOW BOXES

Form pairs of children and distribute one shoebox to each pair. Invite the children to create Good Samaritan shadow boxes illustrating the story of the Good Samaritan. They can draw or paint the background scenery and use clay to create the figures and any other 3-D elements they wish.

OPTION

BAGS OF COMPASSION

Distribute a small paper bag, ribbon, and construction paper hearts to each child. Gather "compassionate gifts," such as Hershey's Kisses chocolates and Hershey's Hugs chocolates (*because everyone needs kisses and hugs*), bandages (*for hurts*), and art (*such as pictures of praying hands to remind us to pray*). Encourage the children to decorate their bags and ask them to write compassionate messages, such as *You are loved,* on each heart. Invite children to fill their bags and use ribbon to tie the bags closed. Encourage them to share their Bag of Compassion with a classmate. Ask children why it is important to show compassion.

RAISING FAITH-FILLED KIDS
a parent page

Focus on Faith

All Are Children of God

In the musical play *South Pacific* one of the songs suggests that prejudice is something that is taught in the family. Jesus faced this issue in telling the story of the Good Samaritan. People had been taught as children not to associate with Samaritans; this group was considered unworthy. In telling the Good Samaritan story, Jesus was attacking such prejudice. Our children are absorbing our prejudices every day—in the stories we tell, in the way we interact with others in public, and in the way we treat their friends. Jesus calls us to treat all people as children of God.

Dinnertime Conversation Starter

Discuss with your child ways he or she can treat others fairly. Do any prejudicial attitudes at home or school call for change?

The Good Samaritan (after Delacroix), Vincent van Gogh

In Our Parish

Organize a group of parishioners to collect blankets for a local charity or parish in need. Encourage volunteers to donate various types and sizes of blankets.

Focus on Prayer

Your child has reflected on the story of the Good Samaritan and on the ways in which he or she can show mercy to others. Share with your child a time when you extended mercy to another person. Discuss how the action made you feel. Then ask God to show you and your child ways to share his mercy.

Hints for at Home

With your child make surprise packages for the children's ward at a local hospital. You will need several rolls of crepe paper, scissors, tape, ribbon, small toys, coins, pencil toppers or erasers, stickers, and other small, inexpensive treats.

Cut a 24-inch length of crepe paper. Place several items on one end of the strip and start rolling it up. Then add several more items and continue rolling in layers. Form a ball and secure its top with a ribbon. With your child deliver the completed surprise packages.

Session 22: We Share God's Life

3-Minute Retreat

Before you prepare for your session, pause for a few moments and quiet yourself. Take three deep breaths and call to mind that you are in the loving presence of God as you foster the children's spiritual growth.

Deuteronomy 30:19–20

I have set before you life and death, the blessing and the curse. Choose life, then, that you and your descendants may live, by loving the LORD, your God, heeding his voice, and holding fast to him.

Reflection

Each day is filled with many choices. It is difficult to imagine anyone would want to choose death over life, but that is what happens when we choose sin over following God. Perhaps the greatest danger is from the small, sinful habits for which we make excuses and accept as okay. We can turn to Jesus to help us make moral choices. Through the Holy Spirit we are better able to choose that which is good, and in unity with Jesus, bring life to the world.

Questions

How can I choose life today? What can I do to help others to know God's mercy and forgiveness?

Prayer

Use these words or those of your own to ask God to help you.

Merciful and loving God, I choose you today. Send your Spirit to guide me.

The Children of Israel Crossing Jordan,
Gustave Doré

Take a few moments to reflect prayerfully before you prepare this session.

Catechist Preparation

Knowing and Sharing Your Faith

Scripture and Tradition in Session 22

We should consider the following factors when making moral choices. There is both good and evil, but we seldom have to choose between pure good and pure evil. Most of our choices involve degrees of good and evil, and the challenge is to choose the greater good and to reject the greater evil. We have free will, which gives us the freedom to make choices, but not a license to do whatever we want. God has placed within each of us a conscience, an inner voice directing us towards what is good. We are obliged to follow our conscience. We are also obliged to seek the truth and to do all in our power to form our consciences properly, giving due respect to such sources as parents, the Church, and the wisdom of people we respect. In making good choices, we and others benefit, and we please God. In making bad choices, we hurt ourselves and others, we damage relationships, and we offend God.

Scripture in Session 22

The Israelites are given a choice by God in **Deuteronomy 30:16–18.** In **John 14:6** Jesus reveals that he is the way to the Father.

Let the scripture and Tradition deepen your understanding of the content in this session.

WINDOW ON THE CATECHISM

The morality of human acts is explored in CCC 1749–1756, and the topic of moral conscience is discussed in CCC 1776–1794.

Moses Smashing the Tablets of the Law, Rembrandt, 1659

Choose to follow God.

Jesus is the way, the truth, the life.

Catechist Preparation

From the Richness of the Tradition

In addition to making moral choices as individuals, we must also help the community make its moral choices. Every four years the American bishops publish guidelines for voting in the presidential elections. Their document is never partisan, telling people how to vote, but it is political in the sense that it promotes moral standards in political participation. In their document preparing for the 2000 elections, the bishops called attention to the major themes of Catholic social teaching, and they asserted as moral priorities for public life the protecting of human life, the promoting of family life, the pursuing of social justice, and the practicing of global solidarity.

✝ Catholic Social Teaching

The following Catholic Social Teaching is emphasized in this session:
Call to Family, Community, and Participation.

GENERAL DIRECTORY FOR CATECHESIS

The role of moral formation in catechesis is treated in *GDC* 85.

Consider in this session how you will invite the children to respond to and prayerfully reflect on God's invitation to love and serve others.

Prayer in Session 22

In this session the children reflect on the guidance of the Holy Spirit in making difficult decisions. In the opening prayer of petition and the closing prayer of thanks, the children will pray for those who help them make right choices.

A special approach to prayer in Session 22 is an extended guided reflection entitled "Making Choices." As you prepare to share this prayer experience with the children, listen to the recorded guided reflection, "Making Choices" (CD 1, Track 10), as a prayerful experience for yourself. Then, when you play the recording during the session, join the children in reflective prayer.

If instead you choose to lead the guided reflection yourself, listen to the recording a second time, following the script (pages 374–375) and noting pauses and tone of voice. You can then use the script or adapt it as you wish. When leading the guided reflection during the session, play instrumental music softly in the background to enhance the sense of prayerfulness.

An alternate approach to prayer in this session is to use the Prayer on the children's page.

Catechist Preparation: Get-Ready Guide

Session 22: We Share God's Life

Session Theme: *God helps us follow our conscience so we can be truly free and happy.*

Before This Session

- For the activity on page 206, you will need to scramble the letters in the words *Choose life!* on index cards (echoso lefi). In advance, prepare one card for every two children.
- To create a powerful visual aid for the activity on page 207, wrap a present containing a model church, Bible, doll, and felt dove.
- Collect tin cans for the option Good Choices Pencil Cans on page 214.
- Bookmark your Bible to Deuteronomy 30:16–18 and John 14:6. Leave the Bible open to the passage from Deuteronomy in the prayer center.
- Set up the CD player so you will be ready to play the guided reflection.
- Display the poster: We Celebrate the Mass (Part I).

Outcomes
At the end of the session, the children should be able to

- understand the importance of making good choices.

- tell why God wants us to choose to follow him.
- explain that God will help us make good moral choices.
- identify basic steps for making good choices.
- define *moral choice.*

- prayerfully reflect on God's presence, his invitation, and our response.

- identify practical ways to act on God's invitation in everyday living.

Steps

DAY 1 **Engage** page 205
We Share God's Life

DAYS 1–3 **Explore** pages 206–211
Choose Life
Guided by God's Gifts
Steps for Making Good Choices
Listening to Your Conscience

DAY 4 **Reflect** page 212
Prayer: The Spirit Helps Us Make Good Choices

DAY 4 **Respond** page 213
Living My Faith: Others Who Can Help Us Make Good Choices

DAY 5 **Extending the Session** page 214
Day 5 offers an opportunity to extend the session with activities that reinforce the session outcomes.

Materials

Required Materials

- Bible
- Writing paper, pens, pencils
- Art materials, such as drawing paper, crayon, markers, scissors, glue
- Index cards (pages 206, 208)
- Wrapped gift box containing model church, Bible, doll, and felt dove (page 207)
- Dessert-sized paper plates, hair-colored yarn (page 210)
- CD 1, Track 10: Making Choices (9:05) (page 212)
- Poster: We Celebrate the Mass (Part I)

Optional Materials

- 6-inch length of string for each child; yellow, blue, green, and heart-shaped beads (page 206)
- Butcher paper, black markers, tempera paints, paint brushes (page 207)
- Tin cans, strips of construction paper, colored paper circles (page 214)
- Blackline Masters 56, 57, 58 (pages 207, 209)

e-resources
www.FindingGod.org

We Share God's Life

Ask the children to spend a few quiet moments with God their Father who loves them.

As you begin this time together, say: *In earlier sessions we learned about living according to the Ten Commandments and about follow-ing our consciences.* Ask: *Who remembers what our conscience is?* (the inner voice that helps us to do what God wants us to do) Continue: *Today we'll learn more about making good choices. Let's sing a song called "Make Good Choices."*

Then sing, to the tune of "Frère Jacques" ("Are you Sleeping?"), the following song:

Make good choices,
Make good choices,
Every day,
Every day.
Holy Spirit, help us,
Holy Spirit, help us,
Show the way,
Show the way.

Invite the children to sing it with you. Then say: *When we follow Jesus, we make good choices and*

Engage

share in God's life as Saint Martin of Tours and the Good Samaritan did.

Say: *Turn to page 205 in your books.* Read the title. Draw atten-tion to the picture. Have the chil-dren describe what they see. (a pair of shoes with stars, dots, and stripes all over them) Then read the words inside the bubbles. Ask: *Do you think the child made a good choice in decorating the shoes?* (no) *Why not?* (She didn't obey her mom.)

Read the paragraph under the pic-ture. Allow the children time to dis-cuss their answers to the question.

Prayer

Say: *Remember the Good Samaritan. He made a good choice. Let's pray to Jesus and ask him to help us to make good choices in our lives. Please pray this prayer of petition along with me.*

Slowly pray the prayer aloud with the children. Then say: *Let's close our eyes, fold our hands, and take a few moments to share with Jesus what is in our hearts.* Pause for 5 to 10 seconds. End the quiet time with Jesus by praying *Amen.*

We Share God's Life Session 22

My mom told me not to decorate my new shoes. But I made them look really cool! Do you like what I did?

I could tell her I like what she did. But she did what her mom told her not to do. I should tell her it was wrong.

Think of a good choice you have made. What helped you make the right choice?

Prayer

Dear Jesus, help me to make good choices in all I do and say.

GOOD CHOICES

On the board, make a list of people the children would ask for help when faced with a difficult choice. The list may include parents, teachers, priests, grandparents, and godparents. Emphasize that the people who can help are usually adults who have experience and wisdom. Discuss choices that might require help and choices that do not require help.

Choose Life

Remind the children: *We make choices every day. We can make one good choice together and promise to follow Jesus!*

Have the children work with partners. Give each pair an index card on which you have scrambled the letters of the words *Choose life!* Have the partners work together to unscramble the message. When they have finished, invite everyone to call out the unscrambled message. Say positively: *Choose life! Choose to follow Jesus!*

Read the title. Say: *We unscrambled an important message. Let's learn about a famous Jewish leader who encouraged people to make this wonderful choice. This story comes to us from the Bible.*

☩ Direct the children's attention to the opened Bible at the prayer center. Then ask three volunteers to each read a paragraph of the story in the student book. Explain: *Moses knew that people could make good choices or bad ones. He was encouraging them to do the right thing and to do as God wanted them to do.*

Continue: *By giving us the freedom to make choices in our lives, God gives us a wonderful gift. He knows that it can be hard to do the right thing. We can always pray, and God will guide and help us.*

Reading God's Word

☩ Read the verse aloud. Say: *These beautiful words remind us that Jesus is our example of love and goodness. By being like him, we are choosing life with God.* Divide the children into three groups and invite them to read the passage as a choral reading. Have everyone read *Jesus said.* Then have the first group read *I am the way,* the second

group read *the truth,* and the third group read *and the life.* Repeat this a couple of times.

Say: *Like Jesus, we are called to be examples of love and goodness in the world.*

"I AM THE WAY" FRIENDSHIP BRACELET

Say: *Let's make friendship bracelets to represent what Jesus means to us!* Give each child a 6-inch length of string and a yellow, a blue, a green, and a heart-shaped bead. Write *yellow, blue, green,* and *heart* on the board.

Tell the children: *The yellow bead represents Jesus as "the way." It reminds us to follow him. The blue bead stands for the truth. Jesus is true blue! The green bead represents life, as we see green in nature. Jesus, our model of love, is represented in the heart!* Ask the children to string their beads in the order indicated on the board (way, truth, life, Jesus). Help the children knot the ends of their string together. Invite them to put on their bracelets. Say: *When you wear your bracelets, remember Jesus' words, "I am the way, the truth, and the life."*

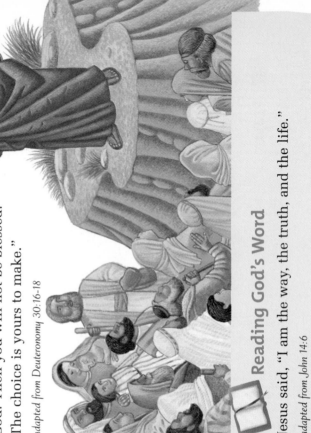

Choose Life

Moses was a great leader of the Jewish people. He led them to freedom. He reminded them of why it was important to do what God wanted.

Moses said, "Good things will happen if you obey the Ten Commandments. Love God and follow his laws. Then you will be blessed.

"You can also choose not to follow God. Then you will not be blessed. The choice is yours to make."

adapted from Deuteronomy 30:16-18

📖 Reading God's Word

Jesus said, "I am the way, the truth, and the life."

adapted from John 14:6

206 God's Invitation

Guided by God's Gift

Tell the children: **We've been blessed by God! He has given us many gifts—and some of those gifts can help us make good choices.**

Display a wrapped gift box. Say: **Inside this box are gifts from God—gifts that help us make good choices.** Ask: **Can anyone guess what these gifts might be?** Allow a variety of responses. Then slowly unwrap the box and reveal a model church (or one cut from felt), a Bible, a doll (or a human figure cut from felt), and a felt dove (or a picture of a dove). Then

say: **Let's read to find out more about these special gifts!**

Read the first paragraph aloud while the group follows along. Draw attention to the term *moral choice* in dark type. Say: **A good moral choice is a choice we make to do what is right because that is what we believe God wants us to do.** Hold up the model church and the Bible, and say: **We found the Church and the Bible in our gift box. How do these help us make moral choices?** (The Bible gives us the example of Jesus; the Church leaders teach us how God wants us to live.)

Ask a volunteer to read aloud the second paragraph. Then hold up the doll. Ask: **Who are the people who help us make moral choices?** (parents, grandparents, teachers, catechists, priests) If you did the option on page 205, compare the children's list with the people mentioned in the book. Then display the dove. Ask: **What does the dove remind us of?** (the Holy Spirit) Then say: **The Holy Spirit is always with us and always helps us.**

✝ *Family and Community*

Steps for Making Good Choices

God has given us the Church and the Bible. These gifts teach us the difference between right and wrong. They help us make a **moral choice.**

We can get help from important people in our lives when making important choices. These people include parents, teachers, catechists, and priests. Praying to the Holy Spirit also guides us in making good choices.

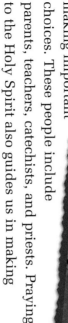

Steps for Making Good Choices

Ask the Holy Spirit to help you make good choices. Then ask yourself these questions before making important decisions.

1. Is the thing I am choosing to do a good thing?
2. Am I choosing to do it for the right reasons?
3. Am I choosing to do it at the right time and in the right place?

Steps for Making Good Choices

Say: **Now we will learn about how to decide whether something is a good choice.** Read the paragraph and the three steps aloud as the group follows along. Say: **The next time you are faced with making a moral choice, ask the Holy Spirit for help as you answer these three questions.**

This might be a good time to remind the children of the additional information on making good choices in the Living Our Faith section at the back of their book.

OPTION

BLM 56: THE TEN COMMANDMENTS

On Blackline Master 56 children create a bookmark to remind them to obey the Ten Commandments.

OPTION

HOLY SPIRIT BANNER

Divide the class into small groups. Provide each group with a large sheet of butcher paper, a black marker, tempera paints, and paint brushes. On the paper have the children paint a large pair of eyes. Then have the children write *Holy Spirit, help me see the right choice!* at the top of their banners with markers. Hang the completed banners around the room.

Listening to Your Conscience

Distribute one index card to each child. Have the children write their names on one side of the card. On the other side, have them write a good choice that they have made. Tell them to consider choices that reflect following the Ten Commandments and being Good Samaritans. When they have finished, have them stand and form a circle, bringing their index cards with them.

Invite volunteers to read their cards. Respect the privacy of students who prefer not to share. When they have finished, say: *We are standing in a circle of good choices! We've learned from one another so many wonderful ways to show that we can make good choices. Thanks for your great suggestions!* Have the children return to their seats and place their index cards aside.

Say: *Now let's read a story together about a girl who listened to her conscience and made a choice.* Read the title. Ask a volunteer to be a narrator and another to read Hannah's words in the first two paragraphs of the story.

Ask: *What is the choice that Hannah has to make?* (whether to take money from her sister's piggy bank or wait for her allowance) Ask: *If Hannah takes her sister's money without her permission, what will she be doing?* (stealing)

Say: *Let's look at the steps for making good decisions on page 207 to see what a good decision would be for Hannah.* Call on a volunteer to read the first step. Then ask: *Is taking money from Hannah's sister's piggy bank a good thing?* (no) Then choose a volunteer to read the second step. Ask: *What is Hannah's reason for wanting to take the money?* (to buy a CD she wants) *Is this a right reason?* (no)

Then have the two volunteers read the final paragraphs of the story. Ask: *What was Hannah's final decision?* (to wait to buy the CD until she has her own money) Ask a volunteer to read the final step on page 207. Ask: *Is Hannah choosing to do this at the right time and in the right place?* (Yes. The right time to buy the CD would be after she earns the money for it herself.) Say: *Hannah knew that her sister probably wouldn't know right away if she had taken money from her bank.* Ask: *Why do you think she didn't take it?* (Hannah listened to her conscience. She knew that it was wrong to take the money.) Conclude: *Hannah did the right thing even though it was hard to do. She made the right choice. It was a choice that allows her to share in God's life.*

Link to Liturgy

Read the sentence aloud. Say: *We pray these special prayers at Mass during the Liturgy of the Eucharist. We ask for mercy and peace before receiving Communion.*

Listening to Your Conscience

Hannah counted all the money she had. She thought, "I need more money to buy the CD I want."

Hannah would not get her allowance until Friday. But if she took money from her sister's piggy bank, she could buy the CD today.

"She will never find out," Hannah thought. Then Hannah listened to her conscience. She knew it was wrong to take what did not belong to her.

Hannah put the bank down. "I will do the right thing. I will wait until I have the money."

Link to Liturgy

At Mass we pray to Jesus, the Lamb of God, for mercy and peace.

A Good Choice

Remind the children: *Hannah listened to her conscience and did the right thing. She made a good choice.* Ask: *How do you think that making that good choice made her feel?* (happy, at peace)

Then say: *Let's imagine for a moment that Hannah decided to take the money from her sister's bank. Then how would she have felt?* (guilty, nervous, afraid to be found out) Continue: *If she had been asked if she knew anything about the money, she might have lied. Then she would have felt even worse.*

Read the activity's title and directions aloud. Clarify that they are to use each word or phrase only once. As they work, walk around the room and offer help if needed. When the children have finished, review their answers.

Then have them answer the question under the piggy banks. Check to see that all wrote *the Holy Spirit.*

Did You Know?

Read the section aloud as the group follows along. Ask the children: *Who remembers what an examination of conscience is?* (thinking about how what we said or did may have hurt our friendship with God or other people) Say: *Once we have made an examination of conscience, we become aware of when we did not make good choices. Then we are ready to confess our sins in the Sacrament of Penance.*

At the end of this time together, remind children that each day will require making choices. They can always depend on the Holy Spirit for help.

OPTION

BLM 57: HOW WOULD YOU FEEL?

Blackline Master 57 requires children to complete an examination-of-conscience-type activity.

OPTION

BLM 58: WE SHARE GOD'S LIFE

Blackline Master 58 is a writing activity that reinforces important themes from the session.

OPTION

CHOICES ROLE-PLAY

Divide the class into three groups. Assign one of the following situations to each group and have them prepare to role-play a good choice that can be made in each situation. When the groups have finished, have them perform their skits. Lead the children in a round of applause after each group performs.

After a long day of work, your father comes home and begins to fold the laundry.

You and your friends are at the store. You see one friend take a candy bar and hide it in his pocket.

On your way to school, your friend says she didn't do her homework. She asks if she can copy yours.

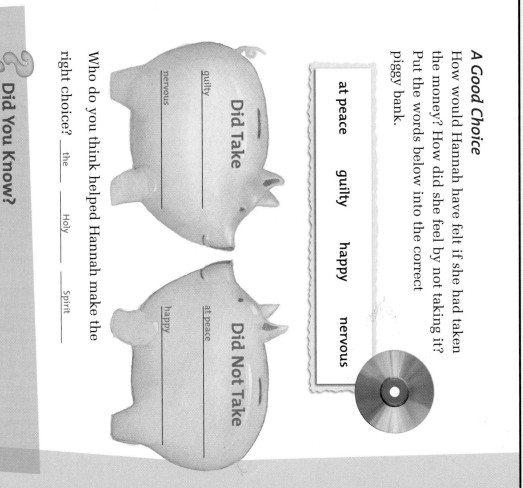

A Good Choice

How would Hannah have felt if she had taken the money? How did she feel by not taking it? Put the words below into the correct piggy bank.

at peace   guilty   happy   nervous

Did Take
guilty
nervous

Did Not Take
at peace
happy

Who do you think helped Hannah make the right choice? __the__ __Holy__ __Spirit__

Did You Know?

We examine our conscience before celebrating the Sacrament of Penance. We think about times when we have not made good choices.

Explore

Make the Right Choice

Smile warmly at the children and ask them how they think you are feeling. (happy) Turn your smile into a frown and ask the same question. (sad, upset) Say: **Our faces often show exactly how we feel! Please show me on your face how you feel when you do not follow your conscience and do not make a good choice.** (frown) Continue: **Now show me how you feel when you pray to the Holy Spirit and follow your conscience to make a good moral choice.** (smile) Say: **Great! You're going to do a good job on today's activities.**

Give each child a dessert-sized white paper plate. Have different colors of hair-colored yarn cut in strips (brown, black, yellow, red). Invite the children to create self-portraits on both sides of their plates, with a smiling face on one side and a sad face on the other. Encourage them to use their markers or crayons to make their eye color and to choose the appropriate color yarn for hair to glue onto both sides of the plate.

When the children have finished, have them clear their desks of everything except their paper-plate faces and their books. Tell the children that you will read a situation in which a child made a decision. Ask them to pretend that they are the child and to hold their paper plate with the face toward you that would show how they felt after making the choice described. Give the following or similar situations and have the children respond with their paper-plate faces. For those requiring a sad face, discuss what a good moral choice might have been.

Examples:
You see your favorite candy at the store. No one is around, so you help yourself to two pieces.

Your mom told you to come right home when the school bus drops you off, but you stop and play at your friend's. Then you tell her that the bus was late.

The new student in your class is having trouble meeting people, so you invite her to your house to play with you and your friends.

Your little sister asks you to help her zip her jacket, but you run out the door.

Your little brother asks you to read to him, and you read his two favorite books to him.

Compliment the children on their thoughtful evaluations of these situations. Say: **Remember that God wants you to keep your happy face.**

Ask the children to open their books to page 210. Read the title and the direction paragraph to the children. Have a volunteer repeat the directions in his or her own words.

Make the Right Choice

God wants us to do what is right. Praying to God will help us make the right choices. Read each of the stories below. Circle the happy face if a right choice was made. Circle the sad face if a wrong choice was made.

1. Susan leaves her jacket at Debbie's house. Debbie thinks about keeping it. Instead, she gives it back to Susan the next day.

2. Rickie and Lisa break their mom's vase while playing. They tell their mom that their little brother broke it.

Read the first situation aloud to the children. Pause to give them time to check the appropriate face. Then invite volunteers to tell and explain their responses.

Read or invite a volunteer to read the second story. After the children have had time to mark their responses, invite a volunteer to suggest what the children might have done to make a good choice.

Continue in the same manner with the third and fourth situations. Encourage discussion of different alternatives children might suggest.

Review all of the ways God helps us to make moral choices by asking questions such as these: **What did Moses tell the people to do to lead blessed and happy lives?** (love God and follow the Ten Commandments) **Where do we find the Ten Commandments?** (in the Bible) **What people in our lives can help us make moral choices?** (parents, teachers, priests) **To whom should we pray for guidance?** (the Holy Spirit) **What questions should we ask ourselves before making important decisions?** (Is what I am choosing to do a good thing? Am I doing it for the right reason? Am I choosing

to do it at the right time and place?) Say: **Hold up the face you want to have after you've made a difficult decision.** (happy face)

Ask the children to think about what they will do the next time they are faced with a difficult decision. Those who wish to do so may share their ideas. Suggest that the children write a sentence about what they will do and take it home with them. Say: **Put this in a safe place where you can find it and use it this week when you have a choice to make between right and wrong. Just like all the things you do, the more you practice the easier it will be.**

---

3. Chloe does not know the answer to a math problem. She glances at her friend's paper and copies the answer.

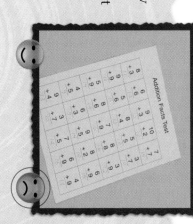

4. Pedro and Rafael said they would be home by five o'clock. When they realize they are late, Rafael suggests that they set their watches back and tell their dad that their watches were wrong. "That is lying!" Pedro says. "I will not do it."

Unit 5, Session 22   **211**

OPTION

MORE CHOICES

Have the children get into small groups and develop additional examples of situations that require choices. Have them vary the outcomes of each situation so that some of the choices are good and some bad. The groups can present their ideas to the class by acting them out in skits. Encourage them to use happy and sad paper-plate faces to show the nature of the choices.

OPTION

WHAT WOULD YOU DO?

Refer the children to the steps for making good choices on page 207. Provide them with a situation and ask them to apply the steps in making a choice. Here are two possible situations:

You find $10 on the ground at school. What do you do?

Your best friend forgot to do his math homework. He knows you are good at math, and he asks you to help by showing him your answers. What do you do?

Prayer

Making Choices: A Recorded Guided Reflection

Remind the children that some choices are easy to make, especially those that are just a matter of preference. Then say: *Even when we make moral choices, some are easy and some are hard. That's why it's good to ask for help from an adult and to pray to the Holy Spirit. Today we will be praying to the Holy Spirit.*

A special approach to prayer in Session 22 is an extended guided reflection titled "Making Choices" (CD 1, Track 10). Refer to pages 374 and 375 for the script and directions for using the recorded guided reflection with the children.

Guided Reflection: An Alternate Approach

An alternate approach to prayer in this session is to use the Prayer on the children's page. The following suggestions will help you guide the children through this Prayer in a reflective manner.

Call attention to the photograph on the page. Ask: *What do you see in the picture?* (a child trying to decide which path to take) Say: *There is a fork in the road. The child must decide which path to follow. He must make a choice.*

Continue: *We have learned that God has given us the gift of the Holy Spirit to help us make good choices. Today, we'll speak to the Holy Spirit and ask for his help.*

Continue: *Let's prepare for our prayer. Please sit comfortably, be very still, fold your hands, silently take a long, deep breath, and then let it out slowly. Close your eyes if you'd like, and listen.*

Read the reflection aloud to the children, pausing after questions, giving the children time to reflect.

At the end of the Prayer, say: *If there's anything else you'd like to tell the Holy Spirit, take time to do that.* Allow the children 20 seconds to complete their prayers. Close by having the children pray the Sign of the Cross.

OPTION

USING THIS PAGE AGAIN

If you have led the children through the recorded guided reflection, you might choose to use this prayer page with them during another session, Day 5, the Review session, or a seasonal session as appropriate.

FYI

PRAYER IN THE REFLECT STEP

Through prayer services that involve spoken parts, you immerse the children in the tradition of vocal prayer. Through guided reflections, in which you invite the children to a deeper understanding of God, you teach meditation. When you invite the children to sit quietly and spend time with the Lord, you lead them into contemplation.

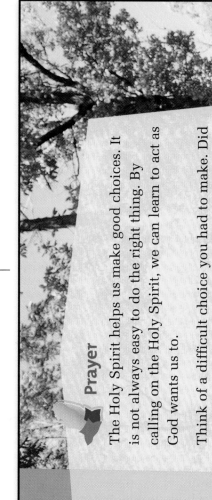

Prayer

The Holy Spirit helps us make good choices. It is not always easy to do the right thing. By calling on the Holy Spirit, we can learn to act as God wants us to.

Think of a difficult choice you had to make. Did you ask anyone for help?

Now think about your choice. Was it the right thing to do? Was it what God wanted you to do?

Take a few moments to speak to the Holy Spirit. Tell him how you feel about your decision.

Now ask the Holy Spirit to guide you the next time you must make a difficult choice. Ask him to help you make the right decision.

212   My Response

Living My Faith

Faith Summary

Ask a volunteer to read the section aloud to the group. Ask: *What are some of God's gifts that help us make moral choices?* (Bible, Holy Spirit, Church, priest, parents, teachers) *What advice did Moses give the people?* (Obey the Ten Commandments and you will be blessed.) Say: *This is still good advice today.*

Word I Learned

Call on a volunteer to define the term. Have the children also look it up in the Glossary and read the definition aloud to the group. Choose another volunteer to use it in a sentence.

Ways of Being Like Jesus

Read the section aloud. Say: *Jesus always made choices that would not hurt others or displease his Father. When we listen to our conscience, we will do what God wants us to do—love him and others.*

With My Family

Read the section. Ask: *Do you know of an organization that helps others?* (parish food pantry, Saint Vincent de Paul Society, Salvation Army, Bread for the World) Call on a child to read the section. Ask: *What are things we can do to help an organization?* (give our time and volunteer, tell others about the organization, make a donation) Say: *You can, together with your family, work to help an organization in one of these ways. What is the family in the picture doing?* (donating new toys to Toys for Tots)

✝ Family and Community

Prayer

Say: *Let's thank God for bringing helpful people into our lives. Fold your hands and pray this prayer of thanks along with me.*

Pray the prayer aloud. Say: *Now close your eyes and take a few moments to tell God whatever is in your heart.* Close by saying: *Let's pray the Lord's Prayer.*

My Response

Read the section. Say: *Every day we make choices. For example, when your dad asks you to set the table for dinner, do you do it joyfully or do you complain? When you see that your teacher is busy, do you help by erasing the board? Think about some of the choices you make every day that affect others. Then write a sentence or draw a picture of a good choice that you want to make that will help another person.*

To end your time together, remind children to think and pray when faced with a difficult choice.

Living My Faith

Faith Summary

Praying to the Holy Spirit helps us make the right choices.

Word I Learned

moral choice

Ways of Being Like Jesus

We are like Jesus when we listen to our conscience and do what God wants us to do.

With My Family

Think of an organization that has made a choice to help others. Help this organization in whatever way you can.

Prayer

🕊 Thank you, God, for the people who help me.

My Response

Make a choice this week that will help another person.

Extending the Session

Choose from the following options to extend the session or to reinforce concepts developed during the week.

Family Involvement

Remind the children to take home the Raising Faith-Filled Kids page to share what they are learning with their families.

Preparation for Sunday Scripture Readings

Lead children in a prayerful discussion of Sunday's readings. Visit www.FindingGod.org/Sunday for more information.

Seasonal Session

Consider the time of the liturgical year and use the appropriate seasonal session. Seasonal sessions may be found on page 241.

Unused Options and BLMs

Incorporate any unused options or Blackline Masters from the week's session.

Web Site Activities

Visit www.FindingGod.org to find additional activities for extending the session.

OPTION

GOOD CHOICES PRAYER

Remind the children of Moses encouraging the people to choose life. Invite the children to write a short prayer to God, asking his help to make good choices. Encourage the children to decorate their prayers with borders, pictures, or cartoons. Encourage creativity. Invite the children to take their prayers home and share them with their families.

OPTION

GOOD CHOICES PENCIL CANS

Gather and bring in enough tin cans for each child to have one. Before the session, cut strips of construction paper that will fit around the cans. You will also need to cut several circles from different colored paper. Distribute a can, a strip, and four circles to each child. Invite the children to decorate the strips before taping them around the cans. Then ask each child to write one of the following phrases in each circle: *Choose Life, Love God, Moral Choice,* and *Pray for Peace.* Have the children tape circles onto the cans as reminders to make good choices. Encourage the children to use their pencil cans in class or bring them home and share them with their families.

OPTION

MORAL CHOICE SCRAMBLE

Write each letter of the words *Moral Choice* on separate pieces of paper and spread them around the room. Call on eleven volunteers to retrieve the letters and ask them to stand in front of the class. Have the remaining children try to unscramble the letters by instructing the volunteers where to move. Provide clues if the children are having trouble figuring out the words.

RAISING FAITH-FILLED KIDS
a parent page

Focus on Faith

Making Choices for Life

Moses knew that he was dying and that he would never see the land God had promised. As the people prepared to cross the River Jordan, Moses delivered one final sermon. He summarized what God wanted of his people. Moses told them to choose to follow God and to obey his commandments. Our children witness our choices every day. Are the choices they see in our lives those that will lead them to choose life in God?

Dinnertime Conversation Starter

Discuss with your child the choices that he or she had to make today in school or at home. Did these decisions affect his or her relationship with God? Help your child develop a method for making good decisions.

Moses Presenting the Tablets of Law, Raphael

Hints for at Home

With your child make a Do the Right Thing display in your home. Trace and cut out doves, using this Holy Spirit pattern. Each time a member of your family makes a good choice, write the person's name on one of the doves. Post the display in a prominent location and watch it grow as your child becomes more aware of the ways in which to do the right thing!

Focus on Prayer

Your child has reflected about the ways in which the Holy Spirit assists him or her in making good choices. With your child offer a prayer of thanksgiving to the Holy Spirit.

Spirituality in Action

Act as a moral barometer for your child. Discuss with him or her daily occurrences that require moral choices to be made. Guide your child to do the right thing through discussion of the issue at hand, its possible outcomes, the way you and God would want your child to act, and the circumstances and repercussions of the choice. Acknowledge and affirm your child's decision when he or she makes a good choice.

Session 23: Following Jesus

3-Minute Retreat

Before you prepare for your session, pause for a few moments and pay attention to your breathing. Take three deep breaths and remember that you are in the loving presence of God as you prepare to help the children continue to grow spiritually.

Matthew 5:8

Blessed are the clean of heart, for they will see God.

Reflection

As Jesus presented the Beatitudes, he told us how God would respond to our actions. We learn that those with a clean heart, concern for justice, and loyalty to the commands of God will see God now and in eternity. Later in the Gospel, Jesus is asked what the most important commandment is. He says the complete love of God and the love of our neighbors as ourselves is the spirit of the Law. Holiness does not come from being removed from the world but rather from engaging it and following the instructions of Jesus to love God, ourselves, and others.

Questions

How might I treat difficult situations as opportunities to practice holiness? Some people are easier to get along with than others. What might I need to change in order to love all my neighbors?

Prayer

Speak to Jesus, using these words or others that come to mind for you. Jesus, you are the champion of the humble, the suffering, and the faithful. Help me to make choices that testify to your loving presence in my life.

Take a few moments to reflect prayerfully before you prepare this session.

Church of the Beatitudes, Mount of the Beatitudes near Tabkha, Israel

Catechist Preparation

Knowing and Sharing Your Faith

Scripture and Tradition in Session 23

The Beatitudes are expressions of praise for people who cultivate certain virtues. People with the spirit of poverty are praiseworthy because they will maintain a solidarity with the poor and acknowledge their need for God. People who are sad because of injustice and the sufferings of others are praiseworthy because they are motivated to action on behalf of justice. The meek are praiseworthy because they will humbly accept their own strengths and weaknesses and keep a proper perspective on things. Those who hunger and thirst for righteousness are praiseworthy because they value justice. People who are merciful are praiseworthy because they forgive the weaknesses of others and show compassion to their brothers and sisters. People who are clean of heart are praiseworthy because they want what is good for others; they don't possess envy or hatred, only love and concern for others. Peacemakers are praiseworthy because they do not perpetuate conflict but rather seek to resolve conflict and create harmony. People who are persecuted are praiseworthy when they are resented by others because they refuse to collaborate with the mistreatment of others.

Scripture in Session 23

Matthew 5:1–10 is the recounting of the Sermon on the Mount.
Matthew 22:37–38 speaks of the primacy of the total love of God.

Let the scripture and Tradition deepen your understanding of the content in this session.

WINDOW ON THE CATECHISM

The Beatitudes are discussed in depth in CCC 1716–1719 and 1725–1728.

The Sermon on the Mount, Fra Angelico

Jesus gives us the Beatitudes.

Jesus teaches us the Great Commandment.

Catechist Preparation

From the Richness of the Tradition

Catholic social teaching challenges us to struggle for justice, to give priority to the poor and vulnerable, to respect the human dignity of every person, and to promote respect for life. It is the same challenge presented in the Beatitudes, for as the American bishops have written, "The Beatitudes tell us that the reign of God belongs to the poor and lowly and to those who stand with the poor, show mercy to them, and hunger and thirst for justice." ("In All Things Charity: A Pastoral Challenge for the New Millennium," November 18, 1999, United States Conference of Catholic Bishops)

✝ Catholic Social Teaching

In this session, these Catholic Social Teachings are integrated:

- **Solidarity**
- **Family, Community, and Participation**
- **Option for the Poor and Vulnerable**

Consider in this session how you will invite the children to respond to and prayerfully reflect on God's invitation to love and serve others.

GENERAL DIRECTORY FOR CATECHESIS

The Beatitudes of Jesus embody the Good News. The message of the Beatitudes is addressed in *GDC* 103.

Prayer in Session 23

In the opening prayer of petition and the closing prayer of thanks, the children acknowledge Jesus' help in their lives and pray for the grace to accept it. In the Reflect step the children reflect on the Beatitudes and the Great Commandment as guides to making moral decisions.

Catechist Preparation: Get-Ready Guide

Session 23: Following Jesus

Session Theme: *We can be like Jesus by treating others fairly and with justice.*

Before This Session

- Bookmark your Bible to Matthew 5:1–10 and Matthew 22:37–38.
- Set up the CD player ahead of time so you will be ready to play the songs and the reflective music.

Steps

DAY 1	**Engage** page 215	
	Following Jesus	

DAYS 1–3	**Explore** pages 216–221	

The Great Commandment
The Beatitudes
Love Your Neighbor
Writing Jesus' Words

DAY 4	**Reflect** page 222	

Prayer: The Beatitudes

DAY 4	**Respond** page 223	

Living My Faith: Choosing a Beatitude to Follow

DAY 5	**Extending the Session** page 224	

Day 5 offers an opportunity to extend the session with activities that reinforce the session outcomes.

Outcomes *At the end of the session, the children should be able to*

- explain what it means to be kind.

- identify the Beatitudes as ways to live a happy life.
- explain that the Bible is composed of the Old and New Testaments.
- identify love of God and neighbors as the Great Commandment.
- define *Beatitudes, Great Commandment, New Testament,* and *Old Testament.*

- prayerfully reflect on God's presence, his invitation, and our response.

- identify practical ways to act on God's invitation in everyday living.

Materials

Required Materials

- Bible
- Writing paper, pens, pencils
- Art materials, such as drawing paper, crayon, markers, scissors, glue
- Index cards or construction paper (page 221)
- CD 2, Track 22: This Little Light of Mine (Instrumental) (page 215)
- CD 2, Track 21: This Little Light of Mine (1:42) (page 217)
- CD 2, Reflective music (page 222)

Optional Materials

- White paper, washable inkpad, wet washcloth (page 218)
- Butcher paper (page 219)
- What Can I Do? index cards, basket (page 222)
- Unlined note cards (page 224)
- Blackline Masters 59, 60, 61 (pages 217, 219)

e-resources

www.FindingGod.org

Following Jesus

Prayer

Jesus, help me to treat others with love and kindness as you do.

Following Jesus

Session 23

Think of a time when someone was kind to you. What did you do? How did you think of this person? How did this person's actions make you want to treat others?

Following Jesus

♪ 💿 While the children get settled, you may wish to have the instrumental version of "This Little Light of Mine" (CD 2, Track 22) playing in the background.

Once settled, tell the children: *We have learned about Jesus and the ways in which his words and actions are models for us to follow. I know you've been working hard to become more like Jesus!*

Let's sing a song we've sung before called "I Can Be Like Him" to remind ourselves to follow Jesus' loving model.

Sing the first verse to the tune of "London Bridge Is Falling Down." Then invite the children to join you as you sing the following verses:

Jesus was a faithful Son, faithful Son, faithful Son, Jesus was a faithful Son, I love Jesus!

Jesus knew God's rules for life, rules for life, rules for life, Jesus knew God's rules for life, I love Jesus!

Jesus listened to God's Word, to God's Word, to God's Word, Jesus listened to God's Word, I love Jesus!

Today we'll learn more about the love and kindness Jesus taught us.

Engage

DAY 1

Hold up the Bible. Say: *Through the Bible, we learn about the life of Jesus. We can learn to be more like him everyday!*

Say: *Open your books to page 215.* Read the title and paragraph aloud. Encourage the children to respond to the questions. Ask: *What does it mean to be kind?* (to care about and be concerned for another's well-being)

Draw attention to the photograph. Ask: *In what way is the boy in the yellow shirt showing kindness?* (He's fixing the other child's bike.)

Prayer

Say: *Jesus treated everyone with love and kindness. He cared for everyone, no matter who they were, where they lived, or what they believed. Let's pray to our role model, Jesus, and ask him to help us treat people as he would. Please pray this prayer of petition aloud with me.*

Lead the children in praying this prayer aloud. Then say: *Now close your eyes and talk to Jesus in your hearts.* Pause and take three deep breaths, allowing the children a few moments to be with Jesus. End the quiet time by praying *Amen.*

The Great Commandment

Draw attention to the illustration. Have the children describe what they see. Say: **Men, women, and children are gathered around Jesus to hear his teaching. Jesus is sharing a very important message with the people. Let's learn about this message.**

Read the title and first paragraph. Call on volunteers to look up the definitions of *Old Testament* and *New Testament* in the Glossary and read them to the group. Hold up the Bible. Show the size of the Old Testament from the book of Genesis to the book of Malachi. Note how long the Old Testament is. Say: **The Old Testament is the story of God's love for Jewish people.** Then show the size of the New Testament from the Gospel of Matthew to the book of Revelation. Note how much shorter the New Testament is in comparison to the Old Testament. Explain: **The New Testament tells about the life of Jesus and about the early church. Now let's read something Jesus taught us in the Bible.**

Choose a child to read the second paragraph. Draw attention to the term *Great Commandment* in dark type. Say: **The Great Commandment is Jesus' teaching that we are to love God and other people.** Ask: **In what part of the Bible do we find the Great Commandment?** (New Testament) Ask: **Who can retell the story of the Good Samaritan that is in the New Testament?** Call on a volunteer to tell the story.

Then say: **The Good Samaritan shared God's love by helping the hurt man. He is an example of someone living the Great Commandment. He shows us how Jesus wants us to live.**

Reading God's Word

Read the verse aloud. Then say: **To follow the Great Commandment is to love God, to love ourselves, and to love our neighbors as much as we love ourselves. This is a good way to live our lives! God wants us to love him and to love others. He wants us to make good choices for him and for others.**

THE GREAT COMMANDMENT

Jesus teaches that the moral life can be summed up in terms of love of God, self, and neighbor. The New Testament understanding of love is based on the Old Testament understanding of covenant love, which is that God's steadfast love will never waver. The Christian who cooperates with the Holy Spirit will not waver in his or her love for God. This is a love of commitment and action to a better personal relationship with God. It shows a true appreciation of how much God loves the person as an individual—as well as the person's willingness to serve the neighbor.

The Great Commandment

The **Old Testament** is the story of God's love for the Jewish people. The **New Testament** is the story of Jesus' life. It also tells how the early Church lived like Jesus.

In the New Testament Jesus gave us the **Great Commandment.** It teaches us how to follow God and care for others. Thinking about the Great Commandment helps us make moral choices. We make the right choice when we love God and others.

Reading God's Word

Love God with all your heart, soul, and mind. Love your neighbor as yourself. This is the greatest commandment.

adapted from Matthew 22:37-38

The Beatitudes

Say: *Today we will find out about the formula for happiness that Jesus gave us.*

Read the title aloud. Then draw attention to the illustration. Have the children describe what they see. (Jesus talking to a crowd) Say: *Jesus was teaching the Beatitudes* (bē at´ ə tōōdz´) *to the people. We'll learn more about the Beatitudes.*

✚ Read the first paragraph aloud. Explain: *Wherever Jesus went, many people came to hear him. With such a large crowd gathered, Jesus had the chance to share very important messages. He taught people the Beatitudes.* Draw attention to the word *Beatitudes* in dark type. Say: *The Beatitudes are ways Jesus gave us to live as his followers.* Ask a volunteer to look up the definition in the Glossary and read it to the group. Continue: *Let's now read some of the Beatitudes that Jesus gave us.*

Read the rest of the page aloud or ask various volunteers to read the different Beatitudes aloud. Explain: *Jesus wants people to know that we will be blessed if we live according to the Beatitudes. He wants us to know how important it is to show mercy to others. Jesus also wants us to work hard to live peacefully with one another.*

♪ Say: *The Beatitudes help us become like bright and shining stars that bring joy to others.* Have the children turn to the song "This Little Light of Mine" in the Songs of Our Faith section in the back of their books. Say: *This song tells about the light that is in each of us. This light is the kindness, love, and generosity that the Holy Spirit gives to us so that we can share it with others.* Play the song on Track 21 of CD 2. You may wish to play it a second time, encouraging the children to sing along with happy voices.

✚ Solidarity

This might be a good time to remind the children of the additional information on the Beatitudes in the Living Our Faith section at the back of their book.

The Beatitudes

Jesus wanted us to be happy. So he taught us the **Beatitudes.**

Jesus said, "Blessed are those who are kind to others. They will be rewarded.

"Blessed are those who do the right thing even when it is difficult. They will be with God one day.

"Blessed are those who are fair to others. They will be treated fairly.

"Blessed are those who work for peace. They are God's children."

When Jesus gave us the Beatitudes, he taught us how to be happy with one another.

adapted from Matthew 5:1–10

Unit 5, Session 23   **217**

OPTION

BLM 59: THE "BEE" ATTITUDES

Blackline Master 59 asks children to create a mobile containing messages reminding children to follow the Beatitudes.

OPTION

BLM 60: MAKING MORAL CHOICES

On Blackline Master 60 children are asked to make moral choices and share their responses with the group.

THE BEATITUDES

The children are learning four of the eight Beatitudes. To read all eight of the Beatitudes, see Matthew 5:3–12.

Love Your Neighbor

Invite the children to stand and join you in an action rhyme. Say each line as you present its accompanying action. Then have the children repeat each line after you.

I can reach out to help my neighbor.
(Shake hands with the person to your right and left.)
I can do a special favor.
(Point to self.)
I can help the weak and small.
(Scrunch down.)
I can help the strong and tall.
(Spring up.)
I can use kind words with everyone.
(Extend arms, make a sweeping motion.)
And love my neighbors, one by one.
(Put hands over heart.)

Conclude: ***Now please have a seat and we'll read about a girl who reached out to help a neighbor.***

Ask a volunteer to read the title and first paragraph aloud. Ask the group: ***What could Tina do?*** Allow a variety of responses. Now read the second and third paragraphs aloud.

Say: ***Tina's mom reminded Tina that Jesus wants us to care for our neighbors. How do you think Amanda felt when Tina asked her to play?*** (happy, excited, grateful) ***How do you think Tina felt about reaching out to Amanda?*** (happy, at peace, close to Jesus) ***Do you think Tina's mom was proud of her?*** (yes) ***Why?*** (because she was showing that she cared for her neighbor, like Jesus did)

Say: ***We can reach out to others too whether they are sad, as Amanda was, or sick, or poor, or lonely.***

✝ *Solidarity*

218   Session 23

THUMB-BODY LOVES YOU CARDS

Explain to the children that they will make greeting cards for a local nursing home or for homebound parishioners as a way of reaching out to their neighbors. Distribute a sheet of white paper to each child. Have them fold the paper in half lengthwise and then again widthwise to create a card. Have the children use their crayons or markers to write a greeting and create a picture on the inside of the card. Remind them to sign their names.

As the children work, visit each individually and have them press their thumbs in a washable-ink pad and then make a thumbprint on the front of the card. Have the child clean his or her thumb with a wet washcloth.

Write *Thumb-body loves you!* on the board. Tell the children to copy the message onto the front of the cards and to turn their thumbprints into self-portraits. When the children have finished, collect the cards. Give the cards to the appropriate parish minister for delivery.

✝ *Family and Community*

Love Your Neighbor

Tina noticed her neighbor, Amanda, looking out the window. Amanda looked sad.

Tina went home and told her mom that Amanda looked sad. Tina wondered what she could do for Amanda.

"Tina," her mom said, smiling, "you are doing what Jesus teaches when you care for your neighbor. Invite Amanda to come over and play."

218   God's Invitation

Doing What Jesus Teaches

Remind the children that as followers of Jesus, we are always looking for ways to be cheerful helpers.

Read the activity's title and directions. Give the children time to complete the activity. Then call on a volunteer to read the first example. Ask: **What beatitude is not being displayed?** (kindness) If the children are unsure, direct them to page 217 for the list of Beatitudes. Then have the child share how Nadia could show kindness. Have a volunteer read the second example and share his or her answer. Ask:

What beatitude is being practiced? (doing the right thing, even when it's difficult) Call on someone to read the third one. Ask: **What beatitude is not being practiced?** (peacefulness) Then have the child share his or her idea for how Arturo and the children could be peacemakers.

✝ The Poor and Vulnerable

Meet a Saint

Slowly read the section aloud as the group follows along. Say: *Even though Saint Elizabeth Ann Seton had a very busy life, she found time to reach out to others! She was a special person.*

Meet a Saint

Elizabeth Ann Seton always found time to help others. She started the first Catholic grade school in the United States. Elizabeth was the first American-born person to be named a saint.

Doing What Jesus Teaches

In the stories below, Nadia, Jerome, and Arturo each have to make a difficult choice. Below each story, write the good choice each person can make to follow the Beatitudes.

1. Will forgets to bring his crayons to art class. Nadia just got new crayons, and she does not want anyone to ruin them.

2. Jerome is helping his sister with an assignment. He really wants to go outside to play.

3. Two children get into a fight on the playground. Arturo and all the other children stop and watch.

✝ The Poor and Vulnerable

FYI

ELIZABETH ANN SETON

Elizabeth Ann Seton (1774–1821) was born to non-Catholic parents. At age 20 she married a wealthy young shipping merchant, and the couple raised five children. Elizabeth's good deeds for the poor and sick earned her the name Protestant Sister of Charity.

Her transformation toward Catholicism began when she and her husband traveled to Italy in hopes of finding a cure for his tuberculosis. He soon died, and she returned with the children to the United States, became a Catholic, and formed a community of sisters whose mission was to open schools and teach children in orphanages. She was declared a saint by Pope Paul VI on September 14, 1975. Saint Elizabeth Ann Seton's feast day is January 4.

✝ The Poor and Vulnerable

Explore

Writing Jesus' Words

Begin with a short time for reflection. Ask the children to pray that they have the right attitude in all that they do this day. Show the children the Bible and invite them to tell you what they have learned about it. (the Old Testament—story of God's love for the Jewish people, the New Testament—story of Jesus' life, Beatitudes, Great Commandment)

Say: *All of the things that our parents, teachers, and the Church teach us about God are contained in the messages of the Bible. The words of the Bible are very important to us.*

Remind the children that Jesus' words to his disciples and to us are recorded in the New Testament.
Say: *We communicate with each other through words too.* Ask: *What do we do when we want someone to remember our words for a long time?* (write them down)

Invite the children to think of something special that they would like to write about following Jesus. Remind them that Jesus used kind, gentle words when he spoke to his friends. Ask the children's help in listing on the board some words that they might find helpful in their writing. (Examples: *love, neighbor, happy, kindness, choices, blessed, Beatitude, Great Commandment*) Suggest that their writing might be a poem, a prayer, or a short paragraph.

Have children write a practice copy first and then use their best handwriting to write it on special lined paper that you have available for them, perhaps border paper or paper they can decorate. Give the children sufficient time to write and copy their work. Gather together for a special sharing time when most have finished.

Examples:

*Jesus teaches me how to live.
Thank you, Jesus, for all you give.*

*I want to live a life blessed by God.
I'll follow Jesus and always help others.*

I love God. I love my neighbor. I want to make good choices and be happy.

Have the children open their books to page 220. Ask the group to read along as you read the title and first paragraph aloud.

Invite the children's comments about the beauty of the sample manuscript page. Read what is on the page and ask if children recognize what it is. (a Beatitude)

Say: *Think of how much care you took to write something very special. Imagine how much time and effort it took people to carefully write by hand all the pages of the Bible!*

Writing Jesus' Words

Hundreds of years ago books were written by hand. Sometimes the pages were also decorated with designs and pictures. Here is an example of how one of the pages might have looked.

Blessed are those who are kind to others. They will be rewarded.

Explore

Read aloud the title and directions. Draw the children's attention to the fancy script used for the Beatitudes.

Slowly read the first beatitude aloud while the children follow along. Pause and call on a volunteer to fill in the missing word. Remind the children that they may try to write the word in fancy writing.

Have children complete the last two beatitudes independently. Suggest that they try to do it without looking back for the words, but if they have difficulty they may look at page 217.

Give each child a 5-by-8-inch index card or a half-sheet of 9-by-12-inch construction paper.

Ask the children to think of one thing they could do at home tonight to live the Beatitudes with their families. (be peaceful with sisters and brothers, obey parents immediately) Suggest that on their index card or paper they write what they will do in the form of a beatitude. For example: Blessed are they who obey their parents, they will

When all have completed the Beatitudes, check them together by having volunteers read them aloud.

may want to use a fancy script and decorate the border.

When most have finished, invite those who would like to do so to share what they have written. Remind the children to take home this card or paper and their special writing from the beginning of today's class to show their families as they explain to them what they have learned this week.

As class ends, ask the children to join you in a prayer. Say:

Thank you, Jesus, for showing us the way to a happy life.

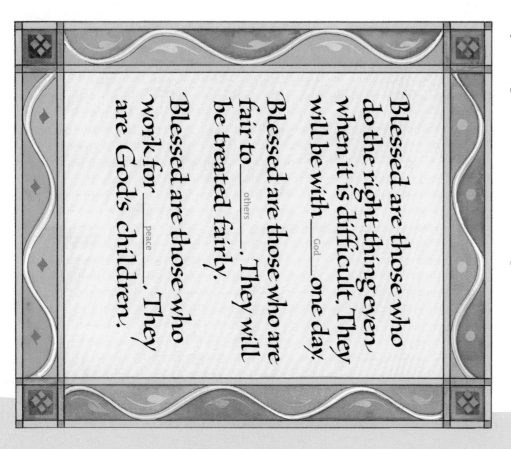

Complete the Beatitudes
Three Beatitudes are written on this page. In fancy writing, fill in the blanks to complete them.

Blessed are those who do the right thing even when it is difficult. They will be with _____ (God) one day.

Blessed are those who are fair to _____ (others). They will be treated fairly.

Blessed are those who work for _____ (peace). They are God's children.

Complete the Beatitudes

Read aloud the title and directions. Draw the children's attention to the fancy script used for the Beatitudes.

BE-GOOD COMICS

Tell the children that they are going to create comic strips. Have each of them divide a piece of paper into three sections. Then say: *In the first section draw someone who needs help. In the second section draw someone coming to assist the person who needs help. In the final section draw the happy conclusion.* Here is an example of what a three-part comic strip may include: A girl drops her ice cream cone; a boy sees the sad girl; the boy gives half of his candy bar to the girl.

Staple the children's comics together into one book. Set it out to be enjoyed by everyone.

Reflect

Prayer

As you begin the day say: *It's time for our special prayer again. Let's be so quiet that we can talk to Jesus in our hearts.*

Reverently say: *We have learned about the Beatitudes, the wonderful message Jesus gave us for living in peace and happiness. Now let's think about how we can practice them in our lives, especially when we have to make difficult choices. Please close your eyes or look at the picture on this page and silently pray along with me.*

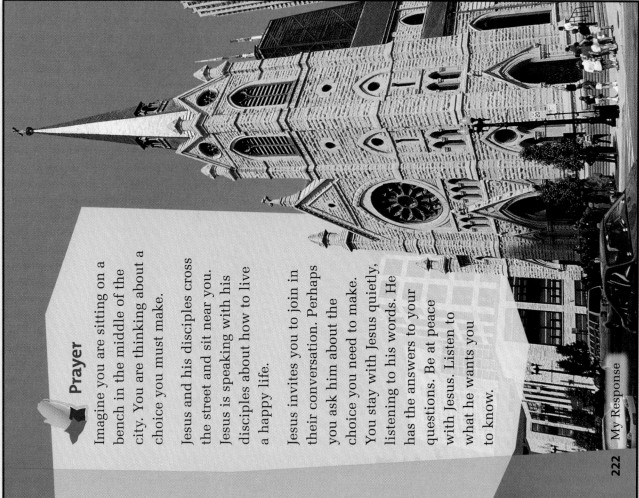

♫ 💿 Softly play the reflective music at the end of CD 2 in the background to create a calming environment. Then read the first paragraph aloud. Pause for a few seconds to give the group time to reflect. Read the second paragraph, pausing after each sentence to give the children time to imagine being with Jesus and his disciples.

Read the final paragraph slowly and then invite the children to remain with Jesus. Pause for 20 seconds and give the children time to speak with Jesus in their hearts. Then close the prayer by inviting the children to pray the Sign of the Cross with you.

OPTION

LOVE AND KINDNESS CHART

On the board create a two-column chart titled Love and Kindness. Label one column *Action* and the other *How I Can Do It*. In the Action column,

222   Session 23

Prayer

🔖 **Prayer**

Imagine you are sitting on a bench in the middle of the city. You are thinking about a choice you must make.

Jesus and his disciples cross the street and sit near you. Jesus is speaking with his disciples about how to live a happy life.

Jesus invites you to join in their conversation. Perhaps you ask him about the choice you need to make. You stay with Jesus quietly, listening to his words. He has the answers to your questions. Be at peace with Jesus. Listen to what he wants you to know.

222   My Response

---

list the following: *Welcome others, Pray for others, Defend others, Do a favor for others, Help others, Use peaceful words.* Then invite the children to think of a specific way in which they can implement each for the How I Can Do It column. (Invite the new girl at school to sit with me at lunch, pray for my grandpa's health, say something nice about my teacher) List their ideas in the second column. When the chart is completed, read it aloud to review the responses. Say: *You've made some great suggestions, and I know that we can all do these things. Remember, reach out to others. Jesus will notice!*

OPTION

WHAT CAN I DO?

Divide the class into small groups. Have one member of each group choose an index card from a basket. The index card will have a situation written on it in which someone needs help. Invite the child to read the card aloud to his or her small group. Have the children in each group discuss what they might do to address the situation on the card. When the groups have finished, have another child from each small group read that group's card to the whole group and explain the group's ideas for how to respond to the situation.

Respond

Words I Learned

Read the section. Ask: *In what ways could we treat people in our lives with love and respect this coming week?* (use gentle words, think about what others want instead of what we want)

Ways of Being Like Jesus

Read the section. Ask: *What is the girl in the picture doing?* (comforting the boy) Have a child read the section. Ask: *What are other ways we could cheer up a family member or neighbor?* (tell them how special they are, help them with their chores, bring them their favorite food)

✝ Family and Community

With My Family

Ask: *What is the girl in the picture doing?* (comforting the boy) Have a child read the section. Ask: *What are other ways we could cheer up a family member or neighbor?* (tell them how special they are, help them with their chores, bring them their favorite food)

Prayer

Say: *We've learned about the ways Jesus told us we are to live if we want to be happy and blessed. Let's thank him for his special words to us. Please pray this prayer of thanks aloud with me.*

Slowly pray the prayer. Say: *Now close your eyes and think about how you can follow Jesus' teachings.* Pause for 10 seconds. To close, say: *Please open your eyes. Let's close with the Sign of the Cross.*

My Response

Say: *Choose one of the Beatitudes that you can follow this week. Turn to page 217 to see the list of the four beatitudes that we have learned.* Say: *After you decide which beatitude you would like to practice and how you will do this, write a sentence about it.*

Conclude today's class, saying: *Remember, happiness is found in following Jesus.*

Living My Faith

Faith Summary

Have a volunteer read the section. Ask: *Who remembers the beatitudes they learned?* (being kind, doing the right thing, being fair, being peaceful) Say: *Jesus gave us special messages to help us live good lives. By living according to the messages of the Great Commandment and the Beatitudes, we can be happy with ourselves and with one another.*

Words I Learned

Call on volunteers to define each word. Then have the volunteers look the words up in the Glossary and read them aloud to the group to check their definitions. Have two children come forward and show the group where to find the Old Testament and the New Testament in the Bible. Choose other volunteers to use the words in sentences.

Faith Summary

In the Great Commandment Jesus told us to love God and others. Jesus gave us the Beatitudes to help us live a happy life.

Words I Learned

Beatitudes   Great Commandment
New Testament   Old Testament

Ways of Being Like Jesus

Treat others with respect in everything you do this week.

With My Family

Comfort a family member or neighbor who is ill or unhappy.

Living My Faith

Prayer

Thank you, Jesus, for the Beatitudes. Thank you for your help in trying to live them every day.

My Response

Choose a beatitude to practice this week.

Extending the Session

Choose from the following options to extend the session or to reinforce concepts developed during the week.

Family Involvement

Remind the children to take home the Raising Faith-Filled Kids page to share what they are learning with their families.

Preparation for Sunday Scripture Readings

Lead children in a prayerful discussion of Sunday's readings. Visit www.FindingGod.org/Sunday for more information.

Seasonal Session

Consider the time of the liturgical year and use the appropriate seasonal session. Seasonal sessions may be found on page 241.

Unused Options and BLMs

Incorporate any unused options or Blackline Masters from the week's session.

Web Site Activities

Visit www.FindingGod.org to find additional activities for extending the session.

OPTION

GREAT COMMANDMENT PRAYER CARDS

Give each child several unlined note cards and tell them that they are going to make Great Commandment prayer cards. Invite children to write the Great Commandment on the note cards and decorate them. Encourage the children to give the cards to people they see who live the Great Commandment.

them to discuss the situations and resolutions.

OPTION

LEARNING THE BEATITUDES

Write each of the Beatitudes mentioned on page 217 on the board. Form four groups of children and assign each group a beatitude. Ask the children to think of a situation that relates to their beatitude and what choices they can make to follow Jesus. For example: *Donating clothes to people who can't buy their own* relates to the first beatitude. *I could start a clothes drive* is a choice that follows Jesus. Assist any children that cannot think of a situation. Then divide the class into new groups, so that each group has one child representing each beatitude. Encourage

OPTION

GETTING TO KNOW THE BIBLE

Organize pairs of children and give each pair a Bible. If it is not possible to give each pair a Bible, you may consider inviting pairs to view the Bible in the prayer center while the children are working on another activity. Work with pairs to thumb through the Bible, noting the various books. Briefly review the Old Testament and the New Testament. Explain to the children that different parts of the Bible are shared during Mass each Sunday.

RAISING FAITH-FILLED KIDS *a parent page*

Focus on Faith

Loving as God Loves

When Blessed Mother Teresa was laboring for the poor, a reporter asked her what she thought about being called a saint. She replied that we are all called to be saints. She was called to be a saint in what she did, and the reporters, cameramen, and producers were called to be saints in what they did. This is the biblical understanding of what it means to be holy. A holy person is someone who responds to God's call to love him and serve others. As parents we are also are called to be holy. We respond to God's call by serving our family members and by showing them God's love.

Dinnertime Conversation Starter

Recall with your family memorable people who have touched your lives. What made them special? How did they serve God and others?

Hints for at Home

With your child create Happy Hand Towels for a homeless shelter. You will need new hand towels and a black permanent marker. Invite your child to draw a smiley face on each towel; ask him or her to write an upbeat message, such as *Jesus loves you* or *Blessed are the clean of heart* on each. With your family deliver the completed towels.

Spirituality in Action

Go with your child to visit a sick or elderly relative, neighbor, or parishioner. Bring along a snack, holy cards, magazines, and a board game. Spend some time visiting, talking, and playing the game with the elderly friend. Afterwards ask your child to share how he or she felt during the visit. Reinforce the idea that when we reach out to those in need, we are loving our neighbors.

Focus on Prayer

Your child has learned the importance of praying for help in making good choices. With your child take a few moments to offer a prayer for help when making difficult choices.

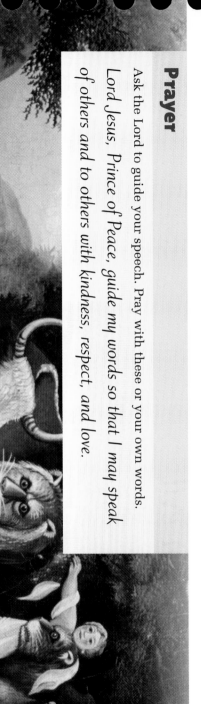

Session 24: Making Choices

3-Minute Retreat

Before you prepare for your session, pause for a few moments and set aside any distracting thoughts. Slowly count to 10 and feel the warmth of God as you continue your journey of faith.

1 Peter 3:10

Whoever would love life
and see good days
must keep the tongue from evil
and the lips from speaking deceit.

Reflection

Speaking about peace brings truth and love into the words we speak to one another. Nearly everyone can recall the sting of unkind words and perhaps even the guilty awareness of the injury caused by unkind words that were spoken. Our love of God is manifest in our speech and our actions toward one another. Respecting people's privacy and possessions is one way to act as people of peace.

Questions

Do my words show a lack of respect for others? How can I reflect the values of peace and respect with the children I serve?

Prayer

Ask the Lord to guide your speech. Pray with these or your own words.

Lord Jesus, Prince of Peace, guide my words so that I may speak of others and to others with kindness, respect, and love.

Take a few moments to reflect prayerfully before you prepare this session.

Peaceable Kingdom, Edward Hicks

Catechist Preparation

Knowing and Sharing Your Faith

Scripture and Tradition in Session 24

When we make moral choices, we show respect for others. When we make bad choices, we show disrespect for others. A boy who is tempted to lie but chooses instead to tell the truth, for example, shows respect for the other person and for that person's desire to know the truth. A girl who steals something shows disrespect for the owner and his right to have property. A boy who allows himself to be overcome with anger for his parents shows disrespect for them, while a girl who chooses to obey her parents, even when it is difficult to do so, shows respect for them and their position in the family.

The well-being of the community is at stake when we make moral choices. In making moral choices, we must consider how those choices will affect individuals and the community.

Scripture in Session 24

1 Peter 3:10–12 urges the Christian community to turn from evil and do good.
Psalm 34:12–15 encourages us to pursue peace.

Let the scripture and Tradition deepen your understanding of the content in this session.

WINDOW ON THE CATECHISM

The morality of human acts is discussed in *CCC* 1749–1756.

Do what is right.

Stay away from evil.

Catechist Preparation

From the Richness of the Tradition

One of the goals of Catholic social teachings is the promotion of an awareness of our social involvement with others in the community and the obligations of belonging to the community. Pope John Paul II made this clear in a 1984 address in Edmonton, Alberta, Canada: "The Second Vatican Council, following the whole of Tradition, warns us not to stop at an 'individualistic' interpretation of Christian ethics, since Christian ethics also has its social dimension. The human person lives in a community, in society. And with the community he shares hunger and thirst and sickness and malnutrition and misery and all of the deficiencies that result therefrom. In his or her own person the human being is meant to experience the needs of others." (*Justice in the Marketplace: Collected Statements of the Vatican and the U.S. Catholic Bishops on Economic Policy, 1891–1984*, p. 355)

✝ Catholic Social Teaching

The following Catholic Social Teaching themes are highlighted in this session:

- **Call to Family, Community, and Participation**
- **Solidarity**
- **Life and Dignity of the Human Person**

Prayer in Session 24

In this session the children pray to Jesus as their model of peace and as their guide in making good choices.

Consider in this session how you will invite the children to respond to and prayerfully reflect on God's invitation to love and serve others.

GENERAL DIRECTORY FOR CATECHESIS

The importance of moral formation in catechesis is explored in *GDC* 85.

Session 24: Making Choices

Session Theme: *God wants us to respect one another's good name and property.*

Before This Session

- Bookmark 1 Peter 3:10–12 and Psalm 34:12–15. Place the Bible in the prayer center open to the first letter of Peter.
- Listen to the reflective music on CD 2 so you can choose an appropriate track for the reflection on page 232.
- Set up the CD player so you will be ready to play the songs and the reflective music.
- Display the posters: We Celebrate the Mass (Part II), Ten Commandments.

Steps

| | Outcomes | *At the end of the session, the children should be able to* |

DAY 1 **Engage** page 225
Making Choices

- understand how to respect others' belongings.

DAYS 1–3 **Explore** pages 226–231
A Community of Believers
Respect Others
Living in Kindness
Making a Moral Choice: A Play

- tell the story of Peter urging people to live in peace.
- explain that God can help us act with kindness.
- describe how God wants us to ask forgiveness for our sins.

DAY 4 **Reflect** page 232
Prayer: Thanking Jesus for Helping Us Grow in Faith

- prayerfully reflect on God's presence, his invitation, and response.

DAY 4 **Respond** page 233
Living My Faith: Showing Respect for Others

- identify practical ways to act on God's invitation in everyday living.

DAY 5 **Extending the Session** page 234
Day 5 offers an opportunity to extend the session with activities that reinforce the session outcomes.

Materials

Required Materials
- Bible
- Writing paper, pens, pencils
- Art materials, such as drawing paper, crayon, markers, scissors, glue
- Numbered index cards with moral choice situations (page 230)
- Post-its, index cards, or small pieces of paper (page 231)
- CD 2, Track 19: Jesus' Hands Were Kind Hands (2:07) (page 229)
- CD 2, Reflective music (page 232)
- Poster: We Celebrate the Mass (Part II)

Optional Materials
- World map or globe (page 226)
- Plastic bags filled with lettered tiles from a word-making game (page 232)
- Craft sticks or twigs, pieces of yarn 5-8 inches in length, paper hearts (page 234)
- Note cards (page 234)
- Blackline Master 62, craft sticks (page 227)
- Blackline Masters 63, 64 (pages 229, 231)

e-resources
www.FindingGod.org

Making Choices

Begin your time together with the Sign of the Cross. Then say: *It has been a privilege to help you learn about God, Jesus, the Holy Spirit, the Church, and what it means to be a child of God.*

Say: *Open your books to page 225. Read the title and paragraph.* Ask: *What does it mean to show respect?* (to be polite, to be kind, to

be considerate, to be careful with others' belongings) Encourage the children to respond to the questions and share their experiences.

Have the group look at the photos. Ask: *How are the children in the picture on the right showing respect for others and their belongings?* (They are working cooperatively to build something out of LEGO-type blocks.) *Are the children in the left-hand picture showing respect for their belongings?* (no) *Why not?* (The child on the right ruined the other child's structure.)

Engage

Prayer

Continue: *Jesus treated everyone with respect. Let's pray to our wonderful role model, Jesus, and ask him to help us respect people by being peacemakers. Please pray this prayer of petition with me.*

Pray the prayer aloud. Then say: *Now close your eyes and ask Jesus to help you be peaceful.* Pause and give the children a few moments to speak with Jesus. End the prayer time by praying *Amen* and asking the children to open their eyes.

Making Choices

Session 24

Think of a time when someone played with your toys. Did this person respect you and your belongings? How can you respect others?

Prayer

Jesus, you want me to live in peace with others. Show me how to be a peacemaker.

OPTION

RULES FOR PEACEFUL PLAY

On the board write *Rules for Peaceful Play.* Ask the children: *What are some ways we can share our toys and games with others and play together peacefully. What rules might we follow?* Encourage a variety of responses. Write the children's suggestions on the board as they are presented. Encourage them to think of these rules the next time they are playing with others.

✝ *Family and Community*

A Community of Believers

Ask the children: *Who remembers who Peter was?* (the leader of the Church, the "rock" on which Jesus built his church) Explain: *As the Church's leader, Peter wanted the first Christians to learn about God and what God had planned for them.*

Bring forward the Bible from the prayer center. Review the two parts of the Bible. Ask: *In what part of the Bible will we read Peter's words? Why?* (He was a follower of Jesus, and Jesus' story is in the New Testament.)

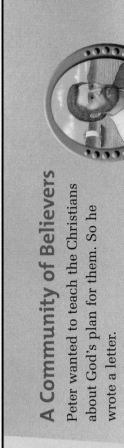

Read the title and first paragraph in the children's book aloud. Then draw attention to the art. Have the children describe what they see. (a picture of Peter, a group of people listening to Peter's letter being read to them) Then read the second paragraph aloud. Explain: *Peter encouraged Christians to act as Jesus would. He wanted them to live in peace.*

Reading God's Word

Ask a volunteer to read the section aloud as the group follows along. Say: *We can work hard to show respect for everyone. We can stop ourselves from saying bad things about people. We can reach out to others in peace.*

Point out that the passage you just read is from the book of Psalms, which is in the Old Testament. Ask: *Is the Old Testament the first or second part of the Bible?* (first)

✝ *Solidarity*

226   Session 24

PEACE PALS

Display a world map or globe. Explain: *We are called to live in peace with all the people in the world. We are called to work together to live in justice and to take good care of God's world.* Challenge volunteers to use the map to point out the continents of Africa, Antarctica, Asia, Australia, Europe, North America, and South America. Explain: *One way to make peace with people around the world is to learn about them. If you would* like to make a friend in another part of the world, you can join ePALS and be a pen pal to someone in another part of the world. On the board write: **www.epals.com**. Have the children copy it down. Say: *With your parents' help you can get on this Web site and make friends all over the world.*

✝ *Solidarity*

A Community of Believers

Peter wanted to teach the Christians about God's plan for them. So he wrote a letter.

Peter wrote, "Whoever loves their life should not tell lies or say evil things. Do what is right and stay away from evil. Bring peace into the world."

adapted from 1 Peter 3:10-12

Reading God's Word

If you want to be happy, do not say bad things or tell lies. Always be peaceful with one another, and do not sin.

adapted from Psalm 34:12-15

226   God's Invitation

Respect Others

Say: *We've discussed how important it is to live and play peacefully with others. We've talked about what it means to show respect for others. Showing respect is an important way to live in peace. When we show respect for someone's good name, we don't say bad things about that person. When we show respect for someone's property, we don't take or misuse what belongs to them. If they lend something to us, we must take care of it as if it were our own and remember to return it.*

✝ *Solidarity*

Invite the children to join you in a song to the tune of "The Farmer in the Dell." Say: *This song reminds us to show respect for others.*

Respecting your good name,
Respecting your good name,
That is how I care,
Respecting your good name!

Respect for property,
Respect for property,
That is how I care,
Respect for property!

Conclude: *Let's read about two children who learn about treating others with respect.*

Explore

Read the title and first paragraph. Have the children describe what they see in the photo. (Benito hearing Ana and Eduardo's saying mean things about him) Ask: *How do you think Benito felt when he heard Ana and Eduardo saying mean things about him?* (upset, sad)

Ask the children to silently read the next paragraph. Ask: *How did Ana and Eduardo feel about what they had done?* (ashamed) Say: *Everyone felt bad about what happened. Only hurt feelings came of it.*

Close this time together by saying: *Gossip is hurtful. Let's avoid it and treat all people with respect.*

Respect Others

Ana and Eduardo said hurtful things about Benito. They did not know that Benito could hear them. Later they wished that they had not said mean things about him.

Harmful words hurt everyone. Benito was hurt by what Ana and Eduardo said. Ana and Eduardo felt ashamed for talking about Benito. They knew that they should never say hurtful things about others.

Like Ana and Eduardo, we can be tempted to say hurtful things about others. But God wants us to treat everybody with kindness. He teaches us that we will be happy if we show respect for others and their feelings.

BLM 62: MAKING PEACE

On Blackline Master 62 children make puppets to retell the story of Ana, Eduardo, and Benito.

THE TELEPHONE GAME

To teach the children how gossip spreads, play the telephone game.

Have the children sit in a circle. Whisper the following story into an ear of one of the children: *The dog across the street from _____'s house bit a child the other day. Some people think the dog has a disease. _____ (same name) is sick and didn't come to school today.* Now have the child whisper the story into the ear of the person next to him or her until your words go all the way around the circle. Ask the last child to tell the group the story he or she heard. Most likely the final version of the story will be quite different from your original one. Tell the group what the original words were. Explain: *See how differently the story ended up. This is one reason why it's important not to gossip and spread rumors.*

Explore

Showing Respect

Say: **God wants us to live in peace with our families and with others. That means we should obey our parents, get along with our brothers and sisters, and respect other people and their belongings.** Say: **Now we'll practice learning more about respect.**

✝ *Life and Dignity*

Read the activity's title and directions aloud. Give the children a few minutes to work.

When they have finished, call on a volunteer to read the first sentence and share his or her answer. Then ask the group: **What beatitude is Tucker not showing?** (He is not being kind.) Allow the children to turn to page 217 if they need to review the Beatitudes.

Call on another volunteer to read the second statement and share his or her answer. Then ask: **What beatitude is Sara not showing?** (She is not doing the right thing.)

Choose another volunteer to read and share the answer for the third statement. Ask: **What beatitude is Kevin showing?** (kindness) Have a volunteer read the fourth statement and give an answer. Then ask: **What beatitude is Yoon-Shoo not showing?** (He is not doing the right thing.)

Finally, have a volunteer read and provide the answer for the final statement. Ask: **What beatitude is Maria showing?** (She is being a peacemaker.)

✝ *Family and Community*

Link to Liturgy

Read the section aloud. Ask the children: **Who remembers what the sign of peace is?** (handshake or hug along with words of peace and fellowship) Demonstrate the sign of peace with a child next to you. Say: **Peace be with you.** Explain that the child should respond: **And also with you.**

Draw attention to the We Celebrate the Mass (Part II) poster. Point out the sign of peace. Ask the children: **In what part of the Mass do we share the sign of peace?** (Liturgy of the Eucharist)

OPTION

NOW IT'S RESPECTFUL!

Review situations 1, 2, and 4 in the Showing Respect activity; these do not show respect for others. Read situation 1 again. Ask the children: **What could have been done to show respect?** Encourage the children to respond. Then read situations 2 and 4 and have the children discuss ways in which they can change the situations to show respectful behavior.

✝ *Life and Dignity*

FYI

THE SIGN OF PEACE

The sign of peace in Mass reminds us of our commitment to love God and one another. Offered before we receive the Eucharist, the sign of peace is frequently shared as a handshake or embrace along with a wish that the other person share the peace of Christ.

Showing Respect

Write **R** on the line if the person is being respectful. Write **NR** if the person is not being respectful.

1. Tucker makes fun of Corey's haircut. _____ NR

2. Sara reads her sister's diary when she is not home. _____ NR

3. Kevin thanks Holly for helping him. _____ R

4. Yoon-Soo takes his brother's candy without asking him. _____ NR

5. Maria cleans her sister's bike after borrowing it. _____ R

Link to Liturgy

The sign of peace at Mass is one way we show respect for others.

228 God's Invitation

Living in Kindness

Remind the children: *Jesus reached out in kindness to everyone he met. We are being like Jesus when we are kind to others.*

[♪] Have the children turn to the song "Jesus' Hands" in the Songs of Our Faith section in the back of their book. Say: *In the second verse, you will say, "Take my hands, Lord Jesus, let them work for you." Pay attention to these words as you ask Jesus to help you do only good with your hands.* Play the song "Jesus' Hands Were Kind Hands" on Track 19 of CD 2 and encourage the children to sing along.

Read the title and first paragraph aloud. Point out the photo, and ask: *In what way is the child showing kindness?* (by helping another child pick up books that were dropped) Say: *This child used his hands to be kind. God encourages us to treat others with the kindness with which we would like them to treat us.*

Read the second paragraph. Say: *In the Showing Respect activity on page 228, look at the first sentence. Ask: What could Tucker do to make up for what he said to Corey?* (say he's sorry, say something nice about Corey's haircut)

Display the Ten Commandments poster and discuss with the children how the commandments help us live in kindness and with respect.

Meet a Saint

Say: *Now we will learn about Saint Francis Borgia* (sänt fran´sis bôr´zha), *who lived a life of doing good for others.* Read the paragraph aloud as the group follows along. Tell the children: *Saint Francis Borgia lived the Great Commandment. He loved God and others. The Church honors this saint on his feast day, October 10.*

Conclude by saying: *As baptized followers of Jesus Christ, we are all called to be saints. Let's be saint-like in our actions today.*

Living in Kindness

God wants us to live in kindness. He wants us to be kind to one another and to enjoy the kindness others show us.

When we steal, lie, or say unkind things about others, we sin. God wants us to make up for what we have done. We ask for forgiveness. We return what was stolen. We stop saying hurtful things. Then we can live in kindness as God wants us to.

Meet a Saint

Saint Francis Borgia was a rich man. One day, Francis gave away his money and became a priest. He helped others and served the Church for the rest of his life.

Unit 5, Session 24   **229**

OPTION

BLM 63: LIVING LIKE JESUS
Blackline Master 63 is a short-answer activity that reviews vocabulary words from Unit 5.

FYI

SAINT FRANCIS BORGIA
Francis Borgia was born into an extremely wealthy and influential Spanish family and married when he was 19. Two deaths affected his life deeply. The death of Empress Isabella showed him that earthly possessions and status are fleeting. The death of his wife in 1546 convinced him to give up all of his possessions and join the Society of Jesus, or Jesuits. He founded a Jesuit College and within a few years became a priest. His subsequent tireless devotion to Jesus Christ and to the Jesuits led many to see him as the Society's second founder. He died in 1572 and was made a Saint in 1671.

Explore

Making a Moral Choice: A Play

Invite the children to join you in an activity that will allow them to practice making good choices.

Divide the class into small groups. Make sure each group has writing paper and a pencil. Have as many moral choice situations written on numbered index cards as there are groups. Distribute the cards and have each group discuss and agree on the best action. Have them write the number of the card and what they would do on their writing paper. Make it a timed activity, and have children rotate cards after three or four minutes.

After the time you have allotted for the activity, encourage the groups to share and comment on each other's responses. In cases of more than one good moral choice, point this out to the children.

Sample situations:

Without thinking, you make some unkind remarks to your friend because you've had a bad day.

You're in a hurry to leave the store when you see a person in a wheelchair approach the door you are near.

Two friends of yours are talking unkindly and making fun of a third friend who got a bad grade on a test.

Your brother needs you to help him with his work, and last night he wouldn't let you watch your favorite TV show.

A classmate forgot his lunch on a field trip day, and you know he's too shy to ask anyone to share.

The same child in your room always shoves and cuts in line.

After the activity, read the title and the first paragraph on page 230 aloud. Choose four volunteers to take the narrator's and children's parts and ask them to read aloud the script on pages 230 and 231. Remind the children that they are role-playing and should try to speak as the character might. Also remind them to read only the words of the speaker.

After the children have finished the reading, repeat the questions posed in the introductory paragraph on page 230, encouraging discussion of each one. Leave the conclusion open-ended, so children will still have to determine the best ending.

Making a Moral Choice: A Play

This play is not finished. You get to write the ending! First read the play with your classmates. Then talk about what Gracie did. Why was it wrong? What will Helena and Paul tell her? What will she say to them? When you have written the ending, share it with your class. Take parts and read your play aloud.

Narrator: Gracie, Helena, and Paul are sitting on a bench.

Helena: Gracie, I thought you were in trouble.

Paul: Yeah, for not doing your homework.

Gracie: I got out of being punished. I told Mrs. Peale that I forgot to bring my homework to school.

Your Ending

Read the heading and directions aloud. Make sure the children understand that the arrows indicate the sequence of speakers.

You might have the children write their endings individually. Then have a volunteer choose two other children to read the play and new ending with him or her. Repeat with other volunteers.

An alternative would be to have the children work in groups of three to write the ending. Then have each group read the play aloud, including their own ending, to the large group. You probably won't need a narrator part because you can have the readers seated on chairs together. Discuss the different endings the groups propose.

Ask the children to try to think of a family member or a friend with whom they need to make up. Say: *Maybe it's just a little disagreement, but wouldn't you feel better if you brought the problem out in the open and forgave or asked forgiveness?*

Give each child a Post-it note, index card, or small piece of paper. Say: *Write the person's name and draw a smiley face next to it. That will remind you that you want to make peace and live*

happily with that person. Can't think of anyone? Great! You're living in kindness! Make a smiley anyway so you'll remember next time!

Ask the children to put their notes inside a book or notebook that they will be taking home today because it's a private reminder. Suggest they put it on a page they'll need for homework.

Say: *Please join me in a prayer of thanksgiving to Jesus for being our teacher and example. Please pray aloud by echoing each part after me.*

Jesus, my friend and example, thank you for teaching me the ways of kindness and respect.

Close the prayer by inviting the children to pray the Sign of the Cross with you.

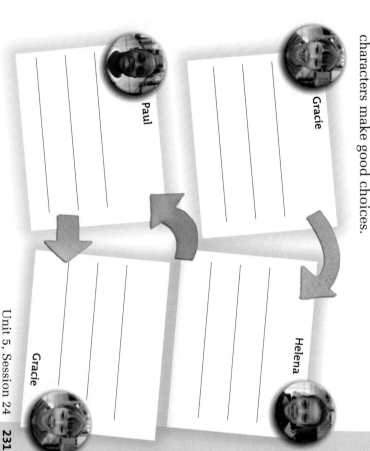

Your Ending

Write your ending to the play. Have the characters make good choices.

Helena: What are you going to do now?

Gracie: She told me I have to bring my homework to school tomorrow.

Paul: So you lied to the teacher. What did she say?

Paul

Gracie

Gracie

Helena

BLM 64: FOLLOWING PETER'S ADVICE

Blackline Master 64 is a matching activity that requires children to apply teachings from Peter's letter to real-life situations.

DOING BETTER

Discuss with the children a few situations that you have observed in the classroom, on the playground, or in the school building. Some possibilities include: bullying, teasing, excluding, rough play, rudeness, or gossip. Pick one or two for the class to discuss. Encourage them to determine a plan to remedy these situations.

Reflect

Prayer

Tell the children: *It's our special time for prayer now. Since prayer is talking and listening to God, it is important that we be very quiet. Sit in a comfortable position as we get ready to talk with God.*

Continue: *We have learned a lot about ourselves and our Catholic faith. Let's spend some time thinking about how close we have grown to Jesus. Please close your eyes, fold your hands, and listen quietly as I read this reflection and give you some things to think about.*

🎵💿 In the background, quietly play the reflective music at the end of CD 2 to create a prayerful atmosphere.

Read the first paragraph aloud for the children, pausing for three seconds after each sentence so the children can imagine Jesus joining them in a quiet place. Then softly say: *How do you feel when Jesus comes to you?* Allow time so the children can think about this.

With a soothing voice read the second paragraph, pausing for a couple of seconds after each sentence. Then say: *What is Jesus doing as you speak to him?* Allow the children time to imagine speaking with Jesus.

Read the third and fourth paragraphs, pausing briefly after each sentence. Count to 10 silently as the children spend quiet time with Jesus. Then softly ask the children to open their eyes. Close by saying: *Let us offer one another the sign of peace.*

OPTION

KIND WORDS

Divide the class into groups. Give each group a plastic bag filled with lettered tiles from a word-making game. Have the groups spell out as many kind words as they can. (please, thank you, may I, nice, happy, helpful) When they have finished, have each group read the words they formed. Say: *Remember to use these kind words when you talk to people. When you use kind words, you are being like Jesus.*

OPTION

WORDS OF RESPECT

Divide the class into groups of three or four and ask each group to sit in a circle. Ask the children to take turns speaking words of kindness and respect to every child in the circle. Encourage them to personalize their words. Show them how to do so by selecting several children from the large group. Speak personalized words of respect, identifying each by name, for example, *Marie, I like the way you're always smiling!* and *Aaron, you're a great artist!* When the groups have finished, say: *When we respect others, we are being like Jesus.*

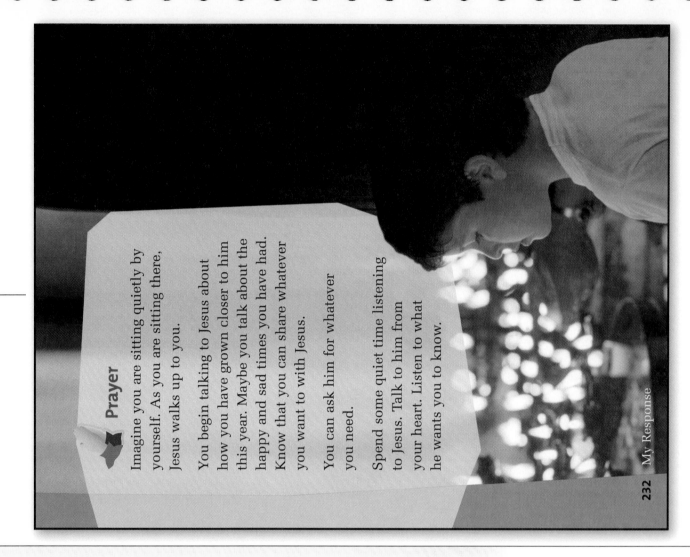

Prayer

Imagine you are sitting quietly by yourself. As you are sitting there, Jesus walks up to you.

You begin talking to Jesus about how you have grown closer to him this year. Maybe you talk about the happy and sad times you have had. Know that you can share whatever you want to with Jesus.

You can ask him for whatever you need.

Spend some quiet time listening to Jesus. Talk to him from your heart. Listen to what he wants you to know.

232   My Response

Living My Faith

Use the following activities to reinforce the importance of putting what the children learned into practice in their lives.

Faith Summary

Read the section aloud. Ask: **How can we show respect for one another?** (by caring for others and their belongings) **Who wrote a letter to teach the early Christians about God's plan for them?** (Peter) **What advice did Peter give to the Christians?** (Do what is right and stay away from evil. Bring peace into the world.)

Ways of Being Like Jesus

Jesus teaches us to respect people and their belongings. We will be happy if we are respectful in our words and actions.

With My Family

Discuss with your family what you can do to live peacefully together.

My Response

Write a way you can show respect for the belongings of others.

Prayer

Thank you, Jesus, for all you have taught me. Help me to respect everyone in my life.

Living My Faith

Unit 5, Session 24   **233**

Ways of Being Like Jesus

Ask the children to read the section quietly. Draw attention to the photo at the right. Say: **These are the children we read about on page 227.** Ask: **How have Benito, Ana, and Eduardo changed? What do you think happened?** (Ana and Eduardo apologized after making the hurtful comments about Benito, and now they all get along.) **What can you do to be kind to people this week?** (say nice things about them and to them)

✝ Family and Community

With My Family

Read the section and then ask: **What are some ways we can live peacefully with our family members?** (help with chores when we are asked, not fight with brothers or sisters)

✝ Family and Community

My Response

Read the section aloud. Say: **We've learned about respecting others and their belongings. Take some time to think about what you can do this week to show respect for the belongings of others. Then write a sentence about it.**

As the children work, observe how well they understand the meaning of respect.

After the children have finished, call on volunteers to share their sentences.

As you conclude today, say: **When you respect another person's belongings, you are respecting the person.**

Prayer

Say: **We've learned so much from Jesus! Please fold your hands and pray this prayer of thanks aloud with me.**

Lead the group in praying the prayer aloud. Then say: **Now close your eyes and take a moment to share what is in your heart with Jesus.** Give the children time to reflect. Then ask the children to open their eyes. Close with the Sign of the Cross.

Session 24   **233**

Extending the Session

Choose from the following options to extend the session or to reinforce concepts developed during the week.

Family Involvement

Remind the children to take home the Raising Faith-Filled Kids page to share what they are learning with their families.

Preparation for Sunday Scripture Readings

Lead children in a prayerful discussion of Sunday's readings. Visit www.FindingGod.org/Sunday for more information.

Seasonal Session

Consider the time of the liturgical year and use the appropriate seasonal session. Seasonal sessions may be found on page 241.

Unused Options and BLMs

Incorporate any unused options or Blackline Masters from the week's session.

Web Site Activities

Visit www.FindingGod.org to find additional activities for extending the session.

OPTION

KINDNESS MOBILE

Give each child two craft sticks or twigs, six pieces of yarn varying in length from 5 to 8 inches, and four paper hearts with a hole punched in the tops. Instruct children to write the following on the hearts: *God* (heart 1) *wants me* (heart 2) *to live* (heart 3) *in kindness* (heart 4). Assist children in tying the craft sticks or twigs together in the shape of a cross, and instruct them to tie one piece of yarn to the four ends of the cross. Then have them tie the paper hearts to the end of each piece of yarn. Use the final piece of yarn to create hangers for the Kindness Mobiles. Invite children to display their mobiles at home.

OPTION

ACTS OF KINDNESS

On note cards, write one situation for every two children, things that might require an act of kindness. Some examples are *You fell down and scraped your knee, You can't find your Mom at the market,* and *You lost your math book.* Form pairs of children and distribute cards to one child of each pair. The other child should not see the card. Have the pairs act out a skit, with the child who has not seen the card responding to the situation in a kind way. When all pairs have performed, have them exchange cards.

OPTION

MAKING IT RIGHT

Review the story of Ana, Eduardo, and Benito on page 227. Ask the children to reflect for a few moments on the story, and then write a sentence or two about what Ana and Eduardo could do to make up for saying mean things about Benito. Some possible answers are *apologize to Benito, go to confession, do something kind for Benito,* and so on. Encourage children to share their answers with the class.

RAISING FAITH-FILLED KIDS

a parent page

Focus on Faith

Our Priorities

Francis Borgia (1510–1572) was a rich nobleman in Spain. He enjoyed being a person of wealth and high social standing. Then one day a close friend died, and Francis realized that his wealth would not last forever or buy him happiness. After his wife died, Francis became a Jesuit priest and was eventually made the head of the order. No longer focused on money and material possessions, Francis had shifted his attention toward serving God. Like Francis, we make decisions every day that teach our children where our priorities lie. They can see how important God is in our lives. If they made a list of what is important to them, where would God rank?

Dinnertime Conversation Starter

Talk about the importance of God in your family life. What are the ways you show that God is a priority in your home?

Hints for at Home

With your family create a Respect poster. You will need watercolor paint, a tin pan, poster board, and a permanent marker. Place the paint in the tin pan and allow each member of your family to take a turn placing his or her hand in the paint. Have each family member place a handprint on the poster board. When each hand is in place, write *Respect* on the poster with the permanent marker. Place the completed poster in a prominent place in your home to remind your family to respect one another's property, good name, and privacy.

The Vision of St. Francis Borgia, with Sts. Aloysius Gonzaga and Stanislaus Kostka, Antonio Salas

Spirituality in Action

With your family make a pledge of peace. Such a pledge encourages respect and forgiveness and opposes the use of violence. With your family join hands in a circle of peace. Recite the pledge "We pledge to respect one another, to listen to one another, and to forgive one another. We pledge to respect all of God's creation. We pledge to oppose violence in all forms and to live our lives in peace."

Focus on Prayer

Your child has learned that the sign of peace is one way we show our care and respect for others. Notice the sign of peace the next time you are at Mass with your child. Discuss the ways in which it strengthens our ties as parishioners and community members.

Session 25: Unit 5 Review
3-Minute Retreat

Before you prepare for your session, pause for a few moments and focus inward. Take three deep breaths, relax, and recognize that you are in the loving presence of God, who is with you as you continue your journey of spiritual growth.

John 14:27

Peace I leave with you; my peace I give to you. Not as the world gives do I give it to you. Do not let your hearts be troubled or afraid.

Reflection

Peace is an action, an attitude, and most of all, a gift from Jesus. The Ten Commandments, the Beatitudes, and the life of Jesus help us know what to do to live in God's peace and in peace with one another. Worry and fear can intrude into our lives and prevent us from knowing God's peace. As we conclude the year, it is important to entrust the children into God's protection and care.

Questions

What situations in my life are causing me to feel fearful or worried?
What can I do to open myself up more fully to the peace of Christ?

Prayer

Prayerfully picture the faces of the children you teach as you speak to Jesus, using these words or others that come to mind for you.

Jesus, you bring your peace into our lives. Watch over the children and guide them with your Spirit. Let them and me know the peace of your presence.

Take a few moments to reflect prayerfully before you prepare this session.

Catechist Preparation: Get-Ready Guide

Session 25: Unit 5 Review

Unit Theme: *Living Like Jesus*

Before This Session

- Bookmark the Bible to John 14:27 and place it open to this passage in the prayer center.
- Set up the CD player so that you will be ready to play the songs and the reflective music.

- For the Prayer Service, choose a child to do the reading from John. Practice the reading with the child before the session begins.

Outcomes *In this session, the children will review*

- that Jesus is God's greatest gift to us.

- that Jesus teaches us the importance of loving everyone.
- that the Holy Spirit helps us make good moral choices.
- that Jesus wants us to love God and others.
- that God wants us to be respectful.

- how to prayerfully reflect on God's invitation in everyday living.

- practical ways to act on God's invitation in everyday living.

Steps

DAY 1 **Engage** page 235
Review

DAYS 2–3 **Explore** pages 236–238
Faith Summary

DAY 4 **Reflect** page 239
Prayer Service: Let Us Walk in Peace

DAY 4 **Respond** page 240
Living My Faith: Ways to Bring Peace to Others

Materials

Required Materials

- Bible
- Writing paper, pens, pencils
- Art materials, such as drawing paper, crayon, markers, scissors, glue
- CD 2, Track 1: Song of Love (4:00) (page 237)
- CD 2, Reflective music (page 238)
- CD 2, Track 11: Friends, All Gather 'Round (2:14) (page 239)

Optional Materials

- Objects that you can make sounds with (keys, whistle, ball, paper) (page 235)
- 3-by-5-inch cards (page 238)
- Blackline Master 65—Unit 5 Show What You Know (pages 235, 236)

e-resources

www.FindingGod.org

Review

Begin by saying: *We have had the chance to learn about God and one another this year. We've also been able to grow in faith together. This week will be a special time for us to think about all that Jesus has taught us and to make a promise to ourselves and to one another that we will bring his peace into the world.*

Continue: *We have learned many things about how we can become more like Jesus.* Ask: *Can you think of one thing that Jesus did that you can do?* Accept all reasonable responses. If the children need

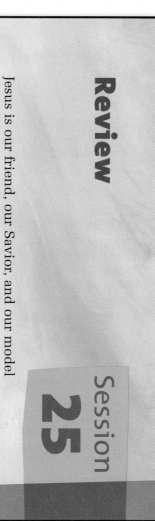

Review

Session 25

Jesus is our friend, our Savior, and our model of love and goodness. He is our greatest gift from God.

Prayer

Jesus, you are my light and my life. May your love help me continue to grow to be more like you.

---

help, allow them to look through the units of their book.

Show What You Know

Distribute BLM 65, Unit 5 Show What You Know, to the children. Explain that it will help the children see how well they understand what was taught.

When the children have finished, ask them to exchange papers and help them correct the objective section. Allow time for them to look over their own corrected papers before collecting the papers.

Review the short-answer and self-assessment items. Provide written feedback and identify concepts needing attention. Use this

Engage

information as you continue the Review on Day 2.

Then say: *Please open your books to page 235.* Read the paragraph aloud. Have the group look at the picture and describe what they see. (Jesus with the children) Remind the children: *Just as Jesus loved children when he was on earth, so does he continue to have a special love for children today.*

Prayer

Say: *Jesus is our greatest gift from God! He is our model of love and goodness. Let's ask Jesus to help us grow through his love.*

Pray the prayer aloud with the group. Then say: *Now close your eyes and invite Jesus into your hearts. Ask for his help as you continue to follow his example.* Then pause so the children can have a few moments to reflect. End by praying **Amen** and asking the children to open their eyes.

LISTEN UP!

Tell the children: *It is very important to listen to Jesus' words because they help us become more like him. Let's play a game in which we have to practice listening very carefully.* Explain: *I will make sounds with certain objects, and you will have to guess what they are. Have the children close their eyes. Then make sounds with a variety of objects such as keys, whistle, crumpling paper, or bouncing ball. After you make each sound, have the children guess what it is. Remind the children to listen just as carefully to the words of Jesus in the Bible.

Explore

Faith Summary

Tell the children that today they will continue their review with the guidance of the Holy Spirit and the example of Jesus.

Show What You Know

Return the assessment, BLM 65, to the children. Review the short-answer questions and any concepts the children did not fully understand.

Say to the children: *We've sung the song "I Can Be Like Him!" when we've been together before. Let's sing it again.*

Sing the first verse to the tune of "London Bridge Is Falling Down." Then invite the children to join you. Sing the remaining verses with the children as well.

Jesus was a faithful Son, faithful Son, faithful Son, Jesus was a faithful Son, be like Jesus!

Jesus listened to God's Word, to God's Word, to God's Word, Jesus listened to God's Word, be like Jesus!

Jesus knew God's rules for life, rules for life, rules for life, Jesus knew God's rules for life, be like Jesus!

Conclude: *You're familiar with the song now and can sing it to yourselves anytime you have choices to make.*

Tell the children: *Let's review what we have learned in this unit.* Ask: *Who is our model of love?* (Jesus) Then read the first paragraph. Ask the group: *Who can tell the story of the parable of the Good Samaritan to the group?* Call on a volunteer to share the story. Ask the group: *What are some ways we can show our love for others?* (help someone who is

sad or injured, reach out to those in need, use kind words)

Now have a child read the second paragraph. Ask: *What are some difficult choices you have had to make?* Be careful that the children's responses do not get too personal. Ask: *Who might be able to help you as you try to make a good choice?* (the Holy Spirit, parents, teachers) *What are the steps for helping us make good or moral choices?* Have the children turn back to page 207 and call on various volunteers to read each of the steps.

Read the third paragraph aloud. Ask: *In what part of the Bible is the Great Commandment?*

(the New Testament) Ask: *What does the Great Commandment teach us?* (to love God and to love our neighbors as we love ourselves) *What do the Beatitudes teach us?* (to be kind and loving to others, to do the right thing even when it's difficult, to be fair with others, to work for peace)

Ask a volunteer to read the final paragraph aloud. Then ask: *How can we show respect to others?* (say nice things about them, take care of their belongings)

End your time together praying the Our Father with the children.

Faith Summary

Jesus shows us how to love others through his words and actions. He gave us an example in the parable of the Good Samaritan.

The Holy Spirit helps us to make moral choices in our lives.

Jesus taught us the Great Commandment and the Beatitudes. They will help us bring peace into our lives and the lives of others.

Jesus wants us to be kind to others. He asks us to respect others and their belongings.

236   My Response

Living Like Jesus

Tell the children that they will continue their review of the unit by doing various activities.

Read the activity's title and directions aloud for the group. Observe how well they are able to remember the concepts taught in the unit. When they have finished, call on volunteers to read the sentences and share their answers.

♪🎵 Now take some time to play "Song of Love" on Track 1 of CD 2. Invite the children to sing along. If they would like to look at the words, they can find them in the Songs of Our Faith section in the back of their book.

OPTION

A HOLY PHRASE

Select a phrase from the Beatitudes (see page 217) that the children have learned, such as "Blessed are those who are kind." On the board create one blank space for each letter of the words in the phrase; include a blank space between the words of the phrase. Then have the children take turns calling out letters until they figure out what the phrase is.

OPTION

PEACE I LEAVE YOU

Have the children draw a picture of themselves with Jesus. Tell them: *Take time to reflect about the peace and love Jesus offers you before you begin to draw.* Encourage the children to hang their drawings in their rooms. Tell them that they can look at their pictures when they wake up in the morning to remind themselves that Jesus is with them every day.

OPTION

SEEING THE GOOD IN OTHERS

Remind the children: *Everyone has good qualities. We should always try to focus on the good things about people.* Provide the group with imagined information about people and ask them to come up with something positive about each person.

Your uncle doesn't visit as often as you would like. (maybe he always remembers to send you a card on your birthday)

Your friend never shares her toys. (maybe she helps you with your homework)

Your sibling always wants to play while you are trying to do your homework. (maybe he helps you with your chores in order to spend time with you)

Your classmate always asks to borrow a pencil. (maybe he wants you to be his friend)

Feel free to add your own situations to the activity, possibly reflecting situations that have occurred in your classroom.

Living Like Jesus

Complete the sentences.
The answers are found in the box.

choices	Commandment	mercy
peace	Samaritan	Testament

1. We make good moral ____choices____ when we ask for God's help.

2. The New ____Testament____ tells the story of Jesus' life.

3. The Good ____Samaritan____ did as Jesus teaches.

4. The Great ____Commandment____ tells us how to love God and others.

5. Showing ____mercy____ is one way to be like Jesus.

6. Jesus said, "Blessed are those who work for ____peace____."

Explore

Prayer for Peace

Read the title and directions. Have the children write a prayer to be shared with another child during the prayer service. Say: *Write a prayer that wishes good things for another child in the group. Encourage him or her to have peace, to stay close to Jesus, and to remember how much God loves each and every person. The child who receives your prayer will read it aloud at our prayer service later in the session.*

The children's book is filled with many prayers. If they are having difficulty writing a prayer, they can look at other prayers in their book for help.

Allow the children time to write their prayers and decorate the hearts.

 You may wish to play the reflective music at the end of CD 2 while the group works. When they have finished, have the children cut out their hearts. Tell the children to place their hearts aside until tomorrow's Prayer Service.

✝ *Solidarity*

Remind the children that although they are completing their year of learning, they will apply what they have learned for the rest of their lives.

OPTION

I WANT TO REMEMBER

Provide each child with a 3-by-5-inch card. Allow time for the children to search through their books and refresh their memories with all that they have learned since the beginning of the year. Tell each child to complete this sentence on their cards: *One thing I want to remember is _____.* When they have finished, gather in a circle and ask them to share their sentences.

OPTION

VOCABULARY CARDS REVISITED

If you made the vocabulary flash cards recommended in an option on page 190, use them now to impress the children with all the words they have learned. You could also have a vocabulary bee as suggested in the same option on page 190.

Prayer for Peace

In the heart write a peace prayer for the prayer service.

Explain to the children: *This is a good time for our group to gather together to remember how much Jesus loves us and how much he wants us to love one another.* Continue: *In today's Prayer Service we will remember the gift of peace that Jesus gave us, and we will share our prayers of peace with others in the group. As we gather, let's make living with the peace of Jesus our goal.*

Have the children look at page 238 of their book. Mention that today one of the children from the group

will do the reading from the Gospel of John. Draw attention to the line that has All in front of it. Remind the children that they will pray this line as a group, saying "Praise to you, Lord Jesus Christ." Have them practice saying this. Then point out that after the Leader part that follows their response, they will exchange peace prayers. Each child will pass the peace prayer to the person to his or her right and say "Walk in peace."

Have the children turn to the song "Friends, All Gather 'Round" in

the Songs of Our Faith section in the backs of their books. Remind them of this song, which they learned in Session 8. Tell them they will sing the song at the end of the Prayer Service.

When all the children are ready, have them gather at the prayer center with their books and prayers of peace. Tell them to insert their peace prayers at the Prayer Service page to serve as a page marker.

Begin the Prayer Service. Read the first two lines and lead the children in the Sign of the Cross.

🕇 Ask the child you chose earlier to proclaim the reading from John. Motion to the group to respond: *Praise to you, Lord Jesus Christ.* Then read the next paragraph. Say: *Now it's time for each of us to present another member of the group with the prayer for peace that we wrote.* Ask the children to pass their peace prayer heart to the person on their right as they say to that person: *Walk in peace.* Read the final paragraph. Then have the children take turns praying their prayers aloud. When all the prayers have been prayed, encourage the children to thank those who wrote their prayers and invite the children to offer one another the sign of peace.

🎵💿 End the service by singing "Friends, All Gather 'Round" on Track 11 of CD 2. Have the children turn to the song in the Songs of Our Faith section in the backs of their books. Encourage the children to sing along. When the song has finished, have the children return to their seats.

Prayer Service

Leader: The Sign of the Cross reminds us that the Holy Trinity is with us.

Reader: A reading from the Gospel of John.

I give you my peace. It is the kind of peace that only I can give.

[adapted from John 14:27]

The gospel of the Lord.

All: Praise to you, Lord Jesus Christ.

Leader: Jesus, our friend and Savior, you gave us your gift of peace. Be with us as we offer our peace prayers to one another, saying, "Walk in peace."

Leader: Because Jesus is in our hearts and minds, let us offer one another a sign of peace.

Respond

Living My Faith

Use the following activities to help reinforce the daily practice of the main themes of this unit.

Ways of Being Like Jesus

Read the section. Say: *We have learned about having peace in our hearts and sharing that peace with others. As you leave this session, share the peace that Jesus gives you by being kind and loving toward others.* Ask: *How does this picture remind you of peace?* (children are joining hands around the world, everyone is happy)

✝ *Solidarity*

With My Family

Ask a volunteer to read the section. Ask: *What things that you have are valuable to you? How do you want others to treat these valuables?* Remind the children to treat the property of their family members with the same respect and care with which they would like their own belongings to be treated.

✝ *Family and Community*

Prayer

Say reverently: *Think about how much Jesus has done for us this past year. We have so much to thank Jesus for. Please pray this prayer of thanks aloud with me.*

Then say: *Now close your eyes and think about how you can make good choices, as Jesus did.* Allow the children time to speak with Jesus. Then ask the children to open their eyes. Close with the Sign of the Cross.

My Response

Read the section. Say: *We can each help bring peace to others. There are many ways we can do this. Think about one way you can bring peace to your family, school, friends, or neighbors.* (volunteer to help parents and siblings with their chores, make friends with new children at school, share with friends, be friendly to neighbors) Have the children write sentences about other things they can do to bring peace to others.

As your time together ends, say to the children: *Remember to live what you have learned.*

Living My Faith

Ways of Being Like Jesus

Jesus gave the world the gift of peace. You are like Jesus when you live in peace with your family, friends, and others.

With My Family

Treat family members and their property with respect. Return the things you borrow.

Prayer

Peaceful Jesus, thank you for all you have done for me. Help me make the right choices in everything I do and say.

My Response

What can you do to bring peace to others?

Seasonal Sessions

The Year in Our Church

Advent 243

Christmas and Epiphany 247

Lent 251

Holy Week 255

Easter 259

Pentecost 263

All Saints Day 267

Catechist Preparation

Welcome to the Seasonal Sessions

The seasonal sessions cover the major feasts and seasons of the liturgical year. Although designed primarily as supplements, with a shorter format than that of the core sessions, they may be used as stand-alone sessions. Each seasonal session follows the same format that you've become accustomed to in the core sessions.

Steps in the Sessions

• Engage—a brief introduction that relates to the children's life experiences
• Explore—an opportunity to explore Scripture and Catholic Tradition
• Reflect—an invitation for children to pray and reflect on the session theme
• Respond—an activity designed to elicit a response to God's transforming word

On the opening page of each session, you will find the theme of that session, a list of outcomes, a list of the required and optional materials, and other preparation suggestions.

Using the Seasonal Sessions

Each seasonal session is designed with flexibility that enables you to use it, depending upon your schedule and calendar, as either a stand-alone session or as a supplement to another session. Here are some options to help you plan your sessions.

As a Stand-Alone Session

By utilizing all the activity options and the additional Blackline Master activities that are provided, you can expand each seasonal session to a full stand-alone session of approximately 45 minutes. You can also creatively enhance the Prayer Service in the Reflect step with local seasonal customs and traditions, for example *Las Posadas* for Christmas. Schedule the seasonal sessions to coincide with the anticipation or actual arrival of each season or feast.

As a Supplement to Another Session

A seasonal session can be used as an introduction to a liturgical celebration that is part of your school program; for example, a Lent session can be used before going to the church for a Lenten prayer service. You can also use a seasonal session as a supplement to any session that occurs when that season or feast is approaching. Simply abbreviate each step in your regular session to allow for incorporation of the seasonal session. You may need to limit or skip the optional activities and Blackline Masters that are available to you.

The Year in Our Church

The liturgical calendar represents the celebration of the mystery of Christ, including the anticipation of his birth; his Incarnation; his death, resurrection, and ascension; and the expectation of his return. The Church marks the passage of time with a cycle of seasons and feasts that invites us, year after year, to deepen our commitment to Jesus. By inviting children into these celebrations, you help them grow in the Catholic way of life.

The Year in Our Church

Liturgical Calendar
The liturgical calendar shows us the feasts and seasons of the Church year.

(Calendar wheel labels: Advent, Christmas, Ordinary Time, Lent, Holy Week, Easter, Ordinary Time, First Sunday of Advent, Christmas, Epiphany, All Souls Day, All Saints Day, Ash Wednesday, Palm Sunday, Holy Thursday, Good Friday, Holy Saturday, Easter Sunday, Ascension, Pentecost, Winter, Fall, Spring, Summer)

Explaining the Liturgical Calendar

Use or adapt the following script to introduce the children to a basic understanding of the liturgical calendar. Repeat this discussion occasionally throughout the year. Ask: *What do you think the diagram on this page represents?* (Accept all reasonable answers.) *It is a liturgical calendar. We normally keep a calendar to mark special days such as birthdays, anniversaries, and holidays. In the same way, the Church keeps a calendar to mark special times in Jesus' life, death, and resurrection.*

Say: *Just as our regular calendar has holidays that commemorate the birthdays of important people or recall important events, the liturgical calendar has feast days and holy days. What feast days are shown on this calendar?* Invite volunteers to name some.

Say: *In our calendar year we have seasons—winter, spring, and so on. The liturgical calendar has seasons too. What seasons are shown on this calendar?* (Advent, Christmas, Lent, Easter, Ordinary Time) *Let's find the season that we are going to learn about today.*

Using the Liturgical Calendar BLM

Every seasonal session invites you to direct the children to locate that season or feast on the liturgical calendar. A Blackline Master of the liturgical calendar that appears on this page can be found on page 376 of this Catechist Guide.

If you choose to use this Blackline Master, distribute copies to the children. Ask them to print their names on their papers. They can color the appropriate section of the calendar with the color of that liturgical season. Refer to the calendar on this page for the correct colors. Ordinary Time can be colored after the Christmas and Easter seasons.

When the children have finished coloring, collect the calendars and save them to use during the next seasonal session. After the last seasonal session, encourage the children to take their completed calendars home.

Liturgical Year

At the beginning of each seasonal session, direct the children to turn to page 242 and to read the paragraph about the season that they will be celebrating. You may use the following summaries to provide additional information about each season.

Advent

Advent is a season of hope and joyful anticipation of the coming of Christ. While we prepare to celebrate the birth of Christ, we also use the season of Advent to anticipate his second coming.

Christmas and Epiphany

At Christmas we celebrate the birth of Jesus. This celebration lasts until the Sunday after Epiphany, which often falls on the celebration of the Baptism of the Lord. On the Epiphany (which means to "show," or "reveal"), we celebrate Jesus being revealed to the whole world.

Lent

Lent is not a somber or sad season but one of sobering joy because we know that the happiness of Easter comes as a result of the pain of the cross. Throughout these 40 days the whole Church prepares by praying, fasting, and giving alms.

Holy Week

Holy Week begins with Jesus' entrance into Jerusalem (Palm Sunday). We celebrate the culmination of the entire liturgical year by marking the Triduum, the three days of Holy Thursday, Good Friday, and Holy Saturday. This period is our celebration of Jesus' death and resurrection.

Easter

In order to properly celebrate Jesus' resurrection, the central feast of Christianity, the Church sets aside 50 days of joyful celebration. These 50 days from Easter to Pentecost are celebrated as one feast day, sometimes called the great Sunday. Easter is celebrated on the first Sunday after the first full moon of spring.

Pentecost

On Pentecost we celebrate the descent of the Holy Spirit upon the disciples 50 days after Jesus' resurrection. As such, Pentecost is our celebration of the birthday of the universal Church.

All Saints Day

The Communion of Saints consists of those who are on earth, those who have died and are being purified, and those who are blessed in heaven. The Communion of Saints is celebrated on the feasts of All Saints Day (November 1) and All Souls Day (November 2).

Ordinary Time

The Sundays of the entire year are counted or set aside as sacred time. Ordinary Time, typically 33 weeks, is celebrated following the Christmas season and then again following Easter.

Liturgical Year

We get our hearts ready to welcome Jesus during **Advent.**

Christmas celebrates Jesus' birth. **Epiphany** celebrates Jesus' coming for all people of the world.

Lent prepares us for Easter. It is a time to do extra good deeds.

During **Holy Week** we remember the suffering and death of Jesus.

On **Easter** we recall with joy Jesus' rising from the dead.

Pentecost is the feast of the Holy Spirit's coming to guide the Church.

All Saints Day celebrates all the holy persons who died and now live with God in heaven.

Ordinary Time is time set aside for everyday living as followers of Jesus.

Advent

Theme

In the season of Advent we prepare to celebrate Jesus' birth.

Outcomes

At the end of the session, the children should be able to

- identify Advent as a time to prepare to celebrate Jesus' birth.
- explain that John the Baptist helped people recognize Jesus.
- prepare for Jesus' coming by praying and doing good deeds.

Required Materials

Bible, paper, pens, pencils, crayons, markers, CD 2, Track 21: This Little Light of Mine (1:42) (page 246)

Optional Materials

Blackline Master 66 (page 244); decorative leafy greens or artificial rope of greens, 4 flashlights, pink and purple cellophane (page 245); and The Liturgical Calendar (page 245)

Before This Session

Bookmark your Bible to both Luke 3:10–14 and Psalm 25:4–5. Place a purple cloth at the prayer center and place the Bible on it, opened to the passage from Luke.

Set up Track 21 on CD 2 ahead of time so you will be ready to play the song.

Check the options for the current session and the materials lists above to prepare for the options you choose.

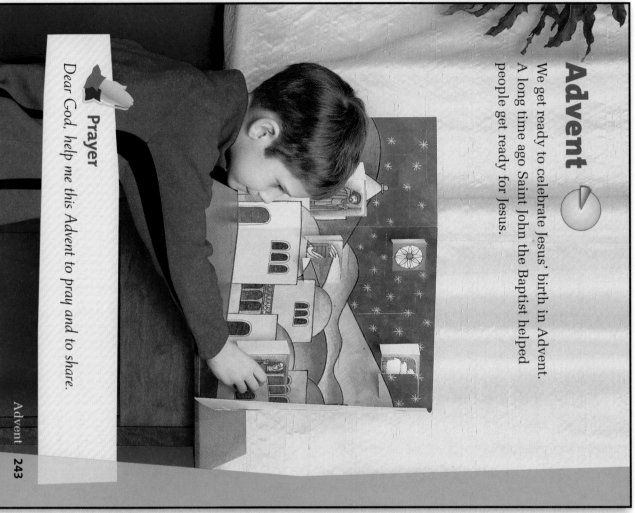

Advent

We get ready to celebrate Jesus' birth in Advent. A long time ago Saint John the Baptist helped people get ready for Jesus.

Prayer

Dear God, help me this Advent to pray and to share.

Advent

Initiate a discussion about getting ready for a special event. Ask: **How do you feel when you're getting ready to celebrate something special?** (excited, nervous) **How can you make it easier to prepare?** (pray to God, ask mom or dad for advice)

Say: **It helps to get advice about how to act and what to do to get ready. John the Baptist gave advice to those who were getting ready to celebrate Jesus' birth.**

Have the children open their books to page 243. Ask them to look at the picture. Briefly explain what an Advent calendar is. Say: **Just as a regular calendar tells us what day it is in a year, an Advent calendar tells us what day it is in a year. An Advent calendar tells us what day it is in Advent. It has a window for each day. Behind each window is a prayer or good deed for the day. Each day we open a window to see what we can do to get ready for Jesus' birth.** Ask the children to describe what they see in the picture. (child opening a window on an Advent calendar) Read the top paragraph while the children follow along silently. Ask: **What is Advent?** (the time when we get ready to celebrate Jesus' birth) **What did John the Baptist help the people to do?** (get ready for Jesus)

Prayer

Say: **Today we are talking about what we can do to get ready to welcome Jesus. Please close your eyes, fold your hands, and play along silently with me. Then quietly talk to God in your hearts.**

Pray the prayer aloud. Pause, giving the children time to talk to God. End the quiet time by asking the children to open their eyes and praying **Amen.**

Explore

Preparing for Jesus' Birth

Read the first two paragraphs aloud as the children follow along. Then ask: *For what do we prepare in Advent?* (Jesus' birth)

Draw attention to the illustration. Have the children describe what they see. Ask: *What is the family doing to prepare for Jesus?* (preparing a manger)

Waiting for Jesus

Read the title aloud. Ask: *What do we call the time when we get ready for Jesus?* (Advent) Say: *We are going to read the story from the Bible about John the Baptist telling the people how to get ready for Jesus.*

Point to the Bible at the prayer center and tell the children that it is opened to read to them. Call to their attention the fact that the Bible is on a purple cloth and that purple is the color of Advent. Ask them to listen for the answers to the question, "What did John the Baptist tell the people to do to get ready for Jesus?"

✝ Read the passage while the children follow along silently in their books. Ask: *What did John the Baptist tell the people to do to get ready for Jesus?* (share and help one another, be honest, don't steal) Give the children time to respond.

Write *Advent is a time of* _____ on the board. Tell the children that you are thinking of a certain word to complete the sentence. Say that you will give them clues until they guess the word. Say: *It's a word that tells something we are doing during Advent. It's something we find hard to do. It's in the title of this section.* Call on volunteers to guess. Write *waiting* to complete the sentence. Then say: *There are lots of other "ing" words that complete our sentence too. Let's make a list of them.* Encourage the

children to provide words. List them on the board as they are offered. (loving, caring, sharing, giving, planning, praying, wanting, hoping, longing)

Have the children copy the sentence beginning, *Advent is a time of* _____ on drawing paper and complete it with one of the words from the list. Then have them illustrate their sentences. As they work, walk around the room and assist anyone who needs help. Ask volunteers to stand and tell the words they chose and show how they chose to illustrate them.

OPTION

BLM 66: TIME OF PREPARATION

Blackline Master 66 involves the children in coloring a tree and writing sentences about how they can prepare for Jesus' birth.

Preparing for Jesus' Birth

Sometimes it is hard to wait. When we have a birthday party, we get ready. Then we wait and wait. We are excited. We celebrate when our birthday guests arrive.

During Advent we get ready to celebrate the birth of Jesus. Advent is our time of waiting.

Waiting for Jesus

People asked John the Baptist how to get ready for Jesus. John told the people to share and to help one another. He told them to be honest. He told them not to steal from one another.

adapted from Luke 3:10-14

The Advent Wreath

Read the title aloud. Ask the children if they have seen the Advent wreath at church or if their family has one at home. Encourage them to tell what they know about the Advent wreath.

Read the first paragraph aloud as the group follows along. Ask: **What is an Advent wreath?** (four candles in a circle of greens) **Why does the Advent wreath have four candles?** (There are four weeks in Advent.) **What do we do during the four weeks of Advent?** (pray and do good deeds) Ask: **What is the name of the man who helped people get ready for Jesus?** (John the Baptist)

Welcoming Jesus

Read the directions aloud. Say: **Jesus' birthday is a special event in our lives. We often decorate our homes to prepare for special events. Ask: How can we decorate our homes to prepare for Jesus?** (wreath, stable/manger without Jesus, Advent calendar, tree without ornaments)

Give the children time to draw their Advent picture, which they can use to decorate their homes. Ask volunteers to share what they

Explain to the children that we continue to prepare for Jesus just as the people John the Baptist spoke to long ago did.

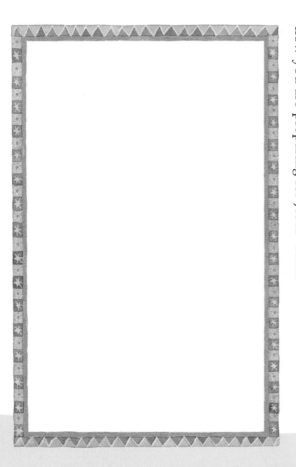

The Advent Wreath

The Advent wreath has four candles. There is one candle for each of the four weeks of Advent. During these four weeks we prepare to celebrate Jesus' birth. We pray and do good deeds for others. This is what John the Baptist told the people to do.

Welcoming Jesus

Draw a picture to put in your home that shows how you are preparing for Jesus' birth.

drew and explain their choices. Invite a round of applause for the group's work.

OPTION

BLM: THE LITURGICAL CALENDAR

This Blackline Master is a liturgical calendar for the children to color. Directions for its use are found on page 241 under the section entitled Using the Liturgical Calendar BLM.

OPTION

ADVENT WREATH

Say: **In a living Advent wreath people stand in a circle to form the wreath. A circle has no beginning and no end, just like God. Sometimes the people in the circle hold decorative leafy greens, which are a sign of life.**

Invite the children to join you in making a living Advent wreath. Have them form a large circle. Use greens or a long artificial rope of greens for the children to hold. Choose four children to hold lit flashlights, three with the light covered in purple cellophane and one with pink cellophane, and stand them in the middle of the circle. The color purple represents waiting; during the third week of Advent, the color pink symbolizes that our waiting is coming to an end. If possible, dim but don't totally darken the room.

Say: **Bow your heads as we pray an Advent prayer.** Pray this prayer: **Jesus, come and live in our hearts. We are waiting to meet you. Light our lives and bless us each day.** Lead the children in praying **Amen.** Say: **Just as our lights brightened our circle, so you can light the world with your good deeds.** Invite the children to share a way they will try to light the world this week using the words **I will light the world when I _____.**

Reflect

Prayer Service

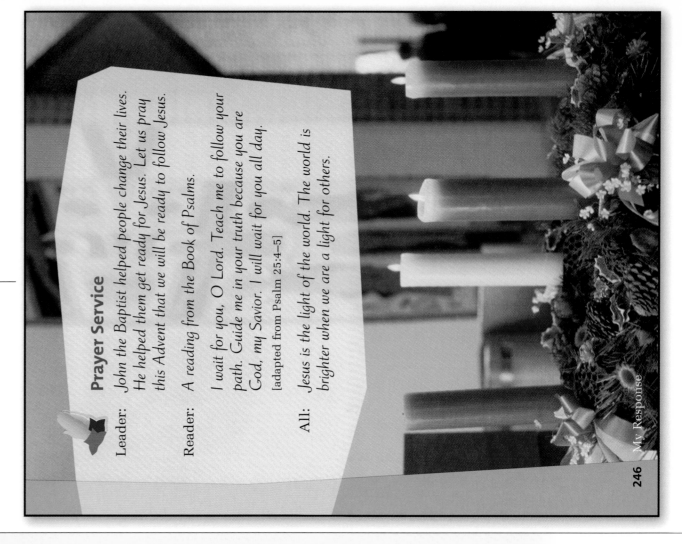

🎵💿 To prepare for the Prayer Service, teach the children the song "This Little Light of Mine" (CD 2, Track 21). Have the children turn to the Songs of Our Faith section in the back of their books and listen to the song on the CD.

Play the first verse once as the children listen. Play the verse a second time and have the children sing along. Follow the same pattern with verses two and three. Then play the entire song through as the children sing along.

Now draw attention to the picture on page 206. Ask the children: *What do you see?* (Advent wreath) *What does each of the candles represent?* (one week of Advent) Say: *Each time an Advent candle is lit, it reminds us that the time to celebrate Jesus' birth is growing near.*

Invite the children to join you at the prayer center with their books opened to "This Little Light of Mine." Say: *As we come to the prayer center, let us sing the song.* Continue: *In this song, tell Jesus how you are going to get ready to celebrate his birth.* Play the song and have the children sing.

✝ Ask the children to turn to the Prayer Service on page 246. Read the adaptation from Psalm 25 with expression, pausing after each sentence. Conclude by reading the final paragraph. Before the children return to their seats, ask them to spend some quiet time talking to God in their hearts about how they can be a light for others. Close by leading them in the Sign of the Cross.

Respond

Divide the class into groups of three or four. Ask the children to write answers to the question you are going to write on the board. They may look at pages 243 through 245 for help. On the board write: *How can we prepare our hearts for Jesus during Advent?* (prepare an Advent calendar, Advent wreath, or empty manger; do good deeds) Give the children time to work quietly in their groups. When all of the groups have finished, ask each group for one answer. Write the answers on the board.

After every group has given an answer say: *Look at all the ways we can get ready for Jesus. Which way will you choose? Say it silently in your heart.*

At dismissal, as each child leaves, say: _____ , *remember to let your light shine.*

Prayer Service

Leader: *John the Baptist helped people change their lives. He helped them get ready for Jesus. Let us pray this Advent that we will be ready to follow Jesus.*

Reader: *A reading from the Book of Psalms.*

I wait for you, O Lord. Teach me to follow your path. Guide me in your truth because you are God, my Savior. I will wait for you all day.

[adapted from Psalm 25:4–5]

All: *Jesus is the light of the world. The world is brighter when we are a light for others.*

Christmas and Epiphany

Theme
During the Christmas season we celebrate Jesus' birth.

Outcomes
At the end of the session, the children should be able to
- understand why the wise men traveled far to see Jesus.
- identify Jesus as God's gift to us.
- appreciate the value of being a gift to others.

Required Materials
Bible, paper, pens, pencils, crayons, markers

Optional Materials
Blackline Master 67 (page 248); yellow construction paper stars (page 250); CD 2, Reflective music (page 250); and The Liturgical Calendar (page 249)

Before This Session
Bookmark the Bible to Matthew 2:1–12. Place the Bible on a white or gold (yellow) cloth.

For the prayer service, cut stars out of yellow construction paper and place the stars at the prayer center. Write a child's name on each star. Select and prepare a child to read at the prayer service.

Check the options for the current session and the materials lists above to prepare for the options you choose.

Christmas and Epiphany

Three wise men traveled far to find Jesus. They wanted to honor him.

Prayer

Jesus, my Savior, help me to be a gift to others as you are to me.

Christmas and Epiphany

Have the children close their eyes and prepare to take an imaginary trip. Ask them to picture someone special to them who lives far away.

Say: *Imagine that you learned you are going to see the special person you are thinking of.* Ask: *How will you get there? Who will go with you? How long will the trip take? Will you take a gift?* Allow the children time to reflect. Have them open their eyes; then ask for volunteers to answer the questions.

Say: *Turn to page 247.* Read the title. Say: *We're going to read about a trip that was made to visit a very special person. Three men made this trip. Do you know who they were and which special person they were going to see?*

Read the top paragraph. Ask: *Who were the visitors?* (the three wise men) *Who was the special person being visited?* (Jesus) *Why did they want to visit Jesus?* (to honor him) Draw attention to the picture. Have the children describe what they see. (the three wise men traveling and following a star)

Prayer

Say: *The three wise men traveled a great distance to see Jesus.* Say: *Jesus is special because he is God's gift to us. Let's ask Jesus to help us be a gift to others. Please fold your hands, close your eyes, and pray along silently in your heart as I pray the prayer aloud. Then be with Jesus for a few moments. Think about how special he is.*

After praying the prayer, silently count to 10 to give the children time to be with Jesus. Say: *Let us close our prayer by praying Amen together.*

Explore

The Three Wise Men

Read the title aloud. Point out the attribution to Matthew below the third paragraph and explain that you are going to read a story from the Bible. Say: *Please follow along in your books while I read the story. Listen carefully for the three gifts the wise men brought to Jesus.* Point to the Bible at the prayer center. Call the white or gold (yellow) cloth to the children's attention and explain that these are the colors for Christmas. Tell them that white or gold is used for times of joy in the Church. Then tell the children that the Bible is opened to the story they are about to hear.

Read the first paragraph. Ask: *For what were the three wise men looking?* (the new king) *What did they want to do when they found him?* (worship him) *How did they find him?* (by following the star)

Read the second and third paragraphs. Ask: *To what city did the star lead the wise men?* (Bethlehem) *Whom did they see when they got there?* (Jesus, Mary, and Joseph) Then ask: *What were the three gifts the wise men brought to Jesus?* (gold, frankincense, and myrrh) Say: *Each of these gifts was very precious, the kind of gift that would only be given to a very special person, like a king.*

Say: *We remember Jesus' birth on a special day called Christmas. We remember the visit of the three wise men on another special day called Epiphany.* Although the children learned the word *Christmas* in grade one, *Epiphany* is a new word for them. Say the word and have them repeat it after you. Say: *Whenever you hear these words, remember what you have learned about the birth of Jesus and the visit of the three wise men.*

Say: *The wise men came from different places. Each one must have been very anxious to share the news of his trip when he returned home. Pretend you are one of the wise men. Ask: What would you tell your family and others about your trip?* Encourage the children to share their ideas.

Some additional questions might help: *How would you describe what led you to Jesus? How would you describe Jesus? Mary? Joseph?* Encourage a variety of responses to these questions.

The Wise Men's Gifts

Read the title and paragraph aloud. Ask: *What gifts did the wise men give to Jesus?* (gold, frankincense, and myrrh) *Why did they give Jesus these gifts?* (They knew he was special.) *How can we be like the wise men?* (by making Jesus special in our lives)

OPTION

BLM 67: SOMEONE SPECIAL

Blackline Master 67 requires children to create a Christmas card to give to someone special.

The Three Wise Men

The wise men were looking for the new king. They wanted to worship him. They saw his star.

The star led the wise men to Bethlehem. There they saw Jesus with Mary and Joseph. They gave Jesus gifts of gold, frankincense, and myrrh.

The wise men then returned home.

adapted from Matthew 2:1-12

The Wise Men's Gifts

Gold, frankincense, and myrrh were very special gifts. The wise men gave these gifts to Jesus because they knew he was special. We can be like the wise men by making Jesus special in our lives too.

248   God's Invitation

Jesus, Our Gift

Read the title aloud for the group. Ask the children how Jesus is a gift to us. Initiate a brief discussion; then present any answers that have not been given. (Jesus shows us how to love one another, which makes us truly happy. This is a far greater gift than material objects such as toys or games.)

Read the first paragraph aloud. Ask the children: *Who gave us the gift of Jesus?* (God) *What does Jesus teach us?* (how to be a gift for others) *How can we do this?* (by bringing Jesus' love into the world)

Then read the second paragraph. Ask the group: *What are some other ways we can be gifts to others?* (respect those who are not popular or rich, be friends with children in need of friends, care for a person who is ill)

Give a Special Gift

Read the activity's title and directions aloud. Say: *Think about how you can be like the three wise men and give a gift to someone you would like to honor. Remember, this should be a gift of yourself, not something you have to buy.* Lead the group in brainstorming what giving a gift of yourself means.

Have the children look at the gift tag in the book. Ask: *Whose name will you put after the word From?* (their name) *Whose name goes after the word To?* (person to whom they will give the gift) Say: *On the lines describe the gift you will give.*

Give the children time to complete the activity. Then invite volunteers to tell the group how giving their gifts will help them to be like Jesus.

BLM: THE LITURGICAL CALENDAR

This Blackline Master is a liturgical calendar for the children to color. Directions for its use are found on page 241 under the section titled Using the Liturgical Calendar BLM.

Jesus, Our Gift

Jesus is God's gift to us. He teaches us how to be gifts to others. We can do this by bringing Jesus' love into the world.

We can respect those who are not popular or rich. We can be friends to children who do not have many friends. We can care for someone who is ill. When we do these things, we are being gifts to others.

Give a Special Gift

Fill out the gift tag. Then on the lines below tell about a gift of yourself that you will give someone this Christmas.

To:

From:

Prayer Service

Say: *Now let's get ready for our Christmas Prayer Service.* Direct the children's attention to the prayer center. Say: *The Bible is opened to the story I will read to you during our Prayer Service.*

Remind the children that white or gold is the color used by the Church for times of joy, and Christmas is a time of joy. Say: *Notice the yellow stars scattered on the table around the Bible. These stars are reminders you will receive as you leave today to help you remember what you have learned.*

Direct the children's attention to the two places where it says *All* on page 250. Tell them that they will be reading those lines. Also tell them that one member of the group will do the reading from the Gospel of Matthew.

 Begin to softly play the reflective music at the end of CD 2. Continue playing it throughout the service. Say: *Please come to the prayer center with your books opened to the Prayer Service.* After the children have gathered, begin by reading the first Leader part.

Have the Reader say: *A reading from the Gospel of Matthew.* Then have the Reader proclaim the reading. Next, have the Reader say: *The gospel of the Lord.* Have the group respond: *Praise to you, Lord Jesus Christ.* Then read the next Leader part. Have the group respond: *Come, let us adore him.*

Say: *The wise men traveled a great distance to adore Jesus. We are also called to honor Jesus.* Have the children silently tell Jesus how much they adore him. Pause for 10 seconds; then lead the group in praying *Amen* before directing them back to their seats.

Say: *Today we've talked about sharing. Now think about how you can share with others the joy of Jesus' coming.* Tell the children they can look at pages 247 through 249 for ideas.

Have the children draw a picture or write a sentence of what they were thinking. When they have finished, ask them to share their work with the group.

When the discussion is finished, say: *Try to do these things to share your joy with others.*

As the children leave, give each of them the paper star with his or her name on it. As you do, say: _____, *make Jesus special in your life this week.*

Prayer Service

Leader: God gave us the greatest Christmas gift, his Son. Let us rejoice and adore Jesus, our Savior.

Reader: A reading from the Gospel of Matthew.

Bethlehem is a small town, but it is very important. A ruler will come from this town.
[adapted from Matthew 2:6]

The gospel of the Lord.

All: Praise to you, Lord Jesus Christ.

Leader: Jesus, God's Son, is born for us.

All: Come, let us adore him.

250   My Response

Lent

Theme

The season of Lent is a time of preparation for the feast of Easter.

Outcomes

At the end of the session, the children should be able to

- understand the importance of depending on Jesus.
- ask for God's help in time of need.
- recognize Lent as a time to make positive changes to live more like Jesus.

Required Materials

Bible, paper, pens, pencils, crayons, markers; CD 2, Track 7: Our Father (1:02) (page 254)

Optional Materials

9-inch-square paper (page 252); Blackline Master 68 (page 253); and The Liturgical Calendar (page 253)

Before This Session

Think of a story to share with the children to share stories about special adults in their lives.

Select and prepare children for Depending on Jesus (page 252) and the Prayer Service (page 254).

Bookmark the Bible to Matthew 18:1–4 and leave it opened at the prayer center on a purple cloth.

Check the options for the current session and the materials lists above to prepare for the options you choose.

Lent

Jesus loves little children.
He tells his disciples to
be like children.

Prayer

Jesus, my friend, teach me this Lent how to live as a child of God. I want to love God as you do.

Lent   **251**

Lent

Begin the session by saying: *Think of an adult in your life who has made you feel special.* Start with a story of your own. Invite the children to share stories about special adults in their lives.

Say: *Today we will read about a special friend of ours who loves children very much.*

Say: *Turn to page 251 in your books.* Draw the children's attention to the illustration and ask: *Who is our special friend?* (Jesus)

Say: *What is Jesus doing in this picture?* (spending time with children) *What do you think Jesus is showing his friends, the disciples?*

Say: *Let's read to find the answer.*

Read the paragraph aloud as the children follow along. Ask: *What is Jesus teaching his friends, the disciples?* (to be like children)

Prayer

Say: *Today we are talking about how Jesus loves children. Let's get ready to talk to Jesus in your hearts.* Say: *Please fold your hands, close your eyes, and follow along in silence as I pray our prayer aloud.* After praying the prayer, say: *Quietly thank Jesus in your hearts for loving children so much.*

Give the children a few moments to be with Jesus. Close the quiet time by asking the children to open their eyes and pray **Amen.**

Lent   **251**

Explore

Depending on Jesus

Read the title aloud. Ask: *What does it mean to depend on someone?* (you trust this person with something important to you) *On whom do we depend in our lives?* (parents, priest, friends, teacher, bus driver)

Point to the Bible at the prayer center. Tell the children that today's story comes from the Bible. Also direct their attention to the purple cloth under the Bible. Explain that purple is the Church's color for Lent.

Read the first paragraph aloud. Ask: *What did the disciples ask Jesus?* (Who is the greatest in the kingdom of heaven?) *Whom did Jesus invite to join them?* (a child)

Read the second paragraph, and ask: *Whom did Jesus say the disciples should be like?* (the child) *What would be their reward for doing what Jesus asked?* (living with God in heaven)

Have three of the children you selected read in unison the disciples' question in paragraph one. Let the fourth child you selected read the words of Jesus. After a short rehearsal, do Depending on Jesus as a short play for the group.

We Depend on God

Read the title and paragraph aloud to the group. Then draw attention to the picture. Ask: *On whom is this girl depending?* (her parents) *If she wasn't holding onto their hands, what could happen?* (She could fall and get hurt.) *Are her parents happy to help?* (yes) *Why?* (They want to protect her.) *On whom do we all depend?* (God, parents, teachers, Church leaders) *Do you think God, our parents, and others are happy to help us?* (yes) *Why?* (They love us. They want us to be safe.)

GOD, BE WITH ME

Ask the children: *When do you need God to be with you?* Have the children write to God and draw pictures showing him times when they especially want him to be with them.

Give each child a 9-inch-square piece of paper. Have the children fold each corner into the center so the points meet and the shape is a smaller square. Write *God, be with me when* on the board. Ask the children to lift the four flaps and copy the words on the inside square. On each flap have them draw a picture of an occasion when they especially want God to be with them. When they have finished, call on volunteers to show and explain their work to the group.

Depending on Jesus

The disciples asked Jesus, "Who is the greatest in the kingdom of heaven?" Jesus called a child to come join them.

He said, "You must become like this child. Then you will live with God in heaven."

adapted from Matthew 18:1-4

We Depend on God

Parents reach out to help their children. Children depend on their parents. We are all God's children. God reaches out to us. We need his help.

Making Changes

Read the title aloud. Say: *We read about Jesus' telling his disciples they must change and be humble like children. Please follow along in your books as I read how Jesus wants us to change.* Read the first paragraph, pausing for a couple of seconds after each question to give the children time to think. Go back and repeat each question, accepting the children's responses for each. Say: *These are questions we can think about during Lent.*

Read the second paragraph.

Then say: *Ashes remind us that Lent is a time to make changes in* our lives so that we can better follow Jesus.

Say: Jesus wanted his disciples to depend on God because they needed his help. During Lent we try to change our bad habits to good ones. Bad and good are opposites. Let's think of some habits that we might want to change to the opposite during Lent. I'll tell you a not-so-good habit and you tell me its opposite: *stingy* (generous); *grumpy* (happy); *mean* (nice); *disobedient* (obedient); *unfriendly* (friendly); *selfish* (unselfish); *impatient* (patient); *uncaring* (caring, kind, loving).

Making Changes

Jesus asked his disciples to change. Lent is a time for change. We ask ourselves questions: How can I help others? How can I stay close to God? How can I be more like Jesus?

We receive ashes on our forehead on Ash Wednesday. This is when we tell God how we will change our lives. These ashes remind us that we should follow Jesus.

Changing for the Better

What could you do to make the bad situations good? Draw a line to connect each box on the top row with its matching box on the bottom row.

Lent **253**

Changing for the Better

Read the activity's title and directions to the group. Pass out pencils if the children don't already have them. Ask them to describe each of the situations on the top row. Then give them adequate time to complete the activity. When most of the children are done, ask them to put down their pencils and have volunteers describe the action in the bottom row that changed the situation in the top row. Say: *Remember, Lent is a time when we can make changes in our lives and follow Jesus.*

OPTION

BLM: THE LITURGICAL CALENDAR

This Blackline Master is a liturgical calendar for the children to color. Directions for its use are found on page 241 under the section entitled Using the Liturgical Calendar BLM.

OPTION

BLM 68: CHANGING TO BE LIKE JESUS

On Blackline Master 68 children create a card that is a personal reminder to change for the better during Lent.

FYI

ASH WEDNESDAY

On Ash Wednesday, either at Mass or at a special celebration, people of all ages receive ashes in the form of a cross on their foreheads. As the persons who are distributing the ashes make the Sign of the Cross, they say: *Turn away from sin and be faithful to the gospel* (adapted from Mark 1:15) or *Remember, man, you are dust and to dust you will return* (adapted from Genesis 3:19). The ashes are made of the palm remaining from the previous year's Palm Sunday of the Lord's Passion.

Lent **253**

Prayer Service

Say: *Now is the time for our Lenten Prayer Service. Let's take a few moments to prepare.* Direct the children's attention to the prayer center, where the Bible is opened to Psalm 97. Show them the Prayer Service on page 254 and direct them to turn to the Lord's Prayer on page 277. Tell them that they will be praying this prayer at the end of the Prayer Service and that they may look at the words if they need to.

[music icon] You may choose to have the children sing "Our Father." If so, set CD 2, Track 7 so it is ready when needed. Ask the children to come to the prayer center quietly with their books.

Begin the Prayer Service by praying the Sign of the Cross with the children. Continue the Prayer Service, reading the Leader part slowly and reverently.

[bible icon] Have the Reader say: *A reading from the Book of Psalms.* Have the child proclaim the reading.

Then say: *The Lord's Prayer is very special because Jesus told us to use this prayer when talking with God our Father.* Then read the final Leader part. Lead the children in praying the Lord's Prayer by singing it or saying it. When finished, ask the children to return to their seats quietly.

FYI

TODAY'S READING

Today's reading is adapted from Psalm 97:10–11. In this psalm the people of Israel rejoice that God loves, protects, and rewards those who are faithful.

254   Lent

Pass out pencils and paper if the children do not already have them. Write the following questions on the board and tell the children to write the answers on their papers: *Who did Jesus tell his disciples to be like?* (children) *When do we receive ashes on our foreheads?* (Ash Wednesday) *Of what do the ashes remind us?* (that we are to follow Jesus, that Lent is a time to make changes)

Give the children time to answer the questions. Explain that they can look back at pages 251 through 253 for help.

After the children have finished, ask for volunteers to share their answers. Then say: *Thank you for sharing your answers! We should also make changes for the better in our lives.*

As you dismiss the children, say: *Remember that Jesus loves children very much. This week try to love all of the children you meet. Treat them as you would want to be treated.*

Prayer Service

Leader: Let us begin our prayer with the Sign of the Cross.

Jesus taught us how to pray to God our Father. Let us tell Jesus that we will listen to him and follow him.

Reader: A reading from the Book of Psalms.

God loves those who hate evil. He protects those who are faithful. He rescues them from the wicked. If you are fair and honest, God will be with you.
[adapted from Psalm 97:10–11]

Leader: Let us close by praying the Lord's Prayer together.

254   My Response

Theme

During Holy Week we remember that Jesus suffered and died for our salvation.

Outcomes

At the end of the session, the children should be able to

- appreciate Jesus' great love for everyone.
- value bringing peace into the lives of others.

Required Materials

Bible, paper, pens, pencils, crayons, markers, unwrapped adhesive bandages (page 256); CD 2, Track 19: Jesus' Hands Were Kind Hands (2:07)

Optional Materials

Blackline Master 69, purple construction paper (page 257); purple construction paper, scissors (page 257)

Before This Session

Think about your own story about forgiving to share with the children on page 256.

Open the Bible to Luke 22:47–51 at the prayer center and place a purple cloth under it. Select and prepare a child to do the reading during the Prayer Service.

Check the options for the current session and the materials lists above to prepare for the options you choose.

Holy Week

Jesus was kind and loving to everyone. Jesus prayed for his enemies. How can you be like Jesus during Holy Week?

Prayer

Jesus, my helper, help me forgive those who hurt me. I want to love others as you did.

Holy Week

Invite the children to join you in a game about feelings called Wow! Say: **We experience many different kinds of feelings each day. Some things make us feel good; others do not.**

Explain that in this game you will present situations. The children will give you a Wow! sign (hold both pairs of middle and ring fingers up to form a *W*) if the situation would give them a good, or "Wow," feeling. If the situation would not give them a good feeling, direct them not to give the Wow! sign, but rather to shake their heads no. Offer the following situations and have the children respond.

A friend invites you to a party. Your mom buys you a great gift for your birthday. You forget your homework.

Discuss how the children would treat the other person(s) in each situation. Say: **Today we are going to learn more about Jesus' life. We will find out what Jesus did when he faced difficult situations.**

Say: **Turn to page 255 in your books.** Read the title and paragraph aloud. Then have the children describe what they see in the picture. (Jesus praying by himself in a garden)

Prayer

Say: *Jesus' life is our example of how to live. Let us ask him to help us be like him and show love for our friends and enemies alike. Please close your eyes and fold your hands. Pray along with me in the quiet of your hearts as I pray this prayer of petition aloud.* After praying the prayer, pause and give the children time to talk with Jesus. End the prayer time by asking the children to open their eyes and pray **Amen** together.

Jesus' Great Love

Read the title aloud. Say: *In the Bible we read about the many times when Jesus showed love to people who did not show love to him. Please follow along in your books while I read one of these stories.*

[Bible icon] Point to the Bible at the prayer center and tell the children that the story you are about to read to them comes from the Bible. Have the children notice the color of cloth you chose to place under the Bible. Remind them that purple is the color of Holy Week, as it is still the season of Lent. Read the two paragraphs aloud while the children follow along. Then draw the children's attention to the art. Have the children describe what they see. (Jesus healing the servant's ear)

Ask: *What were the judge and his servant going to do?* (arrest Jesus) *What did one of Jesus' friends do?* (cut the ear of the servant) *What did Jesus do?* (stopped his friend, healed the servant's ear) *What does this tell you about Jesus?* (He forgives even those who are not his friends.) Say: *Jesus healed the servant's ear. He forgave those who were going to arrest him.*

Have the children come together in a circle or sit on the floor around you. Hold up an unwrapped adhesive bandage and say: *The bandage is a sign of healing for our bodies. Jesus healed the servant's body. He also forgave those who were going to arrest him. Forgiving is a spiritual bandage that we use when others have hurt us.*

Share a forgiving story of your own, and then pass the bandage to those who would like to share a story in which they forgave or were forgiven for something. Advise the children to not tell any stories that are too personal. Have each child pass the bandage to the next volunteer. Let the children know that they are not required to share with the group.

OPTION

SPIRITUAL BANDAGE

Have the children draw an outline of a bandage on drawing paper. Have them draw a heart with the words *I forgive* in the middle gauze part. Have them draw forgiveness pictures on the two adhesive ends. Call on volunteers to share their work with the group. Thank your volunteers.

OPTION

HOLY WEEK PRAYER CHART

Say: *Holy Week is a time to pray for others.* Ask: *What people in our world can we pray for?* Call on volunteers to share their ideas. Write them on the board. (people without jobs, people who don't have a home, people living in places that are at war, people who are sick) Explain: *Just as Jesus prayed for those who hurt him, we can pray for people who need our prayers.*

Jesus' Great Love

Jesus was talking to his friends when a crowd arrived. A judge and his servant were part of the crowd. They came to arrest Jesus.

Jesus' friends rushed to help him. One of them cut the ear of the judge's servant. Jesus told his friend to stop. Jesus touched the servant's ear, and it was healed.

adapted from Luke 22:47-51

256   God's Invitation

The Touch of Love

Read the title aloud. Say: *Jesus healed with a touch.* Let's read *how we can follow Jesus' example.* Read the first paragraph aloud as the group follows along. Say: *Even though Jesus knew he would be arrested, what did he do?* (healed his enemy) *Instead of getting even, what did he do?* (showed love)

Read the next paragraph aloud. Ask: *What should we do if some-one hurts us?* (pray for them, show them kindness, forgive them)

Acts of Love

Read the activity's title aloud. Say: *When we perform acts of love, we are like Jesus. We are peace-makers. Let's think about acts of love we can do on four of the important days of Holy Week to be peacemakers.*

Read the directions to the children. Tell them to begin thinking about their acts of love as you distribute the pencils if the children don't already have them. Give them time to write their answers.

As they work, walk around the room and help them come up with ideas. When they have finished,

The Touch of Love

Jesus knew he would be arrested. Still, he reached out to his enemies with a healing touch. Jesus did not try to get even. He showed love instead.

We are called to be like Jesus. We are not to harm those who do not like us. We can show love by praying for them and by being kind.

Acts of Love

Write acts of love you will do during Holy Week to be like Jesus.

Explore

call on volunteers to share their ideas. Congratulate the children for their fine work.

Refer the children to the liturgical calendar that begins this unit. Direct the children to see that Holy Week is the last week of Lent. During Holy Week we think about how Jesus lived. The last three days of this week have a special name, the Triduum. The Triduum begins with Holy Thursday night and ends with Easter night. It is a hinge between Lent and Easter.

BLM 69: A HEALING TOUCH

Blackline Master 69 asks children to draw pictures of events that happened during Holy Week.

PEACEMAKING HANDS

Explain: *When we make peace with someone, we often shake hands.* Pass out purple construction paper and scissors. Ask each of the children to trace one of their hands on construction paper and to cut out the outline of their hand. On one side of the paper have the children write their names and on the other have them print something they will do to make peace with someone this week. (spend time with a sibling you had a fight with, apologize to mom for not picking up your toys)

When the children finish, ask them to take their Peacemaking Hands home and put them somewhere to remind them to be peace-makers this week.

Reflect

Prayer Service

Say: *Now it's time for our Holy Week Prayer Service.* Point to the prayer center. Show the children that the Bible is opened to the passage from Matthew that is going to be read during the Prayer Service. If you have asked a child to do the reading, make sure this child is prepared. Point to the line that follows *All* and tell the children that this is their response.

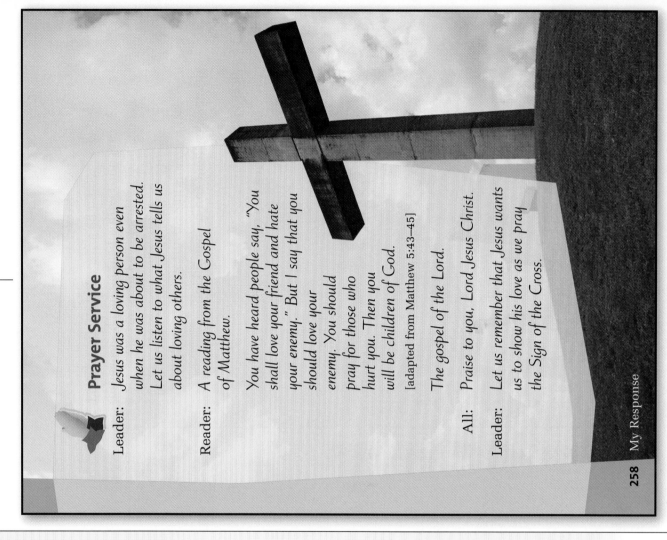

🎵💿 Ask the children to turn to the song "Jesus' Hands Were Kind Hands" (CD 2, Track 19) in the Songs of Our Faith section in the back of their books. If you have not taught the song previously, play the song once as the children listen. Play it a second time and ask them to sing along.

Say: *It is now time to begin our Prayer Service. Please come to the prayer center with your books opened to the song.* Motion for the children to come forward slowly and gather around the prayer center. When they are assembled, begin the prayer service by singing "Jesus' Hands Were Kind Hands" on Track 19 of CD 2. Begin the Prayer Service by reading the Leader part.

✝️ Have the Reader say: *A reading from the Gospel of Matthew.* Then have the child proclaim the reading. Have the Reader then say: *The gospel of the Lord.* Motion to the group to respond: *Praise to you, Lord Jesus Christ.* Then read the final Leader part.

Say: *We have just read about how Jesus wants us to treat those who hurt us. Spend some quiet time with Jesus. Talk to him in your hearts about how you will treat your enemies with love.*

Pause for about 10 seconds; then close by praying the Sign of the Cross and have the children return to their seats.

Respond

Say: *We heard a story today about Jesus healing a man's ear. We can also bring healing into the world, but not in a physical way.* Ask: *What are some ways that you can be a healer?* Invite the children to respond. (say you're sorry, begin a friendly conversation with someone you have recently disagreed with, make up with a brother or sister, admit you were wrong about something)

Write the answers on the board or chart paper. When you are finished, say: *We should try to be healers in what we do and say.*

Before the children are dismissed, say: *Jesus wants us to be peacemakers and to show others acts of love. Before leaving, let us offer one another a sign of peace.* Remind the children that the words for the sign of peace are "Peace be with you." When all have exchanged the sign of peace, dismiss the children peacefully.

Prayer Service

Leader: *Jesus was a loving person even when he was about to be arrested. Let us listen to what Jesus tells us about loving others.*

Reader: *A reading from the Gospel of Matthew.*

You have heard people say, "You shall love your friend and hate your enemy." But I say that you should love your enemy. You should pray for those who hurt you. Then you will be children of God.

[adapted from Matthew 5:43–45]

The gospel of the Lord.

All: *Praise to you, Lord Jesus Christ.*

Leader: *Let us remember that Jesus wants us to show his love as we pray the Sign of the Cross.*

Easter

Theme

During the Easter season we celebrate the Resurrection and Ascension of Jesus Christ.

Outcomes

At the end of the session, the children should be able to

- learn about Jesus' Resurrection.
- identify Easter as a time of joy.
- understand that in serving others they meet Jesus.

Required Materials

Bible, paper, pens, pencils, crayons, markers; CD 2, Track 17: We Come to Your Table (2:12) (page 262)

Optional Materials

Scripture verses on strips of paper, plastic eggs (page 260); Blackline Master 70, craft stems (page 261); and The Liturgical Calendar (page 261)

Before This Session

Think about a joyful event in your life that you can share with the children (page 259).

Open the Bible to Psalm 96 and place a white or gold (yellow) cloth under it at the prayer center.

Check the options for the current session and the materials lists above to prepare for the options you choose.

Easter

Easter is a joyful time. We celebrate that Jesus is risen.

Easter   259

Prayer

Dear Jesus, help me be a person of joy. I want to help others be joyful too.

Easter

Begin this session by saying: *We have many joyful times in our lives.* Tell the children of a special time in your life. Encourage them to share their joyful times.

Say: *Please open your books to page 259.* Have the children look at the picture and describe what they see. Say: *This is a picture of an angel and two women coming towards him.*

Read the top paragraph as the group follows along. Ask: *What is the special time we are learning about?* (Easter) *What feeling do we get during the season of Easter?* (joyful) *Why is Easter so joyful?* (Jesus is risen.) Say: *There is a special word that describes Jesus' rising from the dead. It is Resurrection. Today we're going to learn about Jesus' Resurrection and what it means for us.*

Prayer

Say: *We are talking about joy. Let us pray to Jesus and ask him to help us be joyful and bring joy to others.*

Say: *Please close your eyes, fold your hands, and pray along with me in the quiet of your hearts. Then take a few moments to share with Jesus the joy that is in your hearts.*

Reverently pray the prayer aloud. Pause for a few moments to give the children time to be with Jesus. End by praying **Amen** and asking the children to open their eyes.

Looking for Jesus

Read the title aloud. Direct the children's attention to the picture. Tell them this picture continues the story that began in the picture on the first page. Ask: *What did we see on page 259?* (angel and women) *What do we see here?* (women meeting the angel) Point to the Bible at the prayer center. Tell the children that the story of Jesus' Resurrection comes from the Bible. Direct them to look at the color of the cloth under the Bible. Say: *Whenever we celebrate a joyful season like Easter, the Church uses white or gold. Please listen as I read this story.*

[†] Read Mark 16:1–7. Say: *Let's retell the story we just heard. Let me write two names that are new to us. They will help us tell our story.* Write *Mary Magdalene* on the board. Pronounce it. Say: *Mary Magdalene was one of Jesus' friends.*

Say: *Now, let's retell the story Looking for Jesus.* Ask: *Can you name one of the women who went to Jesus' tomb?* (Mary Magdalene) *Do you know what a tomb is?* (place where a dead person is buried) *What did the women bring to the tomb?* (spices) *What were they going to do with the spices?* (put them on Jesus' body) Tell the children that this was a custom in those days. Spices were used to make the tomb smell good.

Ask: *Whom did they find when they arrived at the tomb?* (an angel) *Who wasn't in the tomb?* (Jesus) *Did the angel speak to the women?* (Jesus) *What did the angel tell the women to do?* (tell Jesus' disciples that he was risen)

Ask if any children would like to retell the story Looking for Jesus. Congratulate the volunteers. Say: *You have just learned a story about Jesus that is very important.* Ask: *Does anyone know what makes this so important?*

(Even though Jesus had died and was buried, he rose from the dead.) Say: *Share this story with your family members. They will be very pleased with you.*

Meeting Jesus in Others

Read the title and first paragraph aloud. Ask: *What did the angel's message mean?* (that when people helped others they would really be helping Jesus) Say: *This is a very important message for all of us.* Read the next paragraph. Invite the group to respond.

OPTION

BIBLE VERSE EGG HUNT

Insert strips of paper with Scripture verses adapted from Mark 16:1–7 inside plastic eggs. Hide these eggs around the room before the session. Have the children hunt for the eggs. After all of the eggs have been found, have the children read to the group the scripture verses inside the eggs. They include the following:
• The women came to the tomb.
• The tomb was empty.
• Jesus is risen.
• Jesus went to Galilee.

Looking for Jesus

Mary Magdalene and other women went to Jesus' tomb. They brought spices to put on his body. When they got there, the tomb was empty. An angel was there. The angel said to them, "Go and tell the disciples that Jesus is risen. He will meet them."

adapted from Mark 16:1–7

Meeting Jesus in Others

The women at the tomb were followers of Jesus. The angel's message meant that the disciples would meet Jesus in the people they would serve.

We meet Jesus in our lives when we help others. Who are the people we can love and serve?

260 God's Invitation

Sunday, the Lord's Day

Read the title and paragraph aloud. Ask the children: **What do we celebrate on Sunday?** (Jesus' Resurrection) **What does Resurrection mean?** (Jesus rose from the dead.) **What special name is given to Sunday?** (the Lord's day) Say: **The Resurrection of Jesus is so special that we remember it on the first day of every week.**

Have the children look at the picture. Ask if they know what it is and what it means. Explain: **The cross is a symbol that reminds us of Jesus' death. The white cloth in the picture, like the white cloth at our prayer center, is the Church color for joy.**

Loving and Serving Others

Read the activity's title and directions aloud. Have the children complete the activity. Walk around the room as the children work and offer assistance as needed. When most of the children are finished, call on volunteers to share what they wrote with the group.

Sunday, the Lord's Day

On this day we remember that Jesus rose from the dead. We celebrate the Resurrection on Sunday, the Lord's day.

Loving and Serving Others

Write ways you love and serve others. These are ways you meet Jesus in your life.

BLM: THE LITURGICAL CALENDAR

This Blackline Master is a liturgical calendar for the children to color. Directions for its use are found on page 241 under the section entitled Using the Liturgical Calendar BLM.

BLM 70: CARING FOR OTHERS

Blackline Master 70 is a craft project that prompts children to care for others during the Easter season.

TRIPLE JOY

Say: *Easter is a time of great joy. To whom did we pray at the beginning of the session to make us persons of joy?* (Jesus) *What are we supposed to do with the joy we have?* (help others be joyful too) Have children make a triple-joy picture.

Give them paper and crayons or markers. Have them position the paper horizontally on their desks. Show them how to fold it into three roughly equal sections. Have them write *Joy* at the top of each section and draw a picture to illustrate three ways they can bring joy into their homes. When they have finished, call on volunteers to hold up and explain their pictures.

Direct the children to return to their seats. Then say: *We have learned that an angel spoke to the women who went to Jesus' tomb. The angel gave the women the good news that Jesus would meet the disciples. This message meant that the disciples would meet Jesus in the people they would serve.*

Say: *Just as the women went to the tomb to serve Jesus, so we are asked to serve others. Think of one way you could serve another person this week. Draw a picture of it.* When the children have finished, ask them to share their work with the group.

As the children prepare to leave, say: *This week let us try to spread the joy of Easter to as many people as we can.*

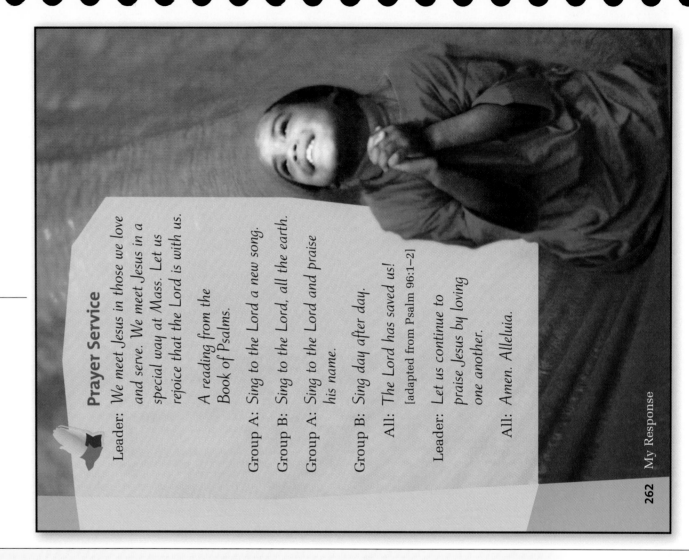

Prayer Service

Leader: *We meet Jesus in those we love and serve. We meet Jesus in a special way at Mass. Let us rejoice that the Lord is with us.*

A reading from the Book of Psalms.

Group A: *Sing to the Lord a new song.*

Group B: *Sing to the Lord, all the earth.*

Group A: *Sing to the Lord and praise his name.*

Group B: *Sing day after day.*

All: *The Lord has saved us!*
[adapted from Psalm 96:1–2]

Leader: *Let us continue to praise Jesus by loving one another.*

All: *Amen. Alleluia.*

262 My Response

Prayer Service

Say: *Now let's get ready for our Prayer Service. Today we will have a special Easter Prayer Service. Please get comfortable as we prepare to meet God in our hearts.*

Pause for five seconds, then ask the children to turn to the song, "We Come to Your Table" (CD 2, Track 17) in the Songs of Our Faith section in the back of their books. If you have not taught the song previously, play it once as the children listen. Play it a second time and ask the children to sing with you.

Make sure the Bible is opened to Psalm 96. Divide the children into Group A and Group B. Have the children look at the Prayer Service. Point out the lines each group will read. Tell them they will read the lines that begin with All as a group. Review parts with the A and B groups.

Invite Group A to come forward and stand together. Then invite Group B to do the same. Remind the children to bring their books with them, opened to "We Come to Your Table."

Once the children have assembled, begin the Prayer Service by singing "We Come to Your Table." Your joyful tone of voice will encourage them to read their parts joyfully.

Read the first paragraph, then motion for Groups A and B to give their responses. Motion for everybody to respond with the All portion.

Close by reading the last sentence by the *Leader* and motioning for all to respond *Amen. Alleluia.*

Pentecost

Theme

At Pentecost we celebrate the coming of the Holy Spirit to bring life to the Church.

Outcomes

At the end of the session, the children should be able to

- celebrate the coming of the Holy Spirit on Pentecost.
- explain why the Holy Spirit came to the disciples.
- realize that the Holy Spirit will help them to help others.

Required Materials

Bible, paper, pens, pencils, crayons, markers; CD 2, Track 9: Jesus in the Morning (Spirit verses) (1:37) (page 266)

Optional Materials

Yellow construction paper, scissors (page 264); Blackline Master 71, hole punch, staples, stiff paper, string (page 265); red construction paper (page 265); construction paper, magazines or newspapers, scissors, glue (page 265)

Before This Session

Bookmark the Bible at the prayer center to Acts of the Apostles 3:1–8 and Galatians 6:2,9. Place the Bible on a red cloth and leave it opened to the passage from Acts of the Apostles.

Pentecost

The coming of the Holy Spirit is celebrated on Pentecost. The Holy Spirit came to Peter and the other disciples. They told everyone about Jesus.

Prayer

Jesus, teach me how to help others the way the disciples did.

Engage

Select and prepare a child to do the reading during the Prayer Service.

Pentecost

Greet the children and say: *I was expecting all of you to be here. But sometimes people surprise us with a visit.* Ask: *Have you ever had a surprise visitor?* Encourage the children to share. Say: *There are many reasons why people visit one another. Today we learn about when the Holy Spirit came to Jesus' friends.*

Say: *Please open your books to page 263.* Direct the children to the picture and ask them to describe what they see. (flames over peoples' heads) Say: *This picture shows Peter and other disciples receiving the Holy Spirit.*

Read the title. Have the children repeat *Pentecost* after you. Read the first paragraph. Ask: *What do we call the day we celebrate the coming of the Holy Spirit?* (Pentecost) *To whom did the Holy Spirit come?* (the disciples) *What did the disciples do after the Holy Spirit came to them?* (told everybody about Jesus) Say: *God's Holy Spirit gave the disciples courage.*

Prayer

Say: *Let's ask Jesus to help us be like the disciples. Please fold your hands, close your eyes, and pray along silently.*

Say: *Pray along with me. Then take a few moments to talk quietly with Jesus.*

After praying, pause to give children time to be with Jesus. Close with **Amen** and ask children to open their eyes.

Explore

Peter Helps

Read the title. Say: *This is a Bible story of how, after the Holy Spirit came to him, Peter helped a man who was crippled.* Point to the Bible at the prayer center and tell the children it is opened to this story. Direct the children's attention to the color of the cloth under the Bible. Tell them that red is the color the Church uses for Pentecost.

✝ Read the first paragraph of the story. Ask: *What did Peter want to do after Pentecost?* (tell people about Jesus)

Then read the second paragraph. Ask: *Where did Peter go to pray?* (the Temple) *Whom did he meet?* (a poor man who couldn't walk) *What did Peter say when the man begged him for money?* (told the man he had no money to give him) *What did Peter do for the man instead?* (told him to get up and walk)

Read the third paragraph while the children follow along. Ask: *How did the man feel?* (excited, happy, grateful) *How do you know?* (He leaped up, walked into the Temple, and praised God.)

Read the question at the bottom of the page. Encourage the children to discuss the answer. Accept all reasonable responses. Explain: *Peter called on Jesus to heal the man. He told the man to walk "in the name of Jesus Christ."*

A GIFT MORE PRECIOUS THAN GOLD

Distribute yellow construction paper. Have the children cut a circle out of the piece of yellow construction paper. The circle is a reminder of a piece of gold. On the circle, have them draw a picture of themselves giving—as Peter did—a gift that is more precious than gold. (helping someone, being kind, spreading Jesus' love)

SPIRIT SLOGAN

Have the children create a group slogan that shows their enthusiasm for the Holy Spirit's living within them. Provide them with a couple of examples. (Yea for God! The Spirit Is With Us! I'm Filled With the Spirit! Go, God!) Call on volunteers to share their ideas. Write them on the board. After there are several suggested slogans, have the children take a vote on their favorite one.

Peter Helps

With the other disciples Peter received the Holy Spirit on Pentecost. He wanted to tell people about Jesus.

Peter was going to the Temple to pray. He saw a poor man who could not walk. The man begged for money. Peter said, "I do not have silver or gold. What I do have, I will give you. In the name of Jesus Christ, get up and walk."

The man leaped up and walked around. He was very excited. He went into the Temple and praised God.

adapted from Acts of the Apostles 3:1-8

How did Peter's actions change the man's life?

What Can You Do?

Read the activity's title. Say: **We have talked about what Peter was able to do with the help of the Holy Spirit. Now we're going to talk about what we can do with the Holy Spirit's help.** Read the directions for the group. Ask if anyone has questions.

Give the children time to complete the activity. Walk around the room and offer assistance if needed.

When the group has finished, read each situation one by one. Call on volunteers to read how they would help the persons in need. Encourage discussion about what each person needs and about what the children would do if they were in these situations. When you have talked about all the scenarios, ask: **What one thing do all the people seem to need?** (the help of other people) **With the help of the Holy Spirit, are we all able to help others?** (yes) Say: **We should remember that we don't always have to have money to help another person.**

What Can You Do?

Like Peter, you have the help of the Holy Spirit. The Spirit leads you to pray and to care for others. Below each situation write what you could do to help the person in need.

1. Justin was absent from school. He needs help with his homework to catch up to the rest of his class.

2. Little Sara is crying. No one will help her learn how to ride her new bike.

3. Mona is feeling sad because the children at her new school do not include her.

4. Jimmy wants to be on the soccer team, but he does not know how to play.

OPTION

BLM 71: THE HOLY SPIRIT SOARS

Blackline Master 71 is a Holy Spirit kite for children to create.

OPTION

I GIVE FROM THE HEART

Tell the children: *Think about a situation in your lives in which you can care for someone who is hurting. Perhaps your brother or sister is upset because he or she doesn't get to spend enough time with you. Or maybe your grandmother isn't feeling well.*

Pass out red construction paper. Have the children cut small paper hearts out of the construction paper. Have them write I at the top of the left arc of the heart and give at the top of the right arc. Ask them to write a sentence or draw on the heart a picture of what they will give to another person. Remind them that it's something you don't buy with money. Encourage the children to put their hearts in a special place at home so they will remember to give from their hearts.

OPTION

PEOPLE HELPING PEOPLE COLLAGE

Say: *When the Holy Spirit came to the disciples, he helped them to tell others about Jesus' love for them. The Holy Spirit lives in us so we can help others.* Distribute construction paper, magazines or newspapers, scissors, glue sticks, and crayons or markers. Have the children look for pictures of people helping others or words that describe how to help others. Ask them to make a collage of the pictures they find. In the middle of their papers have them print People Helping People. When they have finished creating their collages, call on volunteers to share their work with the group.

Reflect

Prayer Service

Say: *It is time to prepare for our Pentecost Prayer Service. Please take a few moments to become still and prepare to pray.* Pause for a few moments.

Say: *We know that, like the disciples, we can spread Jesus' love with the help of the Holy Spirit. Let us pray that the Holy Spirit will help us to show love to others.* Have the children look at the Prayer Service. Draw attention to the parts that say All. Remind the children that they will say those parts. Make sure the child you selected to be the reader is prepared.

♪ ◎ Ask the children to turn to the Songs of Our Faith section in the back of their books and review the words to the song "Jesus in the Morning (Spirit verses)" on CD 2, Track 9.

When finished, invite the children to come to the prayer center with their books opened to the song. Begin the Prayer Service by singing the song. Then pray the Leader part.

✝ The Reader says: *A reading from the letter to the Galatians* and proclaims the reading. After the Reader says *The Word of the Lord,* the group responds *Thanks be to God.* Then read the final sentence in the Leader part.

Ask the children to pray with you the Prayer to the Holy Spirit, which they learned earlier in the year. If they have not memorized the prayer, have them turn to the Prayers to Take to Heart section in the backs of their books for the words. Close the service by inviting the children to offer a sign of peace to one another. After this, ask the children to return quietly to their seats.

Respond

Wait for the children to return to their seats. Then direct their attention to the picture on the page. To help them understand it, refer the children to the second sentence in the letter to the Galatians. Ask a volunteer to read it. Then have all the children repeat, "Do not grow tired of doing good for others."

Ask: *What is the girl imagining?* (all the ways she can do good for others) Say: *Think of one way you can do good.* Tell the children to draw a picture or write a description of how they are going to help another person. Encourage them to share answers and congratulate them on their effort.

Before dismissing the children, say: *Remember that the Holy Spirit lives in you. He will give you the strength to do good for others just as he did for Peter and the other disciples.*

Prayer Service

Leader: *Peter called for Jesus' help in healing the man at the Temple. Let us pray that the Holy Spirit will lead us to serve others in Jesus' name.*

All: *Amen.*

Reader: *A reading from the letter to the Galatians.*

   When you help each other, you obey Jesus' law. Do not grow tired of doing good for others. You will be rewarded if you do not give up.
   [adapted from Galatians 6:2,9]

   The Word of the Lord.

All: *Thanks be to God.*

Leader: *Let us show our love for others every day.*

All Saints Day

Theme

On All Saints Day we celebrate all members of the Church, living and dead, united in Christ.

Outcomes

At the end of the session, the children should be able to

- identify the saints as people who lived model lives.
- discover how to live as children of God.
- recognize that we celebrate the Feast of All Saints every November 1.

Required Materials

Bible, paper, pens, pencils, crayons, markers; CD 2, Track 5: Jesus in the Morning (Jesus verses) (1:37) (page 270)

Optional Materials

Blackline Master 72 (page 268); green construction paper, 8½-by-11-inch white writing paper, stapler (page 269); book of saints (page 269)

Before This Session

Bookmark the Bible to Acts of the Apostles 2:37–39 and 1 John 3:2. Place the Bible, open to the passage from Acts of the Apostles, at the prayer center on a white cloth. Select a child to do the reading for the Prayer Service.

All Saints Day

On the Feast of All Saints we remember the saints in heaven. We want to become saints too. We want to live as children of God.

Prayer

Jesus, my brother, I want to follow you and be close to you.

Check the options for the current session and the materials lists above to prepare for the options you choose.

All Saints Day

Greet the children by saying: *No matter how young or old we are, there is so much to learn.* Ask: *From whom do we learn?* (parents, teachers, others who know things we want to know) Say: *The most important thing we must learn is to love God and others.*

Say: *Open your books to page 267.* Ask the children what they see. What important thing have these children learned? (to love and care for others)

Read the paragraph as the children follow along. Then ask: *Whom do we remember on the feast of All Saints?* (saints in heaven) *How should we live if we want to be saints?* (as children of God) *How do we live as children of God?* (love God and others) Say: *Jesus wants everyone to live as children of God. He wants us to be saints.*

Prayer

Say: *Today we are talking about how to be children of God. Let's pray to Jesus and ask him to help us to be like the saints.*

Say: *Now please pray quietly in your hearts as I pray the prayer aloud. Then take time to talk to Jesus quietly about whatever you would like.*

Pray the prayer. Then pause to give the children time to be with Jesus. Close by praying **Amen.**

Becoming Children of God

Read the title aloud. Point out the source line of the passage and say: *We can read in the Bible what we can do to become saints. This is what Peter told the people.*

Call attention to the color of the cloth under the Bible. Say: *White or gold is the color the Church uses for joyful times, and All Saints Day is a time of joy.*

Read the two paragraphs aloud. Then say: *What two things did Peter tell the people to do if they wanted to be children of God?* (be sorry for their sins and be baptized) *What two things did Peter say would happen if the people were sorry for their sins and were baptized?* (their sins would be forgiven, they would receive the Holy Spirit)

Say: *This is true for us today too. Since we are baptized, the Holy Spirit has come to us. When we are sorry for our sins, they are forgiven.* Ask: *Why is this true?* (because God promised this)

Living as God's Children

Direct the children's attention to the pictures. Say: *Some of these are pictures of saints. The others are people living today.*

Read the title aloud and ask the children to follow along while you read about how to live as children of God.

Read the paragraph aloud to the children. Ask: *What does Jesus give us to help us to be close to him and to one another?* (the grace of the sacraments) *In what sacrament do we become children of God?* (Baptism) *For whom does Jesus want us to pray?* (one another and for those who have died) *How can the saints in heaven help us?* (They can pray for us.)

Say: *All of us who are children of God, whether alive or dead, are part of the Communion of Saints. So, when we die we are still children of God.*

OPTION

BLM 72: MY SPECIAL SAINT

Blackline Master 72 asks children to make a door hanger picturing their favorite saint.

Becoming Children of God

The people wanted to become children of God. So they asked Peter and Jesus' other disciples what they should do.

Peter said, "Be sorry for your sins and be baptized in the name of Jesus Christ. Your sins will be forgiven. You will receive the gift of the Holy Spirit. This promise is made for everyone God calls."

adapted from Acts of the Apostles 2.37-39

Living as God's Children

Jesus wants us to be close to him and to one another. He gives us the grace of the sacraments to help us. He asks us to pray for one another and for those who died. We ask the saints in heaven to pray for us. We are all together in Jesus. This is the Communion of Saints.

268   God's Invitation

Read the title and first paragraph to the group. Ask: **When is the Feast of All Saints?** (November 1) **When we go to Mass, whom do we remember?** (those who have died and live with God)

Read the second and third paragraphs aloud. Say: **Think about someone special in your life who has helped you and shown you how to live a good life by his or her example. Think how happy the person would be to know you are thankful for what he or she has done for you.**

Pass out pencils and crayons or markers. Give the children time to complete the activity. Call on volunteers to explain whose picture is in the frame and what they have written.

Feast of All Saints

On November 1 we celebrate the Feast of All Saints. We go to Mass. We remember those who have died and now live with God.

It is also a good time to think about the special people in your life. Think of how they help you. Think of their good example. Think of their love for you.

In the frame draw a picture of one special person in your life. Write a sentence to tell why this person is special to you.

Explore

OPTION
A THANK YOU TO MY SPECIAL PERSON

Pass out green construction paper and 8½-by-11-inch white writing paper. Have the children fold the two sheets of paper in half together to create cards to send to someone special in their lives. Tell them they will write on the white paper and can decorate it as they wish. As the children work, walk around, stapling the white sheet to the green construction paper. When the children have finished, encourage them to take the cards home and give them to their special persons.

OPTION
MODERN DAY MODELS

Think of people in your parish and community who help others. They might be altar servers who serve Mass whenever needed, volunteer firefighters, people who volunteer at a hospital, or others. Invite one or more of these people to come to speak to your group about what they do and why they do it.

OPTION
MY SPECIAL SAINT IN HEAVEN

Tell the children: **When we think of the saints in heaven, we think of saints who are special to us. Many people are named for special saints. For example, if someone's name is Francis or Anne, his or her special saint would be Saint Francis or Saint Anne.** Ask the children to tell you any saint names they would like you to look up in the book of saints that you have brought to the session. Look up the names and read the stories to the children.

OPTION
FIVE-FINGER PRAYERS

Tell the group that we remember the special people in heaven and in our lives when we pray. Explain that our five fingers serve as reminders of whom to pray for. The thumb reminds us to pray for friends. The index finger reminds us to pray for those who point us to God, such as our parents and family members. The middle finger is the tallest, reminding us to pray for our leaders. The ring finger, our weakest of fingers, reminds us to pray for the less fortunate. The little finger reminds us to pray for ourselves.

Reflect

Prayer Service

Say: *Now it's time to prepare for our All Saints Day Prayer Service.* Say: *We are going to take some time today to pray for those who have died.* Have the children look at the Prayer Service. Remind them that you will read the Leader parts and they will read the All parts.

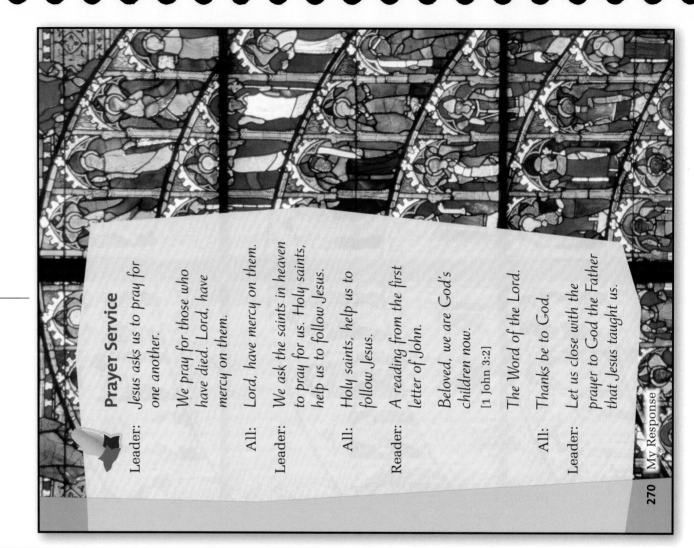 Invite the children to come quietly and join you at the prayer center with their books. When all the children are together, begin the Prayer Service by asking the children to join you in singing the Jesus verses of "Jesus in the Morning" (CD 2, Track 5) in the Songs of Our Faith section in the back of their books.

Begin by reading the first Leader part. Then motion to the children to respond: *Lord have mercy on them.* Read the next Leader part and motion for the children to respond: *Holy saints, help us to follow Jesus.*

Motion to the child selected to read the verse from the first letter of John to begin. When the reading is finished, motion to the children to respond: *Thanks be to God.*

Say: *We have just asked the saints in heaven to pray for us. Now close your eyes and silently in your heart pray to a saint in heaven, asking for help with something important in your lives.* Pause for 10 seconds to allow the children time to pray.

In closing, read the final Leader part. Ask the children to open their eyes and put their books down. Lead the group in praying the Lord's Prayer, as they place their hands in the orans position (hands out with palms up).

Respond

When the children have returned to their seats, say: *We have learned a lot about All Saints Day. Look back through pages 267 through 269 and think of one thing you have learned.*

When the children are ready, call on volunteers to share what they have learned. Write the responses on the board and ask the children to avoid repeating anything that is already listed. When all of the responses have been recorded, direct the children's attention to the board and congratulate them for everything they have learned.

When the children are ready to leave, say: *We are all part of God's family. Let us remember to thank God for making us his children.*

Prayer Service

Leader: Jesus asks us to pray for one another.

We pray for those who have died. Lord, have mercy on them.

All: Lord, have mercy on them.

Leader: We ask the saints in heaven to pray for us. Holy saints, help us to follow Jesus.

All: Holy saints, help us to follow Jesus.

Reader: A reading from the first letter of John.

Beloved, we are God's children now.
[1 John 3:2]

The Word of the Lord.

All: Thanks be to God.

Leader: Let us close with the prayer to God the Father that Jesus taught us.

Prayers and Practices of Our Faith

Prayers and Practices of Our Faith

Grade 2

271

For your convenience the pages of the Prayers and Practices section from the Children's Book are reproduced here.

For your convenience the pages of the Prayers and Practices section from the Children's Book are reproduced here.

273

Knowing and Praying Our Faith

The Bible and You

God speaks to us in many ways. One way is through the Bible. The Bible is the story of God's promise to care for us, especially through his Son, Jesus.

The Bible is made up of two parts. The Old Testament tells stories about the Jewish people before Jesus was born.

In the New Testament Jesus teaches us about the Father's love. The Gospels tell stories about Jesus' life, death, and resurrection.

At Mass we hear stories from the Bible. We can also read the Bible on our own.

274 Prayers and Practices of Our Faith

For your convenience the pages of the Prayers and Practices section from the Children's Book are reproduced here.

For your convenience the pages of the Prayers and Practices section from the Children's Book are reproduced here.

Prayer and How We Pray

Prayer is talking and listening to God. We can talk to God in the words of special prayers or in our own words. We can pray aloud or quietly in our hearts.

We can pray to God often and in many different ways. We praise God. We can ask God for what we need and thank him. We can pray for ourselves and for others.

Prayers to Take to Heart

It is good for us to know prayers by heart. To learn prayers by heart means that we not only learn, or memorize, the words but try to understand and live them.

Knowing and Praying Our Faith

275

Glory Be to the Father

Glory be to the Father,
and to the Son,
and to the Holy Spirit.
As it was in the beginning,
is now, and ever shall be,
world without end.
Amen.

Sign of the Cross

In the name of the Father,
and of the Son,
and of the Holy Spirit.
Amen.

In the name of the Father,   *and of the Son,*

and of the Holy   *Spirit.*   *Amen.*

276   Prayers and Practices of Our Faith

For your convenience the pages of the Prayers and Practices section from the Children's Book are reproduced here.

Lord's Prayer

Our Father,
who art in heaven,
hallowed be thy name;
thy kingdom come;
thy will be done
on earth as it is in heaven.
Give us this day our daily bread;
and forgive us our trespasses
as we forgive those
who trespass against us;
and lead us not into temptation,
but deliver us from evil.
Amen.

Knowing and Praying Our Faith **277**

For your convenience the pages of the Prayers and Practices section from the Children's Book are reproduced here.

Hail Mary

Hail Mary, full of grace,
the Lord is with you.
Blessed are you among women,
and blessed is the fruit of your womb, Jesus.
Holy Mary, Mother of God,
pray for us sinners,
now and at the hour of our death.
Amen.

278 Prayers and Practices of Our Faith

For your convenience the pages of the Prayers and Practices section from the Children's Book are reproduced here.

Act of Contrition

My God,
I am sorry for my sins with all my heart.
In choosing to do wrong
and failing to do good,
I have sinned against you
whom I should love above all things.
I firmly intend, with your help,
to do penance,
to sin no more,
and to avoid whatever leads me to sin.
Our Savior Jesus Christ
suffered and died for us.
In his name, my God, have mercy.

Prayer to the Holy Spirit

Come, Holy Spirit,
fill the hearts of your faithful.
And kindle in them
the fire of your love.
Send forth your Spirit
and they shall be created.
And you will renew
the face of the earth.

Knowing and Praying Our Faith **279**

For your convenience the pages of the Prayers and Practices section from the Children's Book are reproduced here.

Morning Prayer

God, our Father, I offer you today
all that I think and do and say.
I offer it with what was done
on earth by Jesus Christ, your Son.
Amen.

Evening Prayer

God, our Father, this day is done.
We ask you and Jesus Christ, your Son,
that with the Spirit, our welcome guest,
you guard our sleep and bless our rest.
Amen.

280 Prayers and Practices of Our Faith

For your convenience the pages of the Prayers and Practices section from the Children's Book are reproduced here.

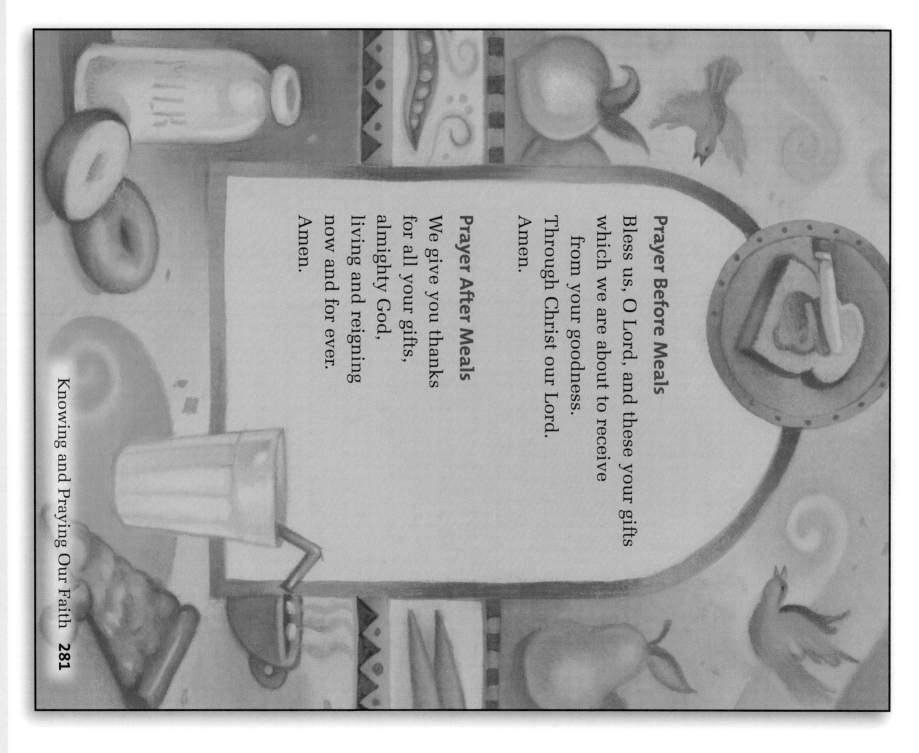

Prayer Before Meals

Bless us, O Lord, and these your gifts
which we are about to receive
from your goodness.
Through Christ our Lord.
Amen.

Prayer After Meals

We give you thanks
for all your gifts,
almighty God,
living and reigning
now and for ever.
Amen.

Knowing and Praying Our Faith **281**

For your convenience the pages of the Prayers and Practices section from the Children's Book are reproduced here.

Prayers and Practices of Our Faith **281**

Apostles' Creed

I believe in God, the Father almighty,
creator of heaven and earth.
I believe in Jesus Christ, his only Son, our Lord.
He was conceived by the power
of the Holy Spirit
and born of the Virgin Mary.
He suffered under Pontius Pilate,
was crucified, died, and was buried.
He descended to the dead.
On the third day he arose again.
He ascended into heaven,
and is seated at the right hand of the Father.
He will come again to judge the living
and the dead.
I believe in the Holy Spirit,
the holy catholic Church,
the communion of saints,
the forgiveness of sins,
the resurrection of the body,
and the life everlasting. Amen.

282 Prayers and Practices of Our Faith

For your convenience the pages of the Prayers and Practices section from the Children's Book are reproduced here.

282 Children's Book Resources

Hail, Holy Queen

Hail, holy Queen, Mother of mercy,
hail, our life, our sweetness, and our hope.
To you we cry, the children of Eve;
to you we send up our sighs,
mourning and weeping in this
land of exile.

Turn, then, most gracious advocate,
your eyes of mercy toward us;
lead us home at last
and show us the blessed
fruit of your womb, Jesus:
O clement, O loving,
O sweet Virgin Mary.

Prayer for Vocations

God, thank you for loving me.
You have called me
to live as your child.
Help all your children
to love you and one another.
Amen.

For your convenience the pages of the Prayers and Practices section from the Children's Book are reproduced here.

The Rosary

The Rosary helps us to reflect on the special events, or mysteries, in the lives of Jesus and Mary.

We begin by praying the Sign of the Cross while holding the crucifix. Then we pray the Apostles' Creed.

We pray the Lord's Prayer as we hold the first single bead. On each of the next three beads, we pray a Hail Mary. Next, we pray a Glory Be to the Father. On the next single bead we think about the first mystery, a particular event in the lives of Jesus and Mary. We then pray the Lord's Prayer.

The five sets of ten beads are called decades. As we pray each decade, we reflect on a different mystery. Between the sets is a single bead on which we think about one of the mysteries and pray the Lord's Prayer. We then pray a Hail Mary as we hold each of the beads in the set. At the end of each set, we pray the Glory Be to the Father.

We end by praying the Sign of the Cross while holding the crucifix.

284 Prayers and Practices of Our Faith

Praying the Rosary

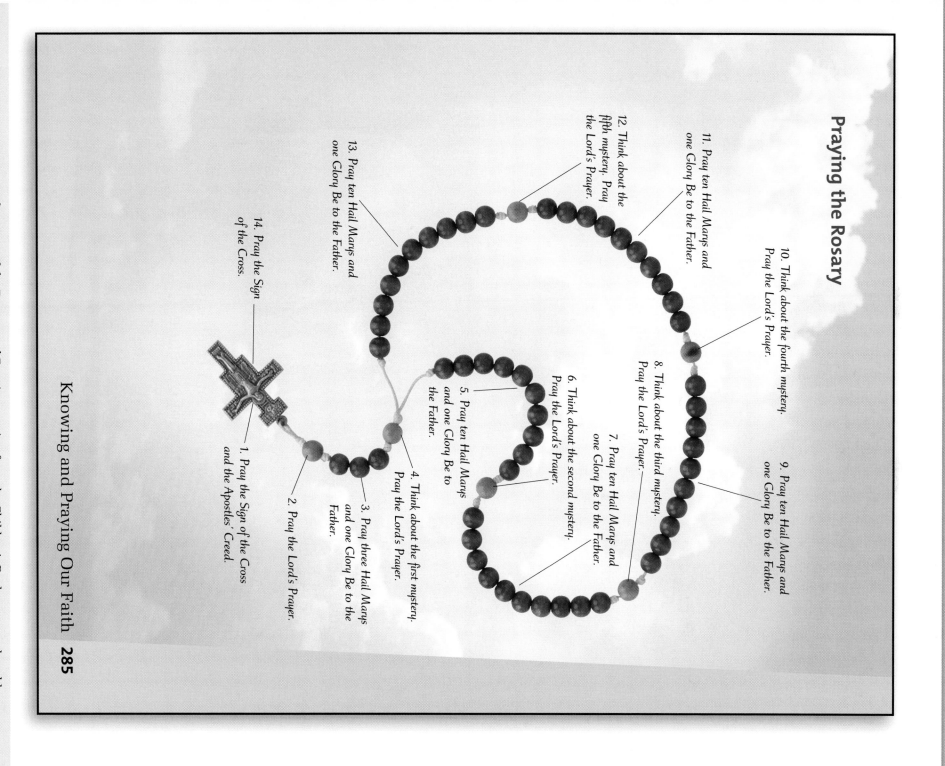

10. Think about the fourth mystery.
Pray the Lord's Prayer.

11. Pray ten Hail Marys and
one Glory Be to the Father.

12. Think about the
fifth mystery. Pray
the Lord's Prayer.

13. Pray ten Hail Marys and
one Glory Be to the Father.

14. Pray the Sign
of the Cross.

9. Pray ten Hail Marys and
one Glory Be to the Father.

8. Think about the third mystery.
Pray the Lord's Prayer.

7. Pray ten Hail Marys and
one Glory Be to the Father.

6. Think about the second mystery.
Pray the Lord's Prayer.

5. Pray ten Hail Marys
and one Glory Be to
the Father.

4. Think about the first mystery.
Pray the Lord's Prayer.

3. Pray three Hail Marys
and one Glory Be to the
Father.

2. Pray the Lord's Prayer.

1. Pray the Sign of the Cross
and the Apostles' Creed.

For your convenience the pages of the Prayers and Practices section from the Children's Book are reproduced here.

Celebrating Our Faith

The Seven Sacraments

The sacraments are signs of the grace we receive from God.

Sacraments show that God is part of our lives. They were given to the Church by Jesus to show that he loves us. The seven sacraments help us to live the way God wants us to live. The sacraments are celebrated with us by priests.

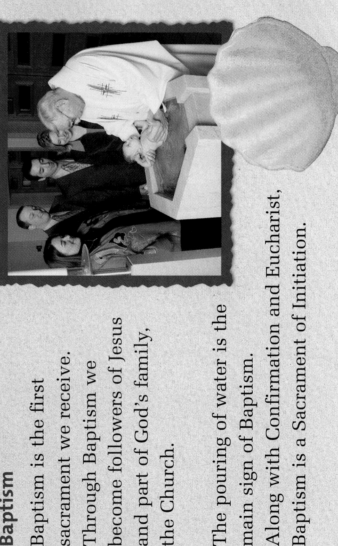

Baptism

Baptism is the first sacrament we receive. Through Baptism we become followers of Jesus and part of God's family, the Church.

The pouring of water is the main sign of Baptism. Along with Confirmation and Eucharist, Baptism is a Sacrament of Initiation.

286 Prayers and Practices of Our Faith

286 Children's Book Resources

For your convenience the pages of the Prayers and Practices section from the Children's Book are reproduced here.

Confirmation

Confirmation is a Sacrament of Initiation.

In this sacrament the Holy Spirit strengthens us to be witnesses to Jesus. Confirmation makes us stronger in faith and helps us become better Christians.

The bishop places holy oil on our foreheads in the form of a cross. This is the main sign of Confirmation.

Eucharist

Eucharist is a Sacrament of Initiation.

At Mass the bread and wine become Jesus' Body and Blood. This happens when the priest says the words of consecration that Jesus used at the Last Supper. Eucharist is also called Holy Communion.

Celebrating Our Faith **287**

For your convenience the pages of the Prayers and Practices section from the Children's Book are reproduced here.

Prayers and Practices of Our Faith **287**

Penance

We ask God to forgive our sins in the Sacrament of Penance. The priest who celebrates this sacrament with us shares Jesus' gifts of peace and forgiveness.

God always forgives us when we are sorry and do penance for our sins.

Anointing of the Sick

In this sacrament a sick person is anointed with holy oil and receives the spiritual—and sometimes even physical—healing of Jesus.

288 Prayers and Practices of Our Faith

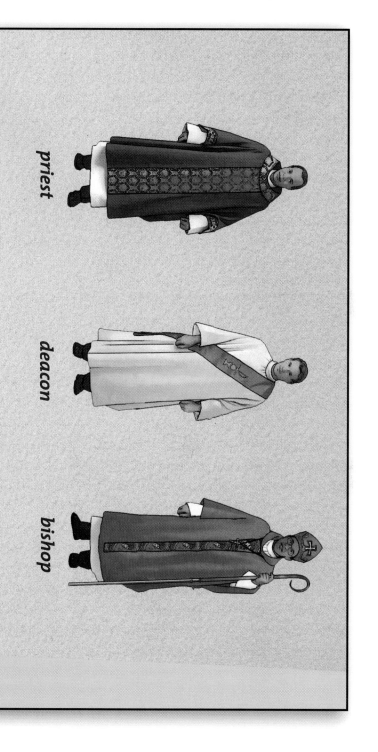

priest

deacon

bishop

Holy Orders

Some men are called to be deacons, priests, or bishops. They receive the Sacrament of Holy Orders. Through Holy Orders the mission, or task, given by Jesus to his apostles continues in the Church.

Matrimony

Some men and women are called to be married. In the Sacrament of Matrimony, they make a solemn promise to be partners for life, both for their own good and for the good of the children they will raise.

Celebrating Our Faith **289**

For your convenience the pages of the Prayers and Practices section from the Children's Book are reproduced here.

Prayers and Practices of Our Faith **289**

Celebrating the Lord's Day

Sunday is the day on which we celebrate the Resurrection of Jesus. Sunday is the Lord's day. We gather for Mass and rest from work. People all over the world gather at God's eucharistic table as brothers and sisters.

Order of the Mass

The Mass is the high point of the Christian life, and it always follows a set order.

Introductory Rite
preparing to celebrate the Eucharist

Entrance Procession and Song

We gather as a community and praise God in song.

290 Prayers and Practices of Our Faith

For your convenience the pages of the Prayers and Practices section from the Children's Book are reproduced here.

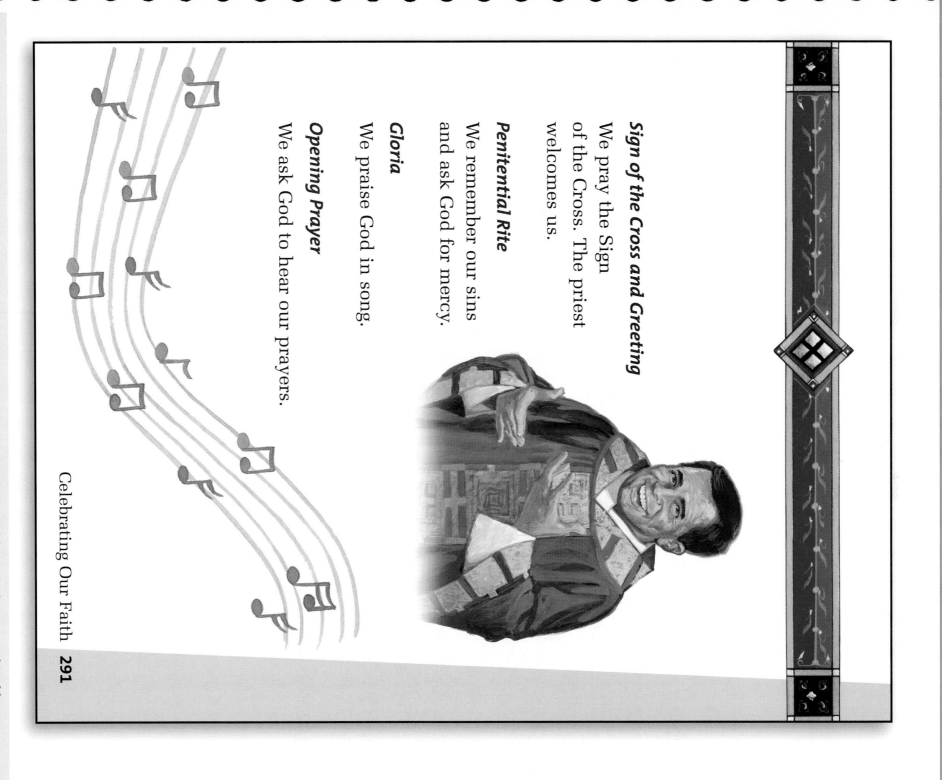

Sign of the Cross and Greeting

We pray the Sign of the Cross. The priest welcomes us.

Penitential Rite

We remember our sins and ask God for mercy.

Gloria

We praise God in song.

Opening Prayer

We ask God to hear our prayers.

Celebrating Our Faith **291**

For your convenience the pages of the Prayers and Practices section from the Children's Book are reproduced here.

Prayers and Practices of Our Faith **291**

Liturgy of the Word
hearing God's plan of salvation

First Reading
We listen to God's Word, usually from the Old Testament.

Responsorial Psalm
We respond to God's Word in song.

Second Reading
We listen to God's Word from the New Testament.

Gospel Acclamation
We sing "Alleluia!" (except during Lent) to praise God for the Good News.

292   Prayers and Practices of Our Faith

For your convenience the pages of the Prayers and Practices section from the Children's Book are reproduced here.

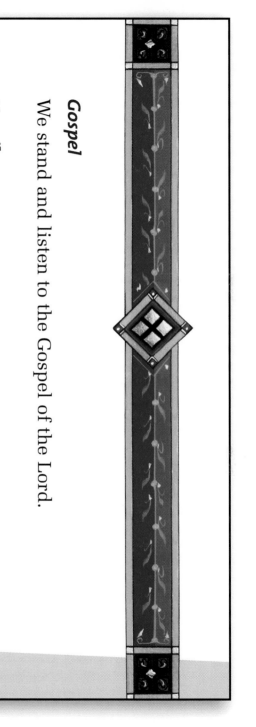

Gospel

We stand and listen to the Gospel of the Lord.

Homily

The priest or deacon explains God's Word.

Profession of Faith

We proclaim our faith through the Creed.

General Intercessions

We pray for our
needs and the
needs of others.

Celebrating Our Faith **293**

For your convenience the pages of the Prayers and Practices section from the Children's Book are reproduced here.

Prayers and Practices of Our Faith **293**

Liturgy of the Eucharist

celebrating Jesus' presence in the Eucharist

Preparation of the Altar and the Gifts

We bring gifts of bread and wine to the altar.

- Prayer Over the Gifts—The priest prays that God will accept our sacrifice.

Eucharistic Prayer

This prayer of thanksgiving is the center and high point of the entire celebration.

- Consecration—
The bread and wine become the Body and Blood of Jesus Christ.

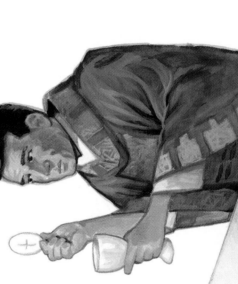

294 Prayers and Practices of Our Faith

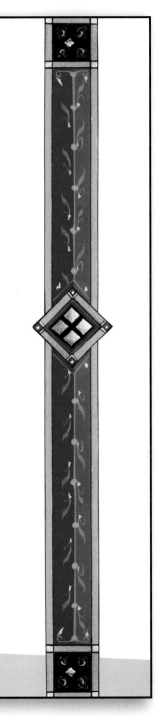

Communion Rite

We prepare to receive the Body and Blood of Jesus Christ.

- Lord's Prayer—We pray the Our Father.
- Sign of Peace—We offer one another Christ's peace.
- Lamb of God—We pray for forgiveness, mercy, and peace.
- Communion—We receive the Body and Blood of Jesus Christ.

Concluding Rite

going forth to serve the Lord and others

Blessing

We receive God's blessing.

Dismissal

We go in peace to love and serve the Lord and one another.

Celebrating Our Faith **295**

For your convenience the pages of the Prayers and Practices section from the Children's Book are reproduced here.

Receiving Communion

When we go to communion, we receive the Body of Christ—in the form of bread—in our hands or on our tongues. The priest or the eucharistic minister says, "The Body of Christ." We reply, "Amen."

We can also receive the Blood of Christ—in the form of wine. The priest or the minister offers the cup and says, "The Blood of Christ." We reply, "Amen." We take the cup in our hands and drink from it, and we then hand it back to the priest or eucharistic minister.

296 Prayers and Practices of Our Faith

For your convenience the pages of the Prayers and Practices section from the Children's Book are reproduced here.

296 Children's Book Resources

Holy Days of Obligation

Holy Days of Obligation are the days other than Sundays on which Catholics gather for Mass to celebrate the great things God has done for us through Jesus and the saints.

Six Holy Days of Obligation are celebrated in the United States.

January 1—Mary, Mother of God

40th day after Easter—Ascension

August 15—Assumption of the Blessed Virgin Mary

November 1—All Saints

December 8—Immaculate Conception

December 25—Nativity of Our Lord Jesus Christ

Celebrating Our Faith **297**

People and Things I See at Mass

processional
cross

altar

paschal
candle

ambo

altar
servers

Eucharistic minister

chalice

paten

298   Prayers and Practices of Our Faith

For your convenience the pages of the Prayers and Practices section from the Children's Book are reproduced here.

298   Children's Book Resources

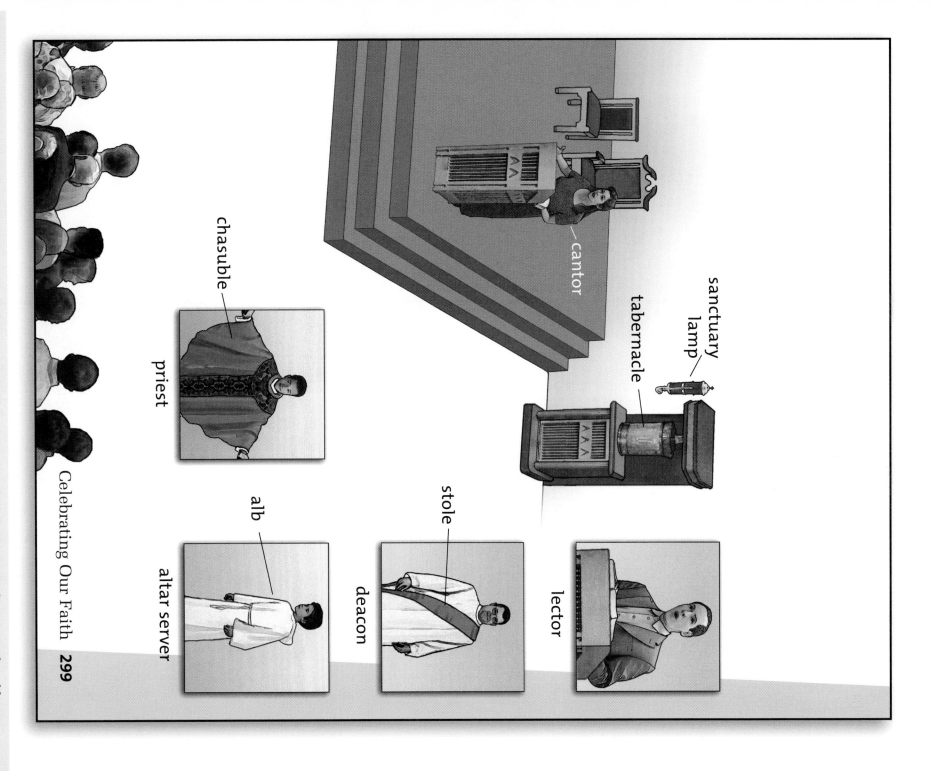

cantor

sanctuary lamp

tabernacle

chasuble

priest

alb

altar server

stole

deacon

lector

For your convenience the pages of the Prayers and Practices section from the Children's Book are reproduced here.

An Examination of Conscience

An examination of conscience is the act of reflecting on how we have hurt our relationships with God and others. Questions such as the following will help us in our examination of conscience:

My Relationship With God

Do I use God's name with love and reverence?

What steps am I taking to grow closer to God and to others?

Do I actively participate at Mass on Sundays and holy days?

Do I pray?

300 Prayers and Practices of Our Faith

For your convenience the pages of the Prayers and Practices section from the Children's Book are reproduced here.

My Relationship With Family, Friends, and Neighbors

Have I set a bad example by my words or actions?
Do I treat others fairly?

Am I loving to those in my family? Am I respectful of my neighbors, my friends, and those in authority?

Do I show respect for my body and for the bodies of others?

Have I taken or damaged anything that did not belong to me? Have I cheated or lied?

Do I quarrel or fight with others? Do I try to hurt people who I think have hurt me?

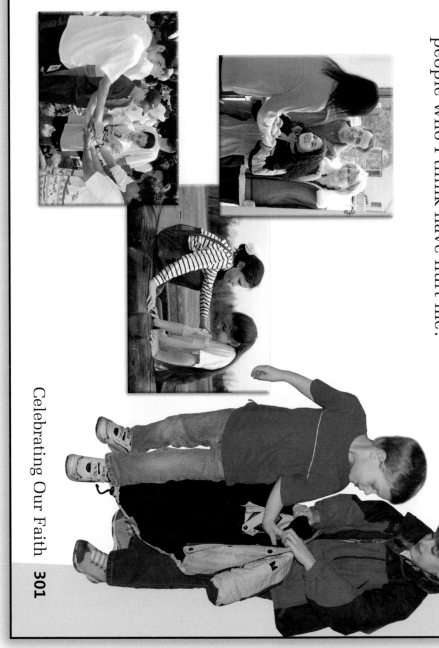

Celebrating Our Faith **301**

For your convenience the pages of the Prayers and Practices section from the Children's Book are reproduced here.

Prayers and Practices of Our Faith **301**

How to Go to Confession

An examination of conscience is an important part of preparing for the Sacrament of Penance. The Sacrament of Penance includes the following steps:

1. The priest greets us, and we pray the Sign of the Cross. He invites us to trust in God. He may read God's Word with us.

2. We confess our sins. The priest may help and counsel us.

302 Prayers and Practices of Our Faith

For your convenience the pages of the Prayers and Practices section from the Children's Book are reproduced here.

302   Children's Book Resources

3. The priest gives us a penance to perform. Penance may be an act of kindness or prayers to pray, or both.

4. The priest asks us to express our sorrow, usually by praying an Act of Contrition.

5. We receive absolution. The priest says, "I absolve you from your sins in the name of the Father, and of the Son, and of the Holy Spirit." We respond, "Amen."

6. The priest dismisses us by saying, "Go in peace." We go forth to perform the act of penance he has given us.

For your convenience the pages of the Prayers and Practices section from the Children's Book are reproduced here.

Living Our Faith

The Ten Commandments

God gave us the Ten Commandments. They teach us how to live for God and for others. They help us follow the moral law to do good and avoid evil.

1. I am your God; love nothing more than me.

2. Use God's name with respect.

3. Keep the Lord's day holy.

4. Honor and obey your parents.

5. Treat all human life with respect.

6. Respect married life.

7. Respect what belongs to others.

8. Tell the truth.

9. Respect your neighbors and your friends.

10. Be happy with what you have.

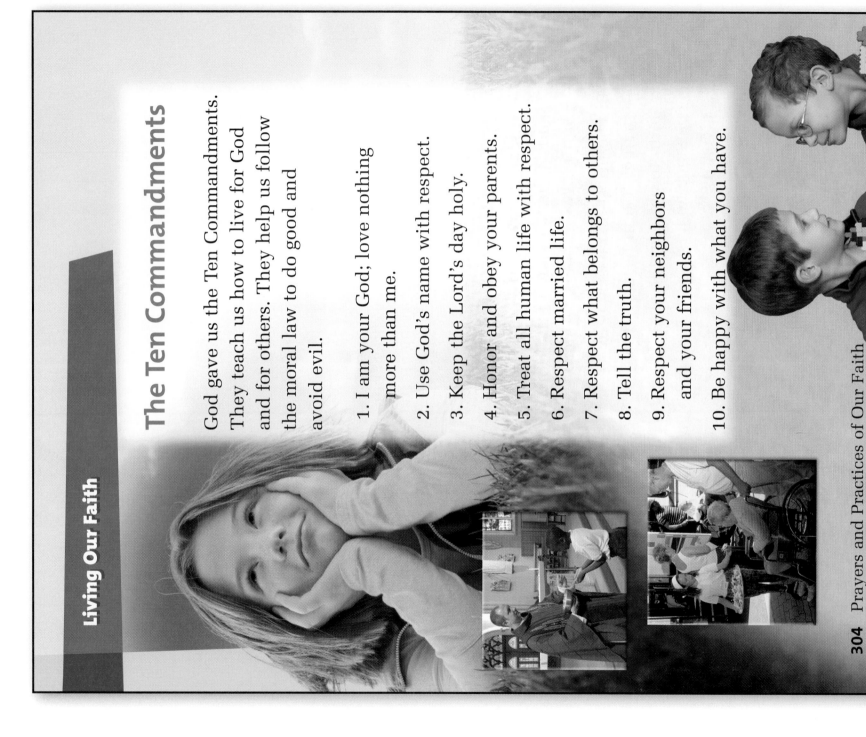

304 Prayers and Practices of Our Faith

The Great Commandment

People asked Jesus, "What is the most important commandment?" Jesus said, "First, love God. Love him with your heart, soul, and mind. The second is like it: Love your neighbor as much as you love yourself."

adapted from Matthew 22:37-39

We call this the Great Commandment.

The New Commandment

Before his death on the cross, Jesus gave his disciples a new commandment: "Love one another. As I have loved you, so you also should love one another."

John 13:34

For your convenience the pages of the Prayers and Practices section from the Children's Book are reproduced here.

Prayers and Practices of Our Faith **305**

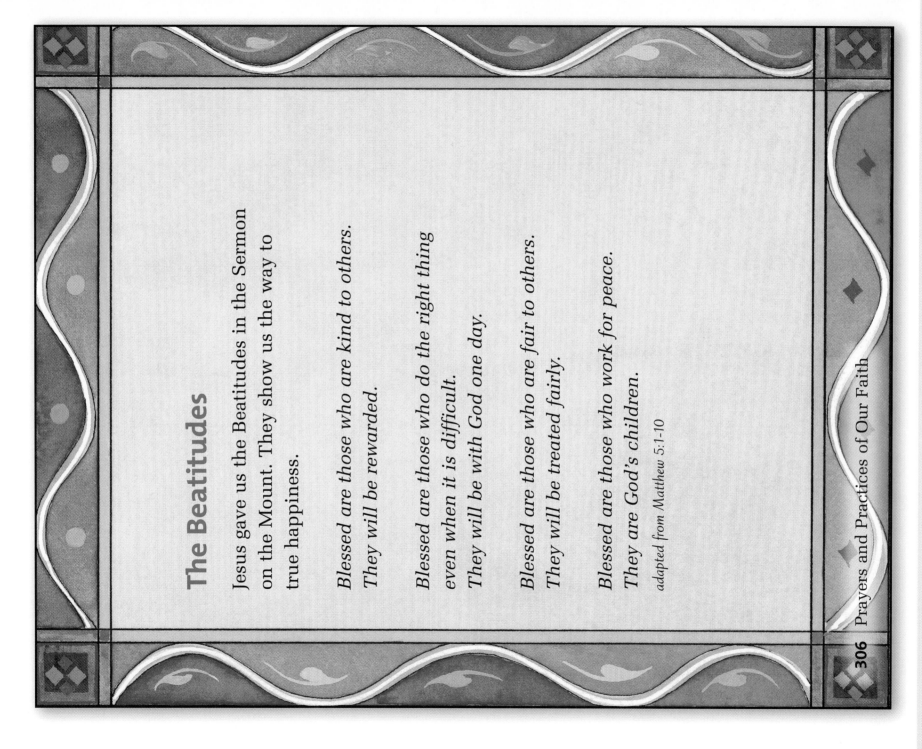

The Beatitudes

Jesus gave us the Beatitudes in the Sermon on the Mount. They show us the way to true happiness.

Blessed are those who are kind to others.
They will be rewarded.

Blessed are those who do the right thing even when it is difficult.
They will be with God one day.

Blessed are those who are fair to others.
They will be treated fairly.

Blessed are those who work for peace.
They are God's children.
adapted from Matthew 5:1-10

306 Prayers and Practices of Our Faith

For your convenience the pages of the Prayers and Practices section from the Children's Book are reproduced here.

Making Good Choices

The Holy Spirit helps us to make good choices. We get help from the Ten Commandments, the grace of the sacraments, and the teachings of the Church. We also get help from the example of the saints and fellow Christians. To make good choices, we ask the following questions:

1. Is the thing I am choosing to do a good thing?
2. Am I choosing to do it for the right reasons?
3. Am I choosing to do it at the right time and in the right place?

Fruits of the Holy Spirit

When we realize that the Holy Spirit lives within us, we live the way God wants us to. The Fruits of the Holy Spirit are signs of the Holy Spirit's action in our lives. They include the following:

love	generosity	peace
kindness	faithfulness	patience
gentleness	self-control	joy

Church Tradition also includes **goodness**, **modesty**, and **chastity** among the Fruits of the Holy Spirit.

Showing Our Love for the World

Jesus taught us to care for those in need. The social teachings of the Church call us to follow Jesus' example in each of the following areas:

Life and Dignity

God wants us to care for everyone. We are all made in his image.

Family and Community

Jesus wants us to be loving helpers in our families and communities.

Rights and Responsibilities

All people should have what they need to live good lives.

FREE HEALTH SCREENING

308 Prayers and Practices of Our Faith

For your convenience the pages of the Prayers and Practices section from the Children's Book are reproduced here.

308 Children's Book Resources

The Poor and Vulnerable

Jesus calls us to do what we can to help people in need.

Work and Workers

The work that we do gives glory to God.

Solidarity

Since God is our Father, we are called to treat everyone in the world as a brother or a sister.

God's Creation

We show our love for God's world by taking care of it.

Living Our Faith **309**

For your convenience the pages of the Prayers and Practices section from the Children's Book are reproduced here.

Songs of Our Faith

Song of Love

Chorus

Thank you Je - sus for help - ing me to

see.

Thank you God for the

heart you've giv - en me.

310 Prayers and Practices of Our Faith

For your convenience the pages of the Prayers and Practices section from the Children's Book are reproduced here.

310 Children's Book Resources

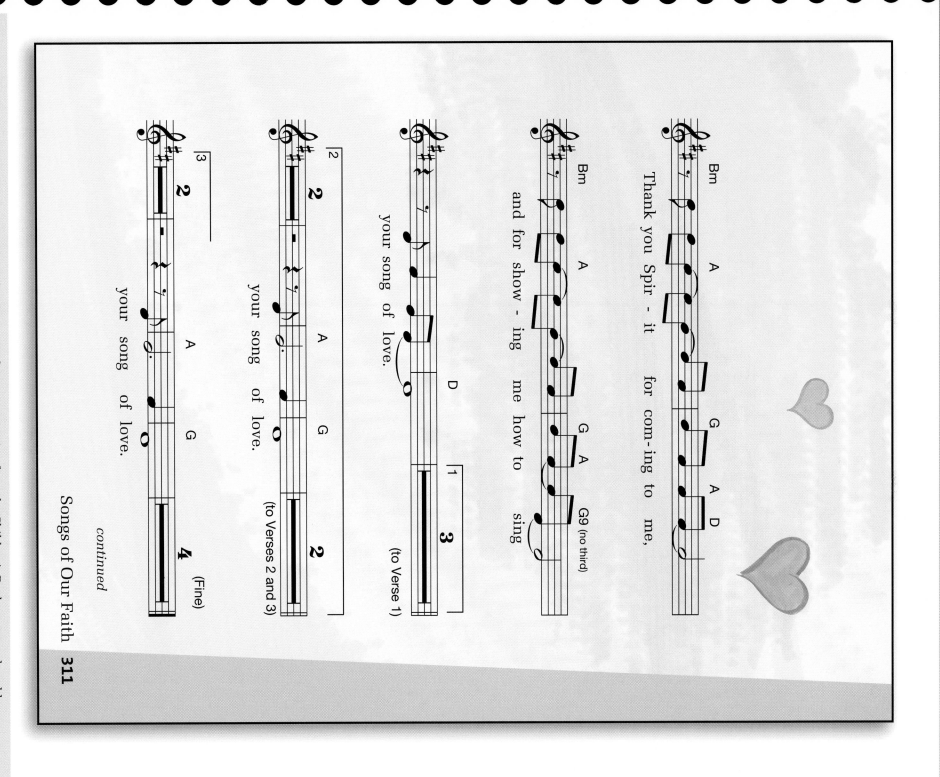

For your convenience the pages of the Prayers and Practices section from the Children's Book are reproduced here.

Bm A G A D

Thank you Spir - it for com - ing to me,

Bm A G A G9 (no third)

and for show - ing me how to sing

D 1 3

(to Verse 1)

your song of love.

2 A G 2

your song of love.

(to Verses 2 and 3)

3 2 A G 4 (Fine)

your song of love.

continued

Songs of Our Faith

311

Song of Love *(continued)*

Verse 1

Bm   G   A   D
I saw some-one lone-ly by the road,

Em   A   G   D
Some-one my age sad-ly all a - lone.

Bm   G   A   D
I shared my friend-ship and we talked a while.

Em   A   G   A   D
I gave a hand, Je - sus gave back a smile. *(to Chorus)*

312   Prayers and Practices of Our Faith

For your convenience the pages of the Prayers and Practices section from the Children's Book are reproduced here.

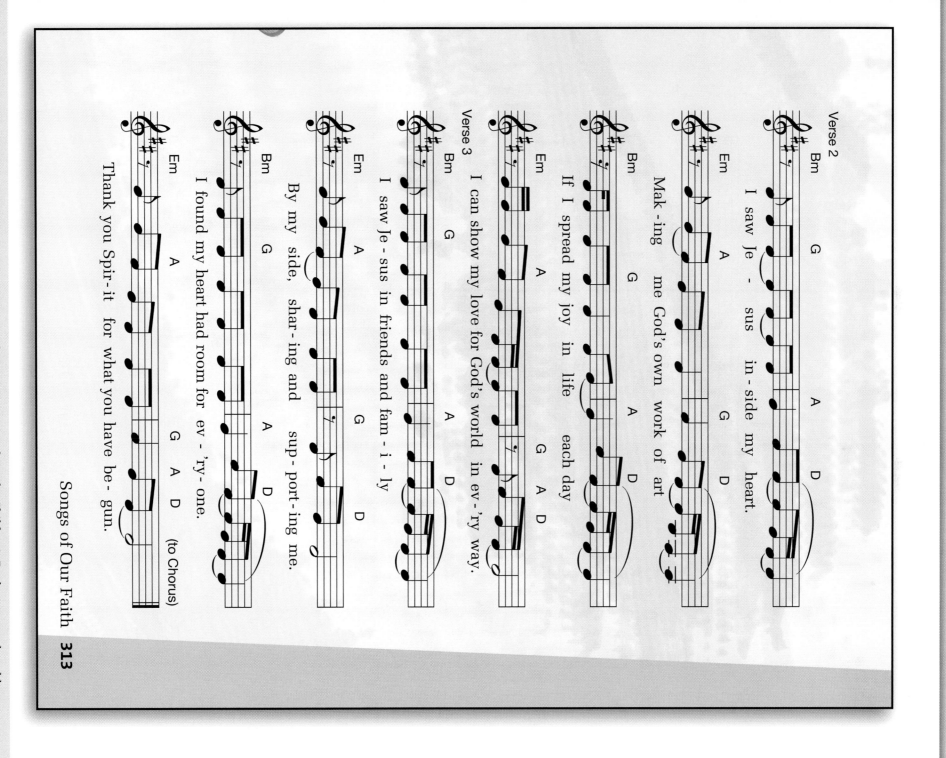

For your convenience the pages of the Prayers and Practices section from the Children's Book are reproduced here.

Songs of Our Faith

"Echo" Holy, Holy

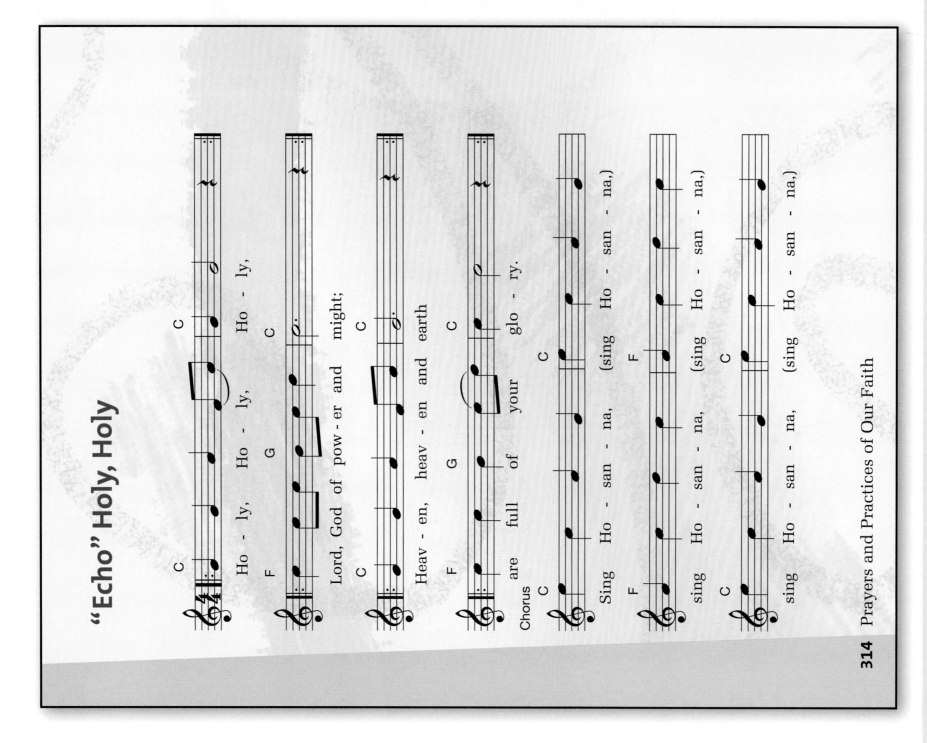

For your convenience the pages of the Prayers and Practices section from the Children's Book are reproduced here.

sing al - le - lu - ia.

(sing al - le - lu - ia.) (Fine)

Bless - ed, bless - ed is He,

(Bless - ed, bless - ed is He,) Who

comes in the Name of the Lord. (Who

comes in the Name of the Lord.) (to Chorus)

Songs of Our Faith **315**

For your convenience the pages of the Prayers and Practices section from the Children's Book are reproduced here.

Jesus in the Morning (Jesus verses)

CAPO 2nd Fret

A

F#m

1. Je - sus, Je - sus,
2. Praise him, Praise him,
3. Love him, Love him,
4. Je - sus, Je - sus,

D

E

1. Je - sus in the morn-ing, Je - sus in the noon-time;
2. Praise him in the morn-ing, Praise him in the noon-time;
3. Love him in the morn-ing, Love him in the noon-time;
4. Je - sus in the morn-ing, Je - sus in the noon-time;

316 Prayers and Practices of Our Faith

For your convenience the pages of the Prayers and Practices section from the Children's Book are reproduced here.

316 Children's Book Resources

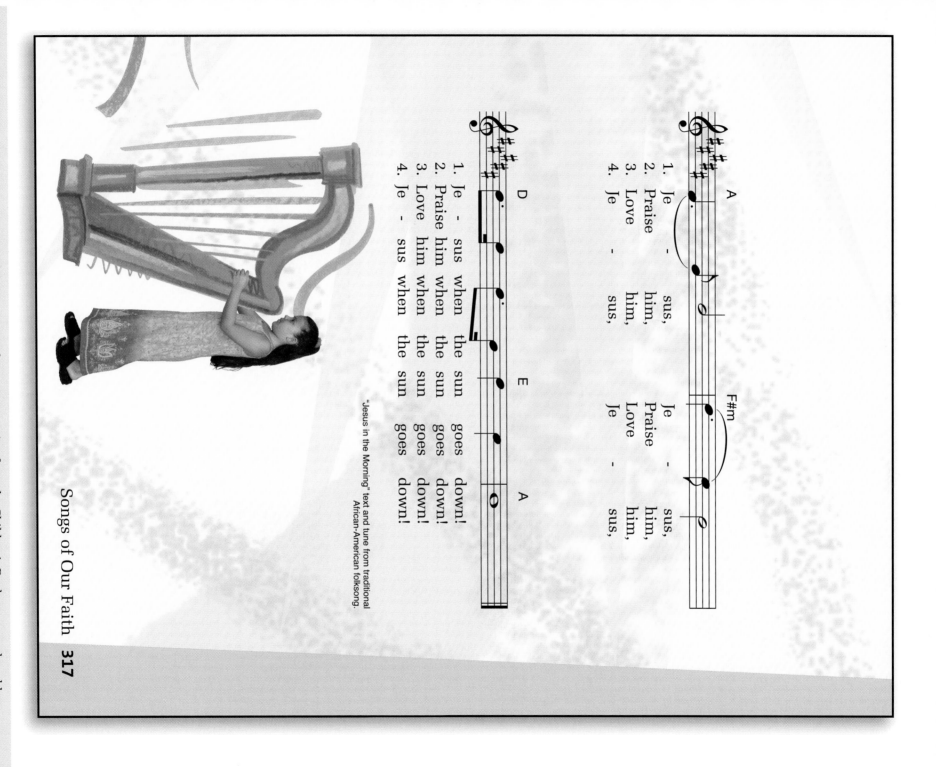

A

1. Je - sus,   Je - sus,
2. Praise   him,   Praise   him,
3. Love   him,   Love   him,
4. Je - sus,   Je - sus,

F#m

D   E   A

1. Je - sus   when   the   sun   goes   down!
2. Praise him when   the   sun   goes   down!
3. Love   him when   the   sun   goes   down!
4. Je - sus   when   the   sun   goes   down!

"Jesus in the Morning" text and tune from traditional
African-American folksong.

Songs of Our Faith   **317**

Jesus in the Morning (Spirit verses)

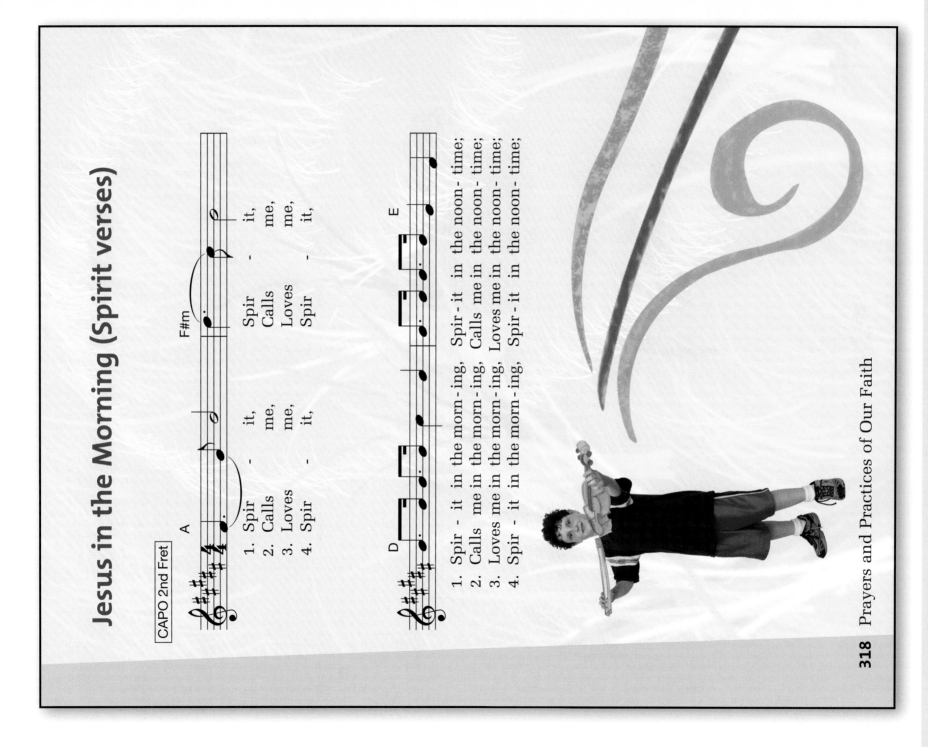

CAPO 2nd Fret

A   F#m

1. Spir - it,   Spir - it,
2. Calls me,   Calls me,
3. Loves me,   Loves me,
4. Spir - it,   Spir - it,

D   E

1. Spir - it in the morn - ing,   Spir - it in the noon - time;
2. Calls me in the morn - ing,   Calls me in the noon - time;
3. Loves me in the morn - ing,   Loves me in the noon - time;
4. Spir - it in the morn - ing,   Spir - it in the noon - time;

318 Prayers and Practices of Our Faith

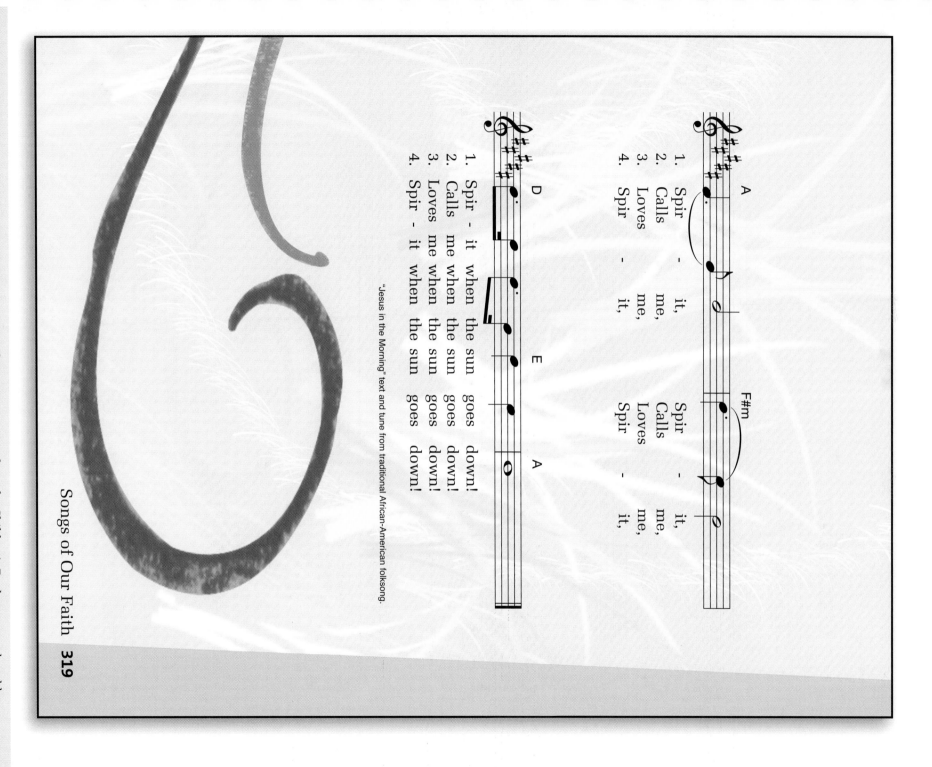

A

1. Spir - it,
2. Calls me,
3. Loves me,
4. Spir - it,

F#m

Spir - it,
Calls me,
Loves me,
Spir - it,

D   E   A

1. Spir - it when the sun goes down!
2. Calls me when the sun goes down!
3. Loves me when the sun goes down!
4. Spir - it when the sun goes down!

"Jesus in the Morning" text and tune from traditional African-American folksong.

Songs of Our Faith **319**

Our Father

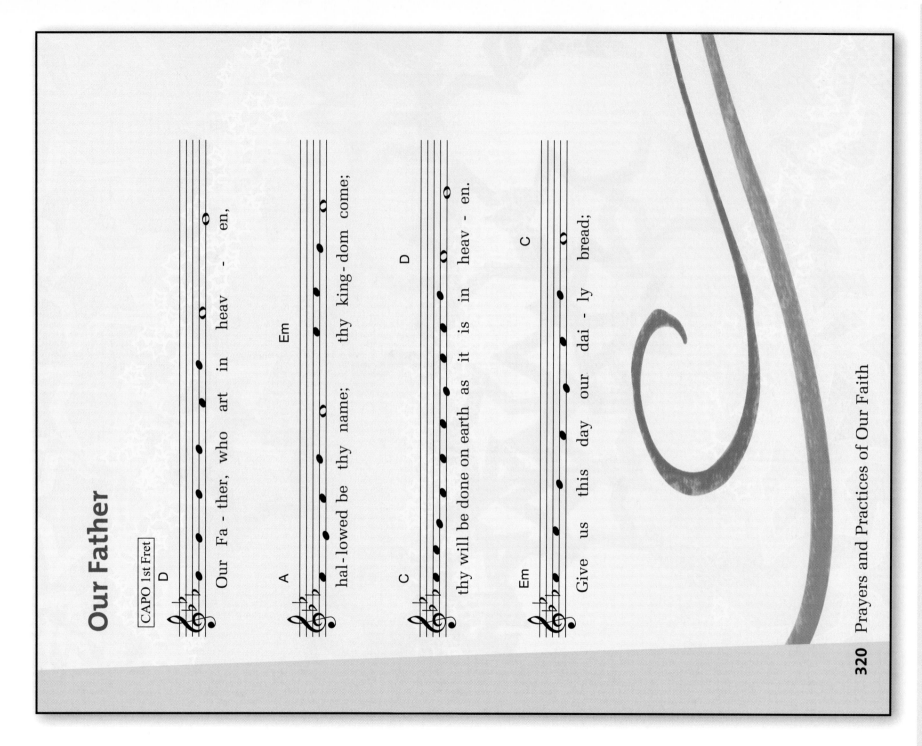

CAPO 1st Fret

D
Our Fa - ther, who art in heav - en,

A · · · · **Em**
hal - lowed be thy name; thy king - dom come;

C · · · · **D**
thy will be done on earth as it is in heav - en.

Em · · · · **C**
Give us this day our dai - ly bread;

320 Prayers and Practices of Our Faith

For your convenience the pages of the Prayers and Practices section from the Children's Book are reproduced here.

320 Children's Book Resources

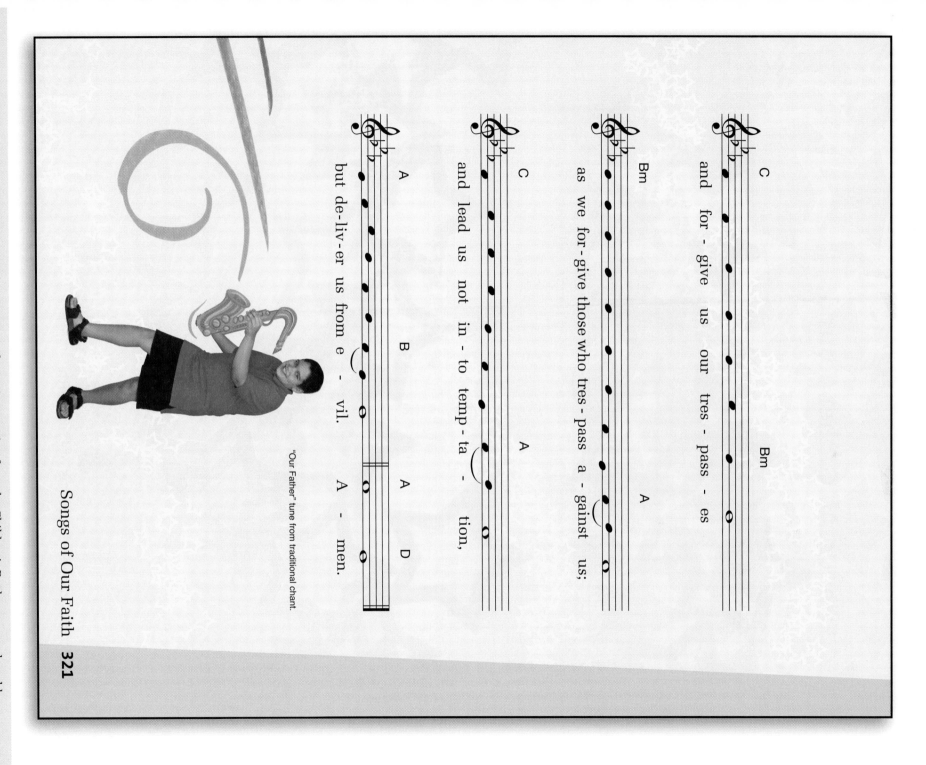

Songs of Our Faith **321**

C   Bm

and for - give us our tres - pass - es

Bm   A

as we for - give those who tres - pass a - gainst us;

C   A

and lead us not in - to temp - ta - tion,

A   B   A   D

but de - liv - er us from e - vil. A - men.

"Our Father" tune from traditional chant.

Friends, All Gather 'Round

Refrain (Repeat Refrain first time only.)

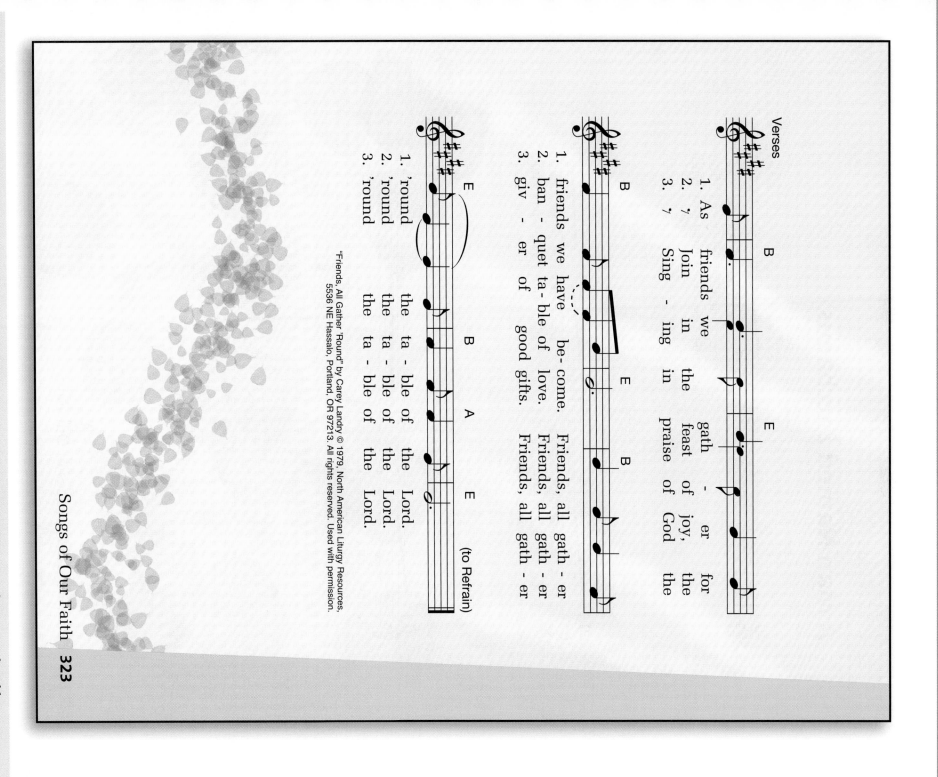

Verses

B   E

1. As   friends   we   gath - er   for
2. %   Join   in   the   feast   of   joy,   the
3. %   Sing - ing   in   praise   of   God   the

B   E   B

1. friends   we   have   be - come.   Friends,   all   gath - er
2. ban - quet   ta - ble   of   love.   Friends,   all   gath - er
3. giv - er   of   good   gifts.   Friends,   all   gath - er

E   B   A   E

1. 'round   the   ta - ble   of   the   Lord.
2. 'round   the   ta - ble   of   the   Lord.
3. 'round   the   ta - ble   of   the   Lord.

(to Refrain)

Songs of Our Faith   **323**

For your convenience the pages of the Prayers and Practices section from the Children's Book are reproduced here.

A Man Named Zacchaeus

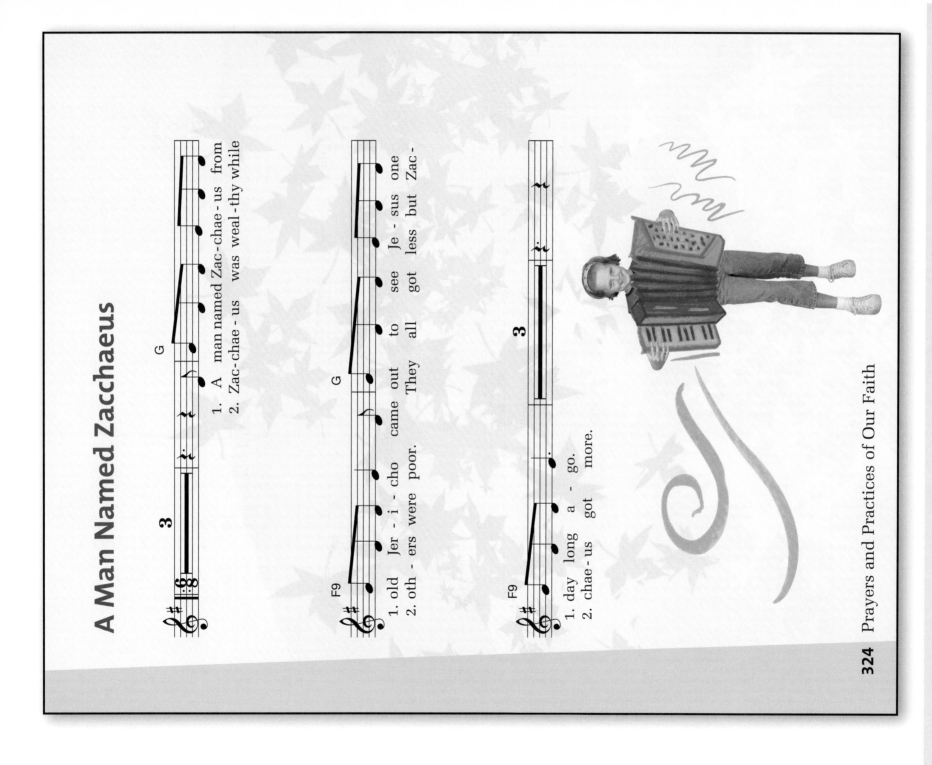

For your convenience the pages of the Prayers and Practices section from the Children's Book are reproduced here.

For your convenience the pages of the Prayers and Practices section from the Children's Book are reproduced here.

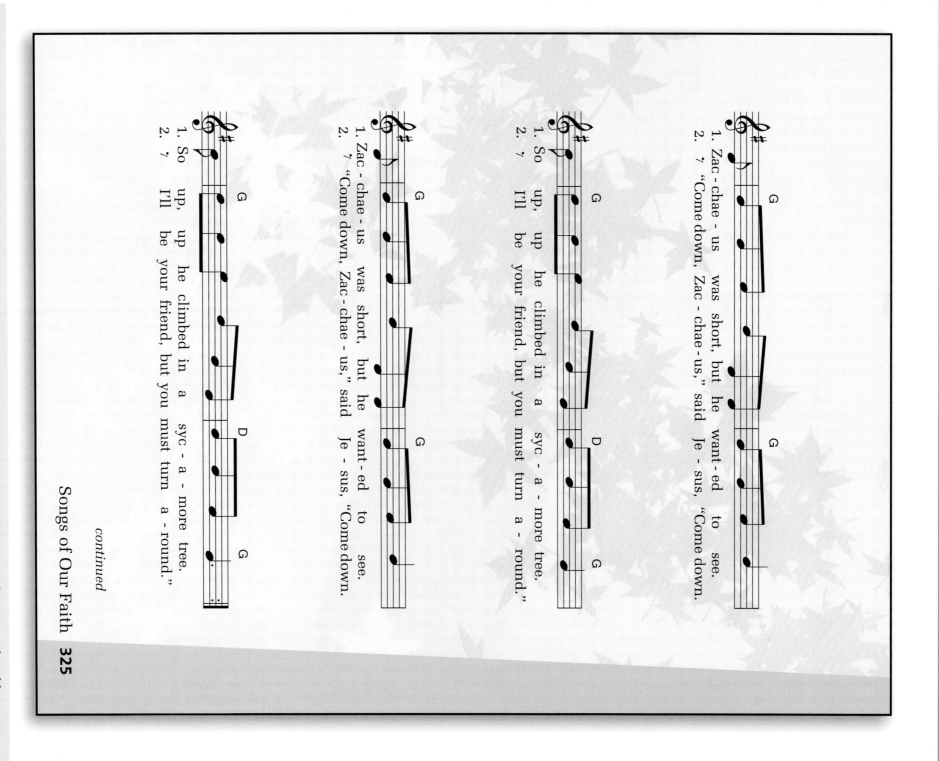

1. Zac - chae - us was short, but he want - ed to see.
2. ⁊ "Come down, Zac - chae - us," said Je - sus, "Come down.

1. So up, up he climbed in a syc - a - more tree.
2. ⁊ I'll be your friend, but you must turn a - round."

1. Zac - chae - us was short, but he want - ed to see.
2. ⁊ "Come down, Zac - chae - us," said Je - sus, "Come down.

1. So up, up he climbed in a syc - a - more tree.
2. ⁊ I'll be your friend, but you must turn a - round."

continued

Songs of Our Faith

325

A Man Named Zacchaeus *(continued)*

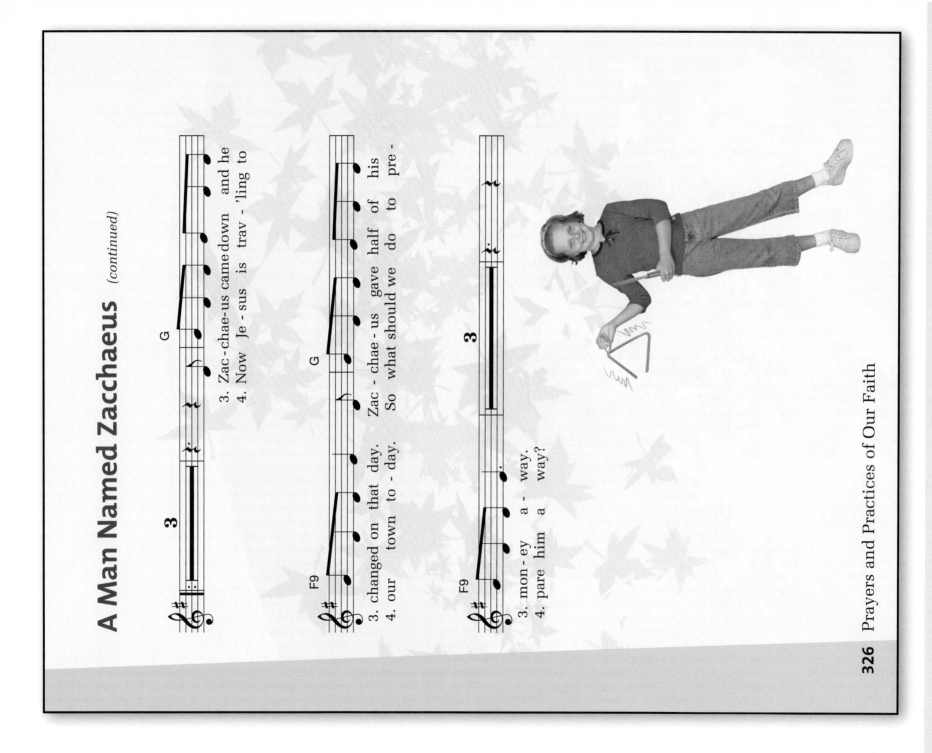

3. Zac - chae - us came down and he
4. Now Je - sus is trav - 'ling to

3. changed on that day. Zac - chae - us gave half of his
4. our town to - day. So what should we do to pre -

3. mon - ey a - way.
4. pare him a way?

For your convenience the pages of the Prayers and Practices section from the Children's Book are reproduced here.

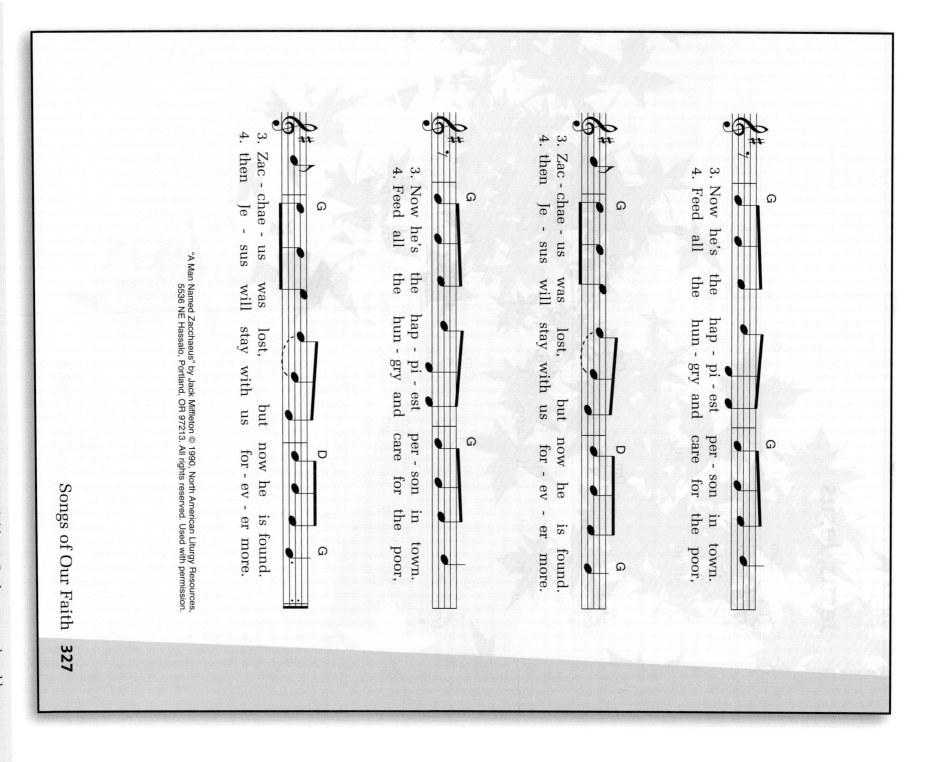

3. Now he's the hap - pi - est per - son in town.
4. Feed all the hun - gry and care for the poor,

3. Zac - chae - us was lost, but now he is found.
4. then Je - sus will stay with us for - ev - er more.

3. Now he's the hap - pi - est per - son in town.
4. Feed all the hun - gry and care for the poor,

3. Zac - chae - us was lost, but now he is found.
4. then Je - sus will stay with us for - ev - er more.

Songs of Our Faith   **327**

For your convenience the pages of the Prayers and Practices section from the Children's Book are reproduced here.

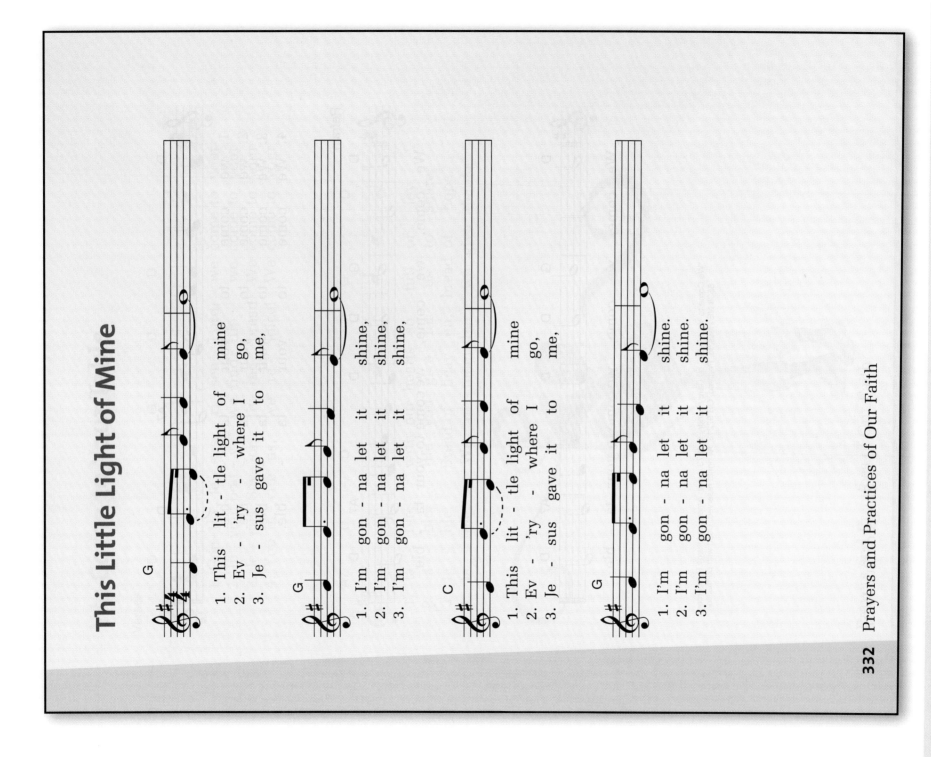

This Little Light of Mine

332 Prayers and Practices of Our Faith

For your convenience the pages of the Prayers and Practices section from the Children's Book are reproduced here.

332 Children's Book Resources

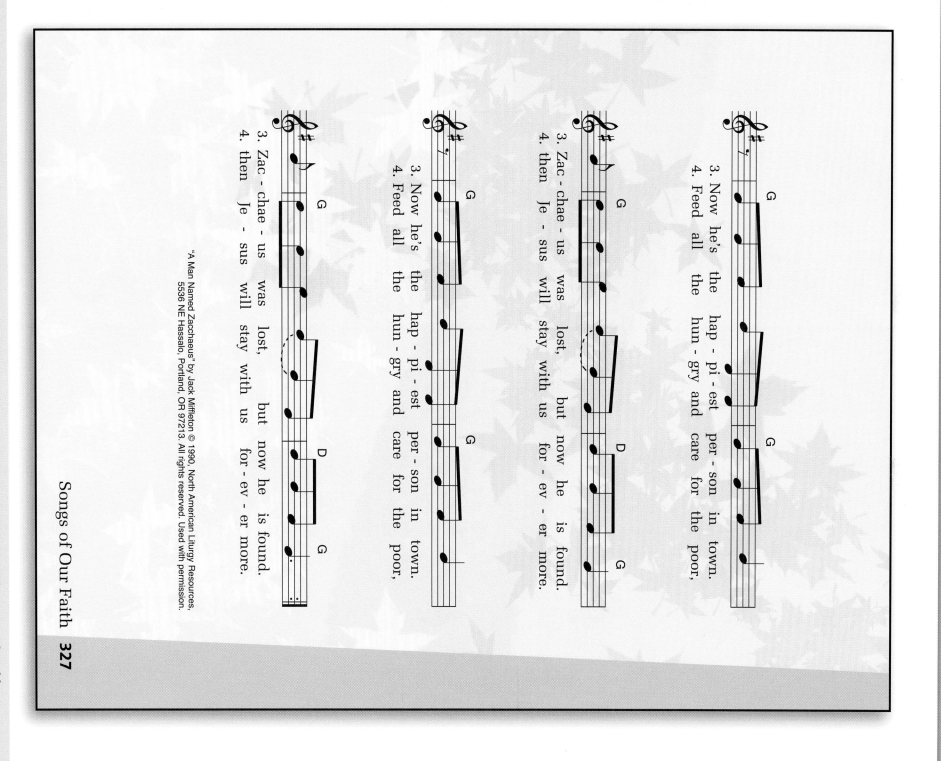

For your convenience the pages of the Prayers and Practices section from the Children's Book are reproduced here.

Jesus, Jesus

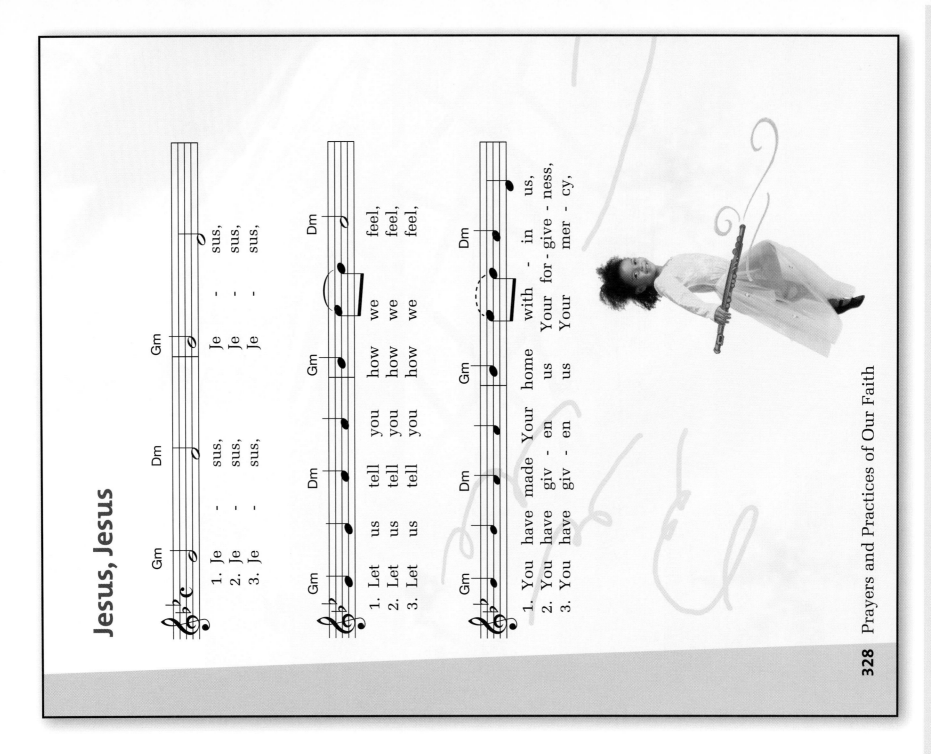

	Gm	Dm	Gm
1.	Je	-	sus,
2.	Je	-	sus,
3.	Je	-	sus,

	Gm	Dm	Gm
1.	Je	-	sus,
2.	Je	-	sus,
3.	Je	-	sus,

	Gm	Dm	Gm	Dm
1.	Let	us	tell	you how we feel,
2.	Let	us	tell	you how we feel,
3.	Let	us	tell	you how we feel,

	Gm	Dm	Gm	Dm
1.	You	have	made Your home with - in us,
2.	You	have	giv - en us Your for - give - ness,
3.	You	have	giv - en us Your mer - cy,

For your convenience the pages of the Prayers and Practices section from the Children's Book are reproduced here.

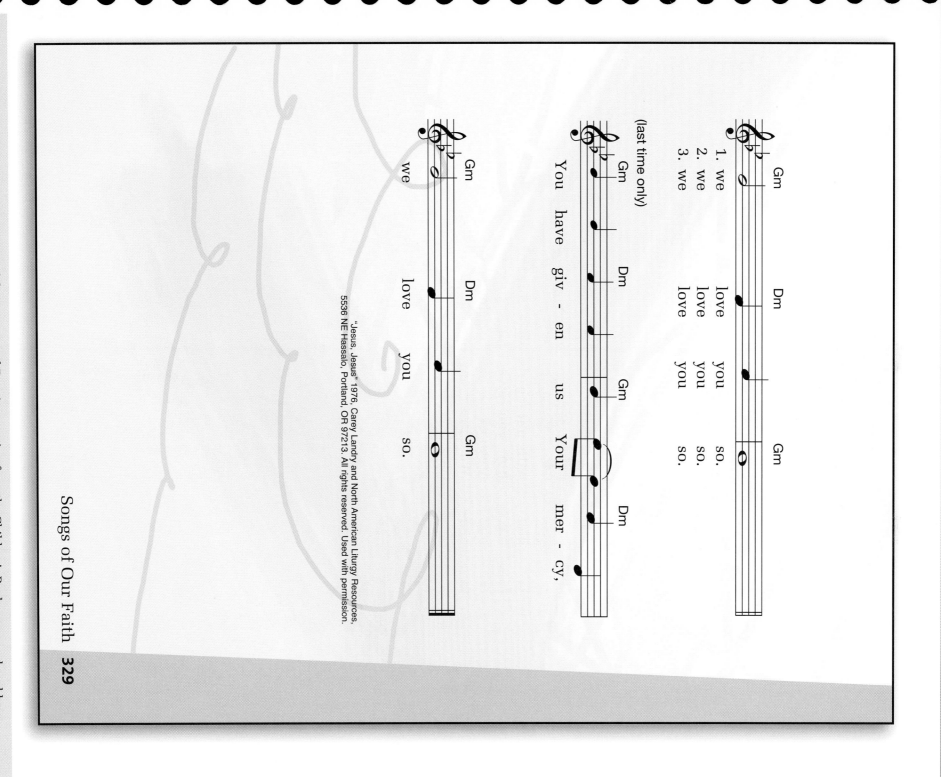

Songs of Our Faith **329**

For your convenience the pages of the Prayers and Practices section from the Children's Book are reproduced here.

Prayers and Practices of Our Faith **329**

We Come to Your Table

Verses

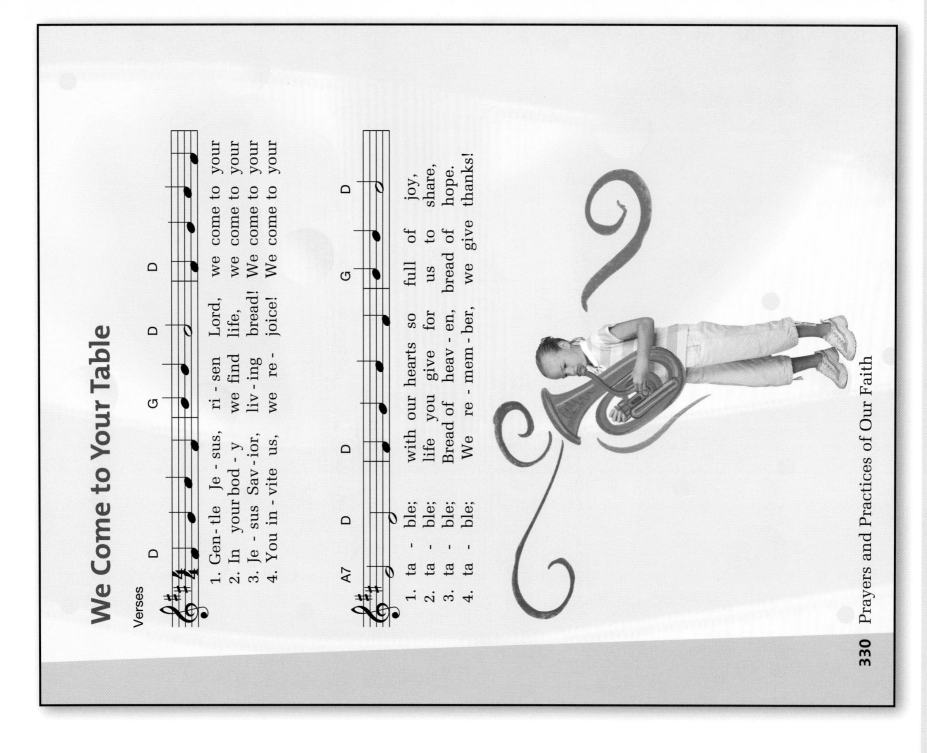

1. Gen-tle Je - sus, ri - sen Lord, we come to your
2. In your bod - y we find life, we come to your
3. Je - sus Sav-ior, liv - ing bread! We come to your
4. You in - vite us, we re - joice! We come to your

1. ta - ble; with our hearts so full of joy,
2. ta - ble; life you give for us to share,
3. ta - ble; Bread of heav - en, bread of hope.
4. ta - ble! We re - mem - ber, we give thanks!

330 Prayers and Practices of Our Faith

For your convenience the pages of the Prayers and Practices section from the Children's Book are reproduced here.

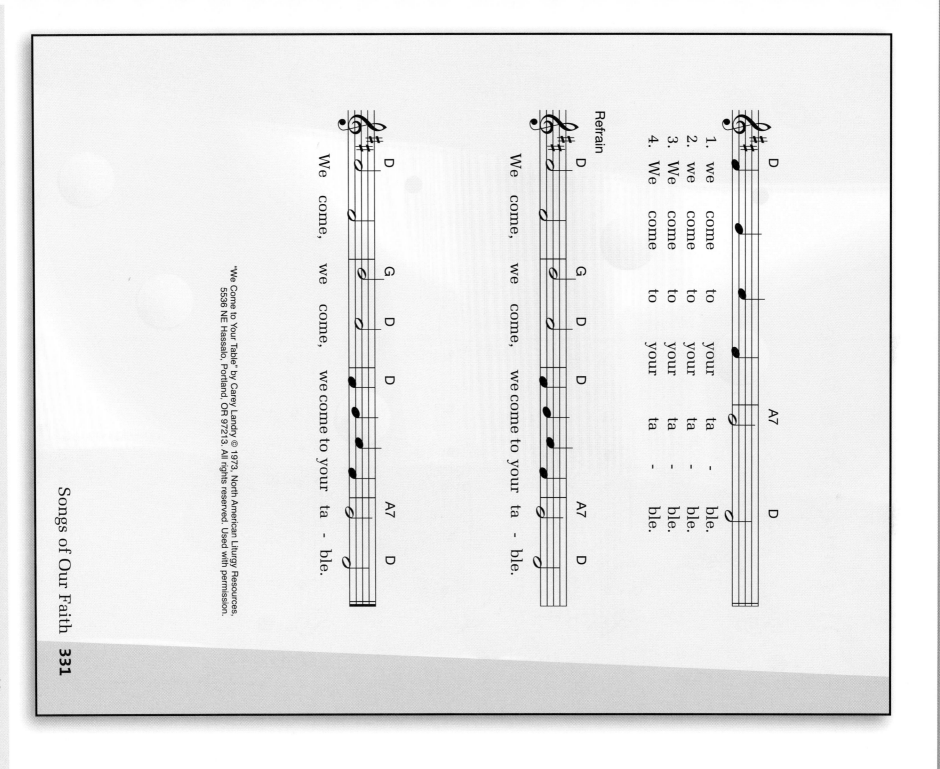

D				A7		D
1. we	come	to	your	ta	-	ble.
2. we	come	to	your	ta	-	ble.
3. We	come	to	your	ta	-	ble.
4. We	come	to	your	ta	-	ble.

Refrain

D ... G D D ... A7 D

We come, we come, we come to your ta - ble.

D ... G D D ... A7 D

We come, we come, we come to your ta - ble.

Songs of Our Faith **331**

This Little Light of Mine

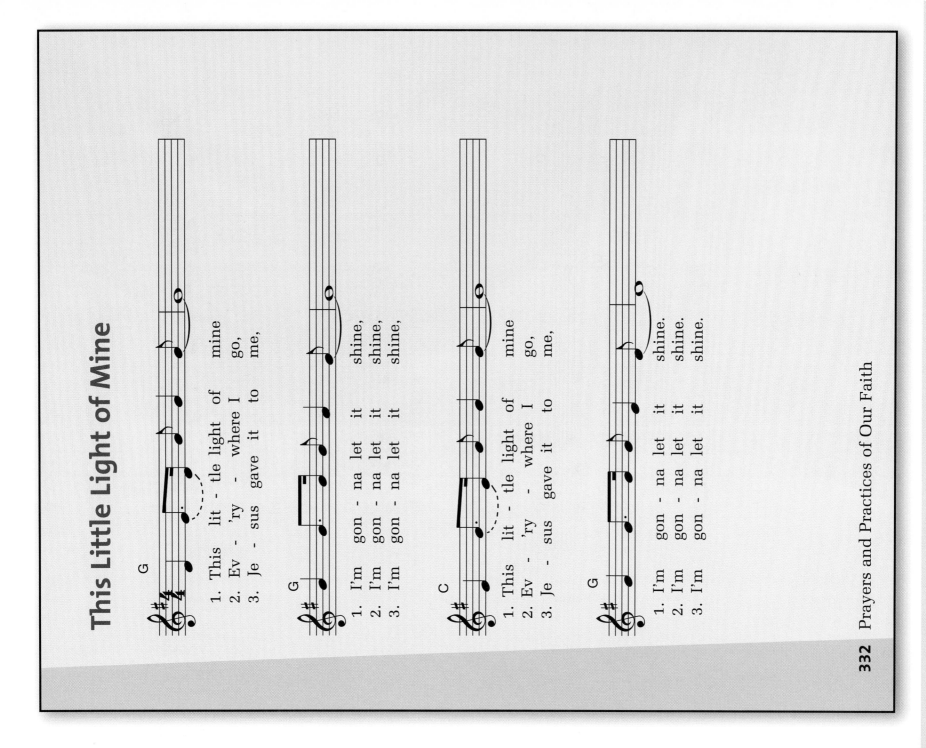

For your convenience the pages of the Prayers and Practices section from the Children's Book are reproduced here.

332 Prayers and Practices of Our Faith

332 Children's Book Resources

For your convenience the pages of the Prayers and Practices section from the Children's Book are reproduced here.

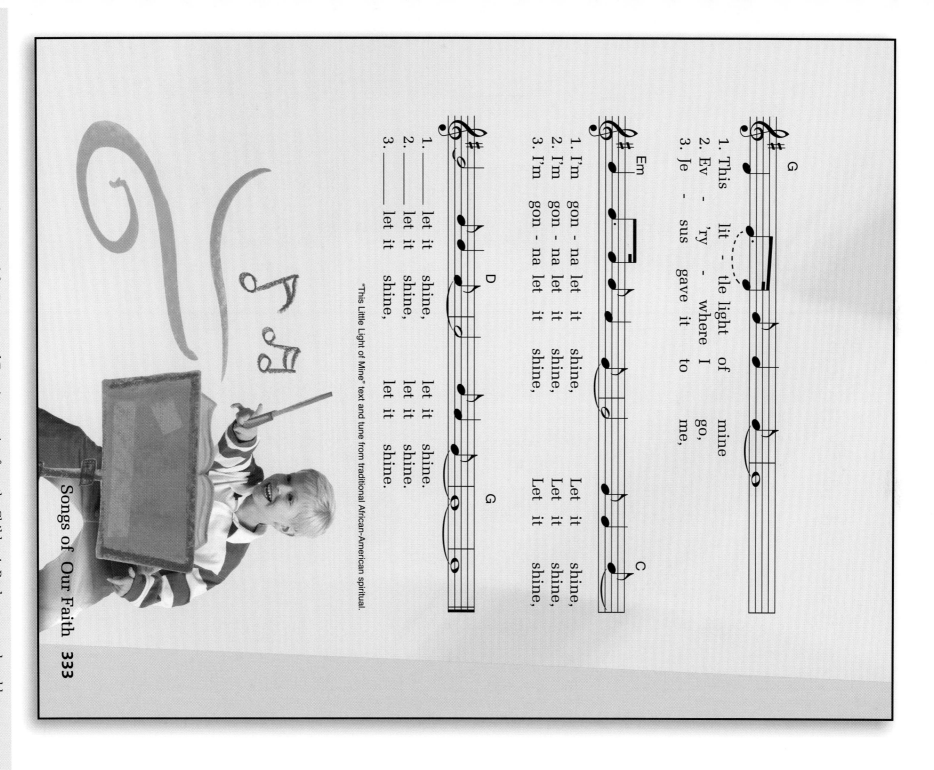

G

1. This lit - tle light of mine
2. Ev - 'ry - where I go,
3. Je - sus gave it to me,

Em

1. I'm gon - na let it shine,
2. I'm gon - na let it shine,
3. I'm gon - na let it shine,

D   G

1. ____ let it shine,   let it shine.
2. ____ let it shine,   let it shine.
3. ____ let it shine,   let it shine.

C

Let it shine,
Let it shine,
Let it shine,

"This Little Light of Mine" text and tune from traditional African-American spiritual.

Songs of Our Faith 333

Jesus' Hands Were Kind Hands

G   G   G   D   G

1. Je - sus' hands were kind hands, do - ing good to all,
2. Take my hands, Lord Je - sus, let them work for you;
3. Je - sus' hands were kind hands, do - ing good to all,
4. Take my hands, Lord Je - sus, let them work for you;

G   G   G   D   G

1. Heal - ing pain and sick - ness, bless - ing chil - dren small.
2. Make them strong and gen - tle, kind in all I do.
3. Heal - ing pain and sick - ness, bless - ing chil - dren small.
4. Make them strong and gen - tle, kind in all I do.

334 Prayers and Practices of Our Faith

For your convenience the pages of the Prayers and Practices section from the Children's Book are reproduced here.

334 Children's Book Resources

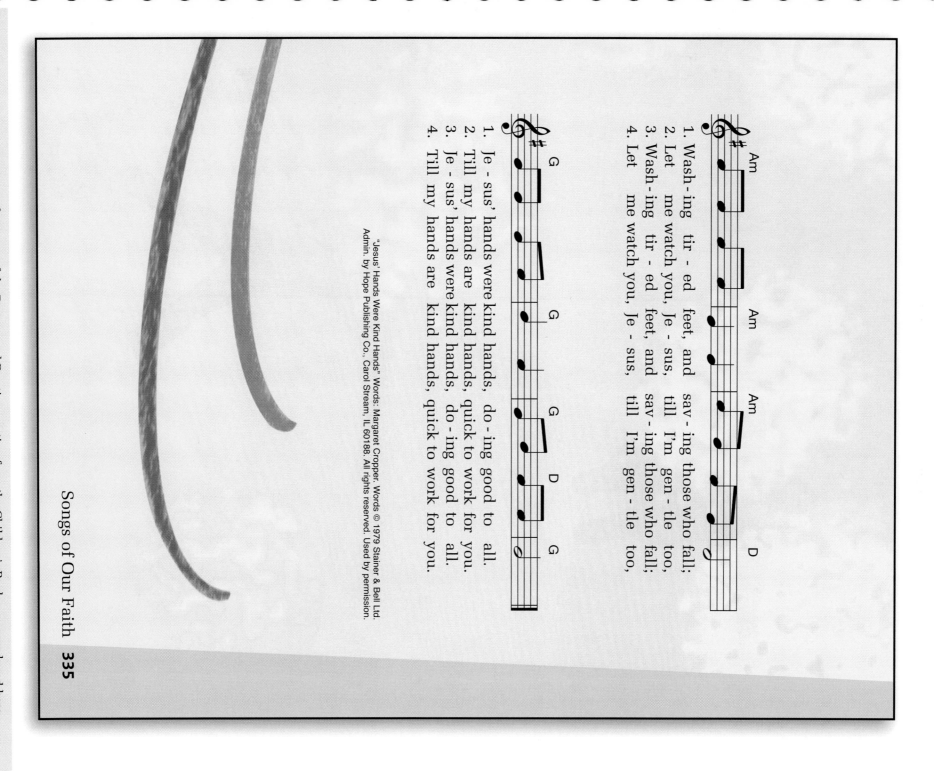

Am   Am   Am   D

1. Wash-ing tir - ed feet, and sav - ing those who fall;
2. Let me watch you, Je - sus, till I'm gen - tle too,
3. Wash-ing tir - ed feet, and sav - ing those who fall;
4. Let me watch you, Je - sus, till I'm gen - tle too,

G   G   G   D   G

1. Je - sus' hands were kind hands, do - ing good to all.
2. Till my hands are kind hands, quick to work for you.
3. Je - sus' hands were kind hands, do - ing good to all.
4. Till my hands are kind hands, quick to work for you.

For your convenience the pages of the Prayers and Practices section from the Children's Book are reproduced here.

Songs of Our Faith

336 Prayers and Practices of Our Faith

For your convenience the pages of the Prayers and Practices section from the Children's Book are reproduced here.

Glossary

A

absolution the forgiveness of God. In the Sacrament of Penance, we say that we are sorry for our sins. Then the priest offers us God's absolution. [absolución]

Advent the four weeks before Christmas. It is a time of joyful preparation for the celebration of Jesus' birth. [Adviento]

Advent wreath

All Saints Day November 1, the day on which the Church honors all who have died and now live with God as saints in heaven. These saints include all those who have been declared saints by the Church and many others known only to God. [Día de Todos los Santos]

All Souls Day November 2, the day on which the Church remembers all who have died as friends of God. We pray that they may rest in peace. [Día de los Muertos]

altar the table in the church on which the priest celebrates Mass. On this table, the bread and wine are offered to God to become the Body and Blood of Jesus Christ. [altar]

ambo a platform from which a person reads the Word of God during Mass [ambón]

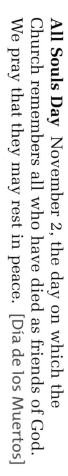

altar

Amen | Blessed Sacrament

Amen the last word in any prayer that we pray. *Amen* means "This is true." We pray "Amen," to show that we really mean the words we have just said. [Amén]

angel a messenger from God [ángel]

Ash Wednesday the first day of Lent, on which we receive ashes on our foreheads to remind us to show sorrow for the choices we make that hurt our friendships with God and others [Miércoles de Ceniza]

B

Baptism the first of the three sacraments by which we become members of the Church. Baptism frees us from original sin and gives us new life in Jesus Christ through the Holy Spirit. [bautismo]

Beatitudes the eight ways we can behave in order to lead a Christian life. Jesus explains that if we live according to the Beatitudes, we are living as his followers. [Bienaventuranzas]

Bible the written story of God's promise to care for us, especially through his Son, Jesus [Biblia]

bishop a leader in the Church. Bishops teach us what God is asking of us as followers of Jesus today. [obispo]

Blessed Sacrament the bread that has been consecrated by the priest at Mass. It is kept in the tabernacle to adore and to be taken to the sick and the dying. [Santísimo Sacramento]

bishop

338   Prayers and Practices of Our Faith

Body and Blood of Christ

Body and Blood of Christ the bread and wine that has been consecrated by the priest at Mass [Cuerpo y Sangre de Cristo]

C

catholic a word that means "all over the world." The Church is catholic because Jesus gave the Church to the whole world. [católico]

Christ a title, like Messiah, that means "anointed with oil." This name is given to Jesus after the Resurrection. [Cristo]

Christian the name given to people who want to live as Jesus taught us to live [cristiano]

Christmas the day on which we celebrate the birth of Jesus [Navidad]

Church the name given to the followers of Christ all over the world. Spelled with a small c, church is the name of the building in which we gather to pray to God. [Iglesia]

commandment a rule that tells us how to live as God wants us to live [mandamiento]

confession the act of telling our sins to a priest in the Sacrament of Penance [confesión]

Confirmation the sacrament that completes the grace we receive in Baptism [confirmación]

conscience the inner voice that helps each of us to know what God wants us to do [conciencia]

Christmas caroling

For your convenience the pages of the Prayers and Practices section from the Children's Book are reproduced here.

consecration | Emmanuel

consecration

consecration the making of a thing or person to be special to God through prayer. At Mass the words of the priest are a consecration of the bread and wine. This makes them the Body and Blood of Jesus Christ. [consagración]

contrition the sadness we feel when we know that we have sinned [contrición]

creation everything that God has made. God said that all of creation is good. [creación]

Creator God, who made everything that is [Creador]

crozier the staff carried by a bishop. This staff shows that the bishop cares for us in the same way that a shepherd cares for his sheep. [báculo]

D

deacon a man who accepts God's call to serve the Church. Deacons help the bishop and priests in the work of the church. [diácono]

disciple a person who is a follower of Jesus and tries to live as he did [discípulo]

E

Easter the celebration of the bodily raising of Jesus Christ from the dead. Easter is the most important Christian feast. [Pascua]

Emmanuel a name that means "God with us." It is a name given to Jesus. [Emanuel]

340 Prayers and Practices of Our Faith

Eucharist the sacrament in which we give thanks to God for giving us Jesus Christ. We receive Jesus Christ in the bread and wine that is blessed at Mass. [Eucaristía]

examination of conscience thinking about what we have said or done that may have hurt our friendship with God or others [examen de conciencia]

F

faith a gift of God. Faith helps us to believe in God and live as he wants us to live. [fe]

forgiveness the act of being kind to people who have hurt us but then have said that they are sorry. God always forgives us when we say that we are sorry. We forgive others the way God forgives us. [perdón]

Fruits of the Holy Spirit the ways in which we act because God is alive in us [frutos del Espíritu Santo]

G

genuflect to show respect in church by touching a knee to the ground, especially in front of the tabernacle [genuflexión, hacer la]

God the Father, Son, and Holy Spirit. God created us, saves us, and lives in us. [Dios]

godparent a witness to Baptism. A godparent helps the baptized person to live as a follower of Jesus. [padrino/madrina de bautismo]

grace the gift of God given to us without our earning it. Sanctifying grace fills us with God's life and makes us his friends. [gracia]

genuflect

For your convenience the pages of the Prayers and Practices section from the Children's Book are reproduced here.

Great Commandment | hope

Great Commandment Jesus' important teaching that we are to love both God and other people [El Mandamiento Mayor]

H

heaven the life with God that is full of happiness and never ends [cielo]

holy showing the kind of life we live when we cooperate with the grace of God [santa]

Holy Communion the consecrated bread and wine that we receive at Mass that is blessed and becomes the Body and Blood of Jesus Christ [Sagrada Comunión]

Holy Days of Obligation those days other than Sundays on which we celebrate the great things God has done for us through Jesus Christ [días de precepto]

Holy Family the family made up of Jesus; his mother, Mary; and his foster father, Joseph [Sagrada Familia]

Holy Spirit the third person of the Trinity, who comes to us in Baptism and fills us with God's life [Espíritu Santo]

holy water the water that has been blessed. It is used to remind us of our Baptism. [agua bendita]

homily an explanation of God's word. A homily explains the words of God that we hear in the Bible readings at church. [homilía]

hope the trust that God will always be with us. We also trust that he will make us happy now and help us to live in a way that keeps us with him forever. [esperanza]

Holy Communion

The Holy Family With Lamb

342 Prayers and Practices of Our Faith

J

Jesus the Son of God, who was born of the Virgin Mary, died, was raised from the dead, and saves us so that we can live with God forever [Jesús]

Joseph the foster father of Jesus, who was engaged to Mary when the angel announced that Mary would have a child through the power of the Holy Spirit [José]

K

Kingdom of God God's rule over us. We experience the Kingdom of God in part now. We will experience it fully in heaven. [Reino de Dios]

L

Last Supper the last meal Jesus ate with his disciples on the night before he died. Every Mass is a remembrance of that last meal. [Última Cena]

Lectionary the book from which the stories from the Bible are read at Mass [Leccionario]

Lent six weeks during which we prepare to celebrate, with special prayers and actions, the rising of Jesus from the dead at Easter. Jesus rose from the dead to save us. [Cuaresma]

liturgy the public prayer of the Church that celebrates the wonderful things God has done for us in Jesus Christ [liturgia]

Liturgy of the Eucharist the second half of the Mass. In this part of the Mass, the bread and wine are blessed and become the Body and Blood of Jesus Christ. We receive the Body and Blood of Jesus Christ in Holy Communion. [liturgia de la Eucaristía]

Lectionary

Liturgy of the Word | mortal sin

Liturgy of the Word the first half of the Mass. During this part of the Mass, we listen to God's Word from the Bible. [Liturgia de la Palabra]

M

Magnificat Mary's song of praise to God. She praises him for the great things he has done for her and planned for us through Jesus. [Magníficat]

Mary the mother of Jesus. She is called "full of grace" because God chose her to be Jesus' mother. [María]

Mass our most important means of praying to God. At Mass we listen to God's Word, the Bible. We receive Jesus Christ in the bread and wine that has been blessed. [Misa]

Messiah a title, like Christ, that means "anointed with oil." *Messiah* also means "Savior." [Mesías]

Mary; The Virgin at Prayer

ministry the service, or work, done for others. Ministry is done by bishops, priests, and deacons in the celebration of the sacraments. All those baptized are called to different kinds of ministry in the liturgy and in serving the needs of others. [ministerio]

moral choice a choice to do what is right. We make moral choices because they are what we believe God wants. [opción moral]

mortal sin a serious choice to turn away from God [pecado mortal]

344 Prayers and Practices of Our Faith

N

New Testament the story of Jesus and the early Church [Nuevo Testamento]

O

Old Testament the story of God's plan for the salvation of all people [Antiguo Testamento]

original sin the result of the sin of Adam and Eve. They disobeyed God and chose to follow their own will rather than God's will. [pecado original]

P

parable one of the simple stories that Jesus told to show us what God wants for the world [parábola]

parish a community of believers in Jesus Christ who meet regularly to worship God together [parroquia]

penance the turning away from sin because we want to live as God wants us to live (See Sacrament of Penance.) [penitencia]

Pentecost the 50th day after Jesus was raised from the dead. On this day the Holy Spirit was sent from heaven, and the Church was born. [Pentecostés]

petition a request of God asking for what we need made with the knowledge that he created us and wants to give us what we need [petición]

pope the bishop of Rome, successor of Saint Peter, and leader of the Roman Catholic Church [Papa]

praise our telling of the happiness we feel simply because God is so good [alabanza]

prayer our talking to God and listening to him in our hearts [oración]

priest | **Sacraments of Initiation**

priest a man who accepts God's special call to serve the Church. Priests guide the Church and lead it in the celebration of the sacraments. [sacerdote]

R

reconciliation making friends again after a friendship has been broken by some action or lack of action. In the Sacrament of Penance, we are reconciled with God, the Church, and others. [reconciliación]

Resurrection the bodily raising of Jesus Christ from the dead on the third day after he died on the cross [Resurrección]

rite the special form followed in celebrating each sacrament [rito]

S

sacrament the way in which God enters our life. Through simple objects such as water, oil, and bread, Jesus continues to bless us. [sacramento]

Sacrament of Penance the sacrament in which we celebrate God's forgiveness of our sins when we say to the priest that we are sorry for them [sacramento de la penitencia]

Sacraments of Initiation the sacraments that make us members of God's Church. They are Baptism, Confirmation, and the Eucharist. [sacramentos de iniciación]

Sacrament of Penance

Prayers and Practices of Our Faith

Sacrifice of the Mass | venial sin

Sacrifice of the Mass the sacrifice of Jesus on the cross. We remember Jesus' sacrifice every time we celebrate Mass. [Sacrificio de la Misa]

saint a holy person who has died as a true friend of God and now lives with God forever [santo]

Savior Jesus, the Son of God, who became human to make us friends with God again. The name *Jesus* means "God saves." [Salvador]

sin a choice we make that hurts our friendships with God and with other people [pecado]

T

tabernacle the container in which the Blessed Sacrament is kept so that Holy Communion can be taken to the sick and the dying [sagrario]

temptation a thought or feeling that can lead us to disobey God. Temptation can come either from outside us or inside us. [tentación]

Ten Commandments the ten rules that God gave to Moses. The Ten Commandments sum up God's law and show us how to live as his children. [Diez Mandamientos]

trespasses acts that harm others [ofensas]

Trinity the mystery of one God, existing in three persons: the Father, the Son, and the Holy Spirit [Trinidad]

V

venial sin a choice we make that weakens our relationship with God or other people [pecado venial]

tabernacle

Glosario

A

absolución perdón de Dios. En el sacramento de la penitencia, después de que decimos que nos arrepentimos de nuestros pecados, el sacerdote nos ofrece la absolución de Dios. [absolution]

Adviento las cuatro semanas antes de la Navidad. Es una época de alegre preparación para la celebración del nacimiento de Jesús. [Advent]

agua bendita agua que ha sido bendecida. Se usa para recordarnos nuestro bautismo. [holy water]

alabanza nuestra expresión de la alegría que sentimos sencillamente porque Dios es muy bueno. [praise]

altar mesa en las iglesias en la que el sacerdote celebra la Misa. En esta mesa, se ofrece a Dios el pan y el vino para que se conviertan en el Cuerpo y Sangre de Jesucristo. [altar]

ambón plataforma desde donde una persona proclama la Palabra de Dios durante la Misa. [ambo]

Amén última palabra de todas las oraciones que rezamos. *Amén* quiere decir "es verdad". Decimos *Amén* para mostrar que lo que acabamos de decir va en serio. [Amen]

ángel mensajero de Dios. [angel]

Antiguo Testamento la historia del plan de Dios para la salvación de toda la gente. [Old Testament]

B

báculo vara que lleva un obispo. Al llevar esta vara, un obispo muestra que cuida de nosotros de la misma forma en que un pastor cuida sus ovejas. [crozier]

Prayers and Practices of Our Faith

bautismo el primero de los tres sacramentos mediante los cuales pasamos a ser miembros de la Iglesia. El bautismo nos libera del pecado original y nos da una vida nueva en Jesucristo por medio del Espíritu Santo. [Baptism]

Biblia historia escrita de la promesa que hizo Dios de cuidar de nosotros, especialmente a través de su Hijo, Jesús. [Bible]

Bienaventuranzas ocho formas en que podemos comportarnos para poder llevar una vida cristiana. Jesús nos explica que, si vivimos según las Bienaventuranzas, vivimos como sus seguidores. [Beatitudes]

C

católica quiere decir "universal". La Iglesia es Católica porque Jesús la ha dado al mundo entero. [catholic]

cielo vida con Dios que está llena de felicidad y que nunca termina. [heaven]

conciencia nuestra voz interior que nos guía a cada uno a hacer lo que Dios nos pide. [conscience]

confesión acto de contar nuestros pecados al sacerdote en el sacramento de la penitencia. [confession]

confirmación sacramento que completa la gracia que recibimos en el bautismo. [Confirmation]

consagración el hacer a una cosa o persona especial ante los ojos de Dios por medio de la oración. En la Misa, las palabras del sacerdote son una consagración del pan y el vino. Esto los convierte en el Cuerpo y Sangre de Jesucristo. [consecration]

For your convenience the pages of the Prayers and Practices section from the Children's Book are reproduced here.

contrición | **diácono**

contrición tristeza que sentimos cuando sabemos que hemos pecado. [contrition]

creación todo lo que hizo Dios. Dios dijo que toda de la creación es buena. [creation]

Creador Dios, quien hizo todo lo que existe. [Creator]

cristiano nombre dado a todos los que quieren vivir como Jesús nos enseñó. [Christian]

Cristo título, que al igual que "El Mesías" significa "el ungido con aceite". Se le dio este título a Jesús después de la resurrección. [Christ]

Cuaresma las seis semanas en las que nos preparamos, con oraciones y acciones especiales, a celebrar en la Pascua la Resurrección de Jesús de entre los muertos. Jesús resucitó para salvarnos. [Lent]

Cuerpo y Sangre de Cristo pan y vino que han sido consagrados por el sacerdote en la Misa. [Body and Blood of Christ]

D

Día de los Muertos el 2 de noviembre, día en que la Iglesia recuerda a todos los que han muerto como amigos de Dios. Oramos por ellos para que descansen en paz. [All Souls Day]

Día de Todos los Santos el 1° de noviembre, día en que la Iglesia recuerda a todos los muertos que pasaron a ser santos y ahora viven con Dios en el cielo. Éstos son todos los muertos que han sido declarados santos por la Iglesia y otros que sólo Dios conoce. [All Saints Day]

diácono varón que acepta la llamada de Dios a servir la Iglesia. Los diáconos ayudan al obispo y a los sacerdotes en el trabajo de la Iglesia. [deacon]

350 Prayers and Practices of Our Faith

For your convenience the pages of the Prayers and Practices section from the Children's Book are reproduced here.

350 Children's Book Resources

días de precepto | examen de conciencia

días de precepto aquellos días que no sean domingos en que celebramos las grandes cosas que Dios ha hecho por nosotros a través de Jesucristo. [Holy Days of Obligation]

Diez Mandamientos diez reglas que Dios dio a Moisés que resumen la ley de Dios y nos muestran cómo vivir como hijos suyos. [Ten Commandments]

Dios Padre, Hijo, y Espíritu Santo. Dios nos creó, Él nos salva, y vive en nosotros. [God]

discípulo persona que sigue a Jesús y trata de vivir de la misma forma en que Él vivió. [disciple]

E

Emanuel nombre que significa "Dios con nosotros". Es el nombre que se le da a Jesús. [Emmanuel]

esperanza confianza de que Dios estará siempre con nosotros. También confiamos en que Él nos dará la felicidad ahora y nos ayudará a vivir de una forma que nos mantendrá con Él para siempre. [hope]

Espíritu Santo tercera persona de la Trinidad, que viene a nosotros en el bautismo y nos llena de la vida de Dios. [Holy Spirit]

Eucaristía sacramento en el cual damos gracias a Dios por habernos dado a Jesucristo. Recibimos a Jesucristo en el pan y el vino que son consagrados en la Misa. [Eucharist]

examen de conciencia el pensar sobre lo que hemos dicho o hecho que pudo haber dañado nuestra amistad con Dios y con otras personas. [examination of conscience]

fe|José

F

fe don de Dios. La fe nos permite creer en Dios y vivir de la forma en que Él quiere que vivamos. [faith]

frutos del Espíritu Santo forma en que actuamos porque Dios vive en nosotros. [Fruits of the Holy Spirit]

G

genuflexión, hacer la forma de mostrar respeto en la iglesia doblando una rodilla y haciéndola tocar el suelo, sobre todo cuando estamos delante del sagrario. [genuflect]

gracia don de Dios que se nos da gratuitamente. La gracia santificante nos llena de la vida de Dios y nos hace sus amigos. [grace]

H

homilía explicación de la Palabra de Dios. Una homilía explica las palabras de Dios que oímos durante las lecturas de la Biblia en la iglesia. [homily]

I

Iglesia nombre que se le da a los seguidores de Jesús por todo el mundo. Si se escribe con "i" minúscula, para referirse al edificio donde nos reunimos para orar. [Church]

J

Jesús Hijo de Dios, que nació de la Virgen María, murió, fue resucitado de entre los muertos, y nos salva para que podamos vivir con Dios para siempre. [Jesus]

José padre adoptivo de Jesús, que estaba desposado con María cuando el ángel anunció que ella tendría un hijo por obra del poder del Espíritu Santo. [Joseph]

352 Prayers and Practices of Our Faith

For your convenience the pages of the Prayers and Practices section from the Children's Book are reproduced here.

L

Leccionario libro del cual se leen en la Misa los relatos de la Biblia. [lectionary]

liturgia oración pública de la Iglesia que celebra las maravillas que Dios ha hecho por nosotros en Jesucristo. [liturgy]

Liturgia de la Eucaristía la segunda de las dos partes de la Misa. En esta parte, se bendice el pan y el vino, que se convierten en el Cuerpo y Sangre de Jesucristo. Luego, recibimos el Cuerpo y Sangre de Cristo en la Sagrada Comunión. [liturgy of the Eucharist]

Liturgia de la Palabra la primera de las dos partes de la Misa. Durante esta parte, oímos la Palabra de Dios en la Biblia. [liturgy of the Word]

M

Magníficat canto de María de alabanza a Dios. Ella lo alaba por las grandes cosas que ha hecho por ella y los grandes planes que ha hecho para nosotros a través de Jesús. [Magnificat]

mandamiento regla que nos muestra cómo vivir de la forma en que Dios quiere que vivamos. [commandment]

El Mandamiento Mayor enseñanza importante de Jesús de amar a Dios y a los demás. [Great Commandment]

María madre de Jesús. Se le dice "llena de gracia" porque Dios la eligió para ser madre de Jesús. [Mary]

Mesías título dado a Jesús, igual que "Cristo", que quiere decir, "ungido". Mesías significa también "Salvador". [Messiah]

Miércoles de Ceniza | oración

Miércoles de Ceniza primer día de Cuaresma en el que se nos coloca ceniza en la frente para que nos acordemos de mostrar arrepentimiento por decisiones que hemos tomado que dañan nuestra amistad con Dios y los demás. [Ash Wednesday]

ministerio servicio, u obra, que se hace para otros. Lo hacen los obispos, sacerdotes, y diáconos en la celebración de los sacramentos. Todos los bautizados son llamados a distintos tipos de ministerio en la liturgia y en el servicio a las necesidades de los demás. [ministry]

Misa la forma más importante de rezar a Dios. En la Misa, oímos la Palabra de Dios en la Biblia y recibimos a Jesucristo en el pan y el vino bendecidos. [Mass]

N

Navidad día en que se festeja el nacimiento de Jesús. [Christmas]

Nuevo Testamento la historia de Jesús y la Iglesia antigua. [New Testament]

O

obispo uno de los líderes de la Iglesia. Los obispos nos enseñan lo que Dios nos pide hoy como seguidores de Jesús. [bishop]

ofensas daño que hacemos a otros. [trespasses]

opción moral el elegir hacer lo que está bien. Elegimos opciones morales porque son lo que creemos que Dios quiere. [moral choice]

oración el hablar con Dios y escucharlo en nuestro corazón. [prayer]

354 Prayers and Practices of Our Faith

padrino/madrina de bautismo

P

padrino/madrina de bautismo testigo de bautismo. El padrino o la madrina ayuda al bautizado a vivir como seguidor de Jesús. [godparent]

Papa el obispo de Roma, sucesor de san Pedro, y cabeza de la Iglesia Católica Romana. [pope]

parábola una de las narraciones sencillas que Jesús contaba que nos muestran lo que Dios quiere para el mundo. [parable]

parroquia comunidad de creyentes en Jesucristo que se reúne regularmente a dar culto a Dios. [parish]

Pascua celebración de la resurrección corporal de Jesucristo de entre los muertos. La Pascua es la fiesta cristiana más importante. [Easter]

pecado decisión que daña nuestra amistad con Dios y con los demás. [sin]

pecado mortal decisión grave que nos aparta de Dios. [mortal sin]

pecado original resultado del pecado de Adán y Eva. Ellos desobedecieron a Dios y decidieron seguir su propia voluntad y no la de Dios. [original sin]

pecado venial decisión que debilita nuestra relación con Dios y los demás. [venial sin]

penitencia el apartarnos del pecado porque queremos vivir de la forma en que Dios quiere que vivamos. (*Véase* sacramento de la penitencia). [penance]

Pentecostés cincuenta días después de la resurrección de Jesús. En este día, el Espíritu Santo fue enviado del cielo y nació la Iglesia. [Pentecost]

perdón | sacramento

perdón acción bondadosa con personas que nos han hecho daño pero que después nos dicen que están arrepentidas. Dios siempre nos perdona cuando decimos que estamos arrepentidos. Nosotros perdonamos a los demás al igual que Dios nos perdona. [forgiveness]

petición pedir a Dios lo que necesitamos, porque Él nos ha creado y quiere darnos lo necesario. [petition]

R

reconciliación volver a ser amigos después de haber roto una amistad por alguna acción o falta de acción. En el sacramento de la penitencia, nos reconciliamos con Dios, la Iglesia, y los demás. [reconciliation]

Reino de Dios dominio de Dios sobre nosotros. Experimentamos hoy el Reino de Dios en parte, pero lo experimentaremos por completo en el cielo. [Kingdom of God]

Resurrección el regreso a la vida del cuerpo de Jesucristo al tercer día después de haber muerto en la cruz. [Resurrection]

rito acciones especiales que hacemos para celebrar cada sacramento. [rite]

S

sacerdote varón que ha aceptado un llamado especial para servir a la Iglesia. Los sacerdotes guían a la Iglesia y presiden la celebración de los sacramentos. [priest]

sacramento forma en que Dios entra en nuestra vida. Por medio de objetos sencillos, como el agua, el aceite, y el pan, Jesús sigue bendiciéndonos. [sacrament]

Prayers and Practices of Our Faith

For your convenience the pages of the Prayers and Practices section from the Children's Book are reproduced here.

sacramento de la penitencia | Santísimo Sacramento

sacramento de la penitencia sacramento en el cual celebramos el perdón de Dios a nuestros pecados cuando decimos a un sacerdote que nos arrepentimos de ellos. [Sacrament of Penance]

sacramentos de iniciación sacramentos que nos hacen miembros de la Iglesia de Dios. Son tres: bautismo, confirmación, y Eucaristía. [Sacraments of Initiation]

Sacrificio de la Misa sacrificio de Jesús en la cruz. Lo recordamos cada vez que celebramos la Misa. [Sacrifice of the Mass]

Sagrada Comunión pan y vino consagrados que recibimos en la Misa, los cuales son bendecidos y se convierten en el Cuerpo y Sangre de Jesucristo. [Holy Communion]

Sagrada Familia familia compuesta por Jesús, su madre María, y su padre adoptivo, José. [Holy Family]

sagrario pieza donde se guarda el Santísimo Sacramento para que la Sagrada Comunión pueda llevarse a los enfermos y a los moribundos. [tabernacle]

Salvador Jesús, el Hijo de Dios, que se hizo hombre para que volvamos a ser amigos con Dios. El nombre *Jesús* quiere decir "Dios salva". [Savior]

santa tipo de vida que vivimos cuando cooperamos con la gracia de Dios. [holy]

Santísimo Sacramento pan que ha sido consagrado por el sacerdote en la Misa. Se guarda en el sagrario para su adoración y para ser llevado a los enfermos y a los moribundos. [Blessed Sacrament]

For your convenience the pages of the Prayers and Practices section from the Children's Book are reproduced here.

Prayers and Practices of Our Faith   357

santo | Última Cena

santo persona virtuosa y ejemplar que ha muerto estando en amistad con Dios y que ahora vive para siempre con Él. [saint]

T

tentación pensamiento o sentimiento que puede llevar a desobedecer a Dios. La tentación puede venir de fuera o de dentro de nosotros mismos. [temptation]

Trinidad misterio de la existencia de un Dios en tres personas: Padre, Hijo, y Espíritu Santo. [Trinity]

U

Última Cena último alimento que compartieron Jesús y sus discípulos en la noche antes de que muriera. Cada Misa es un recordatorio de esa Última Cena. [Last Supper]

358 Prayers and Practices of Our Faith

For your convenience the pages of the Prayers and Practices section from the Children's Book are reproduced here.

Acknowledgments

Excerpts from the English translation of *Rite of Baptism for Children* © 1969, International Commission on English in the Liturgy, Inc. (ICEL); excerpts from the English translation of *The Roman Missal* © 1973, ICEL; excerpts from the English translation of *A Book of Prayers* © 1982, ICEL; excerpts from the English translation of *Book of Blessings* © 1988, ICEL. All rights reserved. Used with permission.

Excerpts from *The New American Bible with Revised New Testament and Psalms* Copyright © 1991, 1986, 1970 Confraternity of Christian Doctrine, Inc., Washington, DC. Used with permission. All rights reserved. No portion of the *New American Bible* may be reprinted without permission in writing from the copyright holder.

115 "Peace of Patience" from *Journey Through Heartsongs* by Mattie Stepanek. Copyright © 2003 by Mattie Stepanek. Reprinted by permission of Hyperion.

Illustration

Peter Church: 14, 15, 16, 18, 34, 35, 38, 50, 52, 53, 54, 62, 64, 72, 73, 82, 83, 86-87, 110, 111, 120, 121, 130, 131, 148, 158, 178, 196-197, 207, 216-217, 226, 247, 248, 251, 255, 256, 263, 264
Doron Ben Ami: 289, 298-299, 308-309
Julie Downing: 9, 63, 65, 101, 104-105, 129, 141, 147, 149, 159, 182-183, 184, 207, 209, 231, 238, 245, 250, 254, 260, 272, 273, 286, 291, 292, 295, 307
Jim Effler: 4, 5, 7, 24, 25, 43, 286-287, 288-289
Tom Foty: 13, 19, 29, 55, 58, 79, 116, 119, 124-125, 134, 136, 142, 153, 157, 161, 162, 163, 164, 167, 168, 169, 170, 180, 187, 190-191, 198, 199, 208, 228, 235, 244, 253, 265, 266, 267, 277, 283, 290, 291, 292, 293, 294
Ed Gazsi: 1, 2, 49, 50, 74, 97, 98, 145, 146, 193, 194, 219, 226, 229
Fran Gregory: 282, 283
Vitali Konstantinov: 241
David LaFleur: 280, 281
John Stevens: 46, 220, 221, 290, 291, 292, 293, 294, 295, 306
Olwyn Whelan: 9, 19, 39, 45, 57, 71, 74, 85, 92, 133, 173, 189, 200, 245, 257, 278

Photography

Unless otherwise acknowledged, photographs are the property of Loyola Press. Page positions are abbreviated as follows: (t) top, (m) middle, (b) bottom, (l) left, (r) right, (l-r) left to right, (bkgr) background, (ins) inset, (cl) clockwise from top right, (all) all images on page.

UNIT 1: 2 (bkgr) © Georg Gerster/Photo Researchers. **3** (cl) photodisc/ Getty Images; © Russell Kaye/Getty Images. **3** © Phil Martin Photography; photodisc/Getty Images; © Royalty-Free/CORBIS. **6** © Stephen Simpson/ Getty Images; (ins) photodisc/Getty Images. **8** (l) photodisc/Getty Images; (m) © Tom & Dee Ann McCarthy/CORBIS; (bkgr) © W. Wayne Lockwood M.D./Getty Images. **9** (bkgr) © W. Wayne Lockwood M.D./Getty Images. **10** Courtesy of Subaru Telescope, National Astronomical Observatory of Japan. **11** © Peter Corez/Getty Images; (ins) photodisc/Getty Images. **12** (bl) photodisc/Getty Images; (tr) © The Crosiers/Gene Plaisted OSC; (mr) © Jeff Greenberg/Index Stock; (br) © Myrleen F. Cate/PhotoEdit. **13** (br) photodisc/Getty Images. **17** © Phil Martin Photography. **20** © Rick Elkin/Getty Images. **21** © Phil Martin Photography. **22** (tl) Fr. William Hart McNichols; (ml) © Tony Freeman/PhotoEdit; (bl) Courtesy Hugo Gutierrez Cordero, Peru; (r) photodisc/Getty Images. **23** © Jose Carillo/PhotoEdit. **26** (l) © Myrleen F. Cate/Index Stock Imagery/PictureQuest. (r) © Peter Cade/Getty Images; (bkgr) Peter Miller/Panoramic Images. **27** (bkgr) Peter Miller/Panoramic Images; (ins) © Phil Deggenger. **28** © Yann Arthus-Bertrand/ CORBIS. **30** Jesse Ceballos/SuperStock. **32** (tl) © Norbert Schaefer/ CORBIS; (bl) © Raoul Minsart/CORBIS; (r) © Myrleen F. Cate/PhotoEdit. **33** (l) © Phil Martin Photography; (r) © Arthur Tilley/Getty Images. **36** (cl) © AJA Productions/Getty Images; (r) © Phil Martin Photography; (m) © Laura Dwight/PhotoEdit; (bkgr) photodisc/ Getty Images. **37** (cl) © Owen Franken/Getty Images; © Mark Segal/Getty Images; © Walter Hodges/Getty Images; (bkgr) photodisc/Getty Images.

40 © Phil Martin Photography. **41** © Robert E. Daemmrich/Getty Images; (leaves) photodisc/Getty Images. **42** (tl) © Cameraphoto/Art Resource, NY; © The Crosiers/Gene Plaisted OSC; (r) photodisc/Getty Images. **43** (ins, r) photodisc/Getty Images; (ins, b) © Myrleen F. Cate/PhotoEdit. **44** Woo Ching Man, 11, Hong Kong. From the worldwide competition: "Children of the World Illustrate the Bible" by MallMedia publishing house, www.bible2000.com. **47** © Phil Martin Photography. **48** © Phil Martin Photography.

UNIT TWO: 51 (tl) © Jeff Greenberg/PhotoEdit. (bl) © David Young-Wolff/PhotoEdit. (r) © Cameron/CORBIS. **56** (t) © Vie de Jésus Mafa/ Images. **59** (t) © Inc. G&J Images/Getty Images. **60** (l) © Don Hammond/CORBIS. (tr) © Hoa Qui/Index Stock Imagery/PictureQuest. **61** (cl) © Ross Whitaker; © Michael Newman/PhotoEdit; photodisc/Getty Images. **65** Dennis DeBasco, Abbot, Inclusive Orthodox Church. **66** (bkgr) © Dave G. Houser/CORBIS; all other photos courtesy family of Carlos Rodriguez Santiago. **67** © Dave G. Houser/CORBIS; all other photos courtesy family of Carlos Rodriguez Santiago. **68** © Myrleen F. Cate/PhotoEdit. **69** (t) © Robert Bremner/PhotoEdit. (m) photodisc/Getty Images. **70** (tl) © Tate Gallery, London/Art Resource, NY; (m) photodisc/ Getty Images; (br) photodisc/Getty Images. **71** (t) photodisc/Getty Images; (tr) © Arthur Tilley/Getty Images. **75** (t) Vittoriano Rastelli/CORBIS. (tr) © Bettmann/CORBIS; (br) SIPA Press. **76** (tl) photodisc/Getty Images; (ml) © Jim Stipe; (r) Reprinted with the Permission of Bread for the World; (bkgr) photodisc/Getty Images. **77** (t) © Margaret Nea; (bkgr) photodisc/Getty Images. **78** © Annie Griffiths Belt/CORBIS. **80** (l) © Jose Luis Pelaez, Inc./CORBIS; (tr) © AFP/CORBIS. (mr) photodisc/Getty Images; (br) © Richard Hutchings/PhotoEdit. **84** © John H. White. **88** © Phil Martin Photography. **89** (t) photodisc/Getty Images. Bridwell/PhotoEdit; (m) photodisc/Getty Images. **90** (l) photodisc/Getty Images; (tr) Elizabeth Lee Hudgins/iconsofthefaith.com; (bl) photodisc/ Getty Images. **91** © Steve Niedorf/Getty Images; (t) © Yellow Dog Productions/Getty Images. **93** (t) © Royalty-free/CORBIS; (bl) © Phil Martin Photography. (r) © Royalty-free/CORBIS. **95** © The Crosiers/Gene Plaisted OSC. **96** © The Crosiers/Gene Plaisted OSC.

UNIT 3: 98 © John Quinn SJ. **99** (t) © Myrleen F. Cate/PhotoEdit; (m) © Richard Hutchings/CORBIS; (b) © Myrleen F. Cate/PhotoEdit. **100** (l) © Myrleen F. Cate/PhotoEdit. (tr) © Phil Martin Photography. **102** (cl) © Myrleen F. Cate/PhotoEdit; photodisc/Getty Images; photodisc/ Getty Images; (br) photodisc/Getty Images. **103** © Stephen McBrady/ PhotoEdit. **106** © Robert Houser/Index Stock Imagery/PictureQuest. **108** (l) Courtesy of The Christophers; (tr) © The Crosiers/Gene Plaisted OSC; (mr) photodisc/Getty Images; (br) photodisc/Getty Images. **109** (br) photodisc/Getty Images. **114** (cl) © Myrleen F. Cate/PhotoEdit. **115** © Steve/Mary Skjold/Index Stock; (bkgr) photodisc/Getty Images. **118** (tl) © Hurewitz Creative/CORBIS; (mr) © Jeff Greenberg/PhotoEdit. (tr) © The Crosiers/Gene Plaisted OSC; (mr) photodisc/Getty Images; (br) photodisc/Getty Images. **126** © Anthony Moreland/Getty Images. **127** © Jim Whitmer Photography. **128** (tl) © James Frank/Stock Connection/PictureQuest; (bl) © Joel Sartore/ CORBIS; (tr) Courtesy of National Library of Greece; (br) © Peter Hince/ Getty Images. **129** (cl) © The Crosiers/Gene Plaisted OSC; (r) © Myrleen F. Cate/PhotoEdit; photodisc/Getty Images; photodisc/Getty Images; (bl) © Jonathan Nourok/PhotoEdit. **133** © The Crosiers/Gene Plaisted OSC. **135** (cl) Archives Charmet/The Bridgeman Art Library; (m) © 2003 Passionist Research Center/Fr. John T. Render C.P., D.Min; (b) © The Crosiers/Gene Plaisted OSC. **138** (t) Scala/Art Resource, NY; (b) © FPG International/Getty Images. **139** (t) photodisc/Getty Images; (r) © David Young-Wolff/PhotoEdit. **143** © Phil Martin Photography. **144** © David Young-Wolff/PhotoEdit.

UNIT 4: 146 (bkgr) © Dennis Degnan/CORBIS. **147** (l) © Bonnie Kamin/ PhotoEdit; (r) © Julie Habel/CORBIS. **149** (br) © Maureen Collins Photography. **150** (m) © Phil Martin Photography. **151** photodisc/Getty Images. **154** © Stephen Frank/CORBIS. **155** © Omni Photo Communications Inc./ Index Stock. **156** (tl) © Tony Hamblin/CORBIS; (ml) © Stephen Derr/Getty Images; (bl) © The Crosiers/Gene Plaisted OSC; (r) photodisc/Getty Images. **160** (l) © The Crosiers/Gene Plaisted OSC. **166** (l) © Regine M./Getty

Acknowledgments

Images; (tr) Vatican Museum of Modern Art; (mr) © The Crosiers/Gene Plaisted OSC; (br) photodisc/Getty Images. **171** (bkgr) photodisc/Getty Images. **173** © Farrell Grehan/CORBIS. **174** © Jim Whitmer Photography. **175** © Phyllis Picardi/Index Stock Imagery/PictureQuest. **176** (tl) © The Crosiers/Gene Plaisted OSC; (bl) © Jeff Greenberg/PhotoEdit; (tr) © Mark E. Gibson/CORBIS; (br) © SW Production/Index Stock. **177** (tl) © John Terence Turner/Getty Images; (tr) © Earl Kowall/CORBIS. **181** (tl) © Chip Henderson/Index Stock Imagery/PictureQuest; (bl) photodisc/Getty Images; (tr) photodisc/Getty Images; (br) © Myrleen F. Cate/PhotoEdit. **182** (t) © Paul Hardy/CORBIS; (b) Thesing/Courtesy of Maryknoll Fathers & Brothers. **183** (tl) Fedora/Courtesy of Maryknoll Fathers & Brothers; (bl) Towle/Courtesy of Maryknoll Fathers & Brothers; (tr) © Cameramann, Int'l/Milton & Joan Mann; (mr) Sprague, Courtesy of Maryknoll Fathers & Brothers; (br) Danaher/Courtesy of Maryknoll Fathers & Brothers. **185** (tr) © Brett Froomer; (mr) photodisc/Getty Images. **186** (tl) © Cameramann, Int'l/Milton & Joan Mann; (bl) V.C.L./Paul Viant/Getty Images; (tr) © The Crosiers/Gene Plaisted OSC; (br) © The Crosiers/Gene Plaisted OSC. **192** (r) © Tony Freeman/PhotoEdit; (m) photodisc/Getty Images.

UNIT 5: 194 (bkgr) © Vanni Archive/CORBIS. **195** (l) © Myrleen F. Cate/PhotoEdit; (r) © Richard Hutchings/PhotoEdit. **201** © Michael Sarnacki/Jesuit Volunteers Corp. **202** photodisc/Getty Images. **204** (tl) © Coll. Kroller-Muller Museum, Otterlo; (bl) © Joe McBride/CORBIS; (tr) © Steve Chenn/CORBIS; (br) photodisc/Getty Images. **207** © Phil Martin Photography. **213** Courtesy Dahri Nelson/Trinity Lutheran School, Waconia, MN. **214** (tl) © Scala, Art Resource, NY; (ml) © The Crosiers/Gene Plaisted OSC; (bl) photodisc/Getty Images; (r) photodisc/Getty Images. **215** © Frank Simonetti/Stock Connection/PictureQuest. **218** © Dave Nagel/Getty Images. **222** © Phil Martin Photography. **223** © Jeff Greenberg/PhotoEdit. **224** (tl) © Ronnie Kaufmann/CORBIS; (bl) © The Crosiers/Gene Plaisted OSC; (tr) © AP/Wide World Photos; (br) © Ronnie Kaufman/CORBIS. **232** © Martin Rogers/CORBIS. **234** (bl) © Phil Martin Photography; (tr) Courtesy Dr. Alex Wengraf, London; (br) © The Crosiers/Gene Plaisted OSC. **236** © Jim Cummins/Getty Images. **238** (bkgr) © Randy Wollenmann. **239** (bkgr) © Randy Wollenmann.

THE YEAR IN OUR CHURCH: 242 (mb) Cameramann, Int'l/Milton & Joan Mann; (b) photodisc/Getty Images. **246** © Jim Whitmer Photography. **249** (t) © Earl & Nazima Kowall/CORBIS. **252** © Tim Pannell/CORBIS. **258** (bkgr) photodisc/Getty Images. **259** (ins) © He Qi, www.heqiarts.com. **261** (t) © The Crosiers/Gene Plaisted OSC. **262** © Doug Menuez/Getty Images. **267** (cl) © Walter Hodges/CORBIS; © Myrleen F. Cate/PhotoEdit; © Michael Newman/PhotoEdit. **269** photodisc/Getty Images. **270** © The Crosiers/Gene Plaisted OSC.

END MATTER: 271 (t) © Myrleen F. Cate/Index Stock Imagery/PictureQuest; (b) Peter Miller/Panoramic Images. **272** (bkgr) Peter Miller/Panoramic Images. **273** (bkgr) Peter Miller/Panoramic Images. **274** © Hot Ideas/Index Stock. **275** © Peter Cade/Getty Images. **276** (tr) photodisc/Getty Images. **277** (tr) © Phil Degginger/Getty Images. **278** (r) © The Crosiers/Gene Plaisted OSC. **284** (bkgr) © Phil Martin Photography. **285** (bkgr) © Phil Martin Photography. **289** (b) © Maureen Collins Photography. **300** (l) © Bill Wittman; (mr) © Bill Wittman. **301** (bl) © Bill Wittman; (m) © Bill Wittman. **304** (bkgr) © Oliver Ribardiere/Getty Images; (bl) © Bill Wittman. **305** (bkgr) © Oliver Ribardiere/Getty Images; (r) © Jonathan Nourok/PhotoEdit.

GLOSSARY: 337 (t) © Mary Kate Denny/PhotoEdit. **339** © Kindra Clineff/Index Stock. **340** © The Crosiers/Gene Plaisted OSC. **342** (t) © The Crosiers/Gene Plaisted OSC; (b) © Archivo Iconografico, S.A./CORBIS. **344** © Christie's Images/CORBIS. **346** © The Crosiers/Gene Plaisted OSC.

All photographs (except tabletop/still life) not listed above were taken by Phil Martin Photography.

All tabletop/still life photographs not listed above were taken by Greg Kuepfer.

For your convenience the pages of the Prayers and Practices section from the Children's Book are reproduced here.

CD Scripts

Based on Matthew 6:25–34

Trust in God

Time: 2 min. 46 sec.

NARRATOR: Wherever Jesus went, people followed to listen to his teachings. One day he sat down on a large hill, and the people surrounded him on the hillside. He looked out at the crowd and spoke loud enough for everyone to hear.

JESUS: Don't worry about everyday life—whether you have enough to eat or drink or enough clothes to wear. Isn't there a lot more to life than food and clothes?

For instance, look at the birds. You don't see them planting gardens or sewing little bird clothes, do you? Of course not! They don't go out and buy lots and lots of food, because God feeds them. He provides bugs and worms and seeds all around them. Now, don't you think you're more important to God than pigeons and crows and sparrows? If you worry all the time, do you think that will help you live longer? Of course it won't.

NARRATOR: Then Jesus motioned to the bright wildflowers in the grass all around them.

JESUS: And why worry about your clothes? Look at how all the flowers grow. They don't work or go

shopping. But the richest person in the world couldn't look more beautiful than the flowers, in all their colors and shapes and sizes. And if God cares so much for the flowers that bloom for just a few days, how much more do you think he cares about you? When you worry so much, you're not really trusting God, are you?

NARRATOR: Many of the people looked a little embarrassed as they thought about how much they did worry about things.

JESUS: So don't worry about having enough food or drink or clothes. Your heavenly Father already knows everything you need, and he will give you those things one day at a time, if you give your life to him. When you live in fear and worry you are acting more like people who don't believe in God at all.

It's silly to worry about tomorrow, because it hasn't even happened yet. When tomorrow comes, you can think about tomorrow and whatever worries or troubles it brings. You have enough to think about today.

Recorded Scripture Stories

Based on Luke 2:41–52

Jesus With the Teachers

Time: 4 min. 11 sec.

NARRATOR: The young boy Jesus lived in Nazareth with his parents, Mary and Joseph. Every year they traveled to the city of Jerusalem, and there they celebrated the Jewish festival called Passover. Mary, Joseph, and Jesus, and many of their friends and family in Nazareth made the trip together. They walked or they rode in wagons or on donkeys, and the journey took three or four days.

When Jesus was 12 years old, the family went to the festival, just like always. They traveled with a large group to Jerusalem. And when the festival was over, Mary and Joseph started the trip back to Nazareth. They didn't notice that Jesus had stayed behind in Jerusalem. They didn't notice that he was missing until they were nearly a day's journey away from the city.

MARY: Joseph, have you seen Jesus?

JOSEPH: No. Not since early this morning when we were packing to go back home.

MARY: I haven't seen him all day.

JOSEPH: He's probably with his cousins.

MARY: I've already asked them. They haven't seen him either.

NARRATOR: So Mary and Joseph looked through the whole group of travelers, but they couldn't find Jesus. Now they were truly worried.

MARY: Joseph, he's only 12. We've got to go find him. Maybe he's hurt or sick.

JOSEPH: You're right. All we can do is retrace our steps, all the way back to Jerusalem if we have to.

NARRATOR: So Mary and Joseph went back to Jerusalem and searched for their son. They looked everywhere they thought a young boy might be. They asked everyone they met, but no one had seen Jesus. Finally, three days later, they went to the Temple where they had worshiped God together. Mary was nearly sick from worry. Joseph was tired and scared.

JOSEPH: Someone must have seen him. So many people come here to the Temple—we'll just stand here and ask every person we see.

NARRATOR: Then Mary's eyes grew wide, and she pointed towards a group of ministers and teachers.

MARY: Is that him?

NARRATOR: She and Joseph ran over to the group. And sure enough, there was Jesus. He was discussing religion with all of these wise teachers! And the teachers were listening carefully to what Jesus had to say.

Mary and Joseph broke into the group and wrapped their arms around their son.

MARY: Son, why have you done this to us? We've been worried sick about you! We've been looking for you for days!

JESUS: Why were you looking for me? Didn't you know I'd be here, in my Father's house?

JOSEPH: What are you saying?

JESUS: Why did you worry? I was right here in my Father's house.

NARRATOR: Joseph and Mary really didn't understand what Jesus was talking about. But Jesus went home with them. Mary thought about all that had happened. As the years went by, she remembered this experience. And she remembered what Jesus had said that day.

Jesus stayed with his parents in Nazareth. He was a good, obedient son. He made friends and studied hard. People had a lot of respect for Jesus. They liked him a lot, and they watched him grow up and become wiser with each passing year. He lived in a way that made God and his parents very happy.

This script is provided for your reference and convenience.

Jesus Heals

Time: 5 min. 30 sec.

NARRATOR: Jesus had been traveling around the country, healing people and teaching them about God. One day Jesus came home to Capernaum, and when people found out that he was home they came to see him. They had heard all about how Jesus could heal the sick. They had also heard that he was a great teacher. They wanted to hear Jesus for themselves. That day so many people gathered in the house where Jesus was teaching that there wasn't even room for one more person. There wasn't even room in the doorways. Outside the house, four men tried to figure out what to do. They had brought their friend with them. He was paralyzed—he couldn't move at all. And his four friends carried him on a stretcher. They hoped that Jesus would heal him.

FRIEND #1: We'll never get through this crowd.

FRIEND #2: Tell people that it's an emergency. We've got a paralyzed man here who needs for Jesus to heal him.

FRIEND #3: No one's paying any attention. They're listening to every word Jesus says. And besides, there are a lot of other people who came for healing too. Everyone is desperate to see Jesus.

NARRATOR: They looked down at their paralyzed friend. They could see that he was very sad. But he tried to make them feel better.

PARALYTIC: That's all right. At least you tried to get me to the teacher. But this is too much trouble. Just take me home.

FRIEND #4: No! We're not turning back now. There's got to be a way.

NARRATOR: Then they saw the ladder. It led up to the roof of the house. All of the houses in that part of the country had flat roofs, and the roofs were made of mud and dried grass. The four men looked at the ladder, and they looked up at the roof.

FRIEND #4: If we can't go through the door, let's go through the roof!

FRIEND #1: I don't know—do we really want to tear up someone's roof?

FRIEND #3: We'll repair it when we're through! We patch our own roofs all the time.

FRIEND #1: He's right. Whatever we damage, we can fix. But our friend's body is much more important than a straw roof—and we can't do anything to help him walk again. Only the teacher, Jesus, can do that.

NARRATOR: So the four friends very carefully carried the man on the stretcher up to the roof of the house. They tore a hole in the straw, big enough

that they could tie ropes to the stretcher and lower it through. As they worked, straw and dried mud fell on the people inside the house. Well, everyone looked up.

PERSON #1: Would you look at that!

PERSON #2: Everyone get out of the way! There's a sick man coming down!

NARRATOR: As the stretcher reached the ground, Jesus stood up and came to stand over the paralyzed man. He looked at the man, and then he looked up at the man's four friends who were looking down through the hole in the roof.

JESUS: My son, God forgives you for all the bad things you've done or said or even thought.

NARRATOR: It happened that some religious leaders were in the room—they had come to hear Jesus teach. But when he told the man on the stretcher that God forgave him, the leaders got upset. They didn't say anything, but they were thinking, *Huh, who is this man who thinks he can speak for God?*

NARRATOR: Well, Jesus knew exactly what they were thinking. He looked straight at the religious leaders.

JESUS: Why are you thinking such things? Which is harder—to tell a man that God forgives him, or to tell him to get off his stretcher and walk? You see, I *do* speak for God. And to prove to you that God has given me the authority to speak for him—

NARRATOR: Jesus turned suddenly to the paralyzed man—

JESUS: I say to you, get up. Then pick up this stretcher and go home.

NARRATOR: And that's exactly what the man did! He listened to what Jesus said to him, and he immediately got up from the stretcher.

PERSON #1: We've never seen anything like this.

NARRATOR: The four men did patch the hole that they made in the roof. But hardly anyone was thinking about the roof anymore. For days, and even years later, they would talk about the man Jesus had healed, the paralyzed man who picked up his own stretcher and walked home.

The man was so full of joy! He laughed and he walked around the room. He waved at his friends up on the roof. They were staring down at him and could hardly believe their eyes.

PARALYZED MAN: Thank you, Teacher.

NARRATOR: He picked up his stretcher then, and the crowd moved aside to let him leave the house and go home.

Recorded Scripture Stories

Based on Luke 24: 13–35

Inviting Jesus to Dinner

Time: 4 min. 53 sec.

NARRATOR: Two of Jesus' followers were walking to the village of Emmaus, about seven miles from Jerusalem. They were talking about all the things that had happened during the past few days.

PERSON #1: What do you think Jesus' special group of disciples will do now that he's gone? For three years they've done nothing but go with Jesus everywhere. They've heard all his teachings and watched his miracles.

PERSON #2: I can't imagine how they feel. They had such hopes for Jesus. In just a day or so he was arrested, taken to trial, and executed. No one expected such a horrible thing to happen to this great man of God.

NARRATOR: While they were talking and debating about what would happen now, Jesus himself came walking up beside them on the road.

JESUS: Excuse me, but you seem to be discussing something very important. What are you talking about?

NARRATOR: Well, the two people were unable to recognize Jesus. When he asked the question, they stopped and looked away sadly.

PERSON #1: Are you the only visitor in Jerusalem who doesn't know about all the things that happened there during the past few days?

JESUS: What things are you talking about?

PERSON #2: All that happened to Jesus the Nazarene. He was a prophet! He performed mighty works and spoke with great wisdom. He was sent from God—

PERSON #1: But our chief priests and leaders turned him over to the authorities, and before anyone could understand what was happening, they sentenced him to death and they crucified him.

PERSON #2: We were hoping that he would be the one who had come to save us. But three days have passed since his death. And some women from our group came to us with an incredible story. They were at Jesus' grave early this morning, and his body was gone. They came back reporting that they saw angels, and the angels told them that Jesus is alive. So some of us went to see for ourselves. And the tomb is indeed empty, but we did not see Jesus.

JESUS: Oh, how foolish you are! How slowly you understand and believe what the prophets have

said! Didn't the Messiah have to suffer all these things before he could do what God had planned for him?

NARRATOR: Then Jesus began with the teachings of Moses and the prophets, and he helped the two disciples understand how the Bible had told about Jesus from the very beginning. As they were coming to Emmaus, where the two disciples lived, Jesus acted as if he would walk on to the next town. But they stopped him.

PERSON #1: Sir, it's nearly dark. Don't go any farther by yourself tonight. We have plenty of room at our home. Please stay with us.

NARRATOR: So Jesus stayed with them. They still did not recognize him, but they gave him a place to sleep, and they prepared an evening meal for the three of them to share.

PERSON #2: We're so glad to have met you. Your wisdom about the Bible helps us understand more about Jesus. We're happy to share this meal with you.

JESUS: And I'm very happy to share it with you.

NARRATOR: Then Jesus took the loaf of bread that was on the table in front of them. He prayed a blessing before the meal, and then he broke the bread into pieces and handed it to both the disciples.

Then they recognized Jesus. But as soon as they recognized him, he disappeared.

PERSON #1: Didn't our hearts pound with excitement while he was talking to us and helping us understand the Bible?

PERSON #2: We've got to go back to Jerusalem and tell the others that we've seen Jesus.

NARRATOR: So even though it was now past dark, the two disciples hurried the seven miles back to Jerusalem. And they went to the place where other followers of Jesus were staying.

When the two entered the house, the others hurried to meet them and started talking excitedly.

DISCIPLE: The Lord truly has been raised from the dead! He appeared to Peter just a while ago!

NARRATOR: Then the two disciples from Emmaus told the rest of them how Jesus had walked on the road with them, and how they didn't even recognize him until he sat at the table and blessed and broke the bread.

This script is provided for your reference and convenience.

The Good Samaritan

Time: 4 min. 6 sec.

NARRATOR: An expert in religious law came to Jesus. He was testing Jesus to see just how much he knew.

EXPERT: Teacher, what must I do to have eternal life?

JESUS: What is written in our law that's in the Bible? What do you understand it to say?

EXPERT: You shall love the Lord your God with all your heart, with all your being, with all your strength, and with all your mind. And you shall love your neighbor as yourself.

JESUS: You've given the right answer. If you do all of that, you will live.

NARRATOR: But that answer wasn't good enough for the expert. He was really trying to start an argument.

EXPERT: If I am supposed to love my neighbor as myself, then who exactly is my neighbor?

JESUS: One day a man—a Jewish man just like you— was attacked by robbers as he walked on the road between Jerusalem and Jericho. They took his clothes and beat him, and left him half dead at the side of the road.

NARRATOR: Everyone listening to this story knew how dangerous it was to walk alone on any of the roads between towns. Robbers often hid in the rocky hillsides and attacked people as they walked by.

JESUS: A religious leader was walking down that road, but when he saw the man all beaten up, he went to the other side of the road to walk around the man. Then a Levite—one of the men who took care of the Temple—came by the man, and he

walked around him too. But a man from Samaria came down that road, and when he saw the man so beaten up, the Samaritan felt compassion for him. He walked over to the man and saw that he was badly hurt. He took oil and wine out of his backpack and poured them on the man's wounds. Then he put the man on his own donkey and took him to a nearby inn.

NARRATOR: When the people heard this part of the story, they were really surprised. Samaritans and Jews didn't even talk to each other. They weren't really enemies, but they stayed away from each other. For a Samaritan to stop on his journey and help out a Jew was very unusual.

JESUS: The Samaritan put the man in a room and took care of him all that night. The next day the Samaritan gave the owner of the inn some money. He said, "Take care of the man I brought here yesterday, and if it costs more than what I've given you, then I will pay you when I return in a few days."

NARRATOR: Jesus paused to look around at the crowd. Everyone looked back at him, waiting to know what happened next. But Jesus ended the story there. He turned to the expert in religious law and asked *him* a question.

JESUS: In your opinion, which of these three was the neighbor to the man who got beaten up—the religious leader, the Levite, or the Samaritan?

EXPERT: The one who showed him mercy. The one who took care of him.

JESUS: You're absolutely right. Now be that kind of neighbor to others.

This script is provided for your reference and convenience.

Recorded Guided Reflections

Unit 1, Session 2

Jesus Is Born

Time: 11 min.

HOW TO USE THE RECORDED GUIDED REFLECTION

A special approach to prayer in Session 2 is an extended guided reflection titled "Jesus Is Born." To prepare to share this reflection with the children, listen to the recording "Jesus Is Born" (CD 1, Track 6) as a prayerful experience for yourself. Then, when you play the recording during the session, join the children in reflective prayer.

If instead you choose to lead the guided reflection yourself, listen to the recording a second time, following the script and noting pauses. You can use the script as is or adapt it as you wish. When leading the guided reflection during the session, play reflective music softly in the background to enhance the sense of prayerfulness.

We all like to imagine. Sometimes we imagine as we play with our friends. Sometimes we imagine stories about our toys. Today we're going to use our imaginations in a very special way.

Let's start by making ourselves as comfortable as possible. Relax. *(Pause.)* Close your eyes if you'd like. *(Pause.)* Let's all be very still. *(Pause.)* That's it. Now breathe deeply, in and out, in and out, in and out. *(Pause.)*

Imagine that you're walking in an open field next to a forest. The weather is just how you like it. Do you feel a breeze? Is it warm or cool? As you walk, you feel happy. You're going to your Heart Home, that place deep inside you where you can talk with Jesus.

You're walking along, and you see an old woman sitting on a rock. She's smiling. You know somehow that you've seen her before, and you can tell that she's kind. "Are you looking for your Heart Home?" she asks.

"Yes," you answer.

"Here, catch!" says the old woman as she tosses you a big ball of red string. Then she says, "If you want to find your Heart Home, hold the ball of red string in front of your heart." *(Pause.)*

You hold the ball of red string just as she says and repeat the words that she tells you to say, "Red string, red string, I will follow you, my red string. Red string, red string, take me to my Heart Home." *(Pause.)*

Then she tells you to toss the string out in front of you and follow it. You throw it, and the ball of red string starts to roll away into the forest. You follow it. At first the string rolls slowly by some tall trees.

It rolls past the trees and stops in a clearing of wildflowers. Can you smell them? Aren't the colors brilliant? *(Pause.)* You look up and watch as the ball of red string amazingly weaves itself into a one-person airplane—just the right size for you. You crawl inside. It's a perfect fit.

You notice gauges and knobs and levers all around you. You're not quite sure what to do. See that green button labeled *start?* Push the button. What do you hear? *(Pause.)*

The power gathers and you see a blinking light. It says *Bethlehem.* Another light starts to blink. It says *A Long Time Ago.* Your airplane takes off.

As you look out the window, you see amazing things—lakes and cities, mountains and deserts. What else do you see? *(Pause.)*

It's a quick flight, and now it's time to land. Your airplane makes a smooth landing and stops. You turn off the engine with a push of the *stop* button and climb outside into the night. As you look around, you see a flock of sheep. The sheep are grazing quietly. Their shepherds are nearby. Then you notice a very bright star in the sky. This must be near Bethlehem.

Right before your very eyes the string airplane unravels and becomes a ball again. It rolls to the shepherds, unwinding a little at a time. You ask the shepherds if they know about a stable where you could find a baby and his parents. (Pause.) They smile and point in the direction of the star's light. The ball of string rolls in that direction and you follow it.

As you follow the string to the stable, you feel quiet and peaceful inside. You see the soft light of the glowing lamps. Then you see Mary and Joseph and the baby. They notice you, of course. They smile and introduce themselves. But you knew who they were before they said *Mary* and *Joseph*, didn't you? (Pause.)

Mary looks down at the baby and tells you his name is Jesus. She might ask you what you've learned about him. Do you tell her that you know he is God's Son? Do you mention that he is a special gift to the world? Take some time to tell Mary what you know. (Pause.)

Mary is smiling at you so lovingly that you have the courage to ask if you could hold the baby. Tell her you'll be very careful. Mary smiles and comes closer. You hold out your arms to receive Jesus. She gives him to you, ever so gently.

You look at him. He looks back and smiles his bubbly little smile. Do you cuddle him? (Pause.) Do you sing to him? (Pause.) You decide and do it. (Pause.)

Joseph shows you how to prop the baby against your left shoulder and pat his back softly. As you are holding him you think, *his little heart is beating right against my heart!* Instead of using words, let your heart love him and let his heart love you. (Pause.) There you are, loving each other. (Pause.)

The time is coming when you will need to leave. Who takes the baby from you, Mary or Joseph? (Pause.) Together they thank you for coming and being nice to their little son. You thank them for letting you hold him. You say goodbye to each other. (Pause.)

At the door of the stable you see the curly end of the red string. You walk toward it, and the string begins to rewind. You follow it.

Just as before, the string weaves itself into an airplane. You climb inside and push the *start* button. The power gathers. You're on your way back.

You fly across the world and time, landing smoothly in the clearing of wildflowers. You climb out and watch as the string airplane becomes a ball of red string once more. The ball of string leads you through the flowers, past the trees, back to where you started. (Pause.)

Slowly come back to the room. Open your eyes. (Pause.) Stretch your arms. (Pause.) Wiggle your fingers. (Pause.) Notice your friends are all around you. (Pause.) Welcome back.

SENSITIVITIES
- The children's awareness of what it means to speak to God in their hearts
- The children's experience with reflective prayer

HINTS
When leading the guided reflection yourself,
- be aware of your voice quality, pacing, and the message
- allow the children time to reflect by pausing at appropriate times throughout the reflection
- gradually decrease the volume of the background music before turning off the CD player

REFLECTIVE RESPONSES
At the close of the guided reflection, say: *Answer just for yourself. What did you tell Jesus while you were holding him?* Allow children time to reflect on their responses. Assure them that they will not be sharing these responses. Then discuss: *What special things do you do when you're asked to take care of someone or something special?*

Recorded Guided Reflections

Unit 2, Session 6

Lost and Found

Time: 8 min. 43 sec.

HOW TO USE THE RECORDED GUIDED REFLECTION

A special approach to prayer in Session 6 is an extended guided reflection titled "Lost and Found." To prepare to share this reflection with the children, listen to the recording "Lost and Found" (CD 1, Track 7) as a prayerful experience for yourself. Then, when you play the recording during the session, join the children in reflective prayer.

If instead you choose to lead the guided reflection yourself, listen to the recording a second time, following the script and noting pauses. You can use the script as is or adapt it as you wish. When leading the guided reflection during the session, play reflective music softly in the background to enhance the sense of prayerfulness.

We all like to imagine. Sometimes we imagine as we play with our friends. Sometimes we imagine stories about our toys. Today we're going to use our imaginations in a very special way.

Let's start by making ourselves as comfortable as possible. Relax. *(Pause.)* Close your eyes if you'd like. *(Pause.)* Let's all be very still. *(Pause.)* That's it. Now breathe deeply, in and out, in and out, in and out. *(Pause.)*

Do you know anybody in the seventh grade? Maybe you have a brother or a sister or a cousin there? If you don't, think about the seventh graders at your school. That's the age Jesus was when Mary and Joseph thought they lost him after the festival. He was one of the "big kids," but he wasn't really grown up yet.

Let's imagine that Jesus and his parents have moved into your neighborhood. That'll make it easy for you to meet him.

In your imagination you're sitting on the front steps, waiting for your friends to come by. Across the street you notice a boy who looks to be about 12 years old. The boy smiles at you and walks over.

You can't believe your eyes! You recognize this 12-year-old. It's Jesus! Jesus calls to you and says hi.

Perhaps he sits down right next to you. You move over on the step to make room. Then elbow to elbow, you sit and chat for awhile. Jesus is so nice, it isn't hard to talk to him. And he really wants to know about you.

He's especially interested in what you've been learning about. Well, there are so many things you learn each day, you can't tell him everything. But you do want to tell him some things. Take the time to tell him now. *(Pause.)*

Jesus smiles because he knows that you learned about how he stayed back in the Temple after the festival, that time when Mary and Joseph couldn't find him. And you've been thinking about it. What do you remember about that story? Jesus is ready to talk about that. He remembers it very well. *(Pause.)*

Why did Jesus stay back in the Temple? You really want to know. *(Pause.)*

Well I'll bet you can remember a time when you got so involved in something that you totally lost track of time. What was it you were doing? *(Pause.)* Were you supposed to be home at a certain time? Were your parents worried? Were they looking for you? *(Pause.)*

Jesus' experience is probably something like yours.

Listen for what Jesus wants you to remember about what happened after Mary and Joseph found him. What does he say? *(Pause.)* Perhaps Jesus goes on to tell you that he left Jerusalem and went home with his parents. And as he grew up, he obeyed them, respected them, and loved them.

Tell Jesus how it is with your parents. Let him know what it's like for you at home. Jesus nods as he listens. (*Pause.*)

Now think about the best part of being a child in your family and share that with Jesus. (*Pause.*) Since it's almost time to return, if there is something you don't understand or have a hard time with, tell Jesus that too. Then be quiet together for a bit. (*Pause.*)

You can tell Jesus likes you. Do you plan to get together again? You can whenever you want. Jesus is always ready to be with you. He loves it when you spend time with him. Make whatever plans you want with Jesus. (*Pause.*)

You and Jesus say goodbye for now. You thank Jesus for spending time with you. You watch as Jesus walks away, waving to you the whole time. (*Pause.*)

Now slowly come back to the room. Open your eyes. (*Pause.*) Stretch your arms. (*Pause.*) Wiggle your fingers. (*Pause.*) Notice your friends all around you. (*Pause.*) Welcome back.

SENSITIVITIES

- The children's awareness of what it means to speak to God in their hearts
- The children's experience with reflective prayer

HINTS

When leading the guided reflection yourself,

- be aware of your voice quality, pacing, and the message
- allow the children time to reflect by pausing at appropriate times throughout the reflection
- gradually decrease the volume of the background music before turning off the CD player

REFLECTIVE RESPONSES

At the close of the guided reflection, say: ***Answer just for yourself. What do you want to remember to talk about with Jesus?*** Allow children time to reflect on their responses. Assure them that they will not be sharing these responses. Then discuss: ***What is it about Jesus that makes him a good friend?***

Unit 3, Session 11

The Vine and the Branches

Time: 10 min. 59 sec.

HOW TO USE THE RECORDED GUIDED REFLECTION

A special approach to prayer in Session 11 is an extended guided reflection titled "The Vine and the Branches." To prepare to share this reflection with the children, listen to the recording "The Vine and the Branches" (CD 1, Track 8) as a prayerful experience for yourself. Then, when you play the recording during the session, join the children in reflective prayer.

If instead you choose to lead the guided reflection yourself, listen to the recording a second time, following the script and noting pauses. You can use the script as is or adapt it as you wish. When leading the guided reflection during the session, play reflective music softly in the background to enhance the sense of prayerfulness.

We all like to imagine. Sometimes we imagine as we play with our friends. Sometimes we imagine stories about our toys. Today we're going to use our imaginations in a very special way.

Let's start by making ourselves as comfortable as possible. Relax. *(Pause.)* Close your eyes if you'd like. *(Pause.)* Let's all be very still. *(Pause.)* That's it. Now breathe deeply and quietly, in and out, in and out, in and out. *(Pause.)*

Imagine that it's late summer. You're taking a walk. It's a warm, breezy day. Sunny now because a storm has just passed. The air smells clean and fresh. Take a whiff. *(Pause.)* There's even a rainbow in the sky. *(Pause.)* You know you should avoid the puddles, but you can't resist a splash or two. *(Pause.)*

You stop to admire a lovely garden, where flowers of all kinds bloom and grow. Yellow and blue, pink and red. They dazzle you with their colors. You bury your nose in one soft bunch of petals and breathe in deeply. How does it smell? Imagine it now. *(Pause.)*

"Go ahead, you may pick one," you hear a voice say. You look up to see a friendly neighbor, who's been there all the time. She's smiling and nodding; she really means what she says.

Now you have a hard decision to make. You look all the flowers over again. The yellow or the blue? The pink or the red? *(Pause.)* Finally you choose. What kind is it? *(Pause.)* You decide that you'd like to take it home. You hold the stem carefully in your hand. The flower is firm and in full bloom.

Continuing your walk, you notice a tree. Its branches have been torn off by the storm. They lie in tangles all around. You pick up a small branch and rub one of its green buds between your fingers, knowing this bud will never get a chance to bloom. Stepping over the branches, you continue your walk. *(Pause.)*

You come to a yard where thick vines are growing on trellises. As you get closer, you notice that the vines are covered with clusters of ripe grapes. You stop to study this miniature vineyard—it's a beautiful thing to see, as beautiful as the flower garden, but in a different way. This neighbor's "flowers" are fruits. *(Pause.)* Everybody loves something different.

Then you notice someone walking toward you admiring the grapes. Must be the gardener. Oh good, it's Jesus. He walks so quietly that you almost feel like whispering when you say hello. As he greets you, Jesus says your name. *(Pause.)* You know that he's happy to see you again. *(Pause.)*

Jesus asks you how you are. He really listens as you tell him what's on your mind or in your heart, or what you've been doing. Tell him whatever you like. *(Pause.)*

Jesus looks thoughtful for a moment. Then he asks about the flower you've picked. *(Pause.)* You look down at your flower. It's not in good

Recorded Guided Reflections

shape. It's limp now, and a few of the petals have fallen off. It's a sad-looking flower. You tell Jesus that you'd planned to take it home, but now you don't think you want to.

Jesus asks you to consider what happened to your flower. (*Pause.*) Do you tell him that it looked pretty for a while, but then it drooped and died? Or have you something else to say? (*Pause.*) Jesus invites you to think again about those tree branches on the ground that you saw.

Why do you think the flower and the tree branches died? Ask Jesus to help you figure out the answer. (*Pause.*)

Jesus tells you that your flower and the broken branches remind him of a story he once told. He walks over to one of the grapevines and tugs on a branch. It doesn't move. You notice how strong and secure the branch is. You see how the fruit is healthy, so juicy and ripe. Jesus asks you if you remember what he once said about vines and branches, something that's written in the Bible. What was it? Do you remember? (*Pause.*)

The two of you talk about how flowers and branches have to be connected to live. The flower has to be connected to its roots. The tree branch has to be connected to the tree.

Jesus tells you that, where he lived, people grew grapes and made wine. (*Pause.*) Just about everybody in Jesus' town knew that the vine branches had to be connected to the vine and its roots. If they weren't, grapes wouldn't grow. Do you understand that? (*Pause.*)

Maybe Jesus takes your hand while he tells you the best part. "When I say I am the vine and you are the branches, I mean you need to stay connected with me."

Maybe this is a hard one for you. Maybe you're also wondering what keeps you connected to Jesus. (*Pause.*)

Love. LOVE is the big answer. Love is what connects you and Jesus. God's love. God's love? In you? Yes! In you. (*Pause.*)

Maybe you want to check it out, just to be sure you understand. If you stay connected with Jesus, he brings you God's love. The more love you have, the more love you can give. With God's love there is no limit! How wonderful is that?

Knowing that you'll be coming back to the room soon, Jesus might ask if the two of you can take a last moment to thank God. Together Jesus and you go down deep into your hearts to that place where God and you meet. (*Pause.*)

After your prayer, you and Jesus say goodbye for now. Before returning to the room, take a moment to tell Jesus anything else you've been thinking about, knowing that he cares. (*Pause.*)

You leave the vineyard and retrace your steps. You again pass the fallen branches. Like your flower, they remind you of the parable of the vine and the branches—Jesus' story about staying connected to him.

Slowly come back to the room. Open your eyes. (*Pause.*) Stretch your arms. (*Pause.*) Wiggle your fingers. (*Pause.*) Notice your friends around you. (*Pause.*) Welcome back.

SENSITIVITIES

- The children's awareness of what it means to speak to God in their hearts
- The children's experience with reflective prayer
- The children's experience with gardening

HINTS

When leading the guided reflection yourself,

- be aware of your voice quality, pacing, and the message
- allow the children time to reflect by pausing at appropriate times throughout the reflection
- gradually decrease the volume of the background music before turning off the CD player

REFLECTIVE RESPONSES

At the close of the guided reflection, say: *Answer just for yourself. What do you still want to talk about with Jesus? When can you do that?* Allow children time to reflect on their responses. Assure them that they will not be sharing these responses. Then discuss: *How do the people who love us help us stay connected to Jesus?*

Recorded Guided Reflections

Unit 4, Session 16

New Life Through Baptism

Time: 11 min. 35 sec.

HOW TO USE THE RECORDED GUIDED REFLECTION

A special approach to prayer in Session 16 is an extended guided reflection titled "New Life Through Baptism." To prepare to share this reflection with the children, listen to the recording the "New Life Through Baptism" (CD 1, Track 9) as a prayerful experience for yourself. Then, when you play the recording during the session, join the children in reflective prayer.

If instead you choose to lead the guided reflection yourself, listen to the recording a second time, following the script and noting pauses. You can use the script as is or adapt it as you wish. When leading the guided reflection during the session, play reflective music softly in the background to enhance the sense of prayerfulness.

We all like to imagine. Sometimes we imagine as we play with our friends. Sometimes we imagine stories about our toys. Today we're going to use our imaginations in a very special way.

Let's start by making ourselves as comfortable as possible. Relax. *(Pause.)* Close your eyes if you'd like. *(Pause.)* Let's all be very still. *(Pause.)* That's it. Now breathe deeply, in and out, in and out, in and out. *(Pause.)*

Imagine your favorite picnic place. *(Pause.)* Maybe it's a park or a playground. It could be the forest or your own backyard. *(Pause.)* Today how about going in your imagination to the beach? Have you ever been there before? *(Pause.)* Maybe you go often, or not at all. No matter, we're going there today.

What do you want to bring with you? A ball? A blanket? A shovel and pail? *(Pause.)* Oh, don't forget your lunch. Will you pack your favorite picnic food? What is it? *(Pause.)*

Hope you're ready now. Let's go. *(Pause.)*

At the beach the sand is hot under your feet. You drop everything you brought and head for the water. At the edge you stand and let the waves lap over your feet. Is the water cold? *(Pause.)*

Someone near you is also enjoying the water. You look over and recognize the person right away. It's Jesus! *(Pause.)* He recognizes you too. In fact, he's been hoping you'd come.

You call out and move toward him. The look on your face tells all. You're so happy to see Jesus. Your visits with him are always so special.

As usual, Jesus asks how you are. Take some time to tell him how things are going. Jesus is not in a hurry, and he likes listening to you. So catch him up with all your news. *(Pause.)*

Jesus looks at you. He looks at you again. He notices you have a fun look on your face. You ask Jesus if he'd like to play a water game with you. You tell him it's not in the water; it's *about* the water. It's a thinking game. And it goes like this: You tell one thing you used water for today. Then Jesus tells you another thing he thinks you used water for today. You try to see how many things you can list.

You go first. For example, you might say, "I brushed my teeth." Jesus might say that you drank a glass of water. The two of you go on. What else do you say? *(Pause.)*

Did you remember watering the plants? How about taking a shower or filling your pet's bowl with water? See how much longer you can keep it up. *(Pause.)*

One thing is for sure. Water is very important and you use an awful lot of it. Do you think you could get along without it? *(Pause.)* Is there anything more you or Jesus want to add to your list? If you think of another thing, just add it on. *(Pause.)*

Jesus asks you if you ever thought about how often you use water for cleaning. What do you tell him? *(Pause.)* Did you mention brushing teeth, washing fruit, cleaning up messes, doing dishes? (*Pause.*) Jesus also reminds you that water is life-giving. People, animals, plants—they all need water.

You nod to show Jesus that you understand. Jesus smiles to see that you really do understand how important water is to life—to our very existence, in fact. He asks you to think about the water of your Baptism. With this water you were given new life in Jesus. How did you react to the water? Did anyone ever tell you? (*Pause.*)

What do you know about your Baptism? Were you a baby? Were you older? Did your family have a party for you? Take some time now to tell Jesus what you know about your Baptism. He wants to hear what you have to say. (*Pause.*)

After you tell him, Jesus wants you to think about what you were given in Baptism—the gift of God's grace. With this grace you became part of God's family and a member of the Church. How does it feel to know that you're part of God's family, that you are a child of God? (*Pause.*) How does it feel to know you are loved by God? (*Pause.*)

Together with Jesus, thank God for your new life. Tell him how happy you are to be his child through Baptism. (*Pause.*) Now be still in your heart. Listen. Does God have a message for you? (*Pause.*)

Your time with Jesus is coming to a close. Take a moment now to share with him anything else you have on your mind. (*Pause.*)

As you get ready to leave, thank Jesus for meeting with you. He promises to always be there when you need him. With this, you say goodbye for now, knowing that you'll see Jesus again very soon.

Now slowly come back to the room. Open your eyes. (*Pause.*) There. Stretch your arms. (*Pause.*) Wiggle your fingers. (*Pause.*) Notice your friends around you. (*Pause.*) Welcome back.

SENSITIVITIES

- The children's awareness of what it means to speak to God in their hearts
- The children's experience with reflective prayer
- The children's experiences with beaches and water

HINTS

When leading the guided reflection yourself,

- be aware of your voice quality, pacing, and the message
- allow the children time to reflect by pausing at appropriate times throughout the reflection
- gradually decrease the volume of the background music before turning off the CD player

REFLECTIVE RESPONSES

At the close of the guided reflection, say: **Answer just for yourself. When will you talk with Jesus again? What do you want to talk about?** Allow children time to reflect on their responses. Assure them that they will not be sharing these responses. Then discuss: **What does it mean to be called a child of God?**

Recorded Guided Reflections

Unit 5, Session 22

Making Choices

Time: 9 min. 6 sec.

HOW TO USE THE RECORDED GUIDED REFLECTION

A special approach to prayer in Session 22 is an extended guided reflection titled "Making Choices." To prepare to share this reflection with the children, listen to the recording "Making Choices" (CD 1, Track 10) as a prayerful experience for yourself. Then, when you play the recording during the session, join the children in reflective prayer.

If instead you choose to lead the guided reflection yourself, listen to the recording a second time, following the script and noting pauses. You can use the script as is or adapt it as you wish. When leading the guided reflection during the session, play reflective music softly in the background to enhance the sense of prayerfulness.

We all like to imagine. Sometimes we imagine as we play with our friends. Sometimes we imagine stories about our toys. Today we're going to use our imaginations in a very special way.

Let's start by making ourselves as comfortable as possible. Relax. *(Pause.)* Close your eyes if you'd like. *(Pause.)* Let's all be very still. *(Pause.)* That's it. Now breathe deeply, in and out, in and out, in and out. *(Pause.)*

Imagine that you go to a favorite place, a place where you are especially comfortable, a place where you can think without being disturbed. *(Pause.)* Maybe it's somewhere you've imagined before, maybe not. It might be in your home—on your bed, in a comfy armchair, or under the dining room table. It might be outside—in an easy-to-climb tree, a playhouse, or the garden. Wherever it is, it's a place where you feel good. Imagine that you are there now. It is your quiet place. *(Pause.)*

You know though that there is one person who is always welcome in your special place. It is Jesus. He is with you now, but you don't mind. You're glad to see him. You're glad that he's here.

Today as a surprise, Jesus has brought a snack for both of you. It's something you love to eat. What has he brought? *(Pause.)* Mmmm. Doesn't it smell good? Together you and Jesus enjoy your snack. It's delicious. You didn't even realize you were hungry until you started eating.

While you're eating, Jesus might ask what you've been learning about today. Tell Jesus what you know, and see his happy face as he listens with love. What do you tell him? *(Pause.)*

Jesus is impressed with what you remember. He might want to know something else now, something about you. He asks you to describe something you've done recently that you feel really good about. Maybe something nice that you said, or how you treated someone kindly. The kind of thing you hope God noticed you doing. What is it you remember doing that was especially nice? Tell Jesus. *(Pause.)* Jesus thinks it was nice too, and he tells you so.

He might go on to ask you if anyone else noticed what you did. Were you praised? How did that make you feel? *(Pause.)* If no one noticed, how did that make you feel? Were you happy anyway? Tell Jesus all about it now. He listens and cares. *(Pause.)*

Jesus is ready to hear more. Is there another time you'd like to tell him about? A time when you were happy with how you acted? Tell Jesus now. *(Pause.)*

When you've finished, Jesus tells you that he has another question for you. Here it is. Perhaps he asks you to think back to yesterday or earlier today. Is there a time when you wish you had acted differently? A time you hope nobody noticed? Can you think of something? Is it something you did or said? *(Pause.)*

Maybe you remember but don't want to talk about it. You sneak a glance at Jesus. You can tell he knows already. Take a deep breath and tell him. Be honest. You're always safe with Jesus. *(Pause.)*

Recorded Guided Reflections

Do you tell Jesus that at the time you didn't know it was a bad choice? That only later you realized you shouldn't have done it? Tell Jesus how things are working out. It doesn't matter if you can't seem to find the right words to explain. Jesus knows and understands what's in your heart. He loves you no matter what. *(Pause.)*

When you're finished, talk with Jesus a little while about choices and the Holy Spirit. What might he say? *(Pause.)* Tell Jesus about the choices you face—the big ones and the ones that aren't so important. *(Pause.)* Jesus reminds you to call on the Holy Spirit for help when you're not sure what to do. Listen to Jesus. *(Pause.)*

Because you're getting ready to come back to the room, Jesus asks you if you'd like to do one last thing together. He suggests that you pray to the Holy Spirit so you can get the help you need. With an open heart, ask the Holy Spirit to guide you. *(Pause.)*

You realize that your time with Jesus is ending. So take just a minute more to share with him anything else that's on your mind. *(Pause.)*

As you get ready to leave your quiet place, thank Jesus for being with you today. Jesus smiles in return. He loves to spend time with you. You both leave happy, knowing that you'll be meeting again soon.

Come back to the room. Open your eyes. *(Pause.)* Stretch your arms. *(Pause.)* Wiggle your fingers. *(Pause.)* Notice your friends all around you. *(Pause.)* Welcome back.

SENSITIVITIES

- The children's awareness of what it means to speak to God in their hearts
- The children's experience with reflective prayer
- The children's experience with having a special or favorite place for prayer
- The children's recent experiences with making choices

HINTS

When leading the guided reflection yourself,

- be aware of your voice quality, pacing, and the message
- allow the children time to reflect by pausing at appropriate times throughout the reflection
- gradually decrease the volume of the background music before turning off the CD player

REFLECTIVE RESPONSES

At the close of the guided reflection, say: *Answer just for yourself.* *What do you want to be sure to talk to Jesus about soon?* Allow children to reflect on their responses. Assure them that they will not be sharing these responses. Then discuss: *What helps you make a good choice?*

Name _____

Date _____

The Liturgical Calendar

The liturgical calendar shows us the feasts and seasons of the Church year. On the liturgical calendar color the current season or feast day.

Finding God

Blackline Masters

God created all the animals.
Now you can make thumbprint animals like the
ones God created.

1. Press your thumb on an ink pad and then into
the box at the end of each sentence.

2. Add legs, arms, tails, and ears to your prints.
Make them look like the animals God created.
Write the names of the animals on the lines.

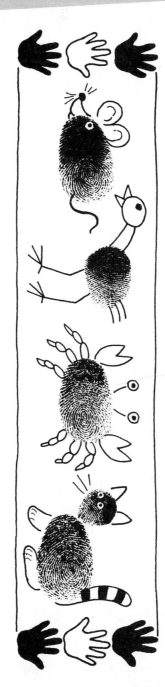

Thank you God for creating _____.

Thank you God for creating _____.

Thank you God for creating _____.

Thank you God for creating _____.

2 God's Blessings

Read each question.
Write or draw the answer.

1. God made the world and everything in it.
What is one of your favorite things that God made?

_____

2. God created you and made you special.
What is one thing that is special about you?

_____

3. God wants us to love one another. What is one way you can show love for another person? Draw your answer.

4. What is one way that someone has shown love for you? Draw your answer.

Finding God, Session 1

3 God's Creation

Fill in the lines to finish each sentence.

1. God made the _____ .

2. God filled the sea with different
   kinds of _____ .

3. God filled the sky with
   _____ .

4. God was _____
   with all he had done.

5. God is Father, Son, and Holy
   _____ .

6. People are part of God's
   _____ .

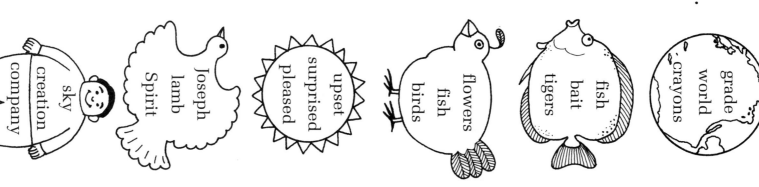

grade
world
crayons

fish
bait
tigers

flowers
fish
birds

upset
surprised
pleased

Joseph
lamb
Spirit

sky
creation
company

Finding God, Session 1

Precious Gifts

1. In each square draw a picture of a gift God has given you.

2. Cut out the pattern, fold on the dotted lines, and tape the sides to make a cube.

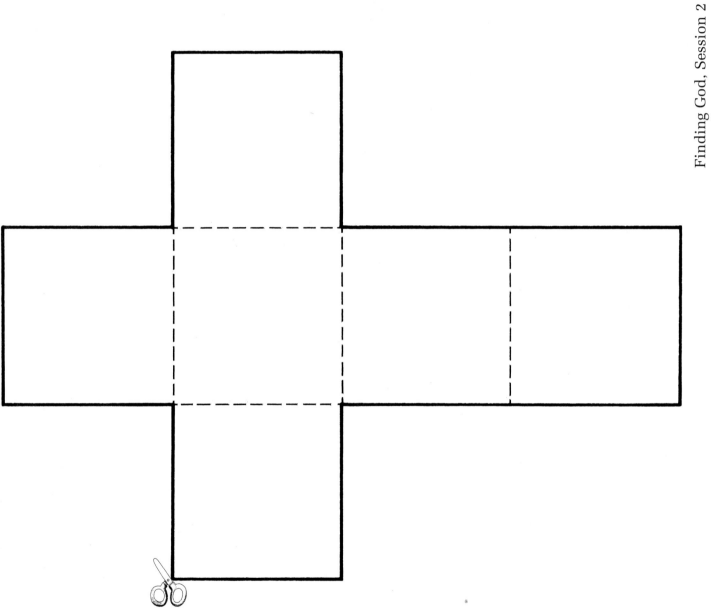

Finding God, Session 2

5 Joseph

Fill in the lines to finish the story of Joseph.
Choose from the words in the box.

Holy	afraid	name	dream	wife	Savior	saves

1. An angel appeared to Joseph in a
   _____.

2. Mary's baby would be from the
   _____ Spirit.

3. The angel said,
   "Do not be
   _____.

4. Joseph was to _____
   to take Mary as your wife,"

5. Jesus means "God
   _____."

6. Jesus is our _____.

7. Joseph took Mary as his _____.

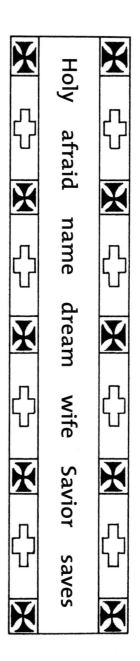

Answers: 1. dream; 2. Holy; 3. afraid; 4. name; 5. saves; 6. Savior; 7. wife

Finding God, Session 2

© Loyola Press

Name _____   Date _____

6 Breaking the Code

Use the code in the box to complete the sentences.

A	B	C	D	E	F	G	H	I
1	2	3	4	5	6	7	8	9

J	K	L	M	N	O	P	Q	R
10	11	12	13	14	15	16	17	18

S	T	U	V	W	X	Y	Z
19	20	21	22	23	24	25	26

1. God gave us his Son, ___ ___ ___ ___ ___ .
                        10 5 19 21 19

2. Joseph first learned of Jesus in a ___ ___ ___ ___ ___ .
                                       4 18 5 1 13

3. Jesus is our ___ ___ ___ ___ ___ ___ .
                19 1 22 9 15 18

4. Jesus is with us in the Blessed ___ ___ ___ ___ ___ ___ ___ ___ .
                                   19 1 3 18 1 13 5 14 20

5. Jesus is with us ___ ___ ___ ___ ___ ___ .
                    1 12 23 1 25 19

Finding God, Session 2

7 God Takes Care

1. On the quilt square draw things that God gives you, such as family and food.

2. Cut out the square.

3. Attach it to the other children's squares to make a quilt.

4. Hang the quilt on the wall.

Finding God, Session 3

8   No More Worries

Joseph had worries. God took care of Joseph.

We have worries too. Write your worries on the slips of paper. Cut them out. Hold them in your hand.

Pray a prayer and give your worries to God. Tear up the papers and throw them out. Trust that God will help you.

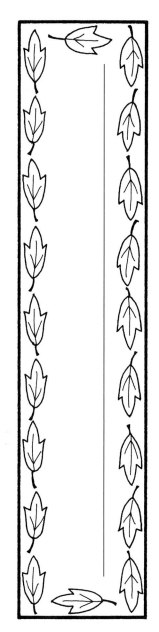

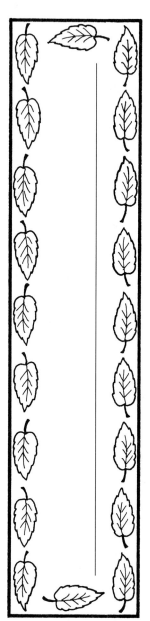

Finding God, Session 3

9 God Is Our Father

Circle **Yes** if the sentence is true.
Circle **No** if the sentence is not true.

1. God takes care of us.   Yes   No

2. Jesus tells us to worry about our lives.   Yes   No

3. Jesus reminds us that God is
   our Father.   Yes   No

4. When we petition God in prayer,
   we give him thanks.   Yes   No

5. Jesus gave us the words to
   the Lord's Prayer.   Yes   No

6. We trust God by placing our cares
   in his hands.   Yes   No

7. We pray the Lord's Prayer during Mass.   Yes   No

Finding God, Session 3

© Loyola Press

10 Holy Spirit

1. On the lines write a sentence about the Holy Spirit.

2. Decorate the dove.

3. Cut out the dove.

4. Pin up your dove to help create a Holy Spirit bulletin board with the rest of the group.

Finding God, Session 4

11 God Loves Us

Complete each word from this unit by adding the missing letters.
Choose from the words in the box.

> Blessed Sacrament   faith   Temple   holy
>
> Messiah   creation   tabernacle   genuflect
>
> praise   petition   Emmanuel   Savior

1. We are part of God's cr — — — ion so we can
   be — — ly.

2. We gen — — — ct to honor the
   — — esse   S — cra — — nt inside the
   — — — erna — le.

3. Jesus is our — av — — — , and we sometimes
   call him — mma — — — l.

4. We can pray prayers of — — t — tion or
   — — ai — — .

5. Simeon had — — ith in God. He knew that the
   Me — — — ah was in the — — mpl — .

Answers: 1. creation, holy; 2. genuflect, Blessed Sacrament, tabernacle; 3. Savior, Emmanuel; 4. petition, praise;
5. faith, Messiah, Temple

12 The Story of Simeon

Number from 1 to 4 the events from the story of Simeon. The words next to each picture tell what is happening.

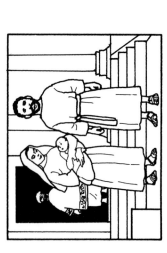

Mary and Joseph enter the Temple with the baby Jesus.

Simeon takes Jesus in his arms, knowing he is the Messiah.

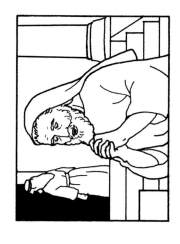

Simeon blesses God and says, "Now, Master, you may let your servant go in peace. My eyes have seen the Savior."

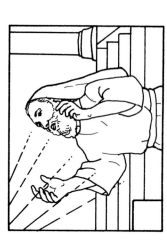

The Holy Spirit promises Simeon that he will see the Messiah.

© Loyola Press

Finding God, Session 4

Answers, top to bottom: 2, 3, 4, 1

13 Unit 1 Show What You Know

Circle **T** for true or **F** for false.

1. God made a man and a woman after he made the sky, the sea, and the animals.   T   F

2. We can be holy because God loves us.   T   F

3. Jesus is our Savior because he taught us to pray.   T   F

4. Emmanuel means "God with us."   T   F

5. Joseph is the Blessed Sacrament.   T   F

6. The Blessed Sacrament is kept inside the tabernacle.   T   F

7. When we petition God in prayer, we ask him for what we need.   T   F

8. We show love for God by caring for the world.   T   F

9. The Holy Spirit guides us to care for ourselves and others.   T   F

10. Jesus reminds us that God is our Father.   T   F

13

Draw a picture of someone caring for God's creation.

Self-Assessment

How well do you understand these things? Rate yourself by writing a letter on each line. The guide below will help you decide which letter to write.

A – I know it very well.

B – I know it, but I have some questions.

C – I do not know it.

___ God's Creation

___ Savior

___ Holy Spirit

Finding God, Session 5

Answers will vary.

1. Color the figures of Jesus, Mary, Joseph, and the Temple.

2. Cut them out and glue them to craft sticks.

3. Use them to tell the story of Jesus in the Temple. Follow the story below for help.

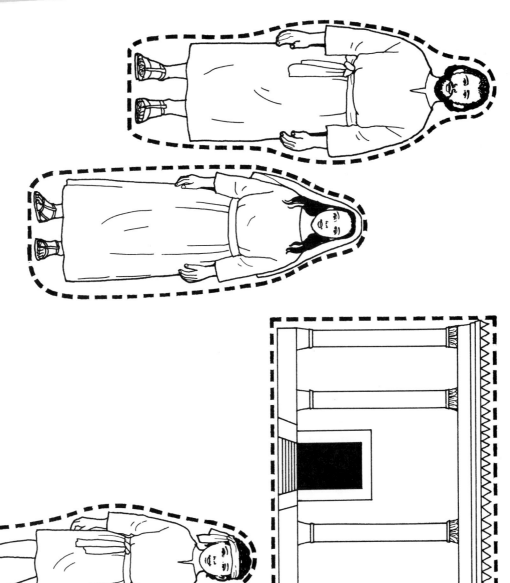

Joseph, Mary, and Jesus go to Jerusalem.

Joseph and Mary cannot find Jesus for three days.

Joseph and Mary find Jesus in the Temple.

Jesus goes home with Mary and Joseph.

Finding God, Session 6

15 Keeping a Commandment Close

1. Decorate and cut out the two pockets.

2. Glue the edges on three sides of the pockets together to make one pocket. Leave the top open.

3. On slips of paper, write ways you obey your parents.

4. Put the papers in the pocket.

5. Tape or pin the pocket to your shirt to remind you to obey your parents.

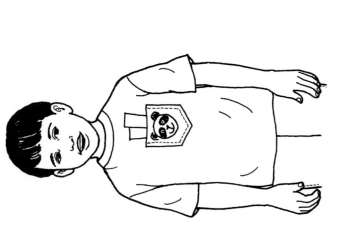

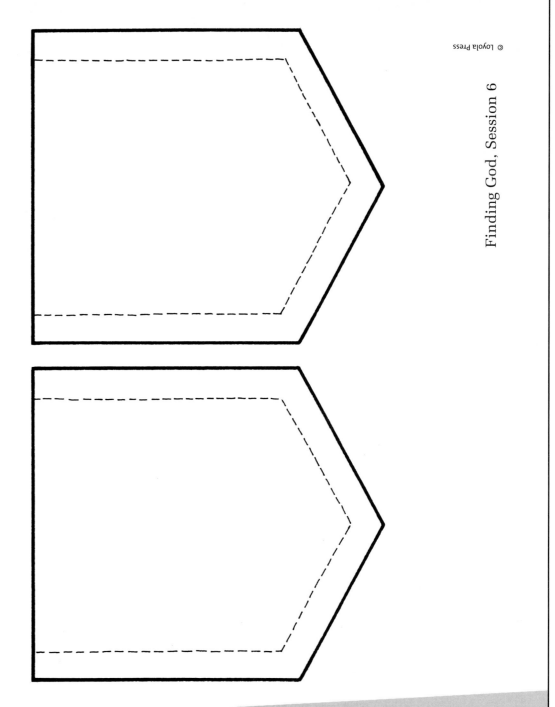

Finding God, Session 6

16 The Holy Family

Unscramble the words.
Write them on the lines to finish the sentences.

1. Mary's mother was Saint (Aenn) _____ .

2. Mary's father was Saint (oJacmhi) _____ .

3. Mary and Joseph found Jesus in the (Telmpe) _____ .

4. Jesus did what his (eparnst) _____ asked.

5. As Catholics, we follow the Ten (Contmsmednam) _____ .

6. Your (coneiencsc) _____ guides you to do what the Commandments tell you.

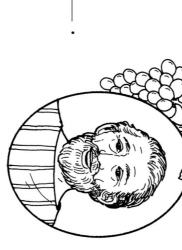

Finding God, Session 6

© Loyola Press

17 Jesus and the Blind Men

Choose parts. Read the play aloud.

Characters: Narrator   Jesus   Two Blind Men   Crowd

Narrator: Jesus and his disciples were leaving Jericho. A crowd followed. Two blind men heard that Jesus was passing by.

Two Blind Men: Lord, have pity on us!

Crowd: (in angry voices) Be quiet! Be quiet!

Narrator: The blind men called out all the more.

Two Blind Men: (louder than the first time) Lord, have pity on us!

Crowd: (in angry voices) Didn't you hear us? Be quiet!

Narrator: Jesus heard the blind men. He stopped and called them. He looked at the men.

Jesus: (in a gentle voice) What do you want me to do for you?

Two Blind Men: Lord, please open our eyes.

Narrator: Jesus was moved with pity. He touched their eyes.

Two Blind Men: We can see! We can see! Lord, we will follow you.

adapted from Matthew 20:29–34

Finding God, Session 7

18 Helping to Heal Others

1. On each bandage draw or write a way you can bring help or healing to someone you know.

2. Cut out the bandages.

3. Give each bandage to a different person.

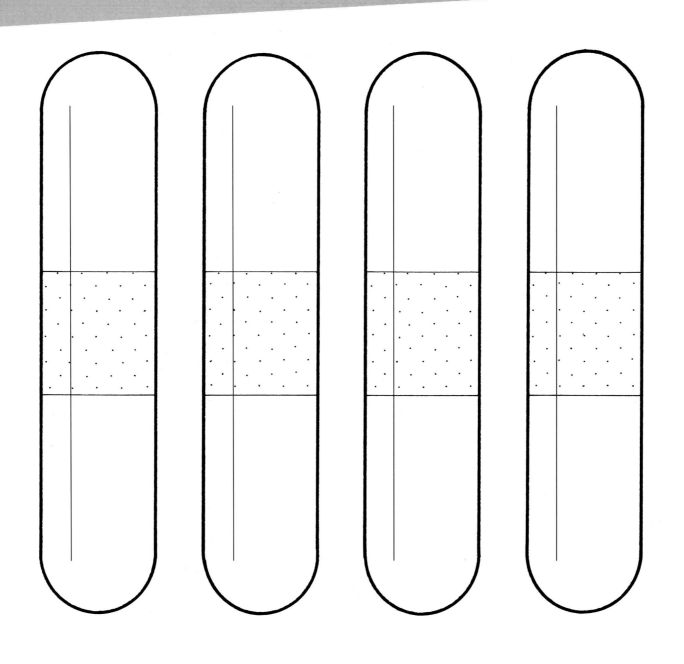

19 Jesus Saves Us

Draw a line to connect the two parts of each sentence.

1. John the Baptist

2. Jesus

3. Jesus helped

4. Jesus wants us to

5. God raised Jesus

6. Jesus is alive

A. from the dead.

B. wanted to know if Jesus was the Messiah.

C. in heaven.

D. people in need.

E. love others.

F. healed the sick.

© Loyola Press

Finding God, Session 7

Answers: 1. B; 2. F; 3. D; 4. E; 5. A; 6. C

1. Color and cut out the puppets.
2. Tape them to fit your fingers.
3. Use the puppets to tell your friends the parable of the banquet.

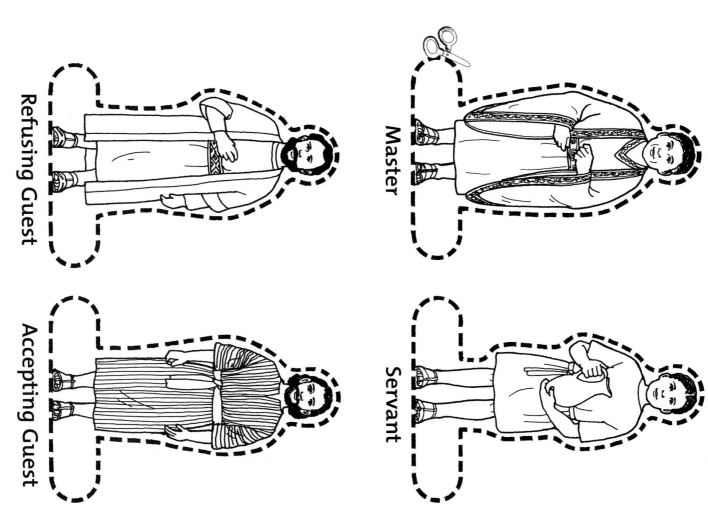

Master

Refusing Guest

Servant

Accepting Guest

Come to God's Banquet

1. Write the names of your family members on the lines on the outsides of the cards.

2. Write Welcome! on the insides.

3. Decorate the cards and cut them out.

4. Fold them in the middle.

5. Take the cards home and place them around the dinner table.

6. Tell your family the parable of the banquet.

Finding God, Session 8

22 Jesus Calls Us to Love

In this session you have learned some of the words below. Cross out the word in each group that does not belong.

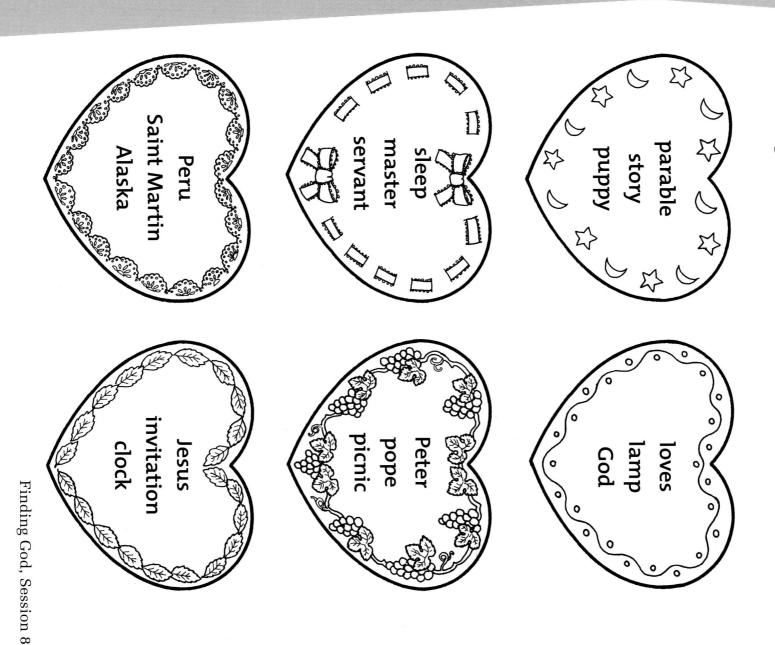

parable
story
puppy

sleep
master
servant

Peru
Saint Martin
Alaska

loves
lamp
God

Peter
pope
picnic

Jesus
invitation
clock

23 God Is My Shepherd

1. Cut out the lamb.

2. Decorate the lamb with cotton balls.

3. Write your name on the tag.

4. Cut out the tag, punch a hole in the top, and add string.

5. Tie the string around the lamb's neck as a reminder that God is your shepherd.

God
is my
shepherd.

_____

Finding God, Session 9

24 Jesus Loves Us

Draw lines.
Match the words on the left with the words on the right.

1. conscience

2. parables

3. Ten Commandments

4. crozier

5. pope

6. deacon

7. bishop

A. stories Jesus told to teach lessons

B. helps priests serve people

C. each bishop carries one

D. guides us to do what the Commandments tell us

E. cares for many parishes

F. leads the whole Church today

G. Jesus, Mary, and Joseph obeyed these

© Loyola Press

25 Jesus Cares for Us

Unscramble the words in dark letters.
Write them on the lines.
One is done for you.

Example:

Jesus teaches God's **olev**. _____love_____

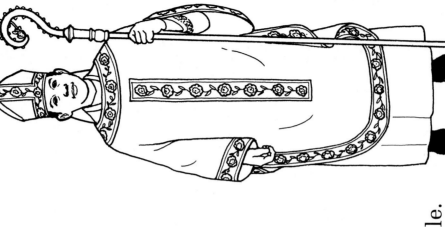

1. God is our **sherdpeh**.

   _____

2. A **ibopsh** cares for many parishes.

   _____

3. Each bishop carries a **czorier**.

   _____

4. Each **nopsre** is important to God.

   _____

5. Priests and **dsaeocn** serve the people.

   _____

6. They lead people in **peryar**.

   _____

Finding God, Session 9

26 Unit 2 Show What You Know

Circle the correct answer.

1. What was Jesus doing when Mary and Joseph found him?
   A. praying the Lord's Prayer
   B. singing with the choir
   C. talking with the teachers

2. What did Jesus, Mary, and Joseph always obey?
   A. angels   B. the pope
   C. the Ten Commandments

3. How did Jesus show John's followers that he was the Messiah?
   A. He healed people who were very sick.
   B. He obeyed his parents.
   C. He prayed to God the Father.

4. Which holy man taught people about the coming of the Messiah?
   A. Saint Isidore   B. Saint Joseph
   C. John the Baptist

5. How did Jesus die?
   A. in a fire   B. on a cross
   C. in jail

6. Who raised Jesus from the dead?
   A. Mary, his mother   B. God
   C. John the Baptist

7. What does the parable of the banquet teach us?

A. God loves us.

B. Food is important to God.

C. God loves people who own land.

8. Who leads the whole Church today as Peter did?

A. a deacon   B. a priest

C. the pope

9. What does a bishop do?

A. teaches shepherds

B. leads the whole Church

C. cares for many parishes

10. What are psalms?

A. songs or prayers

B. priests

C. where Catholic people live

On another sheet of paper write the main idea of the parable of the lost sheep.

Self-Assessment

Rate yourself by writing a letter on each line.

A – I know it very well.

B – I know it, but I have some questions.

C – I do not know it.

___ Ten Commandments

___ pope

___ bishop

Finding God, Session 10

Answers: 7. A; 8. C; 9. C; 10. A. Answers to remaining sections will vary.

27 Saint Ignatius of Loyola

Saint Ignatius read books about Jesus and the saints.
Draw a picture of Jesus on one book page.
On the other page, draw a picture of something you
would like to learn more about.

Growing Good Fruit

Good deeds bring us closer to God.

Inside the apples write good deeds you can do.

Then color the apples.

Finding God, Session 11

29 We Worship God

Finish each sentence. Choose from the words in the box.
When you are finished, the circled letters will spell
a word. Write the word on the line at the bottom.

vine	Spirit	Jesus	sin	poured

1. Saint Ignatius read about ◯ — — — — s and the saints.

2. Jesus said, "I am the v — ◯ — ."

3. The good we find in our words or actions is called the
   Fruits of the Holy ◯ — — — — — it.

4. In Baptism, water is p — ◯ — ed over our heads.

5. Baptism takes away original ◯ — n.

What is the word? _____

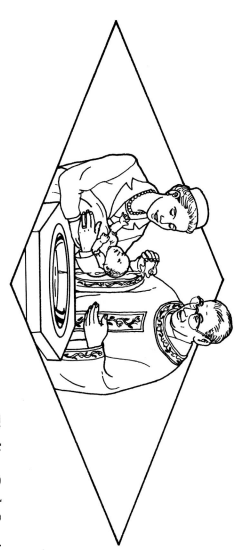

Finding God, Session 11

© Loyola Press

30 Becoming Friends Again

1. Color the pictures.

2. Cut them out.

3. Put them in order to show how the children forgave each other.

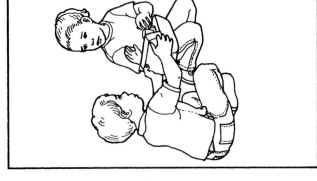

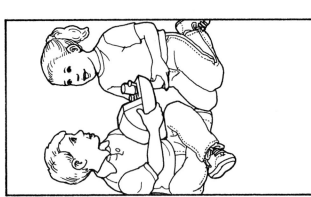

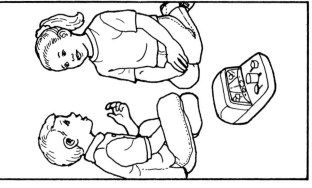

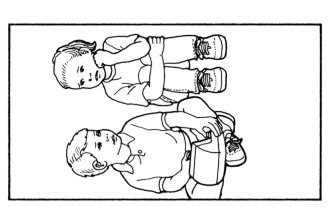

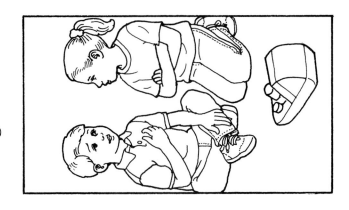

Finding God, Session 12

Answers: top row: 3, 5, 1; bottom row: 6, 2, 4

31 Zacchaeus

Finish the story of Zaccheaus.
Choose from the words in the box.

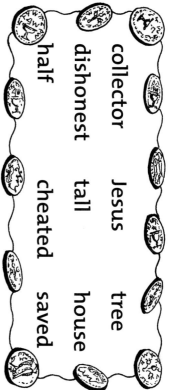

collector	Jesus	tree
dishonest	tall	house
half	cheated	saved

Zaccheaus was a _____ tax

_____ . He had heard that

Zaccheaus wanted to see Jesus. But Zaccheaus

was not _____ .

Zaccheaus ran ahead and climbed up a

_____ .

Jesus told Zaccheaus that he wanted to stay at his

_____ .

Zaccheaus said he would give

of everything he had to the poor. He said he would give

money back to anyone he had _____ .

Jesus said that Zaccheaus was _____

that day.

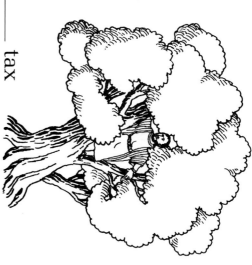

Finding God, Session 12

Answers: dishonest; collector; Jesus; tall; tree; house; half; cheated; saved

32 Celebrating Reconciliation

Complete the crossword puzzle.
Choose from the words in the box.

© Loyola Press

Penance	contrition	mortal sin	venial sin
confession	conscience	reconciliation	

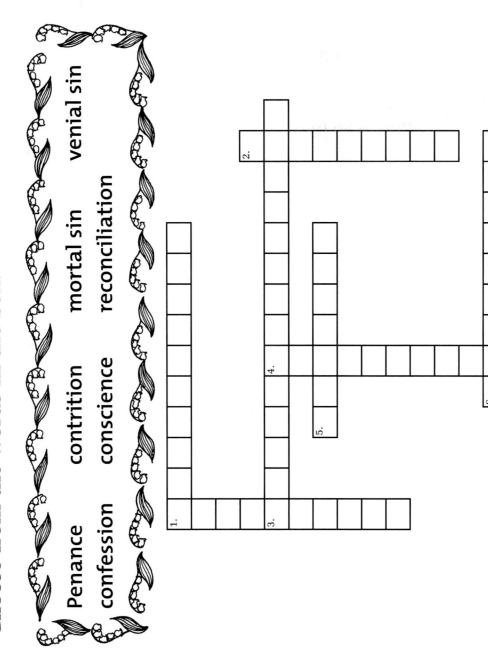

Across

1. telling God we are sorry
3. making peace with God and others
5. the Sacrament when sin is forgiven
6. a less serious sin

Down

1. the sadness we feel when we know we have sinned
2. a very serious sin
4. what we examine to help us think about how we have sinned

Finding God, Session 12

33 Making Peace

Finish the sentences.

One word in each sentence is given, and one whole sentence is done.

Let the sentences show how you can be peaceful.

P ray _____ .

E ach day, I can share.

A lways _____ .

C are _____ .

E ach _____ .

Finding God, Session 13

© Loyola Press

Possible answers: Pray for peace; Each day, I can share; Always be polite; Care for my family; Each day, I can help friends.

34 Jesus Heals

Create a mobile of Jesus healing the man who was paralyzed.

1. Color the objects and glue them onto colored paper.

2. Cut out the objects and punch holes in the top. Tie strings to the man, his friends, Jesus, and the stretcher.

3. Tie the objects to the bottom of the Temple. Make a loop at the top of the Temple. Hang your mobile in a special place.

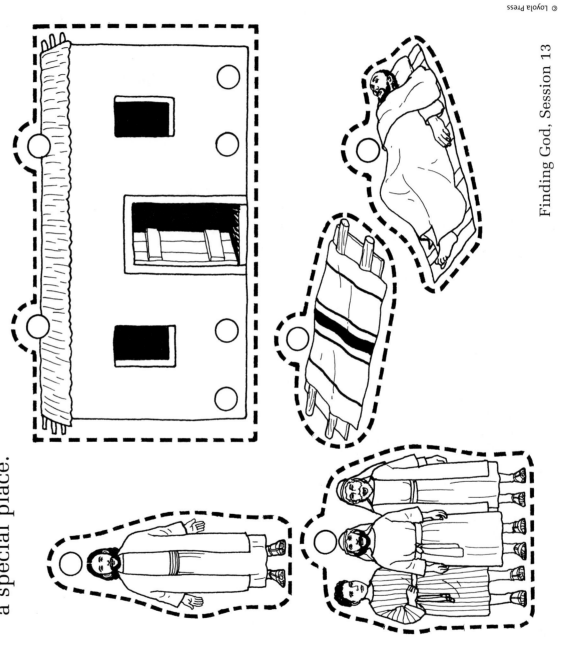

Finding God, Session 13

35 The Sacrament of Penance

What happens in the Sacrament of Penance?
Put the steps in order.
Number them from 1 to 5.

— Tell your sins to a priest.

— Pray a prayer or do a good deed to make up
for your sins.

— Be sorry for your sins.

— Think about what you have done wrong.

— Your sins are forgiven as the priest prays the
prayer of absolution.

Finding God, Session 13

© Loyola Press

413

Answers: (3) Tell your sins to a priest. (5) Pray a prayer or do a good deed to make up for your sins. (2) Be sorry for your sins. (1) Think about what you have done wrong. (4) Your sins are forgiven as the priest prays the prayer of absolution.

36 All Are Welcome

Circle the correct answer to complete each sentence.

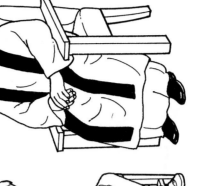

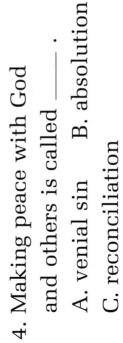

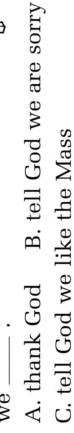

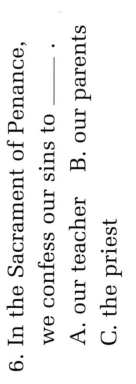

1. Mortal sin is a very serious _____.

   A. confession   B. doubt

   C. wrong

2. Contrition is the sadness we feel
   when we know we have _____.

   A. sinned   B. lost

   C. examined our consciences

3. Baptism takes away original _____.

   A. sin   B. thought

   C. penance

4. Making peace with God
   and others is called _____.

   A. venial sin   B. absolution

   C. reconciliation

5. In the Sacrament of Penance,
   we _____.

   A. thank God   B. tell God we are sorry

   C. tell God we like the Mass

6. In the Sacrament of Penance,
   we confess our sins to _____.

   A. our teacher   B. our parents

   C. the priest

Answers: 1. C; 2. A; 3. A; 4. C; 5. B; 6. C

Finding God, Session 14

© Loyola Press

37 Honoring Mary

1. Color the picture of Mary.
2. Color the letters.
3. Cut out the oval.
4. Glue it to colored paper to make a frame.
5. Hang the picture in your home to honor Mary.

MARY, OUR MOTHER

Finding God, Session 14

38 Your Book of Mary

The pictures show how people around the world honor Mary.

1. Color the pictures.
2. Draw a cover in the blank box. Cut out the cover and pictures to make a book about Mary.

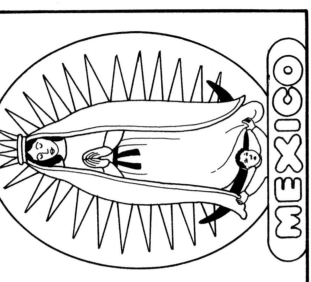

Finding God, Session 14

Name ______________________ Date ____________

39 Unit 3 Show What You Know

Write letters to match the words on the left with the words on the right that tell about them.

____ 1. original sin	A. helps us know if we have done something wrong
____ 2. Fruits of the Holy Spirit	B. promise that priests must keep people's sins secret
____ 3. mortal sin	C. the good we find in our words or actions
____ 4. Sacrament of Penance	D. what Baptism takes away
____ 5. conscience	E. special signs that God is with us
____ 6. reconciliation	F. heals our relationship with God and others
____ 7. Act of Contrition	G. making peace with God and others
____ 8. seal of confession	H. special prayer for telling God we are sorry
____ 9. sacraments	I. the Mother of the Church
____ 10. Mary	J. a very serious wrong

Finding God, Session 15

Answers: 1. D; 2. C; 3. J; 4. F; 5. A; 6. G; 7. H; 8. B; 9. E; 10. I

39

Draw a picture of people making peace with one another.

Self-Assessment

How well do you understand these things? Rate yourself by writing a letter on each line. The guide below will help you decide which letter to write.

A – I know it very well.

B – I know it, but I have some questions.

C – I do not know it.

___ sin

___ confession

___ examination of conscience

Finding God, Session 15

Answers will vary.

40 Pope Saint Pius X

Find the secret word. The clues will help you.
Color the word on the **X** as you read each clue.
The word that is left is the secret word.

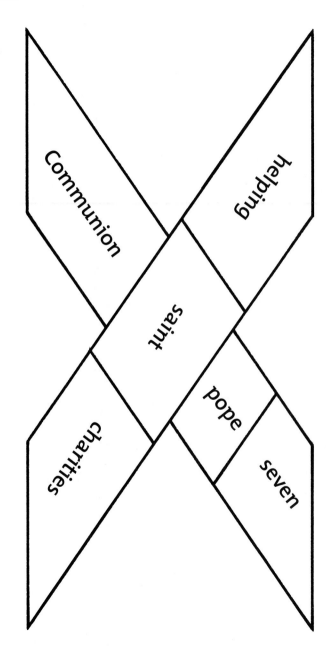

Clues

The secret word is not . . . .

the word that means "aiding" or "assisting."

the word that begins with *p.*

the word we use when we talk about the Eucharist.

the word that tells the age that many children receive their first Holy Communion.

the word that tells what Saint Pius X created to help the poor.

What is the secret word? _____

41 Sacraments of Initiation

1. Color the symbols.

2. Cut out the symbols and the card.

3. Punch holes where shown.

4. Use string to attach the symbols to the Sacraments of Initiation card.

5. Use string to attach the symbols and card to a hanger.

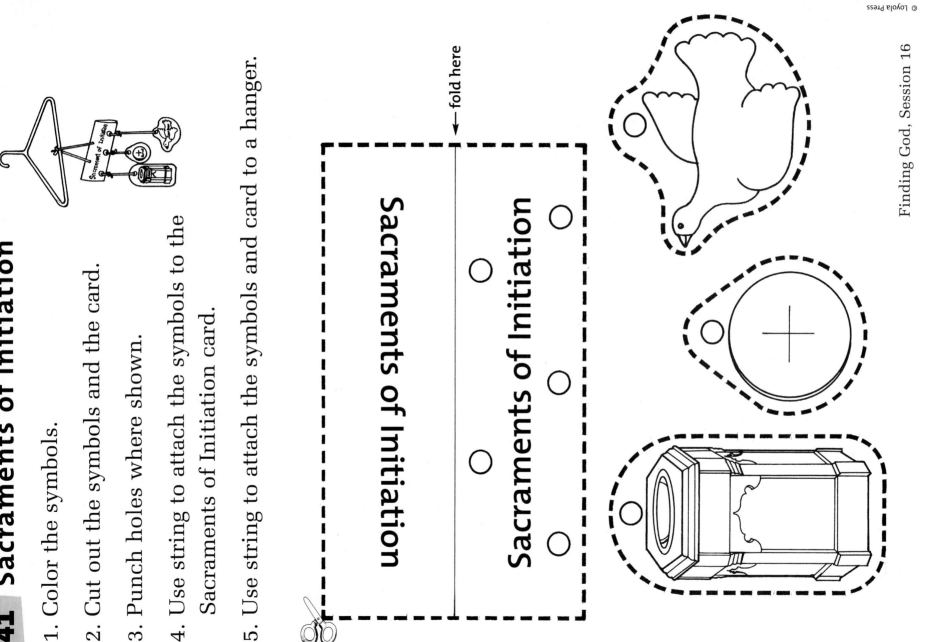

fold here

Sacraments of Initiation

Sacraments of Initiation

42 Meeting Jesus

Circle the correct answers.
Write the circled letters next to the answers in order on the lines at the bottom of the page.

1. Sacraments are ___ that God is with us.

   c signs   **b** friends   **n** houses

2. Sacraments of ___ bring us into God's family.

   e Happiness   **h** Initiation   **i** Help

3. ___ is the beginning of our new life with Jesus.

   m Morning   **g** Breakfast   **u** Baptism

4. Holy Communion is when we receive the ___ .

   l homework   **r** Eucharist   **n** diploma

5. ___ makes us stronger in faith.

   c Confirmation   **h** Laughing   **b** Talking

6. Sacraments give us ___ , which is a gift from God.

   v food   **b** time   **h** grace

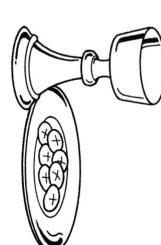

Sacraments were given to the

___ ___ ___ ___ ___ ___ by Jesus.
1   2   3   4   5   6

Answers: 1. signs; 2. Initiation; 3. Baptism; 4. Eucharist; 5. Confirmation; 6. grace; word: Church

Time for Dinner

Create a *Time for Dinner* clock.

1. Color the clock and hands. Cut them out.

2. Fasten the hands to the clock with a brass fastener.

3. Take the clock home. Set the clock to the time your family eats dinner. Pray the Prayer Before Meals and tell the story of Jesus breaking bread with the disciples.

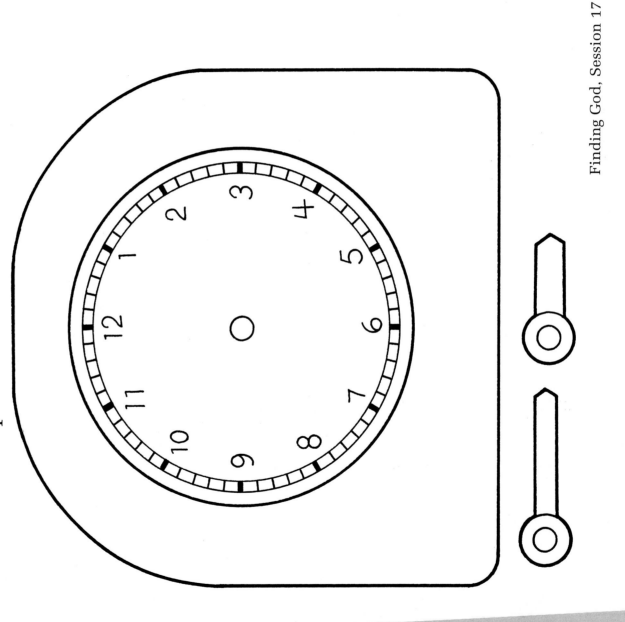

Finding God, Session 17

1. On each dove write one way you can show love to others.

2. Color the doves and cut them out.

3. Glue the doves on a ribbon or long, wide paper strip to make a God's Grace banner.

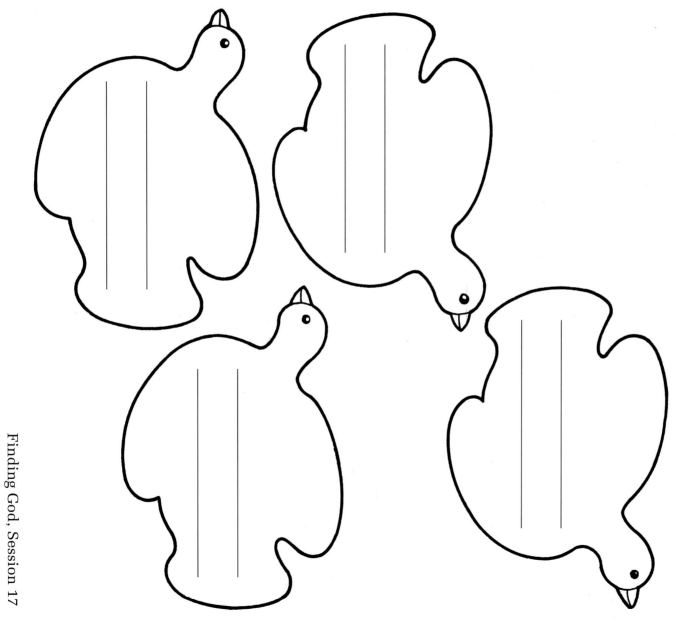

Finding God, Session 17

423

© Loyola Press

45 Inviting Jesus to Dinner

Number the pictures in order. For example, you will write a 1 by the first thing that happened and a 4 by the last thing.

Color the pictures. When you are finished, retell the story of the disciples finding Jesus during the breaking of the bread.

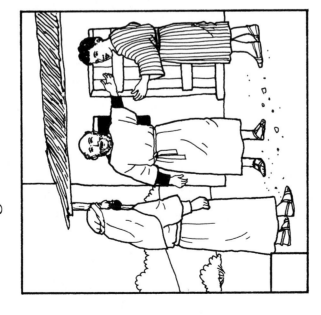

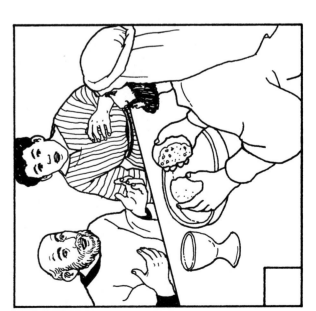

Finding God, Session 17

Answers: top row 3, 1; bottom row 4, 2

We gather at Mass to hear and tell the Good News of Jesus.

1. Decorate the megaphone pattern, glue it to colored paper, and cut it out.

2. Roll it into a cone shape and tape it closed.

3. Use the megaphone to tell your group about the Mass.

Jesus Saves! Spread the Word!

47 **The Liturgy of the Word**

Create a book about the Liturgy of the Word.

1. Decorate and cut out each of the boxes.

2. Punch a hole in the upper-left corner of each box.

3. Put a brass fastener through the holes to bind the book together.

4. Share your book with your family.

OLD TESTAMENT You must know that the Lord is God of heaven and earth, and that there is no other. *adapted from Deuteronomy 4:39*	**LECTIONARY**
GOSPEL Jesus said, "All power in heaven and earth has been given to me. I am always with you, until the end of time." *adapted from Matthew 28:19–20*	**NEW TESTAMENT** People who follow the Holy Spirit are children of God. *adapted from Romans 8:14*

Finding God, Session 18

48 Going to Mass

Use the clues to complete the puzzle.

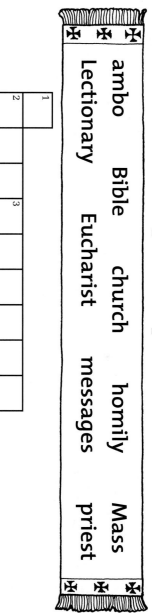

ambo   Bible   church   homily   Mass
Lectionary   Eucharist   messages   priest

Across

2. the Body and Blood of Christ
4. where the Lectionary is read
7. special book with Bible stories read at Mass
9. He explains the readings.

Down

1. God gives us these through the readings at Mass.
3. when the priest explains what the readings mean to us
5. has stories from the Old and New Testaments
6. Attending this brings us closer to Jesus.
8. where we attend Mass

Answers: Across: 2. Eucharist; 4. ambo; 7. Lectionary; 9. priest; Down: 1. messages; 3. homily; 5. Bible; 6. Mass; 8. church

Finding God, Session 18

427

© Loyola Press

Sharing Jesus' Love

1. Cut out the heart pattern and trace it onto three pieces of colored paper.

2. Cut out the hearts, punch holes, and bind the hearts with string to make a book.

3. Decorate the cover with the title *Sharing Jesus' Love.*

4. Decorate each book page with words and pictures that tell how you can share Jesus' love in your family, at school, and in the world.

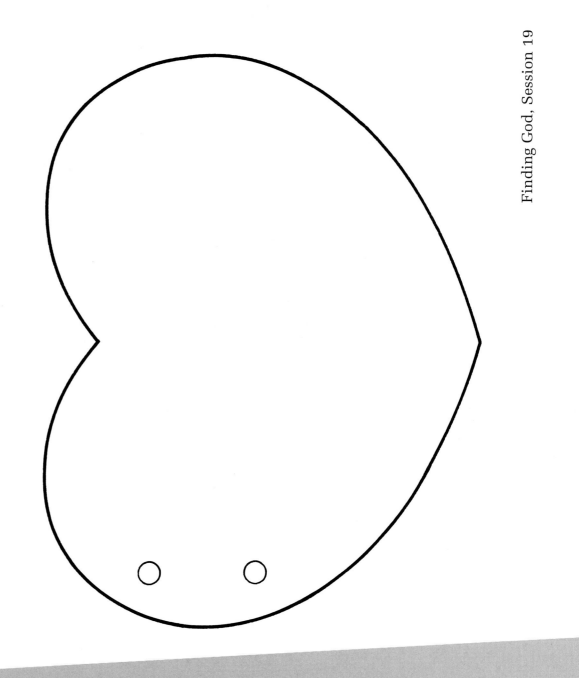

Finding God, Session 19

50 Meeting Jesus

In each sentence cross out the words that do not belong.
The words that remain will make a true sentence.

1. The **(Sacrifice of the Mass) (Lectionary)** is the
   most important way we remember Jesus.

2. Family members sometimes share in the
   (consecration) (ministry) of welcoming people
   to Mass.

3. Bread and wine are brought to the **(altar) (ambo)**.

4. The gifts are presented at the beginning of the
   (Confirmation) (Liturgy of the Eucharist).

5. The bread and wine become the
   (Sacraments of Initiation) (Body and Blood of Christ).

6. We go to Mass on
   (Holy Days of Obligation) (Tuesdays).

7. The Sacraments of Initiation are Baptism,
   Confirmation, and **(Eucharist) (Penance)**.

8. The Bible is read during the
   (ministry) (Liturgy of the Word).

9. The priest explains the readings during the
   (homily) (Holy Communion).

10. The **(Body and Blood of Christ) (Lectionary)**
    contains readings from the Bible.

Answers: 1. Sacrifice of the Mass; 2. ministry; 3. altar; 4. Liturgy of the Eucharist; 5. Body and Blood of Christ;
6. Holy Days of Obligation; 7. Eucharist; 8. Liturgy of the Word; 9. homily; 10. Lectionary

Name ______________________ Date ____________

51 Celebrating the Eucharist

Circle **True** or **False** for each sentence.
Rewrite sentences to make the false sentences true.

1. We do not attend Mass on Holy Days of Obligation.
   True False

   ______________________________.

2. The priest stands at the altar to bless the gifts.
   True False

   ______________________________.

3. At Mass, we celebrate the Liturgy of the Eucharist.
   True False

   ______________________________.

4. Jesus took bread and water at the Last Supper.
   True False

   ______________________________.

5. Mass is the most important way Catholics pray.
   True False

   ______________________________.

Finding God, Session 19

Answers: 1. F; 2. T; 3. T; 4. F; 5. T

52 Unit 4 Show What You Know

Finish the sentences.
Choose from the words in the box.

| homily | Sacrifice | Word | bread | Eucharist |
| Jesus | Baptism | Holy | Mass | Christ |

1. The Sacraments of Initiation are Baptism,
   Confirmation, and _____ .

2. In the Sacrament of Confirmation, we begin our
   new life with _____ .

3. We receive the Body and Blood of
   _____ in the Sacrament
   of Eucharist.

4. The _____ is the most important
   way that Catholics pray.

5. Another name for the celebration of the Eucharist
   is the _____ of the Mass.

6. _____ is the beginning of our
   new life with Jesus.

7. The priest explains how a Bible story fits into
   our lives in the _____ .

Answers: 1. Eucharist; 2. Jesus; 3. Christ; 4. Mass; 5. Sacrifice; 6. Baptism; 7. homily

Name _____ Date _____

8. During the Liturgy of the _____ we listen to God's Word from the Bible.

9. The _____ and wine are brought to the altar for the Liturgy of the Eucharist.

10. We attend Mass on _____ Days of Obligation.

In your own words, write why it is important to receive the Eucharist.

_____

_____

Self-Assessment

How well do you understand these things?
Rate yourself by writing a letter on each line.
The guide below will help you decide which letter to write.

A – I know it very well.
B – I know it, but I have some questions.
C – I do not know it.

___ Liturgy of the Word
___ Sacraments of Initiation
___ Holy Communion

Finding God, Session 20

Answers: 8. Word; 9. bread; 10. Holy. Answers to remaining sections will vary.

53 Saint Martin of Tours

1. Cut out the puzzle pieces and put them together to make a coat.

2. Glue the coat to paper.

3. Use the words on the puzzle pieces to tell a friend about Saint Martin of Tours.

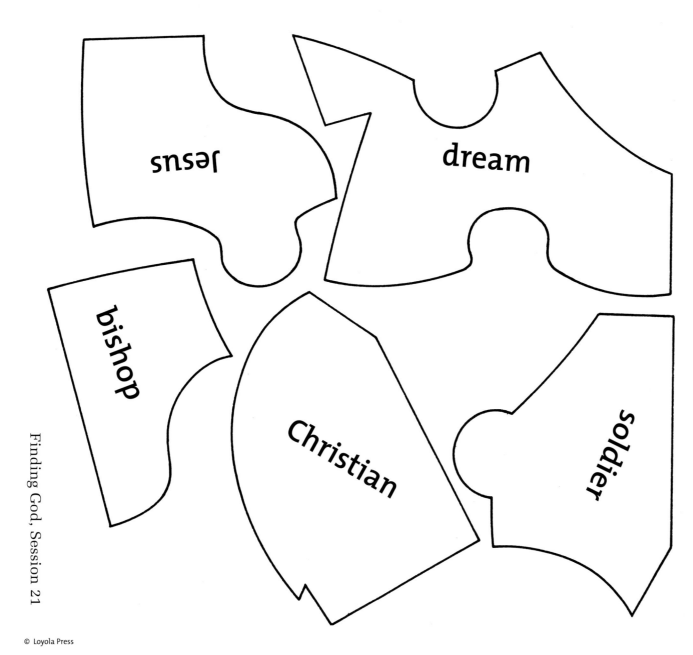

The answer to this activity is found on page 454.

54 The Good Samaritan

Use the code to finish the story of the Good Samaritan.

Retell the story to someone in your group.

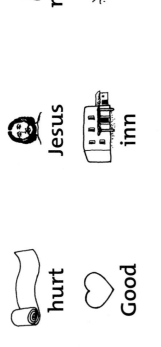 hurt

 Good

 Jesus

inn

robbers

road

A Jewish man was attacked by _____ by the _____ .

They left him _____ Samaritan saw the man.

A _____ Samaritan saw the man.

The _____ Samaritan bandaged the man's

 wounds and took him to an _____ .

_____ said we should be like the

_____ Samaritan.

Answers: robbers; hurt; road; Good; Good; inn; Jesus; Good

Name _____ Date _____

55 Being Like Jesus

Circle the correct answers.
Then write a sentence telling how you can be like
Saint Martin or the Good Samaritan.

1. ____ are people who show mercy.
   God will have mercy on them.
   Blessed   Angry   Acting

2. Saint Martin ____ out to a
   suffering stranger.
   lashed   reached   jumped

3. Leyla ____ Chris after her accident.
   helped   ignored   mocked

4. The Good Samaritan acted with
   ____ and mercy.
   anger   fear   love

5. The priest says, "Go in peace to love
   and ____ the Lord."
   help   serve   remind

_____

_____ .

The Ten Commandments

1. Decorate the pattern to look like a stone tablet.

2. Glue it to colored paper and cut it out.

3. Use it as a bookmark to remind you to obey the Commandments.

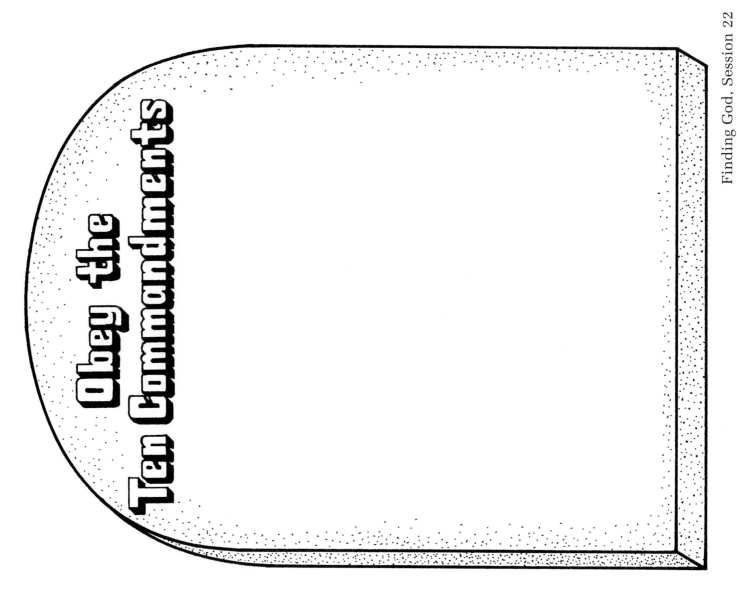

Obey the Ten Commandments

Finding God, Session 22

57 How Would You Feel?

Circle **Guilty** or **Peaceful**
to show how you would
feel in each situation.

Then write a sentence.
Tell how to bring peace to
one of the guilty situations.
Talk to someone about your answers.

How would you feel if you . . .

1. stole candy from a store?   Peaceful   Guilty

_____

2. shared your markers?   Peaceful   Guilty

_____

3. cheated on a spelling test?   Peaceful   Guilty

_____

4. took a toy from your sister?   Peaceful   Guilty

_____

5. made a get-well card for a friend?   Peaceful   Guilty

_____

6. made your bed without
   being asked?   Peaceful   Guilty

_____

Name _____

Date _____

58 We Share God's Life

To make sentences, write the words in order. The first one is done for you.

On the line at the bottom, write ways the Church and the Bible can help you make good moral choices. Talk to the group about your answers.

1. Moses choice told people that they a had.

   Moses told people that they had a choice.

2. They God choose could and blessed be.

   _____

3. Or could not choose they God follow to.

   _____

4. God the us gave Church the and Bible.

   _____

5. They choices moral make help us.

   _____

   _____

Answers: 2. They could choose God and be blessed. 3. Or they could choose not to follow God.
4. God gave us the Church and the Bible. 5. They help us make moral choices. Final answer: Answers will vary.

1. Color and cut out the bees and beehive.
   Be sure to decorate both sides.

2. Tie the bees to string and attach
   them to the beehive.

3. Tie a string to the top of the beehive.
   Hang it in a special place.

the best
way to
BEE-have

"Bee" fair

"Bee" peaceful

"Bee" just

"Bee" Attitudes

"Bee" kind

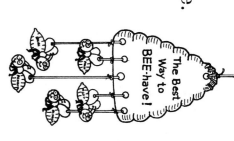

The Best
Way to
BEE-have!

60 Making Moral Choices

Finish the story about Luke by circling the good moral choice. If you make the right choice, Luke will be happy at the end. Talk with the group about your choice.

Luke does not have enough money to buy the video game he wants. He is trying to decide what to do.

He can either

A. work to earn enough money.

B. take money from Nancy's room.

If you circled A, read this.

Nancy asks Luke to help her rake leaves. Luke says, "Sure, I will help you." Luke and Nancy do a great job. Mom decides to reward them. She gives them money. Luke is happy. He is closer to having enough money to buy the game.

If you circled B, read this.

Nancy finds out that Luke took money from her. She tells mom. Mom is very angry. She takes away Luke's video games for a month.

61 Doing What Jesus Teaches

Finish each sentence.
Choose from the words in the box.
Then read your answers aloud as a group.
Volunteer if you would like to share an answer.

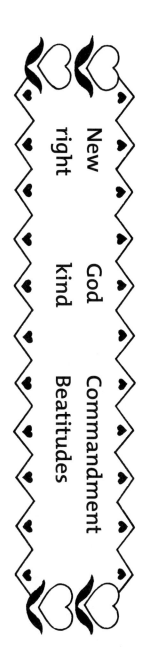

| New | God | Commandment |
| right | kind | Beatitudes |

1. Jesus taught us the _____
   because he wants us to be happy.

2. Blessed are those who are
   _____ to others.

3. People who do the right thing will be with
   _____ one day.

4. The _____ Testament is the
   story of Jesus' life.

5. The Great _____ teaches us
   how to follow God and care for others.

6. We make the _____ choice
   when we love God and others.

On another sheet of paper draw a picture that
shows how you can follow the Beatitudes.

1. Color and cut out the puppets. Make them look like Ana, Eduardo, and Benito.

2. Glue them to craft sticks.

3. Use the puppets to retell the story of Ana, Eduardo, and Benito. Give your story an ending that shows kindness.

4. Create more situations with your puppets. Share with the group.

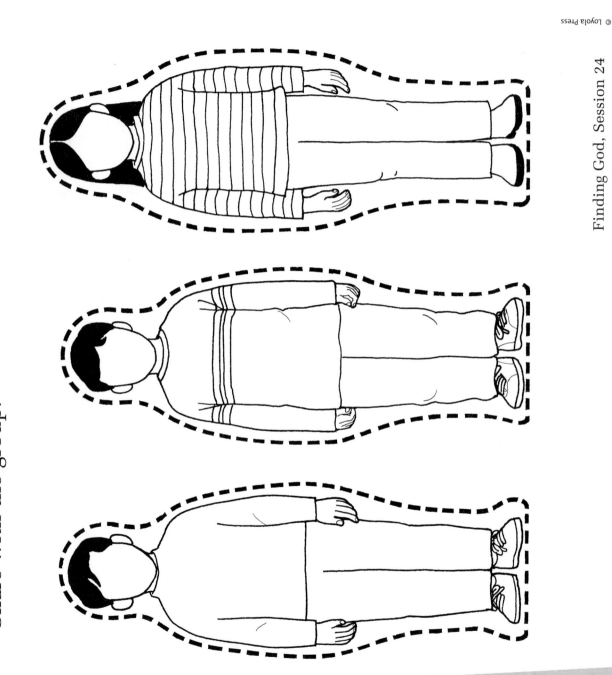

Finding God, Session 24

63 Living Like Jesus

Cut out the word strips and glue them where they belong in the story.

Great Commandment	Beatitudes

moral choice	New Testament

Kelly was thinking about taking her sister's jacket without asking. Then she thought about how Jesus would want her to act. She remembered the

[_____], filled with stories about

how Jesus treated others. Kelly also remembered

how Jesus gave us the [_____]

because he wanted us to be happy. Finally,

she thought about the [_____].

We would not be caring for others if we took

someone's jacket without asking. We would not be

happy. Kelly chose not to take her sister's jacket.

She made a good [_____].

64 Following Peter's Advice

Think about Peter's letter to the Christians.
Draw a line from each part to a picture that shows
someone following his advice.

Then color the pictures. Tell how the people are
following Peter's advice.

1. Tell the truth.

2. Stay away from evil.

3. Bring peace
into the world.

A.

"I have to go home."

B.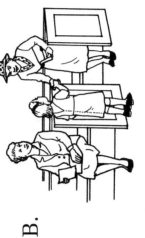

"Peace be with you."

C.

"I did it. I am sorry."

Finding God, Session 24

65 Unit 5 Show What You Know

Circle **T** for true or **F** for false.

1. God will show mercy to people who show mercy to others.   T   F

2. In the parable of the Good Samaritan, the man from Samaria was a good neighbor.   T   F

3. Helping grandma rake leaves is a good moral choice.   T   F

4. Moses was a Temple official.   T   F

5. The Holy Spirit helps us to make good choices.   T   F

6. Jesus gave us the Beatitudes to show us how to be happy.   T   F

7. The Old Testament is the story of Jesus' life.   T   F

8. The Old and New Testaments are in the Bible.   T   F

9. The Great Commandment teaches us to love God and care for others.   T   F

10. Peter wanted to teach the Christians the Sign of the Cross.   T   F

Answers: 1. T; 2. T; 3. T; 4. F; 5. T; 6. T; 7. F; 8. T; 9. T; 10. F

Name _____

Date _____

Draw a picture of something that happened in the parable of the Good Samaritan.

Self-Assessment

How well do you understand these things?
Rate yourself by writing a letter on each line.
The guide below will help you decide which letter to write.

A – I know it very well.

B – I know it, but I have some questions.

C – I do not know it.

___ Great Commandment

___ Beatitudes

___ making moral choices

Finding God, Session 25

Answers will vary.

1. Cut out the ornaments.
2. Glue them to the tree.
3. Decorate the tree and ornaments.
4. The ornaments will remind you of ways to prepare for Jesus' birth during Advent.

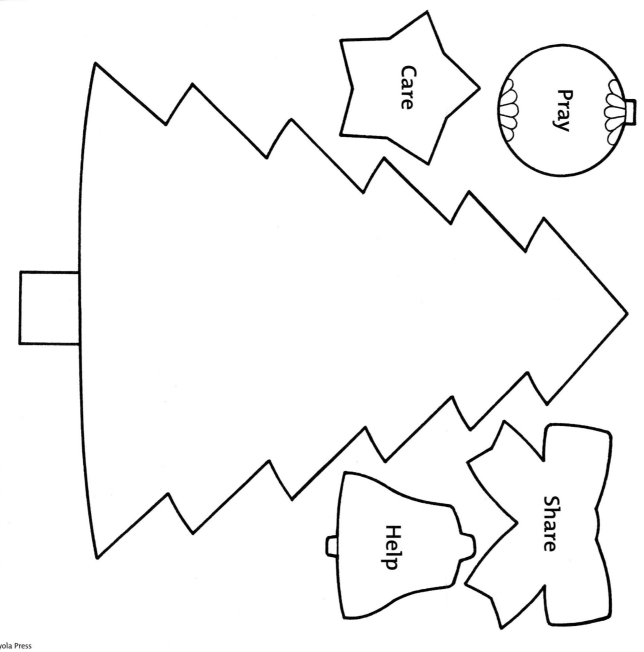

Care

Pray

Share

Help

67 Someone Special

1. Color the picture.

2. Cut out the card and fold in the middle.

3. Write a greeting for your card on the inside.

4. Give the card to someone special. Tell this person the story of the three Wise Men.

Finding God, Christmas and Epiphany

Make a figure of yourself to show a change you will make during Lent.

1. Draw yourself on both sides of the pattern. Put a sad face on one side and a happy face on the other.

2. Color and cut out the pattern.

3. Put the figure by your bed.

4. Every night think, "Was I like Jesus today?" If you were, put the happy side up. If you were not, put the sad side up.

5. Think about what you can do tomorrow to be like Jesus.

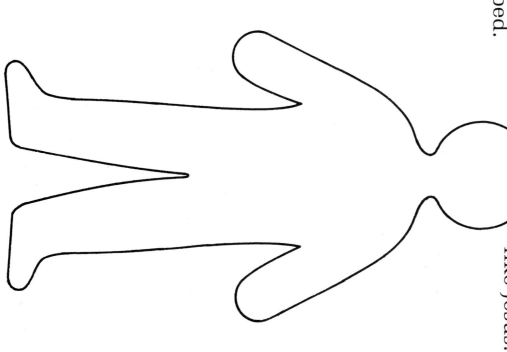

Finding God, Lent

1. In each part of the cross, draw pictures that remind you of what we remember during Holy Week.

2. Color the cross.

3. Cut out the cross and glue it to purple construction paper.

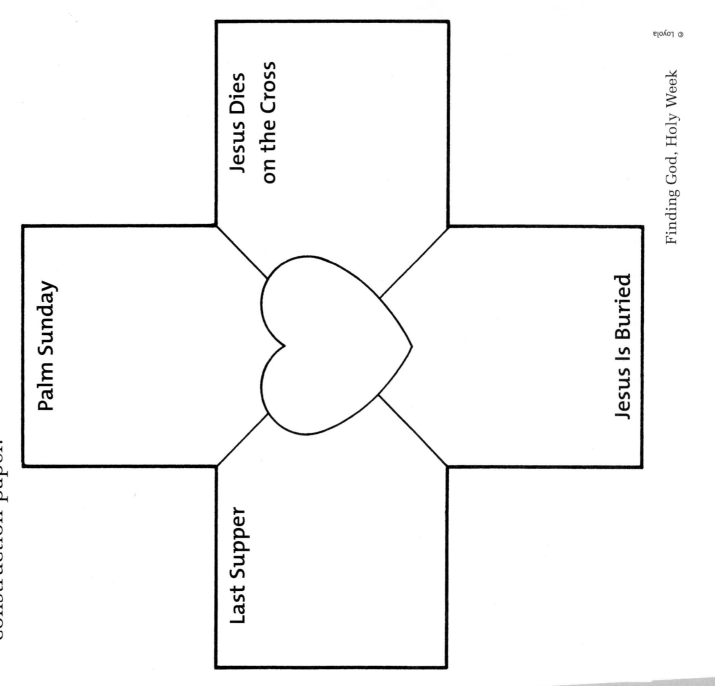

Jesus Dies on the Cross

Palm Sunday

Last Supper

Jesus Is Buried

Finding God, Holy Week

1. On each Easter lily write one thing you will do for another person.

2. Color and cut out the lilies.

3. Make stems by fastening craft stems to the lilies.

4. Keep your lilies.
   Let them remind you of ways to share Easter joy with others.

Finding God, Easter

1. Cut out the dove pattern and trace it onto colored paper.

2. Cut out the dove you traced and fold it down the center.

3. Staple the body together along the fold. Bend the wings down so it looks as if the dove is flying.

4. Punch a hole in the dove and tie a long string to it.

5. Your Holy Spirit kite will remind you that the Spirit is always with you.

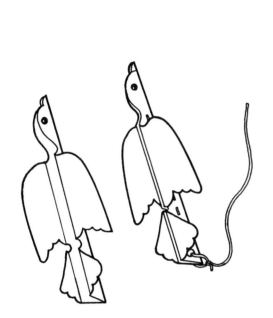

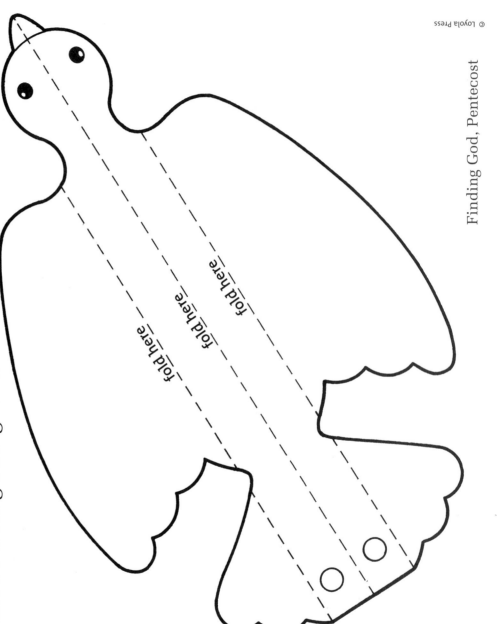

fold here
fold here
fold here

Finding God, Pentecost

Make a door hanger to remind you of your favorite saint.

1. Write the name of your saint on the line.

2. Draw a picture of your saint in the space at the bottom of the hanger.

3. Cut out the hanger and hang it on your door.

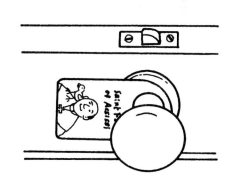

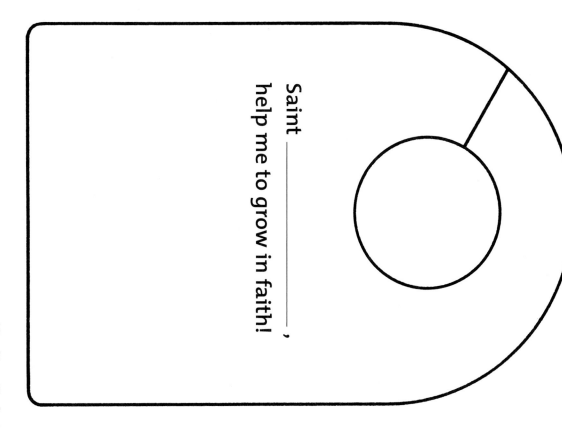

Saint ———————,
help me to grow in faith!

Name _____ Date _____

53 Saint Martin of Tours

1. Cut out the puzzle pieces and put them together to make a coat.

2. Glue the coat to paper.

3. Use the words on the puzzle pieces to tell a friend about Saint Martin of Tours.

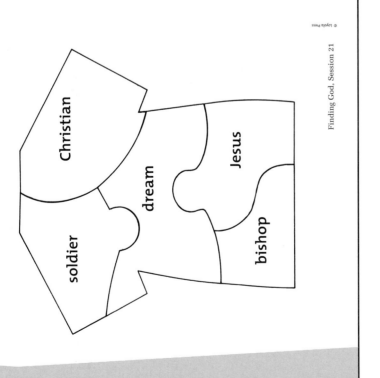

soldier · Christian · dream · Jesus · bishop

Finding God, Session 21

Acknowledgments

Text

Excerpts from the *New American Bible* with Revised New Testament and Psalms Copyright © 1991, 1986, 1970 Confraternity of Christian Doctrine, Inc., Washington, D.C. Used with permission. All rights reserved. No portion of the *New American Bible* may be reprinted without permission in writing from the copyright holder.

Excerpts from the *General Directory of Catechesis* © 1997 Libreria Editrice Vaticana-United States Conference of Catholic Bishops, Inc., Washington, D.C. Used with permission. All rights reserved.

Excerpts from the English translation of the *Catechism of the Catholic Church* for use in the United States of America. Copyright © 1994, United States Catholic Conference, Inc.—Libreria Editrice Vaticana. Used with permission.

Excerpts from "Brothers and Sisters to Us" © 1979; "Economic Justice for All: Catholic Social Teaching and the U.S. Economy" © 1979; "Homelessness and Housing: A Tragedy, a Moral Challenge" © 1988; "In All Things Charity: A Pastoral Challenge for the New Millennium" © 1999; "Resolution on the Pastoral Concern of the Church for People on the Move" © 1976; and "Welcoming the Stranger Among Us: Unity in Diversity" © 2000 United States Conference of Catholic Bishops, Inc., Washington, D.C. Used with permission. All rights reserved.

Kagan, Spencer, and Kagan, Miguel. (1998) *Multiple Intelligences: The Complete MI Book.* San Clemente, Calif.: Kagan Publishing. www.KaganOnline.com/. Used with permission.

Shepherds Speak: American Bishops Confront the Social and Moral Issues That Challenge Christians Today. New York: Crossroads Publishing, 1986.

Loyola Press has made every effort to locate the copyright holders for the cited works used in this publication and to make full acknowledgment for their use. In the case of any omissions, the Publisher will be pleased to make suitable acknowledgments in future editions.

Spoken Word and Music CDs

All CDs were produced and developed by Loyola Press in partnership with Media Creature Music, Los Angeles, California.

Executive Producer: Loyola Press
Producer: Sharal Churchill
Associate Producer: Tony Thornton
Editors: Rogers Masson, Nathanael Lew, and Kathryn Korniloff
Mixed by: Rogers Masson
Mastering: Rogers Masson
Mastered at: Moonlight Mastering
Final Mix: Sharal Churchill and Nathanael Lew, Media Creature Music

Spoken Word CDs

Scripture Stories
Narrators: Martin Sheen and Rita Moreno

Voice-Over Actors:
Jennifer Hale: Mary, Eve, and Woman
R. Todd Torok: Grown Jesus
James Arnold Taylor: Angel, Young Jesus, Friend 1, Son, Adam, Rich Young Man, and Person 2
Nathan Carlson: Peter, Man 2, Isaiah, Joseph, Friend 2, and Angel
Abner Genece: Messenger, Shepherd 2, Elijah, and Father
Earl Boen: Andrew, Court Official, God, Isaac, and Person 2
Cam Clarke: Shepherd 1, Officer, Paralyzed Man, Disciple, Jacob, and Joseph
Jennifer Darling: Mary Magdalene, Mother, Person 1, Person 2, and Rebekah

Lloyd Sherr: Satan, Devil, Philip, Person 1, Friend 4, Jairus, James, and Leader 2
James Horan: Solomon, Person 1, Expert, Friend 3, Leader 4, Man, Man 1, and Angel

Guided Reflections
Voices: Cam Clarke and Jennifer Darling

Music CDs

Musicians:
Arranger: Amanda Kramer
Theme Song Arranger: Paul Gibson
Arranger/Orchestrator: Jeff Gund
Recorded at Media Creature Music and Firehouse Recording Studios
Contractor/Production Manager: Alan A. Vavrin
Music Clearance: Media Creature Music
Instrumental Music: Media Creature Music

Musicians:
Alan A. Vavrin: Drum set and Percussion
Fred Selden: Flute and Bansuri
Christina Soule: Cello
Stefanie Fife: Cello
Robert Matsuda: Violin
David W. Washburn: Trumpet
Laurence D. Greenfield: Violin
Andrew Picken: Viola
Mark Adams: French horn
Joseph Meyer: French horn
Barbara Northcutt: Oboe and English horn

Illustration and Photography

Front Matter
PO38 © Bill Wittman. EC1 © Arthur Tress, Photonica. EC3 © Bill Wittman. EC4 © Jeff Greenberg/PhotoEdit. EC5 © Charles Gupton/Getty Images. EC8 © Royalty-Free/CORBIS. EC9 Courtesy of Nathaniel Weickert. EC10 (b) photodisc/Getty Images. EC11 (t) © Bill Wittman; (b) photodisc/Getty Images. EC12 (t) photodisc/Getty Images. (b) © Bill Wittman. EC13 (t) © Phil Martin Photography; (b) photodisc/Getty Images. EC14 (t-b) photodisc/Getty Images; © Bill Wittman; photodisc/Getty Images. EC15 (all) photodisc/Getty Images. EC16 (t) photodisc/Getty Images. EC17 photodisc/Getty Images. EC18 (t-l) Denise Ortakales; (right, t-b) © Stephen McBrady/PhotoEdit. © Michael Newman/PhotoEdit; © Amy Etra/PhotoEdit. EC19 (t-r) photodisc/Getty Images; (b-r) © Bill Wittman; (b) Denise Ortakales. EC20 (t-b) David LaFleur; Douglas Klauba; John Nava/© Los Angeles Cathedral of Our Lady of the Angels. EC21 (t-b) © Cleve Bryant/PhotoEdit; photodisc/Getty Images; photodisc/Getty Images. EC22 (t, l-r) photodisc/Getty Images; (b) photodisc/Getty Images. EC23 (t, l-r) photodisc/Getty Images; (b) Bill Wittman; photodisc/Getty Images; (b-l) photodisc/Getty Images. EC24 (all) photodisc/Getty Images.

Unit 1
1a © Erich Lessing/Louvre, Paris/Art Resource, NY. 1b © O'Brien Productions/CORBIS. 1c © Jan Kanter. 1d © Dave G. Houser/CORBIS. 1e © David Pollack/CORBIS. 13a © Richard Hutchings/CORBIS. 13b © Stuart Westmorland/CORBIS. 13c © Michael Pole/CORBIS. 23a © John Conrad/CORBIS. 23b © Stuart Westmorland/CORBIS. 23c © Courtesy of East St. Louis Action Research Project. 33a © Douglas Faulkner/CORBIS. 33b © Tim Pannell/CORBIS. 33c © Reuters NewMedia Inc./CORBIS. 43a © Royalty-Free/CORBIS.

Unit 2
49a © Historical Picture Archive/CORBIS. 49b © John Henley/Productions/CORBIS. 49c © Galen Rowell/CORBIS. 49d © Royalty-Free/CORBIS. 49e © Tom & Dee Ann McCarthy/CORBIS. 61a © George B. Diebold/CORBIS. 61b © Bob Krist/CORBIS. 61c © Jose Luis Pelaez, Inc./

Acknowledgments

CORBIS. 71a © Chase Swift/CORBIS. 71b © Araldo de Luca/CORBIS. 71c © East St. Louis Action Research Project/CORBIS. 1a © Children of the World Illustrate the Bible/MallMedia Publishing, www.bible2000.com. 81b © AFP/CORBIS. 81c © Ralf-Finn Hestoft/CORBIS SABA. 91a © Foto World/Getty Images.

Unit 3

97a © Craig Tuttle/CORBIS. 97b © Bob Rowan; Progressive Image/CORBIS. 97c © Galen Rowell/CORBIS. 97e © Ed Bock/CORBIS. 109a © Royalty-Free/CORBIS. 109c © Alison Wright/CORBIS. 119a © D. Boone/CORBIS. 119b © Historical Picture Archive/CORBIS. 119c © Vittoriano Rastelli/CORBIS. 129a © Craig Tuttle/CORBIS. 129b © Scala/Art Resource, NY. 129c © David Lees/CORBIS. 139a © Royalty-Free/CORBIS.

Unit 4

145a © The Crosiers/Gene Plaisted OSC. 145b © Ariel Skelley/CORBIS. 145c © Archivo Iconografico, S.A./CORBIS. 145d © The Crosiers/Gene Plaisted OSC. 157a © Alinari/Art Resource, NY. 157b Courtesy of Old First Church, Newark, NJ. 157c © Jeff Greenberg/PhotoEdit. 167a © The Crosiers/Gene Plaisted OSC. 167c © Rim Light/PhotoLink/Photodisc/PictureQuest. 177a © Alinari Archives/CORBIS. 177c © Ariel Skelley/CORBIS. 187a © The Crosiers/Gene Plaisted OSC.

Unit 5

193a © Archivo Iconografico, S.A./CORBIS. 193b © Bob Daemmrich Photography. 193c © Craig Tuttle/CORBIS. 193d © Ricardo Azoury/CORBIS. 193e © Elio Ciol/CORBIS. 205a Dover Publications. 205b © Bettmann/CORBIS. 205c © Don Hammond/CORBIS. 215a © Buddy Mays/CORBIS. 215b © Massimo Listri/CORBIS.

215c © Bob Daemmrich Photography. 225a © Burstein Collection/CORBIS. 225b © Jim Craigmyle/CORBIS. 225c © East St. Louis Action Research Project. 235a © Bob Krist/CORBIS.

The Year in Our Church

241b © Gabe Palmer/CORBIS.

Staff

Editorial Staff

David Andrews
Sylvia Bace
John Bretzlauf
Elizabeth Fiting
Mandy Gagel
Aaron George
Ann Heesacker
Louise Howe
Amy Joyce
Allison Kessel
Mary Jane Maples
Laura Morley
Martha Morrison
Frank Muschal
Beth Renaldi
Christina Richards
Brian Smith
Elizabeth Strauss

Design/Production Staff

Joan Bledig
Kathleen Burke
David Carothers
Karen Christoffersen
Maureen Collins
Lindaanne Donohoe
Becca Gay
Margo Goia
Rosemary Hunter
Judine O'Shea
Janet Risko
Matthew Taplinger
Vita Schweighart